P9-AQR-822

Correctional Contexts

Contemporary and Classical Readings

Second Edition

Edward J. Latessa
University of Cincinnati

Alexander Holsinger
University of Missouri, Kansas City

James W. Marquart
Sam Houston State University

Jonathan R. Sorensen
University of Texas, Pan American

TECHNICAL COLLEGE OF THE LOWCOUNTRY
LEARNING RESOURCES CENTER
POST OFFICE BOX 1288
BEAUFORT, SOUTH CAROLINA 29901-1288

Roxbury Publishing Company
Los Angeles, California

Library of Congress Cataloging-in-Publication Data
Correctional contexts : contemporary and classical readings / second edition
  Edward J. Latessa, Alexander Holsinger, James W. Marquart, Jonathan R.
Sorensen [editors].
  p. cm.
Includes bibliographical references and index
ISBN 1-891487-53-1
1. Corrections - United States. 2. Corrections - United States - History. 3. Prisons -
United States. 4. Imprisonment - United States. I. Latessa, Edward J. II. Holsinger,
Alexander. III. Marquart, James W. IV. Sorensen, Jonathan R.–
Correctional Contexts, Second Edition
HV9466.C67 2001
365'.973—dc21   00-055282
                                                                                                                CIP

Copyright © 2001 by Roxbury Publishing Company. All rights reserved under International
and Pan American Copyright Conventions. No part of this publication may be reproduced,
stored in a retrieval system, or transmitted in any form or by any means electronic, photo-
copying, recording, or otherwise without prior permission of the publisher.

Publisher: Claude Teweles
Managing Editor: Dawn VanDercreek
Production Editor: Joshua H. R. Levine
Production Assistants: Jamie Elmer, Monica Gomez, Teresa Gonzalez, Casey Haymes,
Todd Kingsley
Typography: Rebecca Evans and Associates with Synergistic Data Systems
Cover Design: Marnie Kenney

Printed on acid-free paper in the United States of America. This book meets the standards
for recycling of the Environmental Protection Agency.

ISBN 1-891487-53-1

ROXBURY PUBLISHING COMPANY
P.O. Box 491044
Los Angeles, California 90049-9044
Tel.: (310) 473-3312 • Fax: (310) 473-4490
E-mail: roxbury@roxbury.net
Website: www.roxbury.net

784.5

To Edward J. Latessa, Sr.
and
Jordan, Lucas, and Elijah

Contents

Part I: History of Punishment and Origins of Imprisonment

Pieter C. Spierenburg
Using a systems approach, Spierenburg explores the origins of the criminal justice system and the rise of the nation-state in pre-industrial western Europe. The criminal justice system at several points throughout history is identified as a tool of governmental repression.

David J. Rothman
Rothman considers urbanization, industrialization, and reform in this piece studying the rise of the American penitentiary. Both the origin and design of early penal institutions are investigated.

Thorsten Sellin
The transition from confinement existing strictly for the purpose of detention, to confinement as the punishment itself is investigated by Sellin. He explores issues surrounding the conditions within the early institutions as well as prison labor.

Nicole Hahn Rafter
Rafter examines the criminal justice system in general, and the Albion, New York, institution for women in particular, as mechanisms of social control for women throughout the early twentieth century.

Part II: Living in Prison

Part IV: Prison Litigation and Inmates' Rights

Part V: Institutional Programming and Treatment

Part VI: Release From Prison and Parole

Part VII: New Directions

Preface

This book traces the history of punishment and the penal institution in the United States, highlighting major developments that have changed the face of corrections. Although the purpose and expectations behind the confinement of human beings may have changed over time, the net effect has not—by and large, individuals who have committed serious crimes are meant to experience punishment of some sort.

The history of punishment has been and remains quite dynamic. The philosophical roots of punishment are explored initially by classic essays in the field. Similarly, the beginnings of the congregate institution, designed for long-term confinement, are also investigated. Other major developments are detailed by researchers who have studied the complex facets of life inside an institution both for individuals and for competing groups. The selections document major changes regarding prisoners' rights as well as the history and proliferation of treatment efforts inside the penal in-

stitution. Moreover, several essays discuss the complexities of parole release and suggest potential directions for the future.

This book is designed as a text for courses in corrections and criminal justice. Each section, and each article within each section, begins with an introduction that presents salient issues regarding the topic at hand, in addition to providing some background. The articles themselves have been ordered to provide the reader with a broad understanding of the intricacies within the section. Finally, study questions at the end of each article will serve to motivate in-class discussion while also providing a study guide for exams.

Several individuals were extremely helpful in the construction and review of this anthology. We wish to extend our sincere thanks to Charlotte Better of the University of Cincinnati.

We also wish to thank the staff members at Roxbury Publishing Company for their assistance, especially Claude Teweles. ✦

Acknowledgements

This anthology traces the history and development of institutional corrections and punishment as they have evolved in the United States over the past few centuries. These articles and essays offer the reader a critical review of where "corrections" in the United States has been in the past, how various facets of the system operate today, and where we may be headed regarding the confinement and treatment of our country's incarcerated population.

Many classical writings are included throughout this volume—particularly those tracing the origin of the institution as it has existed in the United States, along with the various experiences of a confined population, and the major societal influences that have shaped institutional corrections over time. Also included are entire sections highlighting the rehabilitative treatment efforts within institutions, the increasingly critical role of aftercare and parole, and the major influences leading to corrective efforts.

We wish to express our sincere appreciation to those who have given of their time and effort in many different capacities to assist us in assembling this anthology. We especially wish to thank Charlotte Better of the University of Cincinnati; Kristi Holsinger of the University of Missouri—Kansas City; and Claude Teweles and Josh Levine of Roxbury Publishing Company.

We also offer thanks to the following reviewers of the First Edition of this book: Martha Blomquist of Southern Oregon State College; Sue Bourke at the University of Cincinnati; Leo Carroll at the University of Rhode Island; Ron Everett at the University of North Carolina at Wilmington; Mark Fleisher at Illinois State University; Karol Lucken at the University of Central Florida; Eric Poole of Colorado University at Denver; Barbara Sims of Pennsylvania State University at Harrisburg; Joe Spillane of the University of Florida; Robert Weiss of SUNY Plattsburgh; Gregory Wiltfang of the University of Arkansas; and John Wooldredge of the University of Cincinnati. ✦

About the Contributors

D. A. Andrews is Professor of Psychology at Carleton University.

Brandon K. Applegate is a faculty member in the Department of Criminal Justice and Legal Studies at Central Florida University.

James Austin is on the faculty at George Washington University.

Peter J. Benekos teaches in the Administration of Justice program at Mercyhurst College.

James Bonta is Chief of Corrections Research for the Solicitor General of Canada.

Velmer S. Burton, Jr., is Dean of the Graduate School and Professor of Sociology, North Dakota State University.

Todd R. Clear is Professor of Criminal Justice, John Jay College of Criminal Justice.

Donald Clemmer completed pioneer research in 1940 on the prison inmate subculture in his book *The Prison Community*.

Mark B. Coggeshall is a graduate student in the Department of Criminology and Criminal Justice, University of Maryland.

Ben M. Crouch teaches sociology at Texas A&M University.

Francis T. Cullen is Distinguished Research Professor of Criminal Justice at the University of Cincinnati.

Rolando V. Del Carmen is Professor of Criminal Justice in the College of Criminal Justice, Sam Houston State University.

Craig Dowden is a doctoral candidate at Carleton University.

Bonnie S. Fisher is on the faculty of the Division of Criminal Justice at the University of Cincinnati.

Eric J. Fritsch is on the faculty of Criminal Justice, University of North Texas.

Catherine A. Gallagher is in the Department of Public and International Affairs, George Mason University.

Paul Gendreau is Professor and Director of the Institute of Criminal Justice at the University of New Brunswick.

Jurg Gerber is on the faculty of Criminal Justice at Sam Houston State University.

Howard B. Gill was Director, Institute of Correctional Administration, The American University.

Erving Goffman was Benjamin Franklin Professor of Anthropology and Sociology at the University of Pennsylvania and President of the American Sociological Association at the time of his death. His many influential books include *The Presentation of Self in Everyday Life* (1959), *Asylums* (1961), *Relations in Public* (1971), and *Frame Analysis* (1974).

Voncile B. Gowdy is Senior Social Scientist, National Institute of Justice, U.S. Department of Justice.

Gordon C. Nagayama Hall is in the Department of Psychology, Kent State University.

Craig Haney is director of the Program in Legal Studies at the University of California, Santa Cruz.

Eliot S. Hartstone is President of Spectrum Research Associates.

Rodney J. Henningsen is in the College of Criminal Justice, Sam Houston State University.

Peter B. Hoffman is Staff Director (Retired), United States Parole Commission.

Robert D. Hoge is Professor of Psychology at Carleton University.

John Irwin is Professor Emeritus of Sociology at San Francisco State University.

James B. Jacobs teaches in the School of Law at New York University.

Robert Johnson teaches in the Department of Justice, Law, and Society at The American University.

W. Wesley Johnson is Assistant Dean of Undergraduate Studies, College of Criminal Justice, Sam Houston State University.

Reneé Kopache is a former graduate student at the University of Cincinnati.

Edward J. Latessa is Professor and Head of the Division of Criminal Justice, University of Cincinnati.

Lucien X. Lombardo teaches in the Department of Sociology and Criminal Justice at Old Dominion University.

Doris L. MacKenzie is Professor, Department of Criminology and Criminal Justice, University of Maryland.

James W. Marquart teaches in the Criminal Justice Department at Sam Houston State University.

Robert Martinson was a member of the New York State Governor's Special Committee on Criminal Offenders that was responsible for analyzing the effectiveness of treatment programs resulting in the publication of the infamous Martinson Report.

Alida V. Merlo teaches in the Department of Criminology at Indiana University of Pennsylvania.

John Monahan is Professor of Law at the University of Virginia.

Allison Morris is Director of the Institute of Criminology, Victoria University of Wellington, New Zealand. Previously, she was a researcher at the Institute of Criminology, University of Cambridge, England.

Roger H. Peters is Professor in the Department of Mental Health, Law, and Policy, Louis de la Parte Florida Mental Health Institute, University of South Florida.

Joan Petersilia teaches in the School of Social Ecology, University of California, Irvine.

Nicole Hahn Rafter teaches in the College of Criminal Justice at Northeastern University.

Pamela Clark Robbins is Vice President of Policy Research Associates in Delmar, New York.

David J. Rothman is Bernard Schoenberg Professor of Social Medicine and Professor of History at Columbia University.

Thorsten Sellin was Emeritus Professor of Sociology, University of Pennsylvania.

Linda G. Smith is a faculty member at Kennesaw State University.

Pieter C. Spierenburg teaches in the Department of History at Erasmus University in Rotterdam, Holland.

Henry J. Steadman is President of Policy Research Associates in Delmar, New York.

Marc L. Steinberg is on the faculty of the Psychology Department, University of South Florida.

Gresham M. Sykes was director of the Administration of Justice Program in the College of Law at the University of Denver.

Lawrence F. Travis III is Professor of Criminal Justice and Director of the Center for Criminal Justice Research, University of Cincinnati.

Susan Turner is a senior researcher in the Criminal Justice Program at RAND in Santa Monica, California.

Michael S. Vaughn is on the faculty of Criminal Justice, Georgia State University.

Donald H. Wallace teaches in the Department of Criminal Justice at Central Missouri State University.

Terry Wells is in the Department of Government, Georgia College and State University in Milledgeville, Georgia.

Chris Wilkinson is a senior lecturer at the University of Leicester, Leicester, England.

Judith Wilks was Associate Director of the Center for Knowledge in Criminal Justice Planning at City College, City University of New York.

David B. Wilson is a Jerry Lee Assistant Research Professor, Department of Criminology and Criminal Justice, University of Maryland.

Frank A. Zeigler is a doctoral student and instructor in the College of Criminal Justice, Sam Houston State University.

Ivan Zinger is at Carleton University ✦

Introduction

Prior to the nineteenth century in the United States, the facility designed to hold offenders was largely regarded as a vehicle toward an ultimate end—punishment of some form or another for persons who had committed a crime against another individual. The punishment to be carried out was often a publicly held flogging, branding, disfigurement, or execution or a lengthy term in the stocks. After the brutality of these punishments was coupled with a philosophical societal shift (in the form of the Enlightenment), for all intents and purposes the penitentiary was born. From that point forward, punishment in the United States mainly comprised a term in an institution, living in congregate style with many other individuals who had met a similar fate. This is not to say, however, that the birth of the prison meant an end to somewhat brutal practices within the walls of the institution.

The original purpose of the early penitentiaries was to instill repentance in the offender (hence, the root of the term *penitent*). Reform was certainly the goal, but primarily by way of the errant offenders seeking forgiveness from God, through the (at times silent) contemplation of their 'sins.'

Since that time, the penitentiary has undergone many changes in both form and philosophy. Religious atonement was put aside and a concentration on skill development (through educational and vocational programming) took its place. In addition, other changes occurred in the U.S. sentencing structure, perhaps most notably the advent of the indeterminate sentence. This paved the way for what came to be known as the medical model. Offenders would be housed in prison until they "became better" or had been healed. Not surprisingly, this model rested on the assumption that the prison was able to identify, target, and change the factors that had led someone into criminal activity. In many instances, however, the indeterminate sentence has been replaced with a determinate sentencing structure (along with the instigation of the 'justice model') due to disparity in sentencing.

Life inside an institution (regardless of its size) provides a unique set of parameters around which the individual must conform and interact. As such, much study during the twentieth century was directed toward the effect that the institution has on individuals and groups. Similarly, researchers have studied how individuals and groups affect and shape the institution. This has held true for both inmates as well as correctional workers. Several hypotheses have been formulated and investigated regarding what the most important motive factors are in the prison environment. Because the prison is a "total institution," it has provided a somewhat self-contained "laboratory" for the student of human interaction. Until the mid-twentieth century, many never imagined that the offender could have an official impact on the day-to-day routine within the institution.

Although some have argued about details of the true beginning of significant inmate litigation (i.e., the prisoners' rights movement), some important changes occurred during the twentieth century that have influenced both prisons themselves as well as the numbers of individuals sent to them. Perhaps most notably, the courts have shown a willingness to check the conditions inside an institution. This refers to both physical and procedural conditions. The advent of these rights has served to change the prison experience for many offenders and has also brought forth issues regarding the institutions' ability to modify behavior in the long term (postrelease). Besides legislation regarding the rights of prison inmates, sentencing structures for many states have added the possibility of life imprisonment for third-time (usually violent) felony offenders. Introducing an increasingly larger group of 'lifers' will undoubtedly have lasting effects for many U.S. prisons especially in the buildings and grounds, in the daily routines, and in the availability of types of programming.

Legislation throughout the twentieth century (regarding both inmate rights and sentencing structure) has mirrored the public's faith in rehabilitation and treatment. Because the goal of prison has been to change the individuals living within its walls, much has been learned regarding what can invoke change. For example, it has become readily apparent that the rudimentary experience of being confined does little to change behavior in the long term. Not surprisingly, Martinson's research that revealed little to no effect for within-prison programming dealt a welcome blow to rehabilitative efforts during a time when indeterminate sentencing and sentence disparity were at issue in the public eye. Since that time, a significant amount of effort has been put forth toward examining what does work to create positive offender change, with lasting effects after release.

Several studies of offender treatment within institutions and in the community have revealed the efficancy of correctional treatment, provided it is the correct treatment directed toward the correct populations. Advances have been made in the areas of offender classification, and treatment mechanisms, for instance. Treatment programs regarding substance abuse, sexual offending, and educational/vocational training have been examined to specify in detail what works, and how. In addition, specific populations, such as mentally disordered offenders, and the growing number of female offenders that have been scrutinized in the same way.

Moreover, because raw prison populations have been increasing throughout the latter half of the twentieth century, more attention is being paid to the utility and effectiveness of parole release as well as aftercare in general. If parole release and aftercare strategies are kept in place, these populations will continue to burgeon as an echo to the steadily increasing prison population.

The willingness on the part of the American public to continue building prisons, as well as to keep on increasing the number of correctional options in general, may in some ways be a political unifier. Despite one's political affiliation, being tough on crime is regarded as a positive attribute for any candidate. However, being "tough" on crime has translated into new policies, not all of which are beneficial. For example, the proliferation of three strikes legislation may have severe impacts on the characteristics of America's prison population. Similarly, the arrival of the "supermax" prison and its methods of isolation bring many issues not dealt with before (or at least for several generations!). Furthermore, the death penalty continues to present issues that command the attention of the American public. The on-again-off-again relationship of the public with rehabilitative efforts has been "on" throughout the 1990s and beyond. This could change easily provided real results are not forthcoming. In general, America's "imprisonment binge" has forced several challenges to be confronted. This will undoubtedly shape the future of how our country houses and treats its offenders.

When considering the history and present of corrections in America, the only constant appears to be dynamic change. This pattern of change will likely continue to reflect what is going on in greater society in the form of creative new innovations, philosophies, and strategies. The essays in this book represent a sampling of some important works in corrections, both past and current. We believe the best future correctional approach will come from the use of objective scientific discovery, such as that exemplified by this volume. ✦

Part I

History of Punishment and Origins of Imprisonment

Perhaps one of the greatest and most complex social dilemmas has been the processing and treatment of the social deviant. Members of any society who do not follow rules and norms pose a natural threat to the group as a whole. Mechanisms and strategies have long been in place to deal with the errant; but the form and reason behind them have varied greatly over the centuries. However, the underlying goal has remained constant—finding ways in which to respond to and correct what can be a complex set of problems within each individual.

Although the traditional Auburn-style prison is perhaps the most common image representing punishment in the United States, dealing with offenders has a somewhat varied past. Prior to the nineteenth century, for instance, confinement was viewed as a means to an end, rather than an end in and of itself. Large-scale facilities designed to meet any correctional goal did not exist. Instead, confinement occurred briefly, prior to the actual punishment.

Pre-Enlightenment punishments were often Biblically based and corporal in nature. Brandings, whippings, stocks and pillories, ducking stools, thumbscrews, and execution were fashioned and performed to publicly humiliate offenders. Through pain and public humiliation, offenders were expected to atone for their social sins—sins committed against God, a monarch, and/or society. This served an assumed secondary goal of general deterrence. Public punishmen was in part a warning to others of their potential fate should they commit similar offenses.

There is no dispute that pre-Enlightenment punishment in general was severe. What often compunded the severity of the punishment were instances where the punishment clearly did not fit the crime. It was not uncommon for petty thefts, adultery, or vagrancy (just to name a few examples) to carry disproportionate and permanently (physically) disfiguring government responses. One of the social forces that created a correctional conversion was quite possibly public outrage at this disproportionate sentencing structure. Perhaps the desired effect of general deterrence created an unintended consequence of raising public awareness (and outcry) to what was perceived as an unfair state response to relatively minor behavior.

The Enlightenment brought about great change in the application of punishment, due in large part to thinkers such as Beccaria, Bentham, and Voltaire. The net effect of the writings of these philosophers and others was to draw attention to the brutality meted out by the state at that time. As a result, confinement itself was identified as a new "end" in the punishment spectrum. Housing offenders together in large-scale, secure facilities would allow for the accomplishment of different and apparently more humane goals.

In the United States, 1819 saw the birth of the penitentiary in Auburn, New York, with many other states soon implementing this correctional strategy. Although public floggings, drawing and quartering, and other forms of torture were placed aside, the conditions inside this first American prison were in many respects no less destructive.

Originally, prisoners were not afforded opportunities for activity (leisure or labor); they were kept in total isolation from one another and total silence was enforced. Provisions were minimal, conditions were dreary, and offenders were required to contemplate a sin-free (i.e., crime-free) lifestyle. The unfair humiliation and cruel disfiguring punishments largely criticized by Enlightenment philosophers had become a thing of the past. The alternative, however, resulted in punishment turning into a much longer, drawn-out affair with its own set of drawbacks, despite the over-arching goal that offenders should contemplate and ultimately reject a sinful lifestyle. Nevertheless, the Auburn-style prison set the stage for a new era in corrections—one that still determines practices of imprisonment.

In addition to a reconsideration of the delivery of punishment, the Enlightenment brought about other changes in the criminal justice system—principally, the seeds of due process. The nineteenth century also ushered in questions regarding the causation of crime (on both the individual and societal levels). The belief that human beings are indeed free to choose a criminal lifestyle further opened up the possibility that they can just as well choose a crime-free lifestyle.

Although the housing of offenders in large-scale penitentiaries was designed to invoke positive change, offenders were nonetheless viewed largely as slaves of the state.

Issues arose throughout the nineteenth and twentieth centuries, regarding the value of prison industrial labor, the management of increasing populations of offenders, and the challenges of handling a more diverse population with complex needs.

At several points during the nineteenth and twentieth centuries, the purposes and practices of imprisonment were reviewed and critiqued. Propositions were put forth questioning practices that inhibit the accomplishment of offender reform. This is of particular importance (even today) as correctional options thus were reduced to essentially one—imprisonment.

Over the past 200 years, the United States has relied heavily on imprisonment as the general population has swelled and as new crime enforcement strategies have boosted prisoner populations (e.g., the war on crime, the war on drugs, and three-strikes legislation). The dilemma of overcrowded prisons that may not be capable of rehabilitating has called into question the true utility of such a strategy. Hence, America's imprisonment binge is under consideration in hopes of revealing pathways toward improvement. The reader of the following selections is encouraged to take note of the true origins of modern-day punishment, especially the contributions from Enlightenment thinkers. The movement from arbitrary corporal punishment to methods of mass confinement may be viewed as an improvement in some respects. However, the long-term consequences brought on by the accompanying set of problems caused by large-scale imprisonment are deserving of more thought. ✦

1
The Spectacle of Suffering

Pieter C. Spierenburg

Peter C. Spierenburg reveals the origins of the criminal justice system through an investigation of the beginnings of state-enforced punishment. The feudal system in Western Europe provides the backdrop for what ultimately represents a shift away from personal vengeance as the primary impetus for punishment. Criminal behavior came to be viewed as a sin against the state, rather than a sin against another individual. As such, it became the state's responsibility to regulate the processing of offenders. Secondary to the rise of the nation-state as a precursor of state-enforced punishment is urbanization. Although urbanization may have provided an initial opportunity for greater public display of punishment that was rooted in general deterrence, it was ultimately the revulsion of the public that led to what Spierenburg calls the privatization of repression. Above all else, Spierenburg highlights the importance of considering the greater social context when analyzing major changes in a society's punishing mechanisms.

The Emergence of Criminal Justice

From the way in which I have defined repression, it is obvious that its evolution should be intimately connected with the development of the state. The practice of criminal justice was one of the means by which authorities, with or without success, attempted to keep the population in line. As the position of these authorities changed, the character of criminal justice changed. However, before we can speak of criminal justice in any society, at least a rudimentary state organization has to be present. A system of repression presupposes a minimal level of state formation. Differentiation of this system, moreover, also presupposes the rise of towns. This . . .is an attempt to trace the origins of preindustrial repression. . . . It focuses on repression as a system of control, the emergence of which was a function of the rise of territorial principalities and of urbanization.

At the height of the feudal age in Western Europe the state hardly existed at all. Violent entrepreneurs were in constant competition; from his castle a baron would dominate the immediate surroundings and de facto recognize no higher authority. His domain may be called a unit of attack and defense but not a state. Essentially it comprised a network of ties of affiliation and bondage. But in the violent competition between the numerous chiefs of such networks the mechanism was imminent which would eventually lead to the emergence of states. The first units with the character of a state were the territorial principalities which appeared from the twelfth century onwards.

As it happens, the emergence of criminal justice also dates from the twelfth century. Several legal historians have studied the "birth of punishment" or "emergence of public penal law." The most detailed work is by P. W. A. Immink. This author also comes closest to a sociological-historical view of the subject. He placed the origins of punishment in the context of changing relationships of freedom and dependence in feudal society. Thus he avoided presenting an analysis of legal texts alone, which can be very misleading especially for the period in question. From a sociological-historical perspective, the essence of criminal justice is a relationship of subordination. This was noted by Immink:

Excerpts from *The Spectacle of Suffering* by Pieter C. Spierenburg, pp. 1–12, 200–207. Copyright © 1984 by Cambridge University Press. Reprinted by permission.

"In common parlance the term 'punishment' is never used unless the person upon whom the penalty is inflicted is clearly subordinate to the one imposing the penal act." This is the crucial point. This element distinguishes punishment from vengeance and the feud, where the parties are equal. If there is no subordination, there is no punishment.

The earliest subordinates in Europe were slaves. In that agrarian society, from Germanic times up into the feudal period, freemen were not subject to a penal system, but unfree persons were. The lord of a manor exercised an almost absolute authority over his serfs. When the latter were beaten or put to death "or maybe even fined" for some illegal act, this can certainly be called punishment. The manorial penal system of those early ages belonged to the realm of custom and usually did not form part of written law. Therefore we do not know much about it. The Barbarian Codes (*Leges Barbarorum*) were meant for freemen. They only referred to unfree persons in cases where their actions could lead to a conflict between freemen.

Free persons, on the other hand, settled their conflicts personally. There were a few exceptions to this, even in Germanic times. In certain cases, if a member was held to have acted against the vital interests of the tribe, he could be expelled from the tribal community (branded a "wolf") or even killed. But on the whole, as there was no arbiter strong enough to impose his will, private individuals settled their own conflicts. A settlement could be reached through revenge or reconciliation. Vengeance and the feud were accepted forms of private retaliation, but they did not necessarily follow every injury. In a situation where violence is not monopolized, private violence is potentially omnipresent but does not always manifest itself in practice. Notably, it can be bought off. Reconciliation through payment to the injured party was already known in Tacitus' time.

To the earliest powerful rulers who represented an embryonic public authority, encouragement of this custom was the obvious road to be taken if they wished to reduce private violence. This is in fact what the Barbarian Codes are all about. In every instance they fix the amount which can buy off vengeance. These sums are not fines in the modern sense, but indemnities. They were either meant as compensation when a person had been killed, wounded or assaulted (*wergeld*) or as a form of restitution when property had been stolen, destroyed or damaged. Among freemen this remained the dominant system well into the twelfth century.

Criminal justice, however, slowly developed alongside this system. Its evolution during the feudal period was construed by Immink as one argument against the thesis put forward by Viktor Achter. The latter had argued that punishment suddenly emerged in Languedoc in the middle of the twelfth century, from where it spread to the rest of Europe. Although Immink placed the definite breakthrough around the same time, he believed the evolution of punishment was inextricably linked with feudalism. The feudalization of Western Europe had brought about a fundamental change in the notion of freedom. This change eventually led to the emergence of criminal justice.

Before the feudal age the notion of freedom was closely connected to the allod. An allod should not be considered as a piece of property in the modern sense, but rather as an estate which is free from outside interference. Its occupant is completely his own master. His freedom implies a total independence from any worldly power and is similar to what later came to be called sovereignty. Hence the relationship of a freeman with the unfree persons subject to him, and over whom he exercises a right of punishment, is not one of owner-owned but one of ruler-ruled. The development of the institution of vassalage slowly put an end to the notion of freedom based on the allod. The Frankish kings and their successors attached freemen to themselves in a relationship of lord and *fideles*. Hence the latter were no longer entirely independent. By the time the whole network of feudal ties had finally been established, the notion of freedom had been transformed. Freedom meant being bound directly to the king, or to be more precise, there were degrees of freedom depending on how direct the allegiance was.

The feudal transformation of the notion of freedom formed the basis of the emergence of a penal system applied to freemen. The king remained the only free person in the ancient allodial sense, the only sovereign. His reaction to a breach of faith by his vassal (*infidelitas*, felony), usually the imposition of death, can truly be called punishment. The king himself never had a *wergeld*, because no one was his equal. His application of punishment for *infidelitas* resembled the exercise of justice by a master over his serfs. When more and more illegal acts were defined as felonies, the emergence of a penal system with corporal and capital punishments applied to freemen became steadily more apparent.

The implication of Immink's analysis for the study of state formation processes is evident. Absence of a central authority is reflected in the prevalence of private vengeance, the feud or voluntary reconciliation. The development of criminal justice runs parallel to the emergence of slightly stronger rulers. Originally it is only practiced within the confines of a manor; later it is applied by the rulers of kingdoms and territories. But we do not have to accept every part of Immink's story. For one thing, in his description the evolution of criminal justice and the parallel decline of the feud appeared too much as an unlinear process. This follows partly from his criticism of Achter. The latter, for instance, saw the legal reforms of the Carolingian period as a precocious spurt in the direction of a breakthrough of a modern notion of punishment. This would be in line with the fact that this period also witnessed a precocious sort of monopoly of authority. Achter considered the spurt as an isolated episode followed by centuries of silence. This may be too crude. Immink, however, with his conception of an ultimate continuity, seems to go too far in the other direction, playing down the unsettled character of the ninth and tenth centuries. These were certainly times when the vendetta was prevalent, despite whatever intentions legislators might have harbored. On the other hand, we should not overestimate the degree of monopolization of authority around AD 800. The Carolingian Empire and its successor kingdoms were no more than temporary sets of allegiances over a wide geographic area, held together by the personal prestige of an individual king or by a military threat from outside. From Roman times until the twelfth century Europe witnessed nothing approaching a state, but there were certainly spurts in that direction.

In the middle of the twelfth century the first territorial principalities made their appearance and a penal system applied to freemen was established. The symbiosis is evident. Criminal justice emerged because the territorial princes were the first rulers powerful enough to combat private vengeance to a certain degree. The church had already attempted to do so, but largely in vain. I leave aside the question of whether its representatives were motivated by ideological reasons or by the desire to protect ecclesiastical goods. In any case they needed the strong arm of secular powers in order to succeed. The *treuga Dei* only acquired some measure of effectiveness when it became the "country's peace." Two of the earliest regions to witness this development were Angevin England "which can also be seen as a territorial principality" and the duchy of Aquitaine.

Incidentally, the South of France is also the region where, according to Achter, the concept of punishment originated. It is interesting that he reached this conclusion even though he used quite different sources and from a different perspective. Achter considered the element of moral disapproval as the essence of punishment. This notion was largely absent from Germanic law, which did not differentiate between accidents and intentional acts. If a felled tree accidentally killed a man the full *wergeld* still had to be paid. Immink criticized this view and it may be another point where his rejection is too radical. He indicated, in fact, how Achter's view can be integrated into an approach focusing on state-formation processes. For the private avenger redressing a personal wrong, the wickedness of the other party is so self-evident that it need not be stated. As long as the law merely attempts to encourage reconciliation, it is likewise indifferent to a moral appreciation of the acts which started the conflict. When territorial lords begin to administer punishments to persons who have not wronged them personally, their attitudes to the law change as well. Theorizing about the law increases. The beginnings of a distinction between civil and criminal cases become apparent. The latter are *iniquitates*, acts that are to be disapproved of morally and which put their author at the *misericordia* of his lord.

Thus it is understandable that a new emphasis on the moral reprehensibility of illegal acts also dates from the middle of the twelfth century. Indeed this period witnessed an early wave of moralization-individualization, connected to what medievalists have long been accustomed to call the Renaissance of the twelfth century. And yet we should not overestimate this spurt towards individualization, certainly not with regard to penal practice. Before the twelfth century there may have been even less concern for the motives and intentions of the perpetrators of illegal acts, but . . . the practice of criminal justice continued to focus on crimes and their impact on the community rather than on the criminal's personality and the intricacies of his guilt. Up into the nineteenth century repression was not primarily individualized.

There is another aspect of the transformation under discussion which merits attention. When a malefactor finds himself at the mercy (*misericordia*) of a prince, the implication is that a religious notion has entered criminal justice. Mercy was an attribute of God, the ultimate judge. The relationship of all people with God had always been viewed as one of subordination. Hence God was indeed able to punish. Any wrong suffered, such as the loss of a combat, could be seen as a divine punishment, of which another man was merely the agent. Heavenly justice was never an automatic response. The Lord could be severe or show mercy. By analogy this line of thought was also applied to human justice practiced by a territorial lord.

Several authors discussed the "sacred quality" of preindustrial punishment and even considered it an explanatory factor for its character. According to this view, executions, especially capital ones, were a sort of sacrifice, an act of expiation. They reconciled the deity offended by the crime and restored the order of society sanctioned by heaven. This notion may have been part of the experience of executions, although there is little direct evidence for it. But it would certainly be incorrect to attribute an explanatory value to it as being in some way the essence of public punishment. For one thing, during and after the Middle Ages *every* social event also had a religious element. In the absence of a division between the sacred and the profane, religion pervaded life entirely. To note the sacred quality of executions in this context is actually redundant. If a religious view of the world has to "explain" public punishment in any way, it should do so in a more specific sense. But the evolution which gave rise to criminal justice hardly lends support to this view. Criminal justice arose out of changing relationships of freedom and dependence in the secular world. It was extended by powerful princes at the expense of vengeance and the feud. Ecclesiastics had indeed already advocated harsh corporal penalties in the tenth century. But they too favored these merely as alternatives to the vendetta. Their wishes were realized by the territorial princes of the twelfth century. Only then, when powerful lords applied a new form of justice, did notions of mercy, guilt and moral reprehensibility enter the picture; rather as a consequence than as a cause of the transformation. That clergymen should figure in the drama on the scaffold during the next centuries is only natural. As will be argued in this study, the role of the church remained largely instrumental in a spectacle which primarily served the purposes of the secular authorities.

The transformation during the twelfth century was only a small beginning. First, private vengeance had been pushed back to a certain degree, but continued to be practiced throughout the later Middle Ages. Second, generally the various courts were not in a very powerful position. Often they acted merely as mediators facilitating the reconciliation of the parties involved. A resolute practice of criminal justice depended as before on a certain measure of state power and levels of state power continued to fluctuate. But state formation is not the only process to which the further development of criminal justice was linked. A new factor entered the stage: urbanization. During the later Middle Ages the peculiar conditions prevailing in towns increasingly made their mark on the practice of justice. This situation was not equally marked everywhere. In a country such as France alterations in criminal procedure largely ran parallel with the growth of royal power. In the Netherlands, on the other hand, the towns were the major agents of change.

During the early stages of urban development the social context actually formed a counter-influence to the establishment of criminal justice. Originally, relationships of subordination did not prevail in cities. The charters of most towns recognized the inhabitants as free citizens. It has long been commonplace in historiography to note that the urban presence was encapsulated into feudal society. The body of citizens became the vassal, as it were, of the lord of the territory. The town was often a relatively independent corporation, a *coniuratio*. Vis-à-vis each other the citizens were equal. The councils ruling these cities were not very powerful. There were hardly any authorities in a real sense, who could impose their will and control events.

This situation left plenty of room for private violence. As the degree of pacification around the towns was still relatively low, so was the degree of internal pacification. To be sure, the vendetta might be officially forbidden. In the Northern Netherlands the prohibition was legitimized by the notion of a quasi-lineage: the citizens were held to be mutual relatives and a feud cannot arise among relatives. But the fiction of lineage could never prevent actual feuds from bursting out, as the prohibitions, reiterated well into the fifteenth century, suggest. Similarly, proclamations ordering a truce between parties were frequent until the middle of the sixteenth century. An early seventeenth-century commentator gives a good impression of the situation. Speaking of the 1390s, he denounces the lawlessness of the age:

> The people were still rough and wild in this time because of their newly won freedom and practically everyone acted as he pleased. And for that reason the court had neither the esteem nor the power which it ought to have in a well-founded commonwealth. This appears from the homicides, fights and wanton acts which occurred daily and also from the old sentences, in which one sees with what kind of timidity the Gentlemen judged in such cases: for they bargained first and took an oath from the criminals that they would not do *schout*, *schepenen* and burgomasters harm because of whatever sentence they would pass against them. And the most severe, almost, which they imposed on someone, was a banishment or that the criminals would make a pilgrimage here or there before they came in [to town] again, or that they would give the city money for three or four thousand stones. They also often licensed one or the other, if he was under attack from his party, that he might defend himself with impunity, even if he killed the other in doing so. These are things which have no place in cities where the law is in its proper position of power.

Apart from the fact that this situation was considered abnormal in the seventeenth century, we note an acceptance of forms of private violence and the predominance of a reconciliatory stand instead of serious punishment.

Towards the end of the fifteenth century, however, this began to change. The ruling elites finally became real authorities. Patriciates emerged everywhere, constituting a socially superior group. The towns became increasingly stratified. The patrician courts could act as superiors notably towards the lower and lower-middle class citizens. In the towns of the Netherlands this development is clearly reflected in their ways of dealing with criminal cases. For a long time the main business of the courts had been to mediate and register private reconciliations. Around 1500 "corrections" gradually outnumbered reconciliations. The former were measures expressing a justice from above and often consisted of corporal punishment.

Another development in criminal law which took place during the same period, was even more crucial. A new procedure in criminal trials, the inquisitorial, gradually superseded the older, accusatory procedure. This change occurred throughout Continental Europe, but not in England. The accusatory trial, when nothing else existed, was geared to a system of marginal justice. Where the inquisitorial trial prevailed, a justice from above had been established more firmly.

The contrast between the two procedures is a familiar item in legal history. Here it suffices to review briefly the relevant characteristics. The inquisitorial procedure had been developed in ecclesiastical law, and was perfected by the institution which took its name from it. From the middle of the thirteenth century onwards it entered into secular law. Generally speaking, the rules of the accusatory trial favored the accused, while the rules of the inquisitorial one favored those bent on condemning him. The former procedure was much concerned with the preservation of equality between the parties. Thus if the accused was imprisoned during the trial "which was not usually the case" the accuser

was often imprisoned as well. Moreover, if the latter could not prove his case, he might be subjected to the *talion*: the same penalty which the former would have received if he had been convicted. While the proceedings in the older trial were carried out in the open, the newer one was conducted in secrecy. Publicity was only sought after the verdict had been reached.

The most important element of the inquisitorial procedure, however, was the possibility of prosecution *ex officio*. The adage of the older procedure, "no plaintiff, no judge," lost its validity. If it wished to, the court could take the initiative and start an investigation (*inquisitio*). Its officials would collect denunciations and then arrest a suspect, if they could lay hands on him. The court's prosecutor acted as plaintiff. Thus an active prosecution policy was possible for the first time. In the trial the authorities and the accused faced each other and the power distribution between the two was unequal, favoring the former. Under the accusatory procedure the authorities had hardly been more than bystanders. Consequently the rise of the newer form of trial meant a further spread of a system of justice from above.

This is also implicit in the final element to be noted. The inquisitorial procedure brought the introduction of torture. An accused who persisted in denial, yet was heavily suspect, could be subjected to a "sharper examination." It is evident that the principle of equality between parties under the accusatory procedure would have been incompatible with the practice of torture. Torture was not unknown in Europe before the thirteenth century. It had long been a common feature of the administration of justice by a lord over his serfs. Under the inquisitorial procedure torture could for the first time also be applied to free persons. The parallel with the transformation discussed above is obvious.

The retreat of the accusatory before the inquisitorial procedure did not occur at the same pace everywhere. That the older one was originally more common is reflected in the names of "ordinary" and "extraordinary" procedure which the two forms acquired and often retained throughout the *ancien regime*. The gradual establishment of the primacy of the latter took place between the middle of the thirteenth and the beginning of the sixteenth century. Its use in France by Philip the Fair against the Templars paved the way for its further spread. Prosecution *ex officio* increased in importance from the fourteenth to the sixteenth centuries. The growth of royal power was the main force behind it. In the Netherlands, North and South, the cities formed the most important theater. The formation of patrician elites facilitated the shift. But here too the central authorities confirmed it. In 1570, when the Dutch Revolt was already in the process of breaking out, Philip II issued his criminal ordinances, which clearly favored the inquisitorial trial.

In the Dutch towns non-residents were the first to be tried according to the inquisitorial procedure. As outsiders they were more easily subjected to justice from above. Citizens occasionally put up resistance to it, in Malines, for example. In France it was the nobles of Burgundy, Champagne and Artois who protested. Louis X granted them privileges in 1315 which implied a suspension of inquisitorial proceedings. In the end they were unsuccessful. The forces of centralization and urbanization favored the development of a more rigorous penal system.

England forms a partial exception. Criminal procedure in that country remained largely accusatory throughout the preindustrial period. Nevertheless, essentially these developments can be observed there too, and in the end processes of pacification and centralization brought about a firmer establishment of criminal justice. Originally there had been plenty of room for private violence, just as on the Continent. An outlaw or "wolf," for instance, could be captured by any man and be slain if he resisted. This right was abrogated in 1329, but as late as 1397 a group of men who had arrested and beheaded an outlawed felon, were pardoned because they

had thought it was lawful. Around 1400 it was not uncommon for justices to be threatened with violence by the parties in a lawsuit. The power of the courts went up and down with the fluctuations in the power of a central authority. It was the Tudors, finally, who gradually established a monopoly of violence over most of England. Consequently, except in border areas, the feud definitely gave way to litigation. The available literature on crime and justice in early modern England suggests that a system of prosecution of serious crimes, physical punishment and exemplary repression prevailed there, which was basically similar to that on the Continent.

Thus, the emergence and stabilization of criminal justice, a process going on from the late twelfth until the early sixteenth centuries, meant the disappearance of private vengeance. Ultimately vengeance was transferred from the victims and their relatives to the state. Whereas formerly a man would kill his brother's murderer or beat up the thief he caught in his house, these people were now killed or flogged by the authorities. Legal texts from late medieval Germany sometimes explicitly refer to the punishments imposed by the authorities as "vengeance." Serious illegal acts, which up until then had been dealt with in the sphere of revenge and reconciliation, were redefined as being directed not only against the victims but also against the state. In this process the inquisitorial procedure was the main tool. Its increase in frequency in fourteenth-century Venice, for instance, went hand in hand with the conquest of the vendetta. Private violence by members of the community coming to the assistance of a victim was similarly pushed back. In the Netherlands a thief caught redhanded could be arrested by anyone. His captors were obliged to hand him over to the court, but they might seriously harass him and were often excused if they killed him. This "right" retreated too before the increase of prosecution *ex officio*.

It would be incorrect to assume that the state's arm was all-embracing during the early modern period. An active prosecution policy remained largely confined to the more serious crimes. Private vengeance had been conquered, but reconciliation survived in cases of petty theft and minor violence. The mediators were no longer the courts but prestigious members of local communities. The infra-judicial resolution of conflicts prevailed beneath the surface of justice from above. Historians have only recently come to realize this and the phenomenon has only been studied in detail in France.

This "subterranean stream" was kept in motion from two sides. The authorities, though able to take the initiative, restricted their efforts to specific cases. Prosecution policy was often concentrated on vagrants and other notorious groups. The near-absence of a professional police force further limited the court's scope. Hence many petty offenders were left undisturbed. The attitude of local residents also contributed to this situation. Victims of thefts and acts of violence did not often take recourse to the judiciary. One reason was that a trial might be too costly for the potential plaintiff. Another reason was that numerous conflicts arising from violent exchanges or disputes over property were not viewed in terms of crime and the court was not considered the most appropriate place to settle them. Mediation was sought from non-judicial arbiters. This form of infra-judicial reconciliation survived until the end of the *ancien regime*. Thus preindustrial repression was never an automatic response to all sorts of illegal acts.

Relics of private vengeance can also be observed in the early modern period. This is attested by the public's reaction to property offenders in Republican Amsterdam. The archival sources regularly make mention of a phenomenon called *maling*. From it a picture emerges of communal solidarity against thieves. Events always followed a similar pattern. A person in the street might notice that his pocket was picked or he might be chasing after someone who had intruded into his house. Soon bystanders rushed to help him and the thief was surrounded by a hostile crowd. The people harassed and beat him and forced him to surrender the stolen goods. The thief was then usually thrown into a canal. Servants of justice were often said to have saved his life by arresting him, which meant getting him out of the hands of the crowd or out of the water. Memories of the medieval treatment of thieves caught redhanded were apparently still alive. The authorities tolerated it but did not recognize a form of popular justice. In 1718 a man was condemned for throwing stones at servants of justice when they were busy saving a woman, who was in the *maling*, from her assailants. Comparable forms of self-help by the community against thieves existed in eighteenth-century Languedoc.

. . .[T]he emergence of criminal justice was not a function of changing sensibilities. These only started to play a role later. If corporal and capital penalties increased in frequency from the twelfth to the sixteenth centuries, this certainly cannot be taken as reflecting an increased taste for the sight of violence and suffering. It was primarily a consequence of the growth and stabilization of a system of criminal justice. Conversely, whatever resistance may have been expressed against the transformation . . .did not spring from an abhorrence of violent dealings as such. Physical punishment was simply introduced into a world which was accustomed to the infliction of physical injury and suffering. In that sense it was not an alien element. The authorities took over the practice of vengeance from private individuals. As private retaliation had often been violent, so was the penal system adopted by the authorities. Similarly, as the first had always been a public affair, so was the second. Attitudes to violence remained basically the same. Huizinga demonstrated the medieval acceptance of violence more than sixty years ago and recent research confirms his view. Thus "to mention only a few" Barbara Hanawalt gets the "impression of a society in which men were quick to give insult and to retaliate with physical attack." Norman Cohn recalls the violent zeal with which self-appointed hunters of heretics proceeded, such as the two who managed to reverse God's dictum at the destruction of Sodom and Gomorrah: "We would gladly burn a hundred, if just one among them were guilty."

It is understandable that in such a climate of acceptance of violence no particular sensitivity prevailed towards the sufferings of convicts. This arose only later. Urban and territorial rulers had to ensure that people accepted the establishment of criminal justice. But once they had accomplished that, they did not encounter psychological barriers against the full deployment of a penal system based on open physical treatment of delinquents. By the middle of the sixteenth century a more or less stable repression had been established in most of Western Europe. It did not exclusively consist of exemplary physical punishments. Banishment was important as well and confinement would soon appear on the scene. From that time on it was possible for changing sensibilities within society to affect the modes of repression. From that time too the development of states and the ensuing pacification produced domesticated elites and changed mentalities. These would eventually lead to a transformation of repression. . . .

State Formation and Modes of Repression

Modes of repression belong to the history of mentalities. They reflect the elites' willingness to deal in one way or another with persons exhibiting undesirable behavior. The sort of repression which is advocated or tolerated in a particular society is an indication of the psychic make-up of its members. Publicity and the infliction of physical suffering were the two main elements of the penal system of the *ancien regime*. They should be understood as part of the mental atmosphere prevailing in preindustrial Western Europe. Many events in social life, from childbirth to dying, had a more open character, while with

regard to physical suffering in general, a greater lack of concern prevailed than is current today. This mentality was never static; it began to crumble from the seventeenth century onwards. Simultaneously, repression was changed too.

In this study the routine character of seventeenth- and eighteenth-century executions has been demonstrated. From about 1600 the seeds of the later transformation of repression were manifest. The two elements, publicity and suffering, slowly retreated. The disappearance of most forms of mutilation of non-capital convicts constituted the clearest example. An equally important expression of the retreat was the spread of houses of correction; a theme which could not be discussed here. A slight uneasiness about executions among the elites in the second half of the seventeenth century has also been shown. These developments all anticipated the more fundamental change in sensibilities which set in after the middle of the eighteenth century: an acceleration which led to the privatization of repression. The acceleration after the middle of the eighteenth century had a parallel in other areas of the history of mentalities. Processes of privatization are notably reflected in the rise of the domesticated nuclear family.

I am explaining the evolution of modes of repression with reference to processes of state formation. The latter do not of course belong to the history of mentalities; we enter the field of human organization. State formation and such events as the rise and fall of social strata comprise a separate area of societal development. . . . Norbert Elias offered a model for the interdependence of developments in the two fields. I indicate the revisions to be made in the model: notably the shift in emphasis from single states to the rise of a European network of states. In early modern Europe this network extended its influence to areas, such as the Dutch Republic, which lagged behind in centralization. There too a relative pacification produced domesticated elites. On the other hand, the stability of the early modern states remained vulnerable, and this holds true for both patrician republics and absolute monarchies. Ultimately, however, the early modern state was transformed almost everywhere into the nation-state; in Britain, France and the Netherlands among others. These developments provide the key for understanding the evolution of repression in Europe.

This study has continually emphasized the functions which public executions had for the authorities. . . . [L]ate medieval and early modern executions served especially to underline the power of the state. They were meant to be an exemplary manifestation of this power, precisely because it was not yet entirely taken for granted. This explains the two basic elements of the preindustrial penal system. Publicity was needed because the magistrates' power to punish had to be made concretely visible: hence the ceremony, the display of corpses and the refusal to refrain from executions in the tense situation after riots. That public penalties usually involved the infliction of physical suffering is in tune with their function as a manifestation of the power of the magistrates. Physical punishment achieved a very direct sort of exemplarity. The authorities held a monopoly of violence and showed this by actually using it. The spectators, who lived in a relatively pacified state but did not yet harbor a modern attitude towards the practice of violence, understood this. Public executions represented *par excellence* that function of punishment which later came to be called "general prevention."

So far the relationship has been demonstrated largely in a static context: It can be further clarified if we consider the dynamics. . . . [T]he beginnings of criminal justice were intertwined with the beginnings of state formation and, to a lesser extent, with urbanization. Gradually urban and territorial authorities conquered the vendetta and limited private reconciliation. They started to protect their servant, the executioner, and attempted "though unsuccessfully" to raise his status. The magistrates became the agents who exercised justice.

Public executions first served to seal the transfer of vengeance from private persons to the state. The justice which the authorities displayed served to bolster up their precarious position. They were preoccupied with the maintenance of a highly unstable and geographically limited monopoly of violence well into the sixteenth century. When these monopolies became slightly more stable and crystallized into dynastic states or oligarchic republics uniting a larger area, new considerations came to the fore. Control of the monopoly had to be defended against real or imagined incursions. Bandits and armed vagabonds were still omnipresent. Maintaining the dominance over lower strata and marginal groups was another pressing concern.

Thus, the display of physical punishment as a manifestation of authority was still considered indispensable in the early modern period, because the existing states were still relatively unstable in comparison to later times. In other words, the spectacle of suffering was to survive until a certain degree of stability had been reached. The spectacle was part of the *raison d'etat*. I note this in connection with the penalty of sword over head for semi-homicide in the Netherlands. The peace of the community stood more centrally in dealing with crime than today. Hence the existence of a category such as "half guilty," which would be inconceivable in modern criminal law. Similar considerations applied to torture. In the second half of the eighteenth century, when opinions *pro* and *contra* were both expressed, this becomes eminently clear. The reformers, placing an individual person at the center of their considerations, argued that he could be either guilty or innocent. It made torture unnecessary since innocent persons should not be hurt and those found guilty should simply receive their punishment. The defenders of torture argued from a different point of view. They stuck to an intermediate category of serious suspicion. The heavily suspect were dangerous to the community, so that it was lawful to subject them to torture. This argument is based on the *raison d'etat*, where the security of the community takes precedence.

The relative instability was not the sole characteristic of early modern states that explains the nature of repression. A second one, also inherited from the later Middle Ages, was equally important. It is the personal element in wielding authority. . . . In the later Middle Ages the preservation of authority was often directly dependent on the person of the ruler. This was illustrated by urban ordinances which put a higher penalty on acts of violence if committed when the lord was in town. In the early modern period this personal element was not as outspoken as it had been before, but it continued to make its mark on the character of the state. A crime was a breach of the king's peace. Public executions constituted the revenge of the offended sovereign.

The personal element should not be viewed as referring exclusively to the king or sovereign. If that were the case, the fact that public executions in countries ruled by patrician elites "such as the Dutch Republic and eighteenth-century England" did not differ significantly from those in France and in German principalities, would be inexplicable. In France the state meant the king and his representatives; judges in the royal courts, for instance. In the Netherlands the state meant the gentlemen assembled in The Hague, the Prince of Orange or the burgomasters of Amsterdam. Foucault's image of physical punishment as the king's branding-mark is relatively well known. But the marks usually represented the jurisdiction. The symbol was equally forceful in a patrician republic. The reaction to the removal of a body from Amsterdam's gallows field . . .is revealing. The magistrates considered such a body as the property of the city and saw the removal as a theft. The inhabitants of urban and rural communities, also in dynastic states, must have associated authority—perhaps even in the first place—with local magistrates. The conspicuous presence of these magistrates at executions sealed the relationship.

These observations, finally, bring a solution to the problem of the disappearance of public executions. They suggest that a transformation of the state constitutes the explanatory factor. Indeed other transformations are less likely candidates. It would be futile, for instance, to relate the change to industrialization. In many countries the privatization of repression preceded the breakthrough of an industrial society. This chronology is evident in the case of the Netherlands. In England, on the other hand, public executions were still a common spectacle when industrialism was already fully developed. The situation produced hybrid combinations of modern transport and traditional punishment, especially in the larger cities. For a hanging in Liverpool the railway company advertised special trains ("parties of pleasure"), departing from the manufacturing towns. The chronology of industrialization varied from country to country, while the retreat of public executions took place almost everywhere between about 1770 and about 1870. Similarly, the transition from the early modern to the nation-state also occurred in most Western European countries in this period.

Thus, the closing of the curtains can be explained with reference to state formation processes as well. We may schematically divide the inherent transformation of sensibilities into two phases. The first comprised the emergence of an aversion to the sight of physical punishment and a consequent criticism of the penal system among certain groups from the aristocracy and the bourgeoisie. This aversion became manifest in the late eighteenth century and was a result of processes of conscience formation. The relative pacification reached in the early modern states cleared the way for the appearance of domesticated elites. The psychic changes which they underwent first found an expression in a refinement of manners and restraints in social intercourse. But the slight sensitivity to public justice that was already manifest before 1700 prefigured later developments. Originally, psychic controls were largely confined to a context of one's own group. Emotions and aggressive impulses were hardly restrained with regard to inferior classes. This situation altered gradually. In the course of the early modern period mutual dependence between social groups increased. Consequently, the context of psychic controls widened. Once more I should note the importance of the identification aspect: an increase in mutual identification between social groups took place. This increase certainly had its setbacks. . . .[T]he Amsterdam magistrates became "within the confines of the general standard of the period" slightly harsher towards delinquents between 1650 and 1750 due to their increasing social distance from the classes they ruled. This can also be understood as a temporary decrease in identification of rulers with the ruled. But in the long run this identification grew stronger. By the end of the eighteenth century an unknown number of individuals among the elites had reached a new stage and identified to a certain degree with convicts on the scaffold. These delicate persons disliked the sight of physical suffering: even that of the guilty. The first phase of the transformation of sensibilities had set in.

This first phase, so it appeared, resulted from developments that took place within the context of the early modern state. It did not immediately produce a major reform of the penal system. Two ancient features of repression disappeared though: torture and exposure of corpses. Abolition of the latter custom was often part of revolutionary measures. The gallows field symbolized a monopoly of justice particularly within an urban or regional context. The image of the individual city or county as a relatively independent entity had eroded during the seventeenth and eighteenth centuries. The final blow was long overdue. It came everywhere as a direct consequence of the downfall of the *ancien regime.*

The early modern state, however, did not disappear overnight in the Revolutionary period. The final establishment of the nation-state in Western Europe took most of the nineteenth century. The second phase of the transformation of sensibilities set in parallel to it. Repugnance to the sight of physical punishment spread and intensified. In the end the "political conclusion" was drawn and public executions were abolished. The privatization of repression had been completed.

It could be completed because the nation-state lacked the two essential elements of which public executions had been a function. The nation-state, because of closer integration of geographic areas and wider participation of social groups, was much more stable than the early modern state. And the liberal/bourgeois regimes, with their increasingly bureaucratized agencies, had a much more impersonal character. Hence the later nineteenth century witnessed more impersonal and less visible modes of repression. Public executions were not only felt to be distasteful; they were no longer necessary. In its internal affairs the nation-state could largely do without the *raison d'etat.* Beccaria had anticipated the transformation a century earlier. His often-quoted saying that effective prevention of crime depends on the certainty of being caught rather than on the severity of punishment was actually a plea for a stronger state, and in particular for a police force. This was realized in the nation-state. Consequently the authorities could afford to show a milder and more liberal face.

Once more it should be emphasized that absolutes do not exist. Even the privatized repression which emerged in the course of the nineteenth century needed a minimum of exemplarity. We find it expressed, for instance, in the location of prisons on a conspicuous spot where a road or railway entered a town. In an indirect way punishment remained public. L. O. Pike, writing in 1876, reminded his readers that a secondhand impression of a whipping indoors was occasionally brought home to the public by the press. Indirect knowledge of the death penalty, executed within prison walls, remained alive.

National variations in the chronology of the disappearance of public executions must be related to national singularities. The relative importance of the two elements, stability and impersonal rule, may also have varied. In England, for instance, the first half of the nineteenth century was the period of the great public order panic. Thereafter only occasional outbursts of fear occurred and a relative orderliness prevailed. No doubt this situation made the completion of the privatization of repression easier. The kingdom of the Netherlands, on the other hand, was relatively peaceful. The old patrician elites, however, largely dominated the scene until the middle of the nineteenth century. Shortly thereafter the abolition of public executions was a fact. Around the same time the system of public order maintenance was also depersonalized and acquired a more bureaucratic character. These remarks about the specifics of the transformation are of a hypothetical nature and call for detailed research. The continuation of public guillotining in France until 1939 likewise needs a separate explanation.

The fact that the completion of the privatization of repression took about two-thirds of the nineteenth century in most Western European countries adds up to a critique of Foucault's views. He pictures early nineteenth-century imprisonment as suddenly and almost totally replacing a penal system directed at the display of the human body. The new penal system, and especially solitary confinement, was also directed at the mind. It is true that a widespread enthusiasm for "moral treatment" prevailed in the first half of the nineteenth century. But the penitentiary cannot be considered as the successor to public executions. The observations of the present study make the conclusion inescapable: classical nineteenth-century imprisonment represented an experimental phase contemporary to the last days of public executions. Several authors emphasize that the middle of the nineteenth century was the heyday of the penitentiary and solitary confinement, after which the enthusiasm declined. Of course executions were less frequent at the time, but this is not relevant to the argument. From a quantitative viewpoint they had always been in the minority, though they were the pearl in the crown of repression. In the course of the nineteenth century public physical punishment was increasingly questioned. This coincided with experiments in new penal methods such as solitary confinement. The experiments were discontinued and public executions disappeared. Routine imprisonment succeeded "with capital punishment indoors for a few heinous offenses" to the top of the penal system.

Modern imprisonment would need another story. The penal system of today, however, bears the mark of the developments that gave rise to it. On the one hand, it has retained its ancient characteristics to a certain degree. Everyone still has to realize that punishment exists, and this is the essence of the notion of general prevention. And a penalty still involves, in one way or another, the infliction of injury. Feelings of sensitivity, on the other hand, did not vanish after their appearance in the late eighteenth century. Time and again those concerned with the condemned have looked inside prisons and told the public the painful story. The result is a permanent tension. Every modern Western society witnesses the conflict between a perceived necessity of punishment and an uneasiness at its practice. Perhaps this remains inevitable, unless we find a way to do without repression entirely.

Study Questions

1. How did relations among the governing and the governed change between the Germanic and the feudal periods?

2. During this time period, how did inquisitorial procedures change power relations among individuals and between individuals and the state?

3. What purpose did repression, especially caused by the spectacle of public physi-

cal suffering, serve in the early modern states?

4. Exactly how did the transition from an early modern to a nation-state transform sensibilities and make the spectacle of suffering unnecessary? ✦

2
The Discovery of the Asylum

David J. Rothman

In yet another historical account of the development of the penitentiary, David J. Rothman explores the development of the institution, from colonial America to the 1820s. Again, the reader should observe a societal shift from a system based largely on interpersonal settling of disputes in an agrarian setting to an urbanized nation that requires state intervention for punishment. The reader should also take note that, in addition to the rise of the penitentiary, representing confinement as an end in and of itself, society held a belief that the institution could indeed change the individual for the better. Thus, penal institutions were designed to confine the offender while leading him to the skills necessary for a law-abiding life.

The Boundaries of Colonial Society

The colonial attitudes and practices toward . . .the criminal . . .were in almost every aspect remarkably different from those Americans came to share in the pre-Civil war decades. Almost no eighteenth-century assumption about the origins or nature of . . .deviancy survived intact into the Jacksonian era, and its favorite solutions to these conditions also became outmoded. In fact, the two periods' perspectives and reactions

Excerpts from *The Discovery of the Asylum* by David J. Rothman, pp. 3, 15, 16, 18, 48, 51–53, 55–57, 61, 62, 68, 70, 71, 79, 107, 108. Copyright © 1971, 1990 by David J. Rothman. Reprinted with the permission of Little, Brown and Company.

were so basically dissimilar that only a knowledge of colonial precedents can clarify the revolutionary nature of the changes that occurred.

Eighteenth-century Americans did not define. . . crime as a critical social problem. . . . They devoted very little energy to devising and enacting programs to reform offenders and had no expectations of eradicating crime. Nor did they systematically attempt to isolate the deviant. . . . While they excluded some persons, they kept others wholly inside their communities. At times they were . . .willing to allow offenders another chance; but they could also show a callousness and narrow-mindedness that was utterly cruel. From the viewpoint of nineteenth-century critics, their ideas and behavior seemed careless and inconsistent, irrational and injurious, but within their social and intellectual framework, the colonists followed clear and well-established guidelines. . . .

The colonists judged a wide range of behavior to be deviant, finding the gravest implications in even minor offenses. Their extended definition was primarily religious in origin, equating sin with crime. The criminal codes punished religious offenses, such as idolatry, blasphemy, and witchcraft, and clergymen declared infractions against persons or property to be offenses against God. Freely mixing the two categories, the colonists proscribed an incredibly long list of activities. The identification of disorder with sin made it difficult for legislators and ministers to distinguish carefully between major and minor infractions. Both were testimony to the natural depravity of man and the power of the devil—sure signs that the offender was destined to be a public menace and a damned sinner. . . .

To counteract the powerful temptations to misconduct and the inherent weakness of men, the colonists looked to three critical associations. They conceived of the family, the church, and the network of community relations as important weapons in the battle against sin and crime. If these bodies functioned well, the towns would be spared the turbulence of vice and crime and, without frequent recourse to the courts or the gallows, enjoy a high degree of order and stability. To these ends, families were to raise their children to respect law and authority, the church was to oversee not only family discipline but adult behavior, and the members of the community were to supervise one another, to detect and correct the first signs of deviancy. . . .

These attitudes did not stimulate the colonists to new ways of controlling crime. The broad definition of potential offenders and improper behavior did not spur attempts to revise the patently inadequate formal mechanisms of law enforcement. Assemblies created a militia to contain mass disturbances and repel enemy forces but they did not intend it or use it for day-to-day supervision. Towns designated constables to protect their peace, but the force was inadequate both in the number and physical condition of its men. It was understaffed, poorly supervised, and filled with the elderly. Rather, the colonists' perspective on deviancy encouraged a dependence upon informal mechanisms which promoted a localism in many settlements. To an important degree the community had to be self-policing. The citizens themselves would be on guard to report and even apprehend the offender. Just as churchgoers were to be diligent about one another's salvation, so too residents were to protect one another's lives and property. And given the popular sense of man's proclivities to sin and crime, they expected to be busy. . . .

Charity and Correction in the Eighteenth Century

Eighteenth-century criminal codes fixed a wide range of punishments. They provided for fines, for whippings, for mechanisms of shame like the stocks, pillory and public cage, for banishment, and for the gallows. They used one technique or a combination of them, calling for a fine together with a period in the stocks, or for a whipping to be followed by banishment. The laws frequently gave the presiding magistrate discretion to choose among alternatives "to fine or to whip" or directed him to select the applicable one "to use the stocks if the offender could not pay his fine." They included some ingenious punishments, such as having a convicted felon mount the gallows, remain for an hour with a noose around his neck, and then go free. . . . The statutes defined a large number and variety of capital crimes and the courts were not reluctant to inflict the penalty. The gallows was the only method by which they could finally coerce obedience and protect the community. In the absence of punishments in the middle range, they depended extensively upon the discipline of the hangman. . . .

Local jails were found throughout the colonies, and in decent repair. Some towns utilized part of the courthouse building, others erected a separate structure. But regardless of form, these institutions had only limited functions. They held persons about to be tried or awaiting sentence or unable to discharge contracted debts. They did not, however, except on rare occasions, confine convicted offenders as a means of correction. The jails facilitated the process of criminal punishment but were not themselves instruments of discipline. They did not expand in function during the course of the eighteenth century to become a method for penalizing as well as detaining offenders.

The colonists might have adopted a penitentiary system in order to reform the criminal, or to terrify him, or simply to confine him. They could have attempted to mold him into an obedient citizen, or to frighten him into lawful conduct or, at least, to prevent him, if for only a limited period, from injuring the community. But given their conception of deviant behavior and institutional organization, they did not believe that a jail could rehabilitate or intimidate or detain the offender. They placed little faith in the possibility of reform. Prevailing Calvinist doctrines that stress the natural depravity of man and the powers of the devil hardly allowed such optimism. Since temptations to misconduct were not only omnipresent but practically irresistible, rehabilitation could not serve as the basis for a prison program. Moreover, local officials believed that a policy of expulsion offered the community some protection against recidivism. Institutionalization seemed unnecessary when numerous offenders could be marched beyond the town line and not be seen again.

The failure to broaden the functions of the jail also revealed the colonists' dependence upon the family model for organizing an institution. Since life in a prison would perforce duplicate that in a large household, they saw no reason to believe institutionalization would discourage the criminal or even offer the community a temporary respite. A household existence did not seem either painful or corrective. . . .

The institutions already functioning in the colonies did not substantially depart from the family model. The almshouse ran like a large household. Since officials appropriately considered admission a privilege, penalizing anyone who tried to enter it illegally, the poorhouse was hardly an inspiration for a prison system. The occasional workhouse was not a more useful guide; the few to be found in America had not established a disciplinary or punitive routine. . . .

Eighteenth-century jails in fact closely resembled the household in structure and routine. They lacked a distinct architecture and special procedures. . . . True to the household model, the keeper and his family resided in the jail, occupying one of its rooms; the prisoners lived several together in the others, with little to differentiate the keeper's quarters from their own. They wore no special clothing or uniforms and usually neither cuffs nor chains restrained their movements. They walked "not marched" about the jail. The workhouse model was so irrelevant that nowhere were they required to perform the slightest labor.

Jail arrangements so closely replicated the household that some colonists feared that prisons would be comfortable enough to attract inmates. Far from striking terror, they would build a clientele willing to be decently supported in return for a temporary deprivation of liberty. This is why towns frequently required prisoners to provide their own food and "to use such bedding, linen and other necessaries as they think fit, without their being purloined, detained, or they paying [the jailer] for the same." So long as they did not cost the town money, inmates could make living arrangements as pleasant and as homelike as they wished. . . .

The colonial jails were not only unlikely places for intimidating the criminal, but even ill-suited for confining him. Security was impossible to maintain, and escapes were frequent and easy. Conditions were sometimes so lax that towns compelled a prisoner to post a bond that he would remain in the jail, especially if he wished the privilege of exercising in the yard. . . .

No one placed very much confidence in these structures. Even at the close of the colonial period, there was no reason to think that the prison would soon become central to criminal punishment. . . .

The Challenge of Crime

Eighteenth-century notions of . . .deviancy did not survive for very long into the nineteenth, nor did its methods of dispensing . . .correction. The social, intellectual, and economic changes that differentiated the states of the new republic from the several colonies prompted a critical reappraisal and revision of the ideas and techniques of social control. Americans felt compelled to rethink inherited procedures and devise new methods to replace old ones. They devoted extraordinary attention to this issue, hoping to establish quickly and effectively alternatives to the colonial system.

Between 1790 and 1830, the nation's population greatly increased and so did the number and density of cities. Even gross figures reveal the dimensions of the change. In these forty years, the population of Massachusetts almost doubled, in Pennsylvania it tripled, and in New York it increased five times; border and midwestern states, practically empty in 1790, now held over three million people. At Washington's inauguration, only two hundred thousand Americans live[d] in towns with more than twenty-five hundred people; by Jackson's accession, the number exceeded one million. In 1790, no American city had more than fifty thousand residents. By 1830, almost half a million people lived in urban centers larger than that. During these same years factories began to dot the New England and mid-Atlantic rivers. The decade of the 1830s witnessed the first accelerated growth of manufacturing in the nation. At the same time, Enlightenment ideas challenged Calvinist doctrines; the prospect of boundless improvement confronted a grim determinism. But these general trends are not sufficient to explain the very specific reactions to the issue of deviant . . .behavior. To them must be added Americans' understanding of these changes. Under the influence of demographic, economic and intellectual developments, they perceived that the traditional mechanisms of social control were obsolete. The premises upon which the colonial system had been based were no longer valid.

Each change encouraged Americans to question inherited practices and to devise new ones. Inspired by the ideals of the Enlightenment, they considered older punishments to be barbaric and traditional assumptions on the origins of deviant behavior to be misdirected. Movement to cities, in and out of territories, and up and down the social ladder, made it difficult for them to believe that a sense of hierarchy or localism could now stabilize society. When men no longer knew their place or station, self-policing communities seemed a thing of the past. Expanding political loyalties also made colonial mechanisms appear obsolete. Citizens' attachment to state governments promoted

a broader definition of responsibility, so that a sentence of banishment seemed a parochial response. The welfare of the commonwealth demanded that towns no longer solve their problems in such narrow and exclusive ways.

This awareness provoked at least as much anxiety as celebration. Americans in the Jacksonian period could not believe that geographic and social mobility would promote or allow order and stability. Despite their marked impatience and dissatisfaction with colonial procedures, they had no ready vision of how to order society. They were still trapped in many ways in the rigidities of eighteenth-century social thinking. They knew well that the old system was passing, but not what ought to replace it. What in their day was to prevent society from bursting apart? From where would the elements of cohesion come? More specifically, would . . . criminals roam out of control? . . .This question became part of a full, intense, and revealing investigation of the origins of deviant . . .behavior. To understand why men turned criminal . . .would enable reformers to strengthen the social order. To comprehend and control abnormal behavior promised to be the first step in establishing a new system for stabilizing the community, for binding citizens together. In this effort, one finds the clearest indications of how large-scale social changes affected thinking and actions of Americans in the Jacksonian period. And here one also finds the crucial elements that led to the discovery of the [penitentiary].

In the immediate aftermath of independence and nationhood, Americans believed that they had uncovered both the prime cause of criminality in their country and an altogether effective antidote. Armed with patriotic fervor, sharing a repugnance for things British and a new familiarity with and faith in Enlightenment doctrines, they posited that the origins and persistence of deviant behavior would be found in the nature of the colonial criminal codes. Established in the days of oppression and ignorance, the laws reflected British insistence on severe and cruel punishments. . . .

These conceptions had an immediate and widespread appeal. The reform seemed worthy of the new republic, and feasible, so that by the second decade of the nineteenth century, most of the states had amended their criminal codes. The death sentence was either abolished for all offenses save first-degree murder or strictly limited to a handful of the most serious crimes. Instead, the statutes called for incarceration, the offender to serve a term in prison. Construction kept apace with legal stipulations. Pennsylvania led the way, turning the old Philadelphia jail at Walnut Street into a state prison. In 1796, the New York legislature approved funds for building such institutions, and soon opened the Newgate state prison in Greenwich Village. The New Jersey penitentiary was completed in 1797, and so were others in Virginia and Kentucky in 1800. That same year, the Massachusetts legislature made appropriations for a prison at Charlestown, and in short order Vermont, New Hampshire, and Maryland followed suit. Within twenty years of Washington's inaugural, the states had taken the first steps to alter the traditional system of punishment.

In this first burst of enthusiasm, Americans expected that a rational system of correction, which made punishment certain but humane, would dissuade all but a few offenders from a life in crime. They located the roots of deviancy not in the criminal, but in the legal system. Just as colonial codes had encouraged deviant behavior, republican ones would now curtail, or even eliminate it. To pass the proper laws would end the problem.

This perspective drew attention away from the prisons themselves. They were necessary adjuncts to the reform, the substitutes for capital punishment, but intrinsically of little interest or importance. A repulsion from the gallows rather than any faith in the penitentiary spurred the late-eighteenth-century construction. Few people had any clear idea what these structures should look like or how they should be administered—or

even addressed themselves seriously to these questions. To reformers, the advantages of the institutions were external, and they hardly imagined that life inside the prison might rehabilitate the criminal. Incarceration seemed more humane than hanging and less brutal than whipping. Prisons matched punishment to crime precisely: the more heinous the offense, the longer the sentence. Juries, fully understanding these advantages, would never hesitate to convict the guilty, so that correction would be certain. The fact of imprisonment, not its internal routine, was of chief importance.

By the 1820s, however, these ideas had lost persuasiveness. The focus shifted to the deviant and the penitentiary, away from the legal system. Men intently scrutinized the life history of the criminal and methodically arranged the institution to house him. Part of the cause for this change was the obvious failure of the first campaign. The faith of the 1790s now seemed misplaced; more rational codes had not decreased crime. The roots of deviancy went deeper than the certainty of a punishment. Nor were the institutions fulfilling the elementary task of protecting society, since escapes and riots were commonplace occurrences. More important, the second generation of Americans confronted new challenges and shared fresh ideas. Communities had undergone many critical changes between 1790 and 1830, and so had men's thinking. Citizens found cause for deep despair and yet incredible optimism. The safety and security of their social order seemed to them in far greater danger than that of their fathers, yet they hoped to eradicate crime from the new world. The old structure was crumbling, but perhaps they could draw the blue prints for building a far better one.

. . .Although the colonists had blamed inadequate parental and religious training for crime, they were preoccupied with the sinner himself. Convinced that the corrupt nature of man was ultimately at fault, they did not extensively analyze the role of the criminal's family or the church or the general society. Furthermore, they shared a clear understanding of what the well-ordered community *ought to* look like, and this too stifled any inclination to question or scrutinize existing arrangements. Their religious and social certainty covered the discrepancies between ideas and realities, obviating new approaches and theories. Americans in the Jacksonian period stood in a very different position. They learned that men were born innocent, not depraved, that the sources of corruption were external, not internal, to the human condition. Encouraged by such doctrines to examine their society with acute suspicion, they quickly discovered great cause for apprehension and criticism. . . .

Holding such a position, American students of deviant behavior moved family and community to the center of their analysis. New York officials accumulated and published biographies because this technique allowed them to demonstrate to legislators and philanthropists the crucial role of social organizations. Accordingly, almost every sketch opened with a vivid description of an inadequate family life and then traced the effects of the corruptions in the community. . . .

The pessimism and fear underlying this outlook pointed to the difficulty Americans had in fitting their perception of nineteenth-century society as mobile and fluid into an eighteenth-century definition of a well-ordered community. Their first reaction was not to disregard the inherited concept but to condemn present conditions. Hence, in these biographies a dismal picture emerged of a society filled with a myriad of temptations. It was almost as if the town, in a nightmarish image, was made up of a number of households, frail and huddled together, facing the sturdy and wide doors of the tavern, the gaudy opening into a house of prostitution or theater filled with dissipated customers; all the while, thieves and drunkards milled the streets, introducing the unwary youngster to vice and corruption. Every family was under siege, surrounded by enemies ready to take advantage of any misstep. The honest citizen was like a vigilant soldier, well trained to guard against temptation. Should he relax for a moment, the results would be disastrous. Once, observers believed, neighbors had disciplined neighbors. Now it seemed that rowdies corrupted rowdies.

Yet for all the desperation in this image, Americans shared an incredible optimism. Since deviant behavior was a product of the environment, the predictable result of readily observable situations, it was not inevitable. Crime was not inherent in the nature of man, as Calvinists had asserted; no theological devils insisted on its perpetuation. Implicit in this outlook was an impulse to reform. If one could alter the conditions breeding crime, then one could reduce it to manageable proportions and bring a new security to society.

One tactic was to advise and warn the family to fulfill its tasks well. By giving advice and demonstrating the awful consequences of an absence of discipline, critics would inspire the family to a better performance. (The biographical sketches, then, were not only investigations but correctives to the problem.) One might also organize societies to shut taverns and houses of prostitution, an effort that was frequently made in the Jacksonian period. But such measures, while important, were slow-working, and by themselves seemed insufficient to meet the pressing needs of this generation. Another alternative then became not only feasible but essential: to construct a special setting for the deviant. Remove him from the family and community and place him in an artificially created and therefore corruption-free environment. Here he could learn all the vital lessons that others had ignored, while protected from the temptations of vice. A model and small-scale society could solve the immediate problem and point the way to broader reforms. . . .

The Invention of the Penitentiary

Americans' understanding of the causes of deviant behavior led directly to the invention of the penitentiary as a solution. It was an ambitious program. Its design "external appearance, internal arrangement, and daily routine" attempted to eliminate the specific influences that were breeding crime in the community, and to demonstrate the fundamentals of proper social organization. Rather than stand as places of last resort, hidden and ignored, these institutions became the pride of the nation. A structure designed to join practicality to humanitarianism, reform the criminal, stabilize American society, and demonstrate how to improve the condition of mankind, deserved full publicity and close study.

In the 1820s New York and Pennsylvania began a movement that soon spread through the Northeast, and then over the next decades to many midwestern states. New York devised the Auburn or congregate system of penitentiary organization, establishing it first at the Auburn state prison between 1819 and 1823, and then in 1825 at the Ossining institution, familiarly known as Sing-Sing. Pennsylvania officials worked out the details of a rival plan, the separate system, applying it to the penitentiary at Pittsburgh in 1826 and to the prison at Philadelphia in 1829. . . .

The doctrines of separation, obedience, and labor became the trinity around which officials organized the penitentiary. They carefully instructed inmates that their duties could be "comprised in a few words"; they were *"to labor diligently, to obey all orders,* and preserve an *unbroken silence."* Yet to achieve these goals, officers had to establish a total routine, to administer every aspect of the institution in accord with the three guidelines, from inmates' dress to their walk, from the cells' furnishings to the guards' deportment. The common solution was to follow primarily a quasi-military model. The regulations based on this model promised to preserve isolation, to make labor efficient, and to teach men lacking discipline to abide by rules; this regimented style of life would inculcate strict discipline, precision, and instantaneous adherence to commands. Furthermore, a military model in a correctional institution seemed especially suitable for

demonstrating to the society at large the right principles of organization. Here was an appropriate example for a community suffering a crisis of order. . . .

Reformers never spelled out the precise nature and balance of this reformation. They hoped that families, instead of overindulging or neglecting their children, would more conscientiously teach limits and the need for obedience to them. Assuming that social stability could not be achieved without a very personal and keen respect for authority, they looked first to a firm family discipline to inculcate it. Reformers also anticipated that society would rid itself of corruptions. In a narrow sense this meant getting rid of such blatant centers of vice as taverns, theaters, and houses of prostitution. In a broader sense, it meant reviving a social order in which men knew their place. Here sentimentality took over, and critics in the Jacksonian period often assumed that their forefathers had lived together without social strain, in secure, placid, stable, and cohesive communities. In fact, the designers of the penitentiary set out to re-create these conditions. But the results, it is not surprising to discover, were startlingly different from anything that the colonial period had known. A conscious effort to instill discipline through an institutional routine led to a set work pattern, a rationalization of movement, a precise organization of time, a general uniformity. Hence, for all the reformers' nostalgia, the reality of the penitentiary was much closer to the values of the nineteenth than the eighteenth century.

Study Questions

1. How did the American colonists' views on the nature of man and crime shape punishment?

2. Why didn't the colonists conceive of incarceration as a form of punishment?

3. Discuss social changes occurring at the turn of the nineteenth century that would change Americans' thoughts on crime

and punishment within a generation or two.

4. How did Americans' views on the nature of man, crime, and punishment during the Jacksonian era differ from their colonial counterparts?

5. In what way did Jacksonian Americans believe that the trinity of the penitentiary (separation, obedience, and labor) would act as an appropriate example for a community in crisis? ✦

3
A Look at Prison History

Thorsten Sellin

Thorsten Sellin traces the history of punishment and imprisonment from approximately the reformation forward. However, Sellin focuses on the historically relevant view of Radbruch's theory* that punishments were designed to control the underclass (in many cases this meant slaves). As such, prison inmates came to be viewed as slaves of the state. This historical analysis does an excellent job of detailing and describing the societal shift that moved confinement from occurring prior to the "real" punishment (which generally involved severe if not deadly corporal punishment), to actually being the punishment. Although Sellin views moving away from corporal (and public) punishment as a positive shift, he concludes by noting some of the unanticipated consequences that arose from this country's willingness to house offenders of all types en masse. Not the least of these problems includes issues regarding prison labor, and grotesque mistreatment within institutions.

In his symposium, *Elegantiae Juris Criminalis*, Gustav Radbruch published in 1938 an article entitled "Der Ursprung des Strafrechts aus dem. Stande der Unfreien." It is a brilliant exposition of a theory which had been advanced many decades earlier by scholars like Köstlin, von Bar, and Jastrow and it makes the origin of penal imprisonment comprehensible. Rejecting, as illogical or unproved, various explanations of the ori-

Excerpts from *Federal Probation*, Volume 31, Issue 3 (September 1967), pages 18–23.

gin of punishment, Radbruch maintained that the common punishments which came to be introduced in law and applied to all offenders had once been used only for slaves or bondsmen.

> Especially the mutilating penalties. Applied earlier almost exclusively to slaves, they became used more and more on freemen during the Carolingian period and specially for offenses which betokened a base and servile mentality. Up to the end of the Carolingian era, punishments "to hide and hair" were overwhelmingly reserved for slaves. Even death penalties occurred as slave punishments and account for the growing popularity of such penalties in Carolingian times. The aggravated death penalties, combining corporal and capital punishments, have their roots in the penal law governing slaves.[1]

Radbruch believed that earlier penal customs, like feud or compensation, were natural for equals and propertied people who could demand satisfaction or make payments. But the social class system changed greatly during the Frankish era and with it the character of criminality. "Vulgar crime" became looked upon as low-class crime, "vulgar both in the sense of its origin in baseborn people and in its appraisal as being infamous—the crime of another, uncomprehended and despised social layer. . . . The aim of punishment had been clearly stated, in a capitulary of Childebert II in 596 A.D., to be 'to ensure by every means the control of the lower classes.' It was natural that the best means to that end were the punishments that were earlier applied to the very lowest layer of the people—the class of slaves."[2]

The evolution of the penal law until the old slave punishments—death, mutilation, whipping, etc.—were gradually incorporated in the penal law and applied generally needs no further elaboration here.

> The criminal law . . .to this very day reflects its origin in slave punishments. Even now, punishments mean a *capitis deminutio* because it presumes the *capitis deminutio* of

those for whom it was originally designed. Being punished means being treated like a slave. This was symbolically underscored in earlier times when whipping was accompanied by the shaving of the head, for the shorn head, was the mark of the slave."[3]

Penal Slavery

Being concerned mostly with corporal and capital punishments, Radbruch made no mention of penal imprisonment in his essay, yet his theory applies perfectly to that punishment which in its primitive form was slavery of a most abject kind, called penal servitude. Penal servitude was in use in Imperial Rome. Von Bar says that

> since it was customary to punish slaves by hard labor and since the lowest class of freemen were in reality little more respected than were slaves, by the all powerful imperial officials, the idea easily arose of making use of the toil of convicts in the great works being undertaken by the state. This idea was perhaps furthered by an acquaintance with the custom of states annexed to Rome. Thus even Pliny the Younger speaks of the employment of convicts in public works (*opus publicum*), such as cleaning sewers, mending highways, and working in the public baths. A more severe type of this kind of punishment was a sentence 'ad metalla'—labor in the mines—and in 'opus metalli.' The convicts in each of these instances wore chains and as 'servi poenae' lost their freedom. For this reason the punishment was always for life. . . . These punishments were properly regarded as sentences to a slow and painful death.[4]

It is significant that in Imperial Rome the *condamnatio ad opus publicum* was reserved for the *personae humiles*, the humble class of people; it was not applicable to the upper class or *honestiores*. The more severe forms of the *condamnatio* deprived the offender of his liberty (*capitis deminutio maxima*) and hence of his citizenship, reducing his status to that of a penal slave. These punishments, together with exile and death, were classed

by the legists as capital punishments because they incurred civil death. Sentences *ad metalla* meant hard labor, while in chains, in stone quarries, such as the Carrara marble ones, in metal mines, or in sulphur pits. It is obvious that in order to exploit the manpower of these penal slaves it was necessary to keep them imprisoned in some way. Here, then, we find punitive imprisonment in its original form, even though the Romans may not have been its inventors. Therefore, it is curious to be told by George Ives, in his interesting *History of Penal Methods* (1914) that

> imprisonment as a punishment in itself, to be endured under rules made expressly punitive and distressful, may be described as essentially modern and reached its worst phase in the nineteenth century.[5]

"Imprisonment as a punishment in itself" would thus be something new and in essence different from the primitive penal servitude just described. To be sure, historians seem to have adopted that view, but I propose to show that this judgment is questionable.

Parenthetically speaking, it is puzzling to find the great Roman jurist Ulpian categorically declaring that prisons existed only for detention and not for punishment, a phrase which was accepted as a correct definition of prisons until the 18th century. Considering the sentences *ad metalla* common in Ulpian's own day; the later use, mainly in the Mediterranian sea, of convicts as oarsmen in war galleys; the working of convicts in the Spanish mines of northern Africa by the banking house of Fugger to secure repayment of immense loans made to Charles V; the use of convict labor in the arsenals of France and Spain; the transportation of convicts to work in the Siberian mines and lumber camps of Russia; the common use of convicts during the 16th and 17th centuries to build fortifications, etc., one can only conclude that, despite the complete deprivation of liberty characterizing such punitive enterprises, jurists did not look on that element in these punishments as being their distinguishing mark, but placed them, instead, in another category of punishment, that of forced or compulsory labor, to which the deprivation of liberty was merely incidental. As late as 1771, the great French jurist Daniel Jousse still classed penal servitude among the capital punishments. This probably accounts for the view expressed by George Ives that imprisonment as an end in itself is a modern invention.

You will recall that Radbruch claimed that corporal and capital punishments originally imposed only on slaves and bondsmen gradually came to be used for freemen. The same holds true for imprisonment. Originally applied as a punishment for slaves in connection with hard labor, it came to be used for humble folk, who for crime were reduced to penal slaves. In the middle of the 15th century, when France found the supply of free and slave labor on its galley fleets dwindling, beggars and vagrants were first sent to fill the galley crews and, later sturdy felons who had merited the death penalty or corporal punishments. When imprisonment later was applied to all serious offenders, it turned out, on close examination, to be only a variant of the original form of penal servitude.

Punitive Imprisonment

The credit for the gradual substitution of imprisonment for corporal and capital punishments must go to the political philosophers of the 18th century. Experimentation with punitive imprisonment had occurred earlier in the monastic orders and in the houses of correction in many countries, but this involved mostly errant clerics or petty misdemeanants and had not greatly changed the ways of dealing with more serious criminals, who were still being whipped, broken on the wheel, maimed, and hanged. Now the demand arose that nearly all such criminals be sentenced to imprisonment. The most influential voice, so far as penal reform was concerned, was that of Beccaria, who crystallized ideas he had gleaned from the French philosophers, especially Montesquieu.

Beccaria's great essay *On Crimes and Punishments* (1764) is too well-known to you to require any extensive commentary. You will recall that he opposed the death penalty and advocated substituting imprisonment for it, but what may have passed notice is the reason for his proposal and the nature of the substitute. No sentimentality dictated his opposition to capital punishment. As a firm believer in Rousseau's version of the theory of the social contract, he denied the *right* of the state to execute anyone with the possible exception of the leader of a revolt threatening to overthrow the government. No citizen, he said, would have voluntarily agreed to surrender to the state his right to live. When using the death penalty a state was not exercising a right it was not entitled to possess but was engaging in a war against a citizen, whose destruction it believed to be necessary and useful. Beccaria then proceeded to demonstrate the falsity of such beliefs.

Why should imprisonment be preferred to capital punishment? Because

> it is not the intensity but the duration of punishment which has the greatest effect upon man's mind. . . . It is not the terrible but fleeting spectacle of the execution of a scroundrel that is the strongest deterrent to crime but rather the long and painful example of a man deprived of his freedom and become a beast of burden, repaying with his toil the society he has offended. . . . Therefore the intensity of the punishment of perpetual servitude as substitute for the death penalty possesses that which suffices to deter any determined soul. I say that it has more. Many look on death with a firm and calm regard . . .but neither fanaticism nor vanity dwells among fetters and chains, under the rod, under the yoke, or in the iron cage. . . . Were one to say that perpetual servitude is as painful as death and therefore equally cruel I would reply that, adding all the unhappy moments of servitude together, the former would be even worse.[6]

In the last analysis, then, Beccaria, who clearly stated in his essay that the aim of punishment should be to prevent a criminal from repeating crime and to deter others from crime by the example of punishment, did not ask for the abolition of the death penalty for humanitarian reasons but because it (a) had no logical place in a political society based on a social contract and (b) was less of a deterrent than life imprisonment. Such imprisonment was to be served in a prison where the inmate led the existence of a penal slave. Since scores of crimes in the penal laws of his day were made punishable by death, his reform proposal, if accepted, would require the creation of prisons to house large numbers of inmates. It is noteworthy also that Beccaria rarely mentioned imprisonment in his essay except as a substitute for capital punishment. He referred to it in connection with thefts committed with violence, for instance, but when he did mention it he called it temporary or perpetual slavery. Nor was he opposed to corporal punishments.

It is important to remember that Beccaria's essay was, first and foremost, a political tract announcing the principles of a penal code based on the new democratic philosophy of the political equality of men. Older penal law had reflected the views dominant in societies where slavery or serfdom flourished, political inequality was the rule, and sovereignty was assumed to be resting in absolute monarchs. Now the most objectionable features of that law, which had favored the upper classes and had provided often arbitrary, brutal and revolting corporal and capital punishments for the lower classes, were to be removed and equality before the law established. Judicial torture for the purpose of extracting evidence was to be abolished, other than penal measures used to control some conduct previously punished as crime, and punishments made only severe enough to outweigh the gains expected by the criminal from his crime. This meant a more humane law, no doubt, applied without discrimination to all citizens alike in harmony with the new democratic ideas. There was nothing startlingly new, however, in the aims of punishment as advocated by Beccaria. Myuart de Vouglans, who wrote a polemic against him in 1766 and was a leading defender of the old system, believed that the aim of punishment should be (a) to correct the offender; (b) repair the wrong caused by the crime if possible; and (c) deter the evilminded by the example and fear of similar punishments. The aims of these two defenders of different penal philosophies were essentially the same; only the means they advocated differed.

The governments who were influenced by the new philosophy created prison systems that incorporated Beccaria's ideas. Emperor Joseph II of Austria, hailed as a reformer for having eliminated the death penalty from his code of 1787, substituted horrible varieties of imprisonment in dungeons, where prisoners were chained and loaded with irons while working. At about the same time, John Howard observed in a Viennese prison prisoners chained together and awaiting transportation to Hungary where they were to draw barges up the Danube, a task so exhaustive that few survived it. When the French Constituent Assembly in 1791 translated Beccaria's principles into a penal code, different varieties of imprisonment were substituted, the most severe of which provided that the criminal was to have a chain with an iron ball attached to his legs, be confined at hard labor in security prisons, ports or arsenals, or at other public works, and work for the profit of the state. This was, in fact, the way galley slaves had been treated ever since the galleys had been decommissioned as outmoded.

Prison Reform

Concern about the sufferings of prisoners had been expressed in many ways since ancient times. There is both a literature to demonstrate it and organized efforts of relief, engaged in mainly for religious and humanitarian reasons. The outstanding work of John Howard need only be mentioned; it coincided with the period we have just been discussing. But now a new generation of writers appeared. The effects of the movement to make prisons places of punishment rather than of mere detention required not only justification but inventiveness. How should such prisons be organized, what should be the regime, how would they most effectively serve the aims of punishment? The last decade of the 18th and the first half of the 19th century produced an impressive list of writers on prison reform as well as impressive efforts to convert their ideas into practice.

But the roots of imprisonment in penal servitude could not be easily eradicated. When the young American states built penitentiaries for serious offenders who would formerly have been executed, mutilated, or whipped, the law provided that prisoners confined in them should perform labor of the "most harsh and servile kind" (a phrase borrowed from John Howard). The prisons operated on the Auburn plan, in particular, were, most of them, notorious for the maltreatment of prisoners and for the excessive labor required of them in an attempt to meet the demand of legislators that the prisons be self-supporting and even show a profit if possible. These conditions were not reflected in the glowing reports that often emanated from the wardens or overseers of the prisons, but they were amply proved by the many investigations of abuses made from time to time by official commissions. Quite early— in New York in 1817, for instance—the practice began of selling the labor of prisoners to private contractors. This contract system of prison labor spread rapidly to other states and was not completely eliminated until 1934, by act of Congress. As late as 1919 a committee of the American Prison Association reported, after a national survey, that most prisons worked their prisoners in a manner reminiscent of the early forms of penal servitude and that reformation was an empty word.

Let me return to Radbruch for a moment and his theory that in a society where slaves existed, the punishments for slaves tended to be adopted for freemen sooner or later; that, in other words, the institution of slavery placed its stamp on the penal law. Consider the fact that the ancient societies of Greece and Rome were built on a foundation of slavery; that Plato said that all manual labor should be done by slaves; that Aristotle regarded it as an established law of nature that slavery was just and even agreeable to those subjected to it; and that there were times during the Roman Empire when the number of slaves almost equalled the number of free citizens. Consider also that wherever slavery existed the status of a slave was that of chattel property, useful and necessary to his owner, but not permitting the slave to be treated like a free man. In societies where the debtor could be enslaved by his creditor or where the serf was considered practically as a slave, the rise of penal slavery, to use Beccaria's term, and its gradual extension to the members of the lower orders of society who committed crimes and finally to all persons convicted of serious crimes would seem to be a natural evolution. The demonstration of the accuracy of this contention can best be made in the study of the evolution of punishment in the southern states of the United States where slavery was legal until abolished one century ago. Two illustrations will suffice:

The entire history of punishment can almost be said to be recapitulated in the State of Florida in the brief period of a century and a half. Prior to the 1860's punishments were capital, corporal, and financial and the local county jails were detention houses with the kind of inmates that have in historical times been found in such places. There was no interest in prison reform; the State itself had no prison. In 1869 a penitentiary act was adopted by the legislature providing for a state prison to be operated by the Commissioners of Public Institutions. The act authorized the Commissioners to enter into contracts with private persons for the labor of the prisoners. The act emphasized the need to make the prison self-supporting; this nullified another provision of the act, namely, that the contractors must insure the health and safety of the prisoners working for them.

The state penitentiary was located in an arsenal belonging to the Federal Government and for 2 years was governed as a military post where, for the lack of a work program, the prisoners were controlled by chains, muskets, and bayonets. In 1871 the prison was removed from the military, and 6 years later the State transferred the control and custody of the prisoners to private contractors who could now employ them anywhere in the State. Prisoners were leased to individuals and corporations and set to work in phosphate mines and in turpentine camps in the forests. By 1902 there were 30 such convict camps.

"The leasing of convicts," according to a report recently issued by the Florida Division of Correction, from which these data have been culled,

> resulted in incredible acts of brutality to prisoners. The atrocities of the system seem obvious to a modern observer, yet, state officials, conditioned by their culture, could observe that frequent convict camp investigations always found the convicts 'well treated and cared for.'. . . In 1917, the legislature created the State Road Department and also the State Road Convict Force. The Board of Commissioners was authorized to allocate up to 300 convicts for use on the road force (the old *opus publicum*) . . .the remaining convicts were leased to the counties and to private lessees.[7]

Leasing of Prisoners

Prisoners unable to do manual labor—mostly the aged, crippled, and deformed—had to be placed in a state prison, of course. In 1919 the Board of Commissioners were forbidden to lease convicts because public opinion had been aroused and outraged by some of the incidents that had occurred in the convict camps. Now these prisoners had

to be placed in state prisons where they worked on large attached plantations under the guard of specially selected fellow-prisoners, who carried arms. It was not until 1957 that Florida adopted a Correctional Code and set up a State Division of Correction. Since then the State has rapidly joined the mainstream of modern penology.

The particular form of the contract system, known as the lease system described above, flourished in the old slave states of the South after the Civil War, when the slaves had been freed. Can anyone doubt that this kind of penal slavery was not only reminiscent of its most primitive forms but also was adopted as a suitable way of punishing former slaves, their descendants, and poor whites by a dominant group of former slaveowners and their sympathizers? The last state to abolish this system was Alabama, in 1928.

A Recent Prison Scandal

Penal slavery did not disappear when the lease system of prison labor was abandoned; it was merely transplanted into the state penitentiaries. The most recent prison scandal in the United States has just erupted in an old slave state, Arkansas. In 1897 the legislature of that State acquired a large plantation, which now has 15,000 acres and later a subsidiary farm of 4,500 acres, which together constitute the state penitentiary. The aim was to develop a self-supporting institution. That this aim has been realized is shown by the fact that in 1964, the penitentiary showed a net profit from its livestock and its cotton and vegetable acres of nearly half a million dollars. The major cost items were about $91,000 for feeding 1,900 prisoners and $57,000 for feeding the cattle.

This financial success is achieved by working the prisoners from dawn to dusk, guarded by inmate guards, on foot or mounted, and armed with shotguns and rifles. There are only 35 salaried employees in the two institutions combined, including the superintendent and his staff, chaplains, doctors, bookkeepers, and a chief warden and 18 so-called field wardens. Whipping is authorized as disciplinary punishment for a variety of offenses including failure to perform one's quota of work. Nearly half of the inmates are Negroes guarded by inmates of their race. The sentences served are to hard labor and hard labor it is, and unpaid at that. No shops or prison industries exist except those necessary for the maintenance of the buildings, the agricultural machinery, and the trucking equipment.[8]

A few months ago certain incidents at the subsidiary farm known as the Tucker farm resulted in a thorough investigation by the state police of Arkansas. The investigation revealed conditions of corruption, maltreatment, and brutality that are unbelievable. The new state administration which took office 3 months ago is now attempting to remedy the situation.[9]

Conclusion

These examples have not been chosen in order to denigrate the 52 prison systems of the United States, many of which are today acknowledged at home and abroad to be in the forefront of modern correctional treatment methods. I have chosen them to substantiate Radbruch's theory by showing that the primitive form of punitive imprisonment referred to as penal servitude or penal slavery, originally used for slaves (*servi poenae*) and later applied to free men, has not yet been completely stamped out despite the reforms in correctional treatment. I am, of course, aware that I have focused on perhaps the darkest side of the history of punitive imprisonment. Even so, much has been left unsaid. I have made no reference to the prison hulks of England, the treadmills and cranks, the British and French transportation systems, these variants of penal slavery which caused a British judge to say to a convicted murderer: "I shall pass upon you a sentence . . .which in my opinion will be a greater punishment than the momentary pain of death, for you will live like a slave laboring for others and have no reward for your labors. That sentence is that you be kept in penal servitude for life." Shades of Beccaria!

Nor have I referred to the innovations during the 19th century that have generally been regarded as progressive, such as the institutions governed by Obermayer in Bavaria, Montesinos in Spain, or Brockway's reformatory at Elmira, for instance, or the institutions for delinquent children or women that arose in the 19th century on both sides of the Atlantic and even earlier in Europe. From our present viewpoints, most of them were pale shadows of what we regard today as appropriate correctional institutions, even though at the time of their founding they were indeed trailbreakers.

One is tempted to speculate on the motive forces that have operated in producing the gradual progress toward the kind of correctional system we are today visualizing. Improvements in earlier times were and are to some degree even today motivated by humanitarian and religious feelings, but I believe that for penological progress in the last hundred years, slow at first and accelerated only since the second world war, we are indebted chiefly to the behavioral scientists— the psychiatrists, psychologists, and social scientists—whose studies and findings have gradually changed, generation after generation, the intellectual climate into which people, including legal scholars, legislators, correctional administrators, and the behavioral scientists themselves are born.

New ideas do not find easy acceptance, especially when they concern treatment of criminals and therefore meet emotional barriers. Max Planck once said that the only reason a scientific truth is accepted is not that its opponents are converted to it but that they die off and a new generation is born that takes that truth for granted. Perhaps this explains our presence here this week discussing correctional methods which a generation or two ago would have been considered inacceptable.

Study Questions

1. As a policy 'thinker,' Beccaria is often portrayed as a benevolent reformer advocating for mercy on the offender. Make a case for, and against, this portrayal.

2. What were the primary reasons behind the move from public torture and corporal punishment to imprisonment occurring as punishment?

3. What is meant by the phrase "penal slavery?"

4. What were some of the major consequences of moving to a correctional system based on confinement and imprisonment?

Notes

1. Gustav Radbruch, *Elegantiae Juris Criminalis* (2d Ed.). Basel: Verlog fur Recht und Gesellschaft A.G., 1950, p. 5

2. *Ibid.*, pp. 8–9.

3. *Ibid.*, pp. 11–12.

4. Carl Ludwig von Bar, *A History of Continental Criminal Law.* Boston: Little, Brown & Co., 1916 p. 36.

5. Geroge Ives, *A History of Penal Methods.* London: Stanley Paul & Co., 1914, p. 1.

6. Cesare Beccaria, *Dei delitti e delle pene,* xvi.

7. Florida Division of Corrections, *5th Biennial Report, July 1, 1964–June 30, 1966.* Tallahassee, Florida, 1966, p. 5.

8. Robert Pearman, "The Whip Pays Off," *The Nation,* 203:701–704, December 26, 1966.

9. *Tucker Prison Farm Case.* Reprt No. 916–166–66, Criminal Investigations Division, Arkansas State Police, Little Rock, Arkansas.

An address delivered at a Colloquium of the International Penal and Penitentiary Foundation at Ulm, West Germany, April 19, 1967. ✦

4

Partial Justice
Women, Prisons, and Social Control

Nicole Hahn Rafter

Much of what is known regarding the structure and function of the corrective institution has focused on male offenders. Although male offenders make up the majority of the offending population, a very real need exists for more exploration of female offending. Nicole Hahn Rafter's essay provides a historical analysis of an institution designed to house female offenders during the nineteenth and early twentieth centuries. The Albion institution in New York, although housing serious female offenders, also may have served as an extension of formal social control for nonserious female offenders, who for various reasons did not conform to proper norms. Such women were taught the virtues of a "good, womanly life." This essay gives yet another example of how important the greater social context is when studying institutional evolution.

Over the last several decades, historians and sociologists have devoted increasing attention to the phenomenon of social control—the mechanisms by which powerful groups consciously or unconsciously attempt to restrain and to induce conformity, even assent, among less powerful but nonetheless threatening segments of society. Laws, institutions such as schools and prisons, medical policies, informal gestures of approbation or displeasure, even forms of

Excerpts from *Partial Justice* by Nicole Hahn Rafter. Copyright © 1985 by Nicole Hahn Rafter. Reprinted by permission.

language—all may constitute forms of social control. (Social control in this sense should not be confused with criminological control theory . . .which offers an explanation for law-violating behaviors; through a complicated and terminologically unfortunate series of developments in social science, similar terms have been adopted to label different concepts.) The control achieved may be merely external, as when people are forced to do things against their wills; or it may be internal, so thoroughly absorbed by its subjects that they come to monitor and correct their own deviations from prescription. In recent years, research in social control has moved in two directions particularly germane to the study of women's prisons. First, it has come to focus sharply on the political implications of coercion. As David Rothman puts it, "A social control orientation . . .suggest[s] that [institutional] innovations were likely to confer benefits somewhere, and so the question becomes, where? If the prison did not serve the prisoner, then whom did it serve?" In other words, historians and sociologists no longer assume that the narratives of social controllers (who often speak sincerely of the benefits they expect to confer on prisoners and the like) tell the whole story; the picture has been broadened to include the political ramifications of extended controls for both reformers and the subjects of reform. Second, feminist theorists have become sensitive to ways in which social controls are exercised on women *as women*, to encourage conformity to prescribed gender roles.

This chapter analyzes an aspect of the social control of women by focusing on a particular type of prison, the women's reformatory. It explores the conjunction between formal vehicles of social control (in this case the laws establishing reformatories and the institutions themselves) and the internalization of their social control "messages" by the targeted group of inmates. The chapter also deals with social control in terms of social class—the process by which, through establishment and operation of women's reformatories, middle-class crusaders came to impose their definition of womanliness on working-class inmates. This chapter . . . is concerned with the movement's political implications. Without denying the benevolence of the reformers' aims, it attempts to look beyond good intentions to the movement's methods of social control and their results.

The women's reformatory, as we have seen, was unique as an institution for adults. Founded by middle- (often upper-middle-) class social feminists, reformatories extended government control over working-class women not previously vulnerable to state punishment. In addition, the reformatories institutionalized bourgeois standards for female propriety, making it possible to "correct" women for moral offenses for which adult men were not sent to state penal institutions. And reformatories feminized prison discipline, introducing into state prisons for women a program of rehabilitation predicated on middle-class definitions of ladylike behavior. For these reasons, the women's reformatory served special, female-specific functions with regard to social class and social control.

In this chapter, New York's Western House of Refuge at Albion, operated between 1894 and 1931, is used as a case study. Albion built upon experiments by its forerunners to become the first women's prison to realize completely the reformatory plan in architecture, administrative structure, type of inmates and sentence, and program. It established the model adopted by many women's reformatories opened in the early twentieth century. Additionally, Albion adhered to the goals of the women's reformatory movement more consistently than many sister institutions that succumbed to overcrowding, inadequate financing, and routinization. Although it was atypical in this respect, Albion provides a good case for analyzing the ways in which the reformatory movement extended social control just because it did manage to remain relatively "pure." The detailed nature of Albion's prisoner registries and the survival of case files on individual inmates, moreover, make it possible to follow

in some depth the events that brought women to this prison, their institutional treatment, and their reactions to it.

Social Control Functions of the Albion Reformatory

Records of the Albion reformatory indicate that in terms of social control, the institution served two primary functions: sexual and vocational regulation. It attempted the first by training "loose" young women to accept a standard of propriety that dictated chastity until marriage and fidelity thereafter. It tried to achieve the second by training charges in homemaking, a competency they were to utilize either as dutiful daughters or wives within their own families or as servants in the homes of others. In operation, techniques used to achieve these ends were usually indistinguishable. Although they are separated here for analytical purposes, in actuality tactics used to realize the dual goals of sexual and vocational regulation worked together, coalescing and mutually reinforcing one another.

From Sexual Autonomy to Propriety: Preparation for the 'True Good Womanly Life'

To control the sexual activities of "promiscuous" women, the Albion reformatory used several approaches. One was the initial act of incarcerating women who had violated standards of sexual conduct for the "true women." Second was parole revocation if a prisoner showed signs of lapsing back into impropriety while out on conditional release. Third was transfer of intractables to a custodial asylum for "feebleminded" women at Rome, New York, where they could be held indefinitely.

Over the thirty-seven years of its operation as a reformatory, Albion received about 3,150 prisoners. The menial nature of the jobs at which their parents were employed and their own previously high rates of employment at poorly paid, low-skilled jobs indicate that most of these prisoners were working-class women. Three-quarters of them were between fifteen and twenty-one years old, the rest under thirty. The vast majority—over 95 percent—were white. Most had been born in New York State (particularly in the rural western area where the institution was located) of native-born parents; one-third were Catholic, while nearly all the rest were Protestant; and most were single. The composition of the population reflected the desire of Albion's officials to work with cases who appeared malleable and deserving. The institution's commitment law authorized it to receive women convicted of petit larceny, habitual drunkenness, common prostitution, frequenting a disorderly house, or any other misdemeanor. Originally, it could hold them for up to five years; later, the maximum number of years was reduced to three. Less than 2 percent of the prisoners were convicted of violent crimes (and these were mainly second or third degree assault) and but another 14 percent of property offenses (mainly petit larceny). The great majority (over 80 percent) had been sentenced for public order offenses—victimless crimes such as public intoxication, waywardness, and vagrancy.

. . .[F]or at least half (and perhaps up to three-quarters) of Albion's inmates, the act that led to incarceration had actually been sexual misconduct. Some of these women were apprehended for prostitution. Most, however, were merely sexually active, engaging in flirtations and affairs for pleasure instead of money. The efforts of Albion and other reformatories to curb sexual independence by women occurred within the wider context of antiprostitution and other social purity campaigns. Members of the middle and upper classes increasingly committed themselves to the cleansing of society. At the same time, however, some working women became indifferent to traditional definitions of virtue. In rapidly growing numbers, they left home to join the paid labor force. By 1910, a record high of 27 percent of all New York State women were gainfully employed. Even more significantly, nearly 80 percent of Albion's inmates had previously worked for wages. As they acquired a degree of independence, working women turned to new amusements. To smoke cigarettes, frequent dance halls, and become involved in sexual relationships did not strike *them* as depravity; but their disinterest in the ideals of "true" womanhood evoked alarm in those dedicated to the battle against vice. Reformers came to consider any deviation from female sexual propriety, even when it did not involve a financial transaction, as a form of "prostitution."

The sexual misconduct for which women were incarcerated at Albion came to the attention of authorities through a variety of routes. Sometimes irate parents reported sexually active daughters to the police; at others, cuckolded husbands complained to court officials. Premarital pregnancies alerted social control agents in many cases. In yet others, discovery of venereal diseases led to commitment. For many women, a sign of sexual impurity in combination with some other suspicious circumstance seems to have precipitated arrest. For example, Anna H., one of Albion's few black inmates, evidently came to the attention of police when her husband was arrested for attempted burglary. Anna was examined, found to have venereal disease, and sentenced to Albion for vagrancy. There was no question of her fidelity to her husband: reformatory officials accepted Anna's statement that it was he who had infected her, and they later refused to release her on the theory that she would return to him ("the combination is a very bad one"). But Anna had been living apart from her husband, supporting herself as a waitress, and this irregular arrangement may have increased officials' consternation.

Ostensibly, venereal disease was also the ground on which Lillian R., a Coney Islander of orthodox Jewish background, was originally committed; but in her case, too, unseemly independence and bad associates may have contributed to authorities' concern. Having quit school after the seventh grade to help her widowed mother support a large family, Lillian had been variously employed as a messenger, box factory worker, and forewoman in an artificial flower shop. At the age of sixteen she ran off with a soldier for a week and contracted venereal disease. She and her mother decided (according to her record) that "it would not be right for her to remain in her home with the other children. She was . . . put into the Magdalene home. [She] was there one week when sent to the City Hospital for treatment." At the hospital Lillian was charged with "contracting an infectious disease in the practice of debauchery" and sentenced to the Bedford reformatory, from which she was later transferred to Albion.

Some women committed to Albion for sexual misbehavior had in fact been sexually victimized. Such was the case with Anna B., who at the age of fourteen had been charged with ungovernability and sent to the Salvation Army Home in Buffalo, where she bore her first child. Not long after she returned home, her father was sentenced to prison for rape. Anna's case file strongly suggests that she was the victim. While her father was still on trial, Anna was sent to Pennsylvania to live with a grandmother. Within a month, she became pregnant by the sixty-year-old man for whom her grandmother kept house. Anna returned home, where she went to work in a restaurant. Convicted of "running around" when she was seven months into this second pregnancy, Anna seems actually to have been exploited twice by much older men.

Although a handful of cases were, like Anna B., "led astray," most of Albion's inmates appear to have been rebels of some sort—against the double standard of sexual morality; against their families or husbands; or against public regulations such as that prohibiting disorderly conduct. But perhaps "rebels" is not the most accurate term: in officials' view, they defied conventions, but many of these young women may have been acting in accordance with other standards that they themselves considered legitimate. Despite their youth, the majority were independent at the point when police officers plucked them from saloons, hotel rooms,

and street corners to be sent to the reformatory. Four-fifths of them held jobs. Although over 70 percent had not yet married, they were no longer under their parents' control. Whether reacting defiantly against conventional concepts of morality or simply behaving in ways they regarded as acceptable, most clearly had not internalized a view of themselves as "proper" women, demure and asexual. It was this situation that the reformatory, with its goal of imposing and teaching sexual control, sought to remedy.

If incarceration and training within the institution did not teach the prisoner to conform, the reformatory employed another means: parole revocation. Most of Albion's inmates were released on parole before their sentences expired. During the period of parole their behavior was scrutinized by the institution's parole officers, community officials, and employers. . . .When parole was revoked, the violation was frequently sexual in nature.

Some women had parole revoked for overt returns to vice. Such was the case with inmate No. 1899, recalled to Albion after "an officer of Endicott, N.Y., arrested her in a questionable resort." Similarly, inmate No. 1913 was forced to return when, after marrying during parole, she was reported by her husband "for misconduct with men." Women who became pregnant during parole were returned to the institution—unless they quickly married someone "respectable." At other times revocation was triggered not by blatant signs of immorality but rather by indications that a lapse was imminent. One woman was returned to the reformatory because she "became infatuated with a married man named L____. Mrs. L____ wrote us" and, after investigating, reformatory officials decided to recall her. Another parolee was revoked for associating with the father of her child ("they were not married and Washington is a most disreputable character"), and No. 1313 barely escaped revocation when "two former inmates report[ed] seeing her frequently at night with different conductors on the Genesee St. line."

In cases that appeared hopeless to Albion's administrators, a third step was sometimes taken to ensure against relapse: transfer to the State School at Rome or another of New York's institutions for the feebleminded. Such transfers carried an automatic extension of sentence up to life, for according to popular theory of the time, the feebleminded never improve. At the turn of the century, the feebleminded were considered innately promiscuous, so Albion's authorities easily assumed that women who would not reform were feebleminded "defective delinquents." Because intelligence testing was still in a primitive stage, it was not difficult to confirm "scientifically" a suspicion of feeblemindedness and thus establish the basis for a transfer. These transfers, which occurred in cases of women who were disciplinary problems within the institution as well as in instances of overt sexuality while on parole, constituted the final disposition for forty-eight of the sampled cases, or 3 percent of all first releases. In addition, thirteen women who were returned to the reformatory for parole violation (5.2 percent of those who were released a second time), and two women (5.6 percent of the thirty-six sampled cases who returned twice to the reformatory and then discharged a third time) were transferred to institutions for the feebleminded. Case file documents such as school records and letters written by these supposedly feebleminded women indicate that they were not in fact mentally retarded. They were, however, noncompliant. The lesson of their transfer to civil institutions was probably not lost on those left behind at the reformatory.

From Sauciness to Subservience: Preparation for Domestic Service

The second central social control function of the Albion reformatory was to train inmates to become competent housekeepers in either their own homes or those where they were placed as domestics. The institution aimed, in the words of its managers, to re-form "unfortunate and wayward girls" by giving them "moral and religious training . . . and such training in domestic work as will eventually enable them to find employment, secure good homes and be self-supporting." To the achievement of this end, the managers viewed the cottage system, with its "plan of ordinary domestic life," as crucial. Acquisition of decorum was also considered critical; the institution emphasized gentility in all aspects of its program. Within this institutional facsimile of the genteel home, inmates received both academic and domestic training, with by far the heavier emphasis falling on the latter. Albion seldom educated inmates beyond the sixth grade level, but it provided abundant opportunities for perfection of domestic skills, instructing prisoners in dressmaking, plain and fancy sewing, knitting, crocheting, "cookery," cleaning, and "ventilation." A steam-operated washing machine was purchased for the institution's laundry, but the sight of it made visiting prison commissioner Sarah L. Davenport "sorry," for it was "not educating the women . . . for the homes they will go to when they leave Albion." Thereafter, the laundry was washed by hand. A "finely equipped domestic science department," outfitted with dining room furniture, coal and gas burners, and kitchen utensils, was added in 1912, and from then on inmates received instruction in:

> manufacture and source of food supplies, relative cost, and nutritive values; the care of the kitchen, pantry, and dining room; construction and care of the sinks, stoves, (both gas and coal) and refrigerators; table etiquette; the planning and serving of meals; and waitress' duties.

When members of the board of managers met at the reformatory, inmates practiced for future employment by waiting on their table. As Elliott Curie has put it in writing of the Massachusetts reformatory, the institution "trained women to be women."

For middle-class women who lived in its vicinity, Albion provided trained, inexpensive household help. It was the institution's policy "to place our girls in the home of a woman who will take a motherly interest in them." One-quarter of the prisoners were paroled directly to live-in domestic positions. Of the 50 percent paroled to members of their own families, another sizeable proportion also took jobs as domestics. Housekeeping was familiar to Albion's prisoners, many of whom reported their previous occupation as "domestic" or "houseworker." But the reformatory's records suggest that some, at least, had been less than satisfactory servants, given to carelessness, impudence, filching, and running off with young men. The institution tried to turn these and other inmates into competent, submissive domestics.

Attempts by Albion and other reformatories to train domestics took place at a time when the "servant problem" was particularly intense. Difficulties in finding suitable servants became acute after the Civil War and continued to be so well into the twentieth century. As the number of families that could afford servants increased, the interest of working-class women in domestic service declined. The latter came to prefer factory jobs that offered more money, shorter hours, and greater autonomy. Those who had no alternative to domestic service resented the power of the mistress; they also objected to the social restrictions of live-in positions and to expectations of servility. Many reacted to such conditions with impertinence and petty theft. The distaste of working women for domestic service created a predicament for would-be employers. Servants were necessary for the operation of their households, and (equally important) they were a sign of status. Thus in increasing the supply of well-trained domestics, reformatory officials supported the interests of other middle-class women.

Nearly 20 percent of Albion's prisoners had worked before arrest in mills or factories. But as noted earlier, the frequent economic crises of the late nineteenth and early twentieth centuries led to widespread unemployment, and serious labor unrest. Insofar as reformatories removed women from the industrial labor force, they made more jobs available for men. In view of these circumstances, the reformatory's refusal to provide training in skills that might be "unfit" women for domestic service is especially significant. "No industries are maintained," one Albion report declared, "but every inmate is taught to cook and care for a home. This is the most important thing in the work of the institution. Most of the girls when paroled go into homes where this knowledge is necessary." Thus Albion not only provided rigorous training in housekeeping but also tended to discourage inmates from moving beyond the home and earning higher wages. It reinforced the point that women's place was in the home by paroling most women to family situations where they were needed as paid or unpaid domestic help.

Employers and the institution formed a symbiotic alliance over the discipline of women paroled as servants. The reformatory required women released to domestic positions to sign a form agreeing to

> accept the wages agreed upon between the Superintendent . . . and her employer . . . her wages to be retained by employer, excepting such amount as the latter thinks necessary for [the] girl. . . .[C]onsult employer as to her amusements, recreation, and social diversions. To form no friendships, not to visit or receive visits from members of her own family unless approved by the Superintendent. Is not to go out nights excepting when accompanied by a responsible person, and to go very seldom at night. To have one afternoon a week. . . .

Paroled women were also required to send monthly reports to the reformatory, and they were further supervised through visits from a parole officer. If despite these controls a domestic became difficult, the reformatory could revoke parole, a threat that no doubt helped employers maintain discipline. These restraints notwithstanding, many women paroled to domestic positions behaved noncompliantly. Revocations were occasioned by "sauciness," "obscenity," failure to work hard enough, and other demonstrations of independence. Inmate No. 13, for example,

> went to Rochester to work for Mrs. . . .J_____ and for a time did very nicely but finding some girls of her acquaintance she began to visit them too often and to neglect her work. She came back to the institution in Aug. 1897 and there remained till [sentence] expiration.

Inmate No. 2585 was originally paroled to a Mrs. F_____ of Rochester. But, "Jane was a slow worker and very untidy and shiftless. She was very fond of reading. Returned [to the reformatory] for a change of place. . . ." Next Jane was sent to a Mrs. S_____ of Buffalo. This time, "On Oct. 11 went to a movie and did not return until eleven o'clock when she was expected at nine." When Mrs. S_____ threatened to return her to Albion, Jane fled. She was not recaptured, but others on domestic parole were returned to the institution for laziness, disobedience, and running away.

In return for the institution's help with disciplining difficult domestics, employers supervised prisoners. They were "authorized and requested to open and read all mail sent and received by girl" and further charged "to guard her morals, language and actions, and aid her as much as possible by advice as to her present and future conduct. . . . " In the course of aiding fallen women, employers were also aiding themselves by maintaining the quality of the services they received. The entire arrangement, in fact, seems to have been one from which employers benefitted greatly, receiving trained and supervised servants who promised to consult them in all matters and work six and one-half days a week. If the servant became shiftless or impudent, the criminal justice system would step in to do the necessary disciplining.

Techniques of Social Control

Albion developed a variety of techniques to encourage reform. Some have already

been identified: the initial act of incarcerating women for sexual misconduct and other petty offenses; intensive training in domesticity and gentility; a policy of parole to domestic positions; community surveillance; parole revocation; and transfer of the most uncooperative to civil institutions where they could be held indefinitely. Implicit in many of these techniques was another: from the moment of arrest, Albion's inmates were reduced to the standing of children. Like juvenile delinquents, many were detained for status offenses—immorality, waywardness, keeping bad company—for which men the same age were not arrested. At the reformatory they were supervised by motherly matrons, and at parole they were usually released to family situations in which they had a dependent position. Indeed, the very concept of an institution dedicated to the rescue and reform of women under the age of thirty, and operated with an extremely high level of discretionary authority, was rooted in a view of women as childlike creatures. Appropriately, like institutions for juvenile delinquents, Albion was titled a "refuge."

Disruption of inmates' ties with their families was another mechanism used by the reformatory to encourage inmates to conform to its values. Some prisoners, to be sure, had already separated from their families; but being independent through one's own choice was not the same as being severed from one's family by others—and at a time of crisis. Familial disruption was a technique to which women were especially susceptible, their roles being so intimately involved with domestic life. Disconnected from their own families, Albion inmates were more likely to identify with the surrogate "families" of their cottages and, on parole, with those to which they were sent as servants.

Disruption of family life is an inevitable by-product of incarceration, but Albion developed policies relating to mail and visitors that intensified the break. Once in custody, women had immense difficulty contacting families and friends. They were permitted to write letters only once every two months, and these were censored. If the Superintendent decided that either the contents or the designated recipient was unsuitable, she would file the letter in the inmate's folder—quite probably without notifying the writer and certainly without notifying the intended recipient, both of whom might therefore wait in vain anticipation. Incoming mail was also censored and often filed away undelivered. Visits were permitted, but only four times a year. A further restriction limited the pool of potential visitors to close relatives, and even these might be banned if deemed bad influences. Moreover, some approved visitors doubtless were discouraged from visiting by the institution's geographical isolation. For all these reasons, commitment to the reformatory resulted in nearly total severance of ties to former support groups. Isolated in this fashion, prisoners became more susceptible to the institution's staff and its moral advice.

Another aspect of familial disruption, separation from children, was sometimes traumatically final. When women were committed, their children might be sent to orphanages or put up for adoption. Such removals occurred even in instances when inmates had husbands living at home. Thus not only were young mothers severed from their children; they also had to suffer the knowledge that their families had been dissolved. In such cases, moreover, the children were now being cared for by strangers. To judge from Albion's records, its inmates were not informed of the welfare of institutionalized or adopted children.

Occasionally ultimate disposition of children would be left undecided and used to induce the mother to conform. Of a woman committed for vagrancy, for instance, the registry reports,

> Edna made a splendid record while on parole. Mr. Angel, Humane Officer of Courtland County[,] was so well pleased with her that he returned her children to her.

Not to please Mr. Angel, it seems, would have resulted in loss of her children. Another example is provided by the case of Martha, a mother of four, sentenced to Albion for public intoxication. Threat of removal of her children kept Martha sober even in times of great stress:

> Martha returned [on parole] to her husband who had promised every[thing] in the way of reform but who is the veriest hypocrite [*sic*]. She continued leading a true good womanly life hoping to be worthy of her children, as the authorities had promised to restore them when they were satisfied that she would hold out.

In instances like these, there was the initial familial disruption occasioned by commitment and then a threat of further disruption—total loss of children—if the prisoner did not comply with the institution's requirements.

Similar methods of control involved babies who stayed with mothers at the institution. If a woman was nursing at commitment, she was allowed to bring the child with her. Those women who gave birth at Albion were permitted to keep infants. But reformatory policy decreed that all babies had to leave when they reached the age of two. Sometimes the institution decided not to parole a woman until after the baby had been sent away. Mary P___, for example, bore a child a few days after her arrival at Albion in 1922, and in September 1924, two years having expired, the child was sent to the Delaware County Superintendent of the Poor. Mary was paroled just a month later to work in her father's cigar factory. Mary's parents may have refused to let her bring home an illegitimate child. Whatever the reason, the effect of holding her slightly beyond the mandatory release date for the baby was to cut Mary off from the only family she had for two years. She was, moreover, returned to a situation in which she herself was the child.

Some babies brought into or born at the prison were sent to adoption agencies or other institutions before they reached the age of two. How long their mothers might keep them was a matter of administrative discretion, and like all such matters, liable to be used as a mechanism of control. Albion's records do not refer to the practice of using children to coerce institutionalized mothers, but this form of social control is described in a letter from the Superintendent of Maine's State Reformatory for Women to a journalist who had requested information on babies in prison. "The conduct of the mothers," the superintendent informed him,

> decides in a measure the time they are allowed to spend with their babies. . . .They dress and undress and feed their own babies after the baby is six months old. They always have the privilege to kiss them goodnight and to spend an hour in the afternoon with them, unless their conduct precludes the loss [*sic*] of this privilege.

Restricting access to children was probably used as a social control device at Albion and other reformatories as well.

Despite its emphasis on the home as woman's place, Albion developed parole policies that further disrupted some inmates' ties to their former homes. Women who before incarceration lived in stable family situations were frequently paroled not to their own families but to domestic positions in the homes of others. In some instances, the institution deemed the original family unsuitable and wanted to keep the woman away from it as long as possible. In others, officials seem simply to have decided that for a woman to work and save money was the best way for her to pass parole. Often the domestic jobs were in towns distant from the prisoners' families. Women could take infants with them to some domestic live-in positions, but others required them to leave their babies behind.

Many of these dislocating factors were present in the case of Marjorie M., a twenty-year-old of German extraction who, before commitment, lived with her parents and seven siblings in Batavia, where she was employed as a domestic. The mother of a three-

year-old and again pregnant, Marjorie was convicted of disorderly conduct in 1917 and sent to Albion. There she gave birth to her second daughter, Helen. Paroled to a domestic position in Rochester, Marjorie sent five dollars of her eight-dollar weekly salary to the home where Helen was boarded. After parole, she found employment as assistant housekeeper at the Rochester Orphan's Asylum, where Helen was now living. Helen died of diphtheria in the winter of 1920. At this point Marjorie, who at the time of arrest had been living with ten members of her immediate family, was left entirely alone.

The reformatory's policies also perpetuated familial disruption in the case of Henrietta S., a Binghamton woman with two children. After serving time at Albion for intoxication, Henrietta was paroled to a domestic position in Lyndonville, where she earned four dollars a week. When her term was up, she returned to her family with $154 she had managed to save from her wages. The institution interpreted the large sum as a sign of success, but Henrietta and her family paid a high psychological price in return: their family life had been interrupted for three years, and while a Mrs. F_____ of Lyndonville had cheap use of her services, Henrietta's own children had been deprived of her care.

The reformatory's parole policies were not disruptive of family life in all instances, and perhaps some women who *were* returned to parents or husbands would have preferred a less restrictive arrangement. In either case, the institution exercised tremendous control over inmates' social contacts (probably more than any contemporary prison for men), and it used this control to induce conformity. Denying inmates access to mail and visitors, institutionalizing their children or threatening to do so, on occasion probably blocking access to infants within the prison, developing parole policies that frequently prevented contact with families—through such means the prison demonstrated its power and often disrupted the continuity of whatever family life had existed. The effect was to encourage dependency on the institution and increase the likelihood that inmates would internalize the reformatory's teachings about how women like themselves should behave.

'The Best Place to Conquer Girls': The Reformatory's Success

Many women incarcerated at Albion went on to lead lives that met the institution's criteria for success, marrying and maintaining homes of their own or remaining for long terms in domestic placements. No doubt many former inmates would have become more sedate in their mid-twenties or early thirties even without the moral influence of the prison, just as more serious offenders outgrow crime. But the reformatory does seem to have set some formerly wayward women on the path to propriety—to have served, in the words of one inmate's sister, as "the only and best place to conquer girls." Albion appears, that is, to have achieved its goals in some, perhaps even a majority, of cases.

The reformatory worked through kindness as well as coercion, and therein lay the key to its success. Had it merely punished, it would have antagonized; but Albion also performed extensive nurturing functions, alleviating some of the harsher aspects of poverty. It served as a hospital where the diseased could receive treatment, the malnourished food, the pregnant decent care at delivery. It also functioned as a shelter to which women could turn from incestuous fathers and brutal husbands. The superintendent and other staff offered counseling in careers, marriage, and child-rearing. Moreover, the institution provided training in manners that many working-class women may have considered valuable: refined behavior was widely regarded as a sign of female superiority, particularly by people with authority and status.

To be sure, the reformatory did not bring every case to the desired conclusion. It tended to be least successful with women whose families had resisted their commitment. In the case of Anna H., the black woman sentenced for vagrancy, for instance, the reformatory was bombarded with appeals for release from the inmate's frantic parents and their lawyer, the mayor of Newport, Rhode Island; the latter also elicited requests for Anna's discharge from the offices of New York's State Board of Charities and Governor Alfred E. Smith. When the superintendent refused to heed these appeals, Anna attempted to escape. Lillian R., the inmate originally sentenced to the Bedford reformatory for "debauchery," was similarly unappreciative of institutionalization. At Bedford she participated in the July 1920 riots against cruelty to inmates. Subsequently, Bedford's matrons told her she was to be paroled, but as Lillian explained in a letter to her mother, "I knew that parole talk was all a frameup"; she realized she was really being transferred to Albion, at the other end of the state. "[I]f they were any kind of women they would tell us just where we are going and not say that we were paroled. . . . [T]hen they wonder why the girls don't respect them." Lillian's later letters show that she was equally critical of the matrons at Albion. Other inmates demonstrated resistance by misbehaving on parole:

> Julia was a great care throughout her parole . . .deceitful & deceptive. [No. 1581]
>
> She was arrested while on parole and sentenced again to the W.H. of R. But we refused to take her again. [No. 1355]
>
> Minnie gave entire satisfaction [while on domestic parole] for several months[,] saved her money[,] was quiet and unobtrusive. . . . The spirit of unrest [then] took possession of her and she absconded, and no trace of her has been found. [No. 89]

When No. 61 sold her discharge clothes, "bought a telescope," and ran away from the Wayfarers' Lodge in Buffalo, reformatory officials resignedly observed, "[A] perverse nature and bad blood [had] proved too strong for human endeavor."

On the other hand, Albion's records also provide evidence that numerous inmates were grateful for its help. Some, especially those who were very young, alone in the world, or in poor health, seem not to have found incarceration onerous. A few, for example, requested to stay for their full terms, without parole. Inmate No. 1257 resisted leaving Albion for an unpleasant home situation: her mother had been committed to an insane asylum, and there were small children whose care would fall on her. "When it came time for her to go . . . she cried and it was with difficulty that the Parole Officer persuaded her to go." Some parolees ran back to the institution from uncongenial domestic placements. One woman, after having been paroled twice, returned "and asked to be admitted. She was a wreck, physically and morally—her clothing torn and soiled, and evidently [she] had no place to go for the night nor money to pay her way." The reformatory gave her medical attention and sheltered her for another six months. After marrying, some former inmates brought their husbands to visit the reformatory and meet its superintendent. A woman who had escaped later wrote from a distant state to announce that she was happily married; her resentment at being confined, in other words, was not incompatible with a desire to demonstrate that she could achieve the institution's ideals. Many women wrote back after release. "My dear Mrs. Boyd," began a letter received by superintendent Boyd in 1907,

have [you] entirely forgotten Nellie that one time lived in your pleasant Home for Homeless Girls.

I have been thinking for some time that I would write to you. . . .Of course you have heard from Mrs. Green that I am married and have a good Husband. . . .Are any of the Ladies [officers] with you now that were in the years of 1894 or 95 . . . how I would like to see them as well as your self. . . .I have a very pleasant home and appreciate it I think as I ought to. Yours in haste and with love,

Nellie (I am Ever) L_____

Albion succeeded in persuading inmates like Nellie to identify with its standards for correct female behavior. These were, essentially, middle-class standards. While many members of the working class may also have endorsed them, women sentenced to Albion had not—deviations from these values had led to their incarceration. In reforming (and in wanting to demonstrate reformation), successful cases had by definition come to identify with middle-class concepts of female propriety. Class identification was very much in flux at the turn of the century. As Charles Rosenberg has explained,

[S]tatus definitions in 19th century America were . . . particularly labile. . . . A good many Americans must, it follows, have been all the more anxious in their internalization of those aspects of life-style which seemed to embody and assure class status. And contemporaries clearly regard overt sexuality, especially in women, as part of a life-style demeaning to middle-class status.

When women who had been apprehended for sexual misconduct and other signs of independence from middle-class "status definitions" became chaste or sober or (like Nellie) "appreciative" of husband and home, the middle-class won an ideological victory. Its values had been affirmed; its symbols of status had been accorded validity by women of the working-class.

The reformatory probably influenced the values not only of those sentenced to it but also of women in the broader community. Albion's records show that some inmates knew each other before commitment and continued to associate after release. But to be a prisoner was unusual; since acquaintanceship networks existed among inmates, these networks must have been even more extensive between inmates and women never incarcerated. Through such connections, Albion would have come to play a role in the consciousness of working-class women in its area. Women who never set foot inside it would have been aware, through word of mouth, that there existed a state institution prepared to punish them for deviations from middle-class definitions of womanliness.

Informal as well as formal police actions reinforced the social values endorsed by Albion, reminding women in the community of the institution's potential for punishment. This kind of informal social control is almost invisible today since it was seldom noted in official records. Yet glimpses of it can be caught from time to time in reformatory documents. One hint appears in the registry record of inmate No. 2441, a woman confined for vagrancy. She had no previous arrests, according to the registry, but had been "taken to the Police Station twice and talked to for being out late, attending dances." Whereas this particular woman was evidently not influenced by police efforts to get her to behave properly (she did, after all, end up at the reformatory), others so treated may have been. Of No. 1775, paroled in 1919, we are told,

> Edna was very erratic and unreliable during her parole. She was reported [to the reformatory] by the Binghamton police as being on the streets at a late hour very frequently with different men. Chief Cronin was asked several times [by reformatory officials] to arrest her and instructed his men to that effect.

Other police chiefs probably also ordered their men to keep women like Edna in line. Thus, through informal procedures as well as formal arrests, the police helped uphold the reformatory's values; they, too, gave women incentives to submit and behave.

The Definition of Gender

Most other women's reformatories also aimed at rescue and reform and used techniques of social control similar to those of Albion. From Maine to North Carolina, New York to Nebraska, reformatories for women removed errant women from the streets, trained them in domestic skills, and returned them to the home. Through parole supervision they also encouraged inmates on conditional release to maintain "self-control" at work and in sexual relationships; and if located in states with facilities for the feebleminded, they also used transfers to such institutions as an auxiliary disciplinary measure. All prisons of the reformatory type seem to have exercised tight control over mail, visitors, and disposition of children. Like Albion, most other reformatories were multifunctional institutions that served as hospitals, refuges, schools, vocational training and placement agencies, and counseling centers—as well as prisons. Officials at many were rewarded by former inmates who returned, after discharge, to give thanks and demonstrate that they had indeed reformed.

The prisoners of these institutions were burdened by multiple disadvantages. They and their families fell near the bottom of the class hierarchy. In addition to being poor, the prisoners suffered the disability of being women in a society that barred women from many occupations, paid them less than male workers, and imposed male authority everywhere. Race was yet another factor relegating black or Indian women to the base of the social structure, while nativist prejudices pushed the foreign-born toward the margins of society. Most reformatory prisoners were young, a further drawback in terms of status. Those who were single—and they were probably in the majority at other reformatories as well as at Albion—were at another disadvantage in a society that placed a premium on marriage for women.

The prisoners were, then, located at the bottom of many power dimensions in their society, those defined by social class, sex, age, marital status, and (for some) race or ethnicity. But they did not stay put in these lowly positions. They had no authority, yet as the many cases of incorrigible daughters, wandering wives, and unreliable servants in reformatory reports indicate, they balked at obedience. Lacking autonomy, they nonetheless acted independently. Bereft of status, many refused to behave as inferiors. Their very handicaps, in fact, created a situation of some fluidity. As women who had to work, they had achieved a degree (albeit minimal) of economic self-sufficiency. Denied the luxury of being kept, they were to some extent freed from cultural imagery that associated "good" women with fragility and submissiveness. Youth in combination with physical maturity and lack of marital attachment probably encouraged them to seek sexual pleasure outside marriage. Thus their characteristics and situations promoted disengagement from their era's standards for propriety.

Among the factors that fostered establishment of woman's reformatories, two were of special importance: changes in gender roles in nineteenth- and early twentieth-century America and the simultaneous widening of divisions between social classes. During the nineteenth century, as production came to be located outside the family, women were increasingly isolated within the home. Their labor was devalued and a premium came to be placed on feminine characteristics such as domesticity, demureness, purity, and piety. But the ideal of true womanhood was more easily approximated by women of the middle than of the working class. The former were likely to have servants and other aids to gentility, and if they became restless they could take up causes like temperance and prison reform.

Intensification of gender roles had different implications for working-class women, however. For them, true womanhood was more difficult to achieve and less rewarding. As the nineteenth century flowed into the twentieth, some middle-class women (including those who founded and ran reformatories) participated in the gradual break from traditional roles. But for them, activity in the world was more likely to be compatible with respectability; charitable work, for instance, had long been a hallmark of the lady, and social feminism posed no real threat to male authority. But activities available to working-class women in search of self-fulfillment meshed less well with traditional notions of rectitude. Indeed, some of

them, such as drinks in saloons, late night cigarettes with sailors, and casual affairs, became grounds for imprisonment.

Persuaded of innate temperamental differences between the sexes, the reformers naturally set about establishing separate prisons for women run by women; and believing that woman's mission included rescue of the unfortunate, they naturally focused on fallen women—not serious felons or confirmed prostitutes but wayward "girls" who might be saved. Those among them active in social purity campaigns argued against the double standard of sexual morality for men and women. Yet all the reformers worked to found or operate prisons that in fact institutionalized the double standard. Their understanding of "woman's nature" led logically to advocacy of special help for the frailer sex.

This understanding was embodied in laws establishing reformatories that could incarcerate women for minor offenses, mainly "moral" in nature. In many cases, apparently, the understanding came to be internalized by inmates. This internalization provides an instance of the ability of law to perform hegemonic functions—to reproduce the ideological and political conditions of social hierarchy. As Diane Polan has explained, "In respect to patriarchy, a set of ideas . . . operate[s] hegemonically to the extent it succeeds in convincing women that their inferior political, economic, and social status is a result of a *natural* division of the world into separate spheres and *natural* differences between male and female personalities . . . rather than the result of exploitation and domination." From this perspective, inmates' acceptance of reformatory values can be seen as a phase in the process that another writer describes as "the *embourgeoisement* of the working class," its absorption of middle-class attitudes toward status, security, property, the family—and gender roles.

Two groups of women—the working-class offenders and the middle-class reformers—met, so to speak, at the gate of the women's reformatory. The struggle between them was economically functional to the reformers: it helped maintain a pool of cheap domestic labor for women like themselves and, by keeping working women in the surplus labor force, it undergirded the economic system to which reformers owed their privileged positions. But a purely economic explanation does not adequately account for the dedication with which the reformers went about their tasks of rescue and reform. The struggle also involved the definition of gender. The reformers had already absorbed the social controls they sought to instill. These reformers hoped to recast offenders in their own image, to have them embrace the values (though not assume the social station) of the lady. And through reformatories like Albion, some working-class women were taught to accept a new concept of womanhood that restricted their sexual and vocational choices. They were, in fact, reformed.

Study Questions

1. What is meant by social control, and how does it apply to the women's reformatory movement?

2. For what types of offenses were women incarcerated in Albion? By whom? Why?

3. Discuss the types of sexual activities that were likely to land young women in reformatories. How was such promiscuity curtailed by the institution?

4. How did Albion prepare women for their domestic roles?

5. What types of coercive power did reformatories exert on their charges to gain compliance?

6. Discuss the relationship between social class and the reformatory movement. ✦

5
A New Prison Discipline

Implementing the Declaration of Principles of 1870

Howard B. Gill

This article begins with a review of the "old prison discipline." The tenets of what prisons stood for from 1825 to 1925 are elucidated to help define the purposes of confinement over time. Gill points out that, in hindsight, most if not all of these purposes run contrary to what constitutes a healthy well-adjusted personality (e.g., deprivation, subservience, noncommunication, lack of recreation, no responsibility, degradation). After considering how widespread these old principles have become, and what impact they have had on the modern institution, the author suggests a "new prison discipline" aimed at reform. In addition, "operational benchmarks" are listed. These include, but are not limited to, the involvement of the community, a scientific effort toward offender classification, and a redesign of the physical prison and its social structure. The reader should consider the feasibility and utility of implementing these benchmarks.

Several times during recent years, an attempt has been made to revise the Declaration of Principles established by the National Prison Congress in 1870. Such changes as were made were insignificant. No one has ever extolled the revised version of 1930 or of

Excerpts from *Federal Probation*, Volume 34, pages 29–33.

1960. One might as well suggest a revision of the Declaration of Independence! New times call for new manifestos, not revisions of old declarations. What is needed today, 100 years later, is not a revised or a new Declaration of Principles, but a statement implementing the Declaration of Principles of 1870—a statement summarizing what that Declaration has produced through trial and error over the past 100 years; a codification of progress achieved, an affirmation for the future. Let us call it a New Prison Discipline.

There are two types of discipline: One, a set of rules and regulations governing a group; the other, a way of life. There is a discipline in medicine, in religion, in education. So in corrections there is a discipline. It includes rules and regulations, but it is of much broader scope; it is a way of life.

Prison Discipline: 1825–1925

Historically, the prison discipline recognized by prison workers for over 100 years was founded by Elam Lynds, the warden of Auburn Prison, about 1825. It was founded on the basic assumption that the prerequisite for reform was to "break the spirit of the criminal." It prevailed almost universally in the United States from 1825 until 1925. It still is standard operating procedure in some American prisons.

Specifically, this old prison discipline stood for some very concrete things:

Hard Labor.—Through productive work from "making little ones out of big ones" to constructive prison industries, or through nonproductive punitive labor such as the tread-mill and the carrying of cannon shot from one end of the prison yard to the other.

Deprivation.—Of everything except the bare essentials of existence.

Monotony.—Of diet and drab daily routine.

Uniformity.—The warden's proudest boast: "We treat every prisoner alike."

Mass movement.—Mass living in cell blocks, mass eating, mass recreation, even mass bathing. In this monolithic type of program the low of individual personality was characteristic. One watched the dull gray line with its prison shuffle where the faces of men were as if shellacked with a single mask.

Degradation.—To complete the loss of identity prisoners became numbers. Housed in monkey cages, dressed in shoddy nondescript clothing, denied civil contacts even with guards like the one who snarled: "Who the hell are you to wish me a Merry Christmas?" Degradation became complete.

Subservience.—To rules, rules, rules—the petty whims of petty men.

Corporal punishment.—Brutality and force prevailed. In Tennessee the paddle, in Colorado the whip, in Florida the sweat box, etc.

Noncommunication.—Silence or solitary confinement; limited news, letters, visits, or contacts of any normal kind.

Recreation.—At first none; later a desultory or perfunctory daily hour in the yard.

No responsibility.—"No prisoner is going to tell me how to run my prison." Actually prisoners were relieved of every social, civic, domestic, economic, or even personal responsibility for the simplest daily routines.

Isolation.—Often 16 hours a day. Psychologically the admonition to "do your own time" with no thought for the other fellow only increased the egocentricity of the lone wolves.

No "fraternization" with the guards.—The rule found in many prisons that guards must not talk with prisoners about their personal problems or their crimes prevented any attempt at solving the criminal problem.

Reform by exhortation.

The Old Guard Knew What They Wanted

Now that psychology has come of age, we know that such a discipline denied every normal basic need of the human personality and its corresponding opposite essential to a healthy and normal life. These included love and a proper comprehension of its opposite, hate; independence and the right kind of dependence; constructive use of imagination and truth; achievement and learning how to meet failure; identity and a decent humility which recognized the dignity of the individual; intimacy and its opposite—discrimination; creativity and constructive criticism; integration and concentration.

These 16 human needs are recognized today as basic in the making of a healthy personality. Yet the prison discipline which was current for 100 years prior to 1925 denied every one of these basic needs. More than this, such a discipline fostered every pathology which results from a malfunctioning of these needs, namely, rejection, doubt, guilt, inferiority, inadequacy, diffusion, self-absorption, apathy, despair. Is it any wonder that men left prison worse than when they entered?

However, let us give the Old Guard credit. They knew what they wanted. They could tell you just what the "prison discipline" stood for. A young guard learned these concepts in order to be a "good prison officer." And anyone who violated these sacred rules was soon out of a job. There are still a few prison systems—in Arkansas and Mississippi—and in other isolated institutions, described by Dr. Karl Menninger in *The Crime of Punishment*, where such a prison discipline prevails.

'Modern Penology': 1925–1970

During the past 50 years, however, several things have happened which are gradually changing all this:

1. The programs inaugurated at Auburn and Sing Sing prisons in New York and at the Navy prison in Portsmouth by Thomas Mott Osborne, 1916–1920, showed plainly that prisoners knew more about what was going on in prisons than the warden and his officers. This broke the back of the "Old Guard."

2. The individual study of the offender inaugurated by Dr. William Healy in 1915 and followed up by Dr. Bernard Glueck, Dr. W.T. Root, Dr. W.J. Ellis, and Dr. Edgar Doll, resulting in the establishment of the so-called Classification System, destroyed the basic tenet of the old prison discipline that "every prisoner should be treated alike." This was the *coup de grace* that finished the "Old Guard."

3. A new type of correctional institution for tractable prisoners which abandoned the massive, monolithic, monkey cages in favor of small-group cottages or dormitories in an open community, within or without walls, is producing profound changes in climate, personnel, and methods as well as structure. Institutions for women at Alderson, West Virginia, at Dwight, Illinois, and elsewhere, and for men at Lorton, Virginia, Norfolk, Massachusetts, Annandale New Jersey, Algon Farms, Missouri, led the way. The concept of the "therapeutic community" where offenders learn to live like normal, responsible human beings has resulted. The Old Guard are not competent to administer a therapeutic community for offenders.

4. In 1913, Wisconsin, following informal experiments elsewhere, enacted the Huber Law which provided that misdemeanants might serve jail sentence by living in prison at night and working in the community by day. The law was almost forgotten for 50 years. Revived in the past 10 years, 20 states have enacted similar laws and one of the great movements in corrections got underway. Work release is becoming as important in modern corrections as the introduction of probation and parole was 100 years ago.

Since 1925 we have witnessed the development of "Modern Penology"—an attempt to replace the old prison discipline with "programs of rehabilitation"—social work and smug satisfaction, pious platitudes and programs, actually a period of conflict and confusion. The result is that we again have what Samuel L. Parsons, the Quaker superintendent of prisons for Virginia, described in 1826 as a "sickly and mistaken administration of the American penitentiary system."

It can be stated conservatively that over half of the major prisons and reformatories in the United States are just "sweet jails"—institutions where prisoners dawdle at their work, engage in a variety of desultory social and educational activities, receive good medical care, and live under so-called programs of treatment which have little or no relation to the particular criminal problem of any one of them. This is called "bird-shot" penology. We fill the old blunderbuss full of a little work, a modicum of education, a bit of religion, some medical care if necessary, a good deal of recreation—rodeos, radios, baseball, bands, choral groups, and what not—and call it rehabilitation. This is better than what passes for treatment in a minority of our prisons where "machine-gun penology" still prevails, even if the old prison discipline no longer is acknowledged; but it is not good prison discipline.

The difficulty today is that we do not know specifically for what we stand—in structure, in personnel, in method, or even in our basic concepts. What is needed is not a re-statement of fundamental principles, most of which are as applicable now as they were 100 years ago, but rather a formulation of precise, operational, down-to-earth concepts by which we can guide the course of 20th century corrections. At least it may give us a starting point toward a New Prison Discipline.

Ten Basic Concepts

First, then, let us consider some basic concepts for such a discipline.

1. Prisoners go to prison as punishment and not for punishment.

2. The purpose of imprisonment is threefold: (1) To keep prisoners in *security;* (2) to reduce criminality through *problem-solving;* and (3) to adjust prisoners

through *acculturation* to the society to which they will return. These three words—security, problem-solving, acculturation—open the doors to the new discipline.

3. Security must be assured and then assumed. Thus security becomes the primary, but not the ultimate aim of penology.

4. Treatment will begin with restitution to the victim whenever and so far as possible.

5. In the reduction of criminality, problem-solving must precede programming, and programming should be geared to the significant problems affecting criminality in each case. All else is secondary.

6. Since the crime committed is only one symptom of a basic maladjustment, we shall not treat murder, robbery, rape, or treason. Treatment for the reduction of criminality will deal with one or more of five areas of maladjustment, namely, the situational, the medical, the psychological or psychiatric, the antisocial or ethical, and/or the elementary custodial needs of shelter, food, clothing, and well-being.

7. Programs of work, education, medical care, religion, recreation, family welfare geared to solving significant problems of criminality should also be designed to *adjust the offender to the society to which he will return*, i.e., acculturation. Such a concept will revolutionize the structure and the methods of treatment in prisons as well as the personnel. We shall stop erecting massive, medieval, monastic, monolithic, monkey-cage, magnificent monstrosities as prisons. We shall adopt small-group, community-type layouts which resemble as nearly as possible normal living in an American community; and we shall develop halfway houses and residential centers for offenders who can live and work satisfacto-

rily under careful supervision in the community.

8. Treatment through problem-solving and acculturation must proceed whether or not causation can be established or dealt with. While it is helpful to know and understand causation, it is not necessary for treatment. However, causation should be explored as far as possible in environmental, physical, psychological, and characterological areas.

9. The function of the prison will be limited to safe-keeping, observation, diagnosis, planning, and training or treatment. Rehabilitation or re-adjustment will be conducted in the normal community under normal conditions with all the attendant, problems, influences, and responsibilities. This will inevitably lead to the following basic concept.

10. The establishment between the prison and parole of a program of partial or semirelease—what I have called *"social servitude"* or servitude in society as contrasted with penal servitude—under close daily supervision in the community similar to the Intermediate Plan of the Irish System (1850–1870), the Huber Law of Wisconsin (1913), and the work-release programs now in vogue in more than 20 states. This, alone, should reduce the present population of American prisons by 50 percent, remove the necessity for great expansion in prison building, help solve the prison labor problem, reduce the cost of keeping prisoners by millions of dollars, and insure realistic proof of satisfactory adjustment to community life, thus insuring a satisfactory parole program.

Operational Benchmarks

To implement these basic concepts, the following specific operational benchmarks will be essential.

1. *Observation, diagnosis, planning and training or treatment will be based on recognized essentials:* (1) Post-trial and presentence investigation and report; (2) individual case histories and institutional case records; (3) clinical examinations and tests—physical and psychological; and (4) clinical procedures such as counseling to secure change in attitude and action.

2. *Prisoners will be classified primarily in five basic groups for treatment:* (1) New prisoners; (2) tractable—those who desire to change and who respond to mutual trust, cooperation, and normal conditions and relationships; (3) intractable—those who do not desire to change or cooperate and who respond only to fear, force, and deprivation; (4) defective—those who are subnormal or abnormal; and (5) potential work-release prospects.

    Each group will be housed either in separate institutions or in separate sections of the same institution. The indiscriminate mixing of these groups will be avoided in any sound treatment program.

3. *Each of these five basic groups will be further classified for security as:* (1) Maximum custody—requiring close supervision; (2) medium custody—responsible within limits; and (3) minimum custody—free under general supervision.

4. *Treatment of each of these five basic groups will follow well defined lines:* (1) Orientation and preliminary problem-solving for new prisoners; (2) problem-solving and acculturation for tractable prisoners; (3) simple custodial care for intractable prisoners with severely limited privileges and programs; (4) custodial care and limited training under medical supervision for defective prisoners; and (5) treatment and supervision in the free community. Thus shall we eliminate the "sweet jail."

5. *Personnel will develop around five main groups of officers:* (1) Executive personnel; (2) administrative, fiscal, and clerical personnel; (3) professional and technical personnel—medical, industrial, educational, religious, social, recreational, psychiatric, legal—with advisory powers only as regards prisoners; (4) security personnel, especially trained to prevent and handle escapes, contraband, and disorder (such personnel will be the police of the prison community—patrol and inspect the grounds and buildings; conduct search and shakedowns; man the walls, towers, and gates; and direct transportation. They will not undertake training or treatment of prisoners including daily routine or disciplinary matters); and (5) supervisors and others in direct contact with prisoners in living quarters and in work assignments, especially trained in correctional counseling. These officers will be responsible for training and treatment of prisoners including daily routine and disciplinary matters, in cooperation with professional and technical personnel.

    By thus establishing a clear distinction between the advisory powers of the professional and technical staff and the authority for security only of one part of the guard force and for treatment of another part of the guard force, the separation of power and responsibility in the treatment of prisoners and the violent conflict between security and treatment which plagues American prisons today can be resolved.

6. *Institutional design and structure to implement the foregoing will include different types of institutions or sections of institutions, namely:* (1) Reception Center or section for new prisoners; (2) close confinement institution or section for intractable prisoners; (3) community type institution or section for tractable prisoners; (4) custodial-hospital type institution for defectives; and (5) halfway

houses and residential centers for work-release prisoners.

7. *The outside community itself must supplement such a prison discipline with the following:* (1) Supervised probation following suspended sentences; (2) supervised semirelease following a period of penal servitude as preparation for parole, as outlined above; (3) supervised parole; (4) volunteer sponsorship for probationers and ex-prisoners; (5) crime prevention under non-correctional civilian direction; (6) supplementary services in providing employment, medical care, education, family welfare, recreation, and religious counseling not available in correctional agencies.

8. A more elusive but essential element in implementing the basic concepts of a new prison discipline is the *maintenance of an institutional climate* conducive to securing the desired results. Experienced prison workers are fully aware of the importance of climate in the proper functioning of an institution. Climate is something one feels, but it is dependent on very concrete conditions.

   All that has been set forth thus far as essentials in the New Prison Discipline will contribute to the climate. Many things pertaining to structure, personnel, and methods produce climate. In American prisons today three general types of climate may be noted: the custodial, the progressive, and the professional.

   The custodial offers the minimum essentials and a decent routine in a rather grim and barren climate. The progressive satisfies many normal needs with its programs of different activities but falls short of reducing criminality as the recidivism rate shows. The professional seeks to reduce criminality through problem-solving and acculturation. Security must be assured in each.

9. *There are six important elements in producing a professional climate:* (1) *Small-group planning* as applied to structure, to groupings of prisoners, and to treatment methods as contrasted with the indiscriminate massing in all these areas; (2) *one-to-one relationship* in counseling and guidance (whether in individual or group treatment) which is the key to any effective influence on attitudes and behavior; (3) development of *joint participation and joint responsibility* in which both prisoners and the official personnel work together in a common effort to maintain the good life; (4) *normalcy* in relationships between officials and inmates in structure, in methods, in rules and regulations; (5) *community contacts* between the prison and the outside; and (6) *professional training of prison guards-in-contact* as treatment aids to front-office.

   Space does not permit discussion of these six essentials, but their application to an institution program will produce a climate conducive to effective treatment.

10. Finally, such a New Prison Discipline is not the possession or the responsibility only of prison workers. It can only be established under a leadership which recognizes *the whole correctional process as a coordinated unit,* including the police, the courts, probation, prisons, parole, and the public through prevention. It anticipates a rebirth of the old concern of the law for the entire administration of the criminal law. Indeed, until this correctional process from prevention and police work right through to parole is removed from executive-political control and put under the judicial branch of the government, we may not expect the most effective professional understanding or leadership in this field of government.

These 10 basic concepts and these 10 groups of benchmarks furnish the starting point for a New Prison Discipline. They are purposefully definite and precise. They are operational. They are down-to-earth proposals which can be tested in any prison. They offer guideposts for those who want to develop effective treatment for criminals. Moreover, they are an attempt to reflect and to summarize what the Declaration of Principles of 1870 has produced during the past 100 years—the New Prison Discipline of 1970.

Study Questions

1. What two types of prison "discipline" does Gill refer to in his article?

2. What were some of the major goals of the original tenets of the old prison discipline?

3. What were some of the major criticisms of the original tenets of the old prison discipline?

4. Specifically, what changes were brought about with the "Modern Penology" that Gill cites in his article?

5. What does Gill use as measures of success regarding the 10 "Basic Concepts" the author presents? ✦

6
Assessing the Penal Harm Movement

Francis T. Cullen

Part I concludes with a review of the "penal harm" movement. Through historical analyses, the pieces in this section have reviewed the origins and evolution of punishment as well as the ultimate rise of the institution as punishment. Similarly, the preceding articles have revealed some of the consequences of a society that places so much emphasis on confinement. The United States has been described as engaging in an "imprisonment binge." Cullen reviews what has occurred as a result of this binge. The author defines precisely what is meant by "penal harm" and documents major movements resulting from this phenomenon, such as the decline of rehabilitation, the abolition of parole release, and the proliferation of "three strikes" legislation. The utility of penal harm is reviewed, along with the unintended consequences, such as a widening of the racial disparity in U.S. prison populations. Ultimately, one of the components of confinement that remains missing in action is identified as effective efforts toward rehabilitation.

In the aftermath of the Civil War, American corrections had devolved into a state of crisis. Prisons were filled to the brim, populated by the domestic and immigrant poor. Inmates increasingly were seen as coming from the left tail of the bell curve and from

Excerpts from *Journal of Research in Crime and Delinquency,* Volume 32, Number 3, August 1995. Pages 338–358. Copyright © 1995 by Sage Publications, Inc. Reprinted by permission.

the bottom of the evolutionary ladder, and they stood as clear evidence that urban slums were producing a "dangerous class." The idea that prisons should serve the larger social purpose of changing offenders—as the founders of the penitentiary had argued convincingly to a receptive audience only a few decades earlier—was losing credibility. More affluent citizens were tempted to see prisons as effecting "a policy of exclusion and banishment, so the public might be rid of the offender" (Rothman 1980, pp. 24–25). Although "the promise of reform had built the asylums," observes Rothman (1971, p. 240), "the functionalism of custody perpetuated them."

Each historical era has its unique conversation about corrections, but these themes voiced in post-Civil War America resonate remarkably with contemporary discourse about crime and punishment. For over a decade, virtually every contemporary commentary on corrections in the United States has reminded us that the system is in crisis (see, e.g., Blumstein 1989; Colvin 1992; Cullen and Gilbert 1982; Selke 1993; Sherman and Hawkins 1981). Institutions are crowded with at-risk young adults—some would say the less intelligent among us (Herrnstein and Murray 1994)—drawn from the urban underclass. Indeed, it is not uncommon to hear talk of the "return of the dangerous classes" (Gordon 1994; Simon, p. 253). Doubts abound about the reformative powers of correctional facilities. Jails and prisons are now seen as performing a "waste management function" (Feeley and Simon 1992; Irwin 1985; Simon, pp. 259–60) or, in more sanitized language, as "selectively incapacitating the wicked" (Wilson 1983).

The response to the prison crisis—then and now—has been decidedly different, however. In 1870, the leading correctional thinkers and practitioners (the overlap in the groups being considerable at that time) gathered in Cincinnati at the National Prison Congress to design a "new penology" that would rectify correctional failures and challenge the prevailing notion that prisons should function as warehouses with bars or, still worse, as instruments of harm. In issuing their famous "Declaration of Principles," the Congress asserted that "the supreme aim of prison discipline is the reformation of criminals, not the infliction of vindictive suffering" ("Declaration of Principles" 1910 [1870], p. 39).

These new penologists were not moral relativists and did not idealize offenders ("Declaration of Principles" 1910 [1870]): They were defenders of Christian morality and believed in character education; they embraced middle-class values and thought inmates would benefit from them too; they did not mind transforming the urban poor into disciplined workers (though they did reject as exploitive both purposeless hard labor and contract labor in prison); they believed that recalcitrant inmates should not be spared the rod (though they also felt that "rewards, more than punishments, are essential to every good prison system") ("Declaration of Principles" 1910 [1870], p. 39); and they were prepared in defense of public safety to incarcerate incorrigible inmates indeterminately. They also were optimistic that the state could be "changed from its former vengefulness to that of dignified serenity, neither vindictive nor lovelorn, but firmly and nobly corrective" (Brockway 1910, p. 88). Later commentators would criticize them for being class biased and for their naïveté in not anticipating that state power, exercised unfettered behind the high walls of the prison, could be abused and cause more harm than good (Platt 1969; Rothman 1980). I would debate these claims on the grounds that the new penology exerted a restraining influence on punitive sentiments—that the alternative would have been worse (as I believe is now the case). But it is hoped that we can agree not to deconstruct the new penologists' words to the point of ignoring their intent to better, not to hurt, offenders (see Garland 1990).

Today, however, the response to the corrections crisis has turned ugly. In the 1990s, the term *new penology* no longer refers to a correctional philosophy that rejects vengeance in favor of offender reformation, but to an administrative style that seeks depersonalized efficiency in processing increasingly large hordes of inmates in and out of the system (Feeley and Simon 1992). More disquieting, we have entered a "mean season" in which it has become politically correct to build prisons and to devise creative strategies to make offenders suffer. In Todd Clear's words, we are witnessing a movement whose supreme aim is the infliction of "penal harm."

The field of criminology is one of the few remaining bastions in American society in which the advent of the penal harm movement has not been greeted warmly. A few bold colleagues defend the use of prisons (see, e.g., Logan and DiIulio 1992; Wright 1994), but most of us (including me) are sufficiently liberal, fearful of professional disapproval, or (I hope) criminologically astute to caution about the "limits of imprisonment" (see, e.g., Currie 1985; Gordon 1991; Irwin and Austin 1994; Selke 1993; Zimring and Hawkins 1995; see also Forer 1994). We often fret that our research and commentary are ignored by policymakers who seemingly succeed in purchasing the votes of citizens uneasy about crime by offering to effect law and order (see Kaminer 1995). But we are able to console ourselves at conferences through a shared and cathartic excoriation of the get-tough crowd, knowing that their panaceas are doomed to failure and that we stand for truth and justice.

There is a risk, however, that liberal criminologists (like me) will become too professionally insular and complacent in our thinking about corrections—that we will take turns preaching to, and being in, the choir. It is wise, I suspect, to reflect on assumptions that are held too uncritically and to check our biases with some good positivist criminology. An indispensable first step in this intellectual housecleaning is to read the three books informing this essay. Although clearly progressive in orientation, these works are sophisticated attempts to understand and to undermine the penal harm movement. They retain a humanity, which is an integral and worthy side of liberal criminology, but ultimately their strength comes from their rejection of ideology in favor of sharp logic and hard data.

I should warn that these exemplars of liberal correctional thinking—Clear's *Harm in American Penology,* Simon's *Poor Discipline,* and Tonry's *Malign Neglect*—are not immune to reasonable rejoinders by those who see benefits in penal harm; the debates are wonderfully engaged but perhaps not fully settled. But I have a more serious concern about these works: They reflect the tendency in contemporary progressive commentaries to provide incisive criticism of conservative crime policies but then to stop short of articulating a *coherent* alternative *correctional* agenda. Unlike the new penologists of the 1870s, whose "Declaration of Principles" mapped out such an agenda, they thus provide only limited guidance on how to move beyond penal harm—a point I return to at the end of this essay.

Is There a Penal Harm Movement?

Clear does a service in reminding us that an integral part of state punishment is inflicting "penal harm." The "essence of the penal sanction," he observes, is that "it harms . . .it is supposed to hurt" (p. 4). Penal harm is a "planned governmental act, whereby a citizen is harmed, and implies that harm is justifiable precisely because it is an offender who is suffering" (p. 4). We often clothe this reality with respectable-sounding euphemisms, such as "correctional interventions," "offender processing," and "incapacitation." Clear's insistent use of "penal harm" as his organizing concept strips away this comforting language, and forces us to confront the naked truth that corrections is, to a greater or lesser extent, a mean-spirited enterprise.

I suspect that only the culturally illiterate would be unaware that a movement has been afoot to expand the use of penal harm in the United States. In the past 2 years, for example, various versions of "three strikes and you're out" laws, which mandate life sentences for a third felony conviction, have been implemented in 15 states and are under consideration in 22 more (Furrier, Sundt, Applegate, and Cullen forthcoming; see also Benekos and Merlo 1995). Legislators also have publicized their attempts to intensify the pains of imprisonment by reducing such inmate amenities as grants for college education, television privileges, computers in cells, and exercise through weight lifting. Alabama enthusiastically has reinstituted chain gangs. Offenders don white uniforms that display the stigmatizing label "chain gang," are shackled together, and conduct "stoop labor" for 12 hours a day (Bragg 1995; Cohen 1995). Modern technology, it must be admitted, has allowed some escape from penal harm; Alabama officials are able to point "proudly to a new, specially designed toilet that allows the men to relieve themselves in privacy while still linked to their colleagues" (Cohen 1995, p. 26).

Three-strikes laws and chain gangs might merely be part of a symbolic crusade that has affected corrections in visible, but marginal, ways. Is there evidence that penal harm has increased substantively, not just symbolically, in recent years? Clear, with help from Tonry, makes a strong case in the affirmative.

Given the ubiquity of the current get-tough talk about crime, it is easy today to forget that penal harm was not always on the rise. In the half century following 1925, imprisonment rates per 100,000 averaged under 108 per 100,000 citizens, and the number of inmates rose roughly in proportion to the growth in the general population (Clear, p. 44; see also Cullen, Van Voorhis, and Sundt forthcoming). In fact, this remarkable "stability of punishment" was the object of theoretical inquiry (Blumstein and Cohen 1973; see also Blumstein 1995; Scull 1977).

Beginning in the early 1970s, however, a sea change in punishment occurred: The era of stability suddenly ended as the population of offenders under correctional supervision began a rapid, seemingly intractable rise.

Although establishing causal links between policy reforms and correctional populations is difficult (Zimring and Hawkins 1991), over the past two decades politicians certainly intended for penal harm to worsen. Clear documents that between 1972 and 1982, a majority of states restricted or abolished parole release, and mandatory or minimum sentences were widely implemented. "In one way or another," he concludes, "every state altered its penal policy in the direction of greater punitive severity" (p. 50; see also Cullen and Gilbert 1982).

To Clear, the figures on the use of prisons are "astounding": Between 1973 and the beginning of the 1990s, the number of prisoners increased by 332%, and the incarceration rate per 100,000 citizens jumped over 200% (p. 43). The growing punitiveness of sentencing also is apparent: Between 1981 and 1987, the time served for burglary rose 53% and for rape rose 129%; since 1975, the time served for violent offenses has tripled (pp. 54–55).

Michael Tonry echoes these themes and provides a useful cross-cultural perspective (see also Currie 1985). "Americans have a remarkable ability to endure suffering by others," he observes. "We lock up our citizens at rates 5 to 15 times higher than those in other Western countries" (p. 197). He claims that these incarceration rates cannot be explained by America's higher offense rate. Recently conducted international victimization surveys show that crime in the United States is not markedly higher than in other advanced industrial nations, although gun-related violence is a notable exception. Even so, the proclivity to lock up offenders seems less a product of having a larger pool of criminals and more a product of our "national character" (pp. 197–200).

Consider, however, DiIulio's (1994, p. 15) starkly different claim that the "justice system is a revolving door for convicted predatory street criminals"—not a potent instrument for inflicting penal harm—and that "America has not been on an imprisonment binge" (see also Wilson 1995; cf. Irwin and Austin 1994). How can intelligent scholars read the evidence so differently? In fact, there are two divergent cases to be made, and a scholar's intellectual and/or ideological preferences shape which position he or she embraces.

Liberals prefer to cite raw numbers of people in prison and incarceration rates per 100,000 citizens; they also read trends beginning in the early 1970s (Clear, p. 43). In contrast, conservatives, such as John DiIulio (1994) and James Q. Wilson (1995), prefer to cite the amount of punishment meted out per offense committed and to read trend lines dating back to 1960, if not before. This latter methodology reveals that the punishment-per-offense rate declined rapidly throughout the 1960s and 1970s, only to rebound partially in the 1980s.

According to DiIulio (1994, p. 16), for example, the number of people in prison per 1,000 violent crimes dropped from 738 in 1960 to 227 in 1980, only to increase in the 1980s to 423—a point still "42 percent lower than it was in 1960." Wilson's (1995, p. 499) analysis paints a similar portrait: In 1945, the sentence served for all crimes was 25 months, but by 1984 had decreased to 13 months. These statistical patterns, contends DiIulio (1994, p. 16), do not indicate an imprisonment binge, but rather that America "has been recovering from the starvation diet it went on in the late 1960s and stayed on throughout the 1970s."

Using this general approach, the cross-cultural case for America's exceptionalism as a punitive nation also is complicated. Lynch (1995) found that offenders in the United States receive longer sentences than in other advanced industrial nations. In time actually spent in prison, however, the findings were less consistent: Compared to offenders in other nations, offenders in the United States served longer sentences for property and drug offenses but served similar sentences for homicide and serious violence (see also Farrington and Langan 1992).

Where do these competing commentaries leave us? At the very least, we know that in raw numbers, the prison population has grown in the past two decades from about 200,000 to over 1 million inmates. It also is clear that in the past decade, punishment levels have increased considerably. But whether one considers current trends to constitute penal harm or a much-needed, if not overdue, redistribution of governmental resources depends on more than incarceration statistics. In the end, assessing whether penal harm is beneficial or wasteful, and deciding appropriate levels of penal harm, will be influenced by considerations of utility: What does penal harm accomplish? . . . .

The Differential Effects of Penal Harm

"No problem haunts the United States' sense of identity more intractably than race relations," comments Clear (p. 174). "The penal system," he adds, "is part of the problem, because penal harms are inequitably distributed among our racial and ethnic populations." In *Malign Neglect*, Tonry seeks to document how policies central to the ongoing penal harm movement not only have perpetuated but, more significantly, have exacerbated the concentration of punishment on African Americans.

Tonry does not deny that behavioral differences in crime exist between Black and White Americans, and although not dismissing the existence of ill and inequitable treatment of minorities, he does not contend that the racial gap in offending can be explained by the discriminatory practices of criminal justice officials. . . . Even so, he is adamant that "American crime policies since 1980 have had disastrous consequences for Black Americans" and that the penal harms visited on African Americans "do not result from in-

creases in the proportions of serious crimes committed by Blacks" (p. 28).

Indeed, incarceration statistics paint a disquieting portrait: In both 1979 and 1990, African Americans accounted for about 44% of arrests for violent crimes. The Black proportion of admissions to state prisons, however, jumped in this period from 39% to 53% (p. 49). In fact, between 1986 and 1991, the racial mix in prison admissions flip-flopped from 53% White (and 46% Black) to 53% Black (p. 58). By 1991, African Americans were 6.47 times more likely than White Americans to be incarcerated (1,895 to 293 per 100,000) (p. 29). These figures mean that 1 in 50 Blacks are imprisoned on any given day. When the data are disaggregated by gender and age, we learn that 1 in 12 African American men between the ages of 18 and 54 are confined (p. 130). Further, nearly 1 in 4 Black men in their 20s are either behind bars or on probation or parole (p. 4; see also Tonry 1994).

"The rising levels of Black incarceration did not just happen," argues Tonry but were due to "malign neglect"; indeed, the increased penal harms suffered by African Americans after 1980 were the *foreseeable* effects of *deliberate* policies spearheaded by the Reagan and Bush administrations and implemented by many states" (p. 4, italics added). He indicts politicians for using race-based stereotypes about crime (Willie Horton and the like) as a means of stirring up racial enmity, polarizing the electorate, and capturing White votes. "The text may be crime," notes Tonry (p. 6), but "the subtext is race." Most important, he details how the "War on Drugs," which virtually no serious observer felt could be won, was used to increase political capital even though it served to "ruin countless lives and weaken numerous communities" (p. vii; see also Currie 1993; Gordon 1994).

In chapter 3, "Race and the War on Drugs," Tonry details the war's "foreseeable disparate impact on Blacks" (p. 104). The "major fronts in the drug wars were located in minority neighborhoods," in large part because trafficking occurred on the street and officers could more easily make arrests (pp. 105–7). Further, the focus on crack cocaine was especially consequential, because this drug was sold and used disproportionately by minorities and carried substantially longer penalties than powder cocaine—a drug used mainly by Whites. The result of targeting low-level, inner-city, street-level drug dealers and attaching harsh punishments to crack was predictable: In 1985, Blacks made up 30% of drug arrests; by 1989, this figure had jumped to 42%—even though African Americans' use of drugs generally is lower than that of White Americans. Numerically, Black drug arrests more than doubled from 210,298 to 452,574, whereas the number of arrests for Whites increased only 27% (pp. 107–9).

In turn, "drug arrests are a principal reason that the proportions of Blacks in prison . . .have risen rapidly in recent years to . . .extraordinary levels" (p. 110). Data from Pennsylvania are instructive. Between 1980 and 1990, drug commitments rose 1,613% for African American males but only 477% for White males (p. 115). And penal harms such as these have had disturbing consequences. "Poor minority communities cannot prosper," warns Tonry (p. vii), "when so many young men are prevented from settling into long-term personal relationships, getting or keeping jobs, and living conventional lives."

But is the disproportionate allocation of criminal justice resources to minority communities a form of spatial injustice, as Tonry claims, or of spatial justice? In 1989, George Rengert raised this issue, when he used the concept of "spatial justice" to refer "to whether or not citizens are placed at equal risk of victimization as a result of criminal justice practices regardless of where their communities are located—center city, suburb, or rural area" (p. 544). His analysis revealed that burglars received shorter sentences in Philadelphia than in other areas in Pennsylvania and that these offenders were poorly supervised by probation and parole officers burdened with caseloads of 100 to 200 persons. The decisions of officials not to incarcerate or adequately supervise burglars resulted in higher victimization rates for residents of inner-city neighborhoods—those "least able to bear the high physical, economic, and emotional burden of property crime" (p. 557).

Rengert (1989, p. 560) believed that addressing the issue of spatial injustice through imprisonment was the "easy" answer, but "also naive" (he favored intermediate sanctions and crime prevention). Not so for DiIulio (1994), who recently has taken up the issue of "saving Black lives" through penal harm. "If White suburbanites were victimized in disproportionate numbers by convicted criminals out on probation or parole," his essay begins, "then there would be little policy debate about keeping violent or repeat offenders locked up" (p. 3). But this is not the case, he claims. Affluent Whites have the luxury of moving to safer communities in the suburbs and of paying for security devices. Inner-city minorities do not have these options. They must reside, largely unprotected, in neighborhoods populated with predatory criminals whose victimization is mostly intraracial.

To DiIulio, the malign neglect lies in the failure of the criminal justice system to end "revolving door" justice and to lock up these predatory offenders. "No group of Americans would stand to benefit more from policies that kept convicted felons, adult and juvenile, behind bars for all or most of their terms," says DiIulio (p. 15), "than crime-plagued Black inner-city Americans and their children."

I have no reason to doubt DiIulio's sincerity. But his personal character and intent aside, I find it more than a little disingenuous when conservative commentators use the victimization of African Americans to argue for less welfare and more prisons. This new-found concern does not seem to extend to capital investment in inner-city areas; they do not want to improve the "barrel," only take out the "bad apples." I also feel compelled to add a rejoinder to the quote initiating DiIulio's essay: "If White suburbanites were in prison in disproportionate numbers, then there would be little policy debate about reducing imprisonment and investing resources to improve the quality of life in suburban communities."

Tonry (p. 36) takes up the justification of penal harm that he calls the "'We are concerned about Black victims and Black communities' defense." His rebuttal is weakened, I believe, by his firm stance that incapacitation has few meaningful effects on crime—an issue discussed above. But his insights on what African Americans want strike a chord. Tonry agrees that Blacks often want the criminal justice system to crack down on crime when it is an "acute" problem that poses an immediate threat to community order. Blacks also understand, however, that crime is a symptom of "chronic social and economic conditions shaping disadvantaged inner-city communities and the life chances of the people in them" (p. 36). And in large percentages, they endorse social welfare policies that address crime's root causes. Somehow it is no surprise that conservatives hear calls for more police and prisons but turn a deaf ear to calls for help and hope.

Managing Penal Harm

In *Poor Discipline*, Jonathan Simon contributes further to our understanding of the character of the current penal harm movement. Using parole in California as a vehicle for illuminating the larger correctional process, he traces the changing penological models used to control the underclass. He reminds us that "however general the formal commands of the criminal law, the power to punish has always been primarily directed at the poor" (p. 5). A particular strength of his analysis is that he links the meaning and practice of parole to the wider material conditions of the disadvantaged. "The massive expansion of criminal custody over the last decade in the United States," observes Si-

mon, "must be seen in relationship to changes in political economy," including in particular "the restructuring of the labor force away from industrial employment" and "the emergence of an urban underclass living in zones of hardened poverty and made up primarily of minorities" (p. 5).

The emergence and growth of parole release in the late 1800s into the Progressive Era depended on furnishing a persuasive answer—or "narrative" or "account" as Simon would call it—to how it would be possible "to provide control in the community over those defined as dangerous to the community" (p. 38). The response, says Simon, was "disciplinary parole": Make community release contingent on securing and maintaining labor. This narrative (or account) should not strike us as unusual, says Simon, because it is so compatible with long-standing American thinking on corrections (see also Cullen and Travis 1984). "Wherever you look in the development of modernist penality you will find labor," says Simon. "Exhort offenders with religious tracts, but make them work. Subject them to silence, but make them work. Educate them as citizens, but make them work. Treat their pathological features, but make them work" (p. 39).

Having parolees work served to normalize them through the discipline of labor; it provided a test of character, for those who could not keep a job proved their essential criminality; and it implicated private networks of control, because employers had to agree to provide work and to certify that offenders remained on the job in good standing. The plausibility of the disciplinary parole model, of course, rested on having a labor market that could accommodate poor offenders on parole. Until the 1950s, these structural conditions obtained: With the exception of the Depression years, the cities provided a "large labor market . . .for unskilled and semi-skilled labor" (p. 50).

By the 1950s, however, America's deindustrialization undermined the coherence of disciplinary parole: Low-skilled jobs were declining in number, especially for minorities, who, simultaneously, were becoming a growing proportion of the correctional population. We now had offenders who were largely unemployable, who could not be "normalized" by the discipline of the changing workplace but who "must be altered before they could be moved in the labor force" (p. 100). The initial institutional response was the trumpeting of "clinical parole," in which parole officers would function as caseworkers delivering treatment and linking offenders to needed social services. In this narrative, crime was rooted not simply in the failure to work or "idleness," but in a "maladjustment between the individual and the institutions of the community. . . . Such degeneration," continues Simon (p. 104), "could be halted by counseling and treatment which addressed the underlying pathologies that discouraged identification with conventional norms."

The clinical model, however, was rendered implausible by the intersection of three factors. First, the correctional crisis was exacerbated by the continued "hardening of urban poverty" in the inner cities caused by the erosion of the nonskilled labor market in an increasingly postindustrial America. Parole as normalization became "less coherent" when the project of reintegration meant returning underclass offenders to communities burdened by the "tangle of urban pathology" and with "fewer and fewer resources to sustain them" (see chapter 5).

Second, at the same time, legal interventions by the court mandated due process rights for parolees, especially at the revocation hearing. Because discretionary decisions previously made without scrutiny now were rendered visible, pressures emerged to rationalize and introduce uniformity into the application of power (see chapter 4). The need to justify decisions to an external environment was increased further by a third condition: increasing public fears of violent crime and a loss of confidence in criminal justice officials. The challenge was to construct a correctional system in which accountability in the defense of public safety could be demonstrated.

The response to this context over the past two decades has been to rationalize procedures in the pursuit of "risk management" (p. 169). This "managerial model" stands traditional parole on its head by embracing the core principle of the penal harm movement that "custody is the necessary and sufficient solution to criminal risk" (p. 229). The task for parole officers thus becomes not assisting in the community reintegration of offenders but in discerning which offenders in the community should be reincarcerated. "New technologies of control"—risk classification systems, computerized databases, drug testing—increase the capacity for surveillance and for detecting dangerous parolees (see chapter 6). The logical conclusion of the managerial model is the primacy given to the "revocation hearing." Resources are concentrated on administering procedurally correct hearings in which parole's accountability is established by sending risky offenders back to prison at unprecedented rates (see chapter 7).

As Simon recognizes, the success of the managerial model is not complete (see also Cullen, Wright and Applegate forthcoming). It contains the fundamental inconsistency of exacerbating the fiscal crisis in corrections. "Parole has been successful in transforming itself from a system of rehabilitative discipline to one of risk management," observes Simon (p. 229), "and now finds itself criticized for that accomplishment." Further, there is danger in reifying Simon's managerial model to the point of being blinded to the continuing allegiance to offender rehabilitation that exists both among correctional personnel in California and in states that have been less quick to embrace control as the only goal of the criminal sanction.

Still, Simon's *Poor Discipline* is perceptive in identifying the forces that are helping to fuel the penal harm movement. Most disquieting, he reveals that no plausible narrative or account for the correctional enterprise currently exists to challenge the widening hegemony of penal harm. Criminologists, I believe, share a measure of responsibility for this state of affairs. Clear's analysis of "penal science" is sobering (see chapter 3). In recent decades—as authors and as consultants—we have played a large role in delegitimizing the rehabilitative ideal and in providing the intellectual justification and technology for managing penal harm. The challenge now is to help fashion an alternative plausible narrative that can move us beyond harm as the organizing principle of corrections.

Beyond Penal Harm

Unfortunately, the authors stop short of providing a coherent and compelling penological model that rivals the power of get-tough thinking. Let me hasten to blunt this criticism by noting that the books provide useful ideas on how to minimize harm in corrections and, taken together, succeed mightily in showing the importance of engaging in a conversation about the future of corrections. But unlike the "new penologists" who came to Cincinnati in 1870, they do not vigorously advocate the kind of optimistic and confident "Declaration of Principles" that might serve as an alternative narrative to penal harm.

I would like to claim that I do not have the space to outline such a new penological model, but my reticence lies more in a fear that the task is too daunting. Even so, I will take the risk of arguing—as I have for over a decade—in favor of reaffirming rehabilitation as a model to rival penal harm (Cullen and Gendreau 1989; Cullen and Gilbert 1982; Cullen, Van Voorhis, and Sundt forthcoming; Cullen and Wright forthcoming; Gendreau et al. 1994).

A whole generation of criminologists were raised to mistrust state power to do good, to believe that "nothing works" to change offenders, and to embrace "doing justice" as a means of "doing less harm." This pessimistic narrative, which seeks to restrain abuse and not to accomplish good, remains plausible to many criminologists, but it sparks little response from the public and has largely lost its power to humanize corrections. Most important, it fails to capitalize on the generous side of the public's sentiments about corrections; as Tonry (p. 9) notes, "large majorities of Americans . . .want prisons to rehabilitate offenders" (see also Cullen, Cullen, and Wozniak 1988; Cullen, Skovron, Scott, and Burton 1990; McCorkle 1993). In short, rehabilitation is the one liberal correctional narrative that citizens still find plausible.

I would warn, however, that rehabilitation as a form of pure-hearted benevolence is vulnerable to attack. Instead, as the new penologists of the 1870s understood, the *utility* of treatment interventions for the public good must be a central principle if the rehabilitative ideal is to achieve support. Like it or not, American culture is decidedly utilitarian (Bellah et al. 1985), and the failure to take this factor into account will render any liberal correctional model irrelevant. It is instructive that DiIulio and similar advocates of incapacitation do not make this mistake. Indeed, their persuasiveness comes from giving a plausible account of how prisons increase safety while portraying liberal naysayers as having no interest in protecting innocent citizens. The challenge of the utility of penal harm thus must be confronted, not just dismissed. Fortunately, science is on the side of treatment: The research is mounting that shows that rehabilitation "works better" than penal harm in reducing recidivism (see, e.g., Andrews and Bonta 1994; Andrews et al. 1990; Cullen, Wright, and Applegate forthcoming; Lipsey 1992; Palmer 1992; Tonry, pp. 201–3).

Second, rehabilitation should be framed not as a form of governmental entitlement but as a utilitarian exchange. Simon (p. 263) captures this insight with his call for "investing penal resources in community discipline"—a situation in which governmental rewards are tied to offender performance in programs (such as work) that encourage individual responsibility, normalize deviant tendencies, and contribute to the commonweal (such as by providing payment for victims or for the offender's family). Of course, reward systems must be backed up by the threat of negative reinforcement—"behave or you'll suffer the consequences"—which raises the sticky issue of how far to go in enforcing therapy. Although I am not unmindful of the potential for abuse (see Rothman 1980), no liberal correctional narrative will have credibility if offenders are not held accountable for their actions. And consistent with the principles of the 1870 new penologists, it is not clear that offender reform can be effective unless we are willing to assert values and to use "effective disapproval" to encourage conformity (Andrews and Bonta 1994, pp. 202–7).

Third, the rehabilitative narrative should trumpet early intervention. This strategy—a means of diverting much-needed services to vulnerable populations—has marked advantages: It forces attention on conditions, such as the capital disinvestment in inner cities (Currie 1985; Hagan 1994; Short 1991), that place families and children at risk; it focuses on a "deserving" object of attention—children born into difficult circumstances through "no fault of their own"; it embraces the persuasive logic that "you can pay me now or pay me later"; and there is evidence that such interventions can be successful (Greenwood 1995, pp. 112–17).

Some criminologists, I suspect, will find my proposal for reaffirming "utilitarian" rehabilitation misguided. But if so, it is incumbent on these critics and like-minded scholars to move beyond preaching to the criminological choir about the disutility of punishment and to declare their principles for designing a *plausible* and *positive* correctional model. The time for taking up this task is overdue. In chilling detail, Todd Clear, Jonathan Simon, and Michael Tonry illuminate the ideological power and the human costs of penal harm. Unless a better answer can be put forth, this movement promises to gain strength and to permeate more deeply the fabric of the correctional enterprise.

Study Questions

1. Specifically, how does Cullen define the penal harm movement in the United States?

2. What is the primary "utility" of the penal harm movement (from a conservative vantage point) according to Cullen?

3. What is the primary "detriment" of the penal harm movement (from a liberal vantage point)?

4. According to this article, what are the three ways in which the United States should move beyond the penal harm movement?

References

Andrews, D.A. and James Bonta. (1994). *The Psychology of Criminal Conduct*. Cincinnati, OH: Anderson.

Andrews, D.A., Ivan Zinger, R.D. Hoge, James Bonta, Paul Gendreau, and Francis T. Cullen. (1990). "Does Correctional Treatment Work? A Clinically-Relevant and Psychologically-Informed Meta-Analysis." *Criminology*, 28:369–404.

Bellah, Robert N., Richard Madsen, William M. Sullivan, Ann Swidler, and Steven M. Tipton. (1985). *Habits of the Heart: Individualism and Commitment in American Life*. Berkeley: University of California Press.

Benekos, Peter J. and Alida V. Merlo. (1995). "Three Strikes and You're Out!: The Political Sentencing Game." *Federal Probation*, 59 (March):3–9.

Blumstein, Alfred. (1989). "American Prisons in a Time of Crisis." Pp. 13–22 in *The American Prison: Issues in Research and Policy*, edited by L. Goodstein and D. L. MacKenzie. New York: Plenum.

———. (1995). "Prisons." Pp. 387–419 in *Crime*, edited by James Q. Wilson and Joan Petersilia. San Francisco: ICS.

Blumstein, Alfred and Jacqueline Cohen. (1973). "A Theory of the Stability of Punishment." *Journal of Criminal Law and Criminology*, 64: 198–206.

Bragg, Rick. (1995). "Chain Gangs to Return to Roads of Alabama: States Hopes Revival Will

Deter Crime." *New York Times*, March 26, p. Y9.

Braithwaite, John. (1989). *Crime, Shame and Reintegration*. Cambridge, UK: Cambridge University Press.

Brockway, Zebulon R. (1910). "The American Reformatory Prison System." Pp. 88–107 in *Prison Reform: Correction and Prevention*, edited by Charles Richmond Henderson. New York: Russell Sage Foundation.

Bureau of Justice Statistics. (1994). *Criminal Victimization in the United States*, 1992. Washington, DC: U.S. Department of Justice.

Byrne, James M. and April Pattavina. (1992). "The Effectiveness Issue: Assessing What Works in the Adult Community Corrections System." Pp. 281–303 in *Smart Sentencing: The Emergence of Intermediate Sanctions*, edited by James M. Byrne, Arthur J. Lurigio, and Joan Petersilia. Newbury Park, CA: Sage.

Clear, T.R., (1994). *Harm in American Penology: Offenders, Victims, and Theur Communities*. West Sacramento, CA: California Correctional Peace Officers Association.

Cohen, Adam. (1995). "Back on the Chain Gang." *Time*, May 15, p. 26.

Cohen, Jacqueline and José A. Canela-Cacho. (1994). "Incarceration and Violent Crime: 1965–1988." Pp. 296–388 in *Understanding and Preventing Violence: Consequences and Control*, Vol. 4, edited by Albert J. Reiss, Jr. and Jeffrey A. Roth. Washington, DC: National Academy Press.

Colvin, Mark. (1992). *The Penitentiary in Crisis: From Accommodation to Riot in New Mexico*. Albany: SUNY Press.

Cullen, Francis T., John B. Cullen, and John F. Wozniak. (1988). "Is Rehabilitation Dead? The Myth of the Punitive Public." *Journal of Criminal Justice*, 34:379–92.

Cullen, Francis T. and Paul Gendreau. (1989). "The Effectiveness of Correctional Rehabilitation: Reconsidering the 'Nothing Works' Debate." Pp. 23–44 in *The American Prison: Issues in Research and Policy*, edited by L. Goodstein and D.L. MacKenzie. New York: Plenum.

Cullen, Francis T. and Karen E. Gilbert. (1982). *Reaffirming Rehabilitation*. Cincinnati, OH: Anderson.

Cullen, Francis T., Sandra Evans Skovron, Joseph E. Scott, and Velmer S. Burton, Jr. (1990). "Public Support for Correctional Rehabilitation: The Tenacity of the Rehabilitative Ideal." *Criminal Justice and Behavior*, 17:6–18.

Cullen, Francis T. and Lawrence F. Travis, III. (1984). "Work as an Avenue of Prison Reform." *New England Journal of Criminal and Civil Confinement*, 10:45–64.

Cullen, Francis T., Patricia Van Voorhis, and Jody L. Sundt. (Forthcoming). "Prisons in Crisis: The American Experience." In *Prisons 2000: An International Perspective on the Current State and Future of Imprisonment*, edited by Roger Matthews and Peter Francis. New York: Macmillan.

Cullen, Francis T. and John P. Wright. (Forthcoming). "The Future of Corrections." In *The Past, Present, and Future of American Criminal Justice*, edited by Brendan Maguire and Polly Radosh. New York: General Hall.

Cullen, Francis T., John P. Wright, and Brandon K. Applegate. (Forthcoming). "Control in the Community: The Limits of Reform?" In *Choosing Correctional Interventions That Work: Defining the Demand and Evaluating the Supply*, edited by Alan T. Harland. Newbury Park, CA: Sage.

Currie, Elliott. (1985). *Confronting Crime: An American Challenge*. New York: Pantheon.

———. (1993). *Reckoning: Drugs, the Cities, and the American Future*. New York: Hill and Wang.

"Declaration of Principles Promulgated at Cincinnati, Ohio, 1870." 1910 [1870]. Pp. 39–63 in *Prison Reform Correction and Prevention*, edited by Charles Richmond Henderson. New York: Russell Sage Foundation.

DiIulio, John J., Jr. (1994). "The Question of Black Crime." *Public Interest*, 117 (Fall):3–32.

Farrington, David P. and Patrick A. Langan. (1992). "Changes in Crime and Punishment in England and America in the 1980s." *Justice Quarterly*, 9:5–31.

Federal Bureau of Investigation. (1994). *Uniform Crime Reports: Crime in the United States, 1993*. Washington, DC: U.S. Government Printing Office.

Feeley, Malcolm M. and Jonathan Simon. (1992). "The New Penology: Notes on the Emerging Strategy of Corrections and Its Implications." *Criminology*, 30:449–74.

Forer, Lois G. (1994). *A Rage to Punish: The Unintended Consequences of Mandatory Sentencing*. New York: W.W. Norton.

Garland, David. (1990). *Punishment and Modern Society: A Study in Social Theory*. Chicago: University of Chicago Press.

Gendreau, Paul, Francis T. Cullen, and James Bonta. (1994). "Intensive Rehabilitation Supervision: The Next Generation in Community Corrections?" *Federal Probation,* 58 (March): 72–78.

Gordon, Diana R. (1991). *The Justice Juggernaut: Fighting Street Crime, Controlling Citizens.* New Brunswick, NJ: Rutgers University Press.

——. (1994). *The Return of the Dangerous Classes: Drug Prohibition and Policy Politics.* New York: W.W. Norton.

Gramm, Phil. (1993). "Drugs, Crime and Punishment: Don't Let Judges Set Crooks Free." *New York Times,* July 8, pp. B1–B2.

Greenwood, Peter W. (1995). "Juvenile Crime and Juvenile Justice." Pp. 91–117 in *Crime,* edited by James Q. Wilson and Joan Petersilia. San Francisco: ICS.

Hagan, John. (1994). *Crime and Disrepute.* Thousand Oaks, CA: Pine Forge.

Herrnstein, Richard J. and Charles Murray. (1994). *The Bell Curve: Intelligence and Class Structure in American Life.* New York: Free Press.

Irwin, John. (1985). *The Jail: Managing the Underclass in American Society.* Berkeley: University of California Press.

Irwin, John and James Austin. (1994). *It's About Time: America's Imprisonment Binge.* Belmont, CA: Wadsworth.

Kaminer, Wendy. (1995). *It's All the Rage: Crime and Culture.* Reading, MA: Addison-Wesley.

Lipsey, Mark W. (1992). "Juvenile Delinquency Treatment: A Meta-Analytic Inquiry Into the Variability of Effects." Pp. 83–127 in *Meta-Analysis for Explanation: A Casebook,* edited by Thomas D. Cook, Harris Cooper, David S. Cordray, Heidi Hartmann, Larry V. Hedges, Richard J. Light, Thomas A. Louis, and Frederick Mosteller. New York: Russell Sage Foundation.

Logan, Charles H. and John J. DiIulio, Jr. (1992). "Ten Myths About Crime and Prisons." *Wisconsin Interest,* 1:21–35.

Lynch, James. (1995). "Crime in International Perspective." Pp. 11–38 in *Crime,* edited by James Q. Wilson and Joan Petersilia. San Francisco: ICS.

Marvell, Thomas B. and Carlisle E. Moody, Jr. (1994). "Prison Population Growth and Crime Reduction." *Journal of Quantitative Criminology,* 10:109–40.

McCorkle, Richard C. (1993). "Punish and Rehabilitate? Public Attitudes Toward Six Common Crimes." *Crime & Delinquency,* 39:240–52.

Palmer, Ted. (1992). *The Re-Emergence of Correctional Intervention.* Newbury Park, CA: Sage.

Paternoster, Raymond. (1987). "The Deterrent Effect of Perceived Certainty and Severity of Punishment: A Review of the Evidence and Issues." *Justice Quarterly,* 4:173–217.

Petersilia, Joan. (1992). "California's Prison Policy: Causes, Costs, and Consequences." *The Prison Journal,* 72:8–36.

Petersilia, Joan and Susan Turner. (1993). "Intensive Probation and Parole." Pp. 281–335 in *Crime and Justice: A Review of Research,* Vol. 17, edited by Michael Tonry. Chicago: University of Chicago Press.

Platt, Anthony M. (1969). *The Child Savers: The Invention of Delinquency.* Chicago: University of Chicago Press.

Reiss, Albert J., Jr. and Jeffrey A. Roth, eds. (1993). *Understanding and Preventing Violence.* Washington, DC: National Academy Press.

Rengert, George F. (1989). "Spatial Justice and Criminal Victimization." *Justice Quarterly,* 6: 543–64.

Roth, Jeffrey A. (1995). "Achievements to Date and Goals for the Future: New Looks at Criminal Careers." *Journal of Quantitative Criminology,* 11:97–110.

Rothman, David J. (1971). *The Discovery of the Asylum: Social Order and Disorder in the New Republic.* Boston: Little, Brown.

——. (1980). *Conscience and Convenience: The Asylum and Its Alternatives in Progressive America.* Boston: Little, Brown.

Sampson, Robert J. and John H. Laub. (1993). *Crime in the Making: Pathways and Turning Points Through Life.* Cambridge, MA: Harvard University Press.

Scull, Andrew. (1977). *Decarceration: Community Treatment and the Deviant—A Radical View.* Englewood Cliffs, NJ: Prentice Hall.

Selke, William L. (1993). *Prisons in Crisis.* Bloomington: Indiana University Press.

Sherman, Lawrence W. (1993). "Defiance, Deterrence, and Irrelevance: A Theory of Criminal Sanctions." *Journal of Research in Crime and Delinquency,* 30:445–73.

Sherman, Michael and Gordon Hawkins. (1981). *Imprisonment in America: Choosing the Future.* Chicago: University of Chicago Press.

Short, James F., Jr. (1991). "Poverty, Ethnicity, and Crime: Change and Continuity in U.S. Cities." *Journal of Research in Crime and Delinquency,* 28:501–18.

Simon, J. (1993). *Poor Discipline: Parole and the Social Control of the Underclass*. Chicago, IL: University of Chicago Press.

Spelman, William. (1994). *Criminal Incapacitation*. New York: Plenum.

Steffensmeier, Darrell and Miles D. Harer. (1993). "Bulging Prisons, an Aging U.S. Population, and the Nation's Crime Rate." *Federal Probation* 57 (June):3–10.

Tonry, Michael. (1994). "Racial Disproportion in US Prisons." *British Journal of Criminology*, 34: 97–115.

Tonry, Michael. (1995). *Malign Neglect: Race, Crime, and Punishment in America*. New York: Oxford University Press.

Turner, Michael G., Jody L. Sundt, Brandon K. Applegate, and Francis T. Cullen. (Forthcoming). "Three Strikes and You're Out' Legislation: A National Assessment." *Federal Probation*.

Walker, Samuel. (1989). *Sense and Nonsense About Crime: A Policy Guide*, 2nd ed. Pacific Grove, CA: Brooks/Cole.

Wilson, James Q. (1983). *Thinking About Crime*, rev. ed. New York: Random House.

——. (1995). "Crime and Public Policy." Pp. 489–507 in *Crime*, edited by James Q. Wilson and Joan Petersilia. San Francisco: ICS.

Wright, Richard A. (1994). *In Defense of Prisons*. Westport, CT: Greenwood.

Zedlewski, Edwin W. (1987). *Research in Brief: Making Confinement Decisions*. Washington, DC: National Institute of Justice.

Zimring, Franklin and Gordon Hawkins. (1991). *The Scale of Imprisonment*. Chicago: University of Chicago Press.

——. (1995). *Incapacitation: Penal Confinement and the Restraint of Crime*. New York: Oxford University Press. ✦

Part II
Living in Prison

By the beginning of the twentieth century, the use of the prison as a primary form of punishment for offenders was well entrenched in U.S. society. In general the public was satisfied to allow the government to house, feed, clothe, educate, and treat offenders outside of the sight and sounds of most free people. During this time, incarceration also came to the attention of many sociologists, who examined the prison as a self-contained "society of captives," as Sykes called it.

It is important to remember that the prison controls virtually every aspect of an offender's life, but only to an extent. The official existence of the offender—administrative processing, living quarters, job assignments, visiting privileges, and educational and vocational opportunities—falls under the domain of prison officials. However, the unofficial existence of the offender—the development of subculture, social and physical adaptation, economic proliferation, and uprisings—are largely governed by the inmates themselves, either as individuals or as an entire body.

It is perhaps equally important to keep in mind that although prison keeps the offender physically separated from general society, existence within the walls is designed supposedly to prepare the offender for ultimate return to a free life. Given what has been learned about serving time within a secure facility, questions remain as to whether or not prisons currently do (or even can) serve this function. Even so, much has been learned over the last 100 years about human interaction occuring within prisons.

Many of the early efforts geared toward the study of the prison as a separate society focused on the description of the day-to-day regimen. Social scientists were interested in discovering detail regarding virtually every aspect of the institution. Study included basic processes (such as housing, eating, and working) as well as more complex phenomena (such as the creation of subcultures, inmate to inmate communication, and changes in the offender population over time).

The primary characteristic motivating the study of the prison was the fact that it is indeed a total institution. Prisons were assumed to amount to holding a social laboratory of sorts, control over every facet of the offenders' lives. The total institution provides a microcosm of general society, largely cut off from the outside world where various social forces can be observed. Long-term access to a prison community in which minute details can be observed had thus become a coveted position for students of human interaction.

Several phenomena within the operation and development of prisons have provided rich opportunity for discovery. First, research has focused on the pains of imprisonment, such as deprivations from freedom, autonomy, goods and services, and heterosexual contact. Second, the social classification of certain types of offenders has proved deserving of note. Third, the question of whether or not the characteristics of a prison population as a whole were brought in (i.e., imported) by the offenders themselves, or were products of the prison structure (i.e., deprivation), has been studied as well. Fourth, the interaction of subpopulations within a prison, such as between different races or between rival gangs, has provided useful insight. Finally, although the Auburn-style prison is still in existence in many states, the evolution of the prison as a physical structure has been noted.

The populations housed within prisons have evolved perhaps more rapidly than the physical structures themselves. Questions have been raised regarding the needs of special offender groups, such as women, the chronically violent, and gang-affiliated offenders.

Regardless of what has been learned thus far about the characteristics of life inside the confines of an institution, more study is necessary as new phenomena develop. For example, since 1990 the United States has seen the advent of the "supermax" prison designed to house the offender who by and large remains unmanageable in traditional maximum security prison settings. This brings to bear several issues, not the least of which centers on the effects of intensified deprivation of human contact.

By gaining a deeper understanding of how societies within prison operate, knowledge may be gained regarding basic human interaction. More important may be the possibility that through the discovery of why social life within prisons exists as it is, the institutions themselves may become more humane and effective over time.

The reader of the following selections is encouraged to consider what the effects of living in confinement may be on the individual—both short- and long-term. In addition, particular consideration should be given to the increasing diversity and special needs of the offender population. ✦

7
Characteristics of Total Institutions

Erving Goffman

The totality with which the penal institution controls every aspect of the inhabitants' lives is presented in great detail in this selection by Goffman. Although few would argue that the restriction of freedom is the prevailing goal of the total prison institution, the control that occurs there is much more complex than one might imagine. The author begins by presenting some other examples (besides penal institutions) of restrictive institutions in society (e.g., hospitals for the mentally ill or the disabled). The resident of the total institution is portrayed as being at the will of the bureaucracy that governs the facility. In no other institution is this clearer than within the prison. Evidence of the "old life" as it once pertained to the inmates has all but completely been wiped away. This is done by removing all physical traces of the inmates' lives before they arrive at the institution and regulating everything that may be sent in. After that point, all aspects of the offenders' lives are under complete control of the institution, mired in a world of rewards and punishments meted out by prison administrators. The reader should consider what might possibly be the resulting consequences of such a system.

Excerpts from "Characteristics of Total Institutions" by Erving Goffman, *Symposium on Preventive and Social Psychiatry*, pp. 43–64, 84. Copyright © 1957 by Walter Reed Army Institute of Research. Reprinted by permission.

Introduction

Institutions. Social establishments—institutions in the everyday sense of that term—are buildings or plants in which activity of a particular kind regularly goes on. In sociology we do not have an apt way of classifying them. Some, like Grand Central Station, are open to anyone who is decently behaved. Others, like the Union League Club of New York or the laboratories at Los Alamos, are felt to be somewhat "snippy" about the matter of whom they let in. Some institutions, like shops and post offices, are the locus of a continuous flow of service relationships. Others, like homes and factories, provide a less changing set of persons with whom the member can relate. Some institutions provide the place for what is felt to be the kind of pursuits from which the individual draws his social status, however enjoyable or lax these pursuits may be. Other institutions, in contrast, provide a home for associations in which membership is felt to be elective and unserious, calling for a contribution of time that is fitted in to more serious demands.

In this [chapter] another category of institutions is recommended and claimed as a natural and fruitful one because its members appear to have so much in common—so much, in fact, that if you would learn about one of these institutions you would be well advised to look at the others. My own special purpose in examining these institutions is to find a natural frame of reference for studying the social experience of patients in mental hospitals. Whatever else psychiatry and medicine tell us, their happy way of sometimes viewing an insane asylum as if it were a treatment hospital does not help us very much in determining just what these places are and just what goes on in them.

Total Institutions. Every institution captures something of the time and interest of its members and provides something of a world for them; in brief, every institution has encompassing tendencies. When we review the different institutions in our Western society we find a class of them which seems to be encompassing to a degree discontinuously greater than the ones next in line. Their encompassing or total character is symbolized by the barrier to social intercourse with the outside that is often built right into the physical plant: locked doors, high walls, barbed wire, cliffs and water, open terrain, and so forth. These I am calling total institutions, and it is their general characteristics I want to explore. This exploration will be phrased as if securely based on findings but will in fact be speculative.

The total institutions of our society can be listed for convenience in five rough groupings. *First,* there are institutions established to care for persons thought to be both incapable and harmless; these are the homes for the blind, the aged, the orphaned, and the indigent. *Second,* there are places established to care for persons thought to be at once incapable of looking after themselves and a threat to the community, albeit an unintended one: TB sanitoriums, mental hospitals, and leprosariums. *Third,* another type of total institution is organized to protect the community against what are thought to be intentional dangers to it; here the welfare of the persons thus sequestered is not the immediate issue. Examples are: jails, penitentiaries, POW camps, and concentration camps. *Fourth,* we find institutions purportedly established the better to pursue some technical task and justifying themselves only on these instrumental grounds: army barracks, ships, boarding schools, work camps, colonial compounds, large mansions from the point of view of those who live in the servants' quarters, and so forth. *Finally,* there are those establishments designed as retreats from the world or as training stations for the religious: abbeys, monasteries, convents, and other cloisters. This sublisting of total institutions is neither neat nor exhaustive, but the listing itself provides an empirical starting point for a purely denotative definition of the category. By anchoring the initial definition of total institutions in this way, I hope to be able to discuss the general

characteristics of the type without becoming tautological.

Before attempting to extract a general profile from this list of establishments, one conceptual peculiarity must be mentioned. None of the elements I will extract seems entirely exclusive to total institutions, and none seems shared by every one of them. What is shared and unique about total institutions is that each exhibits many items in this family of attributes to an intense degree. In speaking of "common characteristics," then, I will be using this phrase in a weakened, but I think logically defensible, way.

Totalistic Features. A basic social arrangement in modern society is that we tend to sleep, play and work in different places, in each case with a different set of coparticipants, under a different authority, and without an overall rational plan. The central feature of total institutions can be described as a breakdown of the kinds of barriers ordinarily separating these three spheres of life. *First,* all aspects of life are conducted in the same place and under the same single authority. *Second,* each phase of the member's daily activity will be carried out in the immediate company of a large batch of others, all of whom are treated alike and required to do the same thing together. *Third,* all phases of the day's activities are tightly scheduled, with one activity leading at a prearranged time into the next, the whole circle of activities being imposed from above through a system of explicit formal rulings and a body of officials. *Finally,* the contents of the various enforced activities are brought together as parts of a single overall rational plan purportedly designed to fulfill the official aims of the institution.

Individually, these totalistic features are found, of course, in places other than total institutions. Increasingly, for example, our large commercial, industrial and educational establishments provide cafeterias, minor services and off-hour recreation for their members. But while this is a tendency in the direction of total institutions, these extended facilities remain voluntary in many particulars of their use, and special care is taken to see that the ordinary line of authority does not extend to these situations. Similarly, housewives or farm families can find all their major spheres of life within the same fenced-in area, but these persons are not collectively regimented and do not march through the day's steps in the immediate company of a batch of similar others.

The handling of many human needs by the bureaucratic organization of whole blocks of people—whether or not this is a necessary or effective means of social organization in the circumstances—can be taken, then, as the key fact of total institutions. From this, certain important implications can be drawn.

Given the fact that blocks of people are caused to move in time, it becomes possible to use a relatively small number of supervisory personnel where the central relationship is not guidance or periodic checking, as in many employer-employee relations, but rather surveillance—a seeing to it that everyone does what he has been clearly told is required of him, and this under conditions where one person's infraction is likely to stand out in relief against the visible, constantly examined, compliance of the others. Which comes first, the large block of managed people or the small supervisory staff, is not here at issue; the point is that each is made for the other.

In total institutions, as we would then suspect, there is a basic split between a large class of individuals who live in and who have restricted contact with the world outside the walls, conveniently called *inmates,* and the small class that supervises them, conveniently called *staff,* who often operate on an 8-hour day and are socially integrated into the outside world. Each grouping tends to conceive of members of the other in terms of narrow hostile stereotypes, staff often seeing inmates as bitter, secretive and untrustworthy, while inmates often see staff as condescending, highhanded and mean. Staff tends to feel superior and righteous; inmates tend, in some ways at least, to feel inferior, weak, blameworthy and guilty. Social mobility between the two strata is grossly restricted; social distance is typically great and often formally prescribed; even talk across the boundaries may be conducted in a special tone of voice. These restrictions on contact presumably help to maintain the antagonistic stereotypes. In any case, two different social and cultural worlds develop, tending to jog along beside each other, with points of official contact but little mutual penetration. It is important to add that the institutional plant and name comes to be identified by both staff and inmates as somehow belonging to staff, so that when either grouping refers to the views or interests of "the institution," by implication they are referring (as I shall also) to the views and concerns of the staff.

The staff-inmate split is one major implication of the central features of total institutions; a second one pertains to work. In the ordinary arrangements of living in our society, the authority of the workplace stops with the worker's receipt of a money payment; the spending of this in a domestic and recreational setting is at the discretion of the worker and is the mechanism through which the authority of the workplace is kept within strict bounds. However, to say that inmates in total institutions have their full day scheduled for them is to say that some version of all basic needs will have to be planned for, too. In other words, total institutions take over "responsibility" for the inmate and must guarantee to have everything that is defined as essential "layed on." It follows, then, that whatever incentive is given for work, this will not have the structural significance it has on the outside. Different attitudes and incentives regarding this central feature of our life will have to prevail.

Here, then, is one basic adjustment required of those who work in total institutions and of those who must induce these people to work. In some cases, no work or little is required, and inmates, untrained often in leisurely ways of life, suffer extremes of boredom. In other cases, some work is required but is carried on at an extremely slow pace, being geared into a system of minor, often ceremonial payments, as in the case of weekly tobacco ration and annual Christmas presents, which cause some mental patients to stay on their job. In some total institutions, such as logging camps and merchant ships, something of the usual relation to the world that money can buy is obtained through the practice of "forced saving"; all needs are organized by the institution, and payment is given only after a work season is over and the men leave the premises. And in some total institutions, of course, more than a full day's work is required and is induced not by reward, but by threat of dire punishment. In all such cases, the work-oriented individual may tend to become somewhat demoralized by the system.

In addition to the fact that total institutions are incompatible with the basic work-payment structure of our society, it must be seen that these establishments are also incompatible with another crucial element of our society, the family. The family is sometimes contrasted to solitary living, but in fact the more pertinent contrast to family life might be with batch living. For it seems that those who eat and sleep at work, with a group of fellow workers, can hardly sustain a meaningful domestic existence. Correspondingly, the extent to which a staff retains its integration in the outside community and escapes the encompassing tendencies of total institutions is often linked up with the maintenance of a family off the grounds.

Whether a particular total institution act[s] as a good or bad force in civil society, force it may well have, and this will depend on the suppression of a whole circle of actual or potential households. Conversely, the formation of households provides a structural guarantee that total institutions will not arise. The incompatibility between these two forms of social organization should tell us, then, something about the wider social functions of them both.

Total institutions, then, are social hybrids, part residential community, part formal or-ganization, and therein lies their special sociological interest. There are other reasons, alas, for being interested in them, too. These establishments are the forcing houses for changing persons in our society. Each is a natural experiment, typically harsh, on what can be done to the self.

Having suggested some of the key features of total institutions, we can move on now to consider them from the special perspectives that seem natural to take. I will consider the inmate world, then the staff world, and then something about contacts between the two.

The Inmate World

Mortification Processes. It is characteristic of inmates that they come to the institution as members, already full-fledged, of a *home world*, that is, a way of life and a round of activities taken for granted up to the point of admission to the institution. It is useful to look at this culture that the recruit brings with him to the institution's door—his *presenting culture*, to modify a psychiatric phrase—in terms especially designed to highlight what it is the total institution will do to him. Whatever the stability of his personal organization, we can assume it was part of a wider supporting framework lodged in his current social environment, a round of experience that somewhat confirms a conception of self that is somewhat acceptable to him and a set of defensive maneuvers exercisable at his own discretion as a means of coping with conflicts, discrediting and failures.

Now it appears that total institutions do not substitute their own unique culture for something already formed. We do not deal with acculturation or assimilation but with something more restricted than these. In a sense, total institutions do not look for cultural victory. They effectively create and sustain a particular kind of tension between the home world and the institutional world and use this persistent tension as strategic leverage in the management of men. The full meaning for the inmate of being "in" or "on the inside" does not exist apart from the special meaning to him of "getting out" or "getting on the outside."

The recruit comes into the institution with a self and with attachments to supports which had allowed this self to survive. Upon entrance, he is immediately stripped of his wonted supports, and his self is systematically, if often unintentionally, mortified. In the accurate language of some of our oldest total institutions, he is led into a series of abasements, degradations, humiliations, and profanations of self. He begins, in other words, some radical shifts in his *moral career*, a career laying out the progressive changes that occur in the beliefs that he has concerning himself and significant others.

The *stripping processes* through which *mortification of the self* occurs are fairly standard in our total institutions. Personal identity equipment is removed, as well as other possessions with which the inmate may have identified himself, there typically being a system of nonaccessible storage from which the inmate can only reobtain his effects should he leave the institution. As a substitute for what has been taken away, institutional issue is provided, but this will be the same for large categories of inmates and will be regularly repossessed by the institution. In brief, standardized defacement will occur. In addition, ego-invested separateness from fellow inmates is significantly diminished in many areas of activity, and tasks are prescribed that are *infradignitatem*. Family, occupational, and educational career lines are chopped off, and a stigmatized status is submitted. Sources of fantasy materials which had meant momentary releases from stress in the home world are denied. Areas of autonomous decision are eliminated through the process of collective scheduling of daily activity. Many channels of communication with the outside are restricted or closed off completely. Verbal discreditings occur in many forms as a matter of course. Expressive signs of respect for the staff are coercively and continuously demanded. And the effect of each of these conditions is multiplied by having to witness the mortification of one's fellow inmates.

We must expect to find different official reasons given for these assaults upon the self. In mental hospitals there is the matter of protecting the patient from himself and from other patients. In jails there is the issue of "security" and frank punishment. In religious institutions we may find sociologically sophisticated theories about the soul's need for purification and penance through disciplining of the flesh. What all of these rationales share is the extent to which they are merely rationalizations, for the underlying force in many cases is unwittingly generated by efforts to manage the daily activity of a large number of persons in a small space with a small expenditure of resources.

In the background of the sociological stripping process, we find a characteristic authority system with three distinctive elements, each basic to total institutions.

First, to a degree, authority is of the *echelon* kind. Any member of the staff class has certain rights to discipline any member of the inmate class. This arrangement, it may be noted, is similar to the one which gives any adult in some small American towns certain rights to correct and demand small services from any child not in the immediate presence of his parents. In our society, the adult himself, however, is typically under the authority of a *single* immediate superior in connection with his work or uncle's authority of one spouse in connection with domestic duties. The only echelon authority he must face—the police—typically are neither constantly nor relevantly present, except perhaps in the case of traffic-law enforcement.

Second, the authority of corrective sanctions is directed to a great multitude of items of conduct of the kind that are constantly occurring and constantly coming up for judgment; in brief, authority is directed to matters of dress, deportment, social intercourse, manners and the like. In prisons these regulations regarding situational proprieties may even extend to a point where silence during mealtime is enforced, while in some convents explicit demands may be made concerning the custody of the eyes during prayer.

The *third* feature of authority in total institutions is that misbehaviors in one sphere of life are held against one's standing in other spheres. Thus, an individual who fails to participate with proper enthusiasm in sports may be brought to the attention of the person who determines where he will sleep and what kind of work task will be accorded to him.

When we combine these three aspects of authority in total institutions, we see that the inmate cannot easily escape from the press of judgmental officials and from the enveloping tissue of constraint. The system of authority undermines the basis for control that adults in our society expect to exert over their interpersonal environment and may produce the terror of feeling that one is being radically demoted in the age-grading system. On the outside, rules are sufficiently lax and the individual sufficiently agreeable to required self-discipline to insure that others will rarely have cause for pouncing on him. He need not constantly look over his shoulder to see if criticism and other sanctions are coming. On the inside, however, rulings are abundant, novel, and closely enforced so that, quite characteristically, inmates live with chronic anxiety about breaking the rules and chronic worry about the consequences of breaking them. The desire to "stay out of trouble" in a total institution is likely to require persistent conscious effort and may lead the inmate to abjure certain levels of sociability; with his fellows in order to avoid the incidents that may occur in these circumstances.

It should be noted finally that the mortifications to be suffered by the inmate may be purposely brought home to him in an exaggerated way during the first few days after entrance, in a form of initiation that has been called *the welcome*. Both staff and fellow inmates may go out of their way to give the neophyte a clear notion of where he stands. As part of this *rite de passage*, he may find himself called by a term such as "fish," "swab," etc., through which older inmates tell him that he is not only merely an inmate but that even within this lowly group he has a low status.

Privilege System. While the process of mortification is in progress, the inmate begins to receive formal and informal instruction in what will here be called the *privilege system*. Insofar as the inmate's self has been unsettled a little by the stripping action of the institution, it is largely around this framework that pressures are exerted, making for a reorganization of self. Three basic elements of the system may be mentioned.

First, there are the *house rules*, a relatively explicit and formal set of prescriptions and proscriptions which lay out the main requirements of inmate conduct. These regulations spell out the austere round of life in which the inmate will operate. Thus, the admission procedures through which the recruit is initially stripped of his self-supporting context can be seen as the institution's way of getting him in the position to start living by the house rules.

Second, against the stark background, a small number of clearly defined *rewards or privileges* are held out in exchange for obedience to staff in action and spirit. It is important to see that these potential gratifications are not unique to the institution but rather are ones carved out of the flow of support that the inmate previously had quite taken for granted. On the outside, for example, the inmate was likely to be able to unthinkingly exercise autonomy by deciding how much sugar and milk he wanted in his coffee, if any, or when to light up a cigarette; on the inside, this right may become quite problematic and a matter of a great deal of conscious concern. Held up to the inmate as possibilities, these few recapturings seem to have a reintegrative effect, re-establishing relationships with the whole lost world and assuaging withdrawal symptoms from it and from one's lost self.

The inmate's run of attention, then, especially at first, comes to be fixated on these supplies and obsessed with them. In the most fanatic way, he can spend the day in devoted thoughts concerning the possibility of acquiring these gratifications or the approach of the hour at which they are scheduled to be granted. The building of a world around these minor privileges is perhaps the most important feature of inmate culture and yet is something that cannot easily be appreciated by an outsider, even one who has lived through the experience himself. This situation sometimes leads to generous sharing and almost always to a willingness to beg for things such as cigarettes, candy and newspapers. It will be understandable, then, that a constant feature of inmate discussion is the *release binge fantasy*. Namely, recitals of what one will do during leave or upon release from the institution.

House rules and privileges provide the functional requirements of the third element in the privilege system: *punishments*. These are designated as the consequence of breaking the rules. One set of these punishments consists of the temporary or permanent withdrawal of privileges or abrogation of the right to try to earn them. In general, the punishments meted out in total institutions are of an order more severe than anything encountered by the inmate in his home world. An institutional arrangement which causes a small number of easily controlled privileges to have a massive significance is the same arrangement which lends a terrible significance to their withdrawal.

There are some special features of the privilege system which should be noted.

First, punishments and privileges are themselves modes of organization peculiar to total institutions. Whatever their severity, punishments are largely known in the inmate's home world as something applied to animals and children. For adults this conditioning, behavioristic model is actually not widely applied, since failure to maintain required standards typically leads to indirect disadvantageous consequences and not to specific immediate punishment at all. And privileges, it should be emphasized, are not the same as prerequisites, indulgences or values, but merely the absence of deprivations one ordinarily expects one would not have to sustain. The very notions, then, of punishments and privileges are not ones that are cut from civilian cloth.

Second, it is important to see that the question of release from the total institution is elaborated into the privilege system. Some acts will become known as ones that mean an increase or no decrease in length of stay, while others become known as means for lessening the sentence.

Third, we should also note that punishments and privileges come to be geared into a residential work system. Places to work and places to sleep become clearly defined as places where certain kinds and levels of privilege obtain, and inmates are shifted very rapidly and visibly from one place to another as the mechanisms for giving them the punishment or privilege their cooperativeness has warranted. The inmates are moved, the system is not.

This, then, is the privilege system: a relatively few components put together with some rational intent and clearly proclaimed to the participants. The overall consequence is that cooperativeness is obtained from persons who often have cause to be uncooperative. . . .Immediately associated with the privilege system we find some standard social processes important in the life of total institutions.

We find that an *institutional lingo* develops through which inmates express the events that are crucial in their particular world. Staff too, especially its lower levels, will know this language, using it when talking to inmates, while reverting to more standardized speech when talking to superiors and outsiders. Related to this special argot, inmates will possess knowledge of the various ranks and officials, an accumulation of lore about the establishment, and some comparative information about life in other similar total institutions.

Also found among staff and inmates will be a clear awareness of the phenomenon of *messing up*, so called in mental hospitals, prisons, and barracks. This involves a complex process of engaging in forbidden activity, getting caught doing so, and receiving something like the full punishment accorded this. An alteration in privilege status is usually implied and is categorized by a phrase such as "getting busted." Typical infractions which can eventuate in messing up are: fights, drunkenness, attempted suicide, failure at examinations, gambling, insubordination, homosexuality, improper taking of leave, and participation in collective riots. While these punished infractions are typically ascribed to the offender's cursedness, villainy, or "sickness," they do in fact constitute a vocabulary of institutionalized actions, limited in such a way that the same messing up may occur for quite different reasons. Informally, inmates and staff may understand, for example, that a given messing up is a way for inmates to show resentment against a current situation felt to be unjust in terms of the informal agreements between staff and inmates, or a way of postponing release without having to admit to one's fellow inmates that one really does not want to go.

In total institutions there will also be a system of what might be called *secondary adjustments*, namely, techniques which do not directly challenge staff management but which allow inmates to obtain disallowed satisfactions or allowed ones by disallowed means. These practices are variously referred to as: the angles, knowing the ropes, conniving, gimmicks, deals, ins, etc. Such adaptations apparently reach their finest flower in prisons, but of course other total institutions are overrun with them too. It seems apparent that an important aspect of secondary adjustments is that they provide the inmate with some evidence that he is still, as it were, his own man and still has some protective distance, under his own control, between himself and the institution. In some cases, then, a secondary adjustment

becomes almost a kind of lodgment for the self, a churinga in which the soul is felt to reside.

The occurrence of secondary adjustments correctly allows us to assume that the inmate group will have some kind of a *code* and some means of informal social control evolved to prevent one inmate from informing staff about the secondary adjustments of another. On the same grounds we can expect that one dimension of social typing among inmates will turn upon this question of security, leading to persons defined as "squealers," "finks," or "stoolies" on one hand, and persons defined as "right guys" on the other. It should be added that where new inmates can play a role in the system of secondary adjustments, as in providing new faction members or new sexual objects, then their "welcome" may indeed be a sequence of initial indulgences and enticements, instead of exaggerated deprivations. Because of secondary adjustments we also find *kitchen strata*, namely, a kind of rudimentary, largely informal, stratification of inmates on the basis of each one's differential access to disposable illicit commodities; so also we find social typing to designate the powerful persons in the informal market system.

While the privilege system provides the chief framework within which reassembly of the self takes place, other factors characteristically lead by different routes in the same general direction. Relief from economic and social responsibilities—much touted as part of the therapy in mental hospitals—is one, although in many cases it would seem that the disorganizing effect of this moratorium is more significant than its organizing effect. More important as a reorganizing influence is the *fraternalization process*, namely, the process through which socially distant persons find themselves developing mutual support and common *counter-mores* in opposition to a system that has forced them into intimacy and into a single, equalitarian community of fate. It seems that the new recruit frequently starts out with something like the staff's popular misconceptions of the character of the inmates and then comes to find that most of his fellows have all the properties of ordinary decent human beings and that the stereotypes associated with their condition or offense are not a reasonable ground for judgment of inmates.

If the inmates are persons who are accused by staff and society of having committed some kind of a crime against society, then the new inmate, even though sometimes in fact quite guiltless, may come to share the guilty feelings of his fellows and, thereafter, their well-elaborated defenses against these feelings. A sense of common injustice and a sense of bitterness against the outside world tends to develop, marking an important movement in the inmate's moral career. . . .

Adaptation Alignments. The mortifying processes that have been discussed and the privilege system represent the conditions that the inmate must adapt to in some way, but however pressing, these conditions allow for different ways of meeting them. We find, in fact, that the same inmate will employ different lines of adaptation or tacks at different phases in his moral career and may even fluctuate between different tacks at the same time.

First, there is the process of *situational withdrawal*. The inmate withdraws apparent attention from everything except events immediately around his body and sees these in a perspective not employed by others present. This drastic curtailment of involvement in interactional events is best known, of course, in mental hospitals, under the title of "regression." Aspects of "prison psychosis" or "stir simpleness" represent the same adjustment, as do some forms of "acute depersonalization" described in concentration camps. I do not think it is known whether this line of adaptation forms a single continuum of varying degrees of withdrawal or whether there are standard discontinuous plateaus of disinvolvement. It does seem to be the case, however, that, given the pressures apparently required to dislodge an inmate from this status, as well as the cur-

rently limited facilities for doing so, we frequently find here, effectively speaking, an irreversible line of adaptation.

Second, there is the *rebellious line*. The inmate intentionally challenges the institution by flagrantly refusing to cooperate with staff in almost any way. The result is a constantly communicated intransigency and sometimes high rebel morale. Most large mental hospitals, for example, seem to have wards where this spirit strongly prevails. Interestingly enough, there are many circumstances in which sustained rejection of a total institution requires sustained orientation to its formal organization and hence, paradoxically, a deep kind of commitment to the establishment. Similarly, when total institutions take the line (as they sometimes do in the case of mental hospitals prescribing lobotomy or army barracks prescribing the stockade) that the recalcitrant inmate must be broken, then, in their way, they must show as much special devotion to the rebel as he has shown to them. It should be added, finally, that while prisoners of war have been known staunchly to take a rebellious stance throughout their incarceration, this stance is typically a temporary and initial phase of reaction, emerging from this to situational withdrawal or some other line of adaptation.

Third, another standard alignment in the institutional world takes the form of a kind of *colonization*. The sampling of the outside world provided by the establishment is taken by the inmate as the whole, and a stable, relatively contented existence is built up out of the maximum satisfactions procurable within the institution. Experience of the outside world is used as a point of reference to demonstrate the desirability of life on the inside; and the usual tension between the two worlds collapses, thwarting the social arrangements based upon this felt discrepancy. Characteristically, the individual who too obviously takes this line may be accused by his fellow inmates of "having found a home" or of "never having had it so good." Staff itself may become vaguely embarrassed by this use that is being made of the institution, sensing that the benign possibilities in the situation are somehow being misused. Colonizers themselves may feel obliged to deny their satisfaction with the institution, if only in the interest of sustaining the counter-mores supporting inmate solidarity. They may find it necessary to mess up just prior to their slated discharge, thereby allowing themselves to present involuntary reasons for continued incarceration. It should be incidentally noted that any humanistic effort to make life in total institutions more bearable must face the possibility that doing so may increase the attractiveness and likelihood of colonization.

Fourth, one mode of adaptation to the setting of a total institution is that of *conversion*. The inmate appears to take over completely the official or staff view of himself and tries to act out the role of the perfect inmate. While the colonized inmate builds as much of a free community as possible for himself by using the limited facilities available, the convert takes a more disciplined, moralistic, monochromatic line, presenting himself as someone whose institutional enthusiasm is always at the disposal of the staff. . . . In army barracks there are enlisted men who give the impression that they are always "sucking around" and always "bucking for promotion." In prisons there are "square johns.". . . Some mental hospitals have the distinction of providing two quite different conversion possibilities—one for the new admission who can see the light after an appropriate struggle and adapt the psychiatric view of himself, and another for the chronic ward patient who adopts the manner and dress of attendants while helping them to manage the other ward patients with a stringency excelling that of the attendants themselves.

Here, it should be noted, is a significant way in which total institutions differ. Many, like progressive mental hospitals, merchant ships, TB sanitariums and brainwashing camps, offer the inmate an opportunity to live up to a model of conduct that is at once ideal and staff-sponsored—a model felt by its advocates to be in the supreme interests of the very persons to whom it is applied. Other total institutions, like some concentration camps and some prisons, do not officially sponsor an ideal that the inmate is expected to incorporate as a means of judging himself.

While the alignments that have been mentioned represent coherent courses to pursue, few inmates, it seems, carry these pursuits very far. In most total institutions, what we seem to find is that most inmates take the tack of what they call *playing it cool*. This involves a somewhat opportunistic combination of secondary adjustments, conversion, colonization and loyalty to the inmate group, so that in the particular circumstances the inmate will have a maximum chance of eventually getting out physically and psychically undamaged. Typically, the inmate will support the counter-mores when with fellow inmates and be silent to them on how tractably he acts when alone in the presence of staff. Inmates taking this line tend to subordinate contacts with their fellows to the higher claim of "keeping out of trouble." They tend to volunteer for nothing and they may even learn to cut their ties to the outside world sufficiently to give cultural reality to the world inside but not enough to lead to colonization.

I have suggested some of the lines of adaptation that inmates can take to the pressures that play in total institutions. Each represents a way of managing the tension between the home world and the institutional world. However there are circumstances in which the home world of the inmate was such in fact as to *immunize* him against the bleak world on the inside and for such persons no particular scheme of adaptation need be carried very far. Thus some lower-class mental hospital patients who have lived all their previous life in orphanages reformatories and jails tend to see the hospital as just another total institution to which it is possible to apply the adaptive techniques learned and perfected in other total institutions. "Playing it cool" represents for such persons not a shift in their moral career but an alignment that is already second nature. . . .

Culture Themes. A note should be added here concerning some of the more dominant themes of inmate culture.

First, in the inmate group of many total institutions there is a strong feeling that time spent in the establishment is time wasted or destroyed or taken from one's life; it is time that must be written off. It is something that must be "done" or "marked" or "put in" or "built" or "pulled." (Thus in prisons and mental hospitals a general statement of how well one is adapting to the institution may be phrased in terms of how one is doing time whether easily or hard.) As such this time is something that its doers have bracketed off for constant conscious consideration in a way not quite found on the outside. And as a result the inmate tends to feel that for the duration of his required stay—his sentence—he has been totally exiled from living. It is in this context that we can appreciate something of the demoralizing influence of an indefinite sentence or a very long one. We should also note that however hard the conditions of life may become in total institutions harshness alone cannot account for this quality of life wasted. Rather we must look to the social disconnections caused by entrance and to the usual failure to acquire within the institution gains that can be transferred to outside life—gains such as money earned, or marital relations formed, or certified training received.

Second, it seems that in many total institutions a peculiar kind and level of self-concern is engendered. The low position of inmates relative to their station on the outside as established initially through the mortifying processes seems to make for a milieu of personal failure and a round of life in which one's fall from grace is continuously pressed home. In response the inmate tends to develop a storyline[,] a sad tale—a kind of lamentation and apologia—which he constantly tells to his fellows as a means of creditably accounting for his present low estate. While staff constantly discredit these lines inmate audiences tend to employ tact, suppressing at least some of the disbelief and boredom engendered by these recitations. In consequence, the inmate's own self may become even more of a focus for his conversation than it does on the outside.

Perhaps the high level of ruminative self-concern found among inmates in total institutions is a way of handling the sense of wasted time that prevails in these places. If so, then perhaps another interesting aspect of inmate culture can be related to the same factor. I refer here to the fact that in total institutions we characteristically find a premium placed on what might be called *removal activities*, namely, voluntary unserious pursuits which are sufficiently engrossing and exciting to lift the participant out of himself, making [him] oblivious for the time to his actual situation. If the ordinary activities in total institutions can be said to torture time, these activities mercifully kill it.

Some removal activities are collective, such as ball games, woodwork, lectures, choral singing and card playing; some are individual but rely on public materials, as in the case of reading, solitary TV watching, etc. No doubt, private fantasy ought to be included too. Some of these activities may be officially sponsored by staff; and some, not officially sponsored, may constitute secondary adjustments. In any case, there seems to be no total institution which cannot be seen as a kind of Dead Sea in which appear little islands of vivid, enrapturing activity.

Consequences. In this discussion of the inmate world, I have commented on the mortification processes, the reorganizing influences, the lines of response taken by inmates under these circumstances, and the cultural milieu that develops. A concluding word must be added about the long-range consequences of membership.

Total institutions frequently claim to be concerned with rehabilitation, that is, with resetting the inmate's self-regulatory mechanisms so that he will maintain the standards of the establishment of his own accord after he leaves the setting. In fact, it seems this claim is seldom realized and even when permanent alteration occurs, these changes are often not of the kind intended by the staff. With the possible exception presented by the great resocialization efficiency of religious institutions, neither the stripping processes nor the reorganizing ones seem to have a lasting effect. No doubt the availability of secondary adjustments helps to account for this, as do the presence of counter-mores and the tendency for inmates to combine all strategies and "play it cool." In any case, it seems that shortly after release, the ex-inmate will have forgotten a great deal of what life was like on the inside and will have once again begun to take for granted the privileges around which life in the institution was organized. The sense of injustice, bitterness and alienation, so typically engendered by the inmate's experience and so definitely marking a stage in his moral career, seems to weaken upon graduation, even in those cases where a permanent stigma has resulted.

But what the ex-inmate does retain of his institutional experience tells us important things about total institutions. Often entrance will mean for the recruit that he has taken on what might be called a *proactive status.* Not only is his relative social position within the walls radically different from what it was on the outside, but, as he comes to learn, if and when he gets out, his social position on the outside will never again be quite what it was prior to entrance. Where the proactive status is a relatively favorable one, as it is for those who graduate from officers' training schools, elite boarding schools, ranking monasteries, etc., then the permanent alteration will be favorable, and jubilant official reunions announcing pride in one's "school" can be expected. When, as seems usually the case, the proactive status is unfavorable, as it is for those in prisons or mental hospitals, we popularly employ the term "stigmatization" and expect that the ex-inmate may make an effort to conceal his past and try to "pass.". . .

Conclusion

I have defined total institutions denotatively by listing them and then have tried to suggest some of their common characteristics. We now have a quite sizable literature on these establishments and should be in a position to supplant mere suggestions with a solid framework bearing on the anatomy and functioning of this kind of social animal. Certainly the similarities obtrude so glaringly and persistently that we have a right to suspect that these features have good functional reasons for being present and that it will be possible to tie them together and grasp them by means of a functional explanation. When we have done so, I feel we will then give less praise and blame to particular superintendents, commandants, wardens and abbots, and tend more to understand the social problems and issues in total institutions by appealing to the underlying structural design common to all of them.

Study Questions

1. What are some of the common characteristics of total institutions identified by the author?

2. Describe the initial process of self-mortification and the continuing degradations suffered by inmates.

3. How may different inmates adapt to the setting of the total institution?

4. If Goffman is correct about the debilitating effects of the total institution, how might we expect inmates to act upon release? ✦

8
The Prison Community

Donald Clemmer

In this article by Clemmer, the process of "prisonization" is examined closely. After considering the possible effects of the "total institution," the reader should consider how those effects may influence the culture (or subculture) within the walls of the prison. The author describes prisonization as "the process through which an individual will take on the values and mores of the penitentiary." In other words, the prison itself is seen as a world in and of itself—a world with unique characteristics and internal forces that at times mimic the outside world but in many ways are completely different. Because the prisoners, through processes inherent within the prison, have been cut off from outside influences, the potential for the development of new rules, expectations, and economies presents itself. In responding to these new rules, inmates develop ways in which they modify their behavior to fit in and adapt. Such adaptation may help inmates survive in a number of ways. As you read, however, consider whether these behavior modifications inhibit the achievement of any other correctional goals.

Assimilation or Prisonization

When a person or group of ingress penetrates and fuses with another group, assimilation may be said to have taken place. The

Excerpts from *The Prison Community* by Donald Clemmer. Copyright © 1958 by Donald Clemmer and renewed 1986 by Rose Emelia Clemmer. Reprinted with the permission of Holt, Rinehart & Winston, Inc.

concept is most profitably applied to immigrant groups and perhaps it is not the best term by which to designate similar processes which occur in prison. Assimilation implies that a process of acculturation occurs in one group whose members originally were quite different from those of the group with whom they mix. It implies that the assimilated come to share the sentiments, memories, and traditions of the static group. It is evident that the men who come to prison are not greatly different from the ones already there so far as broad culture influences are concerned: All speak the same language, all have a similar national heritage, all have been stigmatized, and so on. While the differences of regional conditioning are not to be overlooked, it is doubtful if the interactions which lead the professional offender to have a "we-feeling" with the naive offender from Coalville can be referred to as assimilation—although the processes furnishing the development of such an understanding are similar to it. . . . [T]he term assimilation describes a slow, gradual, more or less unconscious process during which a person learns enough of the culture of a social unit into which he is placed to make him characteristic of it. While we shall continue to use this general meaning, we recognize that in the strictest sense assimilation is not the correct term. So as we use the term Americanization to describe a greater or lesser degree of the immigrant's integration into the American scheme of life, we may use the term *prisonization* to indicate the taking on in greater or lesser degree of the folkways, mores, customs, and general culture of the penitentiary. Prisonization is similar to assimilation, and its meaning will become clearer as we proceed.

Every man who enters the penitentiary undergoes prisonization to some extent. The first and most obvious integrative step concerns his status. He becomes at once an anonymous figure in a subordinate group. A number replaces a name. He wears the clothes of the other members of the subordinate group. He is questioned and admonished. He soon learns that the warden is all-powerful. He soon learns the ranks, titles, and authority of various officials. And whether he uses the prison slang and argot or not, he comes to know its meanings. Even though a new man may hold himself aloof from other inmates and remain a solitary figure, he finds himself within a few months referring to or thinking of keepers as "screws," the physician as the "croaker" and using the local nicknames to designate persons. He follows the examples already set in wearing his cap. He learns to eat in haste and in obtaining food he imitates the tricks of those near him.

After the new arrival recovers from the effects of the swallowing-up process, he assigns a new meaning to conditions he had previously taken for granted. The fact that food, shelter, clothing, and a work activity had been given him originally made no especial impression. It is only after some weeks or months that there comes to him a new interpretation of these necessities of life. This new conception results from mingling with other men and it places emphasis on the fact that the environment *should* administer to him. This point is intangible and difficult to describe insofar as it is only a subtle and minute change in attitude from the taken-for-granted perception. Exhaustive questioning of hundreds of men reveals that this slight change in attitude is a fundamental step in the process we are calling prisonization. Supplemental to it is the almost universal desire on the part of the man, after a period of some months, to get a good job so, as he says, "I can do my time without any trouble and get out of here." A good job usually means a comfortable job of a more or less isolated kind in which conflicts with other men are not likely to develop. The desire for a comfortable job is not peculiar to the prison community, to be sure, but it seems to be a phase of prisonization in the following way. When men have served time before entering the penitentiary they look the situation over and almost immediately express a desire for a certain kind of work.

When strictly first offenders come to prison, however, they seldom express a desire for a particular kind of work, but are willing to do anything and frequently say, "I'll do any kind of work they put me at and you won't have any trouble from me." Within a period of a few months, however, these same men, who had no choice of work, develop preferences and make their desires known. They "wise up," as the inmates say, or in other words, by association they become prisonized.

In various other ways men new to prison slip into the existing patterns. They learn to gamble or learn new ways to gamble. Some, for the first time in their lives, take to abnormal sex behavior. Many of them learn to distrust and hate the officers, the parole board, and sometimes each other, and they become acquainted with the dogmas and mores existing in the community. But these changes do not occur in every man. However, every man is subject to certain influences which we may call the *universal factors of prisonization.*

Acceptance of an inferior role, accumulation of facts concerning the organization of the prison, the development of somewhat new habits of eating, dressing, working, sleeping, the adoption of local language, the recognition that nothing is owed to the environment for the supplying of needs, and the eventual desire for a good job are aspects of prisonization which are operative for all inmates. It is not these aspects, however, which concern us most but they are important because of their universality, especially among men who have served many years. That is, even if no other factor of the prison culture touches the personality of an inmate of many years residence, the influences of these universal factors are sufficient to make a man characteristic of the penal community and probably so disrupt his personality that a happy adjustment in any community becomes next to impossible. On the other hand, if inmates who are incarcerated for only short periods, such as a year or so, do not become integrated into the culture except insofar as these universal factors of prisonization are concerned, they do not seem to be so characteristic of the penal community and are able when released to take up a new mode of life without much difficulty.

The phases of prisonization which concern us most are the influences which breed or deepen criminality and antisociality and make the inmate characteristic of the criminalistic ideology in the prison community. As has been said, every man feels the influences of what we have called the universal factors, but not every man becomes prisonized in and by other phases of the culture. Whether or not complete prisonization takes place depends first on the man himself, that is, his susceptibility to a culture which depends, we think, primarily on the type of relationships he had before imprisonment, i.e., his personality. A second determinant effecting complete prisonization refers to the kind and extent of relationships which an inmate has with persons outside the walls. A third determinant refers to whether or not a man becomes affiliated in prison primary or semi-primary groups and this is related to the two points already mentioned. Yet a fourth determinant depends simply on chance, a chance placement in [a] work gang, cellhouse, and with [a] cellmate. A fifth determinant pertains to whether or not a man accepts the dogmas or codes of the prison culture. Other determinants depend on age, criminality, nationality, race, regional conditioning, and every determinant is more or less interrelated with every other one.

With knowledge of these determinants we can hypothetically construct schemata of prisonization which may serve to illustrate its extremes. In the least or lowest degree of prisonization the following factors may be enumerated:

1. A short sentence, thus a brief subjection to the universal factors of prisonization.

2. A fairly stable personality made stable by an adequacy of positive and socialized relationships during pre-penal life.

3. The continuance of positive relationships with persons outside the walls.

4. Refusal or inability to integrate into a prison primary group or semiprimary group, while yet maintaining a symbiotic balance in relations with other men.

5. Refusal to accept blindly the dogmas and codes of the population, and a willingness, under certain situations, to aid officials, thus making for identification with the free community.

6. A chance placement with a cellmate and workmates who do not possess leadership qualities and who are also not completely integrated into the prison culture.

7. Refraining from abnormal sex behavior, and excessive gambling, and a ready willingness to engage seriously in work and recreative activities.

Other factors no doubt have an influencing force in obstructing the process of prisonization, but the seven points mentioned seem outstanding.

In the highest or greatest degree of prisonization the following factors may be enumerated:

1. A sentence of many years, thus a long subjection to the universal factors of prisonization.

2. A somewhat unstable personality made unstable by an inadequacy of socialized relations before commitment, but possessing, nonetheless, a capacity for strong convictions and a particular kind of loyalty.

3. A dearth of positive relations with persons outside the walls.

4. A readiness and a capacity for integration into a prison-primary group.

5. A blind, or almost blind, acceptance of the dogmas and mores of the primary group and the general penal population.

6. A chance placement with other persons of a similar orientation.

7. A readiness to participate in gambling and abnormal sex behavior.

We can see in these two extremes the degrees with which the prisonization process operates. No suggestion is intended that a high correlation exists between either extreme of prisonization and criminality. It is quite possible that the inmate who fails to integrate in the prison culture may be and may continue to be much more criminalistic than the inmate who becomes completely prisonized. The trends are probably otherwise, however, as our study of group life suggests. To determine prisonization, every case must be appraised for itself. Of the two degrees presented in the schemes it is probable that more men approach the complete degree than the least degree of prisonization, but it is also probable that the majority of inmates become prisonized in some respects and not in others. It is the varying degrees of prisonization among the 2,300 men that contribute to the disassociation which is so common. The culture is made complex, not only by the constantly changing population, but by these differences in the tempo and degree of prisonization.

Assimilation, as the concept is customarily applied, is always a slow, gradual process, but prisonization, as we use the term here, is usually slow, but not necessarily so. The speed with which prisonization occurs depends on the personality of the man involved, his crime, age, home neighborhood, intelligence, the situation into which he is placed in prison and other less obvious influences. The process does not necessarily proceed in an orderly or measured fashion but tends to be irregular. In some cases we have found the process working in a cycle. The amount and speed of prisonization can be judged only by the behavior and attitudes of the men, and these vary from man to man and in the same man from time to time. It is the excessive number of changes in orientation which the men undergo which makes generalizations about the process so difficult.

In the free communities where the daily life of the inhabitants is not controlled in every detail, some authors have reported a natural gravitation to social levels. The matter of chance still remains a factor, of course, in open society but not nearly so much so as in the prison. For example, two associates in a particular crime may enter the prison at the same time. Let us say that their criminality, their intelligence, and their background are more or less the same. Each is interviewed by the deputy warden and assigned to a job. It so happens that a certain office is in need of a porter. Of the two associates the man whom the deputy warden happens to see first may be assigned to that job while the one he interviews last is assigned to the quarry. The inmate who becomes the office porter associates with but four or five other men, none of whom, let us suppose, are basically prisonized. The new porter adapts himself to them and takes up their interests. His speed of prisonization will be slow and he may never become completely integrated into the prison culture. His associate, on the other hand, works in the quarry and mingles with a hundred men. The odds are three to five that he will become integrated into a primary or semi-primary group. When he is admitted into the competitive and personal relationships of informal group life we can be sure that, in spite of some disassociation, he is becoming prisonized and will approach the complete degree.

Even if the two associates were assigned to the same work unit, differences in the tempo of prisonization might result if one, for example, worked shoulder to shoulder with a "complete solitary man," or a "hoosier." Whatever else may be said of the tempo of the process, it is always faster when the contacts are primary, providing the persons contacted in a primary way are themselves integrated beyond the minimal into the prison culture. Other factors, of course, influence the speed of integration. The inmate whose wife divorces him may turn for response and recognition to his immediate associates.

When the memories of pre-penal experience cease to be satisfying or practically useful, a barrier to prisonization has been removed.

Some men become prisonized to the highest degree, or to a degree approaching it, but then reject their entire orientation and show, neither by behavior nor attitudes, that any sort of integration has taken place. They slip out of group life. They ignore the codes and dogmas and they fall into a reverie or stupor or become "solitary men." After some months or even years of playing this role they may again affiliate with a group and behave as other prisonized inmates do.

Determination of the degree of prisonization and the speed with which it occurs can be learned best through the study of specific cases. The innumerable variables and the methodological difficulties which arise in learning what particular stage of prisonization a man has reached, prohibit the use of quantitative methods. It would be a great help to penology and to parole boards in particular, if the student of prisons could say that inmate so-and-so was prisonized to x^3+9y degrees, and such a degree was highly correlated with a specific type of criminality.

The day will no doubt come when phenomena of this kind can be measured, but it is not yet here. For the present we must bend our efforts to systems of actuarial prediction, and work for refinements in this line. Actuarial procedures do not ignore criteria of attitudes, but they make no effort as yet to conjure with such abstruse phenomena as prisonization. It is the contention of this writer that parole prediction methods which do not give as much study and attention to a man's role in the prison community as is given to his adjustment in the free community cannot be of much utility.

Study Questions

1. What was meant by the term *prisonization*, and what are some of its universal factors?

2. What characteristics of inmates determine the degree and speed with which prisonization occurs?

3. How do the features of the total institution, referred to by Goffman, relate to the process of prisonization? ✦

9
The Society
of Captives

Gresham M. Sykes

Sykes presents a detailed analysis of what he outlines as the "primary pains" of imprisonment. Although the movement from severe public (and at times deadly) corporal punishment to mass imprisonment has been well-documented thus far, Sykes takes an even closer look at the actual punishing features of institutionalization. Specifically, he explores deprivations of liberty, goods and services, heterosexual relationships, autonomy, and security. Sykes maintains that the prison inmate will either rebel against the deprivations (in effect rebelling against the institution itself), or comply, in a manner of speaking, to get along in a world in which resources by definition are scarce. Regarding the latter, the author argues that, in response to these deprivations, inmate adaptations will result. Subcultures and "argot roles" will proliferate, which presents its own set of unique circumstances and problems for the administration of the institution.

The student of human behavior can find many theoretical issues suddenly illuminated by examining this small-scale society where numerous features of the free community have been drastically changed. In the prison, for example, we find the activity of work—so central to the scheme of things in modern industrial society—transfigured by the realities of prison servitude. Race rela-

Excerpts from *The Society of Captives: A Study of a Maximum Security Prison* by Gresham M. Sykes, pp. xiv, xvi, xviii, xix, 63–79, 82, 83, 86–108, 130, 131. Copyright © 1958 by Princeton University Press. Reprinted by permission.

tions take on new forms in the custodial institution where the ratio between Negroes and whites frequently approaches unity and both groups live under conditions of enforced equality. In the prison, as in war, we find men without women and norms concerning the masculine role and the endurance of sexual frustrations take on new guises. In the prison the obvious symbols of social status have been largely stripped away and we find new hierarchies with new symbols coming into play. But what is most important, perhaps, is the fact that the *maximum security prison represents a social system in which an attempt is made to create and maintain total or almost total social control.*

This study, then, concerns itself with a single system of total power—the social system of the New Jersey State Maximum Security Prison. Here more than 300 custodial, clerical, and professional state employees are organized into bureaucratic administrative staff charged with the duty of governing approximately 1,200 adult male criminals held in confinement for periods of time ranging from one year to life.

Of course, the New Jersey State Prison undoubtedly differs from other maximum security institutions in certain respects, such as the proportion of inmates from urban centers, the age of the buildings, the details of the custodial regime, and so on. Such differences are sure to loom large in the minds of those intimately involved in the administration of particular institutions; and such differences must make us cautious in attempting to generalize. Yet it seems that the similarity of the New Jersey State Prison to the other institutions—in terms of social structure—is far more outstanding than the dissimilarity.

When the plans for this study were first constructed, an effort was made to develop a small number of relatively specific hypotheses dealing with the causes and effects of different types of adjustment to the prison environment. As the problem was examined further, however, it became clear that such an effort was somewhat premature; there was far too little knowledge of the variety of roles played by criminals in prison and even less knowledge of how these roles were related to one another and to the social order which the custodians attempted to create in the pursuit of their assigned tasks. In other words, there was a good deal of ignorance about the prison as a social system—as a complex set of interrelated patterns of social behavior—and without a fuller knowledge of the social structure of the prison as a whole, conclusions concerning the causes and effects of particular reactions could be grossly misleading. It was decided, therefore, that an exploratory study of the prison as a social system would be more valuable than the testing of a limited number of propositions whose context remained in doubt.

The Pains of Imprisonment

It might be argued, of course, that there are certain dangers in speaking of the inmates' perspective of captivity, since it is apt to carry the implication that all prisoners perceive their captivity in precisely the same way. It might be argued that in reality there are as many prisons as there are prisoners—that each man brings to the custodial institution his own needs and his own background and each man takes away from the prison his own interpretation of life within the walls. We do not intend to deny that different men see the conditions of custody somewhat differently and accord these conditions a different emphasis in their personal accounting. Yet when we examine the way the inmates of the New Jersey State Prison perceive the social environment created by the custodians, the dominant fact is the hard core of consensus expressed by the members of the captive population with regard to the nature of their confinement. The inmates are agreed that life in the maximum security prison is depriving or frustrating in the extreme.

In part, the deprivations or frustrations of prison life today might be viewed as punishments which the free community deliberately inflicts on the offender for violating the law; in part, they might be seen as the unplanned (or, as some would argue, the unavoidable) concomitants of confining large groups of criminals for prolonged periods. In either case, the modern pains of imprisonment are often defined by society as a humane alternative to the physical brutality and the neglect which constituted the major meaning of imprisonment in the past. But in examining the pains of imprisonment as they exist today, it is imperative that we go beyond the fact that severe bodily suffering has long since disappeared as a significant aspect of the custodians' regime, leaving behind a residue of apparently less acute hurts such as the loss of liberty, the deprivation of goods and services, the frustration of sexual desire, and so on. These deprivations or frustrations of the modern prison may indeed be the acceptable or unavoidable implications of imprisonment, but we must recognize the fact that they can be just as painful as the physical maltreatment which they have replaced. . . . Such attacks on the psychological level are less easily seen than a sadistic beating, a pair of shackles in the floor, or the caged man on a treadmill, but the destruction of the psyche is no less fearful than bodily affliction and it must play a large role in our discussion. Whatever may be the pains of imprisonment, then, in the custodial institution of today, we must explore the way in which the deprivations and frustrations pose profound threats to the inmate's personality or sense of personal worth.

The Deprivation of Liberty

Of all the painful conditions imposed on the inmates of the New Jersey State Prison, none is more immediately obvious than the loss of liberty. The prisoner must live in a world shrunk to thirteen and a half acres and within this restricted area his freedom of movement is further confined by a strict system of passes, the military formations in moving from one point within the institution to another, and the demand that he remain in his cell until given permission to do otherwise. In short, the prisoner's loss of liberty is a double one—first, by confinement to the institution and second, by confinement within the institution.

The mere fact that the individual's movements are restricted, however, is far less serious than the fact that imprisonment means that the inmate is cut off from family, relatives, and friends, not in the self-isolation of the hermit or the misanthrope, but in the involuntary seclusion of the outlaw. It is true that visiting and mailing privileges partially relieve the prisoner's isolation—if he can find someone to visit him or write to him and who will be approved as a visitor or correspondent by the prison officials. Many inmates, however, have found their links with persons in the free community weakening as the months and years pass by. This may explain in part the fact that an examination of the visiting records of a random sample of the inmate population, covering approximately a one-year period, indicated that 41 percent of the prisoners in the New Jersey State Prison had received no visits from the outside world.

It is not difficult to see this isolation as painfully depriving or frustrating in terms of lost emotional relationships, of loneliness and boredom. But what makes this pain of imprisonment bite most deeply is the fact that the confinement of the criminal represents a deliberate, moral rejection of the criminal by the free community. Indeed, as Reckless has pointed out, it is the moral condemnation of the criminal—however it may be symbolized—that converts hurt into punishment, i.e., the just consequence of committing an offense, and it is this condemnation that confronts the inmate by the fact of his seclusion.

Now it is sometimes claimed that many criminals are so alienated from conforming society and so identified with a criminal subculture that the moral condemnation, rejection, or disapproval of legitimate society does not touch them; they are, it is said, indifferent to the penal sanctions of the free community, at least as far as the moral stigma of being defined as a criminal is concerned. For the great majority of criminals in prison, however, the evidence suggests that neither, alienation from the ranks of the law-abiding nor involvement in a system of criminal value is sufficient to eliminate the threat to the prisoner's ego posed by society's rejection. The signs pointing to the prisoner's degradation are many—the anonymity of a uniform and a number rather than a name, the shaven head, the insistence on gestures of respect and subordination when addressing officials, and so on. The prisoner is never allowed to forget that, by committing a crime, he has foregone his claim to the status of a full-fledged, basted member of society. The status lost by the prisoner is, in fact, similar to what Marshall has called the status of citizenship—that basic acceptance of the individual as a functioning member of the society in which he lives. It is true that in the past the imprisoned criminal literally suffered civil death and that although the doctrines of attainder and corruption of blood were largely abandoned in the 18th and 19th centuries, the inmate is still stripped of many of his civil rights such as the right to vote, to hold office, to sue in court, and so on. But as important as the loss of these civil rights may be, the loss of that more diffuse status which defines the individual as someone to be trusted or as morally acceptable is the loss which hurts most.

In short, the wall which seals off the criminal, the contaminated man, is a constant threat to the prisoner's self-conception and the threat is continually repeated in the many daily reminders that he must be kept apart from "decent" men. Somehow this rejection or degradation by the free community must be warded off, turned aside, rendered harmless. Somehow the imprisoned criminal must find a device for rejecting his rejectors, if he is to endure psychologically.

The Deprivation of Goods and Services

There are admittedly many problems in attempting to compare the standard of living existing in the free community and the standard of living which is supposed to be the lot of the inmate in prison. How, for example, do we interpret the fact that a covering for the floor of a cell usually consists of a scrap from a discarded blanket and that even this possession is forbidden by the prison authorities? What meaning do we attach to the fact that no inmate owns a common piece of furniture, such as a chair, but only a homemade stool? What is the value of a suit of clothing which is also a convict's uniform with a stripe and a stencilled number? The answers are far from simple although there are a number of prison officials who will argue that some inmates are better off in prison, in strictly material terms, than they could ever hope to be in the rough-and-tumble economic life of the free community. Possibly this is so, but at least it has never been claimed by the inmates that the goods and services provided the prisoner are equal to or better than the goods and services which the prisoner could obtain if he were left to his own devices outside the walls. The average inmate finds himself in a harshly Spartan environment which he defines as painfully depriving.

Now it is true that the prisoner's basic material needs are met—in the sense that he does not go hungry, cold, or wet. He receives adequate medical care and he has the opportunity for exercise. But a standard of living constructed in terms of so many calories per day, so many hours of recreation, so many cubic yards of space per individual, and so on, misses the central point when we are discussing the individual's feeling of deprivation, however useful it may be in setting minimum levels of consumption for the maintenance of health. A standard of living can be hopelessly inadequate, from the individual's viewpoint, because it bores him to death or fails to provide those subtle symbolic overtones which we invest in the world of possessions. And this is the core of the prisoner's problem in the area of goods and services. He wants—or needs, if you will—not just the so-called necessities of life but also the amenities: cigarettes and liquor as well as calories, interesting foods as well as sheer bulk, individual clothing as well as adequate clothing, individual furnishings for his living quarters as well as shelter, privacy as well as space. The "rightfulness" of the prisoner's feeling of deprivation can be questioned. And the objective reality of the prisoner's deprivation—in the sense that he has actually suffered a fall from his economic position in the free community—can be viewed with skepticism, as we have indicated above. But these criticisms are irrelevant to the significant issue, namely that legitimately or illegitimately, rationally or irrationally, the inmate population defines its present material impoverishment as a painful loss.

Now in modern Western culture, material possessions are so large a part of the individual's conception of himself that to be stripped of them is to be attacked at the deepest layers of personality. This is particularly true when poverty cannot be excused as a blind stroke of fate or a universal calamity. Poverty due to one's own mistakes or misdeeds represents an indictment against one's basic value or personal worth and there are few men who can philosophically bear the want caused by their own actions. It is true some prisoners in the New Jersey State Prison attempt to interpret their low position in the scale of goods and services as an effort by the State to exploit them economically. Thus, in the eyes of some inmates, the prisoner is poor not because of an offense which he has committed in the past but because the State is a tyrant which uses its captive criminals as slave labor under the hypocritical guise of reformation. Penology, it is said, is a racket. Their poverty, then, is not punishment as we have used the word before, i.e., the just consequence of criminal behavior; rather, it is an unjust hurt or pain inflicted without legitimate cause. This attitude, however, does not appear to be particularly widespread in the inmate population and the great majority of prisoners must face their privation without the aid of the wronged man's sense of injustice. Furthermore, most prisoners are unable to fortify themselves in their low level of material existence by seeing it as a means to some high or worthy end. They are unable to attach any significant meaning to their need to make it more bearable, such as present pleasures foregone for pleasures in the future, self-sacrifice in the interests of the community, or material asceticism for the purpose of spiritual salvation.

The inmate, then, sees himself as having been made poor by reason of his own acts and without the rationale of compensating benefits. The failure is *his* failure in a world where control and possession of the material environment are commonly taken as sure indicators of a man's worth. It is true that our society, as materialistic as it may be, does not rely exclusively on goods and services as a criterion of an individual's value; and, as we shall see shortly, the inmate population defends itself by stressing alternative or supplementary measures of merit. But impoverishment remains as one of the most bitter attacks on the individual's self-image that our society has to offer and the prisoner cannot ignore the implications of his straitened circumstances. Whatever the discomforts and irritations of the prisoner's Spartan existence may be, he must carry the additional burden of social definitions which equate his material deprivation with personal inadequacy.

The Deprivation of Heterosexual Relationships

Unlike the prisoner in many Latin-American countries, the inmate of the maximum security prison in New Jersey does not enjoy the privilege of so-called conjugal visits. And in those brief times when the prisoner is al-lowed to see his wife, mistress, or "female friend," the woman must sit on one side of a plate glass window and the prisoner on the other, communicating by means of a phone under the scrutiny of a guard. If the inmate, then, is rejected and impoverished by the facts of his imprisonment, he is also figuratively castrated by his involuntary celibacy.

Now a number of writers have suggested that men in prison undergo a reduction of the sexual drive and that the sexual frustrations of prisoners are therefore less than they might appear to be at first glance. The reports of reduced sexual interest have, however, been largely confined to accounts of men imprisoned in concentration camps or similar extreme situations where starvation, torture, and physical exhaustion have reduced life to a simple struggle for survival or left the captive sunk in apathy. But in the American prison these factors are not at work to any significant extent and Linder has noted that the prisoner's access to mass media, pornography circulated among inmates, and similar stimuli serve to keep alive the prisoner's sexual impulses. The same thought is expressed more crudely by the inmates of the New Jersey State Prison in a variety of obscene expressions and it is clear that the lack of heterosexual intercourse is a frustrating experience for the imprisoned criminal and that it is a frustration which weighs heavily and painfully on his mind during his prolonged confinement. There are, or course, some "habitual" homosexuals in the prison—men who were homosexuals before their arrival and who continue their particular form of deviant behavior within the all-male society of the custodial institution. For these inmates, perhaps, the deprivation of heterosexual intercourse cannot be counted as one of the pains of imprisonment. They are few in number, however, and are only too apt to be victimized or raped by aggressive prisoners who have turned to homosexuality as a temporary means of relieving their frustration.

Yet as important as frustration in the sexual sphere may be in physiological terms, the psychological problems created by the lack of heterosexual relationships can be even more serious. A society composed exclusively of men tends to generate anxieties in its members concerning their masculinity regardless of whether or not they are coerced, bribed, or seduced into an overt homosexual liaison. Latent homosexual tendencies may be activated in the individual without being translated into open behavior and yet still arouse strong guilt feelings at either the conscious or unconscious level. In the tense atmosphere of the prison with its known perversions, its importunities of admitted homosexuals, and its constant references to the problems of sexual frustration by guards and inmates alike, there are few prisoners who can escape the fact that an essential component of a man's self-conception—his status of male—is called into question. And if an inmate has in fact engaged in homosexual behavior within the walls, not as a continuation of an habitual pattern but as a rare act of sexual deviance under the intolerable pressure of mounting physical desire, the psychological onslaughts on his ego image will be particularly acute.

In addition to these problems stemming from sexual frustration per se, the deprivation of heterosexual relationships carries with it another threat to the prisoner's image of himself—more diffuse, perhaps, and more difficult to state precisely and yet no less disturbing. The inmate is shut off from the world of women which by its very polarity gives the male world much of its meaning. Like most men, the inmate must search for his identity not simply within himself but also in the picture of himself which he finds reflected in the eyes of others; and since a significant half of his audience is denied him, the inmate's self-image is in danger of becoming half complete, fractured, a monochrome without the hues of reality. The prisoner's looking-glass self, in short—to use Cooley's fine phrase—is only that portion of the prisoner's personality which is recognized or appreciated by men and this partial identity is made hazy by the lack of contrast.

The Deprivation of Autonomy

We have noted before that the inmate suffers from what we have called a loss of autonomy in that he is subjected to a vast body of rules and commands which are designed to control his behavior in minute detail. To the casual observer, however, it might seem that the many areas of life in which self-determination is withheld, such as the language used in a letter, the hours of sleeping and eating, or the route to work, are relatively unimportant. Perhaps it might be argued, as in the case of material deprivation, that the inmate in prison is not much worse off than the individual in the free community who is regulated in a great many aspects of his life by the iron fist of custom. It could even be argued, as some writers have done, that for a number of imprisoned criminals the extensive control of the custodians provides a welcome escape from freedom and that the prison officials thus supply an external Super-Ego which serves to reduce the anxieties arising from an awareness of deviant impulses. But from the viewpoint of the inmate population, it is precisely the triviality of much of the officials' control which often proves to be most galling. Regulation by a bureaucratic staff is felt far differently than regulation by custom. And even though a few prisoners do welcome the strict regime of the custodians as a means of checking their own aberrant behavior which they would like to curb but cannot, most prisoners look on the matter in a different light. Most prisoners, in fact, express an intense hostility against their far-reaching dependence on the decisions of their captors and the restricted ability to make choices must be included among the pains of imprisonment along with restrictions of physical liberty, the possession of goods and services, and heterosexual relationships.

Now the loss of autonomy experienced by the inmates does not represent a grant of power freely given by the ruled to the rulers for a limited and specific end. Rather, it is total and it is imposed—and for these reasons it is less endurable. The nominal objectives of the custodians are not, in general, the objectives of the prisoners. Yet regardless of whether or not the inmate population shares some aims with the custodial bureaucracy, the many regulations and orders of the New Jersey State Prison's official regime often arouse the prisoner's hostility because they don't "make sense" from the prisoner's point of view. Indeed, the incomprehensible order or rule is a basic feature of life in prison. Inmates, for example, are forbidden to take food from the mess hall to their cells. Some prisoners see this as a move designed to promote cleanliness; others are convinced that the regulation is for the purpose of preventing inmates from obtaining anything that might be used in the *sub rosa* system of barter. Most, however, simply see the measure as another irritating, pointless gesture of authoritarianism. Similarly, prisoners are denied parole but are left in ignorance of the reasons for the decision. Prisoners are informed that the delivery of mail will be delayed—but they are not told why.

Now some of the inmate population's ignorance might be described as "accidental"; it arises from what we can call the principle of bureaucratic indifference, i.e., events which seem important or vital to those at the bottom of the heap are viewed with an increasing lack of concern with each step upward. The rules, the commands, the decisions which flow down to those who are controlled are not accompanied by explanations on the grounds that it is "impractical" or "too much trouble." Some of the inmate population's ignorance, however, is deliberately fostered by the prison officials in that explanations are often withheld as a matter of calculated policy. Providing explanations carries an implication that those who are ruled have a right to know—and this in turn suggests that if the explanations are not satisfactory, the rule or order will be changed. But this is in direct contradiction to the theoretical power relationship of the inmates and the prison officials. Imprisoned criminals are individuals who are being punished by

society and they must be brought to their knees. If the inmate population maintains the right to argue with its captors, it takes on the appearance of an enemy nation with its own sovereignty; and in so doing it raises disturbing questions about the nature of the offender's deviance. The criminal is no longer simply a man who has broken the law; he has become a part of a group with an alternative viewpoint and thus attacks the validity of the law itself. The custodians' refusal to give reasons for many aspects of their regime can be seen in part as an attempt to avoid such an intolerable situation.

The indignation aroused by the "bargaining inmate" or the necessity of justifying the custodial regime is particularly evident during a riot when prisoners have the "impudence" to present a list of demands. In discussing the disturbances at the New Jersey State Prison in the Spring of 1952, for example, a newspaper editorial angrily noted that "the storm, like a nightmarish April Fool's dream, has passed, leaving in its wake a partially wrecked State Prison as a debasing monument to the ignominious rage of desperate men."

The important point, however, is that the frustration of the prisoner's ability to make choices and the frequent refusals to provide an explanation for the regulations and commands descending from the bureaucratic staff involve a profound threat to the prisoner's self-image because they reduce the prisoner to the weak, helpless, dependent status of childhood. As Bettelheim has tellingly noted in his comments on the concentration camp, men under guard stand in constant danger of losing their identification with the normal definition of an adult and the imprisoned criminal finds his picture of himself as a self-determining individual being destroyed by the regime of the custodians. It is possible that this psychological attack is particularly painful in American culture because of the deep-lying insecurities produced by the delays, the conditionality and the uneven progress so often observed in the granting of adulthood. It is also possible that the criminal is frequently an individual who has experienced great difficulty in adjusting himself to figures of authority and who finds the many restraints of prison life particularly threatening insofar as earlier struggles over the establishment of self are reactivated in a more virulent form. But without asserting that Americans in general or criminals in particular are notably ill-equipped to deal with the problems posed by the deprivation of autonomy, the helpless or dependent status of the prisoner clearly represents a serious threat to the prisoner's self-image as a fully accredited member of adult society. And of the many threats which may confront the individual, either in or out of prison, there are few better calculated to arouse acute anxieties than the attempt to reimpose the subservience of youth. Public humiliation, enforced respect and deference, the finality of authoritarian decisions, the demands for a specified course of conduct because, in the judgment of another, it is in the individual's best interest—all are features of childhood's helplessness in the face of [a] superior adult world. Such things may be both irksome and disturbing for a child, especially if the child envisions himself as having outgrown such servitude. But for the adult who has escaped such helplessness with the passage of years, to be thrust back into childhood's helplessness is even more painful, and the inmate of the prison must somehow find a means of coping with the issue.

The Deprivation of Security

However strange it may appear that society has chosen to reduce the criminality of the offender by forcing him to associate with more than a thousand other criminals for years on end, there is one meaning of this involuntary union which is obvious—the individual prisoner is thrown into prolonged intimacy with other men who in many cases have a long history of violent, aggressive behavior. It is a situation which can prove to be anxiety-provoking even for the hardened recidivist and it is in this light that we can understand the comment of an inmate of the New Jersey State Prison who said, "The worst thing about prison is you have to live with other prisoners."

The fact that the imprisoned criminal sometimes views his fellow prisoners as "vicious" or "dangerous" may seem a trifle unreasonable. Other inmates, after all, are men like himself, bearing the legal stigma of conviction. But even if the individual prisoner believes that he himself is not the sort of person who is likely to attack or exploit weaker and less resourceful fellow captives, he is apt to view others with more suspicion. And if he himself is prepared to commit crimes while in prison, he is likely to feel that many others will be at least equally ready. . . . [R]egardless of the patterns of mutual aid and support which may flourish in the inmate population, there are a sufficient number of outlaws within this group of outlaws to deprive the average prisoner of that sense of security which comes from living among men who can be reasonably expected to abide by the rules of society. While it is true that every prisoner does not live in the constant fear of being robbed or beaten, the constant companionship of thieves, rapists, murderers, and aggressive homosexuals is far from reassuring.

An important aspect of this disturbingly problematical world is the fact that the inmate is acutely aware that sooner or later he will be "tested"—that someone will "push" him to see how far they can go and that he must be prepared to fight for the safety of his person and his possessions. If he should fail, he will thereafter be an object of contempt, constantly in danger of being attacked by other inmates who view him as an obvious victim, as a man who cannot or will not defend his rights. And yet if he succeeds, he may well become a target for the prisoner who wishes to prove himself, who seeks to enhance his own prestige by defeating the man with a reputation for toughness. Thus both success and failure in defending one's self against the aggressions of fellow captives may serve to provoke fresh attacks and no man stands assured of the future.

The prisoner's loss of security arouses acute anxiety, in short, not just because violent acts of aggression and exploitation occur but also because such behavior constantly calls into question the individual's ability to cope with it, in terms of his own inner resources, his courage, his "nerve." Can he stand up and take it? Will he prove to be tough enough? These uncertainties constitute an ego threat for the individual forced to live in prolonged intimacy with criminals, regardless of the nature or extent of his own criminality; and we can catch a glimpse of this tense and fearful existence in the comment of one prisoner who said, "It takes a pretty good man to be able to stand on an equal plane with a guy that's in for rape, with a guy that's in for murder, with a man who's well-respected in the institution because he's a real tough cookie. . . . " His expectations concerning the conforming behavior of others destroyed, unable and unwilling to rely on the officials for protection, uncertain of whether or not today's joke will be tomorrow's bitter insult, the prison inmate can never feel safe. And at a deeper level lies the anxiety about his reactions to this unstable world, for then his manhood will be evaluated in the public view.

Imprisonment, then, is painful. The pains of imprisonment, however, cannot be viewed as being limited to the loss of physical liberty. The significant hurts lie in the frustrations or deprivations which attend the withdrawal of freedom, such as the lack of heterosexual relationships, isolation from the free community, the withholding of goods and services, and so on. And however painful these frustrations or deprivations may be in the immediate terms of thwarted goals, discomfort, boredom, and loneliness, they carry a more profound hurt as a set of threats or attacks which are directed against the very foundations of the prisoner's being. The individual's picture of himself as a person of value—as a morally acceptable, adult male who can present some claim to merit in

his material achievements and his inner strength—begins to waver and grow dim. Society did not plan this onslaught, it is true, and society may even "point with pride" to its humanity in the modern treatment of the criminal. But the pains of imprisonment remain and it is imperative that we recognize them, for they provide the energy for the society of captives as a system of action. . . .

Unable to escape either physically or psychologically, lacking the cohesion to carry through an insurrection that is bound to fail in any case, and bereft of faith in peaceful innovation, the inmate population might seem to have no recourse but the simple endurance of the pains of imprisonment. The frustrations and deprivations of confinement, with their attendant attacks on the prisoner's self-image, would strike the prisoner with full force and the time spent in prison would have to be marked down as time spent in purgatory. And to a large extent this is what does happen in reality. There are no exits for the inmate in the sense of a device or series of devices which can completely eliminate the pains of imprisonment. But if the rigors of confinement cannot be completely removed, they can at least be mitigated by the patterns of social interaction established among the inmates themselves. In this apparently simple fact lies the key to our understanding of the prisoner's world.

Frustrated not as an individual but as one of many, the inmate finds two paths open. On the one hand, he can attempt to bind himself to his fellow captives with ties of mutual aid, loyalty, affection, and respect, firmly standing in opposition to the officials. On the other hand, he can enter into a war of all against all in which he seeks his own advantage without reference to the claims or needs of other prisoners. In the former case, the rigors of the environment are met with group cohesion or inmate solidarity. Toleration replaces "touchiness," fellow prisoners are persons to be helped rather than exploited, and group allegiance emerges as a dominant value. The inmate's orientation is "collectivistic." In the latter case, the rigors of the environment elicit an alienated response. Abhorrence or indifference feed the frictions of prison life. Fellow prisoners are persons to be exploited by every expedient that comes to hand; the officials are simply another hazard in the pursuit of the inmate's goals and he stands ready to betray his fellow captives if it advances his interests. The inmate's orientation can be termed "individualistic."

In actuality, the patterns of social interaction among inmates are to be found scattered between these two theoretical extremes. The population of prisoners does not exhibit a perfect solidarity yet neither is the population of prisoners a warring aggregate. Rather, it is a mixture of both and the society of captives lies balanced in an uneasy compromise. . . .

Argot Roles

As group experiences come to differ more and more from those of the larger community of which the group is a part—as new patterns of behavior arise demanding evaluation and interpretation—the language of the group begins to change. Behavior which is not distinguished by the larger community takes on a different importance and receives a special label. New words are invented or old words are applied in a new and often more restricted way; the skein of reality is being cut in an unfamiliar fashion. In short, different experiences mean a different language and the result—in the prison, at least—is argot. The society of captives exhibits a number of distinctive tags for the distinctive social roles played by its members in response to the particular problems of imprisonment. It is these patterns of behavior, recognized and labelled by the inmates of the New Jersey State Prison, which we have chosen to call argot roles and which now occupy our attention.

Rats and Center Men

The flow of information in any social group is always imperfect, if we define perfect communication as the transmission of all information to all group members with equal speed and without error. Of particular interest, however, is the imperfection which arises from two or more "circuits" in the network of communication. Certain types of information are prohibited from flowing across social boundaries erected within the group and deception, hypocrisy, spying, and betrayal emerge as crucial social events.

The most obvious social boundary in the custodial institution is, of course, that which exists between captors and captives; and inmates argue fiercely that a prisoner should never give any information to the custodians which will act to the detriment of a fellow captive. Since the most trivial piece of information may, all unwittingly, lead to another inmate's downfall, the ban on communication is extended to cover all but the most routine matters. The bureaucracy of custodians and the population of prisoners are supposed to struggle in silence.

The word *rat* or *squealer* is a familiar label for the man who betrays his fellows by violating the ban on communication and it is used in this sense in the prison. But in the prison the word *rat* or *squealer* carries an emotional significance far greater than that usually encountered in the free community. The name is never applied lightly as a joking insult—as is often the case with the numerous obscene expressions which lard the conversation of prisoners. Instead, it represents the most serious accusation that one inmate can level against another, for it implies a betrayal that transcends the specific act of disclosure. The *rat* is a man who has betrayed not just one inmate or several; he has betrayed inmates in general by denying the cohesion of prisoners as a dominant value when confronting the world of officialdom.

Most of the *ratting* that occurs in the prison is done for the sake of personal gain, but we can distinguish two different forms.

First, there are those *rats* who reveal their own identity to the officials, who hope to win preferential treatment from their rulers in exchange for information.

Second, there are those *rats* who prefer to remain anonymous, not because their betrayal is an unselfish act committed for the good of the custodians, but because they wish to get rid of a competitor or to settle a grudge. Thus the officials may find themselves being manipulated by their prisoners into a position where they are serving unintentionally as a weapon in the battles taking place among the inmates. There is always the danger that they will be gulled in the process, for the anonymous rat does not need to fear official retaliation if he supplies false information. The rat, in short, may be a liar as well as a betrayer and he threatens the innocent as well as the guilty.

Now to view the *rat* or the *squealer* as a man playing a social role is to view betrayal not as an isolated piece of behavior but as a part of a larger system of action, i.e., the patterns of interaction among guards and inmates. We have suggested that an important aspect of this system is the social boundary separating captors and captives into two "circuits" of communication and that the prisoner who transmits information across the boundary is usually pursuing his own interests at the expense of his fellow prisoners. There is another way of crossing the boundary, however, of being disloyal to the inmate world, which does not involve the disclosure of secrets, which is only partially a matter of personal aggrandizement, and yet which arouses great contempt. An inmate can take on the opinions, attitudes, and beliefs of the custodians. In the New Jersey State Prison, such an inmate is labelled a center man, apparently in reference to the center which serves as the officials' seat of government.

The phenomenon of men identifying themselves with their oppressors—of publicly proclaiming the virtues of the rulers, expressing their values, or, still worse in the eyes of the inmates, obeying them too gladly—may represent a deliberate, Machiavellian attempt to flatter those who have power in order to gain favors. The inmates of the New Jersey State Prison believe, however, that the *center man* is frequently an individual who sides with the officials not because he thinks he can hoodwink his captors but because he actually shares their viewpoint. As one prisoner has said, "The *center man* is a man who's always willing to get along with the institutional officials. He'll bend over backwards to do it. He'll go out of his way. I have one word that seems to fit all of them—servile. They're always bowing and scraping...." It is difficult, of course, to distinguish manipulative fawning from the deference of sincere conviction and the problem is made still more difficult in the prison by the fact that the society of captives is so polarized that anything but unwavering contempt for the guards is defined by the inmates as a sign of abject weakness. But the inmates would seem to be right in believing that disloyalty need not spring from a conscious, deliberate plan to advance one's interests. If the *rat* is a man who pretends to be on the side of the inmates and yet betrays them, the *center man* is a man who makes no secret of where his sympathies lie. His disloyalty is open. And if the *rat* is hated for his deception and his hypocrisy, the *center man* is despised for his slavish submission. But whether a man attempts to escape the rigors of imprisonment by exchanging information for preferential treatment, or, more subtly, by identifying himself with his rulers, he has destroyed the unity of inmates as they face their rejectors. The population of prisoners—the one group to which the inmate can turn for prestige, for approval, for acceptance—has been weakened by his behavior and it is in this light that we must understand his condemnation.

Gorillas and Merchants

The monastic life of the imprisoned criminal is partially relieved by gifts from friends and relatives in the outside world and purchases from the Inmate Store. These legitimate channels for securing extra goods are, however, severely restricted by the custodians' regulations and the prisoners' lack of resources. The inmate, for example, is permitted to spend only $25 per month at the Inmate Store, as we have noted earlier, but even this limit is beyond the reach of most prisoners—the actual expenditure is, on the average, less than $7 per month. The illegitimate channel for securing extra goods, that is, the looting of institutional supplies, is helpful, but it too has obvious defects. The society of captives cannot appreciably improve its material level of existence by wringing additional supplies from its environment, either rightfully or wrongfully.

But if the society of captives cannot improve its lot as a whole, it is possible for an individual prisoner to monopolize the scarce goods possessed by the society, to wrest from his fellow captives their few possessions, and thus soften the hurt of his material deprivation. In the argot of the inmates, an individual who takes what he wants from others by force is known as a *gorilla*. His is a satrapy based on violence and he preys on weaker or more fearful inmates in the cellblock, the industrial shops, or the recreation yard.

Now in many cases the actual use of force is unnecessary for the *gorilla*, for the mere threat of it in the background is sufficient to gain his ends. Unlike the custodians—who are barred from acts of brutality, attuned to the dangers of disorder, and in search of complex patterns of compliance—the man who plays the role of *gorilla* finds coercion or the threat of coercion a potent weapon. He stands ready to use a knife or a piece of pipe, he faces a lone victim, and his demands are simple. And it is this blatant readiness for the instrumental use of violence that often sets the *gorilla* off from other inmates rather than his strength, size or constant use of force. The threatened prisoner has the choice of submitting or fighting and like many others before him he may find discretion the better part of valor. Cigarettes, food, clothing, gestures of deference—all may flow to the man with a reputation for coercive exploitation

once he has established his position in the pecking order which organizes much of the interaction among prisoners.

The prevalence of violence as a means of exploitation is far from new in the New Jersey State Prison—the first investigation of the institution in 1830 indignantly noted the existence of a "Stauch-Gang," a clique of rebellious inmates which intimidated fellow prisoners, cowed the guards, and busily devised numerous plans for escape. At the present time, however, cliques of *gorillas*, in the sense of well-organized and closely knit gangs of men who exploit other inmates by force, have largely disappeared. The *gorilla* of today tends to remain relatively isolated from the bonds of friendship, either because of preference or because he is rejected by other inmates; and if he attempts to form an alliance with other *gorillas*, not on the diffuse basis of friendship but on a narrow calculation of mutual advantage, the current custodial bureaucracy has learned how to cope with his efforts by means of solitary confinement and transfers to other institutions. Yet if there are few cliques at the present time—and these few are but loosely held together and small in size, consisting, perhaps, of a dominant figure and several sycophants—an association of coercive exploiters still poses a fearful threat for the general inmate population: As one prisoner has said, "If you decide to fight one of them you have to fight them all." It is, incidentally, the prevalence of *gorillas* in the prison which partially accounts for the weapons so frequently discovered in the officials' routine searches and surprise raids—the sliver of tin, the razor blade strapped to a toothbrush, the nail inserted in the melted end of a plastic fountain pen. These, as often as not, are seen by the inmates as their last means of defense in a world where the assaults of fellow prisoners are a greater danger than the barbarities of the captors.

The inmate who uses force, then, to gain the amenities of life may find himself in a hazardous position if he drives his victim too far or picks the wrong man to victimize, as a number of would-be *gorillas* have discovered to their sorrow. And, indeed, there is a widespread belief in the inmate population that most *gorillas* are cowards and that tactics of coercion are successful only because the man who lets himself be coerced is somewhat more cowardly than the man who coerces him. In the harsh logic of the prison, the inmate who submits is a *weakling*. "You put a little pressure on a *weakling*," a prisoner has explained, "and he can't take it. You push him into a corner and put a knife against him and he begins to squeal." Be that as it may, there are a number of prisoners who avoid violence as a means of exploitation and turn to manipulating other inmates instead.

A portion of manipulative exploitation in the prison consists of outright fraud and chicanery, such as a simple failure to carry out a bargain in the exchange of goods and services, cheating on gambling debts, and so on. And on occasion fraud can be a more elaborate affair, as when one inmate, working in the center as a sweeper and gaining access to the plans of the officials, was able to cozen his fellow prisoners into believing that he had great influence with the custodians. But as a manipulative mode of adjustment to the rigors of imprisonment, these swindles are overshadowed by the act of selling itself. Confronted by the facts of their material deprivation, the inmates have drawn a sharp line between selling and giving and the prisoner who sells when he should give is labelled a *merchant* or *pedlar*.

Now it is true, of course, that a balanced reciprocity of gifts functions much like a system of barter and that in the prison, as elsewhere, openhanded generosity is apt to be strained by the "free loader," the man who neglects the principle of equivalence, thus underlining the barter aspect of "giving." Yet as Hoebel has pointed out, the exchange of gifts is something more than a disguised version of utilitarian economics. Giving, as opposed to selling for profit, expresses the solidarity of the group and may, indeed, strengthen the social bonds among group

members as contractual barter never can. It is in this light that the inmate population views the *merchant* or *peddlar*, for he is defined as a man so alienated from other prisoners, so selfish in his pursuit of material advantage, that he is willing to thrive on the misery of his companions. In short, he places his own well-being above the well-being of the inmates as a whole. He does not share the goods in short supply but exploits, instead, the need of others.

There are, to be sure, limits placed on the demands for generosity in the inmate population. *Rats, center men, weaklings,* and other figures held in hatred or contempt lie outside the pale and close friends possess a stronger claim than the newly arrived prisoner—the *fish*—or the relative stranger from another cellblock. And the inmates tend to distinguish between gifts from the free community and goods purchased from the inmate store, on the one hand, and material stolen from the institution's supplies, on the other. The former are, in a sense, the prisoner's private possessions and if the prisoner chooses to sell them it is perhaps "understandable" or "excusable" although the practice is not admired. But to sell material that has been filched from the officials is beyond the bounds of condoning, for, in the words of an inmate, "The man stealing stuff from the institution is stealing from me. He shouldn't try and sell it to me." This is quite literally true in the case of food stolen from the supplies for the inmates' mess hall and is true to some extent in other areas as well; and thus there is some tendency for two classes of goods to exist in the prison. In general, however, the generosity of giving or sharing the amenities of life so treasured by the captive population—the cigarettes, the candy, the extra food or clothing, the material to decorate a cell, or the homemade liquor manufactured from fruit juice and rye bread—is normatively demanded by the inmate code, regardless of the source of the goods or the closeness of the bond with the prisoner in want; and the following description of one inmate, given by another, was expressed in the accents of deepest praise:

> My cell partner—he can't say no. He'll have a can of milk. And he knows he ain't going to get no more milk until the next store order. And a complete stranger will come along and say "I ain't got no milk" and he'll give it to him. Or cigarettes. The same way. And a couple of weeks later, the guy will come back and he'll *still* give him cigarettes. He's the kind of guy who'd give you the shirt off his back, if you know what I mean.

The *merchant* or *peddlar*, then, violates this ideal of liberality and is despised as a consequence—not simply because he often drives a hard bargain but also because his impersonal dealings are a denial of the unity of imprisoned criminals. He, like the *gorilla*, treats his fellow captives as objects rather than as persons; and if his tactics of exploitation involve manipulation rather than coercion, his behavior is no less destructive of the solidarity of the rejected.

Wolves, Punks, and Fags

The inmates of the New Jersey State Prison recognize and label a variety of homosexual acts, such as sodomy, fellatio, transvestism, frottage, and so on, although the labels of the inmates are not those of the medical profession or modern psychiatry. And the inmates, too, attempt to distinguish the "true" sexual pervert and the prisoner driven to homosexuality by his temporary deprivation. In the world of the prison, however, the extent to which homosexual behavior involves "masculinity" and "femininity" would appear to override all other considerations and it is this which provides the main basis for the classification of sexual perversion by the inmate population. Homosexuals are divided into those who play an active, aggressive role, i.e., a "masculine" role by the stern standards of the prisoners, and those who play a more passive and submissive part. The former are termed *wolves;* the latter are referred to as *punks* and *fags*.

Now it is true that the society of captives does draw a line between *punks* and *fags*. "*Punks*," it is said, "are made, but *fags* are born." And in this curt aphorism the inmates are pointing to a difference between those who engage in homosexuality because they are coerced into doing so or because male prostitution is a means of winning goods and services in short supply and those who engage in homosexuality because it is preferred. But this division of passive homosexual roles on the basis of motive or genesis is accompanied by—and overshadowed by—the idea that *punks* and *fags* differ in the kind of femininity involved in their sexual aberration. The *fag*—the man who engages in homosexuality because "he likes it" or because "he wants to," according to the prisoners—is a man with a womanly walk and too-graceful gestures; he may, on occasion, dye his underclothing, curl his hair, or color his lips with homemade lipstick. As one inmate, much given to thoughtful analysis, has explained,

> The *fag* is recognizable by his exaggerated, feminine mannerisms. The fag—they call him a queen on the West Coast—employs the many guiles for which females are noted, like playing 'stay away closer' or 'hard to get but getable.'

The *fag*, in short, fills the stereotype of the homosexual as it is commonly held in the free community. He has forfeited his claim to masculinity not only by his reversal of the sexual role per se but also by taking on the outward guise of women.

The *punk*, on the other hand, submits to the importunities of the more active, aggressive homosexuals without displaying the outward signs of femininity in other aspects of his behavior. His forfeiture of masculinity is limited to the homosexual act. But even though the *punk* does not exhibit those mannerisms characterized as feminine by the inmate population, he has turned himself into a woman, in the eyes of the prisoners, by the very act of his submission. His is an inner softness or weakness; and, from the viewpoint of the prisoners, his sacrifice of manhood is perhaps more contemptible than that of the *fag* because he acts from fear or for the sake of quick advantage rather than personal inclination. In the words of the inmate quoted above,

> A *punk* can't fend off the pressure of older, tougher men who may have bullied him, grilled him, put the arm on him in some other institution. He's basically morally weak to begin with, but because he has no source of finances the older, tougher cons ply him with cigarettes, candy, extra food supplies, and maybe even hooch. The weaker ones usually make a deliberate trade, but in some cases the kid may be told that he's not getting it for nothing. He's told he's got to pay up and since he hasn't got the money he's given an alternative—he'll get beaten up or he'll have to submit to an unnatural act. *Punks* are cowards.

The society of captives, then, distinguishes between *punks* and *fags* partly on the basis of differences in the causes or origins of their passive homosexuality. But, more importantly, both *punks* and *fags* fail to be men—the former because they lack an inner core of "toughness" and the latter because they assume the overt, obvious symbols of womanhood. Both are set off from the more active, aggressive, "masculine" *wolf*.

The stress on the "masculinity" of the *wolf's* role is reinforced by the fact that many inmates believe his part in a homosexual relationship to be little more than a search for a casual, mechanical act of physical release. Unmoved by love, indifferent to the emotions of the partner he has coerced bribed, or seduced into a liaison, the *wolf* is often viewed as simply masturbating with another person. By thus stripping the *wolf* of any aura of "softness," of sentiment or affection, his homosexuality loses much of the taint of effeminacy which homosexuality often carries in the free community. His perversion is a form of rape and his victim happens to be a man rather than a woman, due to the force of circumstances.

It would appear, therefore, that the inmates of the New Jersey State Prison have changed the criteria by which an individual establishes his claim to the status of male. Shut off from the world of women, the population of prisoners finds itself unable to employ that criterion of maleness which looms so importantly in society at large—namely, the act of heterosexual intercourse itself. Proof of maleness, both for the self and for others, has been shifted to other grounds and the display of "toughness," in the form of masculine mannerisms and the demonstration of inward stamina, now becomes the major route to manhood. These are used by the society at large, it is true; but the prison, unlike the society at large, must rely on them exclusively. In short, there are primary and secondary sexual characteristics in terms of social behavior just as there are primary and secondary sexual characteristics in terms of biological attributes; and the inmates have been forced to fall back on the secondary proof of manhood in the area of personal relations, i.e. "toughness," since the primary proof, in the form of heterosexual intercourse, is denied them. And the reliance on the secondary proof of manhood is so great that the active, aggressive homosexual—the wolf—almost manages to escape the stigma of his perversion.

By the standards of the free community, the prisoners' definition of masculine behavior may seem excessive with its emphasis on callousness, its flinty indifference to the more tender aspects of human relationships. It is perhaps understandable, however, in light of the fact that the definition of masculine behavior in a society composed exclusively of men is apt to move to an extreme position. But more important for our present analysis is the fact that by changing the criteria of maleness, the prisoners have erected a defense against the threat posed by their involuntary celibacy. The path to manhood has been reopened. However difficult to achieve or however harsh its mode of expression, "toughness"—and thus manhood—is at least possible. The anxieties generated by isolation from women and homo-sexuality lose something of their sting, since the individual's conception of himself as a male no longer depends so completely on his sexual activity. The *fag* and the *punk* must, of course, still bear the burden of the "softness" and the *wolf*—no matter how "tough" he may be—cannot entirely avoid the attitudes commonly elicited by his perversion. But for homosexuals and non-homosexuals alike, the emphasis placed by the society of cap-tives on the accompaniments of sexuality rather than sexuality itself does much to transform the problem of being a man in a world without women.

Ball Busters and Real Men

A group of oppressed men may revolt even if their revolt is almost certain to fail, as we have pointed out before, and the same thing may be said of an individual. Fully aware that the custodians hold the upper hand in the last analysis, knowing that solitary con-finement awaits the inmate who angers the guards beyond the point of endurance, there are some prisoners who nonetheless flare into open defiance. Such men are labelled *ball busters* in the argot of the captives, for as one inmate has said, "That kind of a con is al-ways giving the screws a hard time." Blatant disobedience, physical and verbal assaults on the officials, the constant creation of dis-turbances—these are the patterns of behav-ior of the typical *ball buster* and the following inmate's account is a fair illustration:

> I was sitting in that window yesterday and the officer come over to me, he talked to me like a dog. I said, "Look, I've got a stripe on my britches and a number on my back, but don't forget this. I'm a man." I said, "To you, to you, and to you, and to the warden out there in the Front House and to everyone else in this institution or in this world, I'm a man." I said, "I want to be treated as such and not anything else." He talked to me like a dog. He said, "Get out of that God damned window." I told him, "I have permission to sit here. The warden has said it's alright to

> sit here. I shall continue to sit here. I have been sitting here for seven years and if I'm here seven more years, I'll still be sitting here. I was here before you came and I'll most likely be here when you go. I've got to live here, I've got to put up with it, but I don't have to put up with you."

. . . Such men . . . have, in effect, refused to come to terms with their helplessness, their loss of autonomy, and they continue to shout their defiance despite the ultimate hopeless-ness of their position. And it might seem that such men would win the admiration and ap-proval of their fellow prisoners, since they voice the imprisoned criminal's hostility against officialdom. Weak, dependent, and chafed by a thousand restrictive regulations, the inmate population might be expected to see the figure of the ball buster as a welcome symbol of courageous opposition. In fact, however, this is only partially true, for the *ball buster* is often regarded as a fool. He dis-turbs that delicate system of compromise and corruption which the prisoners have es-tablished with their guards—in the words of the inmates, "He keeps things all shook up." Stricter surveillance, further restrictions, and the alienation of the guardians all flow from his useless, individualistic insurrec-tion. He has sacrificed the well-being of the inmate population as a whole for the sake of a childish, emotional outburst and his fellow inmates view him with contempt. If the *ball buster* has good grounds for his rebellion—if he has been goaded beyond endurance by the standards of the prison world—he may avoid the disparagement of other inmates, particularly if he acts with a cool calculation of the personal consequences rather than with frenzied anger. In general, however, the man who fights back is a man who is viewed as a troublemaker, not only by the guards but by the inmates as well. "A guy who goes out of his way to antagonize an officer," as one prisoner tersely said, "gets all the inmates into a jam. And besides, he's an idiot. He's the sort of person who'll come up and ask you for a stamp when you're washing your hands."

In the prison, then, the open mutiny of a single inmate against the power of the custodians is frequently defined not as an act of heroism but as a thoughtless loss of self-control which calls down the wrath of the rulers. As a result, the role of *ball buster* in the inmate social system is apt to carry little prestige. Instead, the man who can "take it," who can endure the regime of the custodians without flinching, is the man who wins the admiration and respect of his fellow captives.

The ideal of fortitude is, at first glance, the counsel of despair, for it bids us [to] endure that which cannot be avoided. In the prison, however, emphasis is placed not on simple acceptance but on dignity and composure under stress and these are at least partially subject to the individual's control. The rigors of the inmate's world are to be met with a certain self-containment and the excessive display of emotion is to be avoided at all costs. The prisoner should speak slowly and deliberately and he should move in the same fashion. Curiosity, anxiety, surprise—all are to be carefully curbed. Even too great a show of humor must be checked since there is the danger of being thought a clown or a buffoon. The prisoner, in short, is urged to "play it cool," to control all affect in a hard, silent stoicism which finds its apotheosis in the legendary figure of the cowboy or the gangster.

Now it is clear that this concept of fortitude has its roots in a vision of manhood and integrity which far transcends the prison. Self-restraint, reserve, taciturnity, and emotional balance have long been the virtues of the hero in a variety of cultural traditions and they are virtues which feed on adversity. The prisoner who can "take it" plays a part in a drama far older than the custodial institution for the convicted criminal and the value placed on endurance does not simply depend on the conditions of confinement. And it is also clear that the inmate population's view of fortitude as an ideal involves a kind of "toughness" which is linked to the masculine mannerisms and inward stamina so impor-

tant in the area of sexual activities. The important point, however, is that the society of captives has institutionalized the virtue of dignity—the ability to "take it," to maintain the self—in a series of norms and reinforced these norms with a variety of informal social controls. Deprived of their autonomy by the extensive rules of the custodians' regime, the inmates of the New Jersey State Prison have shifted the measure of the individual's worth from rebellion to adjustment. Thus it is not the futile and disturbing defiance of the *ball buster* that is accorded approbation; rather, it is the mute strength to maintain some degree of personal integration.

There is no single, fixed term for the inmate who endures the rigors of imprisonment with dignity, but the label of *real man* is applied, I think, as frequently as any other. The *real man* is a prisoner who "pulls his own time" in the phrasing of the inmate population and he confronts his captors with neither subservience nor aggression. Somewhat aloof, seldom complaining, he embodies the inmates' version of decorum. And if the *real man's* efforts to maintain his integrity in the face of privation have an important psychological utility—for the *real man* regains his autonomy, in a sense, by denying the custodians' power to strip him of his ability to control himself—it is also true that his role is of vital functional significance for the social system of imprisoned criminals. In the emphasis on endurance with dignity, the inmates have robbed the rebel of their support; it is the man who can stop himself from striking back at the custodians that wins their admiration and thus their image of the hero functions wittingly or unwittingly to maintain the *status quo*.

Toughs and Hipsters

It is clear that violence runs like a bright thread through the fabric of life in the New Jersey State Prison and no inmate can afford to ignore its presence. We have spoken of the calculated use of violence in the role of the *gorilla* and the *wolf;* in these we have the employment of violence or the threat of violence for the sake of winning material benefits or sexual favors. And we have spoken of the emotional violence of the *ball buster* who plunges into revolt against the guards. There remains, however, another form of violence which is no less disruptive for the society of captives, namely the violence of the inmate who is quick to quarrel with his fellow prisoners. His assaults flow from the fact that he feels he has been insulted rather than a desire to exploit others and his violence is directed against his companions in misery rather than against the custodians. The inmate population carefully notes the nature of his outbursts and labels him a *tough*. Frequently fighting with a certain cold ferocity and swift to seek revenge for the slightest affront, the *tough* is regarded by other inmates with a curious mixture of fear and respect.

The reason for fearing the *tough* is plain enough. He is marked by a "touchiness" which makes every encounter with him hazardous and he poses a constant danger for the society of captives jammed together in an involuntary community of stone and steel. But on what grounds can he be accorded prestige? It seems paradoxical that the *tough*—the man who explodes into violence directed against fellow prisoners—should be respected, while the *ball buster*—the man who directs his aggression against the officials—is apt to be regarded with contempt. Both the *tough* and the *ball buster* are disruptive forces in the life of the prison and both would appear to lack the self-control which forms such an important basis for the prestige of the *real man*. A part of the answer lies in the fact that some of the respect paid to the *tough* represents the deference of terror, for the *tough*, unlike the *ball buster*, confronts other inmates with the direct and immediate threat of a physical assault. He is a person to be placated and manipulated with homage. Even more importantly, however, the *tough* exhibits the active, aggressive "masculinity" so valued by inmates and he is defined as possessing a raw courage which compensates for his instability. In fact, the prisoners see the *tough's* violence not so much as a matter of wild anger but as cold retaliation and he is slightly more ready to detect a slight than most. The *tough* is not a bully, for he will fight with anyone, the strong as well as the weak. "He won't take anything from anybody," say the prisoners and if the *tough* threatens the personal security of other inmates he also stands prepared to forfeit his own. Thus his vices are his virtues and the inmate population cannot fail to view him with some ambivalence. He is a *real man* turned sour, in a sense, and he has transformed his inward strength from the ability to take it to the ability to hand it out.

The role of the *tough* is obviously based on some rather finely drawn distinctions, particularly in the area of physical courage. For the inmates of the New Jersey State Prison, however, violence is a familiar companion rather than a rare breach in social relationships and they are keenly aware of its different meanings. The prisoners draw a firm line between violence which stems from "real" courage and violence which is part of a pattern of braggadocio. The inmate who pretends to be "tougher than he really is," who "shoots off his mouth" and chooses the victim of his aggression with caution, is singled out and labelled a *hipster*.

This pretence of the *hipster* that identifies him in the eyes of the prisoners—this tendency to erect a false front—is seen as reaching far beyond a simulated bravery. "He wants to be a part of a group that he doesn't belong to," one prisoner has said in describing the man who plays the role of a *hipster*.

> He's always trying to belong to that group and emulating them. He'll hear some fellows saying, 'Hey, did you read so and so? Yeh, that was good wasn't it?' He'll try and get that book so he can tell them, 'Yeh, I read it. It was a good book, wasn't it?' He wants to be like them. He wants to read the things they read, so he can discuss the things they discuss. He sees them lifting weights, he wants to go out there and lift weights. If he sees them out there playing handball, he wants to play handball. He

wants to be part of them. But it's not a natural desire for him to read a certain book, or to act in a certain manner, or to strut around, or to talk out of the side of his mouth. Those things are put on. They are put on by those people we call *hipsters*.

Nonetheless, the major distinguishing characteristic of the *hipster* remains centered on the fact that he is, as another inmate has said, "the bully type—all wind and gum drops." He lays claim to a greater courage than he possesses in fact and his show of toughness, whether assumed to ingratiate himself in his own eyes or in the eyes of others idealizing toughness, remains simply a facade.

Now the *tough* has met the problem of personal insecurity in the prison not by ignoring the irritants of daily life but by reacting to them with violence; he is the problem of personal insecurity from the point of view of many prisoners and his reputation tends to keep others at a distance. Instead of banding together with other inmates and holding group harmony as a value to be advanced at all costs, he follows the individualistic path of depending on his own strength and courage to settle the quarrels in which he becomes involved. Thus he frees himself to some extent from the depredations of the *gorilla* and the *wolf,* for he is a person to be approached with considerable prudence, and many inmates take pains not to give him cause for assault. The solution of the *tough* is far from perfect, however, for there are other *toughs* in the prison who are at least equally ready to fight; and some *hipsters*, intent on building a reputation for toughness, may deliberately provoke him in the belief that he can be beaten.

Quick to anger, then, and slow to cool off, the prisoner addicted to "expressive" rather than "instrumental" violence intensifies the problems of the inmate population as a whole; and he himself, despite his momentary victories, stands as an invitation to further violence. He wins a measure of respect, it is true, but it is the respect of the brutalized and it is apt to reach no further than his fists. It is the *tough* and the *hipster* as much as any other who convert the prison into what one inmate has described as a gigantic playground—a place where blustering and brawling push life in the direction of a state of anomy.

I have presented the patterns of behavior distinguished and named by the inmates of the New Jersey State Prison with a greater simplicity than exists in reality. Argot roles are in fact generalized behavioral tendencies and the playing of a particular role by a particular prisoner is often a matter of degree. Furthermore, some inmates may play one role in the industrial shops, let us say, and another role in the Wing. A prisoner may quickly assume one role on first entering the institution and then shift to another role at a later point in time. But this is simply to reaffirm that the patterns of behavior which I have described are social roles rather than personality traits and that we are interested in the behavior of inmates as a system of action rather than as a collection of individual characteristics. *It is the structure of social relationships formed by imprisoned criminals which concerns us; an inmate may enter these relationships in a variety of capacities for varying periods of time, but it is the structure itself which lays the main claim on our attention.*

I have suggested that the main outlines of this structure, this system of action, are to be found in the inmate behavior patterns classified and named by the prisoners in light of the major problems which confront them. These major problems are, I have argued, five in number and involve deprivation or frustration in the areas of social acceptance, material possessions, heterosexual relationships, personal autonomy, and personal security. From the viewpoint of particular inmates, some of these problems may bite more deeply than others, but in general these problems constitute a common set of pains or rigors of confinement to which almost all prisoners must respond or adapt themselves.

Now the argot terms presented in this chapter largely refer to what I have chosen to call "alienative" modes of response to the specific problems posed by imprisonment. The *rat*, the *center man*, the *wolf*, the *punk*, the *fag*, the *gorilla*, the *merchant*, the *ball buster*, the *tough*, and the *hipster*—all are social roles in which, generally speaking, the inmate attempts to reduce the rigors of prison life at the expense of fellow prisoners and the individual pursues his own interests, his own needs, without regard for the needs, rights, and opinions of others. Inmate cohesion or inmate solidarity is sacrificed for personal aggrandizement; bonds of mutual loyalty, aid, affection, and respect are subordinated to individualistic ends. The variety of "cohesive" responses to the pains of imprisonment, on the other hand, tend to be lumped together under the label of the *real man*, for this term is often extended to cover social roles which involve loyalty, generosity, sexual restraint, and the minimizing of frictions among inmates as well as endurance with dignity. The *real man* appears to form a central cluster of admired behavior patterns from which various types of deviance are measured and the label of *real man* provides a general antonym for the argot terms applied to "alienative" behavior patterns. In any case, it is clear that "cohesive" responses to the harsh conditions of prison life are to be found in the society of captives as well as "alienative" responses, even if prisoners fail to attach distinctive argot terms to each species of the former. *And the greater the extent of "cohesive" responses—the greater the degree to which the society of captives moves in the direction of inmate solidarity—the greater is the likelihood that the pains of imprisonment will be rendered less severe for the inmate population as a whole.* The deprivations and frustrations of prison life cannot [be] eliminated, it is true, but their consequences can be partially neutralized. A cohesive inmate society provides the prisoner with a meaningful social group with which he can identify himself and which will support him in his battles against his condemners—and thus the prisoner can at least in part escape the fearful isolation of the convicted offender. Inmate solidarity, in the form of mutual toleration, helps to solve the problems of personal security posed by the involuntary intimacy of men who are noteworthy for their seriously antisocial behavior in the past. Inmate solidarity, in the form of "sharing" or a reciprocity of gifts and favors, attacks one of the most potent sources of aggression among prisoners, the drive for material betterment by means of force and fraud. It is true that goods in scarce supply will remain scarce even if they are shared rather than monopolized; but scarce goods will at least be distributed more equitably in a social system marked by solidarity and this may be of profound significance in enabling the prisoner to better endure the psychological burden of impoverishment. And a cohesive population of prisoners provides a system of shared, group-supported beliefs and values which will tend to curb forms of behavior such as sexual perversion, useless insurrections which bring only retaliation, and so on.

On the other hand, as the population of prisoners moves in the direction of a warring aggregate the many problems of prison life become more acute. If a war of all against all is apt to make life "solitary, poor, nasty, brutish, and short" for men with freedom, as Hobbes suggested, it would seem to be doubly true for men in custody. Even those who are most successful in exploiting their fellow prisoners will find it a dangerous and nerve-wracking game, for they cannot escape the company of their victims. And insofar as social rejection is a fundamental problem, a state of complete mutual alienation is worse than useless as a solution to the threats created by the inmate's status as an outcast.

The balance struck between the theoretical extremes of perfect solidarity and a war of all against all is, then, of vital significance—not only to the prison officials but to the inmates as well. This balance point, however, is not fixed. Rather, it represents a compromise of a host of competing forces which change through time and thus the structure of social relationships formed by imprisoned criminals is in a constant state of flux. These shifts in the balance point between cohesion and alienation among inmates are in turn part of a larger series of changes embracing the prison as a whole. In short, the social system of the New Jersey State Prison, like every social system, is marked by social change and it is only by examining the nature of this change that we can come to a full understanding of the society of captives. . . .

A Postscript for Reformers

We have seen that keeping men confined is a complex and difficult task, not simply because some men are ingenious in devising ways to escape but also, and more importantly, because the variety of functions which the custodians must perform are often in conflict. Internal order, the organization of prison labor, punishment, and rehabilitation—all must be pursued along with custody within a framework of sharply limited means. The prison officials have attempted to resolve their numerous dilemmas by constructing a vast body of rules and regulations designed to order the activities of the inmate population in minute detail. Such a solution is far from perfect, however, if only on the grounds that the transfer of this intricate and extended control from paper to reality is beset by problems. Unable to depend on a sense of duty among their prisoners as a basis for obedience, barred from the habitual use of force, and lacking an adequate stock of rewards and punishments, the custodians find themselves engaged in a constant struggle to achieve even the semblance of dominance. And the position of the custodial bureaucracy is further undermined by the bonds of friendship which spring up between the guard and his prisoners, by the practices of *quid pro quo* and long familiarity which serve to temper a strict enforcement of the rules.

The fact that the theoretical power of the custodians is imperfect in actuality removes some of the sting of imprisonment as far as the confined criminal is concerned. Yet as much as the power of the custodians may be compromised in the day-to-day routines, the conditions of life posed by imprisonment remain as profoundly disturbing frustrations of the inmate population. Deprived of their liberty, stripped of worldly possessions, denied access to heterosexual relationships, divested of autonomy, and compelled to associate with other deviants, the inmates find that imprisonment still means punishment however much imprisonment may have been softened in this modern era by an accent on humanitarianism and reform. I have suggested that it is these punishing aspects of modern imprisonment, these deprivations or frustrations, which play a crucial part in shaping the inmate social system. It is these deprivations, particularly as they involve a threat or an attack at a deep psychological level, that the inmates must meet and counter. And the inmate population's modes of reactions can be found ranged, I have suggested, between two poles. On the one hand, the prisoner can engage in a highly individualistic war of all against all in which he seeks to mitigate his own plight at the expense of his fellow prisoners; on the other hand, the prisoner can attempt to form a close alliance with his fellow captives and to present a unified front against the custodians. It is the changing mixture of these antithetical behavior patterns and their underlying values which makes up the social system we label so grossly, so overly simply, as the prison community.

Study Questions

1. Describe the pains (i.e., deprivations) of imprisonment identified by the author.

2. How do the various argot roles help inmates to adjust to, or alleviate, these pains?

3. Which of the argot roles represent the most prisonized (in the words of Clem-

mer) response, and which represent the least?

4. In your opinion, would it be possible for prison administrators to alleviate some of these pains? If so, how? What would be the consequences of such an action? ✦

10
Prisons in Turmoil

John Irwin

The changes within the penal institution during the last two centuries have been fairly well documented, both in the greater literature and in the preceding pieces. Irwin examines three major periods in the development of the penal institution. The author first examines a composite of what he terms "The Big House." This amounted to an institutional warehouse in which the goal of doing time was of paramount concern for both administrators and residents. After World War II, however, The Big House evolved into the "Correctional Institution," a clear shift toward the goal of rehabilitation and reform. The indeterminate sentence, offender classification, and treatment were all major portions of this new format. Yet a third shift occurred, defined by Irwin as the "Contemporary Prison." The latter is characterized by severe racial divisions, violence, and gang influence. The reader is encouraged to consider possible next steps in penal institutional evolution, when examining Irwin's ideas.

The Big House

Most of our ideas about men's prisons are mistaken because they fix on a type of prison—the Big House—that has virtually disappeared during the last twenty-five years. A dominant type of prison in this century, the Big House, emerged, spread, and

Excerpts from *Prisons in Turmoil* by John Irwin. Copyright © 1980 by John Irwin. Reprinted by permission.

prevailed, then generated images and illusions and, with considerable help from Hollywood, displayed these to the general society. It caught and held the attention of both the public and sociology. Its images and illusions linger on, surrounding contemporary prisons like a fog and blurring our sight. We must clear the air of false visions, distinguish the Big House as a type, and then move toward an analysis of succeeding types of prisons.

The Big House developed during a long and important phase in the varying history of the prison in the United States. This phase began early in this century and lasted into the 1940s or 1950s and even into the present in some states. Long before this era, the prison had outgrown its infancy as a penitentiary, where the prison planners intended that prisoners be kept in quiet solitude, reflecting penitently on their sins in order that they might cleanse and transform themselves. It also had passed through a half century during which prisoners spent their time in "hard labor," working in prison rock quarries or in profit-making industrial and agricultural enterprises. Eventually, federal legislation and union power forced most convict labor out of the public sector. More recently, prisons in the East, Midwest, and West were touched (most lightly, some belatedly, and a few not at all) by the humanitarian reforms of the "progressive era." Cruel corporal punishment such as flogging, beating, water torture, shackling of inmates to cell walls or hanging them by their thumbs, entombment in small cribs and lone solitary confinement as well as extreme corruption in the appointment of personnel and in the administration of the prison were largely eliminated. The Big House phase followed these reforms.

Although Big Houses appeared in most states, there were many notable exceptions. Many state prison systems never emerged from cruelty and corruption. In a few states, guards unofficially but regularly used brutality and even executions to control prisoners. Some prison administrations continued to engage prisoners in very hard labor throughout the first half of the twentieth century. Even in the eastern, Midwestern, and western states where the Big House predominated, there were many residues of earlier phases; silence systems endured through the 1940s. But in most states outside the South, there emerged a type of prison that was relatively free of corporal punishment and that did not engage most prisoners in hard labor. This prison predominated until the "rehabilitative ideal," a new theory of reform, altered penology and the correctional institution appeared. Since the Big House has been the source of most of our ideas about prisons, I shall construct a composite picture of it and then consider some of the exceptions to the type. This will help us to understand its modern progeny.

Physical Description

The Big House was a walled prison with large cell blocks that contained stacks of three or more tiers of one- or two-man cells. On the average, it held 2,500 men. Sometimes a single cell block housed over 1,000 prisoners in six tiers of cells. . . . Overall, cell blocks were harsh worlds of steel and concrete, of unbearable heat and stench in the summer and chilling cold in the winter, of cramped quarters, and of constant droning, shouting, and clanking noise.

The other prominent physical features of the Big House were the yard, the wall, the mess hall, the administration building, the shops, and the industries. The yard, formed by cell blocks and the wall, was a drab place. . . . Better-appointed yards had a few recreational facilities: a baseball diamond, perhaps basketball courts, tables and benches, and handball courts, which often were improvised by using the walls of the cell blocks. The mess hall had rows of tables and benches and invariably was too small to seat the entire population at one time. The thick granite wall encircled the place and, with its gun towers, symbolized the meaning of the Big House.

This granite, steel, cement, and asphalt monstrosity stood as the state's most extreme form of punishment, short of the death penalty. It was San Quentin in California, Sing Sing in New York, Stateville in Illinois, Jackson in Michigan, Jefferson City in Missouri, Canon City in Colorado, and so on. It was the place of banishment and punishment to which convicts were "sent up." Its major characteristics were isolation, routine, and monotony. . . .

Social Organization

The Big House was like all prisons, a place where convicts lived and constructed a world. This world had divisions and strata, special informal rules and meaning, set of enterprises. Some of the patterns and divisions were built upon external characteristics. The prisoners came from both the city and the country. In Clemmer's study in the 1930s it was about half and half. By and large, they were the poorer and less educated persons, those from the wrong side of the tracks. Many of them were drifters, persons who floated from state to state, looking for work and, when they failed to find it, stealing and then brushing against "the law." About half previously had been in a prison or reform school. The most frequent criminal type was the thief, a criminal who searched for the "big score"—a safe burglary or armed robbery. But most of the prisoners never came close to a big score, and those who were serving a sentence for theft, which was over half the population, were typically convicted of very minor crimes. Clemmer noted that most prisoners were "amateurish and occasional offenders. Most typical of burglars are those who break into a house or store and carry away loot or money seldom exceeding eighty dollars—and not those who tunnel under a street and steal sixty thousand dollars worth of gems from a jewelry store."[1]

Many prisoners were black or other non-white races, but most in the Big Houses outside the South were white. Racial prejudice, discrimination, and segregation prevailed. Blacks (and sometimes other nonwhite prisoners) were housed in special sections, in special cell blocks, or at least with cell partners of the same race; and blacks held menial jobs. By rule or informal patterns, blacks and whites sat in separate sections in the mess hall. In fact, in all facets of prison life, patterns of segregation and distance were maintained.

White prisoners kept blacks and, to some extent, other nonwhites "in their place." They did not accept them as equals in the informal social life of the prison and directed constant hate and occasional violence at them. . . .

According to the formal routine, the prisoners rose early; hurriedly ate breakfast; returned to their cells for one of the four or five daily counts; proceeded to work, school, or the yard for a day of idleness; hurriedly ate lunch; counted; went back to work, school, or idleness; hurriedly ate dinner; and returned to their cells for the night. After count, they read, wrote letters or literary works, pursued hobbies, talked to other prisoners, listened to the radio on their ear phones (when this innovation reached the prison), and then went to sleep when the lights were turned off. . . .

This was the formal, or more visible, routine. Within this general outline a complex, subtle, informal prisoner world with several subworlds was also operating. It pivoted around the convict code, a prison adaptation of the thieves' code. Thieves were not the majority, but they were the most frequent criminal type, and their strong commitment to thieves' values, their communication network—which extended through the thieves' world, inside and out—and their loyalty to other thieves gave them the upper hand in prison. . . .

The central rule in the thieves' code was "thou shalt not snitch." In prison, thieves converted this to the dual norm of "do not rat on another prisoner" and "do your own time." Thieves also were obliged by their code to be cool and tough, that is, to maintain respect and dignity; not to show weakness to help other thieves; and to leave most other prisoners alone. Their code dominated the Big House and generally it could be translated into these rules: Do not inform, do not openly interact or cooperate with the guards or the administration, and do your own time. These rules helped to produce a gap of hostility and unfriendliness between prisoners and guards, a hierarchy of prisoners, a system of mutual aid among a minority of prisoners, and patterns of exploitation among others.

The prisoners divided themselves into a variety of special types. In addition to the yeggs, "Johnsons," "people," "right guys," or "regulars"—thieves and persons whom they accepted as trustworthy—there were several types more indigenous to the prison. There were gamblers, who were involved in controlling prison resources, and prison "politicians" and "merchants," supplying and exchanging commodities. There were prison "queens," who openly presented themselves as homosexuals, and "punks," who were considered to have been "turned out"—that is, made into homosexuals by other prisoners or by the prison experience. There was a variety of prison "toughs," persons who were deeply and openly hostile to the prison administration, the conventional society, and most other prisoners and who displayed a readiness to employ violence against others. These types ranged from the less predictable and less social "crazies" to the more predictable and clique-oriented "hard rocks" or "tush hogs." There was the "character," who continuously created humorous derision through his dress, language, story-telling ability, or general behavior. There were the "masses," who broke into the subtypes of "assholes" or "hoosiers," lower- and working-class persons having little or no criminal skill and earning low respect, and "square johns," persons who were not viewed as criminals by the rest of the population and were oriented to conventional society. There was a variety of "dingbats," who were considered to be crazy, but harmless. Finally, there were "rapos," persons serving sentences for sexual acts such as incest and child molesting, which were repulsive to most prisoners, and "stool pigeons," "rats," or "snitches," who supplied information about other prisoners to authorities.

These types were arranged in a hierarchy of prestige, power, and privilege. At the top of the stack were the right guys, through their propensity to cooperate with each other, their prestige as thieves, and their presentation of coolness and toughness. . . . Very close to the top were the merchants, politicians, and gamblers. They occupied this high position because they largely controlled the scarce prison resources. Characters, when they were accomplished, were awarded a special position with considerable respect and popularity, but not much direct power. Down the ladder were the toughs, who had to be respected because they were a constant threat. The cliques of hard rocks occasionally hurt or killed someone, though seldom anyone with prestige and power. The crazies, who were often very dangerous, were treated with extreme caution, but were avoided and excluded as much as possible. In the middle were the masses who were ignored by the leaders, stayed out of the prison's informal world, and restricted their social activities to small friendship groups or remained "loners." Below them were the queens, punks, rats, and rapos, the latter being at the very bottom of the pile. On the outside of all informal prisoner activities were the dingbats, who were ignored by all.

Most prisoners followed one of three prison careers. The most frequent was that of just doing time. This was the style of the thief and of most other prisoners who shared the thief's primary concern of getting out of prison with maximum dispatch and minimum pain. Doing time meant, above all, avoiding trouble that would place a prisoner in danger or lengthen or intensify his punishment. But in addition, doing time involved avoiding "hard time." To avoid hard time, prisoners stayed active in sports, hobbies, or reading; secured as many luxuries as

possible without bringing on trouble; and formed a group of close friends with whom to share resources and leisure hours and to rely on for help and protection.

Thieves who established this style generally confined their group associations to other thieves. Since they had prestige and power in the prison world, however, they occasionally entered into general prisoner affairs, particularly when they were trying to secure luxuries or favors for themselves or friends. Most of the masses followed the pattern of doing time established by thieves, but their friendship groups tended not to be so closely knit and they tended not to enter into the general prison social activities.

Some prisoners, particularly the indigenous prison types, oriented themselves more completely to the prison and tended to construct a total existence there. Donald Cressey and I once described the style of adaptation of convicts who

seek positions of power, influence and sources of information whether these men are called "shots," "politicians," "merchants," "hoods," "toughs," "gorillas," or something else. A job as secretary to the Captain or Warden, for example, gives an aspiring prisoner information and consequent power, and enables him to influence the assignment or regulation of other inmates. In the same way, a job which allows the incumbent to participate in a racket, such as clerk in the kitchen storeroom where he can steal and sell food, is highly desirable to a man oriented to the convict subculture. With a steady income of cigarettes, ordinarily the prisoner's medium of exchange, he may assert a great deal of influence and purchase these things which are symbols of status among persons oriented to the convict subculture. Even if there is not a well-developed medium of exchange, he can barter goods acquired in his position for equally desirable goods possessed by other convicts. These include information and such things as specially starched, pressed and tailored prison clothing, fancy belts, belt buckles or billfolds, special shoes or any other type of dress which will set him apart and will indicate that the prisoner has both the influence to get the goods and the influence necessary to keep them and display them despite prison rules which outlaw doing so.[2]

Many of the persons who occupied these roles and made a world out of prison—that is, followed the strategy sometimes referred to by prisoners as "jailing"—were individuals who had long experiences with jails and prisons beginning in their early teens or even earlier. Actually, they were more familiar with prison than with outside social worlds. . . .

One last strategy followed by a small number of prisoners I labeled "gleaning" in a later study of the California prison system.[3] An old style, it must be included in the description of the Big House. Gleaning involved taking advantage of any resource available to better themselves, to improve their minds, or to obtain skills that would be useful on the outside. In trying to improve themselves, prisoners in Big Houses read, sought formal education through the prison's elementary and high schools (when these existed) and university correspondence courses, and learned trades in the few vocational training programs or in prison job assignments. In addition, they tried to improve themselves in other ways—by increasing social skills and physical appearance. Generally, in gleaning, prisoners attempted to equip themselves for life after prison.

To a great extent, Big House homosexual patterns were a form of prison improvisation. With no possibility for heterosexual contacts, some prisoners performed homosexual acts as "inserters," although they would not do this on the outside. In addition, many young, weaker, less initiated, and perhaps effeminate prisoners were tricked or forced into the role of "insertee" (that is, they were turned out). Often they were trapped in this role by the knowledge that they had succumbed in the past, and after years of performing as a punk, they developed homosex-

ual identities and continued as homosexuals even after release. Finally, some prisoners, particularly prisoners who were thoroughly immersed in the informal prisoner world—that is, who jailed—performed the role of "wolf" or "jocker." A few of these individuals, after an extended period of continued homosexual activities (ostensibly as the inserter, but actually as both the inserter and insertee in many cases), developed a preference for homosexual relationships and continued in their masculine homosexual role on the outside.

Stupefaction. When I was in the Los Angeles County Jail in 1952, waiting to be sentenced to prison, I met a "four-time loser" who was going back to Folsom, the state's long-term Big House. He advised me, "Don't let them send you to Folsom. It's the easiest place to do time but, man, you leave something there you never get back." He was alluding to Folsom's impact on prisoners' mentality, which prisoners referred to as "going stir." I think the term *stupefaction* catches the sense of this expression. The dictionary defines *stupefaction* as the "state of being stupefied; insensibility of mind or feeling." Serving time in a Big House meant being pressed into a slow-paced, rigid routine; cut off from outside contacts and social worlds; denied most ordinary human pleasures and stimulations; and constantly forced to contain anger and hostility. Many persons were able to maintain their spirit under these conditions, and some were even vitalized by the challenge. But most prisoners were somewhat stupefied by it. They learned to blunt their feelings, turn inward, construct fantasy worlds for themselves, and generally throttle their intellectual, emotional, and physical life. In the extreme they fell into a stupor. Victor Nelson describes an old con:

A trustee in a suit of striped overalls was standing with his arms folded lazily against the handle of the rake, his head resting dejectedly on his arms, his whole attitude that of a man who had worked all day and was very tired although it was only about nine o'clock of a cool spring morning. He seemed almost in a coma. There was an expression of utter indifference on his face and his eyes were glazed with absentmindedness. He was, although I did not know it then, a living example of the total, final, devastating effect of imprisonment upon the human being.[4]

The Big House did not reform prisoners or teach many persons crime. It embittered many. It stupefied thousands.

The Correctional Institution

After World War II, many states replaced Big Houses with correctional institutions, which, when they were newly constructed, looked different, were organized differently, housed different types of prisoners, and nurtured different prison social worlds. Importantly, they had a different effect on prisoners. They spread and became the dominant type of prison in the 1950s, if not in numbers, at least in the minds of penologists. And, like Big Houses, their images live on, blurring our view of contemporary prisons. Consequently, we must distinguish this type of prison to understand the modern violent prison. The correctional institution's emergence was related to broad changes in our society. Briefly, the postwar United States—prosperous, urbanized, and mobile—confronted a new set of pressing social problems. Hard times, natural disasters (floods, droughts, and tornadoes), epidemics, illiteracy, and the "dangerous classes," had been updated to or replaced by poverty, mental health, family disorganization, race relations, juvenile delinquency, and urban crime. Americans faced these with a fundamentally altered posture. The Great Depression and World War II had moved them from their isolationist and individualist position, and they accepted, even demanded, government intervention into conditions that they believed should and could be changed.

Along with all organs of government, agencies whose official function was intervention into domestic social problems grew, gained power, and proliferated. Peopling these agencies and leading the large social services expansion were old and new professionals: physicians, psychiatrists, psychologists, social workers, urban planners, sociologists, and a new group of specialists in penology. The latter group—a growing body of college-educated employees and administrators of prisons, parole, and probation and a few academic penologists whom I will hereafter refer to collectively as "correctionalists"—went after the apparently mushrooming crime problem. These correctionalists were convinced and were able to convince many state governments and interested segments of the general population that they could reduce crime by curing criminals of their criminality. . . .

The innovative penologists kept abreast of the developments in the new social sciences and began constructing a philosophy of penology based on the concept that criminal behavior was caused by identifiable and changeable forces. This led them to the conclusion that the primary purpose of imprisonment should be "rehabilitation" a new form of reformation based on scientific methods. This new penology is generally referred to as the rehabilitative ideal. . . .

The nation's leading penologists agreed as early as 1870, when they formed the National Prison Association, to establish rehabilitation as the primary purpose of prisons and to alter prison routines in order to implement rehabilitation (particularly to introduce indeterminate sentencing). At that time, however, the society was not ready for what appeared to be a nonpunitive approach to crime. Until World War II and the changes described above had occurred, the architects of rehabilitation experimented in juvenile institutions like Elmira, New York, where Zebulon Brockway introduced a full rehabilitative program, and they slipped bits and pieces of rehabilitation into Big Houses—for example, a more elaborate classification system and a small department of rehabilitation. After the war, receiving an okay from the public and various state governments and an infusion of more funds and more college-trained employees, the innovators in penology created the new prison, the correctional institution. In some states, such as Wisconsin and Minnesota, this meant reorganizing the staff structures and introducing new programs into old prisons, but in others, such as California and New York, it also meant constructing many new facilities. In both cases, the correctionalists organized the prisons around three procedures: indeterminate sentencing, classification, and the treatment that they had been developing for decades.

The Indeterminate Sentencing System

According to the early planners of the rehabilitative prison, prison administrators should have the discretionary power to release the prisoner when the administrators or their correctional experts determine that he is cured of criminality. Many early supporters of the rehabilitative ideal, such as Karl Menninger, advocated sentences of zero to life for all offenders so that correctional professionals could concentrate on treating criminals and releasing them when their illness (criminality) was cured. In actuality, no prison system in the United States or any other place achieved this extreme, but California, after thirty-five years of developing an indeterminate sentence routine through legislation and administrative policies, came the closest. After 1950, the Adult Authority—the official name of the California parole board—exercised the power to determine an individual's sentence within statutory limits for a particular crime, to set a parole date before this sentence was finished, and, at any time until the fixed sentence was completed, to restore the sentence back to its statutory maximum or any other length within the margins. It exercised these powers with no requirements for due process or review of decisions. The statutory limits in Califor-

nia—for example, one to ten years for grand larceny, one to fifteen for forgery and second-degree burglary, one to life for second-degree robbery, and five to life for first-degree robbery—gave the Adult Authority large margins within which to exercise their discretion.

Under this system, prisoners remained unsure of how much time they would eventually serve until they completed their sentence. While in prison, they appeared before the Adult Authority annually until the Adult Authority set their release date, invariably within six months of their last board appearance. While individuals were on parole or awaited release, the Adult Authority could refix their sentences back to the maximum and reactivate the process of annual board appearances for violations of the rules of the prison or conditions of parole.

Board appearances were the most important milestones in the inmates imprisonment, and the Adult Authority had full power over their lives. According to the ideal, parole boards should use this power to release prisoners when they were rehabilitated. This presupposed, however, that the correctionalists had procedures for identifying and changing criminal characteristics, which they did not, and that parole boards had procedures for determining when these changes had occurred, which they did not. It also presupposed that rehabilitation of the offender was parole boards' major concern, which it was not. Even in the early planning stages the advocates of indeterminate sentencing intended the discretionary powers to be used to control prisoners and detain indefinitely those who were viewed as dangerous by various authorities (district attorneys, police chiefs, and influential citizens). . . . In addition, although they never admitted this, the advocates of indeterminate sentence systems understood and appreciated that its discretionary powers permitted them to give shorter sentences, or even no sentences, to influence individuals. So, in actual practice, while professing to balance the seriousness of a crime and rehabilitative criteria, parole boards used their discretionary powers to enforce conformity to prison rules and parole routines, avoid criticism from outside authorities and citizens, award higher social status, and express personal prejudice and whim. . . .

Classification

An ideal correctional institution primarily organized to rehabilitate prisoners would require an elaborate, systematic diagnostic and planning process that determined the nature of the individual's criminality and prescribed a cure. Through the decades before the 1950s, the creators of the rehabilitative approach steadily developed more complex classification systems, ostensibly to accomplish these ends. Theoretically, the finished version that they incorporated in the new postwar correctional institutions operated as follows. First, a team of professionals—psychologists, case workers, sociologists, vocational counselors, and psychiatrists—tested the criminal, interviewed him and gathered life history information. Then a team of these correctionalists formed an initial classification committee and reviewed the tests and evaluations, planned the prisoner's therapeutic routine, assigned him to a particular prison, and recommended particular rehabilitative programs for him. In the final stage, classification committees at particular prisons periodically reviewed the prisoner's progress, recommended changes in programs, and sometimes transferred him to another prison.

The classification committees in the first correctional institutions tended to follow this ideal in appearance, but they actually operated quite differently. First, the social sciences never supplied them with valid diagnostic methods and effective cures for criminality. Second, the committees never abandoned control and other management concerns, which classification systems had acquired in the decades when they operated in Big Houses. . . .

Treatment

A variety of effective treatment strategies would complete the ideal correctional institution. As stressed above, none were discovered. What actually existed in the correctional institutions in the 1950s was care and treatment. An administrative branch that coexisted with the custody branch, planned and administered three types of treatment programs—therapeutic, academic, and vocational—and generated reports on prisoners' progress for the institutional classification committees and the parole board.

The most common therapeutic program was group counseling, which, because it was led by staff persons with little or no training in clinical procedures, was a weak version of group therapy. Originally, the plan was to hire psychiatrists and clinical psychologists, but the pay was too small and the working conditions too undesirable to attract those professionals. Some persons with social work training, who were willing to work for the lower salaries, filled in some of the gaps, but in states such as California, where dozens of group leaders were needed, even their numbers were too small. So staff persons with no formal training in psychology led many, if not most, groups in correctional institutions. Most prisoners participated in group counseling programs, because they were led to believe by parole board members and the treatment staff that they would not be granted a parole unless they participated. Also, they believed that unacceptable traits or attitudes revealed in the sessions would be reported by the staffers, and this would reduce their chances of being paroled early. In addition, many prisoners had a strong distaste for discussing sensitive, personal issues and disparaged other prisoners for doing so. The result was that group counseling sessions were invariably very bland. Few prisoners took them seriously or participated sincerely or vigorously.

. . .[F]ew prisoners received individual treatment from psychiatrists or psychologists. Toward the end of the 1950s, the more persistent correctionalists experimented with "milieu therapy" by attempting to convert prisons or units within prisons into "therapeutic communities." More recently, contemporary correctionalists have introduced more intense therapeutic forms, such as "behavior modification" and "attack therapy." However, group counseling, which is inexpensive and easier to implement, was the dominant form of therapy when correctional institutions were at their peak. The academic and vocational education programs had more substance than the therapy treatment programs. All the innovative correctional institutions had formed elementary and high school programs in the 1950s, and many had formed links with universities and were making correspondence courses available to some prisoners. All correctional institutions attempted vocational training. In California during the 1950s, those who desired and were able to enter the programs (there were fewer openings than prisoners) could receive training in cooking, baking, butchering, dry cleaning, shoe repair, sewing machine repair, auto mechanics, auto body and fender repair, small motor repair, sheet metal machining, printing, plumbing, painting, welding, and nursing. All these training programs had inherent weaknesses, and they seldom fully equipped a prisoner for a position in the trade. One of these weaknesses was that some training programs, such as baking and cooking, were appendages of prison housekeeping enterprises and were insufficiently related to outside vocational enterprises. In other cases, the equipment, the techniques, and the knowledge of the instructor were obsolete.

Indeterminate sentences, classification, and treatment were the actualization of the rehabilitative ideal in correctional institutions. As the descriptions indicate, they fell short of the ideal. The reasons for this are varied. In spite of the intentions and efforts of the most sincere visionaries of rehabilitation, they were never able to realize their plans. The public and most government policy makers continued to demand that prisons first accomplish their other assigned tasks: punishment, control, and restraint of prisoners. In addition, the new correctional institutions were not created in a vacuum but planned in ongoing prison systems which had long traditions, administrative hierarchies, divisions, informal social worlds, and special subcultures among the old staff. The new correctionalists were never able to rid the prison systems of the old regime, though often they tried; and the old timers, many of whom were highly antagonistic to the new routines, resisted change, struggled to maintain as much control as possible, and were always successful in forcing an accommodation between old and new patterns. So correctional institutions were never totally, or even mainly, organized to rehabilitate prisoners. Nevertheless, an entirely new prison resulted from the rehabilitative ideal and through its rhetoric, which correctionalists used to defend new programs and disguise other purposes, achieved a temporary unity in the ranks. This type of prison spread throughout the United States, replacing many, perhaps most, Big Houses. In many ways it was a great improvement, and some correctionalists still look on it as the best we can hope for. However, it contained many unnecessary inhumanities, injustices, and idiocies, though for many years these were less visible. Eventually, its own flaws and certain external social changes destroyed it (or at least damaged it beyond repair).

To complete the description of the correctional institution, I shall focus on Soledad, which was opened in 1952, which was planned and operated as an exemplary correctional institution, and in which I served five years during its golden age. All correctional institutions, certainly, had some unique features, but Soledad during the 1950s is a superior example of the type.

Soledad: The Formal Structure

Soledad prison was part of California's very large investment in the new penology.

The state emerged from World War II with a rapidly expanding population, an apparently rising crime rate, relatively full state coffers, and a liberal citizenry. In a few years the state allocated massive sums for higher education, highway construction, and prisons. In the 1950s, in addition to two new "guidance centers," the state constructed six new men's prisons, a new women's prison, and a special narcotics treatment center. Soledad, the first of the men's prisons to be completed after the war, was planned, constructed, and operated as one of the essential parts in a large rehabilitative correctional organization. It was labeled California Training Facility and was intended as the prison for younger, medium risk, more trainable prisoners.

Soledad's physical structure radically departs from that of the Big Houses. It has no granite wall; instead, circling the prison is a high fence with gun towers situated every few hundred feet and nestled in the corners. The nine cell blocks stem over a long hall. Two relatively pleasant dining rooms with tile floors and octagonal oak tables, a spacious library, a well equipped hospital, a laundry, an education building, a gym, several shops, and the administration building connect to this hall. In fact, the entire prison community operates in and around the hall, and prisoners can (and many of them do) live day after day without ever going outside.

Each cell block (called a "wing") had a "day room" jutting off the side at the ground level, and all the inside walls in the prison were painted in pastel colors—pale blue, pale green light yellow, and tan. All blocks originally had one-man cells though many were assigned two occupants later. All cells except those in one small wing used for new prisoners and for segregation and isolation (O wing) had solid doors with a small, screened inspection window. The cells in all cell blocks (except O wing) were in three tiers around the outside of the wings, so each cell had an outside window. Instead of bars, the windows had small panes with heavy metal moldings. All cells originally had a bunk, a desk, and a chair. The close security

cells also had a sink and toilet. In the five medium-security cell blocks, the prisoners carried keys to their own cells. A row of cells could be locked by a guard's setting a locking bar, but in the 1950s, except for regular counts and special lockdowns, prisoners in medium-security wings entered and left the cells at their own discretion.

The formal routine at Soledad was more relaxed than in most Big Houses. On a weekday the lights came on at 7:00 A.M., but there was no bell nor whistle. The individual "wing officers" released their cell blocks one at a time for breakfast. A prisoner could eat or could sleep another hour before work. The food was slightly better than average prison fare, which is slightly inferior to average institution fare and ranks well below state hospitals and the armed services. One pleasant aspect of the dining routine was that prisoners were allowed to linger for ten or twenty minutes and drink unlimited amounts of coffee. After breakfast, prisoners reported to their work or school assignment. Before lunch there was a count, during which all prisoners had to be in their cells or at a designated place where guards counted them, then lunch, a return to work or school, and another count before dinner. During the day the cell blocks were open, and prisoners could roam free, from their blocks, through the hall, to the large yard and its few recreational facilities, and to the library or gym. After dinner the wing officer kept the front door to the cell block locked except at scheduled unlocks for school, gym, library, and, during the summer, "night yard."

On the weekends, prisoners were idle, except for kitchen and a few hospital and maintenance workers. The cell blocks, gym, yard, and library remained open all day. Although they could visit on any day, most visitors came on weekends. The visiting room had clusters of padded chairs around coffee tables, and prisoners could sit close to and even touch their visitors, a relatively pleasant visiting arrangement. On Sunday the highlight of the week occurred: two showings of a three- or four-year-old Hollywood movie.

A few rules were perceived by prisoners as unnecessary, arbitrary, and irksome—rules such as, "no standing on tiers" or "prisoners must walk double file on one side of the hall." But in general, Soledad had a more relaxed and pleasant formal routine than most prisons.

The rehabilitative aspect of Soledad was prominent. As its official name implied, it offered a broad selection of vocational training programs. It also had a good elementary and high school program, through which a prisoner could receive a diploma from the local outside school district. Rounding out rehabilitation was the group counseling program in which the Adult Authority, classification committees, and prisoners' counselors coerced prisoners to participate (if they did not, they were warned that they would not receive a parole). One psychiatrist treated some individuals, but usually only the few whom the Adult Authority referred for special reasons, such as a history of violent or sex crimes. The counseling groups met once a week, and the majority of inmates attended them. In the second half of the 1950s, the treatment staff introduced more intensive counseling programs in which the groups met daily. But weekly group counseling led by relatively untrained guards and other staff members was the total therapy component for most prisoners.

Informal Life. Soledad, like all correctional institutions, developed different group structures, intergroup relationships, and informal systems of social control from those in Big Houses. Some of these differences were a result of changes in the prisoner population, the most important being the shift in ethnic and racial balance. In California the percentages of non-white prisoners had been increasing steadily and, by 1950, had passed 40 percent: about 25 percent Chicano and 15 percent black. This shift towards nonwhite prisoners was occurring in most large eastern, midwestern, and western prison systems. The era of total white dominance in Big Houses was rapidly approaching an end.

More and more Tejanos—Mexicans raised in Texas—were coming to California and its prisons. The Tejanos were different from Los Angeles's Chicanos, who made up the largest group of Mexicans. More Tejanos were drug addicts; in fact, they introduced heroin to the Los Angeles Chicanos. They spoke more Spanish and Calo, the Spanish slang that developed in the United States, and were generally less Americanized. The two groups did not like each other, kept apart in jail, and sometimes fought.

All the Chicanos had experienced extreme prejudice throughout their lives, particularly in the public schools, and were somewhat hostile toward white prisoners. However, many Los Angeles Chicanos had associated with whites, particularly white criminals with whom they had engaged in crime. Heroin, which was spreading from the Tejanos through the Los Angeles Mexican neighborhoods and then into some white neighborhoods, intermixed Chicanos and Anglos even more. While some white prisoners disliked Chicanos, in general they feared and respected them, because whites believed that Chicanos would quickly employ violence when insulted or threatened. Consequently, between the two ethnic groups there was enmity, mixed with respect on the part of whites, but many individuals from both groups crossed over this barrier and maintained friendly relationships.

Black prisoners also divided into two groups: persons raised in Los Angeles or the San Francisco Bay Area and others who had migrated to California from the South and Southwest. Here, too, were prejudice and hostility between whites and blacks, but there were many whites and blacks who had intermixed and cooperated in criminal activities. This was more likely to have occurred between urban blacks and whites. So again, there was a gap between the two racial groups, but considerable crossing over the gap. The gap between Chicanos and blacks was wider, because Chicanos were more deeply prejudiced and hostile than whites were toward blacks.

Still over half of Soledad's population in the 1950s was white. Most white prisoners were working-class and lower-class youths raised in Los Angeles, San Diego, and the San Francisco Bay Area. There was a smaller group of whites from the small cities and towns in California: Fresno, Bakersfield, Modesto, and Stockton. Even though most whites in the prison were descendants of migrants from Kansas, Missouri, Illinois, Oklahoma, Arkansas, and Texas, the heartland of the United States, the prisoners from the smaller towns carried many more rural traditions and were labeled "Okie" in the prisons. The remainder of the white prisoners were a conglomeration of middle-class persons, drifters, servicemen, and state raised youths (individuals who had been raised by state agencies, including the California Youth Authority).

Members of all these different ethnic segments tended to form separate groups and social worlds in Soledad. This differentiation was further complicated by the divisions based on criminal orientations, which were more numerous than in past eras. The thieves were present, but their numbers were diminishing. This system of theft had been carried to California from the East and Midwest, but it was not crossing racial lines and was being replaced by drug addiction among whites. The thieves present in Soledad were very cliquish, practiced mutual aid, did not trust other prisoners, but were respected by them. However, they were not able to dominate the informal world as they had in Big Houses.

A new deviant subculture, that of the "dope fiend" (heroin addict), was spreading in California and became very prominent in the California prisons during the 1950s. Drug addiction brought to Los Angeles by the Tejanos had metastasized in the late 1940s and early 1950s, and most of the Chicanos and a large number of the young, working-class and lower-class white and black prisoners from Los Angeles, San Diego, San Francisco, and Oakland carried the patterns of this special subculture. In the era of the Big House, other prisoners, particularly thieves, did not trust dope fiends, because they believed that drug addicts were weak and would inform under pressure. But in Soledad and other California prisons in the 1950s, dope fiends were the emergent group, had respect, and, in fact, were rather snobbish. While in prison, perhaps in compensation for their individualistic, antisocial, passive, and often rapacious lifestyle while addicted, they were very affable, sociable, active, and verbal. At work and leisure they tended to form small cliques and spend their time telling drug stories Many of them were involved in intellectual anti-artistic activities.

A smaller group of "weed heads" or "grasshoppers" (marijuana users) were present in Soledad. This was before the psychedelic movement and weed heads were urban lower-class or working-class white, Chicano, and black youths who participated in a cultlike subculture; whose carriers lived in "far-out pads," wore "sharp threads," rode around in "groovy shorts," listened to "cool" jazz, sipped exotic liqueurs or wine coolers, and generally were "cool." In prison, weed heads continued to be cool and cliquish. Other prisoners, particularly dope fiends, thought they were silly and stayed away from them. . . .

Most black prisoners who had engaged in systematic theft were not thieves, but "hustlers." Segregation and prejudice cut blacks off from the older tradition of theft. When they migrated to the northern, midwestern, and western cities, blacks developed their own system of thievery, which was fashioned after patterns of early white con men— flimflammers—who toured the United States in the late nineteenth and early twentieth centuries. These flimflammers victimized all categories of rural people and imparted the styles of "short con" to blacks. In the cities, many blacks built on these original lessons and became hustlers. In general, hustling meant making money through one's wits and conversation rather than through force or threat. It involved short con games such as "greasy pig," "three card monte," and "the pigeon drop" [and] rackets such as the numbers, and pimping.

Like the other types of criminals, hustlers formed their own groups. Conversation was a major part of their style of theft, and conversation—"shucking and jiving," bragging about hustling, pimping, and the sporting life—was their major prison activity. An exconvict describes the activities of a black prisoner:

> he was off into that bag—Iceberg Slim [a famous pimp who wrote a successful paperback description of pimping] and all that— wearing their Cadillacs around the big yard.[5]

A special deviant orientation shared by at least 10 percent of the population at Soledad was that of the state-raised youth. Many prisoners had acquired this special orientation in the youth prisons; it involved the propensity to form tightly knit cliques, a willingness to threaten and actually to engage in violence for protection or for increases in power, prestige, and privilege, and a preference for prison patterns and styles as opposed to those on the outside. Many stateraised youths formed gangs in adult prisons, stole from and bullied other prisoners, and participated in the prison sexual world of jockers, queens, and punks.

Most prisoners were not committed "criminals." At least a quarter of the young people in prison in the 1950s were working- and lower-class people who had been "hanging out" in their neighborhoods or drifting around the country, looking for work and a niche for themselves. They had been involved in crime only irregularly and haphazardly, and usually it was very unsophisticated crime. They were often confused about the world and their place in it and saw themselves as "fuck-ups" or losers.

. . . These fuck-ups were the masses in the prison. In the Big Houses they were the hoosiers and in Soledad the assholes, and they were pushed aside and demeaned by other criminals. However, Soledad was a more heterogeneous prison, and the disparagement and exclusion were not as intense or complete. So fuck-ups occasionally rose to positions of power (to the extent that these existed), joined groups of other criminally oriented prisoners, and even began to identify themselves as dope fiends, heads, or hustlers. Thieves were more careful about associating with assholes, but on occasion one might befriend and tutor an inexperienced young person.

In addition to fuck-ups, there were many prisoners, mostly white, who had committed only one felony or a few serious crimes and did not consider themselves, nor were they considered by others, as criminals. Other prisoners referred to them as square johns and ignored them unless they wanted to take advantage of their knowledge or skills. (Many of these square johns were better educated, and a few of them were professionals). In general, however, they were ignored, and they kept to themselves. They either served their time as isolates or formed very small friendship groups with other square johns.

This subcultural mix of prisoners resisted the establishment of a single overriding convict code or the emergence of a single group of leaders. The old convict code did not have the unanimity and force that it had in the Big House. The number of thieves who formerly established and maintained this code was too small, and other criminals—hustlers, dope fiends, heads—with other codes of conduct competed for status and power in the informal realm.

The administrative regime influenced by the rehabilitative ideal inhibited the development of the exploitative, accommodative system, described by Sykes and Messinger, in which politicians' power depended on their control over certain enterprises, allowing them to make important decisions and obtain scarce material, and on their monopoly on information. In this era of professionalism, the staff was much more deeply involved in the day-to-day running of the prison. There was a partially successful attempt to prevent convicts from controlling the prison, and much more information flowed between staff and prisoners. Unlike his counterpart in most Big Houses, a captain's clerk could not autonomously transfer prisoners from one cell to another, squash disciplinary reports, transfer disliked guards to the night watch in a distant gun tower, or place friends on extra movie unlocks. Similarly, the storeroom clerk could not confiscate 20 percent of the prison's coffee, sugar, and dried fruit supply for his and his friends' use or for "wheeling and dealing." These prisoners could manipulate the routine slightly or skim off some commodities, but not enough to elevate them to the levels of power possessed by politicians or merchants in the Big Houses.

Despite the absence of these order-promoting processes, Soledad was still a very peaceful and orderly institution during most of the 1950s. The general mood among prisoners was tolerance and relative friendliness. The races were somewhat hostile toward each other and followed informal patterns of segregation, but there was commingling between all races and many prisoners maintained close friendships with members of their racial groups. During my five years at Soledad there were only a few knife fights, two murders, and one suicide.

Soledad's Ambience. To a great extent, the peace and order at Soledad were the result of a relatively optimistic, tolerant, and agreeable mood. Part of this mood stemmed from the enthusiasm for the new penal routine that the prisoners, returning or returning to prison, experienced in those early years. Most of us who came through the Chino Guidance Center and then moved into Soledad had been raised in the neighborhoods around Los Angeles, where we were involved in a variety of criminal subcultures. Consequently, we had received considerable information about the "joints" before coming to prison. We knew approximately how much time convicts served for a particular crime and how to conduct ourselves in

prison: "don't rap to bulls," "don't get friendly with or accept gifts from older cons," "play it cool," and "do your time." The Chino Guidance Center threw us off track. It was a new institution with physical attires similar to Soledad's. It had pastel-colored cell blocks named Cyprus and Madrone and guards who had been selected for the guidance center because of their ability to relate to prisoners. We were bombarded with sophisticated tests administered by young, congenial, "college types." We were examined thoroughly by dentists and physicians. For six weeks we attended daily three-hour sessions with one of the college types. During the rest of the day we played basketball, sat in the sun, worked out, or engaged in other recreation while we recovered from our profoundly deleterious "dead time" period, the county jail.

In this relatively agreeable environment, we became convinced that the staff members were sincere and were trying to help us. It was implied or stated that they would locate our psychological problems, vocational deficiencies, and physical effects and would fix them. The guidance center staff promised (mostly by implication) and we believed that they were going [to] make new people out of us.

The enthusiasm and the new hope continued into the early years of Soledad and the other correctional institutions. We believed then that the new penal approach was producing a much more humane prison routine. We experienced the new attitudes of many staff persons as a positive outcome of the new era. Although there were many old-school guards, there were many new guards with college experience and a new attitude toward prisons and prisoners. Many of the old guards were even converted or drawn into the new attitude by the new penology, and they tended to see themselves as rehabilitative agents or at least as more humane "correctional officers," as their new job title read.

The physical environment was not as harsh as in older prisons. The one-man cells, modern heating system, dining room, visiting room, gym, and so on were marked improvements over Big Houses. Rules and rule enforcement were not as strict; there was more freedom of movement; and the relationships among prisoners and between staff and prisoners were more tolerant and friendly than in Big Houses. . . .

Tips and Cliques. The peace and order at Soledad also resulted from a system of "tips" and cliques. Tips were extended social networks or crowds that were loosely held together by shared subcultural orientations or preprison acquaintances. Most of the tips were intraracial, and they were overlapping and connected. Consequently, an individual could be involved in more than one tip and usually was related to the tips that connected with his own. For example, I was a member of a large network of Los Angeles young people who had been involved in theft and heroin. My Los Angeles thieves-dope fiends tip was connected to a similar tip of San Francisco thieves-dope fiends through ties established in the youth prisons. There were tips of persons who had experienced the youth prisons together, lived in the same town or neighborhood ("home boys"), and engaged in the same criminal activities. A sense of loyalty existed between members of a tip. A member may not have known other members well, but common membership in the network automatically established some rapport and obligations and increased the possibility of friendship.

Prisoners formed smaller cliques within or across tips. . . . Clique members worked, celled, hung around the tier, yard, and day room, ate, and engaged in the same leisure activities together. The basis of organization varied greatly. Sometimes they formed out of small groups of prisoners who became acquainted at work or in the cell blocks. More often, they developed among persons who shared interest in some activity in prison, preprison experiences, subcultural orientations, and, thereby, tip membership. When clique members were also members of the same tip, the cliques were more cooperative, stable, and cohesive.

Most cliques were constantly transforming. Members were paroled, were transferred, or shifted friendships and interests. Former clique members continued to experience ties of friendships, and this extended friendship bonds outside existing cliques. These clique friendship ties and the ties to other tip members who were interconnected with the cliques established overlapping and extensive bonds of communication, friendship, and obligation through which cooperative enterprises were accomplished and conflict reduced. . . . Many disputes were avoided by indirect negotiations through the tips and cliques. . . . In the absence of more effective social organization, the tip and clique networks established ties and bridged gaps between prisoners, even between races, serving to promote peace and cooperation among prisoners. This system is similar to the clan, extended family, or totem organizations that served as ordering systems among primitive peoples before the establishment of larger, overreaching social organizations.

The Rehabilitative Ideal and Order

The rehabilitative philosophy and its actualizations directly promoted social order. Many of us accepted the altered self-conception contained in the new criminology that underpinned the ideal. We began to believe that we were sick, and we started searching for cures. Many of us adopted Sigmund Freud as our prophet, and we read and reread the *Basic Writings* as well [as] the works of the lesser prophets: Adler, Jung, Horney, and Fromm. Some of us became self-proclaimed experts in psychoanalysis and spent many hours analyzing each other. (Freudian interpretations provided us with new material for the old game of the dozens.)

Accepting this conception of ourselves as sick directed, our attention inward and away from social and prison circumstances. It inhibited us from defining our situation as unfair and from developing critical, perhaps collective, attitudes toward the society and the prison administration. We were divided psychologically by focusing on our own personalities and searching for cures of our individual pathologies.

In attempting to cure ourselves, we involved ourselves in the programs that grew out of the rehabilitative ideal. The formal policy in Soledad was that every prisoner had to have a full-time work, school, or vocational training assignment. The classification committees and the Adult Authority encouraged prisoners to pursue either academic or vocational training. Prisoners were required by policy to continue school until they tested at the fifth-grade level. A few prisoners refused to work or attend school or vocational training programs, but they were usually transferred or placed in segregation. Most prisoners were busy at work or school whether or not they believed in the rehabilitative ideal, and this promoted peace and stability.

The most effective order-promoting aspect of the rehabilitative ideal was more direct. With the indeterminate sentence system and with release decisions made by a parole board that used conformity to the prison routine as a principal indicator of rehabilitation and refused to review a prisoner who had received any serious disciplinary reports within six months, the message was clear: You conform or you will not be paroled. Most prisoners responded to the message.

However, even from the outset there were a few prisoners who were not persuaded to engage seriously in the rehabilitative programs, were not deterred by the threat of the indeterminate sentence system, and continued to get into trouble. This created a special problem for the administration, which was trying to implement the new, ostensibly nonpunitive routine. They solved it by opening up "adjustment centers" in each prison. The adjustment centers were segregation units where prisoners were held for indefi-nite periods with reduced privileges and virtually no mobility. The rationale for the units was that some prisoners needed more intensive therapy in a more controlled situation. In fact, no intensive therapy was ever delivered, and the adjustment centers were simply segregation units where troublesome prisoners could be placed summarily and indefinitely. By the end of the decade, the state could segregate a thousand prisoners in these units. The combination of these and the rehabilitative ideal with all its ramifications kept the peace for ten years.

The Seeds of Disruption

Later this peace was shattered by at least two developments that began in the 1950s in Soledad as well as other correctional institutions. First, black prisoners were increasing in numbers and assertiveness. They steadily moved away from their acceptance of the Jim Crow arrangement that prevailed in prison and began to assume equality in the prison informal world. As stressed above, many black prisoners crossed racial lines, maintained friendships with whites and Chicanos, and participated fully in all aspects of prison life. During most of the 1950s, the racially prejudiced white and Chicano prisoners disapproved of this, but rarely demonstrated their disapproval and prejudice. However, when black prisoners became more assertive and finally militant, racial hostilities intensified and set off an era of extreme racial violence, which disrupted the patterns of order based on tips and cliques.

Second, many prisoners in California and other states with correctional institutions eventually soured on rehabilitation and its artifacts. After years of embracing rehabilitation's basic tenets, submitting themselves to treatment strategies, and then leaving prison with new hope for a better future, they discovered and reported back that their outside lives had not changed. . . .

After prisoners were convinced that treatment programs did not work (by the appearance of persons who had participated fully in the treatment programs streaming back to prison with new crimes or violations of parole), hope shaded to cynicism and then turned to bitterness. The disillusioned increasingly shifted their focus from their individual pathologies to their life situation. They realized that under the guise of rehabilitation the correctionalists had gained considerable power over them and were using this power to coerce prisoners into "phony" treatment programs and "chickenshit" prison routines. In addition, they realized that parole boards arbitrarily, whimsically, and discriminatorily were giving many prisoners longer sentences and bringing them back to prison for violations of parole conditions that most prisoners believed to be impossible.

Rehabilitation inadvertently contributed to mounting criticism of itself by promoting a prison intelligentsia. Partly because of the expanded possibilities and the encouragement stemming from rehabilitation, more and more prisoners began educating themselves. Once we freed ourselves from the narrow conceptions contained in the rehabilitative philosophy, we began reading more and more serious literature. Most of us came from the working and lower-classes and had received very poor, if any, high school education. Our narrow life experience before and after school did nothing to expand our understanding. But in prison in the 1950s, with time on our hands, the availability of books, and the stimulation of the self-improvement message contained in the rehabilitative philosophy, we began to read. At first, we did not know how or what to read, so we read books on reading. Then when we acquired a preliminary sense of the classics, we plowed through them. Malcolm X expressed it well: "No university would ask any student to devour literature as I did when this new world opened to me, of being able to read and *understand*."[6] Most of us started with history, then turned to other areas: philosophy, literature, psychology, economics, semantics, and even mysticism. After several years of intense reading, we developed a relatively firm foundation in world knowledge. It was constructed under peculiar circumstances and in isolation from large intellectual enterprises; consequently, it was somewhat uneven and twisted here and there. But it was broad and mostly solid.

With this new perspective, we saw through things: our culture, society, the prison system, even our beloved criminal careers. They were all stripped of their original meanings, and what we saw made all of us critical and some of us bitter and cynical. . . . Our new understandings guided us in different directions. After being released, some of us "dropped out" and became bohemians or students. Others, particularly many blacks, became activists. Still others, finding no satisfying avenues of expression for their new perspective, returned to old criminal pursuits. But all of us, in different ways, continued to work on a criticism of the "system" and to spread this criticism. This eventually contributed heavily to the great disillusionment with and the eventual dismantling of the rehabilitative ideal. Racial conflict and the sense of injustice that followed this dismantling tore the correctional institution apart. . . .

Division began when black prisoners increased in number and shifted their posture in prisons. The latter change was linked to the civil rights and black movements outside, but it also had very unique qualities. For instance, the civil rights phase was never very important in prison. The tactics of the civil rights protectors were too gentle to catch the imagination of black prisoners, and the central issue, unequal treatment under the law, was not as apparently salient in prison. All convicts, to a greater degree than free citizens, were equally treated and mistreated under the law. Other aspects of the black movement, such as "black is beautiful" and black separatism, were more important in prison than on the outside. . . .

The Contemporary Prison

The reverberations from the 1960s left most men's prisons fragmented, tense, and often extremely violent. The old social order, with its cohesion and monotonous tranquility, did not and perhaps will never reappear. The prisoners are divided by extreme differences, distrust, and hatred. Nonwhites, especially blacks, Chicanos, and Puerto Ricans, have risen in numbers and prominence. A multitude of criminal types—dope fiends, pimps, bikers, street gang members, and very few old-time thieves—assert themselves and compete for power and respect.

Nevertheless, chaos and a complete war of all against all have not resulted. They never do. When human social organizations splinter and friction between the parts increases, people still struggle to maintain old or create new collective structures that supply them with basic social needs, particularly protection from threats of violence. Complex social forms and a high degree of order still exist among prisoners, even in the most violent and fragmented prisons, like San Quentin, but it is a "segmented order."

So it is in prison today. Races, particularly black and white, are divided and hate each other. In general, prisoners distrust most other prisoners whom they do not know well. The strategies for coping with this are similar to those employed in the Addams area. There are virtually no sex strata and much less age stratification in the prison, but increasingly prisoners restrict their interaction to small friendship groups and other small social units (gangs, for example) formed with members of their own race. Other than race, prisoners retreat into small orbits based on social characteristics such as (1) criminal orientation, (2) shared pre-prison experiences (coming from the same town or neighborhood or having been in other prisons together), (3) shared prison interests, and (4) forced proximity in cell assignment or work.

Racial Divisions

The hate and distrust between white and black prisoners constitute the most powerful source of divisions. After being forestalled by the moves toward unity during the prison movement, the conditions and trends discussed [earlier] were reestablished. Black prisoners continued to increase in numbers and assertiveness. Whites, led by the more prejudiced and violent, increasingly reacted. Hate, tension, and hostilities between the two races escalated. . . . White prisoners, whether or not they were racially hostile before prison, tend to become so after experiencing prison racial frictions. . . . Whites hate and, when they are not organized to resist, fear black prisoners.

The divisions and hatreds extend into the guard force and even into the administrations. . . . Black prisoners have consistently testified that white guards verbally and physically abuse them and discriminate against them.[7] Some radical commentators have suggested that guards and administrators have political motivations in their expression of racial hatred. This may be true, in some very indirect fashion. But the discrimination against blacks by white staff has a more immediate source: hatred for black prisoners. In expressing their hate, they sometimes give license to racist prisoners. . . .

White and black prisoners do not mix in informal prisoner groups, and many form groups for the purpose of expressing racial hatred and protecting their friends from the other race. A wife of a San Quentin prisoner described her husband's drift toward organized racial hatred:

> He didn't used to be prejudiced but now he hates blacks. He and some other white friends formed an American National Socialists group which I guess is a nazi group because they hate blacks so much. . . .

Other minority groups, such as Chicanos, Puerto Ricans Chinese, American Indians, and French Canadians, relate to whites and blacks in a more complex fashion. For instance, Chicanos in California prisons are more hostile toward black than toward white prisoners. White prisoners generally fear, distrust, and dislike Chicanos, because Chicanos speak Spanish or Calo and are believed to have a tendency to attack other prisoners with relatively less provocation than members of other groups. However, most white prisoners respect them for their toughness and do not threaten or derogate other white prisoners who befriend, hang around, or identify with Chicanos. Many white and Chicano prisoners have associated with each other in the "streets" and other joints and still maintain close friendship ties, even in the racially divided prison milieu. Puerto Rican, American Indian, French Canadian, and other racial or ethnic minorities have similar ambivalent positions in the complex racial matrix.

Violent Cliques and Gangs

In many men's prisons today, groups of prisoners regularly rob and attack other prisoners and retaliate when members of their clique or gang have been threatened or attacked. This has intensified the fear and widened the gap between prisoners, particularly between prisoners of different races. Presently these groups—which range from racially hostile cliques of reform school graduates, friends from the streets, biker club members, or tough convicts to large, relatively organized gangs—dominate several prisons.

Prisons have always contained violence-prone individuals, who were kept in check by the elders and the code enforced by the elders. In the 1950s and 1960s, small cliques of young hoodlums, such as the lowriders, hung around the yard and other public places together, talked shit (loudly bragged), played the prison dozens, occasionally insulted, threatened, attacked, and robbed unprotected weaker prisoners, and squabbled with other lowrider groups, particularly those of other races. . . . Most of these early

lowriders were young juvenile prison graduates and fuck-ups (unskilled, lower- and working-class criminals) who had low respect among older, "solid" criminals and regular convicts. But they were a constant threat to the other prisoners who were trying to maintain peace. For most of the 1950s and 1960s, other prisoners disparaged, ignored, and avoided the lowriders, whose activities were kept in check by the general consensus against them and the belief (accepted by the lowriders and most other prisoners) that if the lowriders went too far, the older prison regulars would use force, including assassination, to control them.

Lowriders steadily increased in numbers. In the states with large cities whose ghettos bulged during the 1950s and 1960s and whose youth prison systems expanded to accommodate the increase in youth crime, the adult prisons began to receive growing numbers of tough youth prison graduates and criminally unskilled, more openly aggressive young urban toughs. They could no longer be controlled. They entered the growing racial melee and stepped up their attacks and robberies on other prisoners. When there were no successful countermoves against them, they took over the convict world and particularly one of its most important activities: the sub rosa economic enterprises.

In different states the young hoodlums arrived at the adult prisons with different backgrounds and consequently formed different types of groups in the prison. In California the takeover began in 1967 in San Quentin when a tightly knit clique of young Chicanos, who had known each other on the streets of Los Angeles and in other prisons, began to take drugs forcefully from other prisoners (mostly Chicano). The clique gained a reputation for toughness and the label of "the Mexican Mafia." Other aspiring young Chicano hoodlums became interested in affiliating with the Mafia, and, according to rumor, the Mafia members insisted that initiates murder another prisoner. This rumor and the actual attacks aroused and consolidated a large number of "independent"

Chicanos, who planned to eliminate the Mafia members. On the planned day, the other Chicanos pursued known Mafia members through San Quentin, attempting to assassinate them. Several dozen prisoners were seriously wounded and one was killed in this day-long battle, but the Mafia held its ground, won many of the knife fights, and was not eliminated. After this unsuccessful attempt, some of the formerly independent Chicanos, particularly from Texas and the small towns in California who had been in conflict with Los Angles Chicanos for decades, formed a countergroup: La Nuestra Familia. In the ensuing years, the conflict between the two Chicano gangs increased and spread to other prisons and even to the outside, where the gangs have tried to penetrate outside drug trafficking. The attacks and counterattacks between members of the two gangs became so frequent that the prison administrators attempted to segregate the gangs, designating two prisons, San Quentin and Folsom for the Mafia and Soledad and Tracy for La Nuestra Familia. When Chicanos enter the California prison system, they are asked their gang affiliation; if they are to be sent to any of those four prisons (which are the medium- to maximum-security prisons), they are sent to one dominated by their gang.

The Chicano gangs' escalation of robbery, assault, and murder also consolidated and expanded black and white lowrider groups, some of which had already been involved in similar violent and rapacious activities. But on a smaller scale. Two gangs, the Aryan Brotherhood and the Black Guerilla Family, rose in prominence and violent activities. Eventually, the Aryan Brotherhood formed an alliance with the Mafia and the Black Guerilla Family with La Nuestra Familia, and a very hostile and tentative stalemate prevailed. However, peace has not returned. Other racist cliques among the black and white prisoners occasionally attack other prisoners; the Chicano gangs still fight each other; and there seem to be factions within the Chicano gangs themselves. Although the

California prisons have passed their peak of violence, the violence and fear are still intense.

In Illinois, black Chicago street gangs— the Blackstone Rangers (changed later to Black P Stone Nation), the Devil's Disciples, and the Vice Lords—and a Latin street gang named the Latin Kings spread into Stateville and finally took over the convict world. . . . By 1974 the aggressive black and Latin gangs had precipitated counterorganizations among white prisoners who, in their reduced numbers, had been extremely vulnerable to assault, robbery, rape, and murder by the other gangs.[8]

The activities of these violent groups who, in the pursuit of loot, sex, respect, or revenge, will attack any outsider have completely unraveled any remnants of the old codes of honor and tip networks that formerly helped to maintain order. In a limited, closed space such as a prison, threats of attacks like those posed by these groups cannot be ignored. Prisoners must be ready to protect themselves or act out of the way. Those who have chosen to continue to circulate in public, with few exceptions, have formed or joined a clique or gang for their own protection. Consequently, violence-oriented groups dominate many, if not most, large men's prisons.

The New Convict Identity

The escalation of violence and the takeover of the violent cliques and gangs have produced a new prison hero. Actually, the prison-oriented leader has been undergoing changes for decades. In our earlier study, Donald Cressey and I separated the prison world into two systems, one with the ideal type, the "right guy," who was oriented primarily to the prison.[9] In my later study of California prisons, conducted in a period when the right guy was disappearing, the "convict" identity was a blend of various vestigial criminal and prison identities.

This [the convict perspective] is the perspective of the elite of the convict world—the "regular." A "regular" (or, as he has variously called, "people," "folks," "solid," a "right guy," or "all right") possesses many of the traits of the thief's culture. He can be counted on when needed by other regulars. He is also not a "hoosier": that is, he has some finesse, is capable, is levelheaded, has "guts" and "timing."[10]

The upsurge of rapacious and murderous groups has all but eliminated the "right guy" and drastically altered the identity of the convict, the remaining hero of the prison world. Most of all, toughness has pushed out most other attributes, particularly the norms of tolerance, mutual aid, and loyalty to a large number of other regulars. Earlier, toughness was reemphasized as a reaction to the soft, cooperative "inmate" identity fostered by the rehabilitative ideal. . . . [T]he stiff and divisive administrative opposition weakened convict unity, and then the attacks of violent racial groups obliterated it. When the lowrider or "gang-banger" cliques turned on the remaining convict leaders (many had been removed from the prison mainline because of their political activities) and the elders were not able to drive the lowriders back into a position of subordination or otherwise to control them, the ancient regime fell and with it the old convict identity.

Toughness in the new hero in the violent men's prisons means, first, being able to take care of oneself in the prison world, where people will attack others with little or no provocation. Second, it means having the guts to take from the weak. . . .

In addition to threats of robbery, assaults, and murder, the threat of being raped and physically forced into the role of the insertee (punk or kid) has increased in the violent prison: "'Fuck it. It's none of my business. If a sucker is weak, he's got to fall around here. I came when I was eighteen and nobody turned me out. I didn't even smile for two years.'"[11]

Prison homosexuality has always created identity problems for prisoners. Long before today's gang era, many prisoners, particularly those with youth prison experiences, regularly or occasionally engaged in homosexual acts as inserters with queens, kids, or punks, though not without some cost to their own masculine definitions. There has been a cynical accusation repeated frequently in prison informal banter that prisoners who engaged in homosexual life too long finally learn to prefer it and, in fact, become full, practicing homosexuals, both insertees and inserters: "It was a jocular credo that after one year behind walls, it was permissible to kiss a kid or a queen. After five years, it was okay to jerk them off to 'get 'em hot.' After ten years, 'making tortillas' or 'flip-flopping' was acceptable and after twenty years anything was fine." The constant game of prison dozens among friends and acquaintances, in which imputation of homosexuality is the dominant theme, reflects and promotes self-doubt about masculinity. Presently, the threat of force has been added to the slower process of drifting into homosexuality, and fear about manhood and compensatory aggressive displays of manhood have increased drastically.

Today the respected public prison figure—the convict or hog—stands ready to kill to protect himself, maintains strong loyalties to some small group of other convicts (invariably of his own race), and will rob and attack or at least tolerate his friends' robbing and attacking other weak independents or their foes. He openly and stubbornly opposes the administration, even if this results in harsh punishment. Finally, he is extremely assertive of his masculine sexuality, even though he may occasionally make use of the prison homosexuals or, less often, enter into more permanent sexual alliance with a kid.

Convicts and Other Prisoners. Today prisoners who embrace versions of this ideal and live according to it with varying degrees of exactitude dominate the indigenous life of the large violent prisons. They control the contraband distribution systems, prison politics, the public areas of the prison, and any pan-prison activities, such as demonstrations and prisoner representative organizations. To circulate in this world, the convict world, one must act like a convict and, with a few exceptions, have some type of affiliation with a powerful racial clique or gang.

This affiliation may take various shapes. Most of the large racial gangs have a small core of leaders and their close friends, who constitute a tightly knit clique that spends many hours together. Moving out from this core, a larger group of recognized members are regularly called on by the core when the gang needs something done, such as assistance in an attack or display of force. Very often these fringe members are young aspiring initiates who want to be part of the inner core. Then, if the gangs are large, like the Mexican Mafia or the Black P Stone Nation, many more, sometimes hundreds of prisoners, claim an affiliation and are available when a massive display of force is needed.

Most prisoners who circulate in the convict world fall into one of the three categories. However, some highly respected convicts have very loose friendship ties with one or more of the gangs and circulate somewhat independently with immunity from gang attack. . . . A few very tough independents circulate freely, because they have withstood so many assaults from which they emerged victorious. Nevertheless, they still have to be careful with the more powerful gang members, because nobody can survive the attacks of a large group committed to murder.

In some large prisons a few prisoners who refrain from violent and sub rosa economic activities and devote themselves to form organizations and coalitions in order to pursue prisoners' rights and other political goals are tolerated by the gangs and other violent and rapacious prisoners. Occasionally, these organizers are able to create coalitions among warring gangs on particular issues. They have immunity only as long as they stay away from the other activities of the convict world and avoid disputes with the convict leaders.

Finally, other independents circulate freely, because they are viewed as unthreatening to the power of the convict leaders and they supply the convict world with some service. This includes characters and dings, who supply humor, and less desirable homosexuals. Younger, more desired homosexuals, however, must have affiliations with powerful individuals or groups.

In some of the large, more violent prisons, certain groups of prisoners, such as the Muslims and the cliques of "syndicate" men and their friends, are prominent in indigenous prison worlds even though they do not follow the aggressive and rapacious patterns of the gangs. Other prisoners believe that these groups will protect their members and retaliate against attacks; consequently, the other prisoners fear and respect them. These groups often become involved in a prison's informal political and economic activities and sometimes assume leadership in periods of disorder. When these groups are present and prominent, they are a stabilizing force that prevents the complete takeover by the violent cliques and gangs.

Withdrawal. [I]ncreasingly prisoners are shying away from public settings and avoiding the activities of the convict world. Although they occasionally buy from the racketeers, place bets with gamblers, trade commodities with other unaffiliated prisoners, or sell contraband on a very small scale, they stay away from the rackets and any large-scale economic enterprises. They dissociate themselves from the violent cliques and gangs, spend as little time as possible in the yard and other public places where gangs hang out, and avoid gang members, even though they may have been friends with some of them in earlier years. They stick to a few friends whom they meet in the cell blocks, at work, through shared interests, in other prisons, or on the outside (home boys). With their friends they eat, work, attend meetings of the various clubs and formal organizations that have abounded in the prison, and participate in leisure time activities together. Collectively, they have withdrawn from the convict world. . . .

The convicts disrespect those who withdraw, but usually ignore them: "If a dude wants to run and hide, that's all right." They even disrespect formerly high-status prisoners, such as older thieves, who previously received respect even if they avoided prison public life. Prisoners who withdraw occasionally have to display deference or acquiesce subtly in accidental public confrontations with convicts, but they face minimal danger of assault and robbery. This is much less true for young and effeminate prisoners, who will be pursued by aggressive, homosexually oriented convicts, perhaps threatened or raped, even if they attempt to stay to themselves and to avoid the convict world. Segregation may be their only safe niche.

The strategy of withdrawal has been encouraged and facilitated by prison administrations, which have always feared and hindered prisoner unity. The history of American prisons, in a sense, is a history of shifting techniques of separating prisoners. The original Pennsylvania prisons completely isolated prisoners. The Auburn system, which prevailed in the initial era of imprisonment in the United States because of cheap costs, employed the "silence system" to reduce interaction between prisoners and to forestall unity. More recently, the system of individualized treatment, emphasizing individual psychological adjustment, was a mechanism of psychological separation. In the last decade, convinced that large populations of prisoners are unmanageable, prison administrators have recommended, planned, and built smaller institutions for the primary purpose of separating prisoners into smaller populations. In the large prisons that are still used (not by choice, but by economic necessity) some states have split the prison into small units and have formally separated the prisoner population within the large prison. In many prisons these separate units (usually cell blocks with some additional staff and restrictions on access) vary in levels of privilege, some being designated "honor" units that offer many more privileges, more mobility for the residents, and less access for nonresidents.

Since the late 1960s, prison administrations have contravened the movements toward prisoner-organized unity by allowing, even encouraging many small apolitical organizations. . . . Prisoners who withdraw have certain channels provided by the administration to help them and make prison less onerous: if they maintain a clean disciplinary record, they can eventually move to an honor block or unit which houses a preponderance of persons who are withdrawing like themselves, which affords many more privileges, and to which access is restricted. In addition, they may fill in their leisure hours with formal organizational activities located in closed rooms away from the yard and other settings of the convict world.

More recently, in some prisons the administrations are combining the unit structure, segregation, and behavior modification into a system of hierarchial segregation that encourages withdrawal and conformity and greatly reduces contact between prisoners. . . .

This stratification system has succeeded in facilitating withdrawal, but has not eliminated violence in the prison. It has merely concentrated it in the lower levels of the hierarchy. Also, it has produced some added undesirable consequences. Individuals housed in the maximum-security (and more punitive) units become increasingly embittered and inured to violence. Many of them believe that they have been placed and are held there arbitrarily. (Often this is the case, because suspicions and prejudices operate in the classification to various units.) Intense hate between prisoners and guards builds up in the maximum-security units. Different clique and gang members, different races, and guards and prisoners verbally assault each other. Often guards on duty in the units, having grown especially hostile toward particular prisoners, depart from the formal routine and arbitrarily restrict the privileges of certain prisoners (for example, not releasing them for their allowed short exercise period).

All this precipitates regular violent and destructive incidents. San Quentin continues to experience incident after incident in its most secure and punitive units. In February 1978, for several days the prisoners in Max B fought among themselves during exercise periods and defied or even attacked guards who were trying to control them, even though they were risking injury, death, and long extensions of their segregation and prison sentences. More recently, in April 1979, a group of prisoners in the same unit continued to damage their cells for three days. They were protesting not having received their "issue" (toilet paper, tobacco, and the like), showers, or exercise periods for five weeks. They broke their toilets, tore out the electric lights in their cells, burned their mattresses, and pulled the plumbing from the walls. Finally, a large squad of guards (the "goon squad") brought them under control. A guard told Stephanie Riegel, a legal aide who had been informed of the incident by one of the prisoners involved, that "this type of destruction in that section is fairly routine."

Race and Withdrawal. The strategy of withdrawal is more open and appealing to white prisoners. In general, independent black prisoners are not as threatened by gangs. Blacks have more solidarity, and the black gangs tolerate the independents, most of whom are pursuing a more present-oriented expressive mode in prison. . . . Unless several black gangs become very organized and hostile to each other (as in Stateville), unaffiliated blacks participate much more in the convict world and hang around much more in public places, as the big yard.

With few exceptions, Chicanos in the large California prisons—Soledad, San Quentin, Folsom, and Tracy—must have at least a loose affiliation with one of the Chicano gangs. The gangs force this. However, many have token affiliations and actually withdraw and largely avoid the trouble and gang activity that abound in the convict world. However, they may occasionally be called on for some collective action; and if they ignore the gangs' call, they might be attacked. . . .

Concluding Remarks

This is the situation in many—too many—large, men's prisons: not chaos, but a dangerous and tentative order. It is not likely to improve for a while. The sources of conflict are deeply embedded in prisoners' cultural and social orientations. Most male prisoners are drawn from a social layer that shares extremely reduced life options, meager material existence, limited experience with formal, polite, and complex urban social organizations, and traditional suspicions and hostilities toward people different from their own kind. Prisoners, a sample with more extreme forms of these characteristics, are likely to be more hostile toward others with whom they do not share close friendships or cultural backgrounds and less firmly attached to the conventional normative web that holds most citizens together. For decades, the potentially obstreperous and conflictive population was held in a tentative peace by prisoner leaders, a code, and the constant threat of extreme force. When the informal system of peace disintegrated, the formal force was brought in, used (in fact, misused), withstood by the prisoners, and dissipated. For a short period, 1970 to 1973, prisoner organizers pursued the promise of some power for prisoners, mended some of the major rifts that were growing between groups of prisoners, and forestalled further fractionalizing. The administrations, because they fear prisoner political unity more than any other condition, smashed the incipient organizations and regenerated fractionalization. The parts scattered in familiar paths followed by other splintered populations of oppressed peoples: religious escapism, rapacious racketeering, fascism, and withdrawal.

The administrations are not happy with the results, but continue to apply old formulas to restore order. Mostly, they attempt to divide and segregate the masses and to crush the more obdurate prisoners. In California, for instance, the Department of Corrections has continued to search for gang leaders and other troublemakers, transfer those who are so labeled to the maximum-security prisons, and segregate them there in special units. The growing numbers of segregated prisoners are becoming more vicious and uncontrollable. In recent incidents at San Quentin the prisoners in a segregation unit fought among themselves and defied the guards for several days, even though they were risking injury, death, and extensions in their sentences. When the department has succeeded in identifying gang leaders and removing them, new leaders have sprouted like mushrooms. The prisons remain essentially the same.

The violent, hostile, and rapacious situation will probably continue until all prisoners are held in very small institutions of less than one or two hundred or completely isolated (both at astronomical costs) or until administrations begin to permit and cultivate among prisoners new organizations that can pull them together on issues that are important to them as a class. It seems obvious to me that these issues are the conditions of imprisonment and postprison opportunities. Thus, in order for these organizations to obtain and hold the commitment of a number of leaders and thereby to begin supplanting the violent, rapacious group structures, they will have to have some power in decision making. These organizations, however, are political in nature, and presently this idea is repulsive and frightening to prison administrations and the public.

Study Questions

1. Describe The Big House era in American prisons, including their architecture and social organization.

2. Why and how did the purpose of imprisonment in the correctional institutions change after World War II?

3. How were the major tenets of the correctional institutions (indeterminate sentencing, classification, and treatment)

intended to work together in rehabilitating inmates?

4. How did the inmate social system change from The Big House era to the "Correctional Institution" era, particularly in terms of indiginous argot roles as well as those imported from the outside?

5. What factors disrupted the order of the correctional institutions and ushered in the era of "Contemporary Prisons?"

6. Describe race relations throughout the various eras and how black power and gangs have changed the power structure in Contemporary Prisons.

7. How does the new convict identity in the Contemporary Prison differ from that of The Big House and the correctional institution?

Notes

1. Donald Clemmer, *The Prison Community* (New York: Holt, Rinehart & Winston, 1958), p. 7.

2. John Irwin and Donald Cressey, "Thieves, Convicts and the Inmate Culture," *Social Problems*, Fall 1963, p. 149.

3. Claude Brown, *Manchild in the Promised Land* (New York: Macmillan, 1965), p. 412.

4. Victor Nelson, *Prison Days and Nights* (Boston: Little, Brown, 1933), p. 219.

5. *Popeye* (Pamphlet distributed by Peoples' Court Comrades, San Francisco, 1975), p. 6.

6. *The Autobiography of Malcom X* (New York: Macmillan, 1965), p. 173.

7. *Attica: The Official Report of the New York State Special Commission on Attica* (New York: Prager, 1972) has the most convincing reports on such testimony.

8. *Stateville* (Chicago: University of Chicago Press, 1977), pp. 157–158.

9. "Thieves, Convicts, and the Inmate Culture," *Social Problems*, Fall 1963, pp. 145–148.

10. John Irwin, *The Felon* (Englewood Cliffs, NJ: Prentice Hall, 1970), p. 83.

11. Bunker, *Animal Factory* (New York: Viking Press, 1977), p. 32. ✦

11
Responding to Female Prisoners' Needs

Allison Morris

Chris Wilkinson

This article by Morris and Wilkinson continues to study the female offender in prison. The authors use a sample of 200 women who were incarcerated. The women were interviewed at three points—early in their sentence, just before release, and in the community postrelease. Information gathered from the surveys was used to detail the experiences within the walls of the institution, to discuss the major problems experienced (both prior to and during incarceration), and to note which needs were being met. The authors also interviewed prison workers to attain their views about whether the institution was meeting the needs of female offenders. Problems regarding the specific targeting of women (as well as the targeting of specific needs) are revealed and discussed. The reader is encouraged to consider how well today's institution (a) meets the needs of the general offender population and (b) addresses the needs of specific subpopulations.

I had been burgled; I wasn't getting any support. I was being messed around with benefits. I tried all other avenues and I was vulnerable. That's what led to my offense.

I've got a drinking problem; I drink a lot; it's just to get the money to drink—that's why I commit the crimes.

Excerpts from *The Prison Journal*, Volume 75, Number 3 (September 1995). Pages 295–305. Copyright © 1995 by Sage Publications, Inc. Reprinted by permission.

I just needed money, that's basically why I'm in here. I couldn't cope living on the social. I'd just got a new house and I wanted to make it nice.

The public's expectation of imprisonment is not only that it will be made safe but that during the sentence efforts will be made to "rehabilitate" offenders so that when they are released, they will be able to be reintegrated into society (Lee, 1994). This must involve in part addressing the diverse needs that prisoners have and, in particular, addressing those needs that seem to be related to their offending: drug or alcohol use, lack of work skills, and so on. In most countries, arrangements are now in place to do this: analysis of needs on entry to prison, periodic review (for example, by case management or sentence planning), and so on. This article describes some of the difficulties in achieving this on the basis of research recently completed in three women's prisons in England.[1]

We interviewed 200 women.[2] Most were interviewed at three different points: early in their sentence, prerelease, and postrelease in the community. Women who were released after sentences of more than 2 years could only be interviewed at two points, prerelease and postrelease.[3] In all, we were able to make contact with 173 of the women some 3 to 6 months after their release: a follow-up rate of 87%. We were able, therefore, to track many of the women from some point in their sentence through to postrelease and to determine both what they saw as their needs and how the prisons (and the probation service) were responding to these needs.[4]

Because almost a quarter of the women were known to have reoffended within the short follow-up period, it is important also to try to assess the extent to which this reoffending was related to needs that had remained unaddressed or unresolved during their prison sentences. This article attempts to do so. But first it describes the main characteristics of the women, the strategies in place for addressing their needs, and the difficulties the women identified with these strategies.

Characteristics of the Women

The women in this sample were broadly typical, except for their ethnic background,[5] of female prisoners elsewhere. They were relatively young,[6] they were relatively unsophisticated in criminal terms,[7] and they were mainly in prison for property offenses.[8] Over 40% were mothers of dependent children and nearly half of these mothers were single parent mothers. Almost 60% of the women said that they were living solely on benefits prior to their imprisonment. Just under a quarter said they had been in paid work prior to their imprisonment, and more than a quarter of the women who were unemployed said that they had never worked. Almost one half of the women reported having used drugs prior to their imprisonment, and more than half of these women associated their offending with their drug use. Nearly one quarter described themselves as having a drinking problem; two thirds of these women also reported drug use. One third of the women said that they had debts, often the result of their alcohol or drug use. Nearly one quarter of the women reported harming themselves, either by slashing/cutting or by attempting suicide prior to their imprisonment. Nearly half of the women reported having been physically abused prior to their imprisonment, and nearly one third of the women reported having been sexually abused prior to their imprisonment.[9]

This description of the women's characteristics provides clear pointers for penal policy and action: for example, programs to increase women's job skills and, in particular, to address drug and alcohol use. Generally, we expected those women most in need to be targeted for assistance by prison or probation staff. This did not happen.

Work Inside Prison

As we noted above, less than a quarter of the women said they were in paid work prior to their imprisonment. More than a quarter of the women who were unemployed also said that they had never worked. At the same time, more than half of the women in our sample said lack of work was a major factor in their offending. Increasing these women's work skills was, therefore, arguably a priority.[10]

However, the women in this sample seem to have been allocated to jobs in prison on the basis of current vacancies, their interest, and their apparent suitability, but not on the basis of their need for job skills.[11] The emphasis in prison with respect to work seemed to be much more on settling the women into prison routines, passing the time, servicing the institution, and teaching women about the "work habit" than about providing women with the opportunity to acquire skills that might be useful for life after release. Only a minority of the women believed that they had learned any skills in prison,[12] and few left prison with new work skills.

Dealing With Drug Use

We identified about a quarter (47) of the women in the sample as high drug users (regular users of drugs other than cannabis), and slightly more than a fifth (43) as medium drug users (cannabis users or occasional or less frequent users of other drugs). Women who were high drug users tended to have been using drugs for longer, they reported spending considerable sums of money on drugs, and they were also more likely to report that getting into trouble had resulted from using drugs. Even so, there was little difference between the two groups in the way that drugs were paid for: the percentages saying that they had purchased drugs from the proceeds of crime (for example, from shoplifting or other types of theft) were similar.

Only 14 out of the 90 women who admitted drug use had had any kind of drug program during their imprisonment. All but one of these were high drug users. This means that 33 of the 47 women we categorized as high drug users had not been targeted in any way during their prison sentence as in need of treatment or counseling for their drug use.

Dealing With Alcohol Use

Alcohol was viewed as a problem by a quarter of the women we talked with. We categorized one fifth (40) as high alcohol users (women who said they had an alcohol problem, who linked their alcohol use to their offending, and/or spent more than £50 a week on alcohol) and 5% (10) as medium alcohol users (women who said they had an alcohol problem, who did not link their alcohol use to their offending, and who spent less than £50 a week on alcohol). Only 14 of the 50 women who felt they had an alcohol problem said they had had some treatment while in prison: again, all were women in the high problem group. This meant that 26 out of the 40 women we categorized as high alcohol users had never been targeted during their prison sentence for any kind of treatment or counseling.

Strategies for Meeting Women's Needs

The three sample prisons had five overarching strategies for addressing the needs of some of the women, although their practice and emphasis varied. These were:

Personal officer scheme: links an individual prison officer with an individual prisoner with a view to developing a close relationship and providing help and support (at the time of the research, this was primarily aimed at lifers and long-term prisoners but not exclusively so).[13]

Sentence planning: described as ensuring "that the best use is made of an inmate's time while in custody and to provide an op-portunity to keep an inmate's progress under review"; also described as helping offenders "face up to and tackle their offending behavior and give them a planned experience of work, training, and education to help prepare them for release" (primarily at the time of the research aimed at women serving 12 months or more but again this was not exclusively so).[14]

Sentence plans are meant to be prepared within the first month of women's arrival after discussion between the woman and her sentence plan (or equivalent) officer. Targets are set then, such as addressing women's offending behavior, drug addiction, and so on; these targets are meant to be recorded and reviewed at meetings that include the woman and a number of staff members, not necessarily known to the woman, at set intervals.

Shared working: combines the efforts of prison officers and prison-based probation staff to meet prisoners' welfare and social needs. (In operation at the time of the research in two of the three prisons).[15]

Contact with the women's prison-based probation officer.

Contact with the women's home-based probation officer.

In addition, prison staff played a general role in responding to women's needs. We will review each of these in turn.

Personal Officers

Overall, less than half the women in the sample said that they had a personal officer. Although more than half of those who did said they were happy with them, more than 40% had reservations. The reservations had to do with concerns about the prison officer's lack of availability, confidentiality, and a lack of trust; some prisoners dismissed the officers' skills, and others believed that officers could or would do very little. Sometimes there was a clash of personalities in which prisoners had no choice about the officer allocated.

Sentence Planning

Although some women spoke very positively about sentence planning, the women interviewed raised a range of reservations: difficulties in establishing a relationship with the sentence planning (or equivalent) officer allocated; disbelief that something would actually be done as a result of the plan; concerns about the accuracy of the assessments made of them; and concerns about the size of the meetings and their intimidating nature. Both the women and the staff seemed to lack an understanding of the purpose of sentence planning. Women were not given the information they required to consider what might be an appropriate plan for themselves and to actively participate in the planning process. Thus they lacked confidence in the staff's ability to meet the targets identified, in the meaningfulness of the process, and in the confidentiality of the material discussed. The women's view was that sentence planning was largely a paper exercise.

Shared Working

We identified a number of problems with the practice of shared working that arose during our interviews and observations. First, the meaning of shared work and the implications of this were not well explained to the women, demonstrating a lack of communication. Women said they had asked to see a probation officer but ended up seeing a prison officer. From the woman's point of view, this meant confidentiality had been breached at the outset (she may also have deliberately chosen not to speak to an officer or even that particular officer). Women also tended to see this as downgrading their problem.

Second, shared working could also mean that everyone had responsibility and so no one in particular followed up to discover whether or not appropriate (or any) action had been taken, demonstrating a lack of monitoring. Third, there were also logistical difficulties in communicating to members of the shared work team what was going on because of shift work or because staff were pulled off wing duties due to staff shortages or competing demands, demonstrating both a lack of continuity and a lack of commitment.

Women's Contact With Prison-Based Probation Officers

We have already touched implicitly on the role of the prison-based probation officers in our reference to shared working. However, most of the women in the sample had some other contact with prison-based probation officers, even if it was only of a routine nature early in their sentence.[16] A crucial issue for the research was whether or not the women most in need were those who had the most contact with prison-based probation officers. We measured this at two points in the women's sentence: initially and prerelease.

When we compared the women's levels of problems/needs in each of our initial categorizations by the extent of their contact (one to three times, occasional, and regular), in only one category (accommodation) was there significantly more contact when the woman was rated as having a high need. Also, when we divided the women into those with high, medium and low problems or needs, we found no relationship between the level of women's problems and the extent of their contact with the prison-based probation officer.

The same pattern emerged when we compared the extent of contact the women had with probation officers at the prerelease stage: again, only in the accommodation category was there a significant relationship between the two and, indeed, only accommodation needs were significantly lessened at this stage, compared to initial assessments.

Although responses to some problems such as drug use and alcohol use may have been targeted elsewhere within the prison, it is surprising that so many women with identifiable difficulties had had only minimal contact with prison-based probation officers.

Contact With Home-Based Probation Officers

Home probation officers were asked whether or not there were any problems that needed sorting out during the woman's prison sentence. Almost two thirds said there were none. This is a quite remarkable statistic, given the characteristics of the sample. Those probation officers who identified problems rarely mentioned drug or alcohol use, debts, or employment.

Prison Officers' Views on Responding to Women's Needs

We asked prison officers how well they felt they responded to women's needs. Responses varied somewhat according to the prison in which they worked, but about three quarters of the officers we talked with stated that they encountered difficulties in responding to women's needs. Lack of time and lack of resources were the factors most commonly mentioned. Overall, about a third felt that they were not adequately trained for some of the responsibilities expected of them. Sizable minorities thought that cooperation within the prison was itself a problem. Only between a half and a quarter (depending on the prison) felt supported by management. Low morale about future directions within the prison service was also mentioned by some officers. All of this must have had an indirect effect on prisoners and on officers' responses to women's needs.

Specific Preparation for Release

Theoretically, everything done in prison is in preparation for a woman's release. We have already raised questions about the reality of this with respect to work, alcohol and drug abuse, the extent of women's contact with the probation service, and so on. In this section we turn to one further measure of whether or not the women most in need were those who had had the most help in prison: attendance at prerelease courses.

Prerelease Courses

Overall, at the time of the prerelease interview, just over a quarter of the sample had attended or expected to attend a prerelease course in prison. We found no significant relationship between attending or expecting to attend a prerelease course and our categorization in any of the problem areas. In other words, we found no evidence to suggest that women were targeted for such courses according to the problems they might face on release.

Summary

What we have seen from this review is that many of the women in the sample had identifiable needs on entry to prison, but that these needs were not necessarily well met by the strategies then in place. Sometimes nothing much was done in relation to specific and identified needs because a woman's sentence was supposedly too short. Sometimes women with long sentences who were unexpectedly granted parole were released with little having been done to prepare them for release.

Reoffending by the Women

Thirty-three of the 173 women we interviewed postrelease said that they had reoffended, although not all of these offenses were known to the police. Home probation officers were also asked whether or not the women released into their area had reoffended. Ten probation officers reported that a woman had reoffended when the woman herself had not admitted it to the researcher. Another four probation officers reported that women we had been unable to trace had reoffended. If we combine what the women said with what probation officers reported, we find that almost a quarter of the 200 women in the sample were known to have reoffended within a relatively short time—that is to say, within 3 to 6 months of their release.[17]

We looked more closely at those women who had reoffended, and it was immediately apparent that these women had a number of distinctive difficulties:

> Almost half described their accommodations as unsatisfactory, compared with only 14% of those who had not reoffended.

> Almost half said that they were not managing financially, compared with a quarter of those who had not reoffended.

> More than a third said that drug use was a drain on their income, compared with only 3% of those who had not reoffended.

> Almost a quarter said that alcohol use was a drain on their income, compared with 4% of those who had not reoffended

> Only 12% were in paid employment, compared with more than a fifth of those who had not reoffended.

Overall, then, the women who reoffended were more likely to report unsatisfactory accommodation, financial difficulties, drug problems, drugs and alcohol as a drain on their income, and a lack of paid employment.[18] Significantly, more than 40% of the reoffenders were young adults when sentenced, compared with only 15% of those who had not reoffended. Put another way, 20 out of the 39 young adult offenders in the sample had reoffended. These statistics raise questions about whether or not the women's reoffending was both predictable and pre-ventable, given their characteristic and situation before their imprisonment.

Conclusion

A number of specific mechanisms for addressing prisoners' needs exist in English prisons. This research focused in particular on the personal officer scheme, sentence planning, and shared working. Not all of these were in operation in all the sample prisons, and not all prisoners had experience of each. Some strategies were also still in the early days of their development. However, certain points can be drawn from the research.

Women expressed concern about confidentiality, about prison officers' availability, commitment, and skills, and about being able to establish a relationship with a nominated officer. They also felt that they did not have sufficient information to participate actively in the planning process. In addition, the number of people present at sentence planning meetings was seen as threatening, particularly when the woman felt she did not know all those present.

Specific problems (including a lack of communication and a lack of monitoring) were apparent with respect to shared working. Prison officers themselves were aware of many of these difficulties. Overall, about a third of the staff we talked with felt that they were not adequately trained for some of the work expected of them. What this research has indicated, therefore, is that there are difficulties in implementing these various strategies for meeting women's needs and that, at the time of the research, there were limitations in existing systems. No matter how good a particular system looks on paper, it means little if it is not translated into reality.

A crucial issue for the research was whether or not the women most in need were targeted for appropriate help or advice. This was not the case. Specifically, we found that only a minority of the women believed that they had learned any skills within prison, and few left prison with new work skills. More than 70% of the 47 women we categorized as high drug users, and more than two thirds of the 40 women we categorized as high alcohol users, had never been targeted in prison for any kind of treatment or counseling. We also found no relationship between the level of women's problems and the extent of their contact with the prison-based probation officer, and no significant relationship between attending a prerelease course and our categorization in any of the problem areas. This meant that women could leave prison with their needs unaddressed. It would be difficult to argue that this was not a factor in at least some women's reoffending, for example, in the case of those women for whom drug use was a problem.

Some changes have occurred since this research was completed; for example, more prisoners are now subject to sentence planning, more courses leading to a work qualification are available, and more pay phones have been installed. The research does, however, raise more fundamental issues that require consideration. Most of the strategies introduced to address prisoners' needs in English prisons (and the probation service's response to them) are related to the length of a prisoner's sentence. As a result, many of the women in this sample missed out because of their short sentences. Yet there was little evidence that the severity of women's needs or their likelihood of reoffending was linked to sentence length. Given limited resources, it seems self-evident that those most in need, and not those serving a sentence of a particular length, should be among those selected for particular programs, help, or advice. The results of this study underline the importance of both targeting and the need to respond to women's needs proactively. In terms of both preventing reoffense and ensuring that prisoners do not leave prison in a worse situation than they entered, sentence length is an inappropriate guide for practice.

Study Questions

1. Through what method did the authors investigate the population under consideration in this study?

2. What were the primary needs identified by the female prison population?

3. Discuss which of the five "overarching strategies" identified by the authors hold the most promise for meeting the needs of female prisoners.

4. In what ways were female prisoners prepared for release from the institution?

Notes

1. The project was funded by the Home Office Research and Planning Unit.

2. Data were collected primarily between January 1993 and January 1994 from a variety of sources using a number of research methods. In addition to interviewing the women, we observed a number of key stages in the prison process, for example, reception, visits, and sentence planning meetings. We extracted data from prison and probation records, analyzed data from criminal records provided by the National Identification Bureau (NIB), interviewed or received questionnaires from a sample (49) of prison officers, and interviewed most Governor grades, senior probation officers, and education officers in all three prisons. We also carried out a survey of all the women's home-based probation officers (155 responded, a response rate of 78%). In the closing stages of the project, we visited all the other women's prisons (except remand centers), where we interviewed some Governor grades, senior probation officers, and education officers about the issues raised by the research.

3. Slightly more than two fifths of the women in the sample were sentenced to less than 12 months imprisonment (12% were sentenced to less than 3 months) and slightly more than two fifths were sentenced to more than 12 months but less than 4 years. Only 12% of the women in the sample were sentenced to 4 years or more. The sample was not entirely representative of receptions into women's establishments in that it contained, as had been planned, a higher proportion of women serving longer sentences. In terms of the length of

time actually served in prison, almost three quarters of the women in the sample spent less than 9 months in prison (half spent less than 6 months in prison and 13% less than 3 months). One fifth of the women were in prison for more than 12 months, but only 9% were there for 2 years or more.

4. We categorized the women at different stages in their sentence according to a number of potential problems or needs. These included accommodation, drug abuse, alcohol abuse, physical and/or sexual abuse and/or self-harm, as well as problems to do with relationships, child care, financial situation, and employment. At each point, we categorized the women as high, medium, or low/none in need.

5. Prison files described 90% of the sample as White. This over-representation may have been a result of the prisons chosen for the research or the size of the prison population when the samples were drawn. Alternatively ethnic minority women sentenced after October 1, 1992, may have received sentences outside the parameters of the research and the methodology used to determine the sample. A sample based on through put or release dates is by definition nonselective and depends on chance factors. The sample was not targeted.

6. About two thirds were under 30 at the time of their sentence, and just under a quarter were under 21.

7. Almost one third of the women were first offenders and, according to data provided by the NIB, about two thirds were serving their first custodial sentence.

8. Only 20% had committed violent or sex offenses, and 15% had committed drug offenses.

9. It is likely that these are both underestimates, given what we know about violence against women generally.

10. Realistically, it has to be accepted that not all female prisoners want to or are able to work after they are released from prison because of other responsibilities, and so work in prison may take on a different significance for them.

11. What was actually available in terms of work in the three sample prisons varied to some extent, but certain jobs were offered in all prisons: for example, working in the kitchens, laundry, or officers' mess or being an orderly or house cleaner.

12. There was an apparent paradox here between the relatively high percentage of women saying that they were doing the prison job they wanted and the relatively low percentage saying that they had been taught skills in prison. This may reflect the low expectations that the women had of themselves or the low expectations they had of prison work.

13. Women serving 12 months or more were more likely than women serving under 12 months to have personal-officers. Young offenders also tended to have personal officers.

14. None of our sample was officially subject to sentence planning, but some form of sentence planning was in operation in all three sample prisons.

15. In one, individual prison officers (through care officers) were attached full time to the prison's probation department; in the other, prison officers performed welfare tasks in the course of their normal duties in a team that also included probation officers.

16. Methods for making contact with probation officers differed from prison to prison: it was through the shared working scheme in one, through written applications in another, and through surgeries in the third. More generally, prison-based probation officers worked both reactively with individual women (for example, in response to direct requests for help) and proactively (for example, by making women aware of their presence).

17. We have no information for 21 women.

18. We compared women's offending with the ratings in the different problem or needs categories we had identified at the prerelease stage. These findings were broadly but not entirely consistent with the above statistics: drug use and accommodation problems were significantly related to offending, and employment problems only just failed to reach significance. Drug use was the factor that featured most commonly in the women's accounts of their reoffending.

Reference

Lee, A. (1994). Public attitudes towards crime and criminal justice. *Criminal Justice Quarterly*, 8,4–8.

The authors would like to acknowledge the help and support of Andrea Tisi, Jane Woodrow, and Ann Rockley, Nottingham Trent University, in carrying out the research and making this article possible. ✦

12
Supermax Prisons
Panacea or Desperation?

Rodney J. Henningsen

W. Wesley Johnson

Terry Wells

Most penal institutions have developed a portion of the building dedicated to inmates who are experiencing within-institutional punishment, those not able to control themselves satisfactorily in the general prison population. These sections of prisons are generally referred to as "administrative segregation" units. As a recent development, the "supermax" prison represents an institution designed to house nothing but offenders who are not able to control themselves within a general inmate population. The authors discuss how popular these institutions have become within the political realm, as they represent the ultimate "get tough" strategy. Supermax prisons are characterized by solitary confinement, near 24-hour lockdown, and a total lack of congregation and severely limited interaction with other human beings. As such, the model has experienced criticism, particularly regarding the effects of extended solitary confinement. Although true "total control" does appear to be achieved in the supermax institution, the control comes at a cost. The authors identify the costs as including accusations of human rights violations and describe a "psychologically assaultive" environment that creates

long-term damage. The reader is encouraged to contemplate the problems inherent in the creation of a "supermax" prison, while simultaneously considering what "ordinary" prisons should do with those who simply cannot conform, even in a maximum-security setting.

For over a century Americans have sought to find the silver bullet to solve its crime problems. Fads and experiments in corrections have included public humiliation, single-celling, silent systems, 12-step recovery programs, boot camps, electronic surveillance, and now, supermax. Supermax prisons have evolved out of America's love-hate relationship with crime and punishment. A supermax prison has been defined as:

> A free-standing facility, or distinct unit within a facility, that provides for the management and secure control of inmates who have been officially designated as exhibiting violent or seriously disruptive behavior while incarcerated. Such inmates have been determined to be a threat to safety and security in traditional high-security facilities, and their behavior can be controlled by separation, restricted movement, and limited access to staff and other inmates.[1]

At least in theory, this type of prison unit can and should be distinguished from administrative segregation (ad-seg). While most every prison has administrative segregation cells used for holding prisoners in short-term disciplinary or protective custody, supermax units are designed to house prisoners for a much longer period of time. Proponents of supermax prisons contend that they warehouse the worst of the worst, the most violent prisoners who threaten the security of guards and other prisoners while undermining the moral fabric of American society.

While the American public has increasingly turned to government for solutions to its social problems in the last 30 years, its perceptions of the criminal justice system have remained jaundiced. Over 75 percent of respondents in a recent national survey re-

Excerpts from *Corrections Management Quarterly,* Volume 3, Number 2 (1999). Pp. 53–59. Copyright © 1999 by Aspen Publishers, Inc. Reprinted by permission.

ported only "some" or "very little" confidence in state prison systems.[2] Similarly, over 80 percent of people surveyed each year since 1980 have indicated that the courts are too soft on crime.[3]

The American judiciary has responded to public concerns that they are soft on crime and cries for vengeance by placing more people under correctional supervision than ever before. To accommodate the increases in new prison admissions and increases in time served by prisoners, some 168 state and 45 federal prisons have been built since 1990. Today, there are a total of approximately 1,500 state and federal prisons. Between 1990 and 1995, the number of prison beds increased by 41 percent. Despite this tremendous fiscal investment, there are both state and federal prisons that operate in excess of their design capacity, state prisons by 3 percent and federal prisons by 24 percent.[4]

While there are more prisons and prisoners than ever before, there is sustained interest in making prisons even "tougher."[5] This interest may be based on the notion, not strongly supported in the criminological research on recidivism, that prisons deter. Another reason may be simply that victims of crime, and those that see themselves as potential victims, want prisoners to suffer. While harm is a critical component of punishment, its generic application to prison life creates unique challenges for correctional officers, staff, and correctional executives.[6]

Political Popularity of Supermax Prisons

Getting tough on crime has become an increasingly popular campaign platform among elected officials, and support of supermax institutions is a politically popular position in many areas across the country. The American judiciary has also supported the need for supermax prison environments. In *Bruscino v. Carlson*, federal prisoners at Marion, Illinois, sought compensation for the attacks on them by correctional officers during the October 1983 shakedown and relief from the ongoing conditions created by the subsequent lockdown. A 1985 U.S. Magistrate's Report approved by the U.S. District Court for Southern Illinois in 1987 indicated that 50 prisoners who testified to beating and other brutalities were not credible witnesses, and that only the single prisoner who testified that there were no beatings was believable.[7] When the prisoners appealed the decision, the ruling of the Fifth Circuit Court of Appeals described conditions at Marion as "ghastly," "sordid and horrible," and "depressing in extreme," but the court maintained that they were necessary for security reasons and did not violate prisoners' constitutional rights.[8]

The 'New' Controversial Control Models

Today, control units go by many different names. They have been referred to as adjustment centers, security housing units, maximum control complexes, administrative maximum (Ad-Max), special housing units, violence control units, special management units, intensive management units, management control units, or "supermax" prisons. These new units are designed to subdue any and all resistance to order. A survey by the Federal Bureau of Prisons conducted in 1990 found that 36 states operated some form of supermax security prison or unit within a prison.[9] At that time, another six states were planning to build supermax prisons. By 1993, 25 states had specialized control units and control unit prisons were in operation in every part of the country.

> *At Pelican Bay Prison there is no congregate dining or congregate exercise, and there are no work opportunities or congregate religious services. Prisoners are denied standard vocational, educational, and recreational activities.*

The new model for high-security prisons is the security housing unit (SHU) at Pelican Bay Prison in California. Pelican Bay opened in December 1989.[10] Prisoners in such units are kept in solitary confinement in relatively small cells between 22 and 23 hours a day. There is no congregate dining or congregate exercise, and there are no work opportunities or congregate religious services. Prisoners are denied standard vocational, educational, and recreational activities.

The conditions are officially justified not as punishment for prisoners, but as an administrative measure. Prisoners are placed in control units as a result of an administrative decision. Because such moves are a result of an administrative decision, prisoners' ability to challenge such changes in imprisonment is severely limited. Today, throughout the country, conditions in "new" supermax prisons closely resemble those set forth at Pelican Bay.

Since their inception, supermax prison units have had their opponents. Typically, opponents have focused upon conditions that allegedly are illegal or inhumane. In some reports, prison guards have testified to shackling prisoners to their beds and spraying them with high-pressure fire hoses. Other criticisms have centered on issues surrounding

- arbitrary placement/assignment to control unit
- the long-term psychological effects from years of isolation from both prison and outside communities while being housed in solitary or small group isolation (celled 22.5 hours/day)
- denial of access to educational, religious, or work programs
- physical torture, such as forced cell extractions, four-point restraint and hog-tying, caging, beating after restraint, back-room beatings, and staged fights for officer entertainment
- denial of access to medical and psychiatric care

- mental torture, such as sensory deprivation, forced idleness, verbal harassment, mail tampering, disclosing confidential information, confessions forced under torture, and threats against family and visitors[11]

Arbitrary Placement

Prisoners are plated in high-security units for administrative and/or disciplinary reasons.

Such decisions are based on results during (re-) classification hearings. Critics have called the hearings a kangaroo court claiming prisoners are being denied due process. What is called misbehavior is (arbitrarily) decided by the guard on duty and has been known to include refusing to make beds or complaining about clogged and overflowing toilets.[11]

Violations of Human Rights and Abuses

There are many claims of human rights violations and abuses in control units, including denial of medical care to injured and/or sick prisoners (including diabetics and epileptics), extremely cold cells during winter months and extremely hot cells during summer months, arbitrary beatings, psychological abuse of mentally unstable prisoners, illegal censorship of mail, extended isolation and indoor confinement, denial of access to educational programs, and administrative rather than judicial decisions about punishment for misbehaved prisoners.[12,13]

Ability to Reduce Violence in Prisons and Society

Prison officials claim that Marion, Pelican Bay, and the other supermax-type control units reduce violence in the rest of the prison system. All the evidence points to the opposite being true. The creation of control units and increased use of administrative segregation have not reduced the level of violence within general prison populations. In fact, assaults on prison staff nationwide rose from 175 in 1991 [in] 906 to 1993.[14] The number of inmate assaults on prison employees reached 14,000 in 1995. That was up 32 percent from 1990. The number of assaults per 1,000 employees remained stable at 15. It may also be that the potential of supermax prisons to reduce overall prison violence has yet to be realized. As more disruptive inmates are placed in supermax prison cells, assaults in prisons may decline.

While supermax prisons provide correctional executives with another weapon to facilitate order in prison, most supermax prisoners are released back into the general prison population or into society. Conditions in control units produce feelings of resentment and rage and exacerbate mental deterioration.[15] It is anticipated that control unit prisoners who re-enter the general prison population or society will have even greater difficulty coping with social situations than in the past.

The Texas Experience

Overcrowding and the control of violence are critical issues in correctional management, especially in states like Texas where the federal government, in *Ruiz v. Texas,* declared the entire department of corrections unconstitutional. As a result of the Ruiz decision, the federal government actively monitored virtually every facet of the Texas Department of Corrections—Institutional Division for over 20 years. In attempts to shed federal control over Texas prisons, relieve massive prison overcrowding, and avoid future lawsuits, an unprecedented number of new prisons were built in a relatively short period of time. In August 1993, the Texas Department of Criminal Justice, one of the largest correctional systems in the world, operated 54 inmate facilities.[16] By August 1998, the number of correctional facilities in Texas doubled, housing prisoners in 107 correctional facilities.[17]

According to David Stanley, of the Executive Services, Texas Department of Criminal Justice—Institutional Division, Texas prisons will soon be at maximum capacity again. In August 1997, Texas's men's prisons were at 98 percent of their capacity, while women's prisons approached 85 percent of their design capacity. Currently, there are about 126,000 men and 10,000 women incarcerated in Texas prisons. Estimates are that maximum design capacity for housing male inmates will be reached in little more than a year. If current inmate population trends continue, many institutions across the country will be operating above design capacity. These factors, combined with the fact that more violent offenders are now entering prisons at an earlier age for longer periods of time than just a decade ago, affect correctional administrators' ability to maintain order and protect their own staff from assaults.[14]

In attempts to keep the lid on a more volatile prison population, Texas has been one of the first states to make a commitment to new prison construction and new state-of-the-art high-security, supermax correctional facilities. This commitment has required an investment of substantial tax revenues. The new high-security prisons, according to a spokesman for the Texas Department of Criminal Justice-Institutional Division, Larry Fitzgerald, are being built and designed with efficiency and economy in mind. The estimated cost of the some 1,300 beds (double-celled) in the new control units will be a mere $19,000 compared to the current national average of $79,770 per maximum-security bed. Costs are being reduced by using inmate labor for nonsecurity tasks, such as masonry, painting, and welding.

Currently, one high-security unit has been completed near Huntsville, Texas and construction on two other similar units has already begun. Officials estimated that inmate labor saved Texas taxpayers over 2 million dollars in the construction of the new control unit near Huntsville, Texas. Currently, high-security inmates are housed in single-cells.[18]

On August 4, 1997, inmates began arriving at the new $25 million high-security unit of the Texas prison system. The high-security unit is located on the grounds of the Estelle Unit near Huntsville. Similar to high-security units in other states, Texas inmates who are placed in the new high-security unit are put there for one of three reasons: (1) they have tried to escape; (2) they pose a physical threat to staff or inmates; or (3) they are members of disruptive groups, such as an organized gang. Approximately 50 percent to 60 percent of the current residents have been officially classified as belonging to a particular gang.

The Gilbane Corporation, with the help of inmates, began construction on the 65,780 square foot facility in October 1995. Outside, two motion detector fences surround the prison. The exterior of the new unit, although secured by electronic surveillance of the outer fence and certain portions of the building and a patrol vehicle, ironically gives less of the appearance of a traditional fortress prison in that there is no guard tower. Some have likened its appearance to that of a modern high school gym.

Despite its relative benign external appearance, its overall design seeks to provide an alternative for the most recalcitrant inmates. Although two beds per cell are still found in accordance with the original plan, a change from the original purpose of the facility now calls for one inmate per cell. While it would be possible to house 1,300 inmates, the current plan is to house only 650 inmates.

The building has a central corridor with two-story wings on the east and west sides. The east wings contain 63 cells with two beds per cell. The east side recreation yard is 22,451 square feet with 42 individual yards. The west wings have 67 cells with two beds per cell. The west side recreation yard is 24,857 square feet and contains 40 individual yards.

The concern for security prompted the design to establish 8 x 10-foot cells. Unlike the traditional cell with barred doors, all doors on this unit consist of a solid sheet of steel. A slot in the door allows officers to pass items to inmates. An inmate can contact an officer by using an intercom system in his cell. The unit's supporters champion these new doors, convinced that officers will no longer need to fear being assaulted by inmates or their waste products as they walk the unit.[19]

The computerized high-tech design is used to monitor staff as well as inmates. All of the projected 246 employees are required to go through extensive security checks upon entering the building. They are required to place their right hands into a palm print recognition station and then enter their four-digit code. Their name and time of entrance into the unit are recorded and stored digitally.

Once access is authorized, a steel door is opened and shut electronically. The computer keeps a log of all times the door was opened and closed. This feature serves as a source of information for administrators to monitor employee traffic and as an additional source of information when prisoners file allegations of abuse or neglect. All incoming on-duty officers then proceed to a central room near the facility's entrance where monitors with split screens transmit views from the many cameras providing surveillance everywhere both inside and outside the unit.

The central control room, which contains several split-screen monitors, is the hub for internal surveillance. Smaller versions of these computerized nerve centers are found in all prison wings and in the hallways. The setup makes it possible for one officer to monitor each wing.

Operational Conditions in the Texas High-Security Unit

Most of the conditions found in other control units are also found in the new unit in

Texas as well. As in other such units the main objective is to minimize/eliminate an inmates' contact with staff and other prisoners. Such isolation is routine and can be up to 24 hours a day. The inmates in the new Texas control unit will spend most of their time alone in cells. Virtually all their activities both day and night take place in their cells. They eat, shower, and use the restroom in their own cells. The ability to shower the entire unit within a few hours is a major cost- and time-savings procedure, especially compared to showering individual ad-seg inmates under double and sometimes triple custody.

Each cell contains a steel toilet, sink, and showerhead. These are all bolted into the wall. Inmates have the opportunity to shower daily; at other times showers are turned off. Water for the sink and toilet is made available at all times. However, like other "amenities," they can be shut off by the central control system should the cell occupant try to flood his cell block. Inmates receive daily meals in their cells. The food is prepared within the unit by inmates from another institution and is delivered to the inmates by officers.

The high-security unit has no day rooms or television sets other than computer monitors. It does have a visitation room, however, where inmates and their visitors are separated by a thick, impact-resistant glass wall. A steel stool bolted to the floor and a two-way telephone are the only items in the room. No physical contact is possible between inmates and visitors. Likewise, inmates approved for legally prescribed visits may visit other inmates under similar conditions. Such visits are generally conducted in holding cells. Here a wall with a small window, criss-crossed by bars for communication, separates the two inmates who are seated on either side of the wall on a single steel stool bolted to the floor.

Inmates, depending on their level of classification, receive from one hour, three days a week to one hour, seven days a week outdoor recreation time. Often-times the only

real reprieve from their nearly total isolation takes place at these times. During this time, inmates are moved to individual "cages" where they are separated physically from other inmates by (only) fences. There they are able to see and talk to other inmates. The 18' x 20' enclosed recreation yards include a basketball court, a chin-up bar, and a hard wall on which inmates can play handball. Each "cage" is secured by a floor-to-ceiling 35-foot-high mesh steel fence. If other inmates are nearby, they can converse.

While out-of-cell programming is available to supermax inmates in 13 states, in Texas, the intense physical limitations are compounded by the absence of educational, training, or recreational programs. Thus far, supermax imprisonment in Texas has not attempted to include formal rehabilitation programs as part of its daily routine.[20]

Consequences of Total Control

As a result, control unit inmates live in a psychologically assaultive environment that destabilizes personal and social identities. While the same can be said of the prison system as a whole, in control units mind control is a primary weapon, implemented through architectural design and a day-to-day regimen that produces isolation, inwardness, and self-containment. Within this severely limited space, inmates are under constant scrutiny and observation. In the unit, cameras and listening devices ensure constant surveillance and control of not only the inmate but also every movement of the staff.

The rural location of control units increases (or supplements) isolation and makes contact with family and community difficult for many. The difficulty for inmates in maintaining contacts with the outside world is exacerbated by the unit's isolation from major urban centers. This alienation heightens inmate frustration, deprivation, and despair. Over long periods of time, the inevitable result is the creation of dysfunctional individuals who are completely self-involved, socially neutered, unable to participate in organized social activities, and unprepared for eventual reintegration into either the general prison population, or life on the outside. Those inmates who resist less, demand less, and see each other as fierce competitors for the few privileges allowed will fare best in the system. Programs that normally exist in other prisons to rehabilitate are deemed frivolous here.

Discussion

The present system of mass incarceration accompanied by the specter of more and more control units can only be maintained with at least the tacit approval of society as [a] whole. In times of relative economic prosperity, America has had the luxury of focusing its resources on crime reduction. As the new millennium approaches, crime and its control has become a major industry. Despite the lack of valid scientific evidence that massive imprisonment reduces crime, billions of dollars have been spent to build new prisons and satisfy the American public's growing desire for vengeance. While there is some scientific evidence that there is a (weak) negative *correlation* between imprisonment and crime rates, the vast majority of studies indicate that imprisonment is *not causally related* to the variability in crime.[21-24] Critics of current imprisonment trends have argued that imprisoning large numbers of people in order to stop crime has been a spectacular and massively expensive failure.[25] Even prison officials sometimes admit to the reality of the situation.[26]

Supermax prisons, perhaps our most costly prison experiment ever, have been promoted as the new panacea for correctional management problems, a form of deterrence that is guaranteed to work. On the other hand, supermax prisons are symbolic of the desperation Americans face in trying to take out crime using traditional formal control methods. The efficacy of such approaches is generally limited by their reactive nature. As the cost of incarceration continues to increase, public officials may be forced to consider a more balanced approach incorporating a more holistic view of crime control; one which focuses more on community and restoration and less on imprisonment. The challenge of the future lies in the creation of a society and a criminal justice system that is able to thwart violence with less violent means.

What we need, in all seriousness, is a better class of inmates. Such change will take time and substantial resources. As we approach the next century, we have the luxury of a relatively strong economy. While many planners have their eye on the future of the global market, failure to learn from our mistakes of the past and strategically invest in proactive crime control strategies in local communities, will eventually limit our ability to compete with other countries and life in America will become, in the words of Hobbes, even more "short, brutish, and nasty."

Study Questions

1. What are some of the ways in which the supermax prison provides political appeal?

2. What were cited as some of the primary advantages that may have been brought about by the development of the supermax prison?

3. What were some of the primary disadvantages for inmates that are brought about through being housed in a supermax prison?

4. Consider and discuss whether or not the proliferation of supermax prisons has the potential for reducing violent behavior in general population prisons? In greater society?

5. What were identified as some of the primary consequences of "total control" as exemplified by the development of the supermax prison?

Notes

1. National Institute of Corrections. (1997). *Supermax Housing: A Survey of Current Practice*. Washington, DC: Government Printing Office.

2. Flanagan, T.J., and Longmire, D., eds. (1996). *Americans View Crime and Justice*. Newbury Park, CA: Sage.

3. Maguire, K., and Pastore, A.L., eds. (1995). *Bureau of Justice Statistics Sourcebook of Criminal Justice Statistics*. Albany, NY: The Hindelang Criminal Justice Research Center.

4. U.S. Department of Justice. (1997). "Correctional Populations in the United States." *Bureau of Justice Statistics Bulletin*. Office of Justice Programs, June.

5. Johnson, W.W., Bennett, K., and Flanagan, T.J. (1997). "Getting Tough on Prisoners: A National Survey of Prison Administrators." *Crime and Delinquency*, 43(1):24–41.

6. Clear, T. (1994). *Harm in American Penology: Offenders, Victims, and Their Communities*. Albany: State University of New York Press.

7. "Bruscino v. Carlson." (1985). *In Marion Penitentiary—1985*. Oversight Hearing before the Subcommittee on Courts, Civil Liberties, and the Administration of Justice, August 15. Washington, DC: U.S. Government Printing Office.

8. Landis, T. (1988). "Marion Warden Praises Decision." *Southern Illinoisan* July 28.

9. Lassiter, C. (1990). "Roboprison." *Mother Jones*, September/October.

10. Wilson, N.K. (1991). "Hard-Core Prisoners Controlled in Nation's High-Tech Prisons." *Chicago Daily Law Bulletin*, April 25.

11. Prison Activist Resource Center. (1998). "National Campaign to Stop Control Unit Prisons." *Justice Net Prison Issues Desk*. http:///www.igc.apc.org/justice/issues/control-unit/ntscup.html

12. Human Rights Watch. *Cold Storage: Supermaximum Security Confinement in Indiana*. New York: HRW, 1997.

13. *Madrid v. Gomez*, 889 F. Supp. 1146 N.D. Calif. (1995).

14. Prendergast, A. (1995). "End of the Line: In the New Alcatraz, Prisoners Do the Hardest Time of All." *Westword*, 18(46)July:12.

15. Korn, R. (1988). "The Effects of Confinement in the High Security Unit at Lexington." *Social Justice*, 15(1):B–19.

16. Teske, R.H., ed. (1995). "Corrections." *Crime and Justice in Texas*. Huntsville, TX: Sam Houston Press.

17. Stanley, D. (1998). Executive Services, Texas Department of Criminal Justice—Institutional Division. Telephone Interview. Huntsville, Texas.

18. *Huntsville Item*, 26 June 1997, p. 1, 6A.

19. *Huntsville Item*, 3 August 1997, p. 1, 10A.

20. Johnson, W.W., Henningsen, R.J., and Wells, T. (1998). *National Corrections Executives Survey (1998)*. Unpublished Survey Research. Huntsville, Texas: College of Criminal Justice, Sam Houston State University.

21. Blumstein, A., Cohen, J., and Daniel, N., eds. (1978). *Deterrence and Incapacitation: Estimating the Effects of Criminal Sanctions on Crime Rates*. Washington, DC: National Academy of Sciences.

22. Visher, C.A. (1986). "Incapacitation and Crime Control: Does a 'Lock 'Em Up' Strategy Reduce Crime?" *Justice Quarterly*, 4(4):513–514.

23. Krajick, K., and Gettinger, S. (1982). *Overcrowded Time*. New York: The Edna McConnell Clark Foundation.

24. Zimring, F. E., and Gordon, H. (1996). "Lethal Violence and the Overreach of American Imprisonment." Presentation at the 1996 Annual Research and Evaluation Conference, Washington, DC.

25. Irwin, J., and Austin, J. (1994). *It's About Time: America's Imprisonment Binge*. Belmont, CA: Wadsworth.

26. Ticer, S. (1989). "The Search for Ways to Break Out of the Prison Crisis." *Business Week*, May 8. ✦

Part III
Working in Prison

Much has been written about the prisoner's life and adaptation inside the walls of a secure facility. The study of life inside prison has also included investigation about the role of labor. Work and labor inside a prison have taken on many different roles over the decades. Not only has "work for the sake of work" served to occupy idle hands, but prison labor has at times been used to generate profit for both the institution as well as outside agencies.

In recent years, the issues regarding work inside prison have shifted somewhat from the ethics of using inmates for labor to the possibilities of reform and of opportunity. The criminal justice and criminological literature has for decades examined the variable of employment in general and how it may relate to criminal activity. This has been done through both the lens of limited legitimate opportunity, which may cause criminal behavior for profit, and the rubric of lack of skill (and education), which may cause a lack of conformity, to site two examples. Thus, work, education, and vocational programs have all become central to the rehabilitative regimen of many institutions. The issue of "labor" inside a prison has in many ways moved away from whether it is constitutional to use inmate populations for work, to whether working inside a prison has some reformative effect.

When considering work inside an institution, the student of corrections should not overlook the prison guard. In terms of a vocation, the role and function of the prison guard (as well as other professionals inside a secure facility) are perhaps unlike those in any other occupation on the outside. The duties of the correctional officer, both official and unofficial, go far beyond the maintenance of order. Because the prison work environment is naturally hidden from view, the public has remained largely unaware of what life inside the institution is like for those who are greatly depended upon for making it "work."

The prison guard is not subject to the same degree of deprivation as is the inmate. Nonetheless, it would be naïve to think that prison as a work environment does not impose its own unique set of pressures and characteristics on the officers and wardens that have been charged with maintaining smooth daily operation (in addition to other goals, such as reform). Although the relationship that exists between the correctional officer and the prison inmate is by definition adversarial, closer examination reveals a somewhat more codependent situation. Both parties have a vested interest in the maintenance of order inside the institution, and in many ways they need each other to meet this goal.

In some sense, the correctional officers are "doing time" as much as the prison inmates. In fact, research suggests that line officers are misunderstood and under-appreciated by the general public. Perhaps no one would begrudge the necessity of the correctional worker inside the institution, but neither would many aspire to make the direct supervision of serious offenders their life's work.

Because the freedom of movement is by definition limited inside the secure facility, correctional officers' roles and duties tend to be somewhat specialized and in turn appear

151

to define their day-to-day work experience. Similarly, the occupation of correctional officer has become more specialized and more complex as life inside for inmates becomes more technically challenging due to court rulings. It is perhaps natural (and beneficial, in many respects) for correctional officers to become extremely familiar with the individuals they supervise and interact with. This characteristic of institutional living has its advantages. A correctional officer charged with running a print shop, for example, would naturally want to follow basic rules of good management—good communication, fair treatment, and the maintenance of a relaxed work environment. One disadvantage, however, is the potential for inmates' tendency to exploit the good will and familiarity of the prison guard, and by "playing" him or her to thereby compromise security and the guard's professionalism.

In addition to the line officer inside a prison, the administrative body performs functions vital to the daily operation of an institution. Having the final say over both the lives of prison inmates and the guards that supervise them places administrators (in particular, the prison warden) in a unique position of power. Although the line officer may balance the conflicting goals of the prison's upper administration and the inmates, the warden's balancing act is somewhat more complex. The prison warden must consider the desires of the state and balance those with goals of the institution. In addition, the warden must often deal with the public, the press, and the legislature. Finally, this officer must mediate situations that arise between line officers and inmates.

The advent of the private prison has added another wrinkle to the management of prisons. When prison systems were largely state-run, workers were, for the most part, state employees. They were required to hold certain state credentials and follow state regulations. However, when a prison is privatized, a potential Pandora's box is opened regarding who should work within as well as administer an institution housing individuals sentenced by the state. In the following selections, the reader is encouraged to consider the effects of imprisonment on corrections professionals. Like most professions, correctional work has become more complex and specialized over the years. Contemplate some of the challenges of actually running a prison and the critical issues that necessarily exist therein, in which a body of free individuals have been charged with controlling and reforming a body of confined individuals. ✦

13
Guards Imprisoned
Correctional Officers at Work

Lucien X. Lombardo

The complexities of the prison line officer are brought to light in this classic essay by Lombardo. The author brings out the challenges of the correctional officer, such as the extent to which prison guards also experience 'imprisonment' and the consequences of this confinement (such as deprivation). The prison guard's job is often devoid of the respect experienced by others within the administration of an institution. The line officer is charged with maintaining order while managing a population of inmates who often may not wish to comply with the institutional goals of order and productivity. The many roles played by prison guards are identified and discussed in relation to the maintenance of order. Much of the compelling evidence in this essay comes from prison guards themselves—Lombardo uses the actual words of these officers in order to shed light on what may indeed be an undervalued occupation with limited opportunity for advancement.

The traditional portrait of the prison guard has him standing in the prison yard, night stick in hand, or sitting in a tower with his machine gun, observing inmates as they go about their daily routines below. However, such media stereotypes mask the great vari-

Excerpts from *Guards Imprisoned* by Lucien X. Lombardo, pp. 51–71. Copyright © 1989 by Anderson Publishing Company. Reprinted by permission.

ety of tasks and work environments that occupy and surround the working guard. The correction officer's tasks are not so simple or so singular. As in any community, a large number of functions need to be performed if the prison community is to run smoothly. In prison it is the correction officer who performs many of these functions or who supervises the inmates who perform them.

The variety of tasks correction officers perform is compounded by a variety of work environments. He may never come into contact with inmates or they may constantly surround him. His work environment may be highly structured or it may be relatively uncontrolled.

Combinations of these variables create a variety of work environments, each with different demands and expectations regarding the behavior of both inmates and officers. For officers it is less important that they meet inmates in prison than it is *where* in the prison they meet. It is clear that the distribution of tasks and environmental considerations faced by an individual officer depends on his particular job assignment.

The Variety of Job Assignments

Job assignments at Auburn may be classified into seven general categories according to their location within the institution, the duties required and the character of contact with the inmate population. These seven categories are

1. block officers,
2. work detail supervisors,
3. industrial shop and school officers,
4. yard officers,
5. administration building assignments,
6. wall posts, and
7. relief officers.

Each of these assignments has its own duties and its own problems, and it is the men

153

and their tasks that occupy the rest of this chapter.

Block Officers

Perhaps the busiest and most demanding job assignment is that of the block officer. In cell blocks housing between 300 and 400 men, the block officer supervises and cares for inmates and supervises other officers who are assigned to gallery duty within the blocks. During the evening shifts, when inmates are locked in their cells, the tasks of the block officer are fairly routine: making rounds to inspect cells for fires, watching for signs of self-destructive behavior and handling inmate problems as they arise. On day shifts the block officer's tasks become much more complex: a combination of security, supervision, housekeeping and human services:

> In the block my job is to keep the block running orderly and on schedule. Special things to do during the school week and others on weekends. Let them in and out on time, make regular counts. Let those in coming from work. Give out medication. Lock them in and count again. Then let them out into the yard. All the while I have to handle all kinds of problems, personal, plumbing or electrical. I hand out newspapers and mail. I make check rounds to make sure there's no two in a cell. Let some in at seven o'clock and after eight o'clock let those in from the yard. Then I make the final count. There's call-outs and everything else in between. Anything can happen and always does.

Block officers are busy keeping track of 300 to 400 men, solving many personal problems, supervising inmate cleanup crews, all the while attempting to maintain some degree of security. The atmosphere is frequently quite hectic with the officer often sitting at his desk surrounded by five to ten inmates all wanting their own personal problems handled immediately. Requests for passes to other parts of the institution, inqui-

ries about rules or personal concerns are put to block officers in rapid-fire fashion, often creating an atmosphere of confusion. Because of the responsibility they carry and the management and organizational skills they demonstrate, block officers are generally respected by most other officers.

In the block, problems for the officer arise from a lack of stability and consistency, not from the inmates, but from the administration. Changes in rules and regulations create confusion for officers and inmates alike. As one block officer explains:

> [The biggest problem] is the conflict within the administration itself. There's a constant changing of orders brought on by directives from the central office. It creates a state of confusion in the blocks. Among the inmates it's dangerous, among the officers it's chaos. The constant state of turmoil drives everyone crazy. Like the letter writing business, three directives in three days. Everything just keeps changing.

Work Detail Supervisors

Assignments in the clothing room, commissary, hobby shop or store house involve ordering and distributing goods to inmates, supervising a crew of inmates (usually six or seven men), managing inventory and keeping account books. Because these officers often control inmate access to scarce resources and staff access to favors, these positions carry with them both power and frustration. But working with a smaller group of inmates also provides opportunities for satisfaction. One work detail supervisor explains:

> I get a lot of hassle as clothing room officer. I have to issue clothing and I have to refuse to issue it sometimes too. I get sworn at all the time. I could lock guys up every hour. I have to put up with verbal abuse: I'm always a "mother——!" I take it as part of the job. I've got to decide whether to turn inmates down or not. They take my name at least once a day because they don't like it. If I stay one more year, I'll set a record for staying in the clothing room the longest. Sergeants

call and want me to do favors for some inmate hassling them. I've got to turn them down, and they get an attitude toward me. It's a hassle job: fighting and arguing with the inmates. Some days I dread it because certain guys are coming up. But it's all in a day's work. I've got eight guys working for me, seven black and one Puerto Rican. I have a good working relationship with these men. They know what they can and can't do. With some I have a more personal relationship, with others a more officer-inmate relationship.

Supervising work details can be hectic or relaxed. While the pace in the clothing room varies with inmate schedules, cleanup crews can regularly be observed taking their time, often enjoying pleasant weather.

Industrial Shop and School Officers

Officers in these areas perform order maintenance and security functions. However, in these locations they are not alone. Two or three officers are assigned to these areas, where they are in charge of a smaller group of inmates than in the blocks (30 to 40 in an industrial shop and 200 to 300 in the school). Here they must also work with civilian foremen, industrial supervisors and, in the school, with teachers, counselors and school administrative personnel. In addition to taking counts and checking the whereabouts of absentees, the officers, at times, must design and maintain record-keeping systems for inmate payrolls, and at times they must assign inmates to specific tasks and, together with civilians, manage the interactions of the inmate work group. Just as block officers or work detail supervisors, they must handle inmate problems and complaints as well:

The [license plate shop] where I work is like a factory. We tell the men reasons why we do things. We [have the men] punch time cards and try to make it like real conditions. Security-type things? If there's a question,

my job is to let the inmate know why. Sometimes they think it's petty, but I'm in charge of knowing where everybody is and how many there are.

. . .[A]s a new guy comes into the shop that's where they start. If we get two or three guys at a time, the one with the highest number gets the porter's job. It just so happened that two black guys got the toilet area and a white guy got put further up. The black guy asked about this and asked about that. I showed them the number system and they accepted it.

On my job in the school, guys come up to you with personal problems like sickness, a death in the family, and he wants to see a counselor. It might take three to five days before he does. You have to deal with this then and there. You have to pacify. A lot of men are babies, always asking, "Why do I have to do that?" You say, "Rules and regulations say do it like this." The guy blows his top and starts giving you a lot of grief. Now you've got to soft-talk him. Try to keep it calm and keep peace in the school area.

What is the biggest problem you have doing your job?

[In the school] getting them to go back to classes. On my job right now, the inmates aren't going along with the program. They're assigned to the school, but constantly skipping. I get a hassle because I have to account for them. If I can't, I have to put in an infraction. Then they come to me and ask, "Why did you put an infraction report on me? I was here." I say, "you weren't. This gets repetitious. Same thing day after day, but it's my job. I have to know where they are.

When school teachers are out sick, this creates a problem. There are no relief teachers and there might be free periods. They might not be supervised for an hour and a half and I can't get him back to the block. I might get 30 to 50 guys like that and they're hanging around my back with nothing to do. I've got to supervise them and do my routine work at the same time.

Yard Officers

In the blocks inmates are at home; in the school, shops and on work details they are at work; but in the yard inmates are "on the street." For the correction officer, the work environment of the yard is the least structured and provides the inmate the most freedom of action. In the yard the behavioral norms established are those of the inmates and not those dictated by a task, the administration or the officers. Officers working the yard are generally those with the least seniority. They have no specific groups of inmates to supervise nor tasks to complete. Consequently, they spend most of their time concerned with security and maintaining order. Occasionally they may be called upon to direct inmates to the proper channels so that inmate problems can be resolved:

> In the yard it's mainly the observation of key individuals—the supposed troublemakers. You keep an eye on them so they're not causing any trouble that the prison doesn't need or I don't need. There's very little physical labor in the yard, but much mental labor. You've got to be alert to what's going on around you. Inmates are constantly trying to beat you. You have to keep your eyes and ears open to observe them in different situations. You're paid to watch, listen and control.

The yard officer's tasks are characterized by the suspicion that inmates are breaking rules or plotting something devious. The problems of the yard officers are different from those of the officers described above and derive from the unique environment of their assignment:

> My biggest problem is trying to decide if a guy's breaking a rule. Then if I think he is, it's figuring out how to enforce it.

Administration Building Assignments

Correction officers with job assignments in the administration building work under a set of circumstances totally different from that of most other officers. For the most part, these officers have few, if any, contacts with inmates. They are only indirectly concerned with security, having primary responsibility for handling routine administrative tasks. Some of these officers open doors, close doors, check passes in and out of the institution. Others handle routine administrative tasks, often working with civilians. An officer who works in the institution's arsenal describes his work:

> I keep the keys and weapons. Mostly an administrative job. I work the switchboard, handle finances, money that comes to the front hall from the visitors for inmates. I process drafts [inmates transferring to or from other institutions], furloughs and courtmen. You're a doorman, a telephone answerer, you do everything.

An officer who works the night shift in the administration building explains:

> I work with the lieutenant and the watch commander, I cover them when they're out. I answer the phone. [The biggest problem] is answering the phone for outside calls. Relatives and friends of inmates, employees calling in sick. They tell you one thing and a couple of days later they change their story completely and you get stuck in the middle.

For officers in the administration building the day-to-day operations of the prison that affect inmates are of little concern, since they generally have more contact with the public than with inmates. Often they can be seen explaining institutional rules and regulations to complaining, bothered and upset civilian visitors.

Wall Posts

Officers who work on wall towers are concerned almost exclusively with outer-perimeter security. They live in their guard towers for eight hours each day, caring for their equipment, making scheduled security check-ins, eating their meals and otherwise occupying their time. Almost completely removed from the prison's ongoing activities, they readily carry on conversations with inmates or officers passing by on the inside, and often with civilians passing on the outside.

Even upon the walls, out of the daily flow of institutional life, problems arise, but the problems are different from those of their inside counterparts:

> If something happens, it's most important to protect people. You can't shoot till you get the order. By the time you call up, somebody's dead. You're on your own there, actually. You don't know what's coming. You can tell by the climate if something's going to bust loose. I wonder about that. I guess you'll just have to wait till it happens. But I never worry about it. They're always looking for an answer. Today it's right, tomorrow maybe not.

On the wall one has time to philosophize and think deeply about one's situation.

Relief Officers

Relief officers perform a variety of tasks substituting for regular officers on their days off, vacations or sick days. They may have steady relief assignments, working the same two or three jobs on a rotating two-week basis, or they may work a much wider variety of jobs. Not being on any one job for an extended period of time, it is often difficult for relief officers to establish personal relationships with inmates. Moving throughout the institution, performing a variety of tasks, they have no personal identification with any one task and have a more generic definition of their job than does the average officer:

> Naming the biggest problem with this relief job is a tough question because of the varied jobs, I suppose, being a training relief officer, working two to four jobs in the course of a day and having to know what each job consists of. There's supposed to be a written description of every job a guy does in the in-

stitution. I've got to know every man's job. It's my choice. Not knowing fully what the job consists of, I struggle along, I play it by ear, unless the guy I'm relieving carries a notebook on what the guys do and could show me.

On-the-Job Motivations

Even though officers can now bid on the institutional job assignments they perform, it is not the specific duties that are involved in a particular job that seem to be the officer's primary concern. The motivations for working on a particular job assignment are, for the most part, a reflection of individual attempts to relate meaningfully to their work environment, rather than attempts to find positions from which they will be able to make meaningful contributions to the correctional task.

To explore more closely correction officer work motivations, each officer was asked to respond to the question: "If you could have any job in the institution, which job would you pick?" The officer was also asked to indicate why he would pick a particular job. From the responses to the latter question, a number of characteristic motivational concerns emerged.

The most frequently mentioned reason for choosing a particular assignment was that it provided the officer with *activity* and made time pass quickly. According to one officer who works in the kitchen area:

> It's one of the worst jobs and I've got to be crazy to work there. But I worked there before and it's a job where you keep busy. I thought it would make the job go faster.

Officers are not only concerned with putting in "fast" eight-hour days when they bid on "active" jobs, they also want their career as an officer (perceived by many as a "sentence") to pass quickly. One relief officer, for example, relates:

> [I] work a different job every two weeks and get around to see the whole joint. I get to

know what the inmates can and can't have. And it also breaks up my 25-to-life "bit."

A second motivational concern is *autonomy*—a desire to obtain some measure of control over their personal work environment. In order to avoid being subject to perceived inconsistencies of supervisory and administrative directives, some officers want assignments that allow them to make decisions concerning what they do and how they do it. Having autonomy in one's job assignment also means becoming independent of other segments of the institution:

> I worked all the other jobs and didn't want all the hassles. [There are] not as many bosses here. I've got one sergeant to answer to and I take care of most of my problems myself.

Another common concern reflects officers' *desires to contribute* either to the well-being of the inmates or to the overall running of the institution. Although this concern contains some elements of "activity," it is primarily focused upon the positive contribution the activity allows, and not on the activity per se:

> I like working with the misfits. Here [in segregation] you get a good chance to work with the inmates.

> I thought I could be more helpful [in the mess hall]. They requested that I go there. An inmate told a sergeant [that] if he wanted it clean, he should get me.

Another work concern voiced by officers reflects a preference for *privacy* or a *desire to remove themselves* from danger or conflict. Having experienced frustration and conflict in encounters with inmates, the prison administration and supervisors, some officers bid on jobs and shifts that effectively take them out of the action:

> I wanted nights. It's safer than days. No headaches from the brass or from the inmates, but you still have your jobs to do.

A final work concern relates less to the work of the officer inside the prison than to his *life outside* the walls. Arranging shifts to fit family responsibilities and obtaining assignments to obtain weekends off regularly also prompts some officers to bid on certain jobs.

This list of motives is similar to "profiles" of "prison concerns" found among inmates. . . . Like inmates, officers prefer job assignments that "match" their needs for special kinds of social environments.

There is also a discernible tendency for officers who have special motivational concerns to prefer specific job locations. Block jobs, for example, are the most likely to be associated with activity or the desire to help inmates than with any other need. Working in the blocks would thus seem to provide officers with opportunities to keep themselves busy and make the day go by, as well as with opportunities to render services.

For those officers who prefer to work with work gangs of inmates, the primary concern appears to be control over one's environment. The officer in such jobs is less encumbered by interference from supervisory personnel and less distracted by large groups of inmates. He is able to make decisions concerning his men in his own work and also to control specific goods and services to which other institutional personnel might want access. Most officers who express a concern for control do so, indicating they could be their own boss or that they had less interference from others. Work gang jobs also provide a degree of activity, lessening boredom.

Officers expressing a preference for jobs located in the administration building or upon the walls are primarily concerned with decreasing their contact with inmates. Jobs in the administration building are also associated with activity and control over one's environment. For those officers who preferred to work on the wall getting away meant not only getting away from inmates, but also administrative personnel. On the wall the chances of being bothered by anyone are virtually nil.

Other data also point to the importance of these motivational concerns to the officers. When asked if they had received their present job by bidding and if so, why they bid on that particular job, those officers who bid on their jobs indicate that control over their environment and shift were their primary concerns.

The job locations of the 21 officers who did not bid on their jobs again emphasize the importance of special motivational concerns. These officers obtained their jobs by assignment, often prior to the introduction of the bidding system, and they wanted to retain their present jobs. Others who began work and received assignments after the introduction of the bidding system decided to stay with their assignments. From these data it is evident that officers have tended to stay on jobs without bidding on others when their jobs allow for "activity" and "control," such as the assignments of block officer and administration building officers. For younger officers who lack seniority, relief jobs provide for movement throughout the institution, a constant change of environment and diverse "activity," though such jobs are low on "control" since the officer is not permanently assigned to a fixed location.

General Themes in the Guards' Work

The foregoing discussion of specific job assignments and motivational concerns described the range of prison guard duties and the variety of forces motivating these guards to perform them. However, the more general nature of the correction officer's job needs explanation. The variety of facets that form such a general definition provides a look into the operational reality of "being a guard" in more general terms.

In response to inquiries about the general nature of their work, correction officers provide a wide variety of perceptions and definitions with only one theme agreed upon by one-half of the officers. This diversity of definition would seem to indicate that definitions derived from individual experiences take precedence over social definitions provided by the guards as a group, again indicating the weakness of the officer-group tie. However, despite this lack of consensus on any one theme, a number of common themes are evident.

Human Services

The most frequently mentioned theme is that of the provider of human services. Though some officers approach the human service aspects of their work grudgingly, calling themselves "baby sitters" or "playground directors," complaining that "we do everything for the inmates and they never do anything for themselves," most approach the service aspect of their work with a positive attitude. At times officers feel they perform positive services for inmates in spite of perceived pressures against doing so. When they say, "A lot of officers don't like to hear about [providing for inmate needs]," "Others get on me for doing things for the inmates," and "If you try to do too much you get your ass chewed out," these guards underscore the officers' belief that "helping inmates" is not always looked upon favorably by their peers or supervisors, even though they view the human service function positively for themselves. This belief that to provide human services is somehow perceived negatively by others gives the officer a sense of being different from other officers and from supervisors, who in the process become "bad guys." It also provides the officer with a more positive sense of "self as officer" than he might otherwise have had.

As a human services worker, the correctional worker becomes involved with inmate problems and must listen to "sob stories" told to him on a personal level. He is expected to handle institutional adjustment problems and to deal with self-destructive behaviors.

Requests that he "cut red tape" are constantly put to him by inmates. With such, the officer either refers the inmate to a counselor or to a sergeant, or he handles the problem himself. However, no matter how he manages these varying situations, many a correction officer sees himself as the institution's frontline problem solver and referral agency. And, indeed, it is the correction officer who initially encounters nearly every problem in the institution.

The human services theme, as it manifests itself in the correction officers' jobs, has three general aspects, each of which illustrates the characteristics of "people work" put forward by Goffman. Primarily, some officers envision themselves as *providers of goods and services* who see to it that the inmates' basic needs are met. Food, clothing, medication and cleanliness are prime concerns. Inmates locked in their cells for disciplinary or medical reasons must be fed. Occasionally an officer encounters an inmate who refuses to bathe regularly; other inmates often complain to officers about such inmates and the officer will often attempt to have the offending inmate adjust his habits. If the officer can persuade the inmate to tidy up, he reduces the number of problems he must deal with on his gallery. Success in his efforts enhances his status in the eyes of inmates. He is viewed by inmates as an officer who can get things done, gaining more cooperation from those for whom he is responsible. Similar processes appear to be at work as the officer seeks to secure clothing, food or other "necessities of life" for inmates.

Most officers are quite aware of the necessity to keep their word if they say they will take care of a problem for an inmate. Failure to keep one's word is reported to diminish the confidence inmates have in the officer's ability to "take care of business." From the officer's point of view, failure to keep his word can demonstrate to the inmate that the officer does not really care and provides opportunities for what Mathiesen calls "censorious" behavior on the part of inmates.

As one officer put it, "If you say you will do something for an inmate and you don't, you're marked. They'll see you every day and

know who you are. You're in for trouble." Trouble here means that the officer's job becomes tougher. Rather than cooperate, inmates may linger on the gallery before moving into their cells, thus delaying a count. Reportedly, the officer who fails to fulfill his promise must hold back from making an issue of such incidents, lest his failure to live up to his word becomes known to others on the gallery. Here the important thing to note is not that refusal to do a favor causes the officer to lose some of his authority, but rather that failure to live up to one's word once it is given diminishes the value of the officer as a person.

A second aspect of the human service theme deals with the correction officers' handling of inmate institutional problems. Here the officer acts as a *referral agent* or an *advocate*, setting up appointments with counselors, calling the correspondence office or an office to check on the status of an inmate's account. It should be kept in mind that these officers are not required to make phone calls or otherwise intervene on behalf of inmates, and are often discouraged from doing so by administrators and supervisors. All they need to do is to tell the inmate to follow established procedures (i.e., drop a note to the appropriate office and wait for a written reply). Officers, however, know from experience that delay causes problems for them, hence they are motivated to move against the "institutional bureaucracy" in attempts to gain action. Some interview excerpts will illustrate:

> You're dealing with the inmates' everyday problems, money, packages, mail, visits, telephone calls. You've got to call right away and lots of times you can't get the right people. If a guy's borderline, you've got to be careful because he might go into a rage.

> I have a lot of inmates come to me with problems. I try to give help and helpful words. Maybe you call to see how a guy should make arrangements for something. Get the service unit or the chaplain to talk to him. Give some helpful advice. I find myself

doing it a lot. A lot of guys come to me and say, "Mr.——, I've got a problem, maybe you can help." One guy was shaking and upset. He said he was in a big jam and he didn't want to go to the P.K. He gave me a check he'd gotten in the mail (correspondence had overlooked it). I took the check, gave the guy a receipt and put it in his account. It's not a big thing, just little things to take the edge off. Sometimes if you're helpful you can correct things and save trouble. When they can't handle it, they just swing out.

The third, possibly most important, aspect of the human service theme is the role the officer plays in the *institutional adjustment* of inmates. In this role many correction officers see themselves as psychiatrists, doctors, social workers or father figures. The "pains of imprisonment" have been described by Sykes, but it is the correction officer who most closely observes the onset of these "pains" and who, if he desires, can most effectively deal with, or at least aid, the inmate in coping with these pains. When asked what they do when an inmate comes to them with a personal, *noninstitutional* problem, two-thirds of the officers indicated that they try to listen and offer advice, and that they would approach particular inmates if they thought they were having problems with which they might help. Family problems, personal problems and mental health problems come to the attention of the correction officer. This is especially true of officers who work in blocks, industrial shops or with work gangs of inmates. In these situations, officers are involved with the same group of inmates on a day-to-day basis and mutual trust between officer and inmate is more likely to develop. The inmates become dependent on particular officers as sources of support and the officers become dependent on the inmates to provide them with opportunities to "help." In combatting boredom and in seeking to exercise personal control over at least their immediate environment, "helping" proves functional (beyond the benefits of the "help" itself) to both the inmate and the officer:

They've got problems. They get bad news letters, they stay in and brood about it. I call the service unit and get a "it's none of your business." We took care of all these things before the service unit was set up. I can't see why it takes so long to get an answer, to make a decision. I had a guy working for me, a good worker, a Muslim. Everybody was down on him. They said he'd be a bum. I said let's see what he does. I asked what his problem was and he said that he got a bad letter. His little girl had an operation. He didn't know how serious it was, but he was worried. I tried to make arrangements for him to make a phone call. I had a couple of friends up there, you make them after a while. This was like one of those situations you sometimes face yourself, not knowing about these things. He got his phone call and perked up.

This officer's ability to empathize with the inmate makes the offer of assistance less a calculated maneuver designed to secure cooperation and more simply the "human" thing to do.

Occasionally an officer is faced with inmates with serious psychological problems which occasionally become disruptive but must somehow be managed. In these situations officers sometimes enlist the help of inmates in trying to manage the situation:

One group you have is the psychos. There are some in the school. One guy comes to school and takes off all the time. You can't keep him in the school. I didn't know where he was. I saw that he did talk with one of my porters a lot. I asked the porter about the guy and he said he was okay. After a while I teamed him up with the other porter and he stayed on the job. The guy was in [the mental facility for criminals] three or four times. The [other] inmate saw that he had a problem. The inmate tried to talk to this so-called nut, so I asked to see if he could do anything and it worked out pretty well.

Officers working in the Special Housing Unit (Segregation) are particularly aware of inmate problems, being in charge of security, mental health and self-protection cases.

These officers are particularly attentive to the institutional adjustment aspects of their job:

> You never get two alike. Each guy is an individual in mind and thoughts. Different things make them do things. One guy was having problems with his wife and tied a sheet over the bars in back. He had one foot on the bed and one on the toilet and timed it so I was coming around. He didn't want to hang himself. I ran for help and when I came back he was untying the sheet and another officer was folding it up. He did it more for attention. His wife knew he'd be away for a long time and she was playing around and he couldn't stand that.
>
> It could be mail from home, wife, provoked by another inmate, by the staff, to keep from being moved. Sometimes you can't figure out why at the time. One guy stripped down and stood in the center of his cell with his eyes closed. He'd been on drugs and had mental problems. I tried to talk to the guy and he wouldn't answer. We figured out though that he was going back to the population the next day and he didn't want that.

Order Maintenance

This perspective of the correction officer's work is not to be confused with the "restraint" function of keeping inmates "in" or preventing them from getting out. Just as with the human services theme, when an officer acts to protect inmates from one another, he measures his duties in terms of beneficial effects that result for the inmates. Such phrases as "keep them in check," "keep them from going at one another," "keep inmates from killing each other," "keep stealing, gambling and homosexuality to a minimum," illustrate a positive as well as a negative control theme. One officer provided an excellent description of this perspective of his work:

> Security doesn't mean keep them from going over the wall. It means you try to make the guy feel secure, that he's not going to get killed or hurt. You keep the place clean on the block job. You make it so an inmate can sit next to another inmate in the mess hall or the auditorium and feel comfortable. So he doesn't have to worry about something happening. It's so compressed in there. Other than that it's just like the street. If they want to go out they'll find a way. It's not that kind of security.

In this respect, the correction officers see themselves as police officers who intervene in family quarrels to maintain social order:

> If a guy did something to you and you didn't like it, you'd hit him, right? It has nothing to do with prison. It's like a city within a city and we're the policemen. They won't rat on each other normally, unless something will hurt them. I had a guy two years ago, pacing in the shop all day long. Just before he went to the blocks he said, "[Officer], put me on the roof." He said he'd kill a guy in the block if he went back. I called the sergeant and he put him there. Another colored guy was trying to pick on him and he's trying to go along with the program and he wouldn't take any more baloney. He was going to prove he's a man, but he wouldn't do it because "it's not worth it for these animals," he said. He'd escaped from another prison and everyone said he's an escape artist. But I put in a good word for him and gave him a tool room job, only he could go in there. He said I had faith in him and he'd do the job. He respected me for trusting him and so he told me when he was going to do something. It saved him a new sentence and me a hassle.

Here one learns that it is not merely the officer's physical presence as an authority figure which serves to check inmates in their conflicts with one another, but the relationships that develop between an officer and an inmate. A positive relationship allows the inmate to approach the officer when a problem is developing, allowing the officer time to defuse it. Thus one finds a connection between the officer's abilities to maintain order and personal relationships between officers and inmates.

Security (Guard Function)

The security function of the correction officer's role most closely resembles the conventional picture of the "guard" as one who prevents escapes, but only one-sixth of these officers mentioned "keeping inmates in" as part of what they do. One officer saw security as his primary function:

> What do I do? Security. I'm not concerned with why they're in. I just make sure they stay here till the courts let them go. If they rap about their records, okay, but it's not my job to take care of them with talk. I don't push myself on them. I let them alone. If they want to talk or kid or joke, okay. If not, I leave them alone.

Where order keeping and protecting inmates is in many respects an active function of the officer, security is essentially passive. Standing and watching, or sitting and watching, are the principal forms security takes.

Supervision

Correction officers are charged with seeing to it that inmates "do things": that they are ready to leave galleries on time, that they return to their cells on time, that they arrive and leave recreation areas on time. With 1,600 inmates in the institution and each inmate expecting that he will be able to use the limited facilities when he is scheduled to use them, delays in one area cause problems all along the line. This is especially important in an institution like Auburn, where programs for inmates are heavily stressed.

In addition to supervising inmate movement, correction officers also supervise inmates on their various work assignments. Institutional food must be prepared and served and dishes must be washed. Clothing and bedding have to be collected, cleaned and redistributed. Cleanup crews and construction crews must prepare institutional areas for the use of all concerned. It is the inmate who performs these chores and it is the

officer who is responsible for seeing to it that he does.

Rule Enforcement (Police Function)

The enforcement aspect of the correction officer role involves not only citing inmates for rule infractions, but discovering contraband and gathering information concerning possible illicit activities inmates may be engaged in. Though this function receives much attention in prison literature, only 22 percent of the men interviewed include it in their self-definition of the officer role, and none of these officers sees rule enforcement as their only function. Rule enforcement seems to be a concern primarily of younger, relatively less experienced officers. The salience of rule enforcement for those officers indicates that this aspect of their work is a problem with which they are trying to come to grips.

Prison rules say that correction officers must deal with everything from extra helpings of food and smoking in restricted areas to clothing regulations and sanitary conditions of both cells and inmates to fights, gambling and drugs. As the institution's policemen, officers not only enforce regulations, but are also involved in investigatory processes. The gathering of information concerning the entry of drugs or other contraband into the institution, the production of prison "wine" and the conduct of gambling are included within the correction officer's role definition. Skill in the use of inmate informants is seen as a necessary, though not respected, investigatory technique.

Summary—1976

From the guard's perspective, prison guard tasks have nothing to do with rehabilitation, just deserts, corrections or punishments. These are issues for the policy planner and program designer—issues that focus upon the inmate's past or attempt to prepare him for the future. For the prison guard going about his day-to-day business, it is the immediate present that matters, life as it is lived and passes *within the prison community*; the outside has little relevance.

The guard attempts to find assignments that will accommodate his own needs, whether he seeks to make the time pass, to control his work environment or to help or get away from inmates, the guard's work, as he performs it, is often a reflection of his personal preferences. In defining and developing tasks out of the raw materials at hand, guards manage personal conflicts to maintain order or to supervise inmates to get some work done. Most importantly, guards become human service workers dealing with the inmates' personal and institutional adjustment, assisting inmates to cope with the pains of imprisonment.

Task Redefinition: 1976–1986

Over the course of the ten years since the 1976 study, the 32 officers from the original sample who provided information changed job assignment an average of three to four times. The average length of stay on any one assignment was 37 months. While eight of the officers moved from assignments *in* the population to *out* of population assignments, five of these eight and eleven overall moved to positions with increased responsibilities. For many, their new assignments have changed their lives: "I sleep better now"; "Now, I drink a lot less and never before I go to work," and "My family can stand me now" were commonly heard refrains from these experienced officers. Only three of the original sample officers remained on the same post and shifts for the entire ten years. For one officer who did so his assignment (block officer) and shift (11 p.m. to 7 a.m.) reportedly managed to keep him isolated from the changes that were taking place around him. On his preliminary information form he wrote:

I am still on the night shift and not in contact with many of the programs and problems with the department or ACF. I'll be retiring in three years and am in the process of building up my outside business. As you can see, I'm not very interested in my state job but I will help you out if I can.

This officer, however, was unique. Most officers experienced and were forced to cope with new conditions and problems that were reshaping their approaches to their tasks and the tasks themselves.

Re-emergence of Custodial and Law Enforcement Functions

Though the basic outline of correctional officer tasks identified in 1976 has remained fairly constant, some subtle and other not-so subtle changes have occurred in response to organizational changes and to changes in the inmate community. The most dramatic shift that has taken place is in the correctional officers' approach to their tasks. The Human Services functions of correctional officer work had a prominent place in the working lives of the officers in 1976. Though the importance of this function is still recognized, its prominence has been reduced as other functions appear to have gained in importance. As organizational changes have reduced opportunities for *helping* officer/inmate interactions, and as increased drug availability and violence have changed the dynamics of intra-inmate behavior, officer task emphasis has shifted to custodial and law enforcement functions.

Q: *If you had to describe to someone who didn't know anything about the correctional officer's job, how would you describe it?*

The basic thing is security. Make sure they don't get out and make sure they're a ward of the state. Protect themselves against themselves and other inmates. Against the dangers of the institution. Act as a counselor, father figure, chaplain, etc.

The amount of programs has grown enormously. And through the tier system there's

more we have to know about the legal ramifications. The amount of legal knowledge
that you have to have has grown enormously.
Before we just had the facility rule book.
Now there's the facility rule book, state and
facility directives.

Q: *How has the job changed over the last ten
years?*

The CO today has to be more intelligent.
More alert because of the legal issues. Where
before the legal issues were not as important. In society and in the facility you have to
explain why now. Before you had "yes, boss,"
"yes, Captain," "yes, sir." Now you have to explain, you can't just say, "I told you so."

Reduced Expectations

According to many of these officers the
past ten years of correctional evolution have
resulted in *reduced expectations* concerning
the work of correctional officers. While "the
early days" saw officers making individual
discretionary decisions concerning a broad
range of activities, the 1980's have seen the responsibilities of the officer become more circumscribed. *Redeployment* which required
the development of job descriptions and justifications for each correctional officer post
and position (a state mandated activity),
helped contribute to this perception.

With redeployment, every officer's job now
has a description. The Sergeant can't say,
"Hey, this is part of your job," because it's in
the description and this is it. That's all you
have. It's great because in the blocks and on
other posts if you're working a vacation you
don't have to go in blind, you just look up the
job. You've got something to go by. The supervisors can't screw you up and have you do
somebody else's job when they slough off.

Before the officer was right and that was it.
Now you have to show how and why you
were right and you have to be right according to the directives. The inmates get copies
of most of them so they're up to date.

Such specificity may breed structure and
predictability and provide officers with clear

direction. At the same time, however, specificity also reduces the officer's tendency to
"creatively" approach the job. Before 1976,
exercising discretion in determining the
shape of one's tasks was done out of necessity.
Such behavior was tacitly allowed and encouraged by the lack of direction. What appears to be happening now is that officers are
coming to rely on "directives" and directions
to determine job tasks and procedures. While
it was relatively common for officers to alter
verbal orders to fit individual situations and
avoid problems, now the tendency appears to
be one of following directives and using directives to justify one's actions to inmates and to
superiors.

For other officers, reduced expectations relates to a reduced sense of officer self-discipline and is an indication of the lack of professionalism expected from officers.

There's not really different expectations, if
anything there's less. The administration
doesn't deal harshly enough with problem
officers. An officer who has brought booze
into the institution, for example, within six
months he might be back at work. There's
less discipline for the officers now. I remember when you couldn't bring newspapers in.
Now people bring them in and give them to
the inmates. Now you catch officers horsing
around with inmates in the yard and no one
says anything.

Specialization

Another result of redeployment has been
the development of more *specialists* as opposed to the generalist officers of the pre-
1976 period.

There's more specialization now. There are
frisk officers, packing officers, the CERT
team, hostage negotiations, with drug testing you can qualify with the FDA and get
called as an expert witness. The officer of
the year was a frisker.

An officer who is now a sergeant describes
this increased specialization and the associated problems:

Jobs we took for granted ten years ago are now done by specialist officers. Before all officers would be involved in taking care of drafts (movements of inmates in and out of the institution). Now we have special friskers and packers for these things. This has made it worse. I smell booze in one place and tell an officer to look, and he says that the frisker is supposed to do that.

Shift in Responsibilities

Another factor that has had an impact on the human services functions of the Auburn correctional officers is the increase in the number of supervisors and a subtle shift in the control of access to informal service networks from officers with connections to sergeants. Though many officers still report using the grassroots helping networks that they have developed over time, nearly all acknowledge that opportunities to put these networks into action (provided by inmate requests to officers) and officer tendency to utilize personal networks has decreased over time.

From what I hear, ten years ago you had 14 Sergeants, now you have 38. I get lots of calls from officers to have a Sergeant call them to do the officer's job. To make decisions. Today the Sergeant has to make the decisions. The officer doesn't take as much on himself as ten years ago. He takes on very little.

Officers now are better trained than I was. But there's a lack of discipline among them. Why? Well, before you did what you were told. Officers with seniority were looked up to, and you followed the senior officers. Now they look to the Sergeants more, they don't look to the blue shirts.

An officer with three years' experience, however, has a different perspective:

Now we're getting laxity. Auburn's lucky with seniority. So the newer officers can ask officers with 15 years in. At Sing-Sing I was out of the academy two weeks and I was almost a senior officer.

Transfer of Human Service Function to Inmates

Perhaps the change that has had the greatest negative impact on correctional officers' ability to perform human service functions has been the increase in the ability of the inmates to handle such problems themselves, particularly the more personal type of problems. Increased inmate access to telephones (nine in the yard, ten in the gym and ten outside the employees' mess providing virtually unlimited collect calls during the hours they are available) has made it possible for inmates to handle directly and in a timely manner many of the personal problems for which officers had previously served as intermediaries between the inmate and the chaplain and counselors who handled inmate contact with the outside world. Greater use of visitations and state-funded visitations for families living at a distance has closed the gap between family and inmate and made direct contact more likely. Hence, the correctional officers are less likely to play the go-between or personal counselor role that they once did.

This change may also be reinforcing trends in negative inmate behavior. While the pre-1976 world of Auburn reinforced inmates depending on officers, the changes described here appear to enhance inmate dependence. Hence, it should not be surprising to see inmates expressing independence in other areas as well. . . .

Summary—1986

Though the basic components of correctional officer work have stayed essentially the same, changing conditions have led these officers to re-emphasize the security and law enforcement aspects of their work and to reduce their emphasis on human services activities. As sergeants have been given more responsibility and inmates more opportunity to handle inmate problems, as specialization and policy and procedure directives have provided more structure to correctional officer tasks, the individual officer's ability to shape his job has been reduced.

Study Questions

1. What are the various job assignments of prison guards, and what motivates them to perform these services?

2. Describe the various functions and themes in the guard's work.

3. How do the many functions performed by prison guards sometimes complement each other, but at other times conflict? ✦

14
Prison Wardens' Job Satisfaction

Francis T. Cullen

Edward J. Latessa

Reneé Kopache

Lucien X. Lombardo

Velmer S. Burton, Jr.

The authors used a survey administered to a national sample of prison wardens to gather information regarding job satisfaction. Some have assumed that due to the nature of their work, job satisfaction would be relatively low when compared to other administrative positions in other industries. However, the data revealed that prison wardens in fact experience high levels of job satisfaction. Perhaps, surprisingly, organizational conditions were not specifically related to the wardens' ratings of job satisfaction.

In addition, data showed that neither was prior professional experience related to job satisfaction. However, four work-role variables were identified as being influential in predicting levels of job satisfaction for wardens. Positive work-role variables included the existence of social support; provision of treatment/human services; a de-emphasis on custodial issues; and a decrease in the extent to which departments exert centralized authority over the day-to-day business of the institution. The reader is encouraged to consider these variables and how they operate within the institution as well as to note the importance of

Excerpts from *The Prison Journal*, Volume 73, Number 2 (June 1993). pp. 141–161. Copyright © 1993 by Sage Publications, Inc. Reprinted by permission.

prison administration in both everyday and long-term corrections management.

The social science literature on job satisfaction is extensive (e.g., Gruenberg, 1980; Quinn & Staines, 1979), and studies of satisfaction among criminal justice occupational groups are increasing steadily (Blau, Light, & Chamlin, 1986; Cullen, Link, Cullen, & Wolfe, 1989; Cullen, Link, Wolfe, & Frank, 1985; Jurik & Halemba, 1984; Jurik, Halemba, Musheno, & Boyle, 1987; Lindquist & Whitehead, 1986; Talarico & Swanson, 1982; Welch, 1989; Whitehead, 1986). Even so, prison wardens stand out as an occupational group virtually ignored by work satisfaction researchers. This neglect is part of a more general oversight: At present, there is only a beginning academic literature on correctional administration (Colvin, 1992; DiIulio, 1987, 1991; Jacobs, 1977) and, more specifically, on how wardens view their work situations (Cullen, Latessa, Burton, & Lombardo, 1993; Grieser, 1988; Harris & Associates, 1968; Kinkade & Leone, 1992a, 1992b; Miller, 1989). The current study attempts to help fill this void in the literature. Based on a national sample of wardens of state and federal adult prisons, we explore two main issues. First, what is the wardens' overall level of job satisfaction, and how does this level compare with that of other occupational groups? Second; what factors—individual, organizational, role related, contextual—influence wardens' satisfaction with their job? As a prelude to addressing these issues, we use the existing literature to frame the analysis to follow. Because empirical investigations of wardens are scanty, this discussion will draw heavily on previous research on other occupational groups, with a special emphasis on studies of correctional officers.

A comment on the importance of our research is warranted. Given that work is a domain of activity that consumes a major portion of people's lives, it is not surprising that researchers, including criminologists, have taken a deep interest in whether employment is satisfying or, as Karl Marx predicted, inherently alienating. Criminal justice work merits special attention because it involves the distinctive mandate to exercise state power over lawbreakers, especially in corrections where contact with and control over offenders occurs daily. Such work is often painted as "dirty," dangerous, and underappreciated by the public and those doing it are said to pay the price of high stress, cynicism, and dissatisfying job experiences.

As we note later, however, these views may be distorted by the lens of ideology and may mask a more complicated reality. Thus we assess the commonly voiced theme that the dehumanization inherent in institutional life robs workers, in this case wardens, of the satisfactions employment might normally provide. Further, our study presents an opportunity to bring additional data to bear on the relative strengths of two competing models used to explain job reactions, including work satisfaction.

Wardens' Occupational Context

Overall Level of Job Satisfaction

A persistent theme found in prison writings is that correctional institutions are inherently dehumanizing social settings (Irwin, 1980; Mitford, 1974). This indictment of prisons frequently includes the observation that prisons brutalize not only the kept but also the keepers (Zimbardo, Banks, Haney, & Jaffe, 1973). In this view, as Johnson (1987) notes, keepers become "hacks," transformed by their prison experience into "subhuman and senselessly brutal custodians" (p. 120). The end result is that correctional work is alienating, empty of satisfaction. Tannenbaum (1922) voiced this conclusion early on: "The keeper, too, is a prisoner . . . .For him there is little beyond the exercise of power . . . .[Although] this ex-

ercise is a means of escape and outlet, it is not a sufficient means. It does not make the keeper a happy person" (p. 24).

Accounts by and of wardens, admittedly a selective source of data, would challenge the idea that prison administration is devoid of satisfaction (Brockway, 1912/1969; Lawes, 1932; Smolowe, 1992). Further, more empirically based research paints a complicated picture of the satisfaction derived from prison work. Research suggests both that prisons are not uniform but vary in the quality of the work environment (DiIulio, 1987), and that correctional work has the potential, in varying degrees and aspects, to be alienating and satisfying (Johnson, 1987; Lombardo, 1989; Toch & Klofas, 1982).

Surveys report, moreover, that large majorities of correctional officers define their work as "very" or "somewhat" satisfying (Cheek & Miller, 1983; Cullen et al., 1989; Harris & Associates, 1968; Jacobs, 1978; Jacobs & Kraft, 1978; Lindquist & Whitehead, 1986; see also Wright & Saylor, 1992). But these results must be seen in context. Because workers across occupations generally rate their jobs as satisfying (Gruenberg, 1980), these survey data leave open the question of whether correctional officers find their work as satisfying as do other occupational groups. Such comparative occupational research is in short supply, but one study presents beginning insights. Comparing a sample of southern officers to a national sample of workers, Cullen et al. (1989) found that the officers had lower satisfaction scores than did any other occupational category (although officers without a high school diploma reported satisfaction levels similar to other less educated workers).

In assessing the overall level of satisfaction among wardens, it thus seems important to examine both absolute responses and how these ratings compare with other occupational groups. Accordingly, in our analysis we use a measure of job satisfaction that allows us to assess whether wardens are "happy workers," and whether they are as happy as those in other occupational categories, with special attention paid to comparisons with correctional officers and with managers/professionals.

The existing literature suggests several considerations about what we are likely to find. First, we anticipate that wardens will have higher satisfaction levels than do correctional officers and thus, overall, be satisfied with their work. Previous research indicates that job satisfaction is positively related to occupational status (Gruenberg, 1980)—a relationship that appears to hold within corrections. In a study of probation workers, for example, Whitehead (1986) found that managerial personnel reported more satisfaction than did line officers. Although not distinguishing responses for administrators, Blau et al.'s (1986) analysis revealed that compared to other correctional workers, guards had lower satisfaction scores (see also Gerstein, Topp, & Correll, 1987, p. 361). Most instructive, Harris & Associates (1968) reported in a national survey that 70% of correctional administrators as opposed to 56% of line workers rated their jobs as "almost always satisfying " (p. 33).

Second, it is more problematic whether wardens' level of satisfaction will be equivalent to workers in other professional or managerial occupations. Those who characterize prison work as inherently dehumanizing may be guilty of hyperbole, but it is plausible that working in a total institution populated by society's more intractable deviants may be less attractive than other managerial settings and tasks.

Relatedly, there is reason to hypothesize that as an occupation, prison management is declining in its satisfactions. Commentators now portray wardens as caught in the uncomfortable nexus of increasing administrative problems and shrinking administrative authority. "In the good old days," argue Hawkins and Alpert (1989), "wardens ruled with an iron hand, running roughshod over guards as well as prisoners" (p. 357). As prisons have become overcrowded, more violent, racially polarized, and financially strapped (Carroll, 1974/1988; Colvin, 1992;

Irwin, 1980; Jacobs, 1977; Johnson, 1987), wardens have seen not an expansion of their powers but, rather, their role reduced "from a prison czar to a well-constrained manager" (Hawkins & Alpert, 1989, p. 357). Wardens still face the long-standing demand that they insure institutional order and security (Rothman, 1980), but they now must do so with their autonomy eroded by directives passed down by highly centralized state corrections departments, legal mandates and potential liabilities, unionized guards, and the threat of investigative reports by news media (Jacobs, 1977, 1983).

Determinants of Satisfaction

A central thesis of DiIulio's (1987) *Governing Prisons* is that correctional institutions are not all of a piece but vary in their quality and, presumably, in their satisfactions for the employees. If so, we should anticipate variations in job satisfactions that are related to wardens and their work situation. More specifically, our analysis is guided mainly by two models on reactions to correctional work.

The *individual experiences-importation* model suggests that reactions to work are the result of different types of experiences brought to the job. This model typically is operationalized by assessing whether status characteristics (e.g., education, gender, race), which are proxies for social experiences, affect outcome measures. In contrast, the *work environment-prisonization* model hypothesizes that reactions are shaped predominantly by the organizational conditions of prisons and the nature of the work role. This model asserts that work conditions envelop all employees—especially in a total institution like the prison—and thus minimize the effects of individuals' status characteristics (Cullen et al., 1993; Gerstein et al., 1987; Jurik & Halemba, 1984; Jurik et al., 1987; Van Voorhis, Cullen, Link, & Wolfe, 1991).

Previous research on correctional employees suggests support for both perspectives, although the ability of either model to explain variance in job satisfaction has differed across studies (Blau et al., 1986; Cullen et al., 1989; Gerstein et al., 1987; Jurik & Halemba, 1984; Jurik et al., 1987; Lindquist & Whitehead, 1986; Van Voorhis et al., 1991; Wright & Saylor, 1992). Further, the research is still too limited and conflicting to develop clear hypotheses about the effects of specific variables; at best, we can draw expected relations.

Our data set contained two individual characteristics: race and education. (Unfortunately, the survey instrument inadvertently omitted gender; we return to this issue later. Age was not assessed because of its high correlation with another variable, years in corrections.) Previous research is inconsistent on the effects of race: Although some studies of correctional workers report African-Americans to be less satisfied (Cullen et al., 1989; Toch & Klofas, 1982), others find no effect for race on job satisfaction (Blau et al., 1986; Jacobs & Kraft, 1978; Jurik et al., 1987; Wright & Saylor, 1992).

Alternatively, the research is largely consistent in finding that more educated correctional officers are less satisfied with their work (Blau et al., 1986; Cullen et al., 1989; Jurik et al., 1987; but see Walters, 1988). Jurik et al. (1987) attribute this negative relationship to status inconsistency: When their educational attainment outstrips the rewards provided by and skills needed for correctional work, guards will become dissatisfied. If this account is correct, we would not expect educated wardens to be differentially unhappy, because their training would be more commensurate with their occupational status as managers.

The work environment-prisonization model is assessed through variables falling into two subcategories: organizational conditions and the nature of the work role. Organizational conditions are operationalized by measuring (a) institutional age, size, and security level; (b) inmate gender and dangerousness; and (c) whether the prison is in a state or the federal system. The literature does not provide a clear basis for assessing

the impact of these conditions, but several considerations merit attention.

First, one possibility is that wardens who work in more manageable prisons will have higher levels of satisfaction. If so, job satisfaction should be higher in newer, smaller, minimum-security, and female prisons with less disruptive populations. Second, an alternative possibility is that wardens accrue occupational status and rewards by their appointment to posts in more challenging institutions. If so, satisfaction might be higher for wardens of large, potentially volatile institutions—the "Big Houses" or "violent prisons" in Irwin's (1980) terms. Third, the previous literature is consistent in showing that security level per se (e.g., maximum versus minimum) is not a strong predictor of job affects, such as satisfaction, burnout, powerlessness, and stress (Blau et al., 1986; Cullen et al., 1989; Van Voorhis et al., 1991; Walters, 1988). These broad categories may well mask the variability in work conditions within security classifications. Accordingly, we include a measure of inmate dangerousness and assess its effects independent of security level (see Blau et al., 1986). Fourth, compared to many state systems, the Federal Bureau of Prisons is often depicted as having a "better class of inmates" and as being more professionalized (DiIulio, 1991; McKelvey, 1977; Wright & Saylor, 1992). Insofar as qualitative differences in work environments exist, we anticipate that federal wardens would be more satisfied than their state counterparts.

The data set also allowed us to assess the impact on satisfaction of various dimensions of the wardens' work role. First, we include measures of the extent to which the prison's everyday operations are influenced by the courts, state departments of corrections, and the wardens themselves. As noted above, a central theme in correctional writings is that wardens' power has been increasingly constrained by outside forces (Hawkins & Alpert, 1989; Jacobs, 1977)—a condition that presumably would lessen their job satisfaction. Indeed, although limited, evidence on guards suggests that officers with less authority or influence are more likely to manifest negative job affects (Cheek & Miller, 1983; Hepburn, 1987; Jurik & Halemba, 1984). Further, this relationship might be expected to be stronger for wardens, whose managerial status might create higher expectations of job autonomy (cf. Gruenberg, 1980).

Second, we follow previous research on correctional employees and include measures of correctional experience (years in the work role) and the time wardens have spent in their current position. Correctional experience has had conflicting impacts on job outcomes, but when effects have been present, more time working in corrections has resulted in negative job affects (Cullen et al., 1989; Dignam, Barrera, & West, 1996; Jurik & Halemba, 1984; Jurik et al, 1987; Lindquist & Whitehead, 1986; Van Voorhis et al., 1991; Walters, 1988). Tenure in current position has been less studied and not found to be related for correctional workers to job burnout measures (Gerstein et al., 1987). We might anticipate, however, that wardens with more job tenure have shown the capacity to manage a prison effectively, have earned security and status, and reap more certain satisfactions from their work (see Jacobs, 1977; Smolowe, 1992).

Third, although the results are not uniform (Gerstein et al., 1987), supportive work relations have been found to increase job satisfaction (Cullen et al., 1985; Dignam et al., 1996; Lindquist & Whitehead, 1986). Accordingly, we expect that wardens with supportive relations will be more satisfied with their work.

Fourth, there is mounting evidence that correctional workers who have a human services orientation—favor offender rehabilitation, view inmates more positively—are more satisfied with their work (Cullen et al., 1985; Gerstein et al., 1987; Jurik et al., 1987; Walters, 1988; see also Welch, 1989). In the current study, we do not measure attitudes about treatment or offenders, which may well have been preexisting and "imported"

into the prison. Instead, to assess the potential effects of how wardens structure their current work role, we attempt to measure the degree of emphasis that wardens give, in their day-to-day operation of the prison, to treatment/human services and to custodial activities. In line with the research cited above, we anticipate that wardens will derive more satisfaction from a work role that attempts to achieve human services as opposed to custodial ends.

Fifth, we assess the wardens' managerial style, focusing in particular on whether those favoring participatory management by correctional officers find their work more satisfying. DiIulio (1987) suggests that prisons run most efficiently if administered in a bureaucratic, paramilitary style in which authority is hierarchical—from warden, to guard, to inmate. He also proposes that this approach to governing prisons fosters esprit de corps—and, by implication, job satisfaction—among correctional workers by empowering staff vis à vis inmates, creating a sense of teamwork, and reducing the social and physical incivilities of the prison's daily life. In contrast, critics challenge this conclusion by noting that even if bureaucratic authority were one (but not the only) means to producing orderly prisons, over time impersonal, hierarchical management risks eviscerating the quality of human relations, the more enriching or satisfying aspects of correctional work (Toch, 1989; see also Johnson, 1987). Our study, then, attempts to bring beginning data to bear on these divergent views of correctional administration and their effects on wardens' satisfaction.

Related to the work environment perspective, we consider three *previous work roles* of wardens—having been in the military, having been a correctional officer, and having been in a correctional position that delivered treatment—so as to explore whether past work role experiences shape current job satisfaction. Jurik et al. (1987) is one of the few studies to conduct an analysis of this type; they did not find a relationship between previous law enforcement experience and correctional officers' job satisfaction. Even so, given the dearth of existing research, potential influences of previous work experiences on wardens cannot be ruled out.

Finally, we include one measure of *social context:* whether the warden is working in a prison located in the South. With a few exceptions (Wright & Saylor, 1992), research has not examined how the larger context in which wardens are enmeshed influences reactions to correctional work roles. We selected to examine the effects of a southern location because of the distinct historical development of the region's prisons (McKelvey, 1977), current analyses showing the tendency of southern correctional systems to be more punitive toward offenders (Burton, Cullen, & Travis, 1987; Burton, Dunaway, & Kopache, 1992), and the wide use in criminological literature of [the] South as a proxy for contextual differences (Hawley & Messner, 1989).

Method

Sample

The data for this study are drawn from a 1989 national survey of wardens of all 512 state and federal prisons. Using a modified version of Dillman's (1978) Total Design Method, wardens were initially mailed a survey, which was then supplemented by a reminder letter. Nonrespondents received two additional mailings of the survey.[1] In all, 375 wardens, 73.2% of the sample, returned usable questionnaires.

Table 14.1 reports the sample's characteristics. The wardens are predominantly White, college educated, in their mid-40s, and have worked in corrections for nearly two decades, including 5 years at their current institution. Their career history shows that two thirds were in the military, one third were correctional officers, and a majority had held a treatment position in the field of corrections (e.g., counselor in prison, probation officer). They are employed primarily in male and state prisons (not classified solely

Table 14.1
Background and Occupational Characteristics of Wardens (*n* = 375)

Characteristic	Mean/Percentage
Mean age	46.5
Mean years of education	16.6
Percentage White	86.9
Percentage having military experience	67.9
Percentage having been a correctional officer	35.2
Percentage having worked in a treatment position	55.7
Percentage working in a male prison	85.0
Percentage working in a maximum-security prison	6.2
Percentage working in a state prison	93.4
Percentage working in a southern state	40.3
Mean months at current institution	58.0
Mean years working in corrections	19.8
Mean age of institution	31.3
Mean number of inmates at institution	862.1

as maximum security) that are three decades old and house over 860 inmates.

Measures

Job satisfaction measure. To assess job satisfaction, we employed a five-item scale used previously in the Quality of Employment Survey, a national study of workers conducted in 1973 and in 1977 (Quinn & Shepard, 1974; Quinn & Staines, 1979). The items composing this measure are presented in Table 14.2 (see Results section). To compute a respondent's job satisfaction score and overall scale mean, we used the weighting system indicated by Quinn and Shepard

(1974, pp. 54-55). Mean scores on each item could range from 1 to 5, with the five-item scale scores ranging from 5 to 25. The actual mean was 21.3, or an average scale score of 4.26. The Cronbach's alpha for the job satisfaction scale was .81. The reliability was .72 and .77, respectively, for the 1973 and 1977 national worker samples.

The items in the job satisfaction scale are similar to those used in previous studies of correctional workers (Cullen et al., 1989; Jacobs & Kraft, 1978; Jurik & Halemba, 1984; Lindquist & Whitehead, 1986), in that they assess general feelings of satisfaction, ask respondents to compare their current position against other possible occupational alternatives, and ask if respondents would be willing to recommend their work to someone close to them. We also should note that the scale is a "global" measure of job satisfaction; it does not assess attitudes toward specific facets of an occupation, such as financial remuneration, opportunities for advancement, or safety hazards. Global and facet-specific measures of job satisfaction tend to be related positively (Quinn & Staines, 1979, p. 206), and correctional research does not show that studies using the two kinds of scales differ markedly in their findings (see Blau et al., 1986). Even so, caution should be exercised in assuming that our data measure more than generalized feelings of wardens toward their work.

The Quality of Employment Survey satisfaction scale has the added advantage of allowing potentially useful comparisons of how wardens rate their work vis à vis other occupational groups. In Table 14.2, we are able to examine how wardens'levels of job satisfaction compare with both the 1977 national sample of workers (N = 2,242) and a 1983 sample of 155 correctional officers who were employed in a southern state (Cullen et al., 1989). In Table 14.3, we are able to compare wardens' job satisfaction scores with those achieved by other occupational categories (N = 2,042) in the 1973 Quality of Employment Survey (the 1977 survey did not report these data).

These comparisons must, of course, be viewed with a measure of caution. The national data are drawn from the 1970s, and their generalizability to today is undetermined. Given that there is a long-term tendency in the literature for workers to rate their work as generally satisfying, however, it is unlikely that major shifts in satisfaction scores among workers would have occurred—although some fluctuations certainly are possible. For example, between the 1973 and 1977 Quality of Employment Surveys, the mean job satisfaction score declined from 3.79 to 3.66. Similarly, the correctional officer sample is drawn from a single state, though the results for this sample are largely consistent with findings for guards studied in other states and regions (Cullen et al., 1989).

The possible limitations of the comparative occupational analyses also must be balanced against their advantages. First, existing studies present virtually no data on how satisfaction scores (or other job-outcome measures) for correctional workers compare to those employed in other occupations. In the absence of a comparative context, interpreting scores as showing that correctional workers are "highly satisfied" or "a class of alienated workers" is potentially misleading. Second, at the very least the comparisons presented here are useful in deriving operating understandings of wardens' job satisfaction, which, if questioned, can be subjected to reevaluation by future researchers.

Independent variables. The multivariate analysis of the determinants of job satisfaction included several sets of variables. Two *individual variables* were included in the sample: race (I = White; 0 = non-White), and years of education. As noted previously, gender was inadvertently comitted from the survey instrument. Even so, it is not clear whether the results were biased by the failure to control for gender. A consistent finding in the correctional worker empirical literature is that gender is *not* significantly related with job satisfaction (Blau et al., 1986; Cullen et al., 1989; Jurik et al., 1987;

Table 14.2
Frequency Distribution for Job Satisfaction Items for Wardens Compared to Correctional Officer (CO) Sample and National Sample of Employed Adults (in percentages)

Items	Samples		
	Wardens	**COs**	**National**
1. All in all, how satisfied would you say you are with your job?			
A. very satisfied	66.0	25.5	46.7
B. somewhat satisfied	30.5	51.0	41.7
C. not too satisfied	2.9	19.0	8.9
D. not satisfied at all	.5	4.5	2.7
2. With regard to the kind of job you'd most like to have: If you were free to go into any kind of job you wanted, what would your choice be?			
A. I would keep the job I now have.	72.6	31.1	38.1
B. I would want to retire and not work at all.	12.1	9.3	1.0
C. I would prefer some other job to the job I now have.	15.3	59.6	60.0
3. Knowing what you know now, if you had to decide all over again whether to take the job you now have, what would you decide?			
A. I would decide without hesitation to take the same job.	78.4	50.7	63.9
B. I would have some second thoughts about taking my job.	19.5	43.4	28.3
C. I would decide definitely not to take the same job.	2.2	5.9	7.8
4. In general, how well would you say that your job measures up to the sort of job you wanted when you took it?			
A. My job is very much like the job I wanted.	68.3	24.3	52.5
B. My job is somewhat like the job I wanted.	28.0	40.8	35.9
C. My job is not very much like the job I wanted.	3.8	34.9	11.6
5. If a good friend of yours told you he (or she) was interested in working in a job like yours for your employer, what would you tell him (or her)?			
A. I would strongly recommend the job.	72.5	42.8	61.8
B. I would have doubts about recommending the job.	23.6	44.7	29.7
C. I would advise my friend against taking the job.	3.8	12.5	8.6
Mean	4.26	3.12	3.66

Van Voorhis et al., 1991; see also Fry & Glaser, 1987). Furthermore, we attempted to reconstruct the gender variable by matching institutions in the data set with wardens' names from a directory of the American Correctional Association (1989). This process was imperfect: Gender in 26 cases could not be determined from the name listed, and we cannot guarantee that a change in the institution's warden did not occur in the time period covered by the directory. In any case, 35 female wardens were found by this method to be in the sample (9.8% of those coded for gender). The multivariate analysis was run with the reconstructed gender variable included. In no case was a significant relationship found for gender.

The work environment-prisonization model contained both organizational and work-role measures. *Organizational variables* consisted of the number of inmates at the institution, the prison's age, the prison's security classification (1 = maximum only, closed; 0 = all other types), the gender of the inmates housed in the prison (1 = male-only prison; 0 = female, coed),and whether the institution was in a state or federal system (1 = state). The wardens reported the number of inmates, and the other institutional data were obtained from a secondary source (American Correctional Association,1989).

The final organizational variable, inmate dangerousness, was assessed with a three-item measure (alpha = .61). Wardens were asked to state the percentage of the inmates in their institution that they believed "were dangerously violent and should not be released into society," "need to be protected from other inmates," and "might be called chronic 'troublemakers.'"

The work-role variables assessed various aspects of the wardens' influence, relations, and content of daily activities. To assess the wardens' managerial autonomy, the respondents were asked to "indicate what degree of influence each of the following exert on the day-to-day operations of your institution: courts, state central office, themselves." The wardens responded by using a scale ranging from *no influence* (1) to *very great influence* (10). Each item was treated as a separate variable measuring a distinct form of autonomy.

Participatory management (alpha = .58) was measured with two items that wardens were asked to rate using a Likert-type scale ranging from *very strongly agree* (1) to *very strongly disagree* (7): (a) "Generally speaking, correctional officers should have a say in determining procedures designed to implement institutional policy." (b) "Correctional officers should have more opportunities to give me input into the design of institutional procedures." Similarly, *social support* (alpha = .61), was measured with two items, also rated with the agree-disagree scale: (a) "There are few people outside of the institution with whom I can talk about my job." (b) "There are many people on my staff with whom I can openly discuss the problems of my job." In these two measures, responses were coded so that a high response indicates more participatory management and more social support.

Wardens were also asked to rate the emphasis they gave (*no emphasis* [1]; *very great emphasis* [10]) in "the day-to-day operation of your institution" of various custodial and rehabilitative activities. *Emphasis on rehabilitational human services* (alpha = .712) consisted of three activities: (a) providing programs to help inmates learn new skills, (b) providing activities to keep inmates busy, (c) providing adequate space and other needed services to inmates. *Emphasis on custody/institutional order* (alpha = .887) included six items: (a) creating conditions that prevent escapes, (b) ensuring that institutional rules are followed by inmates, (c) ensuring that institutional procedures and regulations are followed by staff, (d) preventing the flow of contraband into prison, (e) preventing the flow or exchange of contraband goods/materials within the prison, and (f) creating conditions that protect inmates from one another.

To assess the possible effect of tenure in work roles, wardens were asked to self-report their years in corrections and months at the current institution.

The analysis included three measures of *previous work roles*: having been in the military (1 = yes); having been a correctional officer (1 = yes), and having worked in a treatment position either in a prison or the field of corrections (e.g., probation officer) (1 = yes). Note that the survey instrument contained space for 10 past positions. Accordingly, the data on having been a guard or worked in treatment are limited to the last 10 previous positions the respondents held.

One social context variable was used: the prison's regional location (coded as 1 = located in [the] South). [The] South was defined as the following states: Alabama, Arkansas, Florida, Georgia, Kentucky, Louisiana, Mississippi, North Carolina, South Carolina, Tennessee, Texas, and Virginia.

Finally, an examination of the correlation matrix revealed no associations to be sufficiently high to warrant concern over multicollinearity among the independent variables. Following Cohen and Cohen (1983), mean values were substituted for missing values.[2]

Results

Overall Level of Job Satisfaction

As the results in Table 14.2 indicate, the wardens in the sample evidenced a high level of satisfaction with their work. Over 90% stated that they were very or somewhat satisfied with their job, and large majorities said that they wished to keep their job, would take the job again without hesitation, felt the job measured up to the expectations they had when they first became a warden, and would recommend their job to a good friend.

Table 14.2 also indicates that wardens' level of satisfaction exceeded that found for the sample of correctional officers and for the 1977 national Quality of Employment Survey sample. Building on this point. Table 14.3 presents data on how wardens' mean satisfaction scores compare with those for other occupational categories (1973 survey data) and for the correctional officer sample. It is instructive that wardens manifested the *highest* mean score, whereas correctional officers had the lowest score on the satisfaction scale.

One caveat about interpreting these results is in order. The results for the national

Table 14.3

Comparison of Mean Job Satisfaction Scores Between Wardens Sample and Other Occupational Categories (scale 1 to 5)

Occupational Category	Mean Score
Wardens	4.26
Farmers and farm managers	4.23
Professional and technical	4.11
Farm laborers and farm foremen	4.08
Managers and administrators (except farm)	4.00
Craftworkers	3.89
Private household workers	3.83
Sales	3.82
Transport equipment operatives	3.81
Service workers (except private household)	3.72
Clerical	3.67
Operatives (except transport)	3.39
Nonfarm laborers	3.28
Correctional officer sample	3.12

sample are for occupational categories (for example, managers and administrators) and not for specific occupations within those categories. Accordingly, it is possible that the satisfaction scores for a given occupation might surpass the wardens' mean. Even so, the general pattern of the results are clear: The wardens sampled showed high levels of job satisfaction both absolutely and in comparison to other occupational groups.

Determinants of Job Satisfaction

Table 14.4 reports the results of job satisfaction regressed on individual variables, organizational variables, work-role variables, previous work roles, and social context. The equation is statistically significant, with 18% of the variance explained.[3]

No individual variables, previous work-role variables, or social context were significantly related to job satisfaction. Among the organizational variables, only number of inmates exerted a significant effect, with wardens working in prisons with more inmates having higher levels of job satisfaction. Three work-role variables, however, had a significant relationship with satisfaction: Wardens with influence over their institutions and with an emphasis on rehabilitation/human services were more satisfied with their work, whereas wardens were less satisfied if they rated as high the influence in their prisons of central offices of state departments of corrections.

Discussion

Perhaps the most noteworthy finding is the high level of job satisfaction evidenced by wardens. In line with previous occupational research, we had anticipated that wardens would be more satisfied with their work than correctional officers would be with theirs—a result to which our data lend credence. More problematic, however, was whether wardens' satisfaction would be consistent with that for managers/administrators generally, or whether it would be depressed by the unique social setting in which they worked. As noted, wardens might have been expected to be relatively unhappy workers if commentators were correct who claim that prisons are dehumanizing to keeper and kept alike and that wardens are an increasingly beleaguered profession. These perspectives do not seem to be borne out by the data: Wardens seemed to derive satisfaction from their work similar to the level found among managers as an occupational category.

Somewhat ironically, the data also suggest that prisons may house not only highly satisfied workers—wardens—but also the least satisfied occupational group—correctional officers. The comparative occupational data are not definitive, but Table 14.4

Table 14.4
Determinants of Wardens' Job Satisfaction

Independent Variables	Beta	Significance Level
Individual variables		
Race (1 = White)	.050	.316
Education	.052	.360
Organizational variables		
Number of inmates	.133	.015
Prison's age	.048	.347
Male prison	−.011	.830
State prison	−.041	.412
Maximum security	−.021	.661
Inmate dangerousness	−.026	.607
Work-role variables		
Warden's influence	.184	.000*
Corrections department's influence	−.160	.002
Courts' influence	−.027	.610
Participatory management	.014	.779
Years in corrections	.070	.203
Months at institution	−.068	.185
Emphasis on custody	.039	.538
Emphasis on rehabilitation	.154	.017
Social support	.108	.031
Previous work roles		
In military	.024	.624
Been a correctional officer	.017	.785
Worked in treatment	.021	.686
Social context		
In [the] South	−.054	.294
Equation F = 3.85; $p < .000$ R^2 = .182		

*$P < .000$.

reveals a rather stark finding: The wardens' mean score was higher, and the correctional officers' mean score was lower, than all other occupational categories (see Cullen et al, 1989). Even if some bias were to exist in the data, this general pattern of results appears too pronounced to be merely a methodological artifact—especially because the correctional officer satisfaction appears similar to guards in other contexts (Cullen et al.,1989). In any case, future researchers might profit from paying closer attention to the potential gap in job satisfaction between wardens and their employees and what role, if any, this gap plays in hindering warden-officer relations and administrative effectiveness.

The attempt to uncover the determinants of variations in wardens' job satisfaction met with only modest success. As a whole, the variables accounted for just under 20% of the variation in satisfaction—an amount not dissimilar to previous studies of correctional workers (Blau et al., 1986; Cullen et al., 1989; but see Jurik et al., 1987). Even so, most of the models and the variables identified were of little assistance in explaining wardens' satisfaction.

It may very well be that these factors simply are not useful in differentiating among wardens who tend, after all, to vary among one another only a limited range in their job satisfaction. The alternative possibility, however, is that better measurement might have increased the explanatory power of the analysis. In this regard, future research might improve on our study in at least four ways.

First, investigators might profit from assessing not only global job satisfaction, as our study did, but also satisfaction with specific facets of the wardens' work situation, such as pay and relations with correctional officers, on which more variation might exist (see Quinn & Staines, 1979). Second, several variables were assessed by either single items or scales that had acceptable, but not strong, reliabilities, and by measures that tapped only a restricted aspect of the underlying construct (e.g., managerial autonomy, participatory management). The analysis would potentially be enhanced by using multiple-item scales less prone to measurement error and by using measures of several dimensions of a given work-related construct. Third, in several instances, we used perceptual measures rather than more objective indicators. For example, we measured inmate dangerousness by asking wardens to characterize the institution's population. Possibly, more objective measures—such as the prison's homicide rate, frequency of lock downs, and number of gang-affiliated inmates—might more adequately assess prison dangerousness and, in turn, more directly affect wardens' satisfaction with their work.

Fourth, more variation might have been explained if we had incorporated measures of intrinsic occupational rewards. Previous research suggests that job satisfaction is higher among workers who see their work role as allowing for personal growth, variety in job tasks, new experiences, and so on (Gruenberg, 1980; Jurik et al., 1987). We did assess one condition that often is conceived as an intrinsic reward—wardens' influence or autonomy (Gruenberg, 1980; Jurik et al., 1987)—and it is instructive that this condition exerted significant effects on job satisfaction. We will revisit this issue later.

Even with these limitations, several useful insights did emerge from the effort to uncover the determinants of wardens' satisfaction. First, although existing correctional officer research shows that education is inversely related to satisfaction, this relationship did not hold for wardens. This pattern of results lends credence to the interpretation that education produces dissatisfaction when correctional workers experience status inconsistency (Jurik et al., 1987). Educated wardens are not happier in their work, but neither, it appears, do they find their educational training inadequately used and compensated.

Second, at least as measured, organizational conditions generally did not affect wardens' job satisfaction. Previous research has not explored a variety of organizational conditions, but those features of prisons that have been assessed (e.g., security classification) have not generally been strongly related to correctional worker satisfaction

(Blau et al., 1986). As such, the findings reported here should be considered as reinforcing the conclusion that worker satisfaction is not rooted in organizational context. The challenge for researchers debating this point is to uncover prison conditions, or more revealing measures of prison conditions, that can in fact explain variation in job satisfaction.

Third, however, one organizational factor—number of inmates—did affect job satisfaction *positively*. It is not clear why working in a larger prison fosters wardens' satisfaction, but we can offer one possible interpretation. Institutional size may be a proxy for scope of administrative responsibility. If so, larger prisons may reflect a step along the path of wardens' occupational mobility, with higher status and commensurate job satisfactions accruing to those chosen from among their colleagues to exercise greater job responsibilities.

Fourth, past occupational experiences, as well as time in the field of corrections, had virtually no effect on job satisfaction. This finding suggests that sources of satisfaction have less to do with previous positions than with the nature of the current work role.

Fifth, and relatedly, four work-role variables were related significantly with job satisfaction. Consistent with past research, social support—having informal relations in which problems can be shared—increased satisfaction (Cullen et al., 1985; Dignam et al., 1996; Lindquist & Whitehead, 1986). Also consistent with much of past research, wardens were more satisfied who emphasized the provision of treatment or human services to inmates (Cullen et al., 1985; Gerstein et al., 1987; Jurik et al., 1987; Walters, 1988). In contrast, emphasizing custodial practices, which may be an essential component of a warden's responsibilities (DiIulio, 1987; Rothman, 1980), did not produce the added advantage of making wardens happier workers.

Perhaps most salient, however, is the finding that wardens' satisfaction decreased when the central department of corrections'

influence over the prison's day-to-day operations was seen as high, and increased when wardens saw their own influence over their institution as high. The key issue, it appears, is the close relationship between wardens' autonomy or authority over their work and their level of satisfaction. As noted, job autonomy is often conceived of as an intrinsic occupational reward; accordingly, the finding for wardens is consistent with research showing that intrinsic rewards are important determinants of job satisfaction (Gruenberg, 1980; Jurik et al., 1987).

More broadly, these results reveal the personal costs of the trend to limit wardens' power and to bureaucratize state and federal corrections (Hawkins & Alpert, 1989; Jacobs, 1977). Highly centralized, hierarchical authority may have organizational benefits, but our data suggest that it may also produce the unintended consequence of diminishing wardens' satisfaction with their work.

Study Questions

1. Discuss the overall level of job satisfaction discovered by the authors through the national survey.

2. Why might the findings regarding the level of job satisfaction be considered surprising?

3. What were used as some of the primary determinants of satisfaction in this study?

4. What were the major correlates of a high level of job satisfaction for prison wardens? Speculate as to why these correlates revealed themselves in these analyses.

Notes

1. For one state, the mailings were distributed, on their request, through the central department of corrections. All wardens in the state completed the survey.

2. The mean number of missing cases for each variable in the analysis was 17. The highest number of missing cases was for the organizational variables. The data were reanalyzed without mean substitution, and the results closely resembled those reported in Table 14.4. In the new analysis, social support became nonsignificant, whereas military background achieved statistical significance (beta = .133). All other significant relationships obtained regardless: of whether mean values were substituted.

3. Because the dependent variable was skewed toward high levels of satisfaction, the data were reanalyzed using a log transformation of the dependent variable. The results closely resembled those reported in Table 14.4: the same variables were significant in both equations (assuming we can count, in the log transformation analysis, social support as significant with p = .054).

References

American Correctional Association. (1989). *ACA directory—1988. Juvenile and adult correctional departments, institutions, agencies, and paroling authorities.* College Park, MD: American Correctional Association.

Blau, J. R., Light, S. C., & Chamlin, M. (1986). Individual and contextual effects on stress and job satisfaction: A study of prison staff. *Work and Occupations, 13,* 131–156.

Brockway, Z.R. (1969). *Fifty years of prison service: An autobiography.* Montclair, NJ: Patterson Smith. (Original work published 1912)

Burton, V. S., Jr., Cullen, F. T., & Travis, L. F., III. (1987). The collateral consequences of a felony conviction: A national study of state statutes. *Federal Probation, 51,* 52–60.

Burton, V. S., Jr., Dunaway, R. G., & Kopache, R. (1992). To punish or rehabilitate? A research note assessing the purposes of state correctional departments as defined by state legal codes. *Journal of Crime and Justice, 16,* 177–188.

Carroll, L. (1988). *Hacks, Blacks, and cons: Race relations in a maximum security prison.* Prospect Heights, IL: Waveland. (Original work published 1974)

Cheek, F. E., & Miller, M. D. (1983). The experience of stress for correction officers: A double-bind theory of correctional stress. *Journal of Criminal Justice, 11,* 105–120.

Cohen, J., & Cohen, P. (1983). *Applied multiple regression/correlation analysis for the behavioral sciences* (2nd ed.). Hillsdale, NJ: Lawrence Erlbaum.

Colvin, M. (1992). *The penitentiary in crisis: From accommodation to riot in New Mexico.* Albany: State University of New York Press.

Cullen, F. T., Latessa, E. J., Burton, V. S., Jr., & Lombardo, L. X. (1993). The correctional orientation of prison wardens: Is the rehabilitative ideal supported? *Justice Quarterly, 31,* 69–92.

Cullen, F. T., Link, B. G., Cullen, J. B., & Wolfe, N. T. (1989). How satisfying is prison work? A comparative occupational approach. *Journal of Offender Counseling, Services and Rehabilitation, 14,* 89–108.

Cullen, F. T., Link, B. G., Wolfe, N. T., & Frank, J. (1985). The social dimensions of correctional officer stress. *Justice Quarterly, 4,* 505–533.

Dignam, J. T., Barrera, M., Jr., & West, S. G. (1996). Occupational stress, social support, and burnout among correctional officers. *American Journal of Community Psychology, 14,* 177–193.

DiIulio, J. J., Jr. (1987). *Governing prisons: A comparative study of correctional management.* New York: Free Press.

DiIulio, J. J., Jr. (1991). *No escape: The future of American corrections.* New York: Basic Books.

Dillman, D. A (1978). *Mail and telephone surveys: The total design method.* New York: Wiley.

Fry, L. J., & Glaser, D. (1987). Gender differences in work adjustment of prison employees. *Journal of Offender Counseling, Services and Rehabilitation, 12,* 39–52.

Gerstein, L. H., Topp, C. G., & Correll, G. (1987). The role of the environment and person when predicting burnout among correctional personnel. *Criminal Justice and Behavior, 14,* 352–369.

Grieser, R. C. (1988). *Wardens and state corrections commissioners offer their view in national assessment.* Washington, DC: National Institute of Justice.

Gruenberg, B. (1980). The happy worker: An analysis of educational and occupational differences in determinants of job satisfaction. *American Journal of Sociology, 86,* 247–271.

Harris, L., & Associates. (1968). *Corrections 1968. A climate for change.* Washington, DC: Joint Commission on Correctional Manpower and Training.

Hawkins, R., & Alpert, G. P. (1989). *American prison systems: Punishment and justice.* Englewood Cliffs, NJ: Prentice Hall.

Hawley, F. F., & Messner, S. F. (1989). The southern violence construct: A review of arguments, evidence, and the normative context. *Justice Quarterly, 6,* 481–511.

Hepburn, J. R. (1987). The prison control structure and its effects on work attitudes: The perceptions and attitudes of prison guards. *Journal of Criminal Justice, 15,* 49–64.

Irwin, J. (1980). *Prisons in turmoil.* Boston: Little, Brown.

Jacobs, J. B. (1977). *Stateville: The penitentiary in mass society.* Chicago: University of Chicago Press.

Jacobs, J. B. (1978). What prison guards think: A profile of the Illinois force. *Crime and Delinquency, 24,* 185–196.

Jacobs, J. B. (1983). *New perspectives on prisons and imprisonment.* Ithaca, NY: Cornell University Press.

Jacobs, J. B., & Kraft, L. J. (1978). Integrating the keepers: A comparison of Black and White prison guards in Minois. *Social Problems, 25,* 304–318.

Johnson, R. (1987). *Hard time: Understanding and reforming the prison.* Monterey, CA: Brooks/Cole.

Jurik, N. C., & Halemba, G. J. (1984). Gender, work conditions, and the job satisfaction of women in a non-traditional occupation: Female correctional officers in men's prisons. *Sociological Quarterly, 25,* 551–566.

Jurik, N. C., Halemba, G. J., Musheno, M. C., & Boyle, B. V. (1987). Educational attainment, job satisfaction, and the professionalization of correctional officers. *Work and Occupations, 14,* 106–125.

Kinkade, P. T., & Leone, M. C. (1992a). Issues and answers: Prison administrators' responses to controversies surrounding privatization. *Prison Journal, 72,* 57–76.

Kinkade, P. T., & Leone, M. C. (1992b). The privatization of prisons: The wardens' views. *Federal Probation, 56,* 58–65.

Lawes, Warden L. E. (1932). *Twenty thousand years in Sing Sing.* Philadelphia, PA: Blakiston.

Lindquist, C. A., & Whitehead, J. T. (1986). Correctional officers as parole officers: An examination of a community supervision sanction. *Criminal Justice and Behavior, 13,* 197–222.

Lombardo, L. X. (1989). *Guards imprisoned: Correctional officers at work* (2nd ed.). Cincinnati, OH: Anderson.

McKelvey, B. (1977). *American prisons: A history of good intentions.* Montclair, NJ: Patterson Smith.

Miller, M. B. (1989, March). *The prison warden study.* Paper presented at the annual meeting of the Academy of Criminal Justice Sciences, Washington, DC.

Mitford, J. (1974). *Kind and usual punishment: The prison business.* New York: Vintage.

Quinn, R. P., & Shepard, L. J. (1974). *The 1972-1973 quality of employment survey: Descriptive statistics.* Ann Arbor: University of Michigan, Institute for Social Research.

Quinn, R. P., & Staines, G. L. (1979). *The quality of employment survey: Descriptive statistics and with comparison data from the 1969–70 and 1972–73 surveys.* Ann Arbor: University of Michigan, Institute for Social Research.

Rothman, D. J. (1980). *Conscience and convenience: The asylum and its alternatives in progressive America.* Boston: Little, Brown.

Smolowe, I. (1992, December 14). Bringing decency to hell. *Time,* pp. 60–62.

Talarico, S. M., & Swanson, C. R., Jr. (1982). Police perceptions and job satisfaction. *Work and Occupations, 9,* 59–72.

Tannenbaum, F. (1922). *Wall shadows: A study in American prisons.* New York: Wiley.

Toch, H. (1989). [Review of *Governing Prisons*]. *Society, 26,* 86–89.

Toch, H., & Klofas, J. (1982). Alienation and desire for job enrichment among correctional officers. *Federal Probation, 46,* 35–44.

Van Voorhis, P., Cullen, P. T., Link, B.G., & Wolfe, N. T. (1991). The impact of race and gender on correctional officers' orientation to the integrated environment. *Journal of Research in Crime and Delinquency, 28,* 472–500.

Walters, S. (1988). Correctional officers' perceptions of powerlessness. *Journal of Crime and Justice, 11,* 47–59.

Welch, M. (1989). Evaluating the sources of job satisfaction among officers: A qualitative and quantitative approach. *The Justice Professional, 4,* 120–140.

Whitehead, J. T. (1986). Job burnout and job satisfaction among probation managers. *Journal of Criminal Justice, 14,* 25–35.

Wright, K. N., & Saylor, W. G. (1992). A comparison of perceptions of the work environment between minority and non-minority employees of the federal prison system. *Journal of Criminal Justice, 20,* 63–71.

Zimbardo, P. G., Banks, W. C., Haney, C., & Jaffe, D. (1973, April 8). A Pirandellian prison: The mind is a formidable jailer. *New York Times Magazine,* pp. 38–56. ✦

15
A Quantitative Review and Description of Corrections-Based Education, Vocation, and Work Programs

David B. Wilson

Catherine A. Gallagher

Mark B. Coggeshall

Doris L. MacKenzie

Although the very existence of treatment options within correctional institutions has had a varied and controversial past, the fact remains that most institutions of all types have some type of educational, vocational, and/or work program in place. The goals of these work programs are often multifaceted and may offer the institution some type of revenue, or at least reduced expenditure, from the labor of the inmates. Educational, vocational, and/or work programs may also provide the inmates with something constructive to fill their time, thereby making the population as a whole more manageable for line officers and prison administrators.

Prison work programs have also been said to offer rehabilitative skills that inmates may

carry with them upon release, thus increasing the likelihood they will "succeed" in the long term. Unfortunately, the effectiveness of these programs has not been explored adequately to determine what precisely works best, if rehabilitation and treatment are at least the primary goals. The authors of this article provide a meta-analysis of educational, vocational, and work programs that exist inside prisons. Ultimately, they determine that, while the presence of these programs do seem to meet several correctional goals (including reductions in recidivism), more effort is needed to identify the specific components of effective programs.

Educational and vocational programs long have been a part of prisons in the United States.[1] A 1995 survey of all state and federal adult correctional facilities conducted by the Bureau of Justice Statistics[2] showed that 94 percent of all such facilities (1,500 in total) had work programs and 87 percent had education programs. Roughly one third of all facilities employed inmates in a prison industry and about half of the facilities provided vocational training. Basic adult education and secondary education [including general equivalency diploma (GED) programs] were offered by more than 75 percent of the facilities. One third of all facilities provided access to college course work. Overall, almost two-thirds of all inmates participated in a work program and slightly less than one quarter of all inmates participated in an education program. Such programs represent a major financial investment on the part of the criminal justice system. It is critical, therefore, to examine the effectiveness of these programs in achieving the rehabilitative goal of reducing future offending.

Although there is theoretical and empirical evidence that academic underachievement and unemployment are related to criminal offending, evidence of the effectiveness of education, vocation, and work programs is less clear. Reviews of evaluative

Excerpts from *Corrections Management Quarterly*, Volume 3, Number 4 (1999). pp. 8–18. Copyright © 1999 by Aspen Publishers, Inc. Reprinted by Permission.

studies of education programs present an equivocal picture of their effectiveness. Gerber and Fritsch[3] concluded that prison education programs were effective. Similarly, Taylor[4,5] concluded that post-secondary educational programs were able to reduce recidivism and argued that they represent a potentially cost-effective method of crime prevention. Looking more broadly at all education program types, Linden and Perry[1] concluded that while such programs clearly have demonstrated their ability to increase academic achievement, they have not demonstrated their ability to increase post-release employment or to reduce offending. In a review of recent studies of adult basic education (ABE) programs, MacKenzie and Hickman stated that "research in the 1990s has failed to reach a definitive conclusion regarding the effectiveness of correctional education on recidivism."[6]

Reviews of vocational and correctional work programs are similarly equivocal. Gerber and Fritsch[3] interpreted the available evidence as supporting the effectiveness of vocational programs in reducing recidivism. In contrast, MacKenzie and Hickman[6] concluded that while some programs appear effective, others appear detrimental. In general, programs that have multiple components, have follow-up programs, and teach skills relevant to the current job market appear to be the most likely to be successful.[7,8]

Taken together, these reviews highlight the lack of a clear consensus from the empirical literature on the effectiveness of education, vocation, and work programs. A potential source of this ambiguity is the heavy reliance on narrative forms of review. Only two of the above-mentioned research summaries are an exception. Gerber and Fritsch[3] used a vote-counting method of synthesis and MacKenzie and Hickman[6] calculated and reported program effect sizes for each reviewed study. The weaknesses of narrative reviews and vote-counting methods have been well documented.[9] Using current quantitative research synthesis techniques,[10] this study addresses the weakness of prior reviews by conducting a meta-analysis of outcome studies of education, vocation, and work programs for adults involved in the criminal justice systems. The authors address the question of the effectiveness of these programs in reducing post-release criminal involvement. Additionally, the study evaluated the methodological adequacy of this body of empirical work and assessed the relationship between observed effects and both methodological and program features.

Overview of Synthesis Approach

The purpose of this study was to quantitatively synthesize the extant evidence on the effects of education, vocation, and work programs using the method of meta-analysis. The authors defined the research space for this synthesis as those studies that (1) evaluated an education, vocation, or work program for convicted adults or persons identified by the criminal justice system (court) and placed in a diversion program; (2) reported on a post-program measure of recidivism (such as arrest, conviction, self-report, technical violation, or incarceration); (3) included a non-program comparison group, that is, a comparison group that did not receive an education, vocation, or work program; and (4) were published or written after 1975 in the English language. The study did not include nonacademic education programs, such as life-skills training, cognitive or behavioral training, and so forth, as those were judged to represent a distinct form of intervention. Note that these criteria exclude many studies of education, vocation, and work programs that did not examine the effects of these programs relative to a comparison group on a measure of post-release offending.

The veracity of the conclusions drawn from a synthesis is related directly to the adequacy of the search for relevant studies. The study goal was to identify and retrieve all, or nearly all, studies meeting the eligibility criteria stated above. The authors did not restrict this study to published works because there is ample evidence that doing so will produce a biased set of studies.[11,12] The study began by examining the reference lists of review articles.[6] This was augmented by searching the following computerized bibliographic databases in the fall of 1998: *Criminal Justice Periodical Index, Dissertation Abstracts Online, ERIC, NCJRS, Psyc INFO, Social SciSearch, Social Sciences Abstracts,* and *Sociological Abstracts.*

The search terms included correctional education, vocational training, vocational education, ABE, GED, general education diploma, secondary education, correctional industries, and correctional work. This search was restricted by including terms specific to evaluative studies (e.g., evaluation, outcome, comparison, etc.), offender populations (e.g., offender, criminal, convict, prisoner, etc.), and recidivism or reoffense. This search strategy identified 143 potential documents, of which the authors retrieved and examined 133. Ten documents remain elusive to these retrieval efforts and a careful read of their titles and abstracts suggests that they are unlikely to meet the above criteria. Thirty-three unique studies were eligible and included in this synthesis.

From each unique research study, the authors extracted a variety of information describing the research participants, program characteristics, research methodology, and detailed results on post-release measures of offending for each group. Many of these studies reported on multiple programs of interest, such as ABE and post-secondary education, contrasting each with a common comparison group. Therefore, the authors treated each program-comparison as the primary unit of analysis. This resulted in 53 program-comparison contrasts across the 33 studies used in this synthesis.

The initial coding protocol was pilot tested by multiple coders, each coding a small sample of studies. Items with poor agreement and/or items that did not map well onto the characteristics of the studies were modified or dropped. This process was repeated until the authors arrived at a coding protocol with acceptable inter-rater agreement that was consistent with the characteristics of the eligible studies.

The data extracted from each study were generally in the form of a proportion of program and comparison participants who recidivated. For purposes of this article, the authors examined only one recidivism outcome per program-comparison contrast. When multiple recidivism data were available from a single program-comparison contrast, the authors selected the data representing reincarceration and the data for the longest follow-up period. In the absence of a measure of reincarceration, preference was given to a measure of conviction, then arrest, then other recidivism measures such as composite indicators. A complete coding protocol is available from the authors.

The recidivism data were converted into an index, the odds-ratio, which measured the differential rate of recidivism between the two groups. This measure was selected due to its desirable properties when analyzing dichotomous data.[13] The odds-ratio was interpreted as the odds of a successful outcome in the experimental group relative to the odds of a successful outcome in the control group. An odds is the probability of success divided by the probability of failure. For example, a success rate of 66 percent translates into an odds (not an odds-ratio) of 2 calculated as $0.66/(1-0.66)$, whereas a success rate of 50 percent translates into an odds of 1 calculated as $0.50/(1-0.50)$. As the name implies, the odds-ratio is the ratio of the respective odds. Using the above two odds produces an odds-ratio of 2. Thus, an experimental group with a success rate of 66 percent has twice the odds of a successful outcome as a comparison group with a success rate of 50 percent. The odds-ratio should not be confused with the risk-ratio. The latter is simply the ratio of the success rate for each group. The success rates of 66 and 50 percent produce a risk-ratio of 1.32 (66/50).

A potential threat to the validity of these findings was the authors' decision to code, when possible, multiple program-comparison contrasts from a single study. This creates statistical dependencies among the effect sizes, potentially biasing the results.[14] The authors concluded that restricting the data set to one program-comparison contrast per study would have obscured valuable data regarding the effectiveness of the programs under consideration. Furthermore, the seriousness of the threat was deemed minimal because the dependencies were across program types (i.e., ABE and vocational training) and the focus of the analyses was on estimating the mean effect size within each program type. The program type mean effect sizes, therefore, were unaffected by these dependencies.

Description of the Research Literature

Table 15.1 presents basic descriptive information for the 33 studies and 53 program-comparison contrasts. Nearly half of these studies were from published sources and nearly one third were local, state, or federal government reports. The remaining documents either were unpublished technical reports or dissertations. Most of the studies were conducted in the United States (31 of the 33). The remaining two studies were conducted in Canada.

The program-comparison contrasts were categorized by the type of program evaluated (see Table 15.1). The most widely examined program types were post-secondary education and vocational education/training programs, with 13 and 17 evaluations of each, respectively. The study's extensive search of the literature identified few evaluations of correctional industries and correctional work programs, greatly reducing the strength of any conclusions that can be drawn about the effects of these programs.

Table 15.1
Description of Studies

Variable	Frequency	Percent
Document type (N = 33)		
Journal	13	39
Book chapter	1	3
Government report	10	30
Technical report/ dissertation	9	27
Program types (N = 53)		
Adult basic education (ABE)	6	11
General equivalency diploma (GED)	3	6
ABE or GED	5	9
Post-secondary education	13	25
Vocational education/ training	17	32
Correctional industries	2	4
Correctional work	2	4
Multi component program	2	4
Other	3	6

Two studies examined multi-component programs: one was a vocational training and correctional industries program and the other combined educational programming, vocational training, and job placement services. Three program-comparison contrasts could not be classified into this study's scheme. However, other program-comparison contrasts from these studies were categorized into these traditional program types.

The methodological quality of these studies varied but generally was weak, as shown by the data in Table 15.2. The typical research design compared naturally occurring groups of program participants with either nonparticipation in the specific program being evaluated or nonparticipation in any education, vocation, or work program. A few studies contrasted offenders who completed the evaluated program with offenders who dropped-out of or were removed from the

Table 15.2

Description of Methodology for the Studies and Program-Comparisons

Variable	Study		Program Comparisons	
	Frequency	Percent	Frequency	Percent
Nature of comparison group				
Nonparticipation in program(s) or management as usual	24	72	42	79
Treatment dropouts or unsuccessful participation	4	12	4	8
Mixture of above	4	12	6	11
Cannot tell	1	3	1	2
Used random assignment to conditions	3	9	3	6
Used initial group differences in statistical analyses	7	21	12	23
Used subject level matching	9	27	14	26
Used statistical significance testing	22	67	30	57
Attrition problem, overall	8	24	10	19
Attrition problem, differential	3	9	4	8

program. Several studies included a mixture of nonparticipants with unsuccessful or limited program participation. More than half made little or no attempt to control for selection bias, that is, differences in the characteristics of offenders who participate in the program relative to those who do not.

Only three studies (six percent of the program-comparison contrasts) used random assignment to conditions. Two-thirds of the studies used statistical significance testing as a basis for inferring differences in post-release offending rates.

Also shown in Table 15.2 is the study's coding of study attrition. Attrition is a potentially serious threat to the validity of inferences from naturalistic field-based evaluative studies.[15] Although the loss of cases due to purely random processes creates no validity threat, it is rare that attrition is of a random nature. Even general attrition across program and comparison groups that is nondifferential, that is, loss of similar cases in both groups, affects the generalizability of the study findings due to the loss of outcome data for that subsample of individuals. Conclusions about the effectiveness of a pro-

gram can be generalized only to individuals with characteristics comparable to those participants who remained in the study. In the study's coding scheme, the authors referred to this as general attrition and, in the authors' judgment, 19 percent of program-comparison contrasts suffered from this validity threat. Attrition that is differential between a program and a comparison group affects the validity of causal inferences regarding the effectiveness of the program. Differential attrition was judged a potential threat in 8 percent of the program-comparison contrasts. Unfortunately, the ability to make these judgments is highly dependent on the information provided in the written report by the researchers. More studies may have been judged problematic with regard to attrition if additional information had been made available. Considering all of the methodological variables simultaneously, only six program-comparison contrasts were judged to have used a methodology allowing for reasonably strong causal inferences regarding the effects of the program.

Not surprisingly, most of the research participants in these studies were men (see Ta-

Table 15.3
Description of Study Participants

Variable	Frequency	Percent
All participants male		
Yes	22	42
No	19	36
Cannot tell	12	23
Program participants were:		
Prison inmates	50	94
Probationers	3	6

Table 15.4
Nature of the Recidivism Measure Used in the Odds-Ratio Analysis

Recidivism Measure	Frequency	Percent
Reincarceration	35	66
Arrest	9	17
Conviction	6	11
Parole revocation	2	4
Composite measure	1	2

ble 15.3). None of the studies included in this synthesis were based solely on a sample of women. Fifteen of the 19 studies known to include women reported sufficient information to determine the actual percentage of men and women. In all 15 studies, women represented 21 percent of the study sample. Thus, the findings from this synthesis cannot be generalized to programs serving women. The vast majority of these studies evaluated programs that were available to the offenders during their period of incarceration. Only three of the program-comparison contrasts evaluated programs for probationers. Slightly less than half (23) of the program-comparison contrasts included offenders from multiple locations within a single system. In general, it appears that the participants in these studies are representative of the general United States and Canadian male prison population.

For purposes of computing the odds-ratio, preference was given to measures of reincarceration rate. More than half of the 53 program-comparison contrasts reported a reincarceration rate (see Table 15.4). For the remaining contrasts, recidivism was measured as arrest rates (17%), conviction rate (11%), parole revocation (4%), and a composite measure that included multiple indicators of recidivism (2%). All studies used official records for determining the outcome status of study participants (for example, no study provided data from a self-report measure of recidivism).

Program-Comparison Contrast Recidivism Outcomes

The vast majority of the findings across the 53 program-comparison contrasts favored the program participants. In 46 of the 53 contrasts, the program group had a lower recidivism rate than the comparison group. In one contrast, the recidivism rate was identical between groups. The mean odds-ratio across these 53 program-comparison contrasts was statistically significant and favored the education, vocation, and work program participants (mean odds-ratio = 1.53, with a 95% confidence interval of 1.36 to 1.72). This mean—and all others reported below—was computed by weighting each odds-ratio by an index of its precision, its inverse variance. This had the result of giving greater weight to studies with larger sample sizes. The authors also assumed that the variance for each odds-ratio had a random effects component.[16–19] This assumption resulted in a more conservative, that is, larger, confidence interval around the mean odds-ratio than under a fixed effects model.

The distribution of odds-ratios was highly heterogeneous, indicating that these effects vary by more than would be expected due to sampling error only, that is, there were real differences in the program effects across studies. These differences may have been due to substantive differences, such as program type, or due to methodological features, such as methodological quality and nature of the outcome measure.

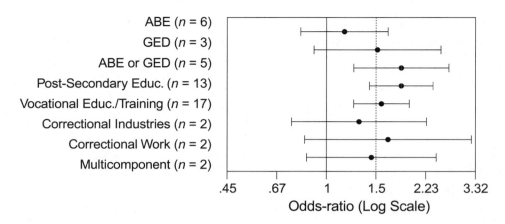

Figure 15.1 Mean Odds-Ratio and 95 Percent Confidence Interval by Program Type. Note: an odds ratio of 1 indicates no difference in recidivism rate, a ratio less than 1 indicates the program increased recidivism, and odds-ratios greater than 1 indicate the program reduced recidivism. The dotted line indicates the overlap between the estimated program effects.

Figure 15.1 presents the mean odds-ratio and associated confidence interval by major program type. Note that an odds-ratio of one indicates no difference in the recidivism rate between the groups being compared; values between zero and one indicate a negative effect such as higher recidivism for the program group and values greater than one indicate a positive effect such as lower recidivism for the program group. As shown in Figure 15.1, the mean odds-ratio for all program types was greater than one. On average, within each program type, program participants recidivated at a lower rate than nonparticipants. The overlap of the confidence intervals across programs (see dotted line in Figure 15.1) indicates that the data do not provide a basis for drawing conclusions regarding the differential effectiveness of the various program types. This was confirmed with a statistical test analogous to a one-way analysis of variance.[9] Unfortunately, several of the confidence intervals extend below one, suggesting that there currently is insufficient evidence to rule out sampling error as an explanation for the observed effect. Thus, all of these programs succeed, some more convincingly than others.

The odds-ratio can be difficult to interpret in practical terms. Is a mean odds-ratio of 1.53 something to get excited about? To facilitate interpretation, the authors have translated the mean odds-ratios into recidivism rates for the program groups, fixing the comparison group recidivism rate at 50 percent. These recidivism rates are shown in Figure 15.2 and range from a low of 36 percent to a high of 46 percent.

Thus, the rate of post-release offending for program participants is, on average, 4 to 14 percent lower than for program nonparticipants. This article will now briefly discuss the findings within each program type, highlighting salient study features.

ABE and General Equivalency Diploma

The results for ABE and GED programs appear contradictory. Taken as a whole, the 14 program-comparisons contrasts[20–30] evaluating either ABE, GED, or both showed positive and statistically significant effects. The overall effect for the six studies evaluating ABE participation was lower than the overall effect for the five studies examining participation in either an ABE or GED pro-

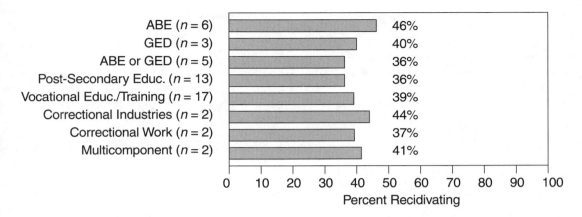

Figure 15.2 Estimated Percent of Program Participants Recidivating Assuming a 50 Percent Recidivism Rate in the Comparison Group

gram. Furthermore, the overall effect for ABE programs was not significant. Individually, only one [26] of the ABE effect sizes was statistically significant and it came from a study that used program drop-outs and those released prior to program completion as the comparison group. A negative effect of ABE was observed by one evaluation,[21] although the effect was small and positive findings were found for women and older inmates. All four of the evaluations of GED programs observed positive effects, with two of the four GED programs reporting statistically significant effects and three of the five ABE/GED evaluations reporting statistically significant effects. The large confidence intervals indicate that this difference between ABE, GED, and ABE or GED may be due to sampling error. Furthermore, other methodological differences between these studies are likely to produce instability in the findings. Although the findings across this collection of studies consistently favor the program participants, all of these studies had weak research methodologies, simply comparing either participants with nonparticipants or program noncompleters, with little to no control or adjustment for selection bias. Thus, it is impossible to rule out selection bias as an explanation for the differential recidivism rate.

Post-Secondary Education

Eleven of the 13 studies[21,22,24,31–40] evaluating the effects of post-secondary education programs demonstrated positive effects, seven of which were statistically significant. The overall mean odds-ratio was positive and statistically significant and translates into a recidivism rate of 36 percent relative to 50 percent for the comparison group, a meaningful reduction in recidivism by most standards. The positive effect remains when the analysis is restricted to five higher quality evaluations. A study by Linden et al.[37] used random assignment to conditions, used volunteers from both a maximum and medium security institution in British Columbia, Canada, and required that all participants had at least an eighth-grade education and were approved by the researchers as being capable of completing the course work. This study found a positive effect of involvement in post-secondary course work with 67 percent of the program group recidivating, relative to 77 percent in the comparison group. This translates into an odds ratio comparable to the mean odds-ratio for this program type. Unfortunately, this effect was not statistically significant given the study's small sample size (33 offenders in each group). The positive finding across this collection of studies is encouraging but the generally weak methodology does not allow for the attribution of the lower rates of recidivism to the post-secondary programs rather than to unique characteristics of inmates who chose to participate in them.

Vocational Education and Training

The largest collection of evaluations was of vocational education/training programs.[20,21,24,28, 41-48] The overall mean odds-ratio for these evaluations was positive and statistically significant (see Figure 15.1). Of the individual effects, 14 were positive and seven of these were statistically significant. As with other program areas, the typical evaluation of vocational programs was methodologically weak. There were, however, two exceptions. Lattimore et al.[45] conducted a randomized evaluation of an integrated vocational training and reentry program with close to 300 participants and found that participants in the integrated program had a lower rate of rearrest than did control group members. Saylor and Gaes,[47] using a high-quality propensity score-based quasi-experimental design, evaluated a vocational training and apprenticeship program, also finding positive program effects. Combining these two high-quality studies yields a statistically significant mean odds-ratio of 1.49 with a 95 percent confidence interval of 1.35 to 1.65. Although these two evaluations provide strong evidence that vocational programming can reduce post-release offending, both represent better-integrated and more intensive programs than are typically found throughout the criminal justice system. Thus, the generalizability of this finding to typical vocational programs is unwarranted.

Correctional Industries and Correctional Work

Only four studies were identified that evaluated the effects of work programs on recidivism, two evaluating correctional industries programs[47,49] and two evaluating correctional work.[50,51] Both types of programs had positive mean odds-ratios roughly comparable in magnitude to the other program types. Unfortunately, neither mean odds-ratio was statistically significant. Analyzing the four studies together, however, the overall mean odds-ratio was significant due to the boost in statistical power. All four of these studies observed lower rates of recidivism in the offenders participating in the work program than the comparison offenders. Two of the observed effects were statistically significant, one for each type of work program.

The sole randomized design examining a correctional work program was conducted by Van Stelle et al.[51] Although the study found small positive effects, the design was compromised severely by a high level of attrition. Furthermore, the generalizability of this finding to other work programs is limited because this program included job placement and community follow-up services in addition to the correctional work.

Although not a randomized design, the study by Saylor and Gaes[47] used the propensity score method to adjust for selection bias and as such, it represents a high-quality quasi-experimental design. This study contrasted participants in a correctional industries program with nonparticipants in either correctional industries or vocational programs. The adjusted effect, controlling for measured group differences, was statistically significant, resulting in an odds-ratio of 1.31, or an estimated recidivism rate for the correctional industries group of 43 percent, relative to a 50 percent rate in the comparison group. Although the propensity score method is unlikely to account for all of the important differences between those offenders participating in work programs and those not participating, the careful attention of this study to the problem of selection bias reduces the likelihood that the finding is an artifact of the participation process rather than an effect of the program. These findings are promising but are insufficient to draw any strong conclusions regarding the effects of correctional work programs on future offending rates for prison inmates.

Multi-Component Programs

Two evaluations examined multi-component programs. Menon et al.[52] studied the impact of Project RIO in Texas, a program incorporating an individualized Employability Development Plan for each inmate, encouraging participation in existing education, vocation, and work programs within the prison system, providing job preparation and job search assistance, and encouraging employers in the community to hire releasees. The participants in this program had higher rates of employment and lower rates of recidivism than nonparticipants, even after adjusting for background characteristics of the offenders.

> These findings are promising but are insufficient to draw any strong conclusions regarding the effects of correctional work programs on future offending rates for prison inmates.

The Saylor and Gaes[47] study discussed above also contrasted offenders who participated in both vocational training and correctional industries programs. The outcomes were positive, favoring program participation, and were highly similar to the outcomes for participation in only vocational training or correctional industries. In other words, there appeared to be no additional advantage to participation in both programs, at least in terms of future recidivism.

Job Placement Services

Three studies evaluated programs that included job placement services.[45,51,52] Unfortunately, the authors were unable to identify any study that evaluated the sole effect of job placement services, either by contrasting an education, vocation, or work program with and without job placement services or by examining job placement services as a single program. Although all three of these evaluations had positive findings, no conclusions specific to the important topic of job placement services could be drawn from this collection of studies.

Summary and Conclusions

There is strong support for the claim that participants in corrections-based education, vocation, and work programs recidivate at a lower rate than nonparticipants, with roughly comparable overall effects across the different types of programs. However, the current level of evidence does not allow for conclusions regarding differential effects of these programs.

The typical study included in this meta-analysis was quasi-experimental and compared naturally occurring groups of program participants with nonparticipants. Few studies made any serious attempt, in the authors' opinion, to control for biases produced by this self-selection into programs. Although space restrictions may create some randomness in who participates and who does not in some of the programs evaluated, it seems highly plausible that, as a whole, the comparison individuals differ from the program individuals in ways likely to affect recidivism. For example, the program participants may be more motivated toward positive life changes. It may be this motivation and the engagement in a set of behaviors perceived by the offender as improving their chances at finding satisfactory employment upon release that are critical to success rather than the specific skills learned. Furthermore, the denial of programs to motivated individuals may have detrimental effects, even if it is not the program per se that facilitates positive changes. Unfortunately, the serious potential for self-selection bias in the vast majority of these studies does not allow for a resolution of this issue or the attribution of observed reduction in post-release offending to the activities of the programs.

Focusing specifically on the higher-quality studies revealed promising findings but does not provide sufficient foundation to support a general statement of the effectiveness of these programs. The six program-comparison contrasts that were rated as having a strong methodology came from four studies that consistently found positive effects. Unfortunately, the interventions examined by two of the contrasts were not typical education, vocation, or work programs. The study by Lattimore et al.[45] evaluated a vocational education program that included an individualized plan based on each inmate's vocational interests, aptitudes, and post-release placement. The *Specialized Training and Employment Project* evaluated by Van Stelle et al.[51] included correctional work, job placement services, and community follow-up services. Participants also could receive ABE and/or vocational training services if needed. It is impossible to determine from these studies whether the positive findings were a result of the more enhanced nature of the programming and the findings thus may not generalize to more typical vocational and work programs found throughout the criminal justice system. These higher-quality studies suggest, however, that at least under certain program configurations, education, vocation, and work programs can lead to reductions in the rate of future offending.

It should be stressed that this review did not examine other potential benefits of education, vocation, and work programs. A common goal of these programs is to increase the employability of offenders, which was not the focus of this analysis. It also can be argued that any effect of these programs on recidivism is mediated by the program's success in increasing both the employment and wage rate for the participants. Furthermore, rehabilitation is not the sole justification for these programs. For example, a nontrivial function of these programs is the reduction of disciplinary problems by providing an incentive for good behavior[53] and reduction of idleness.[47] The large financial investment in these programs and the current public concerns over government spending underscore the need for these programs to demonstrate their effectiveness not only in improving prison life but also in increasing the likelihood that the prisoner will become a productive member of society upon release. As a whole, the current evidentiary base fails to establish a clear causal connection between these programs and future offending. The authors believe, however, that the evidence is encouraging and that it therefore would be unethical to deny motivated inmates the potential benefits of these programs.

Future research that merely compares participants with nonparticipants of these programs is not needed to resolve the questions of the effectiveness of these programs, for it is well established that participants do reoffend at a lower rate than nonparticipants. Rather, the field needs high-quality evaluation studies that can provide a strong basis for establishing a causal connection between the activities of the programs with future positive changes in inmate behavior. A prison system with demand for these programs that exceeds available resources has a natural opportunity to implement a randomized experiment.[54] Furthermore, the randomization of persons to programs with and without supplemental components, such as job placement or individualized employment planning, is generally both feasible and ethical in these settings. Also, two strong quasi-experimental designs that may be well suited to prison systems include the propensity score method [55] and the regression discontinuity design.[15] Only after the collection and synthesis of several high-quality studies of typical corrections-based education, vocation, and work programs will the issue over the effectiveness of these programs be resolved.

Study Questions

1. What were identified as the primary goals of educational/vocational/work programs within prisons?

2. Of the programs reviewed, which types appeared to have the largest impact on postrelease recidivism?

3. What were some of the primary weaknesses of the study, as cited by the authors?

4. Discuss what new directions may be explored regarding programming in prison, on the basis of findings presented in this study.

References

1. R. Linden and L. Perry, "The Effectiveness of Prison Education Programs," *Journal of Offender Counseling Services and Rehabilitation* 6 (1983): 43–57.

2. J.J. Stephan, *Census of State and Federal Correctional Facilities, 1995*. Washington, D.C.: Bureau of Justice Statistics, 1997.

3. J. Gerber and E.J. Fritsch, "Adult Academic and Vocational Correctional Education Programs: A Review of Recent Research," *Journal of Offender Rehabilitation* 22 (1995): 119–142.

4. J.M. Taylor, "Should Prisoners Have Access to Collegiate Education? A Policy Issue," *Educational Policy* 8 (1994): 315–338.

5. J.M. Taylor, "Post-Secondary Correctional Education: An Evaluation of Effectiveness and Efficiency," *Journal of Correctional Education* 43 (1992): 132–141.

6. D.L. MacKenzie and L.J. Hickman, *What Works in Corrections? An Examination of the Effectiveness of the Type of Rehabilitation Programs Offered by Washington State Department of Corrections: Report to the State of Washington Legislature Joint Audit and Review Committee*. College Park, MD: University of Maryland, 1998.

7. S. Bushway and P. Reuter, "Labor Markets and Crime Risk Factors," in *Preventing Crime. What Works, What Doesn't, What's Promising*, eds. L.W. Sherman, et al. Washington, D.C.: Office of Justice Programs, U.S. Department of Justice, 1997.

8. C. Tracy and C. Johnson, *Review of Various Outcome Studies Relating Prison Education to Reduced Recidivism*. Austin, TX: Windham School System, 1994.

9. L.V. Hedges and I. Olkin, *Statistical Methods for Meta-Analysis*. Orlando, FL: Academic Press, 1985.

10. H. Cooper and L.V. Hedges, eds., *The Handbook of Research Synthesis*. New York: Russell Sage Foundation, 1994.

11. H.C. Kraemer, et al., "Advantages of Excluding Underpowered Studies in Meta-Analysis: Inclusionist Versus Exclusionist Viewpoints," *Psychological Methods* 3 (1998): 23–31.

12. M.W. Lipsey and D.B. Wilson, "The Efficacy of Psychological, Educational, and Behavioral Treatment: Confirmation from Meta-Analysis," *American Psychologist* 48 (1993): 1181–1209.

13. J.L. Fleiss, "Measures of Effect Size for Categorical Data," in *The Handbook of Research Synthesis*, ed. H. Cooper and L.V. Hedges. New York: Russell Sage Foundation, 1994.

14. L.J. Glesser and I. Olkin, "Stochastically Dependent Effect Sizes," in *The Handbook of Research Synthesis*, ed. H. Cooper and L.V. Hedges. New York: Russell Sage Foundation, 1994.

15. T.D. Cook and D.T. Campbell, *Quasi-experimentation: Design and Analysis Issues for Field Settings*. Boston: Houghton Mifflin, 1979.

16. L.V. Hedges and J.L. Vevea, "Fixed- and Random-Effect Models in Meta-Analysis," *Psychological Methods* 3 (1998): 486–504.

17. M.W. Lipsey and D.B. Wilson, *Practical Meta-Analysis*. Thousand Oaks, CA: Sage, forthcoming.

18. R.C. Overton, "A Comparison of Fixed-Effects and Mixed (Random-Effects) Models for Meta-Analysis Tests of Moderator Variable Effects," *Psychological Methods* 3 (1998): 354–379.

19. S.W. Raudenbush, "Random Effects Models," in *The Handbook of Research Synthesis*, ed. H. Cooper and L.V. Hedges. New York: Russell Sage Foundation, 1994.

20. K. Adams, et al., "A Large-Scale Multidimensional Test of the Effect of Prison Education Programs on Offenders' Behavior," *The Prison Journal* 74 (1994): 433–449.

21. S.V. Anderson, *Evaluation of the Impact of Correctional Education Programs on Recidi-*

vism. Columbus, OH: Office of Management Information Systems Bureau of Planning and Evaluation, Ohio Department of Rehabilitation and Correction, 1995.

22. M.D. Harer, "Recidivism among Federal Prisoners Released in 1987," *Journal of Correctional Education* 46 (1995): 98–127.

23. K.A. Hull, *Analysis of Recidivism Rates for Participants of the Academic/Vocational/Transition Education Programs Offered by the Virginia Department of Correctional Education.* Richmond, VA: Commonwealth of Virginia Department of Correctional Education, 1995.

24. Z.D. Maciekowich, "Academic Education/Vocational Training and Recidivism of Adult Prisoners," dissertation. Phoenix, AZ: Arizona State University, 1976.

25. A.M. Piehl, *Learning While Doing Time.* Cambridge, MA: John F. Kennedy School of Government, Harvard University, 1995.

26. F.J. Porporino and D. Robinson, *Can Educating Adult Offenders Counteract Recidivism?* Portland, OR: Annual Meeting of the ACA Winter Conference, 1992.

27. C. Ramsey, *The Value of Receiving a General Education Development Certificate While Incarcerated in the South Carolina Department of Corrections on the Rate of Recidivism.* Columbia, SC: South Carolina Department of Corrections, 1988.

28. R.E. Schumacker, et al., "Vocational and Academic Indicators of Parole Success," *Journal of Correctional Education* 41 (1990): 8–12.

29. G.R. Siegel and J. Basta, *The Effect of Literacy and General Education Development Programs on Adult Probationers.* Tucson, AZ: Adult Probation Department of the Superior Court in Pima County, 1997.

30. A. Walsh, "An Evaluation, of the Effects of Adult Basic Education on Rearrest Rates among Probationers," *Journal of Offender Counseling, Services, and Rehabilitation* 9 (1985): 69–76.

31. M.E. Batiuk, et al., "Crime and Rehabilitation: Correctional Education as an Agent of Change," *Justice Quarterly* 14 (1997): 167–180.

32. F.S. Blackburn, *The Relationship between Recidivism and Participation in a Community College Associate of Arts Degree Program for Incarcerated Offenders.* Costa Mesa, CA: Annual Meeting of the Correctional Education Association, 1981.

33. D.D. Clark, *Analysis of Return Rates of the Inmate College Program Participants.* Albany, NY: New York State Department of Correctional Services, 1991.

34. C. Gaither, *An Evaluation of the Texas Department of Corrections' Junior College Program.* Huntsville, TX: Department of Correction Treatment Directorate, Research and Development Division, 1976.

35. J. Holloway and P. Moke, *Post-Secondary Correctional Education: An Evaluation of Parolee Performance.* Wilmington, Ohio: Wilmington College, 1986.

36. M. Langenbach, et al., "Televised Instruction in Oklahoma Prisons: A Study of Recidivism and Disciplinary Actions," *Journal of Correctional Education* 41 (1990): 87–94.

37. R. Linden, et al., "An Evaluation of a Prison Education Program," *Canadian Journal of Criminology* 26 (1984):65–73.

38. D. Lockwood, "Prison Higher Education and Recidivism: A Program Evaluation," in *Yearbook of Correctional Education.* Burnaby, British Columbia: Institute for the Humanities, Simon Fraser University, 1991.

39. C.J. McGee, *The Positive Impact of Corrections Education on Recidivism and Employment.* Springfield, IL: Illinois Department of Corrections and Illinois Council on Vocational Education, 1997.

40. M. O'Neil, "Correctional Higher Education: Reduced Recidivism?" *Journal of Correctional Education* 41 (1990): 28–31.

41. D. Anderson, "The Relationship between Correctional Education and Parole Success," *Journal of Offender Counseling, Services, and Rehabilitation* 5 (1981): 13–25.

42. B.B. Coffey, "The Effectiveness of Vocational Education in Kentucky's Correctional Institutions as Measured by Employment Status and Recidivism," dissertation. Lexington, KY: University of Kentucky, 1983.

43. S. Davis and B. Chown, *Recidivism among Offenders Incarcerated by the Oklahoma Department of Corrections Who Received Vocational-Technical Training. A Survival Data Analysis of Offenders Released January 1982 through July 1986.* Oklahoma City, OK: Oklahoma State Department of Corrections, 1986.

44. E.A. Downes, et al., "Evaluating the Effects of Vocational Education on Inmates: A Research Model and Preliminary Results," in *The Yearbook of Correctional Education*, ed. S. Duguid. Burnaby, British Columbia: Simon Fraser University, 1989.

45. P.K. Lattimore, et al., "Experimental Assessment of the Effect of Vocational Training on Youthful Property Offenders," *Evaluation Review* 14 (1990):115–133.

46. J.T. Luftig, "Vocational Education in Prison: An Alternative to Recidivism," *Journal of Studies in Technical Careers* 1 (1978): 31–42.

47. W.G. Saylor and G.G. Gaes, *PREP: Training Inmates through Industrial Work Participation and Vocational and Apprenticeship Instruction*. Washington, D.C.: Federal Bureau of Prisons, 1996.

48. J.L. Winterton, *Transformations: Technology Boot Camp*. Summative Evaluation. Unpublished.

49. K.E. Maguire, et al., "Prison Labor and Recidivism," *Journal of Quantitative Criminology* 4 (1988): 3–18.

50. K.M. Lee, "The Wichita Work Release Center: An Evaluative Study (Kansas)," dissertation. Manhattan, KS: Kansas State University, 1983.

51. K.R. Van Stelle, et al., *Final Evaluation Report: Specialized Training and Employment Project (STEP)*. Madison, WI: University of Wisconsin-Madison Medical School, Department of Preventive Medicine, Center for Health Policy and Program Evaluation, 1995.

52. R. Menon, et al., *An Evaluation of Project RIO Outcomes: An Evaluative Report*. College Station, TX: Texas A and M University, Public Policy Resources Laboratory, 1992.

53. J.J. DiIulio, Jr., *No Escape: The Future of American Corrections*. New York: Basic Books, 1991.

54. R.F. Boruch, *Randomized Experiments for Planning and Evaluation: A Practical Guide*. Thousand Oaks, CA: Sage, 1997.

55. P.R. Rosenbaum and D.B. Rubin, "The Central Role of the Propensity Score in Observational Studies for Causal Effects," *Biometrika* 70 (1983): 41–55. ✦

16
Should We Privatize Our Prisons?
The Pros and Cons
Voncile B. Gowdy

A recent development in the housing and treatment of offenders has been the issue of institutional privatization. For some systems, privatization appears as a natural extension because many public institutions already contract with the private sector for numerous services—not the least of which include maintenance, rehabilitative services, and the provision of food.

Conversely, some see privatization as providing too many opportunities for the decline of accountability and the increase of abuses of various sorts. Opponents to privatization argue that when profit becomes a primary motivating factor in prison development and offender treatment, corruption will not be long to follow. Gowdy traces the history of prison privatization and identifies current trends regarding this issue. Conventional wisdom maintains that the state has grown weary of building and managing offender institutions that ultimately become overcrowded and outmoded.

Similarly, many public institutions already use private industry in vital capacities—turning over total control seems to be a very short step in some cases. On the other hand, accountability, logistics, and related concerns regarding prisoners' rights are the bedrock on

which opponents object to prison privatization. The reader is encouraged to consider the potential benefits and complications, should private prisons continue to gain a foothold in American correctional strategies.

As crowding in the nation's prisons and jails continues to intensify, the private sector is increasingly viewed as a viable option to help resolve this problem.[1-4] This movement toward the transfer of full management or ownership to private entrepreneurs who are in business for profit is unique to the criminal justice system.

Few proposals in the field of corrections have stimulated as sharply divided opinions as the privately operated approach, leading to considerable and sometimes heated debate.[2,5-8] While the National Sheriffs' Association (NSA) has expressed disapproval and opposition to the concept of private jail facilities, the past executive director of the American Correctional Association (ACA) endorses the concept stating "We ought to give business a try."[9] Other organizations, such as the American Bar Association and the National Governors' Association, urge careful study of the complex issues involved before proceeding with this kind of contractual arrangement.[10]

The President's Commission on Privatization recommends that contracting be regarded as an effective and appropriate form for the administration of prisons and jails at the federal, state, and local levels. The commission believes that contracting for the operation of entire facilities, and not just particular problems within them, is an appropriate government option. At the same time, the commission notes that there are legitimate concerns about accountability and liability relative to the private prisons.

Privatization proponents foresee the chance to introduce efficiency and innovation to a field laboring under the burden of outmoded facilities, staff costs, declining resources, increasing executive and judicial

Excerpts from *Corrections Management Quarterly* (1997), Volume 1, Number 2. pp. 56–63. Copyright © 1997 by Aspen Publishers, Inc. Reprinted by permission.

demands for improved services, and public calls for more prisoners at half the price.[1,11-13] On the other hand, their opponents fear that the profit motive will interfere with professional corrections practice and question whether any part of the administration of justice is an appropriate market for economic enterprise.[14,15] The claim that imprisonment is an inherently and exclusively governmental function, and therefore should not be performed by the private sector, has surfaced as the most adamant objection to the delegation of authority for custody control.[2]

The theoretical basis for delegating the imprisonment of criminals to private parties can be traced to the English philosopher John Locke. He argued that individuals have the right to punish those who egress against them. Through the social contract, they form a state and transfer to it the power and authority to govern and to punish. Thus, the power and authority to imprison do not originate with the state, but they are delegated to it. Presuming that the consent of the people is possessed, that authority can be delegated by the state to private parties or agents. These agents, like state employees, are governed by rules of law in administering this authority.

Support for delegation of this kind of authority can be found with an analysis of federal law, which remands violators of federal laws to the custody of the Attorney General for confinement in "any available, suitable, and appropriate institution or otherwise."[16] The federal Bureau of Prisons (BOP) interprets this statute to include private contractors as well as other levels of government. The BOP uses private contractors now in its community treatment centers and is planning to contract with a private agency to operate a prison in California.[17,18] The Immigration and Naturalization Service (INS) contracts out the operation of several facilities for its detainees. That the state may delegate the authority to imprisonment was affirmed in Medina v. O'Neill with the notation that while the authority to incarcerate may be delegated, the responsibility is retained by the government entity.[19]

As of 1995, there were 104 private facilities in operation with a total capacity of approximately 65,000. This total represents less than 5 percent of all U.S. jails and prisons.[1] Of this number, approximately 34,000 are secure prison beds. Nonetheless, the concept continues to grow as public officials consider the benefits of privatization.[18]

Historical Context of Privatization

The private sector involvement in corrections affairs is not a new movement. The earliest examples of privatization can be traced to the era of the Romans.[20] During the late 16th century resemblance to the current contract system was operating on the Amsterdam when wood rasped by the inmates was sold to private entrepreneurs. The proceeds from these sales were used to offset institutional expenses incurred and to provide income for inmates whose production exceeded the cost of their confinement.[20]

This private sector involvement continued into the 17th century when the English adopted transportion as a replacement for specific capital and corporal sanctions.[21] England used a variety of colonial and American locations for deposit of transported prisoners. Private merchants were used to transport prisoners, and the "merchants made their profit by selling convicts as indentured servants in the colonies. It was thus essentially a private business, with which the colonial authorities had little or no concern."[22]

As early as 1634, American colonies involved the private sector in corrections affairs. A fort established on Castle Island in Boston Harbor, created for military purposes, held criminals too difficult to manage in less secure facilities.[23] This installation, which was created through private subscriptions, exemplifies the private financing of public facilities.

During the 19th century, prisoners were frequently hired out to private companies, and some prisons were financed exclusively from the fees derived from contract prison labor. Abuses of such arrangements and lobbying by prison reform groups led to the prohibition of such a practice. Although this practice was abandoned and privately operated jails and prisons were replaced by public facilities, the private sector was never eliminated from corrections affairs. Moreover, during the latter half of the 19th century public institutions turned to the private sector with renewed interest for assistance in meeting their obligations.[24]

Trends Leading to the Current Use of Privatization of Corrections

As the U.S. prison population began to expand rapidly in the 1970s, coupled with court mandates to improve prison conditions and operations, corrections agencies found it increasingly difficult to provide the necessary variety and quality of services on their own. As public resources became more scarce, there was a growing interest in the use and cost-effectiveness of the private sector as a service provider.

Concern about the cost of incarceration has been important since its inception as a significant American penal tool. Beginning as early as the mid–19th century, concern relative to the cost of providing care for so many criminals at the expense of the state has been prevalent. Prison construction and operating costs have always been enormous. The cost of building a single medium security cell can exceed $80,000.[25] Annual operating costs per inmate average $15,513.[26]

During the last decade, privatization has gained broad recognition and widespread acceptance. The federal government has spearheaded much of the current move toward privatization. President Reagan's 1988 reform initiative encouraged the goal of restructuring government operations to resemble more closely the procedures and principles embodied in contemporary business management. The President's 1988 task force on privatization, designed to identify promising efforts and to promote private sector involvement in government operations, was also instrumental in promoting this movement. For example, one finding of this task force was that the United States is experiencing a renewed interest in the systematic examination of the boundary between public and private delivery of goods and services. Furthermore, this commission declared that "the interest also reflects a belief that new arrangements between the government and the private sector might improve efficiency while offering new opportunities and greater satisfaction for the people served."[27]

The modern movement expanding the private sector role into corrections began to generate considerable interest and controversy in the early 1980s. This movement is unique in that it includes the transfer of full management and/or ownership responsibilities of corrections institutions from governments to private entrepreneurs who are in business for profit.

The Debate: Pros and Cons

The debate surrounding the prospect of contracting with the private sector for the management of prison facilities has been ongoing for the last decade, and it continues to be a subject for extensive discussion. Opposition to contracted prisons has come from the NSA; the American Civil Liberties Union (ACLU); and the American Federation of State, County, and Municipal Employees (AFSCME). The American Bar Association (ABA) and the National Governors' Association called for careful study of the complex issues involved before proceeding with this kind of contractual arrangement.

> The federal government has spearheaded much of the current movement toward privatization.

In 1984, the NSA adopted a resolution opposing for-profit jails and prisons.[11] Since this time, there has been no change in this opposition. In a 1984 survey of corrections agencies, 75 percent indicated they would not consider contracting the management of an entire facility, while only 21 percent said they would. Four percent remained unsure.[28]

The AFSCME position states that "for the public for correctional personnel, even for the inmates, contracting out is a terrible idea—it's bad policy, and it's bad government."[29] Unions continue to oppose private prisons largely because contracting poses threat to union jobs and union power.[30]

The ACLU has opposed private prisons since the inception of this concept, fearing that such facilities threaten prisoners' due process rights.[31] Furthermore, the ACLU and other prisoner advocacy groups worry that privatization will further escalate the use of prisons.

In February 1986, the ABA called for a moratorium on private prisons and recommended that "Jurisdictions that are considering the privatization of prison and jails not proceed . . .until the complex constitutional, statutory, and contractual issues are satisfactorily developed and resolved."[10]

In February 1984, *The Wall Street Journal* endorsed the private corrections concept and stated, "Where some people see problems, others see opportunities." Again in 1987, in an editorial continuing to favor the idea, *The Wall Street Journal* predicted that "Faced with swelling inmate populations, riots, court orders to improve prison conditions, and tight budgets, more states may be inclined to find out for themselves whether private prisons work."[32]

The ACA has endorsed the use of profit and nonprofit organizations to develop, fund, build, operate, and provide corrections services, programs, and facilities since the idea surfaced. Past executive director, Anthony P. Travis, suggested that "We ought to give business a try."[33]

The President's Commission on Privatization recommends that contracting be regarded as an effective and appropriate form for the administration of prisons and jails at the federal, state, and local levels. The commission believes that contracting for the operation of entire facilities—not just particular programs within them—is an appropriate government option. At the same time, the commission noted that there are legitimate concerns about accountability and liability relative to the private operation of prisons, many of which cannot be resolved at this time.

Logan identified ten controversial issues that are often at the forefront of any debate relative to the use of the private sector as a service provider. These issues include the following:

1. Propriety—Who has the right to manage these institutions?

2. Cost—How much will it cost to operate these institutions?

3. Quality—Are privately run prisons operated better than public sector facilities?

4. Quantity—Will cheaper and more efficient prisons mean more imprisonment?

5. Flexibility—Will the private sector respond more readily to immediate needs with greater flexibility and speed than are typically possible under government operation?

6. Security—What are the appropriate roles and liabilities of the state and its private providers?

7. Liability—Will public agencies and officials be allowed to avoid or diminish their responsibilities because services have been delegated to private vendors?

8. Accountability—Will the private sector or the public sector be in charge of these facilities?

9. Corruption—What, if any, will be the extent of corruption in corrections privatization?

10. Dependence—Will the public sector become dependent on the private sector for operation of these facilities, and if so, what changes may occur?[2]

Logan makes the case for commercial operation of prisons and jails as an alternative to the public sector's monopoly. Although critics of private prisons argue that imprisonment is an exclusively governmental function that may not be delegated, Logan notes that the authority of the state to imprison is derived originally from the consent of the governed and may therefore, with similar consent, be delegated further. He goes on to state that the authority to imprison is not owned by the state and is not an absolute authority, but subject to the provisions of law, whether it is exercised by salaried state employees or by contracted agents.[2]

DiIulio, on the other hand, objects to the proprietary argument for privatizing prisons. He points out that the notion of private prisons is undesirable, as a matter of principle. He further states, "The power to punish those who transgress on our rights must, if it is to remain legitimate, reside in the hands of duly constituted public authorities. This power may not be freely delegated to contractually deputized private individuals or groups. Yet the privatization of corrections is predicated on just such an illegitimate delegation of state authority."[6]

The first and foremost argument for privatizing prisons is that it is more cost-effective and cost-efficient. Unlike the state and federal governments, private firms are basically free from politics, bureaucracy, and costly union contracts. Private contractors are accountable to their investors and therefore are motivated to satisfy the terms of their contract.

Although the proponents of privatization claim that public costs are 20 percent to 40 percent greater than private costs, the evidence is not yet persuasive.[18,34] Two studies that evaluate the cost issue are worth noting. In one research project it was estimated that by contracting out prison management to a private firm, Hamilton County, Tennessee, saved from 4 percent to 15 percent annually on its county penal farm costs.[35] Logan further noted that although careful comparisons were made in Tennessee, the many variables made precise savings difficult to calculate.

The other study compared a public adult minimum security institution with a privately operated prison in Kentucky and two pairs of public and private facilities for violent youths in Massachusetts.[36,37] The researchers concluded that the private operations in both states appeared to be managed more successfully than the public ones in a number of ways.

However, these studies, as well as many others, have significant methodological problems. The most comprehensive review of all studies completed to date was recently conducted by the GAO. In that report, GAO identified five studies that have been completed since 1991 on privately operated systems in Texas, New Mexico, California, Tennessee, and Louisiana. Of these studies only two were deemed sufficiently well designed to make meaningful cost comparisons. The results showed minimal or no differences between the public and privately operated facilities.[18]

Despite these research findings, the private sector continues to assert its superiority in reducing prison costs. The Corrections Corporation of America (CCA), one of the most prominent companies in the incarceration industry, estimates that private management of corrections facilities should lead to operational costs 10 percent to 25 percent below those of public corrections bureaucracies. Beyond promising to deliver the same service cheaper, Ted Nissan, the corporate chairman of Behavioral Systems Southwest, promised that he could provide more efficient and innovative services.[38]

Because the private entrepreneur is under competitive pressure to perform and is free of bureaucratic restrictions and administrative procedures, proponents contend that the quality of privately provided services is likely to be superior. Although it may be the case in the short run, whether there will be adequate market pressure to maintain these improvements over a long period remains unclear. For example, the Louisiana study reviewed by the GAO found that there were initial savings for the privately operated facility but that these savings disappeared over time.[21] Adequate monitoring is a critical mechanism available to ensure that the private provider is continuing to perform satisfactorily.[36,37]

Opponents of privatization worry that the private provider may cut corners to save costs and thereby lower the quality of service. A CCA executive complains, "This cutting corners idea attributes to manning only the bases of motives. It does not recognize that there are good, responsible, pillars-of-the-community type people who want this concept to work as an industry for the long term."[39] Contrary to this belief, Donahue notes that the integrity of the service provider is not the real issue. What must be considered is quality control. He bases his premise on the fact that if the central goal of privatization is about saving money, if incarceration contracts are awarded on the basis of cost, and if it is possible to cut costs by lowering standards, the quality control issue inevitably becomes an urgent matter.[14]

> Critics of privatization claim that it is immoral to profit from the imprisonment of others.

Another concern is the profit-making issue. Critics of privatization claim that it is immoral to profit from the imprisonment of others and that it is likely to interfere with professional corrections practice. They further contend that it provides no incentive to reduce crowding, and they question whether any part of the administration of justice is an appropriate market for economic enterprise. Because prisons have traditionally been financed through tax-exempt general obligation bonds, privatization encourages prison construction.

Administrative issues such as flexibility and accountability and legal issues including security and liability are among other controversial concerns. Although many of these issues surfaced very early in the study of the private prison concept, they continue to be debated. In 1985, the National Institute of Justice (NIJ) commissioned a study to examine the experience of those governments that had decided to privatize.[40] The goals of the study were to discuss trends in contracting for state corrections facilities and to review important issues that had developed in the privatization effort. Findings reported by the researchers from the Council of State Governments and the Urban Institute, provide 23 practical recommendations for officials who are thinking about contracting with private organizations. They included ways and means of dealing with inmate protection, the contracting process, new and existing facilities, the selection of inmates, and level of authority. One of the major recommendations that is consistent with the recommendation of others[2,12,14,41–44] was the importance of giving special attention to monitoring both in the contract itself and in the correction agency's subsequent administration of the contract.

Accountability requires an understanding of clearly defined roles. The importance of including evaluation and monitoring mechanisms to ensure the adequate completion of this task cannot be emphasized too much. Critics charge that contracting reduces accountability; that is, private entrepreneurs are insulated from the public and are not subject to the same set of political regulations as their public sector counterparts. On the other hand, proponents claim that properly written contracts are specific and identify expectations and performance. Logan believes that contracting increases accountability because the government is more willing to monitor and control a contractor than it is to monitor and control itself. Logan further notes that the most obvious form of accountability in corrections is legal, "If the Rule of Law can limit and constrain the power of the state, surely it can hold a private firm at least equally accountable."[2]

Although the liability debate has raised a number of questions for consideration, it does not seem to have slowed the pace to privatize corrections. Critics and proponents of privatization agree that while the contractor is willing to accept responsibility to operate or manage a prison facility, the government will not escape liability and will retain overall authority. According to the President's Commission Report on Privatization, the liability issue depends on the nature of state tort laws and specific provisions within the contract.

Proponents of private prisons posit that the advantage in speed and flexibility of construction has merit. Financing and construction of these facilities by the private sector have been attractive to state governments, as it has afforded them an opportunity to have this task completed without having to raise the capital. The private sector builds the prison with private financing and operates it. The state then makes installment payments to the private owner under a lease-purchase agreement.[34] The term *lease* is used mainly because the government usually does not have a title to the property until it has completed payments sufficient to buy the property and pay interest to the lenders who financed the purchase.[45]

The Future of the Private Prisons

Despite the continuing controversy surrounding private prisons and their limited track record, their future seems to be promising. However, private prisons are likely to be increasingly seen as a complement to and an expansion of the public sector as opposed to its replacement. This view is different from the way the concept was originally framed.

To develop private prisons that are problem free and of value to the corrections system, more jurisdictions will have to conduct studies demonstrating the cost-benefits of privatized facilities. Moreover, each jurisdiction will need to decide whether to privatize or not. The limited experience and research on privatized prisons limit our capacity to make meaningful assessments. Thus, the option to privatize may become riskier than implementing other traditional corrections programs. In making these decisions, it will be important to answer the following five questions:

1. What factors led managers to adopt the privatization concept?

2. What distinguished public sector managers that adopted this concept from others?

3. Why do some managers privatize and others do not?

4. Is this innovation characteristic of legislation and the state or the public sector manager?

5. How did these managers make the decision to privatize?

Thus far, those studies are rare and tend to show little if any differences between publicly and privately operated facilities. Nonetheless, the public's unsatisfactory view of today's penal system in terms of its costs and high recidivism rates are two factors that are likely to encourage further expansion of the private sector's role. But the tentative nature of support by corrections officials remains absent more concrete evidence. As stated by the BOP director:

> I know that the Attorney General and . . .[the Office of Management and Budget] are very interested in working carefully with us in the Bureau of Prisons to track,

on these new contracts, very carefully, what cost impact truly is, because there are a lot of hidden costs in privatization. . . . [T]here has never been, we don't believe, a real good cost analysis to determine, apples to apples, what is the cost of a traditional prison system and private contracting. The private contractors claim they can do it at great savings, and so we are very interested in monitoring the ones that we have projected for the next few years and determining . . .how well the taxpayers are being served on either side.

The many issues and concerns identified in this article will have to be continually explored, and resolutions will have to be sought through experiences gained from the use of the private sector. As the industry grows and thereby establishes track records for its usage, the demand on corrections officials to consider using privatization as a means of quickly and economically addressing prison crowding problems is likely to become more prominent. Whether private prisons can deliver what they promise remains an open question.

Study Questions

1. Why might some argue that the movement toward private institutions comes as no surprise? Base your response on the evidence presented in this article.

2. What primary trends were identified as leading to the current use of privatized prison institutions?

3. Discuss the primary pros and cons for the proliferation of privatized prisons as identified by the authors.

4. Based on the author's conclusions, what is a future concern of managing private prisons?

References

1. Thomas, C. *Private Adult Correctional Facility Census.* Gainesville, Fla.: University of Florida, 1995.

2. Logan, C.H. *Private Prisons: Pros and Cons.* New York, N.Y.: Oxford University Press, 1990.

3. Greenwood, P. *Private-Enterprise Prisons? Why Not? The Job Would Be Done Better and at Less Cost.* Santa Monica, Calif.: Rand Corporation, 1981.

4. Hutto, T.D. "Corrections Partnership: The Public and Private Sectors Work Together." *Corrections Today,* 50(1988):20, 22.

5. Robbins, I.P. *The Legal Dimensions of Private Incarceration.* Washington, D.C.: American Bar Association, 1988.

6. DiIulio, J. "Prisons, Profits and Public Good: The Privatization of Corrections." *Research Bulletin no. 1.* Huntsville, Tex.: Sam Houston State University Criminal Justice Center, 1986.

7. Miller, J. "The Private Prison Industry: Dilemmas and Proposals."*Journal of Law, Ethics, and Public Policy,* 2(1986):465–477.

8. Camp, C., and Camp, G. "Correctional Privatization in Perspective." *The Prison Journal* 65, no. 2 (1985):14–31.

9. National Sheriffs' Association. *National Sheriffs' Association Position Paper on Privatization of Adult Local Detention Facilities.* Alexandria, VA: 1996.

10. Robbins, I.P. "Privatization of Corrections: Defining the Issues." *Judicature* 69, no. 6 (1986): 326.

11. Savas, E.S. "Privatization and Prisons." *Vanderbilt Law Review,* 40(1987):889–99.

12. Ring, C. *Contracting for the Operation of Private Prisons: Pros and Cons.* College Park, MD: American Correctional Association, 1987.

13. Brakel, S.J. *Privatization in Corrections: Federal Privatization Project Issue Paper* no. 2. Santa Monica, Calif.: Reason Foundation, 1989.

14. Donahue, J. *The Privatization Decision: Public Ends, Private Means.* New York, N.Y.: Basic Books, 1989.

15. DiIulio, J. "What's Wrong with Private Prisons?" *The Public Interest,* 92(1988):66–83.

16. 18 U.S.S.S. 4082.

17. U.S. General Accounting Office. *Private Prisons.* Washington, D.C.: GAO, 1991.

18. U.S. General Accounting Office. *Private and Public Prisons: Studies Comparing Opera-*

tional Costs and/or Quality of Service. Washington, D.C.: GAO, 1996.

19. *Medina v. O'Neill,* 589 F. Supp. 1028.

20. Sellin, J.T. *Slavery and the Penal System.* New York, N.Y.: Elsevier, 1976.

21. Hughes, R. *The Fatal Shore.* New York, N.Y.: Alfred A. Knopf, 1987.

22. Smith, A.E. *Colonists in Bondage.* Boston, Mass.: Peter Smith, 1965.

23. Powers, E. *Crime and Punishment in Early Massachusetts.* Boston, Mass.: Beacon Press, 1966.

24. McKelvey, B. *American Prisons: A History of Good Intentions.* Montclair, N.Y.: Patterson Smith, 1977.

25. McDonald, D. *Private Prisons and the Public Interest. Research and Corrections.* Boulder, Colo.: National Institute of Corrections, National Information Center, 1990.

26. Bureau of Justice Statistics. Washington, D.C.: U.S. Department of Justice, 1992.

27. Linowes, D. *Privatization toward More Effective Government.* March 1988.

28. National Institute of Corrections. *Private Sector Involvement in Prison Services and Operations.* Washington, D.C.: U.S. Department of Justice, 1985.

29. Keating, J.M. *Seeking Profit in Punishment: The Private Management of Correctional Institutions.* Washington, D.C.: American Federation of State, County and Municipal Employees, 1985.

30. Poole, R.W. "Objections to Privatization." *Policy Review,* 24(1983):105–119.

31. American Civil Liberties Union. "Board Minutes." *Policy Guide,* 243(1986).

32. "Prison for Profit." *The Wall Street Journal,* (5 February 1987).

33. *Public Correctional Policy on Private Sector Involvement in Corrections.* Lanham, MD: American Correctional Association, 1985.

34. Logan, C., and Rausch, S. "Punish and Profit: The Emergence of Private Enterprise Prisons." *Justice Quarterly,* 2(1985):303–318.

35. Logan, C.H. *Looking at Hidden Costs: Public and Private Corrections.* Washington, D.C.: National Institute of Justice Reports, 1989.

36. Hackett, J. et al. *Contracting for the Operation of Prisons and Jails.* National Institute of Justice Research in Brief. Washington, D.C.: Department of Justice, 1987.

37. Hackett, J. et al. *Issues in Contracting for the Private Operation of Prisons and Jails.* Washington, D.C.: Department of Justice, 1987.

38. Tolchin, M. "As Privately Owned Prisons Increase, So Do Their Critics." *The New York Times,* 11 February 1985.

39. Crane, R. Testimony before the House Committee on the Judiciary, U.S. Congress, 13 November 1985 hearings.

40. *Corrections and the Private Sector: A National Forum.* National Institute of Justice, 1985.

41. Mullen, J. "Corrections and the Private Sector." The Prison Journal, 65, no. 2 (1985): 1–13.

42. Mullen, J. *Corrections and the Private Sector.* Research in Brief. Washington, D.C.: Department of Justice, 1985.

43. Mullen, J. *Corrections and the Private Sector.* Washington, D.C.: National Institute of Justice Reports, 1985.

44. Thomas, C.W. "The Background, Present Status, and Future Potential of Privatization in American Corrections." Paper based on presentation at Privatization: Promise and Pitfalls Conference, Wayne State University, Detroit, Michigan, 31 March 1989.

45. Chaiken, J., and Mennemeyer, S. *Lease-Purchase Financing of Prison and Jail Construction.* National Institute of Justice Research in Brief. Washington, D.C.: Department of Justice, 1987.

Suggested Readings

American Bar Association. *Private Prisons.* Washington, D.C.: ABA, 1984.

American Bar Association. Section of criminal justice 1986 report to the House of Delegates, 10 December 1985. Amended and approved as ABA policy by the ABA House of Delegates.

American Correctional Association. *Private Sector Operation of a Correctional Institution.* Washington, D.C.: U.S. Department of Justice, National Institute of Corrections, 1985.

American Correctional Association. "American Correctional Association National Correctional Policy: Private Sector Involvement in Corrections." *Corrections Today,* 46(1985):48.

American Correctional Association. *Directory of Juvenile and Adult Correctional Departments, Institutions, Agencies, and Paroling Authorities.* College Park, Md.: ACA, 1987.

Chi, K.S. "Prison Overcrowding and Privatization: Models and Opportunities." *Journal of State Government* 50, no. 2 (1989): 70–76.

Churchman, C.W. *The Systems Approach.* New York, N.Y.: Dalecort Press, 1968.

Coalition for a Moratorium on Private Prisons. *Privatization of Correctional Facilities.* Philadelphia, Pa.: The Pennsylvania Prison Society, 1985.

Cook, T., and Reichardt, C. Council of State Governments and Urban Institute. *Issues in Contracting for the Private Operation of Prisons and Jails: Executive Summary and Final Report.* Washington, D.C.: Department of Justice, 1987.

Logan, C.H. (1987). "The Propriety of Proprietary Prisons." *Federal Probation*, 53(3):35–40.

Miller, J. "The Private Prison Industry: Dilemmas and Proposals." *Journal of Law, Ethics and Public Policy* 2(1986):465–477.

Schoen, K.F. "Private Prison Operators." *The New York Times*, 28 March 1985.

U.S. Department of Justice. *Prisoners in 1983.* Bulletin. Washington, D.C.: Bureau of Justice Statistics, 1984.

The views expressed in this article are those of the author and do not necessarily represent the views of the National Institute of Justice or the U.S. Department of Justice. ✦

Part IV
Prison Litigation and Inmates' Rights

Until the beginning of the 1960s, the rights (constitutional or otherwise) afforded to prison inmates were largely at the discretion of institutional administration. In early America, *Ruffin v. Commonwealth* had established that prison inmates were to be regarded as "slaves of the state." The concept of slavery denotes unpaid, forced labor. In effect history translated into exactly that for many inmates throughout the United States for much of the nineteenth and twentieth centuries.

Prior to the 1960s, the courts maintained a "hands-off" doctrine regarding the administration of prisons. This approach was fueled by a desire to keep executive-level powers separate, in addition to a deference of the court system toward correctional professionals. The institutions themselves were physically out of sight of the general public, and conceptually out of sight of litigators. With very little sympathy for the plight of prisoners, conditions inside institutions were ignored on all counts. Prison was intended to be a "punishment" in and of itself, which stymied motivation to improve conditions or policies. The movement toward humane punishment had ended with the retirement of the stocks and the implementation of mass warehousing for offenders. Not surprisingly, however, due to an apparent lack of executive oversight, institutions were often allowed to deteriorate in both physical condition and the interaction between inmates and correctional officers.

In large-scale penal institutions, efforts are placed toward making life as uniform as possible. In essence, it is advantageous to allow for very few, if any, exceptions in the daily lives of inmates. This is readily apparent when the history and development of the U.S. prison is examined. The hands-off doctrine reinforced this concept because prison inmates were believed to have experienced a complete civil death. That is, due to their crimes against society, offenders were no longer entitled to any of the "basic" human rights enjoyed by free citizens, as demonstrated by the deprivations outlined by Sykes in Part II. Most significantly, however, the concept of civil death was perceived to include deprivation of many of the rights outlined in the Bill of Rights of the U.S. Constitution. In addition, and perhaps most importantly, inmates were not afforded rights to the very court system that had committed them in the first place.

Although many of the societal and legal changes that marked the beginning of the Prisoners' Rights movement are widely believed to have occurred throughout the 1960s, the seeds of this movement were undoubtedly planted during the 1940s. Perhaps the first effort toward breaking through the hands-off doctrine was seen in *Ex Parte Hull* (1941). Through the review of this court case, the Supreme Court declared that prisoners have the unrestricted right of access to the federal court system. Similarly, three years later, *Coffin v. Reichard* (1944) established that inmates had the right of court re-

209

view when challenging the conditions of confinement. Both of these court cases, while significant in what they later came to symbolize, applied only to federal prisoners. Precedent was set, however, for similar cases that would apply to state level prisons and other institutions designed to house offenders.

Many of the initial challenges to the conditions of confinement occurred in the area of freedom to practice individual religion. Several religions (both Eastern and Western) require access to materials that may be considered contraband by a prison system. Similarly, many religions require certain facilities, clothing, movement, and celebration that may disrupt the desired uniformity that make prisons easier to manage. In *Cooper v. Pate* (1964) the U.S. Supreme Court maintained that denial of the inmates' right to practice their religion was indeed a violation of their First Amendment rights of expression. *Cooper v. Pate* was brought to the Supreme Court under Section 1983 of the federal Civil Rights Act and later became the primary avenue through which conditions of confinement would be challenged.

Although attention to freedom of religion was seen by many as a major victory in prisoner rights, this did not address the physical conditions of confinement. The 1970s and 1980s brought numerous cases before the Supreme Court under the Eighth Amendment, claiming that the current state of many prisons constituted cruel and unusual punishment. Judges often determined that finding grotesque filth, vermin infestations, inadequate heating and ventilation, fire hazards, and noise levels prohibited anything that resembled a peaceful environment. A number of these court cases did result in the improvement of physical conditions inside prison walls. Currently, prisoners' rights and protections generally include religious freedom, freedom of speech, rights to medical

treatment, physical protection from attack and assault, due process prior to (additional) institutional punishment, and equal treatment regarding institutional jobs and educational opportunities.

It is important to note that although conditions inside prisons have greatly improved since the 1960s, the rights outlined above (as well as others not mentioned) are still considered to be provisional. Because prison administrators are responsible first and foremost to confine the convicted offender, the Supreme Court in most cases has ruled that rights be upheld only as much as possible without compromising the security of the prisons' charges. This is not to say that the advances and changes brought about by prison litigation have been meaningless—far from it. However, a significant amount of discretion naturally lies within official hands.

Litigation and court activity regarding prisoners' constitutional rights has settled many critical issues. However, the issue of inmate rights is far from over. The burgeoning prison population that spurred many of the initial legal inquiries is still increasing at dramatic rates in many states. In addition, the population of the prison system is changing. Every year, women have been constituting a larger portion of the total prison population. Because the vast majority of major cases before the courts have concerned male inmates, many of the old issues need to be revisited to apply to females in custody. Moreover, new issues regarding women prisoners may bring about other conditions not previously reviewed. Similarly, the prison population is aging rapidly. Because countless characteristics of inmates mimic basic trends in the general population, future litigation will likely surround issues such as the conditions of geriatric inmates and the specific needs (medical and otherwise) characteristic of the aged. ✦

17
The Prisoners' Rights Movement and Its Impacts

James B. Jacobs

Throughout the previous sections, aspects of life inside institutions have been explored. Essays have identified and defined the total institution and discussed their dynamics, both social and physical. In the latter half of the twentieth century, the prison systems within the United States have experienced what has been called the prisoners' rights movement. Not surprisingly, this movement came about and gained momentum during a time when the rights of many subgroups within greater society were receiving national-level attention. Jacobs overviews the prisoners' rights movement and lists the very real ways in which it changed life inside America's institutions. Even though the right to religious freedom has been perhaps the most often challenged, the seedlings of the prisoners' rights movement should not be overlooked.

For example, it was during the 1950s that federal prisoners first gained simple access to the federal court system, which represented the first challenge to prisoners' previous status as "civilly dead." Affording prisoners even basic rights has been interpreted by some as a potential affront to security. Although security (both within the institution and outside in the public realm) remains of paramount concern, there is little argument that prison conditions, both physical and social, were greatly improved due to court intervention. Readers are encouraged to consider the utility of the "ma-

jor" rights that have been established and put into practice for America's prison population. Specifically, review whether the court has perhaps gone too far, or perhaps not far enough, in regarding the terms of confinement, the practice of religion, and access to rehabilitation, for example.

During the past two decades prisoners have besieged the federal courts with civil rights suits challenging every aspect of prison programs and practices. It is as if the courts had become a battlefield where prisoners and prison administrators, led by their respective legal champions, engage in mortal combat. Although the war has dragged on for almost twenty years, and shows no sign of abating, strangely enough there seems to be no agreement on which side is winning.

It frequently appears that both sides are trying to convince the public and themselves that their own defeat is imminent. Prison officials complain that the demands of litigation and court orders have pressed their beleaguered staffs and limited resources to the verge of collapse; they decry the naïvete of judges who cannot see the deadly struggle for power which lies behind the disingenuous facade of legal petitions that ask "only" for "humane treatment" and "basic civil rights." Even worse, from the perspective of prison officials, judges have not been content merely to resolve limited conflicts, but have made Herculean efforts, by use of structural injunctions (see Fiss, 1978, 1979), special masters (see, e.g., Nathan, 1979), and citizens' visiting committees, to restructure and reorganize prisons according to their own value preferences. Legal attacks and judicial interference have, according to some prison officials, fatally undermined these officials' capacity to administer their institutions and to maintain basic order and discipline.

Activist prisoners and their advocates are equally despondent. Each victory seems to accentuate how far their cause still has to go

Excerpts from *Crime and Justice, Vol II* by James B. Jacobs. Copyright © 1980 by The University of Chicago Press. Reprinted by permission.

to attain its goals. And unfavorable court rulings, especially those of the Supreme Court, seem to harbinger the final demise of all prisoners' rights. One decision heralded as apocalyptic is *Bell v. Wolfish* (1979). The Supreme Court, in an opinion by Justice William Rehnquist, reversed a sweeping injunction condemning a multitude of conditions and practices at the Federal Bureau of Prisons' Metropolitan Correctional Center in New York City. The Court rejected the Court of Appeals standard for review of jail conditions, under which pretrial detainees could "be subjected to only those 'restrictions and privations' which inhere in their confinement itself or which are justified by compelling necessities of jail administration." Instead, the majority required only a showing that jail practices are reasonably related to a legitimate governmental objective. Applying this less restrictive standard, the Court upheld a prohibition on receiving books and magazines from any source other than the publisher as well as a restriction on receipt of packages, double-bunking, unannounced cell searches, and mandatory visual inspection of body cavities.

With both sides claiming defeat, who is the real winner and who the real loser in the war over prisoners' rights? So put, the question is too simplistic to be useful. What is needed is a holistic understanding of the role of litigation and law reform in creating and sustaining a prisoners' rights movement, which includes prison reform efforts of all sorts, by prisoners and others. . . .

Prisoners' Rights as a Sociopolitical Movement

In speaking of the prisoners' rights movement I refer to far more than the sum total of court decisions affecting prisoners. We are dealing with a broadscale effort to redefine the status (moral, political, economic, as well as legal) of prisoners in a democratic society. The prisoner's rights movement, like other social movements—the civil rights

movement, the women's movement, the student movement—includes a variety of more or less organized groups and activities; there is also wide variation in the extent and intensity of individual participation. What is decisive, however, is a shared sense of grievance and the commitment to enhanced rights and entitlements for prisoners.

The prisoners' rights movement must be understood in the context of a "fundamental democratization" (Mannheim, 1940) that has transformed American society since World War II, and particularly since 1960. Starting with the black civil rights movement in the mid-1950s, one marginal group after another—blacks, poor people, welfare mothers, mental patients, women, children, aliens, gays, and the handicapped—has pressed for admission into the societal mainstream. While each group has its own history and a special character, the general trend has been to extend citizenship rights to a greater proportion of the total population by recognizing the existence and legitimacy of group grievances.

Prisoners, a majority of whom are now black and poor, have identified themselves and their struggle with other "victimized minorities," and pressed their claims with vigor and not a little moral indignation. Various segments of the free society linked the prisoners' cause to the plight of other powerless groups. To a considerable extent the legal system, especially the federal district courts, accepted the legitimacy of prisoners' claims.

To recognize the prisoners' rights movement as part of a larger mosaic of social change is not to deny this movement's own sociopolitical history. The drive to extend citizenship rights to prisoners must be placed in the context of two hundred years of effort at prison reform. The issues being argued today in constitutional terms have previously been debated on religious and utilitarian grounds (see, e.g., Rothman, 1980). Reformers of earlier generations did not pursue their objectives in the courts because, until recently, the courts were unreceptive to such complaints. The rule of law did not apply to prisoners; their status placed them "beyond the ken of the courts" (*Yale Law Journal*, 1963).

Before the 1960s prisoners were a legal caste whose status was poignantly captured in the expression "slaves of the state" (*Ruffin v. Commonwealth*, 1871). Like slaves, prisoners had no constitutional rights and no forum for presenting their grievances. But unlike slaves, prisoners were invisible, except perhaps for occasional riots, when they captured public attention.

Until the 1960s the federal judiciary adhered to a "hands off" attitude toward prison cases out of concern for federalism and separation of powers and a fear that judicial review of administrative decisions would undermine prison security and discipline. A prisoner who complained about arbitrary, corrupt, brutal, or illegal treatment did so at his peril. Until recently, protest to the outside world was severely repressed (Hirschkop and Millemann, 1969). Prisoners were, therefore, isolated from the rest of society; the possibility of forming alliances with groups outside prison was very limited. The precondition for the emergence of a prisoners' rights movement in the United States was the recognition by the federal courts that prisoners are persons with cognizable constitutional rights. Just by opening a forum in which prisoners' grievances could be heard, the federal courts destroyed the custodians' absolute power and the prisoners' isolation from the larger society. And the litigation in itself heightened prisoners' consciousness and politicized them.

The new era of prisoners' rights began in the early 1960s in the wake of the civil rights movement. In prisons, it was the Black Muslims who carried the torch of black protest. The Muslims succeeded with the assistance of jailhouse lawyers, and in turn provided an example for using law to challenge officialdom. A rights movement clearly had appeal for a generation of minority youth that had become highly conscious of its rights and entitlements. But the movement was not comprised solely of prisoners. It depended heavily on the involvement and efforts of free citizens, particularly lawyers and reinvigorated prison reform groups. Of course, the prisoners' rights movement would not have been possible without activism in the federal judiciary and some stamp of approval by the justices of the United States Supreme Court. Nor is prison reform the sole prerogative of courts; a complete sociopolitical history of the prisoners' rights movement would have to take federal and state legislative and administrative activity into account.

The Black Muslims and the Religious Freedom Controversy

A high priority for building a body of research on prisoners' rights is to document fully the activities of the Black Muslims in American prisons and jails. The Black Muslims filed lawsuits throughout the country in the early 1960s asserting denial of racial and religious equality. (By my count, there were sixty-six reported federal courts decisions pertaining to the Muslims between 1961 and 1978.) The issues raised by the Muslims were timely and likely to appeal to federal judges. The legitimacy of demands by blacks for equal protection under the law in other contexts was becoming well-established. The rights asserted—to read religious literature and to worship as one wishes—are fundamental in American values and constitutional history and difficult to deny. The only posture available to prison officials was to deny the Muslims' sincerity. Prison officials often disputed the Muslims' claim to religious legitimacy, but the result was to strengthen Muslim resolve and intensify their struggle.

The Supreme Court's first modern prisoners' rights case, *Cooper v. Pate* (1964), was an appeal from a lower court ruling upholding the discretion of prison officials to refuse Muslim prisoners their Korans and all opportunities for worship. The Supreme Court's decision was narrow: the Muslim prisoners had standing to challenge religious discrimination under Section 1983 of the resurrected Civil Rights Act of 1871. But for the prisoners' movement it was not the breadth of the decision that mattered but the Supreme Court's determination that prisoners have constitutional rights; prison officials were not free to do with prisoners as they pleased. And the federal courts were permitted, indeed obligated, to provide a forum where prisoners could challenge and confront prison officials. Whatever the outcome of such confrontations, they spelled the end of the authoritarian regime in American penology.

Once disputes between prisoners and prison officials were seen by outsiders to be religious controversies and not simply struggles for institutional control the result was inevitable (Rothman, 1973). The success of the Muslims on the constitutional issue of free exercise of religious rights brought the federal courts into the prisons. The abominable conditions in American prisons kept them there. Prisoners and their advocates presented their grievances in constitutional terms and federal courts became more deeply involved in disputes over prison practices, policies, and conditions.

The Black Muslims are undoubtedly the best organized and most solidary group to exist for any length of time in American prisons. They set an example for other prisoners, who soon began organizing themselves in groups and blocks, in contrast to the cliques of former times (Clemmer, 1958; Irwin, 1980). In place of the subcultural norm "do your own time," the Muslims introduced a new morality—group time (see Jacobs, 1976). They showed how, through legal activism, prisoner groups could achieve solidarity and some tangible successes.

The issue of religious freedom was picked up by diverse prisoner groups who saw the opportunity to formulate as a religious controversy their objections to prison life and their opposition to prison officials. The most dramatic example was the Church of the New Song, a "religion" begun by federal pris-

oners in Marion, Illinois, which soon spread to other federal and state facilities. The church earned nationwide media attention: its leader proclaimed himself the Bishop of Tellus, prophesied in the Book of Revelations; its "liturgy" required porterhouse steaks and Harvey's Bristol Cream; its agenda called for the wholesale destruction of the American prison system. The status of the Church of the New Song was vigorously litigated in the Fifth and Eighth federal judicial circuits; the prisoners achieved several legal victories requiring correction departments to afford them the same opportunities and prerogatives as traditional religions. (See, e.g., *Theriault v. Silber*, 1977; *Remmers v. Brewer*, 1976.)

Jailhouse Lawyers and Access to the Courts

The traditional role of the jailhouse lawyer had been to assist fellow prisoners in preparing postconviction petitions asserting defects in their prosecution or conviction. Prison officials often were hostile to jailhouse lawyers because of their status among, and influence over, fellow inmates (*Washington and Lee Law Review*, 1968). There were also not unwarranted fears that jailhouse lawyers might abuse their power over other prisoners (Brierley, 1976). It was not uncommon for prison rules to prohibit giving legal assistance of any kind; punishments could be very severe. Consequently, jailhouse lawyers often functioned "underground." Official hostility to jailhouse lawyers intensified as prisoners' rights actions succeeded and as the jailhouse lawyers became judicially recognized adversaries.

The Supreme Court's decision in *Johnson v. Avery* (1969) ushered in a new age in jailhouse lawyering (Wexler, 1971). The Court held that when prison officials are not providing prisoners with adequate legal services, prisoners cannot be punished for providing legal assistance to one another. The decision marked another triumph for a class of prisoners whom the officials disliked and feared. More victories followed. In 1972, the Court held, in *Haines v. Kerner* (1972) that prisoners' *in forma pauperis* petitions had to be treated in a manner most advantageous to prisoners; where there was a glimmer of a federal cause of action in the complaint, the case could not be dismissed. *Wolff v. McDonnell* (1974) extended the jailhouse lawyer's authority of representation to civil rights suits attacking institutional conditions and policies. The Court went even further in *Bounds v. Smith* (1977), holding that the constitution imposed upon the states an affirmative obligation to provide prisoners with either adequate law libraries or adequate assistance from persons trained in the law. These decisions have established the jailhouse lawyer as an institutionalized adversary and have undoubtedly contributed to the popularity of litigation as a prisoner avocation.

Prisoners

By the late 1950s and early 1960s blacks constituted a majority of the prisoners in many northern prisons and in some states. Their consciousness aroused by the civil rights movement, it was only natural that this generation of minority prisoners would demand its rights even behind bars; it was not about to accept being invisible. By the late 1960s some black prisoners, such as Eldridge Cleaver, George Jackson, and Martin Sostre, had achieved extraordinary prominence. Their ties to outside groups, and to batteries of lawyers, could not be severed. And they may well have politicized their lawyers as much as their lawyers politicized them. Riots and law reform were paths to political change in the larger society during this period and the same phenomena became increasingly evident in the prisons.

The Prisoners' Rights Bar

A platoon, eventually a phalanx, of prisoners' rights lawyers, supported by federal and foundation funding, soon appeared and pressed other-than-religious constitutional claims. They initiated, and won, prisoners' rights cases that implicated every aspect of prison governance. In many cases the prisoners' attorneys were more dedicated and effective than the overburdened and inexperienced government attorneys who represented the prison officials (Bershad, 1977, quoting Supreme Court Justice Lewis Powell).

Many of the leading prisoners' rights lawyers had earlier gained considerable experience working for black civil rights (Bronstein, 1977). Herman Schwartz, a professor at the State University of New York at Buffalo, Alvin Bronstein of the American Civil Liberties Union's National Prison Project, William Bennett Turner and Stanley Bass of the NAACP Legal Defense Fund, and others brought both national perspective and some minimal coordination to the prisoners' rights litigation.

Notwithstanding the role played by a few national prisoners' rights groups and institutions, day-to-day advocacy has been carried on by hundreds of lawyers and paralegals on the state or local level. Many of these groups were founded and supported under the auspices of OEO Legal Services (see, e.g., Welch, 1979). Prisoner Legal Services in Illinois, begun in the early 1970s by a nonlawyer activist, had nine full-time attorneys, several social workers, and a staff of forty by the mid-1970s, and was a potent force in the life of northern Illinois prisons. Prison administrators viewed the organization as a powerful and omnipresent watchdog. Consideration of policy decisions always involved some attention to the likely reaction of the Legal Services staff. A number of prisoners' rights projects were established in law schools (Cardarelli and Finkelstein, 1974) and contributed to the flow of outside legal actors into the closed prison world. A 1973 report by the Council on Legal Education for Professional Responsibility listed sixty-three law schools as providing some form of legal assistance to prisoners.

Many of these law students and prisoners' advocates identified strongly with the prisoners' interests, thereby building up the prisoners' hopes and encouraging their protests. In turn, the prisoners gave these legal personnel a "cause" and strong personal reinforcement. At times legal services personnel went well beyond even far-reaching class actions and worked on such "political" tasks as establishing prisoner unions (e.g., *Jones v. North Carolina Prisoners' Union*, 1977). Many lawyers began to see themselves no longer as technicians but instead as prisoners' rights advocates working for the reform or abolition of the prison system. The most extreme example was a small but influential group of radical lawyers and law collectives.

The American Bar Association gave the prisoners' movement the imprimatur of the established legal community. It created in 1970 the Commission on Correctional Facilities and Services for the purpose of advancing correctional reform. With Ford Foundation funding, the Commission opened full-time offices in Washington. Its Resource Center for Correctional Law and Legal Services was a central clearinghouse for information and coordinated effort and resources among prisoners' rights groups and litigators. Legal periodicals on prisoners' rights were established, including one published for an ABA section. At least seven sections of the ABA later formed prisoners' rights committees, and, as of 1974, twenty-four state bar associations had special committees working on prison reform (American Bar Association, Commission on Correctional Facilities and Services, 1975). The most active ABA Committee is the Joint Committee on the Legal Status of Prisoners. Its *Tentative Draft of Standards Relating to the Legal Status of Prisoners* (1977) prescribes, among other things the minimum wage for prisoner laborers, a right to form prisoner organizations, and a limited right to privacy. While not yet adopted by the ABA, that such standards are being seriously considered is an indication of the degree of legitimacy which the prisoners' rights movement has attained

(see also U.S. Dept. of Justice, 1978; National Council on Crime and Delinquency, 1966, 1972).

Federal funding for prisoner legal services has lately become more difficult to obtain, in part because of the displacement of OEO Legal Services by the Legal Services Corporation. The ABA Resource Center for Correctional Law and Legal Services ran out of money in mid-1978. Illinois Prisoner Legal Services for all practical purposes went out of existence because of lack of funds at about the same time. Increasingly, those government grants that are available prohibit civil rights suits and class actions (American Bar Association, Resource Center on Correctional Law and Legal Services, 1974, p. 407).

The luster of the prisoners' rights movement may also be fading. The image of the prisoner as hero, revolutionary, and victim is disappearing. Other minority rights movements, such as that associated with the handicapped, are increasingly attracting resources and the energies of young attorneys. The path breaking prisoners' rights litigation is behind us. The nitty-gritty of more routine legal services may be less attractive to young lawyers with reformist aspirations. Whether a viable prisoners' rights movement at the grass roots level can survive funding cutbacks, judicial retrenchment, and other social and political change is unclear.

It would be wrong, however, to conclude that the prisoners' rights movement is dying. Increasing numbers of cases are filed each year; 11,195 prisoners' rights petitions were filed in federal district courts in the year ending June 30, 1979, a 451.5 percent increase since 1970 and a 15 percent increase over 1978 (U.S. Administrative Office of the United States Courts, 1979; see also McCormack, 1975). The vast majority of these cases are filed *pro se*, without legal representation. Most of the cases are dismissed at the pleading stage or on summary judgment (Turner, 1979), but if only a small percentage survive, the number of litigated cases will continue to be substantial.

Fewer prisoners' rights lawyers are now available, but many of those are experienced and highly skilled. The ACLU's National Prison Project has only seven full-time attorneys but carries on major litigation across the country, often supporting cases originally brought by a local ACLU chapter. The project effectively employs the services of a cadre of expert witnesses including such ex-correctional officials as David Fogel and John Conrad. The experience that this litigation team has accumulated over years in lawsuits around the country makes it a formidable opponent. The project's director, Alvin Bronstein, exerts influence in many ways beside litigation: for example, by lobbying, accepting speaking engagements, and maintaining a high profile at national meetings and conferences.

It is possible that the U.S. Department of Justice will emerge as a crucial force in the reconstituted prisoners' movement of the 1980s. The Special Litigation Section has intervened in a number of important cases in the last few years, most notably a massive challenge to the Texas Department of Corrections. The Civil Rights of Institutionalized Persons Act, passed by Congress in 1980, clarifies and broadens the Justice Department's authority to represent prisoners in institutional litigation.

The Supreme Court

Any analysis of the prisoners' rights movement must acknowledge the crucial role of the United States Supreme Court. The prisoners' rights movement required at least the passive acquiescence of the Court. The movement also needed the symbolic energizing that *Brown v. Board of Education* provided to the civil rights movement. The crucial prison case was *Cooper v. Pate* (1964). Although a *per curiam* opinion, lacking the powerful language of *Brown v. Board of Education*, it left no doubt that prisoners have rights that must be respected.

Many legal victories followed after *Cooper v. Pate*. Each contributed to the strength,

self-confidence, and momentum of the prisoners' rights movement. A high-water mark was reached in *Wolff v. McDonnell* (1974), which raised issues about the procedural protections to which prisoners are entitled at disciplinary hearings. The Supreme Court finally provided the kind of clarion statement that could serve as a rallying call for prisoners' rights advocates. Speaking for the Court, Justice Byron White said:

> [The State of Nebraska] asserts that the procedure for disciplining prison inmates for serious misconduct is a matter of policy raising no constitutional issue. If the position implies that prisoners in state institutions are wholly without the protections of the Constitution and the Due Process Clause, it is plainly untenable. Lawful imprisonment necessarily makes unavailable many rights and privileges of the ordinary citizen, a "retraction justified by the considerations underlying our penal system" [citations omitted]. But though his rights may be diminished by the needs and exigencies of the institutional environment, a prisoner is not wholly stripped of constitutional protections when he is imprisoned for crime. There is no iron curtain drawn between the Constitution and the prisons of this country.

Since *Wolff*, prisoners have won several important victories in the Supreme Court—e.g., *Estelle v. Gamble* (1976) (deliberate indifference to serious medical needs constitutes cruel and unusual punishment); *Hutto v. Finney* (1978) (approving a wide-ranging structural injunction against certain practices and conditions in the Arkansas prisons)—but none equals *Wolff* for eloquence.

I stress the symbolic importance of Supreme Court prisoners' rights decisions, not to belittle the holdings, but to emphasize that from a sociopolitical perspective what is critical is the psychological impact of court decisions, the feeling of those in the field, in this case prisoners' advocates, prison officials, and their respective lawyers, that the Supreme Court and the Constitution are for them or against them. The negative impact of court decisions on morale is nicely captured in a case study of protracted litigation involving Louisiana's Jefferson Parish Prison (Harris and Spiller, 1977, pp. 213–214):

> The one negative factor that unquestionably did flow from the suit involved the aggravation and adverse personal effects associated with it. Overall, it appears that the worst effects of the judicial intervention may have been psychological ones. It was psychologically very difficult for the defendants to accept that what they had been doing was wrong or inadequate when they believed that they were doing a decent job. It was psychologically very difficult for the defendants to accept that a federal judge who had never operated a correctional facility could dictate what would be done. It was psychologically very difficult for defendants to have their job performances criticized by persons who were not believed to understand their problems. It was psychologically very difficult for the defendants to accept blame for defects for which they saw others as being responsible. Acceptance of all of these things was made even more difficult by the fact that they were imposed publicly.

The positive impact of court decisions on movements such as the prisoners' is more sharply grasped by Stuart Scheingold (1974, p. 131) than by any other writer with whom I am familiar:

> Regardless of the problems of implementation, rights can be useful political tools. It is possible to capitalize on the perceptions of entitlement associated with rights to initiate and nurture political mobilization—a dual process of activating a quiescent citizenry and *organizing* groups into effective political units. Political mobilization can in its fashion build support for interests that have been excluded in existing allocations of values and thus promote a realignment of political forces. . . . Since rights carry with them connotations of entitlement, a declaration of rights tends to politicize needs by changing the way people think about their discontent.

The symbolic and psychological significance of being "vindicated" or "repudiated" by a court explains wildly exaggerated reactions to court decisions—exaggerated, that is, when viewed through the lawyer's detached lens. But once the potential of court decisions and even litigation itself to power a movement or to demoralize its opposition is understood, then the relationship of courts to sociopolitical movements becomes much more complicated than simply looking at the "holding" of each new judicial decision.

It is hardly surprising that such decisions as *Bell v. Wolfish* (1979) and *Rhodes v. Chapman* (1981) are being heralded by prisoners' rights advocates as a fatal blow to the movement and by prison officials as a vindication of their authority and competence. What makes *Wolfish* more than just another case is Justice Rehnquist's rhetoric: for example, his quip that the Constitution embodies no "one man, one cell" principle and his repeated emphasis on the need for judicial deference to prison officials.

> The deplorable conditions and draconian restrictions of our Nation's prisons are too well known to require recounting here, and the federal courts rightly have condemned these sordid aspects of our prison systems. But many of these same courts have, in the name of the Constitution, become increasingly enmeshed in the minutiae of prison operations. Judges, after all, are human. They, no less than others in our society, have a natural tendency to believe that their individual solutions to often intractable problems are better and more workable than those of the persons who are actually charged with the running of the particular institution under examination. But under the Constitution, the first question to be answered is not whose plan is best, but in what branch of the Government is lodged the authority to initially devise the plan. This does not mean that constitutional rights are not to be scrupulously observed. It does mean, however, the inquiry of federal courts into prison management must be limited to the issue of whether a particular system vio-

lates any prohibition of the Constitution, or in the case of a federal prison, a statute. The wide range of "judgment calls" that meet constitutional and statutory requirements are confided to officials outside the Judiciary Branch of Government.

Neither prison officials nor prisoners' rights lawyers are much impressed by the facts that *Wolfish* is only one case, that it can be distinguished from many prison cases on its facts, that it is arguably applicable only to modern jails like the Metropolitan Correctional Center, or that a later case, such as *Vitek v. Jones* (1980), scores a victory for prisoners by establishing a right to a hearing before transfer to a mental health facility.

This Supreme Court has demonstrated its concern that the prisoners' rights movement, or more specifically, the involvement of federal courts in matters of state prison administration, not go too far. The Court has not signaled a return to the "hands off" doctrine or a redefinition of prisoners as nonpersons. But prisoners' rights activists should not in the foreseeable future expect highly dramatic decisions that will mobilize social and political energies on behalf of prisoners. If there is to be a stimulus for further momentum in the prisoners' rights movement it probably will not come from the Supreme Court. Having liberated prisoners from being slaves of the state, this Court seems unwilling to establish them as citizens behind bars.

The Lower Federal Courts

The significance of Supreme Court decisions notwithstanding, it would be a grave error, as Jerome Frank admonished three decades ago, to rely too heavily on appellate decisions as indicators of what lower courts are doing. Frank (1949) spoke of "the myth that upper courts are the heart of the courthouse government." Frank was right. Most legal analysts of the prisoners' rights movement are transfixed by Supreme Court decisions. Each new decision generates intense exami-

nation of the opinion's language, new doctrinal syntheses, and unending critiques of judicial logic. Hardly any attention is paid to what the trial courts are doing in prisoners' rights cases (but see Turner, 1979).

Prisoners' rights cases are won and lost on the record. The Supreme Court has not effectively hemmed-in activist federal judges (Frankel, 1976). Most complaints deal with access to lawyers and legal materials, property loss or damage, brutality, censorship of mail, and medical care (Turner, 1979). All of these fall within the ambit of recognized constitutional violations or are controlled by state law or previous consent decrees. Many prisoners' complaints can be redressed without breaking new ground.

Justice Brennan pointed out in *Rhodes v. Chapman* (1981, p. 353) that "individual prisons or entire prison systems in at least 24 states have been declared unconstitutional under the Eighth and Fourteenth Amendments, with litigation underway in many others." *Bell v. Wolfish* failed to prevent major judicial interventions into the operation of state prisons, such as *Ramos v. Lamm* (1979), which shut down "old Max," Colorado's Canon Correctional Facility, and *Ruiz v. Estelle* (1980), which declared the entire Texas prison system to be in violation of the Constitution. And even a cursory glance through the *Criminal Law Reporter* will bolster the spirits of those who fear that the prisoners' rights movement is dead. Consider *Cooper v. Morin* (1979), a post-*Wolfish* decision by New York's highest court, which held that while *Wolfish* forecloses the argument by pretrial detainees that they have a federal constitutional right to "contact visits" with family and friends, such a right is guaranteed by the state constitution's due process clause.

Many prisoners' rights cases are not decided in the courts. Settlements are negotiated, sometimes with the approval and even the collusion of reform-minded administrators. These administrators are not averse to admitting that facilities are dilapidated and poorly maintained, or that medical care is inadequate; a court-approved consent decree on such matters may greatly improve their leverage in the executive budget competition and with the legislature (Herman Schwartz, 1972, p. 791; Harris and Spiller, 1977, pp. 92–96). Furthermore, rules and practices can be liberalized and then blamed on the courts, thereby blunting criticism from rank-and-file guards.

Legislatures

The federal courts have been the most important redefiners of the legal status of marginal groups, with lawyers and federal judges the key implementers. However, to focus only on litigation would be too limited. Legislatures and executive agencies have also had key roles to play. Correctional politics is as much a legislative as a judicial game. Prisoners' rights advocates have frequently encountered intransigence and hostility among legislators, but they have also sometimes won support for important new programs. Increased legal activism focuses attention on prisoners and on prisons and may bring some legislators to the realization "that something must be done."

Some states moved to codify the basic requirements set forth in the landmark cases. The Illinois legislature, in 1973, enacted a comprehensive Unified Code of Corrections, addressing issues ranging from procedures for disciplinary action to availability of radios, televisions, and legal materials, and the treatment of prisoners with mental health problems (Illinois Ann. Stat. Ch. 38, Section 1001–1–1 et seq. [1973]).

Other states, while continuing to delegate their rule-making authority for prisons to their correctional agencies, adopted strict rule-making procedures, including provisions for public input and court review. California law, for example, until 1975 permitted the director of corrections to prescribe rules and regulations for the administration of the prison system and change them at his pleasure. Under the current statute he may promulgate new rules only in accordance with California's Government Code, which requires notice and public hearing prior to an exercise of rule-making authority. Furthermore, copies of proposed rules must be posted in the state's penal institutions (Ca. Penal Code, Section 5058 [1970 and 1979 Supp.]). Until 1968, California Law (Penal Code, Section 2800) provided that a sentence to prison suspended an individual's civil rights. The section was amended in 1968 to provide what has come to be called an inmate bill of rights (*U.C.L.A. Law Review*, 1973, p. 481).

In many states, legislation was necessary to establish halfway houses, work release programs, home furloughs, and grievance procedures (see, e.g., N.Y. Correc. Law, Sections 22–A, 22–B, 26, 139 [McKinney's Supp., 1978]). To take another example, the Minnesota legislature established an ombudsman for the department of corrections in 1973. The point is that a preoccupation with the courts should not blind us to the role of legislatures in both stimulating and impeding the goals of prisoners' rights advocates and their allies.

Departments of Corrections

When the federal courts began to involve themselves in prison disputes, some officials realized that written, uniform, and, most important, reasonable rules would reduce charges of unfairness, and reduce the chance of judicial intervention. Today, for example, because of a decision by a federal district judge, every rule of the Arizona Department of Corrections must be approved by the federal court (*Harris v. Cardwell*, 1977). The court-approved rules cover every aspect of prison operations.

Connecticut's rules and regulations run to more than four hundred pages. Some regulations track Supreme Court or lower federal court decisions, others go substantially beyond the courts. For example, prisoners are entitled to a hearing and an appeal in cases of disciplinary transfer from a minimum to a maximum security prison, despite a 1976

Supreme Court decision, *Meachum v. Fano* (1976), holding that the Constitution does not require such procedures. And despite approval in *Bell v. Wolfish* for rectal and genital searches whenever pretrial detainees meet visitors in person, Connecticut rules limit such searches to admissions from outside the institution and instances where officials have probable cause to believe that a prisoner is hiding contraband in a body cavity. *Bell v. Wolfish* itself noted that during the pendency of the case the Federal Bureau of Prisons liberalized one of the policies in dispute in the lawsuit, regarding receipt of books and magazines from sources other than the publisher. I suspect that litigation has frequently led to agency reconsideration and liberalization of policies and rules, even when not constitutionally compelled.

National Institute of Corrections; American Correctional Association

The National Institute of Corrections (NIC), a federal agency, has in the past few years played an increasingly important role in the prisoners' rights movement. NIC has sponsored research, conferences, and training programs of all sorts to institutionalize progressive legal reforms. For example, in conjunction with the Center for Community Justice, NIC provides training and technical assistance in the development and implementation of inmate grievance procedures. Recently it launched an ambitious project to train special masters to carry out more effectively their role of monitoring court decrees in prison cases.

It is not far-fetched to consider prison officials' key professional association, the American Correctional Association (ACA) as playing a role in the prisoners' rights movement, at least now. The ACA leadership and permanent staff are fully aware of legal developments, and through a variety of activities help to disseminate and clarify the legal requirements of prison officials.

From 1977 to 1981, for example, with funding from the National Institute of Corrections, ACA sponsored a Corrections Law Project, which exposed prison officials and state attorneys general from all over the United States to legal scholars and practicing attorneys who specialize in prisoners' rights. More important is the ACA's substantial accreditation project (see American Correctional Association, 1978), which attempts to hold state and local prisons and jails to comprehensive and progressive confinement conditions and practices.

Identifying and Evaluating the Impacts of the Prisoners' Rights Movement

The Problem of Assessing Compliance

Simply to measure the extent to which a particular prison administration complies with a particular court decision is not a satisfactory way to assess the impacts of the prisoners' rights movement on institutions; the most important impacts may operate indirectly. But even in measuring compliance with court decrees we encounter substantial conceptual difficulty. How can one tell whether an injunction has been complied with? Initially one needs to know what the decision required. But many declaratory judgments, consent decrees, and injunctions in prison cases are ambiguous. Many details are deliberately left to the parties to resolve. The court may retain jurisdiction for several years. What is required is often not apparent for some time after the initial decision. Reasonable persons may differ sharply on what a decree "really means."

Neither is it clear when compliance should be measured. Immediately following a decree there may be confusion, limited resources, and lack of organizational skill. Considerable time must pass before we can know whether inactivity is merely the temporary product of inefficiency and turmoil or is instead a "failure of compliance." As time passes, however, intervening variables emerge to confound evaluation. Initial compliance may quickly be eradicated by new events. No directed social change can be expected to persist in perpetuity. That more lawsuits are later necessary to vindicate previously declared rights or to establish new ones need not mean that the original court intervention "failed."

Hypotheses on the Impacts of the Prisoners' Rights Movement

One way to think about the impacts of the prisoners' rights movement is to determine the extent to which changing legal norms have been implemented. Another way is to consider how the changing legal status of prisoners is reflected in social, political, and organizational change. This second approach requires a good deal of speculation and imagination, even intuition, but in the end it may provide a more profound understanding of the prisoners' rights movement. Based on my own reading and research, the following hypotheses suggest the kinds of empirical research and theory building which need to go on if we are to increase our understanding of the impact of legal change on prisons:

1. *The prisoners' rights movement has contributed to the bureaucratization of the prison.* As Max Weber (1954) pointed out, there is a close relationship between law and bureaucracy. Until recently, prisons operated as traditional, nonbureaucratic institutions. There were no written rules and regulations, and daily operating procedures were passed down from one generation to the next. Wardens spoke of prison administration as an "art"; they operated by intuition. The ability of the administration to act as it pleased reinforced its almost total dominance of the inmates.

Early lawsuits revealed the inability of prison officials to justify or even to explain their procedures. The courts increasingly demanded rational decision making processes and written rules and regulations; sometimes they even demanded better security procedures. The prisons required more support staff to meet the increasing demand for "documentation." New bureaucratic offices and practices began to appear. Lawrence Bershad (1977, p. 58) notes: "Court-imposed due process requirements have made extensive and time consuming documentation a necessity." Harris and Spiller (1977, p. 24) draw the following conclusion from their comprehensive study of four cases of protracted jail and prison litigation:

> By focusing attention on the severe deficiencies of the correctional system, the litigation created pressure for management reforms. Contemporaneously with the litigation, or soon thereafter, a broad range of important changes occurred. Those changes assumed different forms—new organizational structure, increased funding, new administrators, changes in personnel policies, new facilities, additional personnel, improved management procedures, etc. These changes were generally considered beneficial.

2. *The prisoners' rights movement has produced a new generation of administrators.* Litigation created pressures to establish rational operating procedures, to clarify lines of authority, and to focus responsibility. Wardens were required to testify in court. Their rules and practices were subject to blistering cross-examination. The despotic wardens of the old regime were neither temperamentally nor administratively suited to operate in the more complex environment fostered by court judgments and gradually have been replaced by a new administrative elite, which is better educated and more bureaucratically minded (Alexander, 1978).

3. *The prisoners' rights movement expanded the procedural protections available to prisoners.* The Supreme Court, in *Wolff v. McDonnell* (1974), ruled that prisoners were entitled to rudimentary procedural protections when faced with forfeiture of good time or with special punitive confinement. The extension of procedural due process to prisoners continues, despite setbacks (see, e.g., *Meachum v. Fano*, 1976). *Vitek v. Jones* (1980), affirms the prisoner's right to a hearing before transfer to a mental hospital.

Many legislatures and administrative agencies responsible for operating prisons also mandated more procedures in a variety of decision-making contexts. Many corrections departments have instituted prison grievance procedures that provide a formal and orderly mechanism for dispute resolution; some provide for final step arbitration by a neutral outsider (Breed, 1976; Breed and Voss, 1978; Singer and Keating, 1973; Keating, 1975, 1976). Federal legislation now requires the attorney general to promulgate "minimum standards" for inmate grievance proceedings and to certify whether the states are in substantial compliance.

4. *The prisoners' rights movement has heightened public awareness of prison conditions.* Prison cases are increasingly brought to the attention of the public through the mass media. In 1976 the *New York Times* reported on prisoners' rights litigation on seventy-eight different occasions, accounting for 16 percent of its total prison coverage. Prisoners' rights cases made the CBS national news on eight separate occasions. . . . Prison litigation may be the peaceful equivalent of a riot, in bringing prisoners' grievances to public attention and in mobilizing political support for change. On this point the observations of Harris and Spiller (1977, p. 26) are instructive:

The litigation sensitized public officials and public servants to correctional deficiencies and increased responsiveness to correctional needs. Legislative, regulatory, and supervisory bodies adopted rules, provided funds, and took other actions that facilitated correctional improvements. Changes were initiated that had not been ordered by the courts. In each jurisdiction, progressive administrators were able to take advantage of the general climate change that accompanied the litigation. In a sense, the court was used as a "scapegoat" and the court orders as a tool for improving correctional programs.

5. *The prisoners' rights movement has politicized prisoners and heightened their expectations.* The availability of judicial forums encouraged prisoners to believe that their grievances would be redressed. But it is not clear that the movement has assuaged prisoners' discontent; to the contrary, it may have intensified it. Indeed, it would be surprising in light of historical experience if rising expectations did not outpace the realities of reform. A high level of prisoner pressures for continued improvements in prison conditions is accompanied by a high level of frustration and tensions. Fred Cohen (1972, p. 864) provides the following insight on the prisoners' rights movement's psychological impact on prisoners:

In my own experience in visiting and talking with numerous inmates (adult and juvenile) and parolees, there can be no doubt that their self-image has been dramatically altered. Where two or three years ago the questions asked of me would be almost exclusively concerned with defects in the conviction or, with regard to prison conditions, loss of good time and the vagaries of detainers, now the discussion focuses on rights. . . . *Advances that are not attributed to prison rebellions seem most closely linked to successful litigation.* That this may prove to be dangerously romantic and disillusioning is the one point that I hope remains with the reader. [Emphasis added.]

6. *The prisoners' rights movement has de-moralized prison staff.* There is some ba-is to believe that today's correctional of - ficers are more insecure, both morally and legally, about their position vis-a-vis inmates . . .than were their predecessors. Staff resents the inmates' access to the courts (*U.C.L.A. Law Review,* 1973, p. 494). They resent even more the im-pression that courts believe the prisoners and "favor them" over the guards. Leo Carroll's (1974, p. 54) research at Rhode Island's maximum security prison led him to observe:

The result of these [judicial] intrusions upon the coercive powers of the custodians has not only been normlessness in the area of job performance, but also a deterioration of the working relationships among the cus-todians. Like the police in the case of the Miranda decision, the officers view the court decisions as placing the law and the courts on the side of the inmate and in op-position to them. By extending legal rights to inmates, restricting the power of the offi-cers and placing the institution on eighteen months probation, the decision makes the prisoners the "good guys." In short, the offi-cers feel themselves betrayed and "sold out" by agencies that should support their au-thority. These agencies are not only the courts but the Department of Corrections it-self. The nature of the court ruling was in the form of a consent decree, a compromise agreement between counsel for the plain-tiffs and the Department of Corrections. The officers interpret this action as a be-trayal by their own superiors.

Not only the officers but the top adminis-trators also may resent being "second guessed" by the courts. It takes a high degree of professionalism to accept that courts have their job to do and must test administrative practice against statutory and constitutional requirements. Thus, Lawrence Bershad (1977, p. 61) notes:

Courts define correctional staff consistently as defendants—a startling role change for

people who entered prison work ostensibly for a combination of law enforcement and social work reasons. Correctional adminis-trators no longer live in obscurity; rather their thoughts are memorialized in court transcripts and their careers become the subject of debate in the media. Added to the psychological impact of frequent publicity is the consistent failure to persuade the courts of the wisdom and "rightness" of cor-rectional methodology. Thus, frustration, bitterness, confusion, and demoralization inevitably result, although usually without public expression.

7. *The prisoners' rights movement has made it more difficult to maintain control over prisoners.* The prisoners' rights move-ment has brought about significant limi-tations on the punishments that can be used against prisoners. Starvation, whip-ping, standing at attention, and exposure to freezing temperatures have been elim-inated. There are also restrictions on the reasons for which a prisoner can be pun-ished. Guard brutality may also have been deterred (although hardly stamped out) by the threat of liability for money damages in a suit for prisoner abuse. The net result is that prisoners are harder to control. More staff may be necessary to maintain order. Less punitive but possi-bly more intrusive mechanisms of con-trol are now becoming more popular— closed-circuit televisions, more frequent use of tear gas, sophisticated locking sys-tems, and unit management that seeks to limit inmate movement and contact.

8. *The prisoners' rights movement has contrib-uted to a professional movement within corrections to establish national standards.* At least among the top correctional lead-ership, there is a strong desire to avoid the embarrassment of judicial scrutiny and denunciation. These officials do not want to be rebuked in federal court for poor administration and maintenance of inhumane institutions. Like workers generally, they place a high value on au-tonomy—they would strongly prefer to

run the prisons without outside intervention. There is a growing feeling that good administrators stay "ahead of the courts." Professional rule making and standard setting is seen as an opportunity to increase correctional resources, improve conditions, and shield the profession from scathing outside criticism. The American Correctional Association, the professional organization of American prison officials, has recently embarked upon a concerted accrediting process, based upon rigorous standards covering almost all aspects of prison management (American Correctional Association, 1978). If, as appears likely, most states voluntarily agree to subject their penal facilities to accreditation review, the process could have an enormous influence on corrections in the next decade.

Assessing the Significance of the Prisoners' Rights Movement

Many prison observers, including lawyers, express misgivings over the benefits brought by the prisoners' rights movement. Perhaps some prisoners' rights advocates hoped that the recognition and vindication of constitutional rights would dismantle the entire American prison system. To their disappointment, the same facilities and many traditional problems remain; even the best run, most benign prison remains an institution of punishment. They have therefore concluded that expansion of prisoners' rights and judicial reform will not significantly change the "system."

The indirect effects of the prisoners' rights movement are difficult to identify and difficult to evaluate. Is it better or worse that today's prison is more fully bureaucratized than the prison of a decade ago? Some of the autocratic wardens may have been rooted out of corrections, but excessive bureaucratization has its own dysfunctions. Prisoners

may find something insensitive and inhuman about administration by the book. While bureaucratization was a response to an earlier form of organization which could not justify its decisions or focus responsibility, excessive bureaucratization may lead to the same result: a mass of offices and office holders insulated from effective outside scrutiny.

Closely related to the advent of bureaucratization is the proliferation of due process. Here, too, one can legitimately question whether more and better procedures have led to higher quality and better outcomes. The Harvard Center for Criminal Justice (1972) found positive prisoner reaction to the disciplinary procedures implemented by *Morris v. Travisono* (1970), although the researchers themselves doubted the significance of the procedural changes. My Stateville study (Jacobs, 1977) revealed no change in the numbers of prisoners sent to disciplinary confinement or in the offenses charged after the establishment of disciplinary due process. That the same personnel continued to make the decisions under the new rules undercut the value of the improved procedures. But the involvement of the central office of the Illinois Corrections Department in final-step grievance resolution has produced a credible administrative vehicle for dealing with complaints. While the "justice model" (Fogel, 1975) remains to be fully elaborated and tested, it is yet an intriguing possibility for a new organizational model built upon the rule of law.

It is a speculation worth pursuing that the prisoners' rights movement has made the provision of welfare benefits to prisoners more logical and legitimate (see, e.g., *New York University Law Review*, 1976). A study by Abt Associates documents the large increase of noncustodial service-type personnel in American prisons since 1950, especially in the past decade. Therapists, teachers, counselors, and medical technicians have become visible members of the prison regime. Schooling has almost achieved the status of a right. The prisons constitute school districts in some states (see Miller, 1978). Availability of a school education seems to be nearly universal. Tuition-free programs in which prisoners can earn college credits are also common (Seashore and Haberfeld, 1976). At Attica one-sixth of the prisoners are enrolled in college or junior college programs.

In the last several years, and particularly since the Supreme Court's decision in *Estelle v. Gamble* (1976), there has been substantial improvement in prison medical services (Neisser, 1977). In 1975, at Stateville, there was only a handful of medical personnel. In 1979 the Illinois Department of Corrections and Prison Legal Services signed a consent decree that called for a medical staff of forty-eight persons (*Cook v. Rowe*, 1979). Care is to be provided around the clock and includes the services of medical technicians stationed in each cell house, fully qualified nurses, a half-dozen dentists, several doctors, a physical therapist, and an X-ray technician. The American Medical Association sponsors an influential prison medical services project and publications program to improve medical care and health services in correctional institutions. As in other prison areas, suits over medical care have spurred the development of American Correctional Association accreditation standards.

The direct effects of the prisoners' rights movement are easier to identify, if difficult to quantify. In practically every prison in the United States one could point to concrete improvements in administrative practices and living conditions directly attributable to the prisoners' rights movement. Inmates who previously were not permitted to have the Koran, religious medallions, political and sociological monographs, and law books now possess them. Inmates once afraid to complain to relatives and public officials about their treatment are now less afraid. Censorship of outgoing mail has been all but eliminated. Censorship of incoming mail is less thorough and intrusive, increasing the privacy of written communication. Prisoners in isolation, segregation, and other disciplinary confinement suffer less from brutal punishments, cold, hunger, infested and filthy cells, and boredom. In some cases, Arkansas, for example, unspeakable tortures have been stopped. In some jails and penitentiaries, prisoners are spared the misery of greater overcrowding than already exists because court decrees limit the number of inmates. In numerous institutions major advances in the quality and delivery of medical services can be directly attributed to court decisions.

None of this denies the considerable suffering still imposed upon those who are incarcerated in the United States. The question is whether the prisoners' rights movement has made things significantly better. One's answer depends upon one's definition of "significantly" and some standard of reform against which current efforts can be compared. An exploration of the legal rights of prisoners inevitably leads to philosophical questions about the nature of imprisonment in a democratic society. To what extent must it be punitive and impose suffering? In my opinion, neither the extension of the rights of citizenship to prisoners nor judicial scrutiny of prison conditions and practices will alter the punitive reality of imprisonment any more than expansion of the franchise and passage of equal employment legislation will alter the reality of the ghetto. In neither case am I ready to conclude that legal reform is not significant or important, although, to be sure, one must recognize the limits of legal reform. The prisoners' rights movement has not transformed the American prison into a utopian institution and will not.

Prisons are too often dilapidated, overcrowded, underfunded, and poorly governed. Still, the impact of prisoners' rights must be judged in light of social and political realities, and in my view, seen in that light, the movement has contributed greatly to the reduction of brutality and degradation, the enhancement of decency and dignity, and the promotion of rational governance.

Study Questions

1. Discuss prisoners' rights as a sociopolitical movement and how certain groups contributed to this movement.

2. How has the Supreme Court changed its posture toward prisoners' rights over the past few decades?

3. Was the prisoners' rights movement successful, according to the author? If so, how?

References

Alexander, Elizabeth. 1978. "New Prison Administrators and the Court: New Directions in Prison Law." *Texas Law Review* 56:963–1008.

American Bar Association. 1977. "Tentative Draft of Standards Relating to the Legal Status of Prisoners." *American Criminal Law Review* (Special Issue).

American Bar Association, Commission on Correctional Facilities and Services. 1975. *When Society Pronounces Judgment.* Washington, DC: American Bar Association.

American Bar Association, Resource Center on Correctional Law and Legal Services. 1974. "Providing Legal Services to Prisoners." *Georgia Law Review* 8:363–432.

American Correctional Association. 1978. *Accreditation: Blueprint for Corrections.* College Park, MD: American Correctional Association.

Bershad, Lawrence. 1977. "Law and Corrections: A Management Perspective." *New England Journal of Prison Law* 4:49–82.

Breed, Allen F. 1976. "Instituting California's Ward Grievance Procedure: An Inside Perspective." *Loyola of Los Angeles Law Review* 10:113–125.

Breed, Allen F., and Paul H. Voss. 1978. "Procedural Due Process in the Discipline of Incarcerated Juveniles." *Pepperdine Law Review* 10:641–71.

Brierley, J.R. 1976. "The Legal Controversy as It Relates to Correctional Institutions—A Prison Administrator's View." *Villanova Law Review* 16:1070–76.

Bronstein, Alvin J. 1977. "Reform without Change: The Future of Prisoners' Rights." *Civil Liberties Review* 4:27–45.

Cardarelli, Albert P., and M. Marvin Finkelstein. 1974. "Correctional Administrators Assess the Adequacy and Impact of Prison Legal Services Programs in the United States." *Journal of Criminal Law and Criminology* 65:91–102.

Carroll, Leo. 1974. *Hacks, Blacks, and Cons: Race Relations in a Maximum Security Prison.* Lexington, MA: D.C. Heath Co.

Clemmer, Donald. [1940] 1958. *The Prison Community.* New York: Holt, Rinehart, & Winston.

Cohen, Fred. 1972. "The Discovery of Prison Reform." *Buffalo Law Review* 21:855–87.

Fiss, Owen. 1978. *The Civil Rights Injunction.* Bloomington: Indiana University Press.

———. 1979. "The Forms of Justice." *Harvard Law Review* 93:1–58.

Fogel, David. 1975. '. . .We are the Living Proof. . .': *The Justice Model for Corrections.* Cincinnati: Anderson Publishing.

Frank, Jerome. 1949. *Court on Trial: Myths and Reality in American Justice.* Princeton: Princeton University Press.

Frankel, Marvin. 1976. "The Adversary Judge." *Texas Law Review* 54:465–87.

Harris, M. Kay, and D.P. Spiller, Jr. 1977. *After Decision: Implementation of Judicial Decrees in Correctional Settings.* Washington, DC: U.S. Department of Justice, Law Enforcement Assistance Administration.

Harvard Center for Criminal Justice. 1972. "Judicial Intervention in Prison Discipline." *Journal of Criminal Law and Criminology* 63:200–228.

Hirschkop, Philip, and M.A. Millemann. 1969. "The Unconstitutionality of Prison Life." *Virginia Law Review* 55:795–839.

Irwin, John. 1980. *Prisons in Turmoil.* Boston: Little, Brown, & Co.

Jacobs, James B. 1976. "Stratification and Conflict among Prison Inmates." *Journal of Criminal Law and Criminology* 66:476–82.

———. 1977. *Stateville: The Penitentiary in Mass Society.* Chicago: University of Chicago Press.

Keating, J.M. 1975. "Arbitration of Inmate Grievances." *Arbitration Journal* 30:177–90.

———. 1976. "The Justice Model Applied: A New Way to Handle the Complaints of California Youth Authority Awards." *Loyola of Los Angeles Law Review* 10:126–48.

Mannheim, Karl. 1940. *Man and Society in an Age of Reconstruction.* New York: Harcourt Brace Jovanovich.

McCormack, Wayne. 1975. "The Expansion of Federal Question Jurisdiction and the Prisoner Complaint Caseload." *Wisconsin Law Review* 1975:523–51.

Miller, L.M.P. 1978. "Toward Equality of Educational Opportunity through School Districts in State Bureaus: An Innovation in Correctional Education." *Harvard Journal of Legislation* 15: 221–96.

Nathan, Vincent M. 1979. "The Use of Masters in Institutional Reform Litigation." *University of Toledo Law Review* 10:419–64.

National Council on Crime and Delinquency. 1966. *Standards Act for State Correctional Services.* Paramus, NJ: National Council on Crime and Delinquency.

National Council on Crime and Delinquency. 1972. *National Council on Crime and Delinquency—Policies and Background Information.* Rockville, MD: National Institute of Justice.

Neisser, Eric. 1977. "Is There a Doctor in the Joint? The Search for Constitutional Standards in Prison Health Care." *Virginia Law Review* 63:921–73.

New York University Law Review. 1976. Note. "Workers' Compensation for Prisoners." *New York University Law Review* 51:478–92.

Rothman, David. 1973. "Decarcerating Prisoners and Patients." *Civil Liberties Review* 1:9–30.

——. 1980. *Prison Reform in the Progressive Era.* New York: Harper & Row.

Scheingold, Stuart A. 1974. *The Politics of Rights.* New Haven: Yale University Press.

Schwartz, Herman. 1972. "Comment on Sostre v. McGinnis." *Buffalo Law Review* 21:775–93.

Seashore, Marjorie, and Steven Haberfeld. 1976. *Prisoner Education: Project Newgate and Other College Programs.* New York: Praeger.

Singer, Linda R., and J.M. Keating. 1973. "Prisoner Grievance Mechanisms." *Crime and Delinquency* 19:367–77.

Turner, William B. 1979. "When Prisoners Sue: A Study of Prisoners' Section 1983 Suits in Federal Courts." *Harvard Law Review* 92:610–63.

UCLA Law Review. 1973. Note, "Judicial Intervention in Corrections: The California Experience—An Empirical Study." *UCLA Law Review* 20:452–575.

U.S. Administrative Office of the United States Courts. 1979. *Annual Report of the Director.* 1979. Washington, DC: U.S. Administrative Office of the United States Courts.

U.S. Department of Justice. 1978. *Federal Standards for Corrections: Draft, 1978.* Washington, DC: U.S. Government Printing Office.

Washington and Lee Law Review. 1968. Note, "The Regulated Practice of the Jailhouse Lawyer." *Washington and Lee Law Review* 25:281–86.

Weber, Max. 1954. *On Law in Economy and Society.* Cambridge, MA: Harvard University Press.

Welch, Robert. 1979. "Developing Prisoner Self-Help Techniques: The Early Mississippi Experience." *Prison Law Monitor* 2:105, 118–22.

Wexler, David B. 1971. "The Jailhouse Lawyer as a Paraprofessional: Problems and Prospects." *Criminal Law Bulletin* 7:39–56.

Yale Law Journal. 1963. Note, "Beyond the Ken of the Courts: A Critique of Judicial Refusal to Review the Complaints of Convicts." *Yale Law Journal* 72:506–58.

Cases

Bell v. Wolfish, 441 U.S. 520 (1979).

Bounds v. Smith, 430 U.S. 817 (1977).

Brown v. Board of Educ., 347 U.S. 483 (1954).

Cook v. Rowe, No. 76C2224 (N.D. Ill. 1979).

Cooper v. Morin, 398 N.Y.S.2d 928, 50 A.D.2d 32 (1979).

Cooper v. Pate, 378 U.S. 546 (1964).

Estelle v. Gamble, 429 U.S. 97 (1976).

Haines v. Kerner, 404 U.S. 519 (1972).

Harris v. Cardwell, C.A. No. 75–185–PHX–CAM.D. Ariz. (1977).

Holt v. Sarver, 442 F.2d 304 (8th Cir. 1971), *on remand;* 363 F. Supp. 194 (1973), *rev'd, Finney v. Ark. Bd. of Corrections*, 505 F.2d 194 (1974), *on remand*, 410 F. Supp. 251, *aff'd*, 548 F.2d 740 (1977), *aff'd, Hutto v. Finney*, 437 U.S. 678 (1978).

Johnson v. Avery, 393 U.S. 483 (1969).

Jones v. N.C. Prisoners' Union, 433 U.S. 119 (1977).

Meachum v. Fano, 427 U.S. 215 (1976).

Morris v. Travisono, 310 F.Supp. 857 (D.R.I. 1970), *further relief granted*, 373 F. Supp. 177 (1974), *aff'd*, 509 F. 2d 1358 (1st Cir. 1975).

Ramos v. Lamm, 485 F. Supp. 122 (D. Colo. 1979), *aff'd in part, set aside in part*, 639 F.2d 559 (10th Cir. 1980), *cert. den.*, 450 U.S. 1041 (1981).

Remmers v. Brewer, 529 F.2d 656 (8th Cir. 1976).

Rhodes v. Chapman, 452 U.S. 337 (1981).

Ruffin v. Commonwealth, 62 Va. 790 (1871).

Ruiz v. Estelle, 503 F. Supp. 1265 (S.D. Tex. 1980).

Theriault v. Silber, 547 F.2d 1279 (5th Cir. 1977), *cert. denied*, 434 U.S. 871 (1977).

Vitek v. Jones, 445 U.S. 480 (1980).

Wolff v. McDonnell, 418 U.S. 539 (1974). ✦

18
Prisoners' Rights
Historical Views

Donald H. Wallace

The era prior to the advent of the prisoners' rights movement was largely characterized by a "hands-off" doctrine upheld by the federal government. That is, government did not interfere with the management decisions of the professionals working within the system. Reinforcing this view was the notion that prisoners were indeed considered "slaves of the state" having lost their rights as members of society. The prisoners' rights movement is largely believed to have changed both the "hands-off" doctrine as well as the view that prisoners are slaves of the state. Jacobs, however, challenges this view on both counts. He systematically cites and discusses the major tenets of the prisoners' rights movement and puts forth examples in which the government supported their issues of concern long before cases were brought about in the 1960s and beyond. Wallace raises some important points regarding the actual origin of the prisoners' rights movement. The reader should consider what effect these early cases may have had during the times when inmate litigation was more frequent and had farther-reaching effects.

A leading textbook on prisoners' rights (Krantz & Branham 1991) states that the 19th-century case of *Ruffin v. Commonwealth* (1871) reflects the prevailing view of the 19th and early 20th centuries that prisoners in the U.S. had no rights. Many present-day courts and other texts have cited the Virginia Court of Appeals observation that a prisoner had, at this point in history,

Copyright © 1997 by Roxbury Publishing Company.

as a consequence of his crime, not only forfeited his liberty, but all his personal rights except those which the law in its humanity accords to him. He is for the time being the slave of the State. (*Ruffin v. Commonwealth,* 1871, p. 796)

Consequently, "[l]ittle or no help could be expected from the bench" (DiIulio, 1990, p. 3); a prison warden's exercise of authority over inmates was unreviewable in the courts.

The present-day conventional view of the history of the development of legal rights of prisoners generally envisions a four-stage process: (1) the *Ruffin*-exemplified slave of the state era; (2) a so-called "hands-off" period, considered by present-day courts and commentators as an evolutionary development from the bleak slave of the state era; (3) a period of judicial activism in the 1960s and 1970s; and (4) the present day.

This chapter will discuss other cases from the late 19th and early 20th centuries which indicate that this conventional history needs to be revised. In my view, the "slave of the State" reference in *Ruffin v. Commonwealth* does not actually represent a once held general view that prisoners were considered slaves of the state. Further, the hands-off period does not necessarily represent an evolutionary development from a time where prisoners were equated with slaves; instead, it constitutes a time of retrenchment from the earlier period. This chapter concludes with a discussion of the need to correct the conventional but, in my opinion, erroneous historical view of the legal status of prisoners.

Ruffin Reevaluated

Considering the strong language equating the legal status of prisoners with that of slaves and how the case has been referred to by later courts and commentators (see Wallace, 1992, for a detailed discussion), it would seem that this case must deal with allegations of cruel conditions or discipline over prisoners, calling upon a court to intervene in the administration of a prison. Yet, counter to the present-day conventional view of this case, the underlying facts of *Ruffin* and its holding show that the case was not concerned with the role of the judiciary in overseeing the discretion of prison administrators.

While serving a criminal sentence, Woody Ruffin had been contracted by the prison to work on the Chesapeake and Ohio railroad. At the work site, he killed a guard in an escape attempt. Ruffin was found guilty of murder in the first degree and sentenced to be hanged. The appeal of this trial formed the basis of the oft-quoted decision by the Virginia Court of Appeals. The court viewed the case as limited to the issue of the proper venue of Ruffin's trial. Ruffin contended that the Virginia statute that gave the circuit court of the City of Richmond jurisdiction to try offenses committed by convicts of the Virginia penitentiary conflicted with the state constitutional guarantee that trials be held at the place of defendant's "vicinage."

The language referring to the slave of the state status was minimized by the Virginia court within this opinion. The Court acknowledged that it had "intimated" (*Ruffin v. Commonwealth*, 1871, p. 798) that the bill of rights applies to freemen and not to convicted felons. But, instead of refusing to entertain the appeal of Ruffin, as one who has no cognizable legal rights, the Virginia Court of Appeals did reach the merits of this prisoner's legal claims. The Court concluded that the constitutional guarantee was not violated by Ruffin's trial occurring at the location of the prison, as this was construed to be Ruffin's vicinage. Importantly, in arriving at this conclusion the Court did not have to explicitly determine that a prisoner has no legally cognizable rights. In fact, by construction, the Court upheld this prisoner's right to be tried in his vicinage.

> If he can be said to have a *vicinage* at all, that vicinage as to him is within the walls of the penitentiary, which (if not literally and actually) yet in the eye of the law surround

him wherever he may go, until he is lawfully discharged. (p. 798)

Above all, the issue on appeal did not concern the issue of a court's oversight of prison restrictions on its inmates. Thus, a closer reading of the *Ruffin* case indicates that the "slave of the State" language is clearly not a controlling influence on the result in this case.

Nineteenth- and Early Twentieth-Century Decisions Regarding Prisoners' Rights

In 1917, the legal encyclopedia, *Corpus Juris* (1917), observed that the slave of the state position was considered to be "not a correct statement of [the prisoner's] relation toward society" (p. 914). Cases from the late 19th and early 20th centuries indicate that the slave of the state view was not generally held, if it was ever held by any court. For example, in *Westbrook v. State* (1909), the Georgia Supreme Court found that, being powerless against the state, a prisoner is owed some affirmative obligation from the state:

> The convict occupies a different attitude from the slave toward society. He is not mere property, without any civil rights, but has all the rights of an ordinary citizen which are not expressly or by necessary implication taken from him by law. While the law does take his liberty, and imposes a duty of servitude and observance of discipline for the regulation of convicts, it does not deny his right to personal security against unlawful invasion. (p. 585)

There are cases dating from this era that did specifically accept prisoner grievances and found conditions of institutions and actions of custodians to violate legal norms.

Cases on Physical Conditions

Prisoners' allegations of unsanitary and unhealthy conditions in places of incarceration were reviewed by the courts of the 19th and early 20th centuries. Although it should first be observed that courts held unanimously that a county was not liable for injuries to a prisoner received by being confined in an unhealthful or unfit prison (Annotation, 1927), here governmental immunity prevented this cause of action. But, for municipalities the rule of immunity was not so unanimous regarding liability for unsanitary or improper conditions of a jail (Annotation, 1927). For example, an exception to governmental immunity was found where city authorities in North Carolina provided "a place of imprisonment which is so badly constructed that a prisoner cannot be reasonably comfortable" (*Shields v. Durham*, 1894, p. 795). Here, the North Carolina Supreme Court found that where the city jail had been for "months in a terrible, filthy, wet, and frozen condition, with window glass broken out as far back as December, 1892, [the municipal authorities] are presumed to know it, and will be held responsible, whether they actually know it or not" (p. 795). Other reported appellate cases supporting municipal liability include *Topeka v. Boutwell* (1894), *Peters v. White* (1899), *Lamb v. Clark* (1940), and *Ratliff v. Stanley* (1928).

Cases on Excessive Discipline and Assaults by Custodians

Caselaw from this period also shows that the authority of the prison administration to select a mode of inflicting discipline was reviewable and could not be arbitrary (*American Jurisprudence*, 1942). Thus, there were cases where relief was held obtainable against the officer in charge of the inmates. Custodians were held liable for damages in *Topeka v. Boutwell* (1894). Here, the prisoner claimed that he was beaten with gross excess after having been subdued and placed under custodial control. The majority of the Kansas Supreme Court stated that it is the duty of custodians to treat prisoners "humanely . . . . [K]eepers of city prisoners have

no warrant authority in law to be harsh and brutal in the management of those in their custody" (*Topeka v. Boutwell*, 1894, p. 822). The concurrence was more explicit in finding a constitutional dimension in this situation:

> [T]he constitution of the state forbids cruel or unusual punishments, and the courts have ample power to prevent such punishments from being inflicted. In making arrests and in the treatment of prisoners, in or out of city prisons, no police or other officer is justified in using unnecessary harshness or excessive violence. (p. 825)

In *Peters v. White* (1899), the superintendent of a county workhouse was held liable for the illegal and unauthorized infliction of corporal punishment on a prisoner. The court found no statutory authority for the county commissioners to delegate their authority to inflict corporal punishment to a superintendent. The court observed that since the use of the whipping post and lash as means for punishment of criminal offenses had long been abolished in Tennessee,

> It would be an anomaly to hold that, when a criminal had been thus convicted and sentenced by a court, he could not be corporally punished, and yet if he has been sentenced for some crime, he might be so punished, at the discretion of one man, for another offense or fault, without even the form or semblance of a trial. (pp. 726–7)

Other cases supporting the principle of liability include *Bartlett v. Paducah* (1906) and *Rose v. Toledo* (1903).

Beyond tort liability, state and federal constitutional prohibitions on cruel and unusual punishment were successfully invoked in state and federal cases where the imposition of discipline was litigated. In 1889, the federal district court in Georgia in the case of *In re Birdsong* found that chaining a prisoner by the neck to the grating of his cell to force him to stand through the night was cruel and unusual punishment. This case has been viewed (Berkson, 1975) as the most famous judicial ruling during the 19th century dealing with the chaining of prisoners. After reading about the custodian's actions in a local newspaper, the district court judge undertook to investigate the circumstances:

> [I]t is clear to any unprejudiced mind, that had the prisoner swooned—a natural result of such inhumanity—his death from strangulation would have been inevitable. It was, in fact, punishment by the pillory, but a pillory where the links of the trace chain and the padlock encircling the bare neck of the prisoner were substituted for the wooden frame. (p. 602)

In 1925, the Arizona Supreme Court applied the state's constitutional ban on cruel and unusual punishment to prison deprivations in *Howard v. State* (1925). For a remedy, the court directed the lower court to initiate injunctive orders. If these orders were not obeyed, then the lower court would have been able to punish the prisoner's custodian in a contempt proceeding. Precedent for this procedure was found in *In re Birdsong* (1889), where the federal court had held that attachment for contempt was the proper proceeding.

In addition to these civil cases regarding abusive disciplinary scenarios during the late 19th and early 20th centuries, there are reported cases of prison administrators and guards subjected to criminal prosecution for flogging prisoners. Almost without exception, these courts held that whipping may not be levied by custodians of prisoners, in the absence of established regulations and legislative approval (*Smith v. State*, 1882; *State v. Nipper*, 1914). The Tennessee Supreme Court in 1881 (*Cornell v. State*) upheld the conviction for assault and battery of a manager of the lessee of convicts for the whipping of two prisoners who had behaved in clear violation of prison rules. The court observed that at the time of this decision, whipping of prisoners had "fallen under the ban of modern civilization, as tending to degrade the individual and destroy the sense of personal honor" (p. 624).

Procedural Hurdles

If there were cases during the so-called slave of the state era that recognized legal rights of prisoners and enforced these rights, the question remains as to why this period is characterized by brutal and inhumane conditions and treatment. While the courts of the late 19th and early 20th centuries cannot be seen as accepting the slave of the state doctrine, this period cannot be equated with the judicial activism of the 1960s and 1970s. The probable answer is not that the courts refused to recognize the substantive rights of prisoners, but rather in the lack of procedural rights or methods available to enforce these substantive rights. Thus, it should be recognized that substantive rights are of little value without accompanying procedural guarantees to implement them.

These rulings in the late 19th and early 20th centuries were made in the face of some major procedural barriers encountered by prisoners. Without the procedural protections of the 1960s and 1970s (that stemmed from the revitalized Civil Rights Act, its concomitant attorneys' fees awards, and the expanded role of the federal courts in enforcing federal constitutional rights against state governmental actors), the prisoners of the late 19th and early 20th centuries had to rely upon the traditional available remedies. The following paragraphs outline various traditional remedies and the accompanying hurdles that have historically hindered these remedies for prisoners. These go beyond the practical difficulties of an indigent person attempting to obtain legal assistance.

Tort Remedies

Several of the above described rulings involved tort actions. As has been observed, tort remedies against the custodians of prisoners were made problematic by doctrines of governmental immunity. The general rule was that in the absence of a statute, the state was not liable to a prisoner for injuries sustained by him as a result of the negligence of a prison employee (American Jurisprudence, 1942; Ruling Case Law, 1929). This rule did not depend upon the status of prisoners being that of slaves but upon a notion of governmental immunity that was generally applicable to anyone (Ruling Case Law, 1929).

Contempt Proceedings

Contempt of court could be enforced by attachment as used in *In re Birdsong* (1889) and *Howard v. State* (1925). Contempt has an advantage over tort remedies in that immunity doctrines which would disqualify a prisoner from suing do not apply to these proceedings (Note, 1950). Limitations with contempt as a remedy lay in the difficulties in persuading a court to imply a direction not to abuse the prisoner from a typical custodian's instruction to "receive and safely keep" him, and in maintaining a court's subject-matter jurisdiction which was deemed to be lost when the court term, at which the prisoner's sentence had been pronounced, expired (Note, 1950, p. 801).

Habeas Corpus Relief

Habeas corpus represents another possible remedy for prisoners. Yet, application of this remedy to address deplorable conditions was difficult. Three limitations on the availability of habeas corpus have traditionally existed: (1) the requirement of exhaustion of alternative remedies; (2) the restriction to contesting the legitimacy of confinement and not to allow challenging of the manner of confinement; and (3) the limitation of a remedy to a total release of the inmate (Comment, 1963).

The last of these limitations prevented relief in *Ex Parte Ellis* (1907), where a county jail inmate sought release on habeas corpus because of the facility's squalid conditions. The Kansas Supreme Court held that it could not release the prisoner merely because of the conditions of the jail. The release of the prisoner was seen as an impermissible rem-

edy, and further "[t]o do so would require us on similar applications to order the release of all prisoners confined there" (p. 83).

In the 1940s and continuing into the 1960s, the federal courts began a process of modifying these three limitations. For example, in *Coffin v. Reichard* (1944), the court allowed for habeas corpus challenges to the manner or mode of confinement. Habeas corpus was used in *Johnson v. Dye* (1949) to challenge extradition; here, the prisoner was successful in establishing that he had been subjected to cruel and unusual punishment at the institution from which he had escaped.

Mandamus

Historically, this device of a court's order to require action by a government agency has been of only limited use as a remedy. For example, in the federal courts, only in recent times has this remedy been given any general application. Prior to 1962, the only federal courts authorized to issue writs of mandamus on original jurisdiction were those in the District of Columbia (Berkson, 1975). In 1962, all federal district courts were empowered to "compel an officer or employee of the United States or any agency thereof to perform a duty owed to the plaintiff" (Berkson, 1975, p. 114).

Injunctive Relief

As a court's order to a government agency to cease an activity, injunctive relief was available in state courts but was limited if any statutory remedies were available. For example, in *Stuart v. La Salle County* (1876), the investigation of physical conditions and sanitation by a grand jury concluded "that it is absolutely cruel and inhuman to confine a human being in the present La Salle county jail for any length of time" (p. 344). The Illinois Supreme Court, however, dismissed the claim for injunctive relief on the use of the jail, not because of a notion of prisoners as slaves, but because the court found that an adequate remedy was provided by a statute.

The Hands-Off Era as a Period of Retrenchment

The conventional history of prisoners' rights is that, prior to the hands-off period, prisoners had no rights. Thus, the hands-off period under this view represents some progress for prisoners' rights advocates, and under this conventional view, there need be no exploration of prisoners' rights jurisprudence before the hands-off era of the 1940s and 1950s.

A revised historical view of the caselaw shows that in this second period of prisoners' rights history, the federal courts may have regarded prisoners as having rights but, for policy reasons unrelated to the legal status of prisoners, these courts would deny relief (Krantz & Branham, 1991). (Cases said to represent the hands-off era were predominantly if not entirely federal court decisions.) Among the policy and jurisdictional reasons for denying relief was a concern for federalism. In *Siegel v. Ragen* (1950), the state prisoners were seeking redress under the Civil Rights Act. The 7th Circuit Court of Appeals found this statute inapplicable:

> The Government of the United States is not concerned with, nor has it power to control or regulate the internal discipline of the penal institutions of its constituent states. All such powers are reserved to the individual states. (p. 789)

A further policy concern raised by these federal courts in the hands-off era was a concern regarding the separation of powers, that the judiciary should not interfere in matters that reside within the discretion of the executive branch of government. Thus, in *Powell v. Hunter* (1949), the 10th Circuit Court of Appeals reminded the prisoner:

> The [federal] prison system is under the administration of the Attorney General . . . and not of the district courts. The court has no

power to interfere with the conduct of the prison or in discipline. (p. 332)

A third policy concern was the need of the federal courts to defer to the expertise of prison administrators and consequently avoid interfering with the complexities of institutions. Thus, prison operations were considered exclusive concerns of corrections officials. For example, the decision as to the appropriate site for a prisoner's mental health care was considered not to be one for the federal courts in *Garcia v. Steele* (1951). The 8th Circuit Court of Appeals determined that it was

> not conceivable to us that every inmate of the [United States] Medical Center [for federal prisoners at Springfield, Missouri] who considers himself to be sane and ineligible for confinement in that institution, can, by asserting that to be the fact, require the District Court to conduct a hearing and investigation to determine whether the prisoner should be in the Medical Center or in some penitentiary or correctional institution. (p. 196)

This result should be compared to *Vitek v. Jones* (1980), where the U.S. Supreme Court recognized the need for procedural protections prior to transfers of prisoners to a mental hospital.

There were other cases from the hands-off era that rejected claims that would raise constitutional issues today. For example, an allegation of interference with access to the courts was alleged in *Sarshick v. Sanford* (1944). The inmate in *Sutton v. Settle* (1962) unsuccessfully sought relief concerning electric shock treatment, solitary confinement, use of the mails, purchase of law books with his own money, use of the prison library, storage space for his property, and suppression of psychiatric treatment. Thus, this was an era where, particularly in the federal courts, inmates had difficulty obtaining relief.

From Judicial Activism to Retrenchment

The judicial activism of the 1960s and 1970s ended the era of the hands-off doctrine. These courts recognized many of the claims of prisoners due to the legal developments involving expansive readings given to the Civil Rights Act and the Fourteenth Amendment by the U.S. Supreme Court (*Cooper v. Pate*, 1963; *Robinson v. California*, 1962).

The judicial activism of the 1960s and 1970s has been credited with significant improvements in prison living conditions and administrative practices (Clear & Cole, 1986, p. 497). This prison litigation has resulted in increased funding for prisons. Substantial appropriations of money have been spent responding to court orders that likely would not have occurred without this judicial activism (Samaha, 1988, p. 655). After noting that individual prisons or entire prison systems in at least 24 states have been declared unconstitutional, Justice Brennan observed (concurring in *Rhodes v. Chapman*, 1981):

> [T]he lower courts have learned from repeated investigation and bitter experience that judicial intervention is indispensable if constitutional dictates—not to mention considerations of basic humanity—are to be observed in the prisons. (p. 354)

It has been the activism of the federal judiciary based upon expanded procedural avenues opened to prisoners in the 1960s and 1970s that has made significant differences in prison conditions. The judicial activism of the lower federal courts during this period precedes the present-day period. From the 1970s onward, the present period has seen the U.S. Supreme Court formally, yet narrowly, recognizing many of the rights of prisoners. Arguably, the gains of prisoners in the 1960s and 1970s have been turned back to a significant extent due to a retrenchment conducted by the U.S. Supreme Court. There have been significant restrictions on procedural protections, such as those involving the Civil Rights Act (Smith, 1995). Further, there have been reversals of the substantive rights won in the lower federal courts in the 1960s and 1970s.

There are numerous examples of Supreme Court decisions that have narrowed prisoners' rights. In *Jones v. North Carolina Prisoners' Labor Union* (1977), the Court held that the prisoners had to show conclusively that prison officials were wrong in their mere belief that the union would be detrimental to prison security and order. In *Turner v. Safley* (1987), the Court rejected any call for a heightened scrutiny for any particular type of prisoner claim; all that is necessary to determine the validity of a prison regulation which impinges on the constitutional rights of prisoners is a reasonable relationship to legitimate penological interests. The Court has required that an inmate must prove that any force used upon him must have been accomplished maliciously and sadistically in order to establish an Eighth Amendment claim (*Hudson v. McMillian*, 1992). In *Hudson v. Palmer* (1984), the Court held that there was no Fourth Amendment protection for prison cell searches.

Beyond this retrenchment, two Supreme Court justices have adopted a view that the Eighth Amendment has no application at all to deprivations suffered by prisoners beyond what was inflicted by their sentences. (Apparently, they do not see the anomaly seen in 1899 in *Peters v. White* that this interpretation of the Eighth Amendment would allow a prison official to do to an inmate what a sentencing court could not do.) Under this view, it is only recently that the Eighth Amendment's ban on cruel and unusual punishment was deemed not applicable "at all to deprivations that were not inflicted as part of the sentence for a crime" (*Hudson v. MacMillian*, 1992, p. 173 [Thomas, J., with Scalia, J., dissenting]; *Helling v. McKinney*, 1993 [Thomas, J., with Scalia, J., dissenting]).

> [H]istorically, the lower courts routinely rejected prisoner grievances by explaining

that the courts had no role in regulating prison life. . . . It was not until 1976—185 years after the Eighth Amendment was adopted—that this Court first applied it to a prisoner's complaint about a deprivation suffered in prison [*Estelle v. Gamble*, 1976]. (*Hudson*, p. 174)

There are two problems with this view (see Wallace, 1994, for a detailed discussion). One of them involves the implied historical importance placed upon the hands-off era. The preceding section has indicated that the hands-off period represents a departure from a tradition of courts recognizing the need to protect prisoners. The other problem concerns the U.S. Supreme Court's first expressed decision, regarding the propriety of the manner in which a sentence is imposed. To suggest that it was only in the era following the hands-off period (the 1960s and 1970s) that the U.S. Supreme Court first applied the Eighth Amendment to the manner in which punishment was carried out is misleading. In *Louisiana ex rel. Francis v. Resweber* (1947), the Supreme Court reviewed whether a second attempt at an execution by electrocution would be cruel and unusual punishment. The Court did not indicate that the ban on cruel and unusual punishment was limited to prescribing the proper contours of the criminal sentence; instead, the Court determined that the very manner in which the sentence is carried out comes within the parameters of the Cruel and Unusual Punishment Clause. This view of *Resweber* was approved in *Ingraham v. Wright* (1977). Here, the Court stayed with the broader view of the ban on cruel and unusual punishment and observed that "prison brutality . . .is a proper subject for Eighth Amendment scrutiny" (*Ingraham v. Wright*, 669).

Robinson v. California (1962), which explicitly applied the Eighth Amendment to the states through the Fourteenth Amendment Due Process clause eclipsed the importance of *Resweber*. Yet, prior to the *Robinson* decision, *esweber* was viewed as extending to

the states the prohibition of cruel and unusual punishment, either by Eighth Amendment "or a similar one . . .extended to the states by the due process clause of the Fourteenth" (Note, 1962, p. 1003).

Conclusions

The generally accepted notion of the evolution of prisoners' rights has pernicious effects. This conventional notion supports the view of the two justices that the courts have not historically been concerned about deprivations suffered by prisoners. This conventional notion allows lower courts to deny prisoners' claims and yet take comfort from the idea that progress in prisoners' rights can be measured by a harsh jurisprudence of the past. For example, in *Buscino v. Carlson* (1989), the Seventh Circuit Court of Appeals detailed the effects on conditions of imprisonment resulting from the permanent lockdown at the U.S. Penitentiary in Marion, Illinois. The court postulated that such "sordid and horrible" conditions "would have raised few eyebrows a hundred years ago" (p. 164). The litigating inmate in *Azeez v. Fairman* (1986) was explicitly reminded of the accepted view of the *Ruffin* case, when it ruled against the inmate.

Yet, the restrictive view of the historical development of the rights of prisoners needs to be rebutted in order to raise the overall level of the current Supreme Court discussion of prisoners' rights. The lack of direct rebuttal by other members of the Supreme Court to the Thomas view of history should not be surprising, since present-day courts and commentators have given such short shrift to the prisoners' rights jurisprudence of the 19th and early 20th centuries. Thus, under the traditional view of the evolution of prisoners' rights, the activity of the judiciary in the 1960s and 1970s seems out of place and artificially created by activist judges. But, more properly viewed, it is really the hands-off era that should be described as incongruous, since the preceding historical era displayed a measurable judicial concern for the rights of prisoners without the self-imposed policy reasons created to deny relief to prisoners.

In delineating the content of the Eighth Amendment, the Supreme Court has stated that this constitutional provision "must draw its meaning from the evolving standards of decency that mark the progress of a maturing society" (*Trop v. Dulles*, 1958). Thus, underlying the ban on Cruel and Unusual Punishment is the concept of the continuing development of the dignity of humankind. A corrected history of prisoners' rights jurisprudence requiring the dropping of the unsupportable slave of the state view would suggest a different starting point for measuring the growth of a maturing society. It should be placed at a much higher level.

Rather than repeat the baseless view that the courts of the 19th century viewed all prisoners as nothing more than slaves of the state, the starting point for determining the growth of a maturing society could consider the aspirations of a 19th-century decision (from the so-called slave of the state era) regarding the likely support from the general public for improvement of conditions in jail facilities. In *Topeka v. Boutwell* (1894; see also *Stuart v. La Salle County*, 1876), where concern was indicated that improvements should be made to the city jail, the Court observed:

> Jails are never desirable places in which to remain; but the dictates of humanity demand that some consideration should be given to the comfort, and especially to the health of those compelled to occupy them. As communities become more enlightened and prosperous, the tendency is in favor of bettering the condition of all classes of unfortunate persons who are committed to the care of the public. (p. 164)

Study Questions

1. Contrary to popular opinion and according to the author, what were the courts' views on prisoners' rights during the mislabeled "slaves of the state" era?

2. What remedies have traditionally been used by prisoners in asserting their rights?

3. Why does Wallace assert that the so-called "hands-off" period was one of retrenchment in prisoners' rights? In other words, why wasn't the hands-off policy a logical step, as most assert, in the evolution from "slaves of the state" to judicial activism?

4. What does the period of judicial activism in the 1960s and 1970s have to do with the availability of particular judicial remedies?

5. In what ways are the arguments in the Wallace and Jacobs articles compatible and yet divergent?

References

American Jurisprudence (1942). *Prisons and Prisoners, 41*, 37. San Francisco, CA: Bancroft Whitney.

Annotation (1927). Liability for Death of or Injury to Prisoner. *American Law Reports, 46*, 94.

Berkson, L. (1975). The Concept of Cruel and Unusual Punishment. Lexington, MA: Lexington Books.

Branham, L.S., & Krantz, S. (1994). Sentencing, Corrections, and Prisoners' Rights. St. Paul, MN: West Publishing.

Clear, T., & Cole, G. (1986). American Corrections (2nd ed.). Pacific Grove, CA: Brooks/Cole Publishing.

Comment (1963). Beyond the Ken of the Courts: A Critique of Judicial Refusal to Review the Complaints of Convicts. *Yale Law Journal, 72,* 506–558.

Corpus Juris (1917). *Convicts, 13*, 914. St. Paul, MN: West Publishing.

DiIulio, J. (1990). Courts, Corrections and the Constitution—The Impact of Judicial Intervention on Prisons and Jails. New York: Oxford University Press.

Krantz, S. & Branham, L.S. (1991). *The Law of Sentencing, Corrections and Prisoners' Rights* (4th ed., p. 263). St. Paul, MN: West Publishing.

Note (1950). Prisoners' Remedies for Mistreatment. *Yale Law Journal, 59,* 800.

Note (1962). Constitutional Rights of Prisoners: The Developing Law. *University of Pennsylvania Law Review, 110,* 163–191.

Ruling Case Law (1929). Prisons and Prisoners, vol. 21. Rochester, NY: Lawyers Co-operative Publishing Co.

Samaha, J. (1988). *Criminal Justice* (p. 633). St. Paul, MN: West Publishing.

Smith, M.R. (1995). Law Enforcement Liability Under Section 1983. *Criminal Law Bulletin, 31,* 128–150.

Wallace, D.H. (1992). *Ruffin v. Virginia* and Slaves of the State: A Nonexistent Baseline of Prisoners' Rights Jurisprudence. *Journal of Criminal Justice, 20,* 333.

Wallace, D.H. (1994). The Eighth Amendment and Prison Deprivations: Historical Revisions. *Criminal Law Bulletin, 30,* 5–29.

Cases

Azeez v. Fairman, 795 F.2d 1296 (7th Cir. 1986).

Bartlett v. Paducah, 28 Ky. L. Rep. 1174, 91 S.W. 264 (1906).

Birdsong, In re, 39 F. 599 (S.D. Ga. 1889).

Buscino v. Carlson, 854 F.2d 162 (7th Cir. 1989).

Coffin v. Reichard, 1944, 143 F.2d 443 (6th Cir. 1944).

Cooper v. Pate, 378 U.S. 546 (1963).

Cornell v. State, 74 Tenn. (6 Lea) 624 (1881).

Estelle v. Gamble, 429 U.S. 97 (1976).

Ex Parte Ellis, 76 Kan. 368, 91 P. 81 (1907).

Garcia v. Steele, 193 F.2d 276 (8th Cir. 1951).

Helling v. McKinney, ___ U.S. ___, 113 S.Ct. 2475 (1993).

Howard v. State, 28 Ariz. 433, 237 P. 203 (1925).

Hudson v. McMillian, ___ U.S. ___, 117 L.Ed.2d 156 (1992).

Hudson v. Palmer, 468 U.S. 517 (1984).

Ingraham v. Wright, 430 U.S. 651 (1977).

Johnson v. Dye, 175 F.2d 250 (3rd Cir. 1949), *rev'd per curiam on other grounds,* 338 U.S. 864.

Jones v. North Carolina Prisoners' Labor Union, 433 U.S. 119 (1977).

Lamb v. Clark, 282 Ky. 167, 138 S.W.2d 350 (1940).

Louisiana ex rel. Francis v. Resweber, 329 U.S. 459 (1947).

Peters v. White, 103 Tenn. 390, 53 S.W. 726 (1899).

Powell v. Hunter, 172 F.2d 330 (10th Cir. 1949).

Ratliff v. Stanley, 224 Ky. 819, 7 S.W.2d 230, 61 A.L.R. 566 (1928).

Rhodes v. Chapman, 452 U.S. 337 (1981).

Robinson v. California, 370 U.S. 660 (1962).

Rose v. Toledo, 24 Ohio C.C. 540 (1903).

Ruffin v. Commonwealth, 62 Va. 790 (1871).

Sarshick v. Sanford, 142 F.2d 676 (5th Cir. 1944).

Shields v. Durham, 118 N.C. 450, 24 S.E. 794 (1894).

Siegel v. Ragen, 180 F.2d 785 (7th Cir. 1950).

Smith v. State, 76 Tenn. (8 Lea) 744 (1882).

State v. Nipper, 81 S.E. 164 (N.Car. 1914).

Stroud v. Swope, 187 F.2d 850, 851–2 (9th Cir. 1951), *cert den* 342 U.S. 829.

Stuart v. La Salle Co., 83 Ill. 341 (1876).

Sutton v. Settle, 302 F.2d 286 (8th Cir. 1962).

Topeka v. Boutwell, 53 Kan. 20, 35 P. 819 (1894).

Trop v. Dulles, 356 U.S. 86, 101 (1958).

Turner v. Safley, 482 U.S. 78 (1987).

U.S. ex rel. Wakeley v. Pennsylvania, 247 F.Supp. 7 (E.D. Pa.1965).

Vitek v. Jones, 445 U.S. 480 (1980).

Westbrook v. State, 133 Ga. 578, 66 S.E. 788 (1909). ✦

19
Resolving the Paradox of Reform
Litigation, Prisoner Violence, and Perceptions of Risk

Ben M. Crouch

James W. Marquart

This section examines the prisoners' rights movement and some of its potential impacts. Ben M. Crouch and James W. Marquart examine the influence of litigation on a specific incarcerated population. The authors surveyed a population of male prisoners at nine institutions under the jurisdiction of the Texas Department of Corrections to investigate effects of prisoner litigation regarding the level of safety felt by the inmates. The survey respondents indicated that they felt safer after the intervention of litigation, although despite the uncertainty of correctional officers, a brief increase in institutional violence occurred during initial implementation.

The turmoil and prisoner violence that frequently follow court efforts to improve prison conditions have been called the "paradox of reform," in which the very process

Excerpts from "Resolving the Paradox of Reform Litigation, Prisoner Violence, and Perceptions of Risk" by Ben M. Crouch and James W. Marquart, *Justice Quarterly Volume* 7: 103–122. Copyright © 1990 by Academy of Criminal Justice Sciences. Reprinted by permission.

intended to make the prison better can make it a more dangerous place. This argument implies that prisoners are often safer before the reforms and that high rates of violence and fear become a normal element of postreform prison life. The present analysis examines violence rates and prisoners' perceptions of risk before and through nearly a decade of litigated reform in the Texas prison system. Results show that prisoners did not feel at all safe in the "old days" and that the paradox exists only in the short term.

In recent decades prison organizations and the informal social order of prisoners have undergone considerable change as the result of sociopolitical and humanitarian reforms (Carroll, 1974; Irwin, 1980; Jacobs, 1977; Stastny and Tyrnauer, 1982). Of these reforms, the most consequential has been the intervention of federal courts to define and guarantee prisoners' rights. Since the mid-1960s, courts have intervened extensively in prison operations on behalf of prisoners (see Feeley and Hanson, 1986; Jacobs, 1980; J. Thomas, 1988). Court-mandated reforms of prison policies and structures have improved prison conditions and services (Brakel, 1986; Harris and Spiller, 1977). At the same time, those reforms appear to have promoted some unintended consequences, especially increased unrest and violence among prisoners (Irwin, 1980; Jacobs, 1977; Marquart and Crouch, 1985). A more dangerous prison environment resulting from reforms is especially significant because prisoners' safety frequently was a specific reason for court intervention in the first place.[1]

Personal safety is a critical concern for prisoners. Indeed, feeling free from exploitation and victimization is a key index of the quality of institutional life (Toch, 1977). Yet personal safety for prisoners is at best uncertain; there is always some risk of injury or material loss at the hands of aggressive or unbalanced fellow prisoners and prison gangs (Bowker, 1982; Davidson, 1974; Lockwood, 1980). Yet the organizational changes following reforms can create a much more pervasive threat to prisoners' safety. As many researchers and commentators have noted, the environment may become increasingly dangerous when those changes undermine the informal, established norms and alliances through which prisoners negotiate a predictable environment (Carroll, 1974; Colvin, 1982; DiIulio, 1987; Irwin, 1980; Jacobs, 1977; Marquart and Crouch, 1985; McCleery, 1961; Silberman, 1979; Statsney and Tynauer, 1982; Thomas, 1980; see also Gaylin, Glasser, Marcus, and Rothman, 1978).

The tendency of reforms to promote greater violence has been lamented by some as the "paradox of reform" (Engel and Rothman, 1983). John Conrad (1982, 319) writes:

> Prisoners are not longer so isolated, so poor, so celibate or so restricted in permissible initiatives. Without minimizing the importance of these improvements, they lose most of their significance in prisons where sudden and unpredictable violence has to be expected as a natural part of daily living.

Engel and Rothman (1983, 105) state the paradox of reform more directly: "The overall effects of the reform movement have been the dissolution of the inmate social order and heightened violence." These conclusions raise a number of questions about the consequences of litigation for violence rates and prisoners' safety, and how these are related and change over time. Research on such questions is relevant both to theories of social control within the prisoners' social system and to the policy of reforming prisons through judicial intervention. Yet despite the growing body of literature on the impact of prison litigation (see Feeley and Hanson, 1986), relatively little systematic research has addressed such questions, especially with a longitudinal approach.

Our purpose in the following analysis is to examine the long-term implications of litigated reform for violence among prisoners, prisoner's perceptions of safety (or risk), and

the "paradox of reform" argument generally. Specifically, we address two fundamental questions. First, what is the relationship between recorded violence (homicides and assaults) and perceptions of personal safety by prisoners before and through the reform process? The "paradox of reform" argument assumes implicitly that prison environments were less violent before the implementation of reforms and that prisoners generally felt safer (albeit more deprived) in those environments. We will examine this assumption in light of data on prisoners' perceptions of danger and actual levels of violence across years of decree implementation. In the process we will examine how perceptions of risk are influenced by prisoners' race, ethnicity, and age and by the changing control structure of the Texas Department of Corrections.

Second, if court-ordered reforms promote disorder and prisoner violence, then do greater danger and fear become a permanent feature of prison life or, in Conrad's terms, a "natural part of daily living?" Many analyses of prison reform, frequently written during the early years of transition and disorder in a particular prison, suggest that once reforms set off disorder, heightened violence becomes institutionalized and all prisoners suffer accordingly into the future.[2] Such a short-term focus may provide a distorted view of the true consequences of litigation for prisoner violence and safety. Only a longitudinal analysis can offer a balanced assessment of how litigated reform actually affects the fundamental issue of prisoners' safety.

The present research reports the experience of prisoners in the Texas Department of Corrections (TDC), a prison system that has undergone massive court-ordered reform since the early 1980s. The focus is on prison conditions, violence levels, and perceptions of safety before, during, and in the final phases of decree implementation. We begin by describing briefly the transformation of TDC in the wake of rulings by a federal district Judge in *Ruiz v. Estelle* (503 F. Supp. 1265 [S.D. Tex., 1980]). In the second part of the analysis we examine the issue of inmates' safety before and throughout nearly a decade of reform litigation.

Methodology

The analysis of prisoners' safety presented here is part of a larger case study of the mandated reform of Texas prisons (Crouch and Marquart, 1989). Conclusions are informed by extensive interviews of prisoners and staff as well as by participant observation. Data on actual prisoner violence came both from prison records and from reports prepared by court monitors. Data on prisoners' perceptions of safety, the primary basis from the analysis reported here, came from a survey of TDC prisoners.

Sample and Data Collection

In early spring 1987 we conducted a survey of male prisoners on nine of TDC's 27 prison units.[3] Each of these units is a large (between 1200 and 2500 prisoners) maximum-security prison. This strategy of going directly to the prisoners to assess the impact of *Ruiz* follows Dolbeare's (1974, 218) admonition that "[l]aw should be analyzed not only from the perspective of the lawgiver but also from the perspective of the consumer . . .the individual should be taken as the focus for at least some of the analysis."

Our plan was to ask these legal-reform "consumers" about personal safety throughout the course of court activism in TDC (from approximately 1978 to 1987). This plan required us to limit our sample to prisoners who had been incarcerated in Texas throughout that period. Thus, we purposely excluded men who had been incarcerated in TDC for five years or less because they would not have been able to make personal, comparative judgments about safety and violence before and in the early phases of reform. Consequently, nearly all our respondents had begun to serve time before

1981; approximately 40 percent had begun to serve before 1978.[4]

We drew the sample by using the discrete TDC numbers assigned permanently to each prisoner. These six-digit numbers are consecutive and remain with a prisoner throughout his incarceration, even if he changes units. After identifying the range of numbers assigned to prisoners between 1978 and 1981 (an arbitrary though reasonable prereform period), we obtained a list of all the men on each unit with numbers in that range. From each of these lists we drew a simple random sample of 60 to 120 prisoners per prison unit (a 5 percent sample); the total sample drawn across the nine units was 614. Of these, 123 were not available at the time of data collection (e.g., because of bench warrant, solitary, job, furlough, or illness); 30 refused to participate. These refusals showed no pattern that would bias the sample.

Racial percentages in the sample for blacks, whites, and Hispanics (50, 33, and 18 respectively) generally parallel those in the TDC system (43, 35, and 22 respectively). The somewhat higher proportion of blacks in our sample probably reflects the fact that our data came from prison units for more serious offenders and that blacks are convicted of violent crimes more frequently than members of the other groups. Not surprisingly, then, prisoners in our sample (regardless of race/ethnicity) had committed more crimes of personal violence. Finally, though our sample ranged in age from the early twenties to the mid-seventies, respondents are somewhat older than average; their median age is 32 years, compared to a system wide median age of 27.

Administration of the questionnaires presented a number of problems. The first considerations were instrument readability and validity. We pretested the questionnaire with prisoner informants at the Eastham unit and revised it accordingly. We administered the questionnaire in whatever space could be made available on a unit. Consequently prisoners completed questionnaires in classrooms, gyms, libraries, and a cafeteria under renovation.

Despite less than optimal research conditions, questionnaire completion was monitored carefully. No more than 15 to 20 prisoners at a time filled out the questionnaires, always under the direct supervision of at least four members of the research team. This arrangement ensured that instructions and items were understood and that each prisoner provided his own answers.

Prison staff members brought prisoners from work or housing wings in small groups. As they arrived, the researchers explained the purpose of the study, answered all questions, assured the prisoners that results were confidential, and disassociated themselves from the court and TDC. The research team included several graduate students who helped answer inmates' questions and read questions to illiterate inmates. A Hispanic graduate student assisted Spanish-speaking prisoners.

Measuring Prisoners' Perceptions of Safety

To ascertain the impact of the *Ruiz* litigation and the resulting organizational changes on prisoners' definitions of their own safety, data on safety perceptions before and during decree implementation are required. Ideally, a panel of prisoners should be asked how safe they feel at regular intervals throughout the reform period. Such data, however, are not available in Texas, or anywhere else to our knowledge. Thus, to address this important question, we had no alternative but to ask prisoners to recall how safe they had felt at various points.

We know that data based on respondents' recollections are always subject to problems of faulty and selective memory; our data on prisoners' recollections of their personal security are no exception. We contend, however, that recall problems are min-imized if the issues or conditions being recalled are central to the respondent's life and are associated with significant events in time or "landmarks" (see Converse and Presser, 1986, 20–23). Because safety is a very basic prisoner concern, we reasoned that the prisoners should be able to recall meaningfully this feature of the environment, especially if asked to use as cues periods of major changes in the prison. Accordingly we asked prisoners to describe their perceptions of personal safety in time periods that coincided with milestones in the prison reform process, milestones that should stand out sharply in their minds.[5] These five periods, which we believed prisoners should be able to differentiate reliably, are defined below:

1. 1970–1978: period before the trial;[6]

2. 1979–1981: period of trial, initial court order, and very preliminary changes in TDC;

3. 1982–1983: period in which TDC initially fought some portions of the ruling, lost, and then began to implement the majority of reforms, most of which occurred in 1983;

4. 1984–1985: period of unprecedented inmate violence, death, and general disorder;

5. 1986 and 1987: the 13 to 16 months before the administration of the questionnaire.

Of necessity we determined these periods before data collection; they were not defined statistically after the fact.

We asked respondents to indicate on a 10-point scale how safe they felt in each of the periods. On that scale 1 represented a very dangerous and unsafe prison environment and 10 represented a very safe one. For the analysis we defined responses from 1 through 4 as reflecting a generally unsafe environment and responses in the 7 to 10 range as reflecting a generally safe environment.

Overview of the *Ruiz* Litigation

Ruiz v. Estelle is a complex and wide-ranging civil suit which ultimately altered almost every aspect of Texas prison operations. In his December 1980 ruling, Judge William W. Justice declared that TDC operating procedures in such areas as health care, access to courts, fire and safety, sanitation, and inmate discipline were totally unacceptable. He concluded: "Their aggregate effects upon TDC inmates undeniably contravene the constitution" (Justice, 1980, 190).

Inmate safety was a critical concern to Judge Justice. In his ruling he wrote:

In essence, TDC has failed to furnish minimal safeguards for the personal safety of the inmates. Primarily because the civilian security force is insufficient in number and poorly deployed, inmates are constantly in danger of physical assaults from their fellow prisoners. . . . Simply put, inmates live in a climate of fear and apprehension by reason of constant threat of violence. (Justice, 1980, 26)

To TDC officials, this portion of the ruling was beyond comprehension. For decades TDC had prided itself on its ability to ensure inmates' safety. During the *Ruiz* trial, prison officials had pointed in their defense to the prison's low homicide, assault, and disturbance rates. They noted, for example, that between 1970 and 1978 only 16 prisoners had been murdered, a homicide rate far lower than in other large state prisons (Sylvester, Reed, and Nelson, 1977). Other witnesses for the state called TDC a paragon of prisons because of its apparent ability to protect prisoners (see Krajick, 1976).

The plaintiffs, however, drew a very different picture of TDC's safety record. They described a system in which inmates were subjected to daily physical coercion by guards. They described how the guards for years had coopted a cadre of tough prisoners, called "building tenders," to enforce order through fear and physical coercion (Marquart and Crouch, 1985). The plaintiffs claimed that this control system, which relied on an often capricious use of force, created an unsafe environment. This picture of fear and abuse prompted the judge to make the dismantling of that control system a prominent part of his order.

As the traditional system of social control was first weakened and then eliminated under court pressure, TDC began to experience the disorder which has been called paradoxical. The court's efforts to create a constitutional and presumably safe environment created disorganization, fear, and violence among prisoners in the process. Officials and prisoners generally agreed that extortion rackets flourished more openly, homosexual rape became more common, and prison gangs emerged rapidly to promote and control contraband, especially narcotics. Even more significantly, homicides and serious assaults rose dramatically in comparison to prereform days (see Ekland-Olson, 1986). In 1984 and 1985, for example, a total of 52 inmate deaths and over 600 nonfatal stabbings took place.

This marked rise in violence among prisoners appears to substantiate the "paradox of reform" thesis, but figures on homicide and assaults such as these are limited. They do not tell us how general-population prisoners define their own risk levels in light of violence or whether high rates of violence persist as reform implementation continues. We now turn to these questions.

Prisoners' Perceptions of Safety Over Time

. . .These data provide answers to the questions we raised initially: (1) Does a low rate of violence before reform mean that prisoners also felt safe then? (2) Do post-reform violence and perceptions of danger continue unabated, as the "paradox of reform" argument suggests?

First, the majority of prisoners in TDC did not view the prison as a safe place before

1978. This finding is not consistent with the contention made by TDC officials at trial that in the "old days" prisoners were free from fear. Instead, though deaths and stabbings may have been relatively rare before the court's intervention, most prisoners did not feel at all safe on the TDC units. Prisoners primarily feared the coercion employed by building tenders and staff. In addition and more to the point, these data do not square with the "paradox" assumption that prisoners felt relatively safe before reforms, despite an official record of stability and relatively low rates of serious violence.

Generally the proportion of all prisoners stating that they felt safe remained relatively low from the 1970s through 1985. Prisoners continued to perceive their world as dangerous even after the prison began to comply with the court orders (e.g., by removing building tenders, hiring more guards, and curtailing the use of force by staff). Thus through the early years of decree implementation there was relatively little change in prisoners' perceptions; the prison population viewed the environment as becoming neither more safe nor more dangerous. After 1985, however, a dramatic shift took place as prisoners began to feel much safer in TDC than ever before.

Before examining these broad patterns further, however, we must determine whether a consensus exists across various prisoner groups. Accordingly we focus on racial/ethnic and age status. We reasoned that these characteristics, representing quite different social locations in the prison world, might produce different perceptions of risk among prisoners. First, race clearly influences how prisoners experience and react to incarceration (Carroll, 1982; Jacobs, 1977) and has been shown to affect patterns of prisoner violence (Lockwood, 1980). Similarly, age and the aging process affect involvement in criminal and violent behavior. As offenders grow older, they become less threatening to others and probably less likely to be the target of violence in return (Farrington, 1986; Lockwood, 1980). Older

prisoners may feel safer at any time than younger prisoners.

Differences by Prisoner Race and Ethnicity

. . .We found a clear consensus among TDC prisoners, regardless of racial/ethnic status, on the level of personal risk or danger over time. Some differences exist, however, which should be examined more closely, if somewhat speculatively. We will trace each racial and ethnic group across time.

In the earliest period, 1970 to 1978, blacks were the least likely to report having felt safe. Only 27 percent felt secure, compared to 38 percent of white and 45 percent of Hispanic respondents. Although only a minority of each group felt safe, the difference in these proportions are notable. The greater fear reported by black prisoners is due largely to the fact that they were most frequently the targets of physical coercion both by building tenders and by staff (Marquart, 1986). At the same time white inmates were a favored class in the prereform era. This favoritism flowed primarily from the prejudiced attitudes of the predominately white, rural prison staff toward minorities, especially blacks. In addition, the inmate power structure on these large units was dominated by white convicts in the 1970s. White building tenders and bookkeepers were the most powerful men in the inmate social system. The ordinary white, and even Hispanic, prisoners benefitted from this arrangement. For example, at the Eastham unit at that time the top tier of cells in the blocks contained mostly black prisoners. In the summer, the top tier was always the hottest and least desirable. Lower and perhaps slightly cooler tiers were "reserved" for white and Hispanic prisoners. In addition, disputes between white and black inmates frequently ended with the minority inmate's receiving some form of physical punishment from officials or at their behest.

Significantly, Hispanic prisoners throughout the 1970s felt the least threatened. This feeling of relative security most probably was due to the Hispanics' strong sense of in-group solidarity, a solidarity strengthened by culture and language. Hispanics tended to defend and control their own and to rely on each other for social and economic support much more than did the other two inmate groups. For Hispanics, there was quite literally safety in the group. One 54-year-old Hispanic convict incarcerated since 1964 described inmate life in the 1970s:

> See, we [Hispanics] took care of ourselves. You know, we got a lot of pride, we looked out for each other. Now that don't mean all was cool. We had dudes that killed or cut each other, but it was Mexican against Mexican. I mean, it was our business, not nobody else's. I know it don't make sense to you [interviewer], but Mexicans just stick together outta need. Mexicans are just different than your whites or blacks.

During the period from 1979 to 1981, prisoners still generally viewed their world as dangerous, but the proportion of whites reporting that they felt safe in this period dropped markedly, compared to the other groups. This tendency of whites to feel less safe and of blacks to feel slightly safer is probably due at least in part to the court-mandated desegregation of TDC, which occurred in 1979.[7] Until that time Hispanics, blacks, and whites were housed in separate living areas and worked in segregated work squads in the fields. Because blacks constituted a majority on most farms, white prisoners in particular were apprehensive about integration and thus may have felt less secure in this second period. Further, many minority prisoners, especially blacks, who had suffered the most from official discrimination also were heartened in this period by the *Ruiz* trial and by the media attention it received. Experiencing rising expectations about immediate change, minority prisoners may have begun to be less subservient and

more aggressive, especially toward white prisoners (Alpert, Crouch, and Huff, 1984).

In the 1982–1983 period reforms began to be imposed; yet traditional alliances and control structures still were in effect. As a result, prisoners were receiving mixed signals. On the one hand, court officials and the media emphasized new rights and freedoms; on the other, prisoners seldom encountered those rights and freedoms in daily prison operations. This was a period of organizational flux, and prisoners continued to feel uncertain and unsafe. Indeed, from 1979–1981 to 1982–1983, the percentage of blacks reporting that they felt safe in TDC dropped from 32 to 24; possibly this change reflected their fear of the white gangs which were emerging to meet the presence of and pressure from blacks after desegregation of the prison.

As we noted above, the mid-1980s were especially traumatic as violence and prisoner deaths rose dramatically. Yet despite this violence the ordinary prisoners in our sample felt no more at risk at this time than in the previous period; indeed, whites and Hispanics even seemed to feel somewhat more secure through 1984 and 1985. These results suggest that the lethal violence which marked this period did not affect all members of the population equally. Indeed, evidence developed in the larger transition study indicates that this violence (especially homicide) was primarily gang-related and was confined largely to the lockdown wings of the units. Thus, somewhat surprisingly, the violence of the mid-1980s did not produce a drop in the proportion of prisoners feeling safe. Apparently the gang-nongang ecology of the prison world tended to keep ordinary prisoners from sensing that they were any more at risk at that time than they had been in the past.

The most dramatic shifts in prisoners' perceptions of safety occurred in 1986 and early 1987. After 1985, all racial and ethnic groups felt much safer in TDC than in previous years. The increase in the percentage of prisoners feeling safe in 1986 in comparison to 1984–1985 was greatest for blacks (30 points) and least for Hispanics (11 points); the percentage increase for whites fell exactly between those for the other groups. By 1987 the perception of safety had increased even further; approximately two-thirds of all groups reported that they felt personally safe within the prison.

Although each racial and ethnic group reflected the same general pattern of perceptions of safety over time, it is possible that a prisoner's age at the onset of the reform may have affected his perceptions of risk and safety in some way. We explore this possibility below.

The Effects of Prisoner Age

Prisoners' ages may confound the general pattern of risk perceptions. Respondents may recall being unsafe in earlier years simply because they were younger and (at least statistically) more vulnerable to violence at that time. In a similar vein, it is more likely that older prisoners, by virtue of their greater experience (in prison as well as in life), have found a "niche" in prison, which provides a sense of safety and stability in an uncertain environment (see Seymour, 1977).

Our research plan called for sampling prisoners who had been locked up continuously from a time before the court order through most of the reform period. Consequently most of the respondents had been incarcerated for similar lengths of time. Thus we were not able to assess directly whether prisoners who had served more time might be less likely to feel at risk. We reasoned, however, that older prisoners would be more inclined and even more able to find whatever safe niches were available in TDC. If this were the case, prisoners at different ages might be expected to report quite different perceptions of personal risk in TDC across time.

Results, however, reveal that a prisoner's age makes relatively little difference in perceptions of personal safety. We compared the perceptions of prisoners in three age groups: 22–31, 32–44, and 45–72. All of these respon-

dents had experienced the period of litigated reform in TDC (approximately nine years), but they were at different ages when those reforms began. Although prisoners in the middle group felt safer in all periods, this difference is slight; the perception of risk over time for each age group is very similar. These results echo those from the racial/ethnic status analysis.

Clearly, prisoners' perceptions of their own safety throughout the reform process are not influenced by age or by racial/ethnic status. This finding suggests that the pattern of risk perceptions in our sample is general and is reflected across important prisoner subgroups. If this pattern is general, we must look to structural changes in the prison environment for an explanation.

Control Structure Changes Affecting Prisoners' Safety

Judge Justice's order to dissolve TDC's traditional but unconstitutional control system altered directly two fundamental elements in the prisoners' world. The presence and then the absence of these two elements had important implications for prisoners' safety.

The first control element altered by court order was the building tender system. Building tenders were inmate guards who worked for the staff and maintained order through fear and intimidation (see Marquart and Crouch, 1985). Although most officials and even some prisoners lamented the dismantling of this control system, most prisoners (60 percent) disagreed with the following statement: "Actually the building tenders were not all that bad." Similarly, a majority (58 percent) of respondents disagreed with the statement, "Overall, inmates were better off under the old system than they are today." These sentiments prevailed across racial and ethnic groups. For example, a black inmate commented:

> Getting rid of the BTs, turnkeys, and count-boys was a very good thing because in the old days it was a simple matter for them

[BTs] to "cross out" [lie about another inmate to the staff] somebody they didn't like. They did that shit all the time. . . . Most people were tense all the time.

Although the following statement by a Hispanic prisoner is somewhat more ambivalent, he, too, was glad to see the BTs go.

I never felt another convict should be over another convict. They (BTs) done some pretty bad shit on the streets and they told us what to do in here. That wasn't right. I never supported it but like I went along with it because you couldn't fight them. In some respects it was good because they kept the noise down and them niggers in line.

A white prisoner stated:

The building tender system was terrible and getting rid of it's been one of the best things to come out of the *Ruiz* case. It was bad when they were here because they stole your property and they also ran protection scams. . . . The people in grey (guards) never did nothin' about it neither.

The second element of the control structure that was ordered changed to improve prisoners' safety was the behavior of correctional officers. Beginning in 1984, TDC administrators charged the Internal Affairs (IA) division with ensuring that guards treated prisoners in accordance with a detailed use of force policy drafted at the court's direction. Inmates' reports of guards' violations of this policy regularly brought IA officers out to the various units to investigate. Disciplinary actions for offending officers included reprimands, transfers, and even dismissals. As a result many officers, especially veterans, backed off; they merely "put in their eight" each day and went home. That is, they became less inclined to intervene among prisoners or to interact with them. This guard-force position of distance from prisoners also was promoted by the introduction of well over 1,000 new officers in 1983 to replace the building tenders and to improve further the officer-inmate ratio.

That ratio, which was 1:12.5 at the time of the trial, had fallen to 1:6 by 1986.

These changes in TDC's control system created an authority vacuum. In 1983 the building tenders were gone; by 1984 the guards had backed off, to a large extent. Thus officials no longer penetrated into the cell blocks through building tenders' snitches or by their own presence. As a consequence, rather suddenly there was no one to enforce an old order, and a new order was yet to emerge.

With no one apparently in charge in the cell blocks, and with a chance for anyone to take charge, the more aggressive prisoners, previously held in check by the "authorities," began to seize opportunities to establish their own dominance. At this time (late 1983 and 1984) exploitation of the weak became blatant, racial tensions rose, and gang activity became a major concern of officials, prisoners, the court, and the media.

Prisoner Reactions to Structural Changes

Because no building tenders were present to settle disputes authoritatively among ordinary inmates and because officials lacked advance information of weapons or vendettas, there was little structural restraint on conflict. To control their own immediate environments, prisoners increasingly had to rely on themselves. This self-help as a form of social control sometimes involved violence. In this connection Black (1984, 1) argues that crime and even violence sometimes are the result of the offender's engaging in self-help: "Far from being an intentional violation of a prohibition, much crime is moralistic, and involves the pursuit of justice. It is a mode of conflict management, possibly a form of punishment, even capital punishment." It is a reasonable hypothesis that much of the aggression among prisoners during the reform years, particularly 1984 and 1985, was defensive, aimed at protecting egos, statuses, property, and bodies. By this time many prisoners in TDC were experiencing a "crisis of personal safety" (Alpert et al., 1984).

Indirect evidence for this pattern of fear-triggered aggressiveness among prisoners is found in the distribution of rule violations involving weapons possession. For the nine major units included in the prisoner survey the numbers of official weapons possession violations by year are as follows: 1983, 637 cases; 1984, 825 cases; 1985, 870 cases; 1986, 564 cases; 1987, 170 cases.[8] This pattern of violations, we believe, reflects prisoners' recognition, especially through 1984 and 1985, that they had to rely on themselves for protection, and that for many, prison seemed to be an increasingly dangerous place. Prisoners made or obtained weapons overwhelmingly for self-defense; as they saw others arming, they felt compelled to do the same.

We are now in a position to reexamine . . .the perceptions of safety from the 1970s through 1985. Although there are some variations across these years, perceptions of personal safety generally did not change very much. How can we explain the fact that prisoners' definitions of their risk remained fairly constant despite the increase in assaults, homicides, and even weapons possession?

One explanation is that shifts in levels of violence through 1985 reflect manipulation of statistics by TDC officials rather than changes in prisoners' behavior. After all, unit wardens and officers could have overreported violence to strengthen their claims that judicial intervention was not only unwelcome but detrimental to prison safety. In this way, overreporting violent conditions would benefit the agency. We reject this explanation because of the trend in homicide statistics; these numbers are very difficult to inflate or to dampen, regardless of official desires to do so. Prisoners' deaths at the hands of other prisoners rose markedly during the reforms. These statistics, combined with extensive qualitative data on prisoner and staff actions, convince us that the vio-

lence was the result not of statistical tinkering by officials but of changes in prisoners' behavior.

If the increase in violence and danger in TDC in the early and mid-1980s was real, why did prisoners not suddenly perceive their world to be more dangerous than it had been before the tumultuous reforms? Our hypothesis is that prisoners simply experienced a shift during these years from one threat to another; they feared official violence before reform and peer violence during reform. As court pressure eliminated brutality by staff and building tenders, a new threat emerged, namely aggressive fellow prisoners using the diminished official control and the court-guaranteed "freedoms" to expand their dominance, gang extortion, and drug activity. This shift in the source of threat dampened any sense among prisoners that the place had become appreciably safer after officials quit using coercion in late 1983.

Implications of Official Reactions to Prisoner Violence

To regain some control of a prison that outsiders (and many insiders) felt was almost out of control in 1984 and 1985, TDC's administration instituted a number of strategies. In addition to increasing the regular guard force, they created a Special Operations and Response Team (SORT), with contingents assigned to each large prison unit. Unfortunately, many regular officers were ill-prepared, for whatever reason, to enter very crowded cell blocks and to confront abusive and often aggressive prisoners. Though trained for such duty, SORT members were few and basically reactive; they entered the scene only after a death, a stabbing, or a disturbance.

More effective at controlling violence was a new classification plan. This plan was implemented at the court's behest by the prison's "reform" director, Raymond Procunier, who took command in May 1984.

Among other things, the new plan directed that prisoners who were likely to be assaultive or otherwise troublesome be identified and then locked down indefinitely. In late 1984 special "administrative segregation" cellblocks were constructed on several units. These "admin. seg." blocks at first were not used extensively. In Fall 1985, however, in response both to escalating prisoner violence and to strong political pressure to "do something" about it, the administration ordered a massive lockdown of all known gang members and of inmates who had assaulted guards or other inmates. By December 1985 this dragnet had caused nearly 3,200 men to be confined indefinitely in single cells under very tight security (Fong, 1987).

This lockdown strategy produced the desired effect. In 1986 there were five homicides (versus 25 in 1985); in 1987 there were only three. Prisoners as well as a beleaguered staff praised the strategy; 80 percent of the prisoners in the survey pointed to administrative segregation as the main reason for the dramatic drop in prisoner assaults and deaths. A sizable percentage (43 percent) also believed that if those currently locked down were returned to the general population, the violence would begin again.

By removing assaultive prisoners from the general population into the administrative segregation wings, officials made the regular prisoners feel safer, but in the process they also concentrated the violence. Of the 52 homicides committed in 1984 and 1985, 44 were gang-related and in most cases occurred in the "admin. seg." cellblocks. Thus the removal of the most assaultive prisoners from the population did not eliminate danger for those in "admin. seg.," but it did permit more general-population prisoners to feel increasingly safe.

Conclusions

The "paradox of reform" argument questions implicitly whether broad court intervention really makes life better for prisoners. If intervention heightens violence and if prisoners thus are exposed not only to the danger of assault and death but also to the stresses created by greater risk, perhaps intervention is not worth the pain to prisoners. This argument might have some validity if it could be shown that increases in violence and risk in fact become the norm in a postreform prison environment. Unfortunately, however, data on the long-term effects of litigation on violence and on prisoners' definitions of risk have not been available. As a result, neither assumption of the paradox argument has been tested: that prisoners were or felt safer in an ostensibly stable prereform environment and that violence becomes the norm after reforms. Examining these assumptions has been the primary objective of the present analysis.

In the 1970s, before court intervention, TDC was reputed to be a stable, safe prison; official statistics reveal that assaults, homicides, and escapes were relatively infrequent (see DiIulio, 1987, 5263). The implication is that few prisoners in such a place should feel that they are at personal risk. Our data show clearly, however, that only a minority of prisoners actually felt safe; blacks felt the most threatened. Clearly, TDC was safe and predictable only from the viewpoint of officials, who could report little trouble in the very tightly controlled Texas prisons. Indeed, particularly throughout the 1970s, the very control regime that created TDC's often-vaunted stability was the chief reason why prisoners felt unsafe.

This conclusion moves our understanding of prereform Texas prisons beyond that offered by DiIulio (1987). His account (influenced strongly by the TDC of the 1960s and early 1970s under Director Beto) presents a control model of Texas prisons that offered all prisoners a safe, predictable environment. Yet the data presented here reveal that although in the "old days" powerful directors may have been able to limit official violence and to maintain a level of order envied by prison managers and researchers, most TDC prisoners did not share this perception of safety and order in the years before the court-ordered reforms.

Our data make it apparent that perceptions of risk and actual rates of violence in a prison do not covary; low rates of violence before reforms did not mean that prisoners felt safe. Similarly, after the reforms, when violence increased dramatically, prisoners' perceptions of their own safety in TDC remained rather close to those reported for the prereform period. Despite some variations in perceptions by race, ethnicity, and age, this broad continuity of perceptions was true for all prisoners. The reason, we suggest, is that greater prisoner aggressiveness and gang activity, spurred by changes in the control structure, replaced official coercion (from building tenders and guards) as a daily risk. Because of that coercion, the prison had been dangerous in the past; because the reforms provided opportunities for aggressive prisoners, the prison remained dangerous in the early years of reform.

If aggressive prisoners and gang violence had continued unchecked, then the reforms might be said to be paradoxical. Our analysis, however, shows that high violence rates do not continue in the long term, and prisoners begin to feel less fearful for their personal safety. After 1985, violence in TDC dropped markedly. When reforms, and especially a new, constitutional control system, became institutionalized in the prison, a majority of prisoners reported feeling safe.

In TDC the introduction of standardized procedures, legal discipline, adequate numbers of officers and supervisors, and the extensive use of administrative segregation meant that most prisoners for the first time feared neither the staff nor other prisoners. Of course, although approximately two-thirds of TDC prisoners reported feeling quite safe by 1987, a sizable minority still felt somewhat less secure; prison, after all, is never a completely safe world. Nonetheless, the present analysis argues that although intervention is painful in the short term, that pain does not negate the reform effort. In time, low rates of violence and feelings of real security among prisoners have been achieved.

A final issue is whether the paradox of reform might also be resolved in other state prisons. We argue that the course and the consequences of court-ordered reforms in TDC would be reflected in other prisons; indeed, the Texas experience in many respects is a microcosm of broad changes in American corrections. Texas prison history and operation contain many somewhat unique elements, including the extensive BT system, acreage for a plantation prison, and decades of political autonomy. Yet in its court-mandated move from a paternalistic, repressive order toward bureaucratic order and professional management, TDC mirrors the transitions in California (Irwin, 1980) and Illinois (Jacobs, 1977) prisons, for example. Each of these prison systems, like TDC, experienced significant judicial intervention which moved it from autonomy through turmoil and violence into a period of renewed stability. In view of these similarities, it is reasonable to argue that prisoners in other states (perhaps including those in Alabama, Mississippi, and Arkansas prisons, where much less research has been conducted) would report a greater sense of safety in the postreform period. Yet because data such as those reported above are not available from other states, prisoners' perceptions of risk through the reform process can only be hypothesized. A clearer picture awaits further research.

Study Questions

1. What do the authors mean by the "paradox of reform"?

2. How do the authors rebut the "paradox of reform" regarding inmate violence and disarray after the *Ruiz* case?

3. Describe the methodology (sample, research design, data collection methods, and measures) used by the authors to come to their conclusions regarding or-

ganizational change before, during, and after the court-ordered change.

4. What were the initial effects of the *Ruiz* decision on the inmate social system, and how were the problems remedied?

5. Do you believe that anyone could have prevented the violence and disarray that resulted from the court-ordered reform? If so, who? How?

Notes

1. See, for example, *Gates v. Collier*, 501 F.2d 1291 (5th Cir. 1974) and *Holt v. Sarver*, 300 F.Supp. 825 (ED Ark. 1969); *Ruiz v. Estelle*, 503 F.Supp. 1265, 1277–1279 (S.D. Texas 1980).

2. Jacobs' (1977) account of the reforms at Stateville (Illinois) prison is an exception. Rather than leaving the impression that disorder and danger prompted by reforms remained high, he suggested that some degree of stability was reemerging at the close of his study.

3. The following prisons were included in the study: Eastham, Ellis I, Coffield, Ferguson, Wynne, Darrington, Retrieve, Ramsey I, and Ramsey II. Because limited resources precluded a survey of prisoners on all TDC units (27, including three for female prisoners), we selected a subset. We chose to survey those TDC units which were, and essentially remain, primarily for more experienced and more violence-prone prisoners. It is here that safety has been most problematic for inmates. For these reasons, these nine units also have received the greatest attention from the court.

4. Prisoners in administrative segregation (permanent lockdown) were excluded from the sample. Security considerations and logistics of questionnaire administration made it impossible to include them.

5. In the view of the prisoners who participated in the pretesting of the instrument, these periods were sufficiently distinguished so that most prisoners would have no trouble recalling their own sense of safety during each.

6. The relatively longer time for the 1970–1978 period reflects a post hoc analysis decision. Anticipating that some respondents actually would have been incarcerated before 1978 despite our sampling plan, we included on the questionnaire a "before 1978" category in which prisoners could indicate their sense of safety or risk. We reasoned that respondents locked up before 1978 would have been in prison for only two or three years before the reform trial. This was generally the case for the 180 who had TDC experience before 1978; except for a small minority, those responding about the pre-1978 period actually were referring to a period from the mid-1970s to 1978. A few respondents, however, had been in TDC continuously since as early as 1970. To include their characterizations of safety "before 1978," we expanded the category accordingly for reporting the data.

7. This order, unrelated to *Ruiz v. Estelle*, was the result of *Lamar v. Coffield*, Civil Action No. 72–H–1393 (United States District Court, Southern District, 1979).

8. These figures are limited to the years 1983 through 1987 because comparative data is not available from TDC for earlier years.

References

Alpert, Geoffrey, Ben M. Crouch, and C. Ronald Huff (1984). "Prison Reform by Judicial Decree: The Unintended Consequences of *Ruiz v. Estelle.*" *Justice System Journal* (9):291–305.

Black, Donald (1984). "Crime as Social Control." In D. Black (ed.), *Toward a General Theory of Social Control*. Volume 2. New York: Academic Press, pp. 1–27.

Bowker, Lee (1982). "Victimizers and Victims in American Correctional Institutions." In R. Johnson and H. Toch (eds.). *The Pains of Imprisonment*. Beverly Hills: Sage, pp. 63–76.

Brakel, Samuel (1986). "Prison Reform Litigation: Has the Revolution Gone Too Far?" *Judicature* (70):1–8.

Carroll, Leo (1974). *Hacks, Blacks, and Cons.* Lexington, MA: Lexington Books.

——. (1982). "Race, Ethnicity, and the Social Order of the Prison." In R. Johnson and H. Toch (eds.), *Pains of Imprisonment*. Beverly Hills: Sage, pp. 313–30.

Colvin, Mark (1982). "New Mexico Riot." *Social Problems* (29):449–63.

Conrad, John (1982). "What Do the Undeserving Deserve?" In R. Johnson and H. Toch (eds.), *Pains of Imprisonment*. Beverly Hills: Sage, pp. 313–30.

Converse, Jean and Stanley Presser (1986). *Survey Questions: Handcrafting the Standardized Questionnaire.* Beverly Hills: Sage.

Crouch, Ben, and James W. Marquart (1989). *An Appeal to Justice: Litigated Reform of Texas Prisons.* Austin: University of Texas Press.

Davidson, Theodore (1974). *Chicano Prisoners: The Key to San Quentin.* New York: Holt, Rinehart.

DiIulio, John (1987). "Prison Discipline and Prison Reform." *The Public Interest* (Fall):71–90.

Dolbeare, Kenneth (1974). "Law and Social Consequences: Some Conceptual Problems and Alternatives." In J. Pennock and J. Chapman (eds.), *The Limits of Law.* New York: Lieber-Atherton, pp. 211–29.

Ekland-Olson, Sheldon (1986). "Crowding, Social Control and Prison Violence: Evidence from the Post-Ruiz Years in Texas." *Law and Society Review* (20)3:389–421.

Engel, Kathleen, and Stanley Rothman (1983). "Prison Violence and the Paradox of Reform." *The Public Interest* (Fall):91–105.

Farrington, David (1986). "Age and Crime." In Michael Tonry and Norval Morris (eds.), *Crime and Justice: An Annual Evaluation of Research. Volume 7.* Chicago: University of Chicago Press, pp. 189–250.

Feeley, Malcolm, and Roger Hanson (1986). "What We Know, Think We Know and Would Like to Know about the Impact of Court Orders on Prison Conditions and Jail Crowding." Presented to the Working Group on Jail and Prison Crowding, Committee on Research on Law Enforcement and the Administration of Justice, National Academy of Sciences, October 15–16, Chicago.

Fong, Robert (1987). "A Comparative Study of the Organizational Aspects of Two Texas Prison Gangs: Texas Syndicate and the Mexican Mafia." Unpublished doctoral dissertation, Sam Houston State University, Huntsville, TX.

Gaylin, Willard, Ira Glasser, Steven Marcus, and David Rothman (1978). "Doing Good." New York: Pantheon.

Harris, M. Kay, and Dudley P. Spiller (1977). *After Decision: Implementation of Judicial Decrees in Correctional Settings.* Washington, DC: American Bar Association.

Irwin, John (1980). *Prisons in Turmoil.* Boston: Little, Brown.

Jacobs, James (1977). *Stateville.* Chicago: University of Chicago Press.

——. (1980). "The Prisoners' Rights Movement and Its Impacts: 1960–1980." In Norval Morris and Michael Tonry (eds.), *Crime and Justice: An Annual Review of Research. Volume 2.* Chicago: University of Chicago Press.

Justice, William W. (1980). "Memorandum Opinion." United States District Court for the Southern District of Texas, Houston Division, December 12.

Krajick, Gary (1976). "They Keep You In, They Keep You Busy and They Keep You from Getting Killed." *Corrections Magazine* (1):4–8, 10–21.

Lockwood, Daniel (1980). *Prison Sexual Violence.* New York: Elsevier.

Marquart, James (1986). "Prison Guards and the Use of Physical Coercion as a Mechanism of Prisoner Control." *Criminology* Volume 24 (May): 347–366.

Marquart, James W., and Ben M. Crouch (1985). "Judicial Reform and Prisoner Control: The Impact of *Ruiz v. Estelle* on a Texas Penitentiary." *Law and Society Review* (19):557–86.

McCleery, Richard (1961). "The Governmental Process and Informal Social Control." In Donald Cressey (ed.), *The Prison: Studies in Institutional Organization and Change.* New York: Free Press, pp. 179–205.

Seymourt, John (1977). "Niches in Prison." In Hans Toch (ed.), *Living in Prison: The Ecology of Survival.* New York: Free Press, pp. 179–205.

Silberman, Charles (1979). *Criminal Violence, Criminal Justice.* New York: Random House.

Stastny, Charles, and Gabrielle Tyrnauer (1982). *Who Rule the Joint?* Lexington, MA: Lexington Books.

Sylvester, Sawyer F., John Reed, and David Nelson (1977). *Prison Homicide.* New York: Spectrum.

Thomas, Charles (1980). "The Impotence of Correctional Law." In Alpert (ed.), *Legal Rights of Prisoners.* Beverly Hills: Sage, pp. 243–260.

Thomas, Jim (1988). *Prisoner Litigation: The Paradox of the Jailhouse Lawyer.* Totowa, NJ: Rowan & Littlefield.

Toch, Hans (1977). *Living in Prison: The Ecology of Survival.* New York: Free Press. ✦

20
Constitutional Issues Arising From 'Three Strikes and You're Out' Legislation

Frank A. Zeigler

Rolando V. Del Carmen

Perhaps the most significant pieces of litigation regarding the offender population within the last decade have been in the form of "three strikes" laws. The basic premise of three-strikes legislation, which came into its modern form in 1994 in California, is that the courts will systematically identify the small proportion of offenders who commit a disproportionate amount of serious crime, thereby incapacitating a significant portion of the offender population. The public (both in California and in many other states in which three-strikes legislation has been passed) enthusiastically supports life sentences for what the court considers to be "habitual" offenders. The authors in this chapter examine three-strikes legislation through what is perhaps its most formidable challenger—the Eighth Amendment protection against cruel and unusual punishment. Through a review of four major court cases, the proportionality of three-strikes legislation is challenged. The issue at hand is whether prior offenses should serve as factors in deciding the court's response to a current offense. The reader is encouraged to consider the proportionality argument pre-

Excerpts from *Three Strikes and You're Out: Vengeance as Public Policy* (1996), pp. 3–23. Copyright © Sage Publications, Inc. Reprinted by permission.

sented in this chapter. Should the role of an offender's prior record be taken into account, and are limitations on judicial discretion a benefit or a detriment to the sentencing system in the United States?

Seated at counsel table after an adverse jury verdict, the lawyer turned to the defendant to offer consolation. The client, realizing that all that could be done had been done, gave a wan smile and said, "You do the crime, you do the time." With that, the sheriff escorted the convicted felon away to serve a life sentence.

Over the years, that scenario has become familiar and is replayed daily in courts throughout the country. In contemporary language, the above aphorism might be more aptly stated: "You do the third crime, you do a lifetime." This reformulation is derived from the "three strikes and you're out" legislation passed in 1994 in California that is gaining momentum across the United States ("Recent Legislation," 1994).[1] The constitutional limits on these mandatory minimum sentencing schemes are left for the courts to resolve primarily by interpreting the "cruel and unusual punishments" clause of the Eighth Amendment and similar state constitutional provisions.

How the words *cruel and unusual* are defined by the courts reflects an evolving standard based on a developing societal view on punishment for crime. In *People v. Romero* (1995), the first constitutional test of California's new statute, the appellate court's decision reflects this public view in upholding three-strikes punishment. The opinion states that the ultimate test whether the statute is cruel and unusual or disproportionate can be determined by the results of California's initiative referendum (Proposition 184) conducted November 1994, in which the voters approved the new three-strikes law by a 72% to 28% margin. The judicial attitudes appear to be that the public has spoken; the appellate court defers to the will of the public. It is not always that simple, however.

This chapter examines, through decisions of the U.S. Supreme Court, the constitutional conflict presented when habitual offender statutes are challenged on Eighth Amendment grounds as being cruel and unusual. First, a brief historical background traces the origins of repeat offender provisions and the term *cruel and unusual punishment* and tracks their ultimate collision in the landmark case of *Rummel v. Estelle* (1980). Next, the chapter analyzes a trilogy of cases in the decade that followed that found the Supreme Court clearly divided on the constitutionality of three-strikes measures. Another section summarizes current applications of proportionality laws. A final section discusses the emerging constitutional challenge under the doctrine of separation of powers.

It must be noted at the outset that the legislative power to enact habitual offender laws similar to current three-strikes statutes has rarely been rejected by the courts on a constitutional basis, but when they have, it has been on disproportionality grounds. Given this, the main thrust of this chapter is on the proportionality doctrine as it relates to the cruel and unusual punishments clause of the Eighth Amendment. In essence, the proportionality doctrine prohibits a punishment more severe than that deserved by the offender for the harm caused or the acts committed. Over the years, the Supreme Court has woven an uneven tapestry of standards for evaluating three-strikes provisions, as the cases discussed below illustrate.

Background

James Madison borrowed the phrase "cruel and unusual" from the English Bill of Rights of 1689 and incorporated these words into the Eighth Amendment to the U.S. Constitution in 1791. It is essentially a term of enlightenment—that government is obliged to respect the human dignity of its citizens.

Traditionally, the framers were thought to have been concerned only with torturous punishment methods. The accepted view today, however, is that the framers' intention was to create a right to be free from excessive punishment ("The Effectiveness," 1961). Despite its importance as a constitutional protection, the debate on the inclusion of the phrase "cruel and unusual" at the Constitutional Convention involved just two speakers and featured fewer than 200 words.[2] From such inauspicious beginnings, this clause has evolved to become the major constitutional limitation on today's three-strikes legislation.

Serving as backdrop to the constitutional conflict between cruel and unusual punishment and the enhancement of the length of sentences for repeat offenders are two cases decided by the U.S. Supreme Court almost nine decades ago but whose effect is felt up to the present. These cases are seminal on the issue of cruel and unusual punishment.

Cruel and Unusual Punishment: *Weems v. United States*

The constitutional principle that the punishment should fit the crime was first articulated by the Supreme Court in *Weems v. United States* (1910). As sometimes happens in developing law, unusual circumstances gave birth to precedent. William Weems was convicted of falsifying a public document and was sentenced to 15 years of hard labor. His punishment included shackling at the ankle and wrist and permanent loss of a multitude of civil rights, including parental authority, property ownership, and permanent surveillance for life (*Weems*, 1910, p. 364).

The majority opinion began with unusual candor by admitting that there was no precedent, and little commentary, on the meaning of the words cruel and unusual from which to fashion an interpretation of the Eighth Amendment. Nevertheless, the Court went on to say that justice required that punishment for crime be graduated and proportioned to the offense (*Weems,* 1910, p. 367). Reasoning that the Constitution must be read in light of contemporary social needs, the Court took the course of a broad interpretation of the Eighth Amendment. Thus, the doctrine of proportionality was born. The test used to reverse the conviction was an objective comparison of punishments of similar crimes in other jurisdictions and a comparison with punishments for more serious crimes within the same jurisdiction (*Weems,* 1910, p. 380).

The decision can be read as the first pronouncement by the Supreme Court on the basic conflict between legislative enactment of punishment measures and judicial interpretation of their constitutionality. The power of the legislature to define crime and punishment is vast, but not absolute; therefore, constitutional limits exist. The Court, in sweeping language, recognized the evolutionary potential for humaneness in a broad application of the cruel and unusual punishments clause. *Weems* was a landmark holding in Eighth Amendment law; most scholars commenting on the decision were surprised by the ruling (Fredman, 1910). There had been little prior indication that the Court was inclined to expand the cruel and unusual punishments clause into the area of sentencing—using the proportionality rationale.

The proportionality doctrine enunciated in *Weems* must be viewed as the most important limitation on present three-strikes legislation. This Eighth Amendment protection, however, had to wait more than 50 years to be held applicable to state criminal proceedings. This came about in *Robinson v. California* (1962), where the defendant was given a 90-day sentence by the trial court for narcotics addiction. The Supreme Court nullified the sentence, saying that any imprisonment for merely being addicted, as opposed to being found in personal possession or selling a specific controlled narcotic, was disproportionate. The importance of *Robinson* is twofold: First, it placed limitations on the states to criminalize a person's status (e.g., addic-

tion to drugs or vagrancy, having no money); second, for purposes of this chapter, it made proportionality review of criminal sentences applicable to the states through the due process clause of the Fourteenth Amendment. Prior to this, an Eighth Amendment analysis was used only for federal crimes.

Graham v. West Virginia and Early Habitual Offender Statutes

The Supreme Court's first review of habitual offender laws came in *Graham v. West Virginia* (1912). In that case, the Court traced their beginnings to English statutes that "inflicted severer punishment upon old offenders" (*Graham* 1912, p. 625). The record does not disclose how "old" John H. Graham was. It does indicate he had previously been convicted of grand larceny and burglary before his final grand larceny conviction resulted in a life sentence under a forerunner three-strikes provision enacted in Virginia in 1796 and later codified when West Virginia was partitioned and entered statehood in 1863.

In the 19th century, a majority of states had statutes that enhanced punishment for previous felons (*Graham,* 1912, p. 622). The Court in *Graham* first disposed of the former jeopardy argument of twice being punished for the same crime (using the former convictions) before indicating that habitual offender laws did not constitute cruel and unusual punishment.

Early repeat offender statutes were cumbersome, requiring the warden of the receiving penitentiary to investigate a person's criminal history and return him for a second indictment and jury trial on his previous convictions. The sole issue at this trial was whether the "convict is the same person mentioned in several records."[3] With the Baumes Act (1926)[4] passed by New York and adopted by other states, the procedure was simplified into one proceeding with the defendant's prior record determined at his initial trial and his sentence enhanced accordingly.

California enacted a forerunner three-strikes provision in 1927.[5] Its purpose was more remedial than deterrent. The theory that a small number of offenders committed a majority of crimes was yet to be known and was not the rationale for the statute. Eleven other states in that era had similar statutes in effect that were designed to sentence nonviolent third offenders to life imprisonment. Criminal punishment at that time did not reflect the public frustration that currently drives three-strikes legislation, hence these early statutes were seldom used to incapacitate a certain category of offenders. California repealed its early version in 1935. By 1980, when the Supreme Court first fully examined the conflict between three-strikes laws and cruel and unusual punishment, only West Virginia, Washington, and Texas still had nonviolent three-strikes statutes in their penal codes (*Rummel* 1980, p. 296, n. 13).

The Collision: Proportionality and Three Strikes

Rummel v. Estelle (1980) was the first of four Supreme Court cases between 1980 and 1991 that yield seemingly inconsistent holdings on proportionality review. These decisions exemplify the struggle within the Court to clarify the parameters of punishment under three-strikes provisions and cruel and unusual punishment. This collision between criminal and constitutional law is discussed in the cases that follow.

Rummel v. Estelle: The Turning Point

William Rummel was convicted in Texas in 1964 of credit card fraud to obtain $80.00 worth of goods; was convicted in 1969 of passing a forged check for $28.36; and, in 1973, was convicted of obtaining money ($120.75) by false pretenses. All three nonviolent offenses were classified as felonies under Texas law. Rummel was prosecuted for his third "strike" offense under the Texas equivalent three-strikes provision. Within the statute, a third-strike conviction would result in a mandatory life imprisonment. Pursuant to the statute, the trial judge imposed the obligatory life sentence (*Rummel* 1980, pp. 264–266).

Thereafter, an intense constitutional debate ensued within the appellate courts on the proportionality of Rummel's sentence. The Texas Court of Criminal Appeals affirmed his conviction in *Rummel v. State* (1974). A divided panel of the Fifth Circuit reversed his conviction as disproportionate in *Rummel v. Estelle* (1978). On rehearing, the circuit court, sitting en banc, rejected the panel's ruling and affirmed the conviction in *Rummel v. Estelle* (1978). On appeal, the Supreme Court, Justice Rehnquist writing for a 5–4 majority, held that the state of Texas could constitutionally impose a sentence of life imprisonment for three sequential nonviolent felonies.

The Court justified the *Rummel* (1980) result by distancing it from the precedent of proportionality in *Weems* (1910), stressing that recent applications had been limited to death penalty cases such as *Coker v. Georgia* (1977) because of their finality. A "bright line" was thereby drawn between death and imprisonment. The majority reasoned that to do otherwise would invite imprecision in future cases in attempting to draw a clear line on different lengths of imprisonment (*Rummel* 1980, p. 275). *Weems* was characterized as limited by its particular facts (shackling at the wrist and ankles); the Court emphasized the highly subjective character of legal analysis used in establishing constitutional limits on amounts of punishment. The Court concluded that punishment is traditionally a state instead of a federal concern and is purely a matter of legislative judgment (*Rummel* 1980, p. 282).

In a dissent, premised on *Weems* and the humanitarian intent of the framers of the Constitution Justice Powell opined that proportionality analysis is an inherent aspect of the cruel and unusual punishments clause.

He felt a constitutional obligation to measure "the relationship between the nature and number of offenses committed and the severity of the punishment inflicted upon the offender" (*Rummel* 1980, p. 288). Justice Powell laid out three objective criteria, earlier announced in *Weems*, for reviewing proportionality challenges to the length of criminal sentences: (a) the nature of the offense, (b) comparison with sentences imposed in other jurisdictions for commission of the same crime, and (c) comparison with sentences imposed in the same jurisdiction of commission of other crimes (*Rummel* 1980, p. 295).

Applying these criteria, the dissent concluded that Rummel's sentence violated the Constitution. First, the strike offense of false pretenses was found to be nonviolent. Next, the dissent established that Texas punished repeat offenders dramatically harsher than other jurisdictions. Finally, within the Texas statutory equivalent three-strikes scheme, Rummel's sentence for three nonviolent felonies was harsher than for those first and second offenders who committed more serious crimes, such as murder or rape (*Rummel*, 1980, pp. 295–303). The majority conceded in a footnote that one could imagine extreme examples when the doctrine of proportionality would be an issue (*Rummel* 1980, p. 274, n. 11).

The *Rummel* decision is best understood in the context of Justice Rehnquist's statement that defendant Rummel had been well informed of the consequences of repeated criminal conduct (two prior prison sentences) and given every opportunity to reform. Therefore, the early three-strikes statute was nothing more than a "societal decision that when such a person commits yet another felony, he should be subjected to the admittedly serious penalty of incarceration for life, subject only to the state's judgment as to whether to grant him parole" (*Rummel* 1980, p. 278). To the dissenters, however, evolving standards of decency necessitated the Court's exercise of its historic role as the final interpreter of the cruel and unusual punishments clause and felt that under the circumstances of this case, the Court ought to have rejected the punishment as unconstitutional.

The battle to delineate the precise contours of proportionality was fought again 2 years later in *Hutto v. Davis* (1982). The decision exemplifies the intensity of the continuing debate over the three-strikes legislation.

Hutto v. Davis: Anarchy in the Fourth Circuit

In *Hutto v. Davis* (1982), the Supreme Court upheld the power of the states to punish repeat offenders with severe sentences, including first offenders. Although not a three-strikes decision, *Davis* (1982) is instructive because it set the stage for a reversal of *Rummel* (1980) a year later in *Solem v. Helm* (1983).

Roger Davis's first offense in 1976 resulted in conviction on two counts of both possessing with intent and distributing 9 ounces of marijuana. A Virginia jury set his sentences at 20 years on each charge to run consecutively, or a 40-year prison term. *Davis's* procedural history resulted in the Fourth Circuit reversing his conviction on proportionality grounds in 1979 (*Davis v. Davis*, 1979). Two weeks after issuing its mandate in *Rummel* (1980), the Supreme Court ordered *Davis* (1979) vacated and remanded for further consideration in light of *Rummel*.

On remand, the Fourth Circuit reaffirmed its earlier reversal, reasoning that Davis's sentence fell within that narrow group of "rare" cases the majority in *Rummel* had conceded in a footnote that the doctrine of proportionality might apply (*Davis v. Davis*, 1981). In the protocol of the Supreme Court's supervisory powers over the circuit courts, this rejection of *Rummel* was almost unprecedented, prompting the Court to again grant review and state that "unless we want anarchy to prevail within the federal judiciary, a precedent of this Court must be followed by the lower federal courts no matter how misguided the judges of those courts may think it to be" (*Hutto v. Davis*, 1982, p. 375).

In affirming Davis's punishment, Justice Burger defended the bright line drawn in *Rummel* between death penalty cases and varying lengths of imprisonment. *Davis's* major premise was that an Eighth Amendment review should not be subjective; the Court also concluded that the 40-year sentence was beyond the constitutional range of the federal courts (*Davis*, 1982, p. 373). Once again, the Court stressed that federal courts should be reluctant to review legislatively mandated terms of imprisonment, be it within a habitual offender scheme or otherwise. This reluctance is based on the Tenth Amendment, which reserves to each state the power to determine varying lengths of sentences for the same criminal violation. (Using this approach, grand larceny may carry a 10-year maximum for a first offense in one state and 2 years in another.)

Justice Powell concurred and followed the precedent of *Rummel* perhaps in an effort to quell the uprising in the Fourth Circuit. He pointed out, however, that neither the majority in *Rummel* nor the majority in *Davis* had laid the doctrine of proportionality to rest (*Davis*, 1982, p. 377). In retrospect, Justice Powell's concurrence was the fulcrum for his opinion 1 year later in *Solem v. Helm* (1983), which would reverse an almost identical three-strikes provision in South Dakota.

Three justices dissented in *Davis*, distinguishing *Rummel* as a three-strikes case that was not applicable to the first offense before the Court. The dissent also refused to go along with the Court's criticism of the mischief of the Fourth Circuit Court of Appeals. Moreover, the dissent argued that this was one of those exceedingly rare cases where the disparity of Davis's punishment, in comparison to other sentences in Virginia for marijuana offenders, required reversal on proportionality grounds. To support this, the dissent alluded to an unusual letter from Davis's trial prosecutor, included in the record, which characterized the sentence as "grossly unjust" (*Davis*, 1982, p. 385).

The *Davis* decision resulted in uncertainty in the Eighth Amendment analysis of the length of legislative sentences for both repeat and first offenders. With the majority of the Court demanding objective criteria (while rejecting all proffered criteria as too subjective), the two leading opinions in *Rummel* and *Davis* resulted in legal confusion within various circles regarding the applicability and scope of proportionality review ("The Eighth Amendment," 1982). State courts were equally confused; some chose to disregard Supreme Court interpretation and proceeded instead to decide similar cases under their parallel state constitution's cruel and unusual punishments clause.[6]

Solem v. Helm: Three-Factor Proportionality for Three Strikes

Just three terms after *Rummel* the Supreme Court, by a 5–4 majority in *Solem v. Helm* (1983), demonstrated that no constitutional precedent is safe from revision. In a dramatic departure, the Court reversed a three-strikes life imprisonment sentence.

Jerry Helm had spent much of his life in the penitentiary and had six previous nonviolent felony convictions. In 1979, he pleaded guilty to writing a bad check for $100. Instead of asking the trial court to sentence Helm under the South Dakota general criminal statute, which carried 5 years for the offense charged, the prosecutor proceeded under an equivalent three-strikes provision. This resulted in a life sentence (*Helm*, 1983, p. 280).

The trial court record reveals that the sentencing judge indicated to Helm that it would be up to him and the parole board when he would be released. Unknown to the judge, a buried provision in the statute provided that Helm was not eligible for parole.[7] This proved crucial to the reversal of the sentence by the Eighth Circuit in *Helm v. Solem* (1982) and provided the rationale for the majority decision in the Supreme Court.

Justice Powell, who dissented in *Rummel* (1980), began the majority opinion by tracing the origin of the cruel and unusual punishments clause and proportionality back to English common law and *Weems* (1910). The opinion stressed the need for deference to both the legislature and the sentencing courts. Such deference meant that successful proportionality challenges would be rare, but no sentence was beyond constitutional scrutiny. As he did in dissent in *Rummel* Justice Powell opined that when sentences are reviewed under the Eighth Amendment, courts should be guided by three objective factors or the "Helm test": (a) a comparison of the gravity of the offense and the harshness of the penalty, (b) a comparison with sentences imposed for other crimes in the same jurisdiction, and (c) a comparison with sentences imposed for the same crime in other jurisdictions (*Helm* 1983, pp. 291–292). Although these factors are relative, they are not purely subjective. Judges are assumed competent to make broad comparisons of crime, relative harm, and culpability; moreover, legal line-drawing has always been a standard technique of the judicial art.

Applying the *Helm* test to the facts, the majority concluded that the three-strikes sentence was cruel and unusual. The strike crime of writing a $100 check was nonviolent and involved a small amount. The statute carried heavy penalties for two prior convictions that the court also viewed as nonviolent, minor offenses. Life imprisonment without possibility of parole was the most severe punishment available in South Dakota, hence the first factor suggested an imbalance between crime and punishment. Second, the court reviewed punishment for other crimes in the state and found that only a few much more serious crimes were mandatorily punished by life imprisonment without parole. Thus, the Court concluded that Helm's life sentence was more severe than sentences that South Dakota imposed for far more serious crimes. Finally, the majority considered the sentence in the national context and concluded that Helm would have been punished less severely for

his third offense in every other state (*Helm*, 1983, pp. 298–300).

Because *Rummel* (1980) and *Helm* (1983) were essentially the same case (involving three-strikes life imprisonment punishment for nonviolent offenders), Justice Powell distinguished the facts by emphasizing the difference between life imprisonment with and life imprisonment without parole. Parole is a regular part of the rehabilitative process, is governed by legal standards, and assuming good behavior, is the normal expectation of a defendant like Rummel. On the other hand, Helm's only possibility of release was executive clemency, which lacked articulable standards (*Helm*, 1983, p. 303).

The dissenters were outraged that the majority would apply the three-factor test that *Rummel* had categorically rejected as imprecise while rejecting the bright-line rule of *Rummel* (proportionality review only for death sentences). Chief Justice Burger's dissent further high-lighted the intra-Court dissonance that mandatory minimum sentencing evokes and that would reoccur in *Harmelin v. Michigan* (1991). In conclusion, the dissent reiterated its concern that proportionality review of length of sentences would open the floodgates to lower courts making subjective determinations of excessive sentences.

This prediction proved to be false, however, in the 8 years that followed. Lower courts had little difficulty in applying Eighth Amendment proportionality to cases involving legislative determinations. During this period, only four state cases were reversed on the basis of the *Helm* three-factor test and none in the federal courts. These cases were *Clowers v. State* (1988), in which there was a reduction of a 15-year sentence without parole for a forged check; *Ashley v. State* (1989), in which there was a reduction of sentence for a defendant who burgled a home of $4.00 to pay for food eaten in a store; *Gilham v. State* (1988), in which the court struck down a felony conviction for using a vehicle in a criminal endeavor when the defendant had engaged in the lesser crime of prostitution;

and *Naovarath v. State* (1989), in which the court set aside a life sentence without parole for an adolescent who killed an individual who repeatedly molested him.

The Eighth Amendment balance between crime and punishment in *Helm* would again change 8 years later when a divided Supreme Court issued a decision that would result in another reversal of precedent and a narrowing of the constitutional principle of proportionality review.

Harmelin v. Michigan: Proportionality 'Strikes Out'

The war on drugs served as the catalyst for a third 5–4 Supreme Court decision on the constitutionality of three-strikes measures and similar mandatory minimum sentencing schemes. In *Harmelin v. Michigan* (1991), the Court again reversed itself on when proportionality review can be applied and returned full circle to principles announced a decade earlier in *Rummel*. The disagreement over the contours of the Eighth Amendment, as applied to legislative punishment, is evidenced by the five separate opinions the decision generated.

Ronald Harmelin was stopped for a routine traffic violation. A search of his vehicle revealed 672 grams of cocaine. Michigan's statute required that Harmelin be sentenced to life imprisonment (for possession of more than 650 grams) with no possibility of parole even though he had no prior felony record. Review was granted by the Supreme Court to consider the issue of whether a mandatory life sentence constitutes cruel and unusual punishment.

Justice Scalia rejected the principle that the Eighth Amendment requires a proportionality review for non-death penalty cases and called for the overruling of *Helm* (1983). Only Chief Justice Rehnquist, however, shared this view. The other three members of the plurality, led by Justice Kennedy, discerned a narrow proportionality doctrine in the Eighth Amendment, even though they

agreed with Justice Scalia that there was nothing unconstitutional about Harmelin's sentence (*Harmelin*, 1991, p. 1008). The four dissenting justices argued, in three separate opinions, that mandatory sentences or three-strikes provisions like *Helm* called for more searching analysis.[8]

The decision's balance tilted in the direction of Justice Kennedy's concurrence. It began with a recognition of *Helm's* three-factor test and a narrow proportionality doctrine. To provide guidance in limiting appellate review of sentences, the concurring opinion rejected Harmelin's contention that full comparative analysis under *Helm's* three factors was required. Justice Kennedy stated that under the first prong—severity of the crime and harshness of penalty—Harmelin's sentence was proportionate. With that threshold determination, an analysis of the second and third prongs of *Helm* became unnecessary. This conclusion was rested on the three-part severity of Harmelin's drug offense: (a) A drug user may commit crime because of drug-induced changes in cognitive ability, (b) a drug user may commit crime to buy drugs, and (c) a violent crime may occur as part of the drug culture (*Harmelin*, 1991, p. 1002).

To support its position, the plurality cited results from *Drug Use Forecasting* (National Institute of Justice, 1990), in which a vast majority of arrestees had tested positive for illegal drugs. Therefore, Justice Kennedy reasoned that the Michigan legislature could conclude that because of the link between drugs, violence, and crime, the possession of large amounts of cocaine warranted the deterrence and retribution of a life sentence.

The decision in *Harmelin* (1991) represents a subtle shift in the balance between severity of crime and harshness of punishment from one of disproportionality to that of gross disproportionality. In conceding the harmful effects of drug trafficking on the nation, the Court failed to take into account defendant Harmelin's low position in the drug hierarchy or his first-offense status. In *Rummel* (1980), *Davis* (1982), and *Helm* (1983), the Court examined the nature of the crimes and the history of the individual defendants. In *Harmelin* (1991) the focus was on the abhorrent nature of the drug problem and its current status as "one of the greatest problems affecting the health and welfare of our population" (p. 1002).

The Implications of *Harmelin*: Current Applications of Proportionality to Three-Strikes Legislation

Federal Courts

The four cases analyzed above constitute a roller-coaster ride in Supreme Court proportionality review. Seldom has a constitutional amendment generated such closely split decisions as the cruel and unusual punishments clause has in defining the legislative parameters of three-strikes laws and mandatory sentences. Using the antidrug justification in *Harmelin*, the Court stripped the Eighth Amendment of much of its potential to prohibit the lifelong imprisonment of individuals for one offense and, correspondingly, of three-strikes offenders (see, generally, Vandy, 1993).

Under the last-decided-best-decided theory of legal precedent, only the extremely rare case wherein the punishment is grossly disproportionate to the crime will the threshold of *Harmelin* be crossed. Although the Court has not completely retreated to the bright-line rule of applying the Eighth Amendment only to death penalty cases, three-strikes measures similar to the California statute appear well poised to withstand constitutional challenges. Federal courts have cited *Harmelin* as the dispositive case in Eighth Amendment challenges, and three recent circuit court opinions appear to have settled the issue at the federal level at least for now.[9]

California's Three-Strikes Statute and Proportionality

The preceding discussion has highlighted the Supreme Court's view of proportionality under the Eighth Amendment of the U.S. Constitution. The California three-strikes statute has prompted other jurisdictions to implement similar legislation that will likely result in legal challenges.

As proportionality challenges develop, each state must chose between the holding of *Harmelin* under federal law or interpret its three-strikes measure under its own state constitution's cruel and unusual punishments clause. In *Romero* (1995), mentioned earlier, the California Court of Appeals looked to the California Constitution in holding the statute constitutional (*Romero*, 1995, p. 378). In a departure from *Harmelin*, the court applied the three-factor *Helm* test while mandating defendant Romero's sentence of 25 years to life for his third conviction.

In another departure, the Michigan Supreme Court, a year after *Harmelin*, reconsidered its 650-gram "lifer" law and held in *People v. Bullock* (1992) that such sentences for simple possession for first offenders were disproportionate to the crime under the Michigan state constitutional provision against cruel and unusual punishment. The decision used the three-objective criteria of *Helm* to examine the individual circumstances of defendant Bullock and concluded that it would be unfair to impute full responsibility of the defendant for any unintended consequences that might be later committed by others in connection with the seized cocaine (*Bullock*, 1992, p. 876). The decision applied only to those convicted of simple possession, which meant Ronald Harmelin's earlier sentence was reduced to life, with eligibility for parole in 10 years.

Summary of Current Varying Interpretations of the Proportionality Review

In general, federal courts are currently in accord with the "grossly disproportionate" approach announced in *Harmelin* (1991). In contrast, at the state level, *Romero* (1995) retains the objective comparison criteria of *Helm* (1983) in applying a somewhat cursory proportionality review. Finally, *Bullock* (1992) totally rejects *Harmelin* by engaging in extended proportionality review using the three factors of *Helm*, along with the individual circumstances of the defendant, to find Michigan's 650-gram life statute cruel and unusual. *Bullock* represents that rare situation where in-depth analysis favors the defendant (*Helm*, 1983, p. 285).

The difference in the above approaches is central to determining the balance between crime and punishment and the constitutionality of three-strikes laws. Proportionality of the length of sentence is determined by each court's application of the three-step sequence of objective criteria of *Helm* to Eighth Amendment review. As with most balancing analyses, the difficulty remains in identifying important variables, assigning them a weight, and deciding their cumulative effect (*Helm*, 1983, pp. 292–295).

Although *Harmelin* appears to severely limit the three criteria in *Helm*, chances are that most initial state court decisions will follow the extended analysis of *Helm* in reviewing their respective three-strikes legislation. This is evident in the *Romero* and *Bullock* state court decisions. The fact that *Harmelin* was divided on a 5–4 plurality lessens its precedential value. A comparison between the gravity of the offense and the harshness of the penalty is a matter of judicial determination. The other two factors in *Helm*—comparison of sentences for other crimes in the same jurisdiction and comparison with sentences for the same crime in other jurisdictions—induce a deference to preferences expressed by the state legislature. It is within this framework that three-strikes statutes will likely be decided. Rare, then, will be a case that will favor the defendant. Even in that case, a successful proportionality challenge does not set the defendant free; instead, it merely obliges the state to resentence within broad constitutional limits.

Perspective: Mandatory Sentencing and the Emerging Constitutional Issue of Separation of Powers

It is evident from court decisions that currently the Eighth Amendment is a limited source for invalidating three-strikes statutes.

Solem v. Helm (1983) stands as the only Supreme Court decision declaring a criminal sentence disproportionate. The opinion, however, was based on the nonviolent nature of Helm's three offenses coupled with a no-parole provision within the early South Dakota three-strikes statute.[10]

The new California law,[11] learning well the lesson of *Helm*, requires that prior strike crimes be "violent" or "serious"[12] (the current offense can be any felony). The statute also provides for parole release, but increases the length of imprisonment for offenders with one prior by reducing the "good time" credits prisoners can earn from one half to only one fifth of the total sentence and mandating a minimum of 25 years for those with two or more prior convictions.

At first glance, the California law appears to comport with the essentials of *Helm*. A closer examination, however, reveals an important distinction. The South Dakota trial judge who sentenced defendant Helm had the option to dismiss from the record Helm's previous nonviolent crimes, thereby avoiding the imposition of a life sentence without parole if the court was persuaded that such punishment was not proportionate to the offense of writing a $100 bad check. Under the California three-strikes scheme, this individualized, proportionate review does not exist. Only the prosecution is vested with the power to dismiss a prior strike conviction(s).[13] This legislative change in the balance of power in the sentencing process is emerging as a second constitutional challenge to three-strikes legislation.

In the context of criminal punishments, our system of checks and balances separates the power to punish the offender within three constitutional functions. The legislature has inherent power to define and provide punishment for crime, the executive has the power to prosecute criminal conduct, and the judiciary has the duty to provide a remedy for legislative and executive excesses (*People v. Tenono*, 1970).

Other three-strikes laws in various states include statutory provisions, similar to those in the California law, that abrogate the long-standing historical power of judges to discretionarily impose criminal punishments. Not unexpectedly, Proposition 184 represents the public's displeasure with the judicial system's "revolving door" and "soft on crime" judges, who use loopholes to reduce punishment (*Romero*, 1995, p. 377).

The emerging separation-of-powers constitutional challenge is exemplified in *Romero* (1995), the first appellate decision on California's three-strikes statute. Jesus Romero had five previous felony convictions when he was arrested for possession of one tenth of a gram of cocaine. Two of the prior convictions were for residential burglary, qualifying Romero with two strikes ("life priors") and a mandatory sentence of 25 years to life imprisonment. The trial judge dismissed from the record Romero's two strikes and imposed a sentence of 6 years, reasoning that the mandatory sentence constituted cruel and unusual punishment under the California Constitution. The trial court further opined that the three-strikes provision that allowed only the executive (prosecutor) to dismiss prior convictions violated separation of powers (*Romero*, 1995, p. 371).

On review, the California Court of Appeals rejected the trial court's determinations and returned the case with instructions to sentence Romero in accordance with three strikes (25 years to life imprisonment). Addressing the issue of separation of powers, the court found the narrowing of judicial discretion to dismiss strike convictions as consistent with the public's pronouncement in Proposition 184 that the judiciary keep its "hands off three strikes" and the certainty of the statute's punishment for repeat offenders (*Romero*, 1995, p. 377).

The decision was also premised on a narrowing of prosecutorial discretion contained within the law. Whereas three strikes grants the prosecutor sole authority to dismiss strike convictions "in the interest of justice," other provisions[14] require the executive to plead and prove all prior convictions available on a defendant, thus eliminating a valu-

able tool from a prosecutor's plea bargaining arsenal. The appellate court found a balance in the statute because the legislature had placed limitations on the use of discretion on both the judicial and executive branches of government (*Romero*, 1995, p. 373). As this chapter goes to press, *Romero* is pending before the California Supreme Court.

The U.S. Supreme Court has yet to determine the constitutionality of state statutes that curtail the traditional authority of judges in the sentencing process. Interestingly, the Court has previously affirmed prosecutorial discretion on the use of prior convictions in the plea bargaining process. In *Bordenhircher v. Hayes* (1978), the defendant was offered a 5-year sentence by the prosecutor in exchange for a plea of guilty. Hayes did not plead guilty and was charged with being a habitual offender under Kentucky law. He was convicted and sentenced to life imprisonment. The Supreme Court upheld Hayes's conviction and concluded, in a 5–4 decision, that the prosecutor's alleged vindictiveness was within the sound discretion of prosecutorial authority (*Hayes*, 1978, p. 358).

Hayes would appear to be inconsistent with three-strikes limitations on a prosecutor's discretion to use prior strike convictions in the plea bargaining process. The narrowing of both judicial and executive authorities in three strikes, therefore, may result in legal challenges from both branches of government as state legislatures across the nation expand their power to punish offenders who "strike out" for the third time.

Conclusion

Over the years, the Supreme Court has struggled with the concept of cruel and unusual punishment as applied to sentencing. The standard is proportionality. The Court has shown deference to punishment choices made by state legislatures, sometimes bowing to political realities when resolving constitutional dilemmas. In *Rummel* (1980), the majority sought to develop havens behind which to retreat. In *Davis* (1982), the majority had difficulty implementing its policy decision. In *Helm* (1983), a new majority of those present at *Rummel* recognized the inability of some state criminal justice systems to guard constitutional rights under the Eighth Amendment. In reaffirming principles of proportionality in sentencing, the *Helm* majority reasserted its role as final arbiter of the Constitution. The emergence of the drug wars brought with it the *Harmelin* (1991) plurality and ushered in three-strikes legislation and a return to legislative deference.

These four Court decisions first clarified and then confused proportionality review. Even if the states retain the objective criteria of the three-factor test of *Helm* after *Harmelin*, it is unlikely that there will be many three-strikes reversals. With mandatory sentencing severely hampering judicial discretion, the appellate courts might assert their authority and reject, under the doctrine of separation of powers, legislative provisions within three-strikes statutes that transfer sentencing discretion to the executive branch. Because the contest is being played in their ballpark and because they make the crucial calls, courts may ultimately find a way to limit three-strikes punishments and the courts' assumption that prior convictions contain all the information needed for justice to be served. Should that happen, the judiciary will then have redefined its role in society's continuing search for a system of justice where the punishment truly fits the crime.

Study Questions

1. What are the origins of the term "cruel and unusual punishment" as it is used in the Eighth Amendment?

2. What are some of the historical roots of "three strikes" legislation (that is, for what reasons may this legal strategy have been formulated)?

3. What is meant by the term "proportionality" regarding challenges to three strikes legislation?

4. How are issues of "mandatory sentencing" and "separation of powers" linked in this chapter?

Notes

1. Seventeen other states have implemented similar three-strikes measures in which the third strike results in a calculated low end (usually 25 years) to life imprisonment, with differing parole restrictions. Five other states are debating similar measures. See also *People v. Romero*, 37 Cal. Rptr.2d 364, 381 (1995) for a list of states with three-strikes laws.

2. *Annals of the Congress of the United States* (J. Bales, Ed., Vol. 1), 754 (1789).

3. Code of West Virginia, chap. 165, sec. 4 (1863).

4. New York Penal Laws, para. 1941 et seq. (1926).

5. California Statutes, chap. 634, para. 1, p. 1066 (1927).

6. See, for example, *State v. MuLally*, 127 Ariz. 92, 618 P.2d 586 (1980); *State v. Fain*, 94 Wash. 2d. 387, 517 P.2d 720 (1980).

7. South Dakota Codified Laws, para. 24–15–4 (1979). See also Aked (1984).

8. Justice White dissented, joined by Justices Blackmun and Stevens, Justice Marshall filed a separate dissenting opinion, Justice Stevens also filed a dissenting opinion in which Justice Blackmun also joined.

9. See *United States v. Kramer*, 955 F.2d 479 (7th Cir. 1992); *United States v. Lowden*, 955 F.2d 128 (1st Cir. 1992); *United States v. Hopper*, 941 F.2d 419 (6th Cir. 1991). But compare in *Austin v. United States*, 113 S. Ct. 2801 (1993), the Court reversed a civil forfeiture as disproportionate under the excessive fines clause of the Eighth Amendment.

10. South Dakota Comp. Laws Ann., para. 22–6–1 (1969).

11. California Penal Code, sec. 667(b)-(i).

12. California Penal Code, sec. 667(d).

13. California Penal Code, sec. 667(f)(2).

14. California Penal Code, sec. 667(f)(1) and (g)(1).

Cases

Ashley v. State, 538 So.2d 762 (Miss. 1989).

Bordenkircher v. Hayes, 434 U.S. 357 (1978).

Clowers v. State, 522 So.2d 762 (Miss. 1988).

Coker v. Georgia, 433 U.S. 584 (1977).

Davis v. Davis, 601 F.2d 153 (4th Cir. 1979) (en banc).

Davis v. Davis, 646 F.2d 123 (4th Cir. 1981).

Gilham v. State, 549 N.E.2d 555 (Oh. 1988).

Graham v. West Virginia, 224 U.S. 616 (1912).

Harmelin v. Michigan, 501 U.S. 957 (1991).

Helm v. Solem, 684 F.2d 582 (8th Cir. 1982).

Hutto v. Davis, 454 U.S. 370 (1982).

Naovarath v. State, 779 P.2d 944 (Nev. 1989).

People v. Bullock, 485 N.W.2d 866 (Mich. 1992).

People v. Romero, 37 Cal. Rptr.2d 364 (1995).

People v. Tenono, 473 P.2d 933 (Cal. 1970).

Robinson v. California, 370 U.S. 660 (1962).

Rummel v. Estelle, 568 F.2d 1193 (5th Cir. 1978).

Rummel v. Estelle, 587 F.2d 651 (5th Cir. 1978) (en banc).

Rummel v. Estelle, 445 U.S. 263 (1980).

Rummel v. State, 509 S.W.2d 630 (Tex. Crim. App. 1974).

Solem v. Helm, 463 U.S. 277 (1983).

Weems v. United States, 217 U.S. 349 (1910).

References

Aked, J. (1984). Solem. v. Helm: The Supreme Court extends the proportionality requirement to sentences of imprisonment. *Wisconsin Law Review*, pp. 1401–1430.

The effectiveness of the Eighth Amendment: An appraisal of cruel and unusual punishment [Note]. (1961). *New York University Law Review*, 36, 846.

The Eighth Amendment: Judicial self-restraint and legislative power [Note]. (1982). *Marquette Law Review*, D65, 434–443.

Fredman. (1910). Comment on recent judicial decisions—Cruel and unusual punishment. *Journal of Criminal Law*, 1, 612.

National Institute of Justice. (1990, June). Drug use forecasting annual report (Vol. 9). Washington, DC: Author.

Recent legislation: California enacts enhancement for prior felony convictions [Note]. (1994). *Harvard Law Review*, 107, 2123.

Vandy, K. (1993). Mandatory life sentences with no possibility of parole for first time drug possessors is not cruel and unusual punishment, *Harmelin v. Michigan*, 501 U.S. 957 (1991) [Note]. *Rutgers Law Review*, 23, 883. ✦

Part V

Institutional Programming and Treatment

"With few and isolated exceptions, the rehabilitative efforts that have been reported so far have not had an appreciable effect on recidivism."

—Robert Martinson

After examining more than two decades of correctional research, Martinson's now famous conclusion had a tremendous impact on the field of corrections. Whatever the limitations of the Martinson study, and there were many, the conclusion drawn by many was that treatment or rehabilitation is not effective. Thus, what became known as the "nothing works" doctrine led to renewed efforts to demonstrate the effectiveness of correctional programs. The effectiveness of correctional programs has been debated and studied for many years. Evaluating their effectiveness is challenging even under the best of circumstances. For example, political, ethical, and programmatic reasons may not permit the researcher to develop adequate control groups or measures. Furthermore, tracking offenders after they have been released from prison is time consuming and difficult. Despite these constraints, many studies have been conducted on the effectiveness of correctional programming and treatment.

There are three ways that research is reviewed: the traditional literature review, the ballot counting approach that Martinson used, and meta-analysis. The articles in this section illustrate all three approaches. During the past decade, however, it has been meta-analysis that has taken center stage as the best tool for determining effectiveness. Meta-analysis has greatly facilitated our ability to examine the large body of research that exists on correctional effectiveness; this approach uses a quantitative synthesis of research findings in a body of literature. Meta-analysis computes the "effect sizes" between the treatment and outcome. The effect size can be negative (treatment increases recidivism), zero, or positive (treatment reduces recidivism).

Meta-analysis also has its limitations. First, like the literature review and ballot counting approaches, meta-analysis is affected by "what goes into it." In other words, what studies are included in the analysis? Second, how factors are coded can also be an important issue. There are major advantages, however, to this approach. For instance, it is possible to control for factors that might influence the size of a treatment effect (e.g., size of sample, length of treatment, quality of research design). In addition, results can be quantified, replicated, and tested by other researchers. Meta-analysis also helps build knowledge about a subject, such as correctional treatment, in a precise and parsimonious way.

The articles in Part V reflect how far we have come in learning about the effectiveness of correctional programs. In some ways they also illustrate the debate over rehabilitation, some of which centers around institutional programming. We know that programs are an important part of a correctional institution. What we want is for the most effective programs to be operated and supported. ✦

21
What Works?— Questions and Answers About Prison Reform

Robert Martinson

The tremendous increase of crime during the 1960s heralded a shift in the way Americans would come to view criminals in the next decade, leading to a law-and-order movement in the early 1970s. The Martinson Report, a massive study undertaken at that time to determine the most effective means of rehabilitating prisoners, concluded that, "with few and isolated exceptions, the rehabilitative efforts that have been reported so far have had no appreciable effect on recidivism." These words were interpreted to mean that "nothing works" as far as rehabilitating prisoners was concerned and that a new direction needed to be found. In 1974, a summary of the study's findings was presented by Robert Martinson in The Public Interest. Other research studies supported Martinson's conclusion and, by the end of the decade, a paradigm shift had occurred in corrections from rehabilitation to deterrence and just deserts. The influence of Martinson's article, the first published account of the above survey, cannot be underestimated—it was "the straw that broke the camel's back." Support for the rehabilitative ideal and the medical model of corrections decreased substantially after its publication.

Excerpts from "What Works?—Questions and Answers About Prison Reform" by Robert Martinson, *The Public Interest* 35:22–54. Copyright © 1974 by National Affairs, Inc. Reprinted by permission.

In the past several years, American prisons have gone through one of their recurrent periods of strikes, riots, and other disturbances. Simultaneously, and in consequence, the articulate public has entered another one of its sporadic fits of attentiveness to the condition of our prisons and to the perennial questions they pose about the nature of crime and the uses of punishment. The result has been a widespread call for "prison reform," i.e., for "reformed" prisons which will produce "reformed" convicts. Such calls are a familiar feature of American prison history. American prisons, perhaps more than those of any other country, have stood or fallen in public esteem according to their ability to fulfill their promise of rehabilitation.

One of the problems in the constant debate over "prison reform" is that we have been able to draw very little on any systematic empirical knowledge about the success or failure that we have met when we *have* tried to rehabilitate offenders, with various treatments and in various institutional and non-institutional settings. The field of penology has produced a voluminous research literature on this subject, but until recently there has been no comprehensive review of this literature and no attempt to bring its findings to bear, in a useful way, on the general question of "What works?" My purpose in this [chapter] is to sketch an answer to that question.

The Travails of a Study

In 1966, the New York State Governor's Special Committee on Criminal Offenders recognized their need for such an answer. The Committee was organized on the premise that prisons could rehabilitate, that the prisons of New York were not in fact making a serious effort at rehabilitation, and that New York's prisons should be converted from their existing custodial basis to a new rehabilitative one. The problem for the Committee was that there was no available guidance on the question of what had been shown to be the most effective means of rehabilitation. My colleagues and I were hired by the committee to remedy this defect in our knowledge; our job was to undertake a comprehensive survey of what was known about rehabilitation.

In 1968, in order to qualify for federal funds under the Omnibus Crime Control and Safe Streets Act, the state established a planning organization, which acquired from the Governor's Committee the responsibility for our report. But by 1970, when the project was formally completed, the state had changed its mind about the worth and proper use of the information we had gathered. The Governor's Committee had begun by thinking that such information was a necessary basis for any reforms that might be undertaken; the state planning agency ended by viewing the study as a document whose disturbing conclusions posed a serious threat to the programs which, in the meantime, they had determined to carry forward. By the spring of 1972—fully a year after I had re-edited the study for final publication—the state had not only failed to publish it, but had also refused to give me permission to publish it on my own. The document itself would still not be available to me or to the public today had not Joseph Alan Kaplon, an attorney, subpoenaed it from the state for use as evidence in a case before the Bronx Supreme Court.[1]

During the time of my efforts to get the study released, reports of it began to be widely circulated, and it acquired something of an underground reputation. But this article is the first published account, albeit a brief one, of the findings contained in that 1,400-page manuscript.

What we set out to do in this study was fairly simple, though it turned into a massive task. First we undertook a six-month search of the literature for any available reports published in the English language on attempts at rehabilitation that had been made in our corrections systems and those of other countries from 1945 through 1967. We then picked from that literature all those studies whose findings were interpretable—that is, whose design and execution met the conventional standards of social science research. Our criteria were rigorous but hardly esoteric: A study had to be an evaluation of a treatment method, it had to employ an independent measure of the improvement secured by that method, and it had to use some control group, some untreated individuals with whom the treated ones could be compared. We excluded studies only for methodological reasons: They presented insufficient data, they were only preliminary, they presented only a summary of findings and did not allow a reader to evaluate those findings, their results were confounded by extraneous factors, they used unreliable measures, one could not understand their descriptions of the treatment in question, they drew spurious conclusions from their data, their samples were undescribed or too small or provided no true comparability between treated and untreated groups, or they had used inappropriate statistical tests and did not provide enough information for the reader to recompute the data. Using these standards, we drew from the total number of studies 231 acceptable ones, which we not only analyzed ourselves but summarized in detail so that a reader of our analysis would be able to compare it with his independent conclusions.

These treatment studies use various measures of offender improvement: recidivism rates (that is, the rates at which offenders return to crime), adjustment to prison life, vocational success, educational achievement, personality and attitude change, and general adjustment to the outside community. We included all of these in our study; but in these pages I will deal only with the effects of rehabilitative treatment on recidivism, the phenomenon which reflects most directly how well our present treatment programs are performing the task of rehabilitation. The use of even this one measure brings with it enough methodological complications to make a clear reporting of the findings most difficult. The groups that are studied, for instance, are exceedingly disparate, so that it is hard to tell whether what "works" for one kind of offender also works for others. In addition, there has been little attempt to replicate studies; therefore one cannot be certain how stable and reliable the various findings are. Just as important, when the various studies use the term "recidivism rate," they may in fact be talking about somewhat different measures of offender behavior—i.e., "failure" measures such as arrest rates or parole violation rates, or "success" measures such as favorable discharge from parole or probation. And not all of these measures correlate very highly with one another. These difficulties will become apparent again and again in the course of this discussion.

With these caveats, it is possible to give a rather bald summary of our findings: *With few and isolated exceptions, the rehabilitative efforts that have been reported so far have had no appreciable effect on recidivism.* Studies that have been done since our survey was completed do not present any major grounds for altering that original conclusion. What follows is an attempt to answer the questions and challenges that might be posed to such an unqualified statement.

Education and Vocational Training

1. *Isn't it true that a correctional facility running a truly rehabilitative program—one that prepares inmates for life on the outside through education and vocational training—will turn out more successful individuals than will a prison which merely leaves its inmates to rot?*

If this *is* true, the fact remains that there is very little empirical evidence to support it. Skill development and education programs are in fact quite common in correctional facilities, and one might begin by examining their effects on young males, those who might be thought most amenable to such efforts. A study by New York State (1964)[2] found that for young males as a whole, the degree of success achieved in the regular prison academic education program, as measured by changes in grade achievement levels, made no significant difference in recidivism rates. The only exception was the relative improvement, compared with the sample as a whole, that greater progress made in the top 7 percent of the participating population—those who had high I.Q.'s, had made good records in previous schooling, and who also made good records of academic progress in the institution. And a study by Glaser (1964) found that while it was true that, when one controlled for sentence length, more attendance in regular prison academic programs slightly decreased the subsequent chances of parole violation, this improvement was not large enough to outweigh the associated disadvantage for the "long-attenders": Those who attended prison school the longest also turned out to be those who were in prison the longest. Presumably, those getting the most education were also the worst parole risks in the first place.[3]

Studies of special education programs aimed at vocational or social skill development, as opposed to conventional academic education programs, report similarly discouraging results and reveal additional problems in the field of correctional research. Jacobson (1965) studied a program of "skill re-education" for institutionalized young males, consisting of 10 weeks of daily discussions aimed at developing problem-solving skills. The discussions were led by an adult who was thought capable of serving as a role model for the boys, and they were encouraged to follow the example that he set. Jacobson found that over all, the program produced no improvement in recidivism rates. There was only one special subgroup which provided an exception to this pessimistic finding: If boys in the experimental program decided afterwards to go on to take three or more regular prison courses, they did better upon release than "control" boys who had done the same. (Of course, it also seems likely that experimental boys who did *not* take these extra courses did worse than their controls.)

Zivan (1966) also reported negative results from a much more ambitious vocational training program at the Children's Village in Dobbs Ferry, New York. Boys in his special program were prepared for their return to the community in a wide variety of ways. First of all, they were given, in sequence, three types of vocational guidance: "assessment counseling," "development counseling," and "pre-placement counseling." In addition, they participated in an "occupational orientation," consisting of role-playing, presentations via audio-visual aids, field trips, and talks by practitioners in various fields of work. Furthermore, the boys were prepared for work by participating in the Auxiliary Maintenance Corps, which performed various chores in the institution; a boy might be promoted from the Corps to the Work Activity Program, which "hired" him, for a small fee, to perform various artisans' tasks. And finally, after release from Children's Village, a boy in the special program received supportive after-care and job placement aid.

None of this made any difference in recidivism rates. Nevertheless, one must add that it is impossible to tell whether this failure lay in the program itself or in the conditions under which it was administered. For one thing, the education department of the institution itself was hostile to the program; they believed instead in the efficacy of academic education. This staff therefore tended to place in the pool from which experimental subjects were randomly selected mainly "multi-problem" boys. This by itself would not have invalidated the experiment as a test of vocational training for this particular type of youth, but staff hostility did not end there; it exerted subtle pressures of disapproval throughout the life of the program. Moreover, the program's "after-care" phase also ran into difficulties; boys who were sent back to school before getting a job often received advice that conflicted with the program's counseling, and boys actually looking for jobs met with the frustrating fact that the program's personnel, despite concerted efforts, simply could not get businesses to hire the boys.

We do not know whether these constraints, so often found in penal institutions, were responsible for the program's failure; it might have failed anyway. All one can say is that this research failed to show the effectiveness of special vocational training for young males.

The only clearly positive report in this area comes from a study by Sullivan (1967) of a program that combined academic education with special training in the use of IBM equipment. Recidivism rates after one year were only 48 percent for experimentals, as compared with 66 percent for controls. But when one examines the data, it appears that this difference emerged only between the controls and those who had successfully *completed* the training. When one compares the control group with all those who had been *enrolled* in the program, the difference disappears. Moreover, during this study the random assignment procedure between experimental and control groups seems to have broken down, so that towards the end, better risks had a greater chance of being assigned to the special program.

In sum, many of these studies of young males are extremely hard to interpret because of flaws in research design. But it can safely be said that they provide us with no clear evidence that education or skill development programs have been successful.

Training Adult Inmates

When one turns to adult male inmates, as opposed to young ones, the results are even more discouraging. There have been six studies of this type; three of them report that their programs, which ranged from academic to prison work experience, produced no significant differences in recidivism rates, and one—by Glaser (1964)—is almost impossible to interpret because of the risk differentials of the prisoners participating in the various programs.

Two studies—by Schnur (1948) and by Saden (1962)—*do* report a positive difference from skill development programs. In one of them, the Saden study, it is questionable whether the experimental and control groups were truly comparable. But what is more interesting is that both these "positive" studies dealt with inmates incarcerated prior to or during World War II. Perhaps the rise in our educational standards as a whole since then has lessened the differences that prison education or training can make. The only other interesting possibility emerges from a study by Gearhart (1967). His study was as one of those that reported vocational education to be non-significant in effecting recidivism rates. He did note, however, that when a trainee succeeded in finding a job related to his area of training, he had a slightly higher chance of becoming a successful parolee. It is possible, then, that skill development programs fail because what they teach bears so little relationship to an offender's subsequent life outside the prison.

One other study of adults, this one with fairly clear implications, has been performed with women rather than men. An experimental group of institutionalized women in Milwaukee was given an extremely comprehensive special education program, accompanied by group counseling. Their training was both academic and practical; it included reading, writing, spelling, business filing, child care, and grooming. Kettering (1965) found that the program made no difference in the women's rates of recidivism.

Two things should be noted about these studies. One is the difficulty of interpreting them as a whole. The disparity in the programs that were tried, in the populations that were affected, and in the institutional settings that surrounded these projects make it hard to be sure that one is observing the same category of treatment in each case. But the second point is that despite this difficulty, one can be reasonably sure that, so far, educational and vocational programs have not worked. We don't know why they have failed. We don't know whether the programs themselves are flawed, or whether they are incapable of overcoming the effects of prison life in general. The difficulty may be that they lack applicability to the world the inmate will face outside of prison. Or perhaps the type of educational and skill improvement they produce simply doesn't have very much to do with an individual's propensity to commit a crime. What we do know is that, to date, education and skill development have not reduced recidivism by rehabilitating criminals.

The Effects of Individual Counseling

2. *But when we speak of a rehabilitative prison, aren't we referring to more than education and skill development alone? Isn't what's needed [is] some way of counseling inmates or helping them with the deeper problems that have caused their maladjustment?*

This, too, is a reasonable hypothesis; but when one examines the programs of this type that have been tried, it's hard to find any more grounds for enthusiasm than we found with skill development and education. One method that's been tried—though so far, there have been acceptable reports only of its application to young offenders—has been individual psychotherapy. For young males, we found seven such reported studies. One study, by Guttman (1963) at the Nelles School, found such treatment to be ineffective in reducing recidivism rates; another, by Rudoff (1960), found it unrelated to *institutional* violation rates, which were themselves related to parole success. It must be pointed out that Rudoff used only this indirect measure of association, and the study therefore cannot rule out the possibility of a treatment effect. A third, also by Guttman (1963) but at nother institution, found that such treatment was actually related to a slightly *higher* parole violation rate; and a study by Adams (1959b and 1961b) also found a lack of improvement in parole revocation and first suspension rates.

There were two studies at variance with this pattern. One by Persons (1966) said that if a boy was judged to be "successfully" treated—as opposed to simply being subjected to the treatment experience—he did tend to do better. And there was one finding both hopeful and cautionary: At the Deuel School (Adams, 1961a), the experimental boys were first divided into two groups, those rated as "amenable" to treatment and those rated "non-amenable." Amenable boys who got the treatment did better than non-treated boys. On the other hand, "non-amenable" boys who were treated actually did worse than they would have done if they had received no treatment at all. It must be pointed out that Guttman (1963), dealing with younger boys in his Nelles School study, did not find such an "amenability" effect, either to the detriment of the non-amenables who were treated *or* to the benefit of the amenables who were treated. But the Deuel School study (Adams, 1961a) suggests both that there is something to be hoped for in treating properly selected amenable subjects and that if these subjects are not properly selected, one may not only wind up doing no good but may actually produce harm. There have been two studies of the effects of individual psychotherapy on young incarcerated *female* offenders, and both of them (Adams, 1959a; Adams, 1961b) report no significant effects from the therapy. But one of the Adams studies (1959a) does contain a suggestive, although not clearly interpretable, finding: If this individual therapy was administered by a psychiatrist or a psychologist, the resulting parole suspension rate was almost two-and-a-half times *higher* than if it was administered by a social worker without this specialized training.

There has also been a much smaller number of studies of two other types of individual therapy: counseling, which is directed towards a prisoner's gaining new insight into his own problems, and casework, which aims at helping a prisoner cope with his more pragmatic immediate needs. These types of therapy both rely heavily on the empathetic relationship that is to be developed between the professional and the client. It was noted above that the Adams study (1961b) of therapy administered to girls, referred to in the discussion of individual psychotherapy, found that social workers seemed better at the job than psychologists or psychiatrists. This difference seems to suggest a favorable outlook for these alternative forms of individual therapy. But other studies of such therapy have produced ambiguous results. Bernsten (1961) reported a Danish experiment that showed that socio-psychological counseling combined with comprehensive welfare measures—job and residence placement, clothing, union and health insurance membership, and financial aid—produced an improvement among some short-term male offenders, though not those in either the highest-risk or the lowest-risk categories. On the other hand, Hood, in Britain (1966), reported generally non-significant results with a program of counseling for young males. (Interestingly enough, this experiment *did* point to a mechanism capable of changing recidivism rates. When boys were released from institutional care and entered the army directly, "poor risk" boys among both experimentals *and* controls did better than expected. "Good risks" did worse.)

So these foreign data are sparse and not in agreement; the American data are just as sparse. The only American study which provides a direct measure of the effects of individual counseling—a study of California's Intensive Treatment Program (California, 1958a), which was "psychodynamically" oriented—found no improvement in recidivism rates.

It was this finding of the failure of the Intensive Treatment Program which contributed to the decision in California to de-emphasize individual counseling in its penal system in favor of group methods. And indeed one might suspect that the preceding reports reveal not the inadequacy of counseling as a whole but only the failure of one *type* of counseling, the individual type. Group counseling methods, in which offenders are permitted to aid and compare experiences with one another, might be thought to have a better chance of success. So it is important to ask what results these alternative methods have actually produced.

Group Counseling

Group counseling has indeed been tried in correctional institutions both with and without a specifically psychotherapeutic orientation. There has been one study of "pragmatic," problem-oriented counseling on *young* institutionalized males by Seckel (1965). This type of counseling had no significant effect. For adult males, there have been three such studies of the "pragmatic" and "insight" methods. Two (Kassebaum, 1971; Harrison, 1964) report no long-lasting significant effects. (One of these two did report a real but short-term effect that wore off as the program became institutionalized and as offenders were at liberty longer.) The third study of adults, by Shelley (1961), dealt with a "pragmatic" casework program, directed towards the educational and vocational needs of institutionalized young adult males in a Michigan prison camp. The treatment lasted for six months and at the end of that time Shelley found an improvement in attitudes; the possession of "good" attitudes was independently found by Shelley to correlate with parole success. Unfortunately, though, Shelley was not able to measure the *direct* impact of the counseling on recidivism rates. His two separate correlations are suggestive, but they fall short of being able to tell us that it really is the counseling that has a direct effect on recidivism.

With regard to more professional group *psychotherapy*, the reports are also conflicting. We have two studies of group psychotherapy on young males. One, by Persons (1966), says that this treatment did in fact reduce recidivism. The improved recidivism rate stems from the improved performance only of those who were clinically judged to have been "successfully" treated; still, the overall result of the treatment was to improve recidivism rates for the experimental group as a whole. On the other hand, a study by Craft (1964) of young males designated "psychopaths," comparing "self-government" group psychotherapy with "authoritarian" individual counseling, found that the "group therapy" boys afterwards committed twice as many new offenses as the individually treated ones. Perhaps some forms of group psychotherapy work for some types of offenders but not others; a reader must draw his own conclusions on the basis of sparse evidence.

With regard to young females, the results are just as equivocal. Adams, in his study of females (1959a), found that there was no improvement to be gained from treating girls by group rather than individual methods. A study by Taylor of borstal (reformatory) girls in New Zealand (1967) found a similar lack of any great improvement for group therapy as opposed to individual therapy or even to no therapy at all. But the Taylor study does offer one real, positive finding: When the "group therapy" girls *did* commit new offenses, these offenses were less serious than the ones for which they had originally been incarcerated.

There is a third study that does report an overall positive finding as opposed to a partial one. Truax (1966) found that girls subjected to group psychotherapy and then released were likely to spend less time reincarcerated in the future. But what is most interesting about this improvement is the very special and important circumstance under which it occurred. The therapists chosen for this program did not merely have to have the proper analytic training; they were specially chosen for their "empathy" and "non-possessive warmth." In other words, it may well have been the therapists' special personal gifts rather than the fact of treatment itself which produced the favorable result. This possibility will emerge again when we examine the effects of other types of rehabilitative treatment later in this article.

As with the question of skill development, it is hard to summarize these results. The programs administered were various; the groups to which they were administered varied not only by sex but by age as well; there were also variations in the length of time for which the programs were carried on, the frequency of contact during that time, and the period for which the subjects were followed up. Still, one must say that the burden of the evidence is not encouraging. These programs seem to work best when they are new, when their subjects are amenable to treatment in the first place, and when the counselors are not only trained people but "good" people as well. Such findings, which would not be much of a surprise to a student of organization or personality, are hardly encouraging for a policy planner, who must adopt measures that are generally applicable, that are capable of being successfully institutionalized, and that must rely for personnel on something other than the exceptional individual.

Transforming the Institutional Environment

3. *But maybe the reason these counseling programs don't seem to work is not that they are ineffective per se, but that the institutional environment outside the program is unwholesome enough to undo any good work that the counseling does. Isn't a truly successful rehabilitative institution the one where the inmate's whole environment is directed towards true correction rather than towards custody or punishment?*

This argument has not only been made, it has been embodied in several institutional programs that go by the name of "milieu therapy." They are designed to make every element of the inmate's environment a part of his treatment, to reduce the distinctions between the custodial staff and the treatment staff, to create a supportive, non-authoritarian, and non-regimented atmosphere, and to enlist peer influence in the formation of constructive values. These programs are especially hard to summarize because of their variety they differ, for example, in how "supportive" or "permissive" they are designed to be, in the extent to which they are combined with other treatment methods such as individual therapy, group counseling, or skill development, and in how completely the program is able to control all the relevant aspects of the institutional environment.

One might well begin with two studies that have been done of institutionalized adults, in regular prisons, who have been subjected to such treatment; this is the category whose results are the most clearly discouraging. One study of such a program, by Robison (1967), found that the therapy did seem to reduce recidivism after one year. After two years, however, this effect disappeared, and the treated convicts did no better than the untreated. Another study by Kassebaum, Ward, and Wilnet (1971), dealt with a program which had been able to effect an exceptionally extensive and experimentally rigorous transformation of the institutional environment. This sophisticated study had a follow-up period of 36 months, and it found that the program had no significant effect on parole failure or success rates.

The results of the studies of youth are more equivocal. As for young females, one study by Adams (1966) of such a program found that it had no significant effect on recidivism; another study, by Goldberg and Adams (1964), found that such a program did have a positive effect. This effect declined when the program began to deal with girls who were judged beforehand to be worse risks.

As for young males, the studies may conveniently be divided into those dealing with juveniles (under 18) and those dealing with youths. There have been five studies of milieu therapy administered to juveniles. Two of them—by Lavlicht (1962) and by Jesness (1965)—report clearly that the program in question either had no significant effect or had a short-term effect that wore off with passing time. Jesness does report that when his experimental juveniles did commit new offenses, the offenses were less serious than those committed by controls. A third study of juveniles, by McCord (1953) at the Wiltwyck School, reports mixed results. Using two measures of performance, a "success" rate and a "failure" rate, McCord found that his experimental group achieved both less failure *and* less success than the controls did. There have been two positive reports on milieu therapy programs for male juveniles; both of them have come out of the Highfields program, the milieu therapy experiment which has become the most famous and widely quoted example of "success" via this method. A group of boys was confined for a relatively short time to the unrestrictive, supportive environment of Highfields; and at a follow-up of six months, Freeman (1956) found that the group did indeed show a lower recidivism rate (as measured by parole revocation) than a similar group spending a longer time in the regular reformatory. McCorkle (1956) also reported positive findings from Highfields. But in fact, [as] the McCorkle data show[s], this improvement was not so clear: The Highfields boys had lower recidivism rates at 12 and 36 months in the follow-up period, but not at 24 and 60 months. The length of follow-up, these data remind us, may have large implications for a study's conclusions. But more important were other flaws in the Highfields experiment: The populations were not fully comparable (they differed according to risk level

and time of admission); different organizations—the probation agency for the Highfield boys, the parole agency for the others—were making the revocation decisions for each group; more of the Highfields boys were discharged early from supervision, and thus removed from any risk of revocation. In short, not even from the celebrated Highfields case may we take clear assurance that milieu therapy works.

In the case of male youths, as opposed to male juveniles, the findings are just as equivocal, and hardly more encouraging. One such study by Empey (1966) in a residential context did not produce significant results. A study by Seckel (1967) described California's Fremont Program, in which institutionalized youths participated in a combination of therapy, work projects, field trips, and community meetings. Seckel found that the youths subjected to this treatment committed more violations of law than did their non-treated counterparts. This difference could have occurred by chance; still, there was certainly no evidence of relative improvement. Another study, by Levinson (1962–1964), also found a lack of improvement in recidivism rates—but Levinson noted the encouraging fact that the treated group spent somewhat more time in the community before recidivating, and committed less serious offenses. And a study by the State of California (1967) also shows a partially positive finding. This was a study of the Marshall Program, similar to California's Fremont Program but different in several ways. The Marshall Program was shorter and more tightly organized than its Fremont counterpart. In the Marshall Program, as opposed to the Fremont Program, a youth could be ejected from the group and sent back to regular institutions before the completion of the program. Also, the Marshall Program offered some additional benefits: the teaching of "social survival skills" (i.e., getting and holding a job), group counseling of parents, and an occasional opportunity for boys to visit home. When youthful offenders were released to the Marshall Program, either directly or after spending some time in a regular institution, they did no better than a comparable regularly institutionalized population, though both Marshall youth and youth in regular institutions did better than those who were directly released by the court and given no special treatment.

So the youth in these milieu therapy programs at least do no worse than their counterparts in regular institutions and the special programs may cost less. One may therefore be encouraged—not on grounds of rehabilitation but on grounds of cost effectiveness.

What About Medical Treatment?

4. *Isn't there anything you can do in an institutional setting that will reduce recidivism, for instance, through strictly medical treatment?*

A number of studies deal with the results of efforts to change the behavior of offenders through drugs and surgery. As for surgery, the one experimental study of a plastic surgery program—by Mandell (1967)—had negative results. For non-addicts who received plastic surgery, Mandell purported to find improvement in performance on parole; but when one reanalyzes his data, it appears that surgery alone did not in fact make a significant difference.

One type of surgery does seem to be highly successful in reducing recidivism. A twenty-year Danish study of sex offenders, by Stuerup (1960), found that while those who had been treated with hormones and therapy continued to commit both sex crimes (29.6 percent of them did so) and non-sex crimes (21.0 percent), those who had been castrated had rates of only 3.5 percent (not, interestingly enough, a rate of zero; where there's a will, apparently there's a way) and 9.2 percent. One hopes that the policy implications of this study will be found to be distinctly limited.

As for drugs, the major report on such a program—involving tranquilization—was made by Adams (1961b). The tranquilizers were administered to male and female institutionalized youths. With boys, there was only a slight improvement in their subsequent behavior; this improvement disappeared within a year. With girls, the tranquilization produced worse results than when the girls were given no treatment at all.

The Effects of Sentencing

5. *Well, at least it may be possible to manipulate certain gross features of the existing, conceptional prison system—such as length of sentence and degree of security—in order to affect these recidivism rates. Isn't this the case?*

At this point, it's still impossible to say that this is the case. As for the degree of security in an institution, Glaser's (1964) work reported that, for both youth and adults, a less restrictive "custody grading" in American federal prisons was related to success on parole; but this is hardly surprising, since those assigned to more restrictive custody are likely to be worse risks in the first place. More to the point, an American study by Fox (1950) discovered that for "older youths" who were deemed to be good risks for the future, a minimum security institution produced better results than a maximum security one. On the other hand, the data we have on youths under 16—from a study by McClintock (1961), done in Great Britain—indicate that so-called Borstals, in which boys are totally confined, are more effective than a less restrictive regime of partial physical custody. In short, we know very little about the recidivism effects of various degrees of security in existing institutions; and our problems in finding out will be compounded by the probability that these effects will vary widely according to the particular *type* of offender that we're dealing with.

The same problems of mixed results and lack of comparable populations have plagued attempts to study the effects of sentence length. A number of studies—by Narloch (1959), by Bernsten (1965), and by the State of California (1956)—suggest that those who are released earlier from institutions than their scheduled parole date, or those who serve short sentences of under three months rather than longer sentences of eight months or more, either do better on parole or at least do no worse.[4] The implication here is quite clear and important: Even if early releases and short sentences produce no improvement in recidivism rates, one could at least maintain the same rates while lowering the cost of maintaining the offender and lessening his own burden of imprisonment. Of course, this implication carries with it its concomitant danger: the danger that though shorter sentences cause no worsening of the recidivism rate, they may increase the total amount of crime in the community by increasing the absolute number of potential recidivists at large.

On the other hand, Glaser's (1964) data show not a consistent linear relationship between the shortness of the sentence and the rate of parole success, but a curvilinear one. Of his subjects, those who served less than a year had a 73 percent success rate, those who served up to two years were only 65 percent successful, and those who served up to three years fell to a rate of 56 percent. But among those who served sentences of *more* than three years, the success rate rose again—to 60 percent. These findings should be viewed with some caution since Glaser did not control for the pre-existing degree of risk associated with each of his categories of offenders. But the data do suggest that the relationship between sentence length and recidivism may not be a simple linear one.

More important, the effect of sentence length seems to vary widely according to type of offender. In a British study (1963), for instance, Hammond found that for a group of "hard-core recidivists," shortening the sentence caused no improvement in the recidivism rate. In Denmark, Bernsten (1965) discovered a similar phenomenon: That the beneficial effect of three-month sentences as against eight-month ones disappeared in the case of these "hard-core recidivists." Garrity found another such distinction in his 1956 study. He divided his offenders into three categories: "pro-social," "anti-social," and "manipulative." "Pro-social" offenders he found to have low recidivism rates regardless of the length of their sentence; "anti-social" offenders did better with short sentences; the "manipulative" did better with long ones. Two studies from Britain made yet another division of the offender population, and found yet other variations. One (Great Britain, 1964) found that previous offenders—but not first offenders—did better with *longer* sentences, while the other (Cambridge, 1952) found the *reverse* to be true with juveniles.

To add to the problem of interpretation, these studies deal not only with different types and categorizations of offenders but with different types of institutions as well. No more than in the case of institution type can we say that length of sentence has a clear relationship to recidivism.

Decarcerating the Convict

6. *All of this seems to suggest that there's not much we know how to do to rehabilitate an offender when he's in an institution. Doesn't this lead to the clear possibility that the way to rehabilitate offenders is to deal with them outside an institutional setting?*

This is indeed an important possibility, and it is suggested by other pieces of information as well. For instance, Minet (1967) reported on a milieu therapy program in Massachusetts called Outward Bound. It took youths 15½ and over; it was oriented toward the development of skills in the out-of-doors and conducted in a wilderness atmosphere very different from that of most existing institutions. The culmination of the 26-day program was a final 24 hours in which each youth had to survive alone in the wilderness. And Miner found that the program did indeed work in reducing recidivism rates.

But by and large, when one takes the programs that have been administered in institutions and applies them in a non-institutional setting, the results do not grow to encouraging proportions. With casework and individual counseling in the community, for instance, there have been three studies; they dealt with counseling methods from psycho-social and vocational counseling to "operant conditioning," in which an offender was rewarded first simply for coming to counseling sessions and then, gradually, for performing other types of approved sets. Two of them report that the community-counseled offenders did no better than their institutional controls, while the third notes that although community counseling produced fewer arrests per person, it did not ultimately reduce the offender's chance of resuming to a reformatory.

The one study of a non-institutional skill development program, by Kovacs (1967), described the New Start Program in Denver, in which offenders participated in vocational training, role playing, programmed instruction, group counseling, college class attendance, and trips to art galleries and museums. After all this, Kovacs found no significant improvement over incarceration.

There have also been studies of milieu therapy programs conducted with youthful male probationers not in actual physical custody. One of them found no significant improvement at all. One, by Empey (1966), did say that after a follow-up of six months, a boy who was judged to have "successfully" completed the milieu program was less likely to recidivate afterwards than was a "successful," regular probationer. Empey's "successes" came out of an extraordinary program in Provo, Utah, which aimed to rehabilitate by subjecting offenders to a non-supportive milieu. The staff of this program operated on the principle that they were not to go out of their way to interact and be empathetic with the boys. Indeed, a boy who

misbehaved was to be met with "role dispossession": He was to be excluded from meetings of his peer group, and he was not to be given answers to his questions as to why he had been excluded or what his ultimate fate might be. This peer group and its meetings were designed to be the major force for reform at Provo; they were intended to develop, and indeed did develop, strong and controlling norms for the behavior of individual members. For one thing, group members were not to associate with delinquent boys outside the program; for another, individuals were to submit to a group review of all their actions and problems; and they were to be completely honest and open with the group about their attitudes, their states of mind their personal failings. The group was granted quite a few sanctions with which to enforce these norms: They could practice derision or temporary ostracism, or they could lock up an aberrant member for the weekend, refuse to release him from the program, or send him away to the regular reformatory.

One might be tempted to forgive these methods because of the success that Empey reports, except for one thing. If one judges the program not only by its "successful" boys but by all the boys who were subjected to it—those who succeeded and those who, not surprisingly, failed—the totals show *no* significant improvement in recidivism rates compared with boys on regular probation. Empey did find that both the Provo boys and those on regular probation did better than those in regular reformatories—in contradiction, it may be recalled, to the finding from the residential Marshall Program, in which the direct releases given no special treatment did *worse* than boys in regular institutions.

The third such study of non-residential milieu therapy, by McCravy (1967), found not only that there was no significant improvement, but that the longer a boy participated in the treatment, the worse he was likely to do afterwards.

Psychotherapy in Community Settings

There is some indication that individual psychotherapy may "work" in a community setting. Massimo (1963) reported on one such program, using what might be termed a "pragmatic" psychotherapeutic approach, including "insight" therapy and a focus on vocational problems. The program was marked by its small size and by its use of therapists who were personally enthusiastic about the project; Massimo found that there was indeed a decline in recidivism rates. Adamson (1956), on the other hand, found no significant difference produced by another program of individual therapy (though he did note that arrest rates among the experimental boys declined with what he called "intensity of treatment"). And Schwitzgebel (1963, 1964), studying other, different kinds of therapy programs, found that the programs *did* produce improvements in the attitudes of his boys—but, unfortunately, not in their rates of recidivism.

And with *group* therapy administered in the community, we find yet another set of equivocal results. The results from studies of pragmatic group counseling are only mildly optimistic. Adams (1965) did report that a form of group therapy, "guided group interaction," when administered to juvenile gangs, did somewhat reduce the percentage that were to be found in custody six years later. On the other hand, in a study of juveniles, Adams (1964) found that while such a program did reduce the number of contacts that an experimental youth had with police, it made no ultimate difference in the detention rate. And the attitudes of the counseled youth showed no improvement. Finally, when O'Brien (1961) examined a community-based program of group psychotherapy, he found not only that the program produced no improvement in the recidivism rate, but that the experimental boys actually did worse than their controls on a series of psychological tests.

Probation or Parole Versus Prison

But by far the most extensive and important work that has been done on the effect of community-based treatments has been done in the areas of probation and parole. This work sets out to answer the question of whether it makes any difference how you supervise and treat an offender once he has been released from prison or has come under state surveillance in lieu of prison. This is the work that has provided the main basis to date for the claim that we do indeed have the means at our disposal for rehabilitating the offender or at least decarcerating him safely.

One group of these studies has compared the use of probation with other dispositions for offenders; these provide some slight evidence that, at least under some circumstances, probation may make an offender's future chances better than if he had been sent to prison. Or, at least, probation may not worsen those chances.[5] A British study, by Wilkins (1958), reported that when probation was granted more frequently, recidivism rates among probationers did not increase significantly. And another such study by the state of Michigan in 1963 reported that an expansion in the use of probation actually improved recidivism rates—though there are serious problems of comparability in the groups and systems that were studied.

One experiment—by Babst (1965)—compared a group of parolees, drawn from adult male felony offenders in Wisconsin, and excluding murderers and sex criminals, with a similar group that had been put on probation; it found that the probationers committed fewer violations if they had been first offenders, and did no worse if they were recidivists. The problem in interpreting this experiment, though, is that the behavior of those groups was being measured by separate organizations, by probation officers for the probationers, and by parole officers for the parolees; it is not clear that the definition of "violation" was the same in each case, or that other types of uniform standards were being applied. Also, it is not clear what the results would have been if subjects had been released directly to the parole organization without having experienced prison first. Another such study, done in Israel by Shoham (1964), must be interpreted cautiously because his experimental and control groups had slightly different characteristics. But Shoham found that when one compared a suspended sentence plus probation for first offenders with a one-year prison sentence, only first offenders under 20 years of age did better on probation; those from 21 to 45 actually did *worse*. And Shoham's findings also differ from Babst's in another way. Babst had found that parole rather than prison brought no improvement for recidivists, but Shoham reported that for recidivists with four or more prior offenses, a suspended sentence was actually *better*—though the improvement was much less when the recidivist had committed a crime of violence.

But both the Babst and the Shoham studies, even while they suggest the possible value of suspended sentences, probation, or parole for some offenders (though they contradict each other in telling us *which* offenders), also indicate a pessimistic general conclusion concerning the limits of the effectiveness of treatment programs. For they found that the personal characteristics of offenders—"first offender status, or age, or type of offense"—were more important than the form of treatment in determining future recidivism. An offender with a "favorable" prognosis will do better than one without, it seems, no matter how you distribute "good" or "bad," "enlightened" or "regressive" treatments among them.

Quite a large group of studies deals not with probation as compared to other dispositions, but instead with the type of treatment that an offender receives once he is on probation or parole. These are the studies that have provided the most encouraging reports on rehabilitative treatment and that have also raised the most serious questions

about the nature of the research that has been going on in the corrections field.

Five of these studies have dealt with youthful probationers from 13 to 18 who were assigned to probation officers with small caseloads or provided with other ways of receiving more intensive supervision (Adams, 1966 [two reports]; Feistman, 1966; Kawaguchi, 1967; Pilnick, 1967). These studies report that, by and large, intensive supervision does work—that the specially treated youngsters do better according to some measure of recidivism. Yet these studies left some important questions unanswered. For instance, was this improved performance a function merely of the number of contacts a youngster had with his probation officer? Did it also depend on the length of time in treatment? Or was it the quality of supervision that was making the difference, rather than the quantity?

Intensive Supervision: The Warren Studies

The widely reported Warren studies (1966a, 1966b, 1967) in California constitute an extremely ambitious attempt to answer these questions. In this project, a control group of youths, drawn from a pool of candidates ready for first admission to a California Youth Authority institution, was assigned to regular detention, usually for eight to nine months, and then released to regular supervision. The experimental group received considerably more elaborate treatment. They were released directly to probation status and assigned to 12-man caseloads. To decide what special treatment was appropriate within these caseloads, the youths were divided according to their "interpersonal maturity level classification," by use of a scale developed by Grant and Grant. And each level dictated its own special type of therapy. For instance, a youth might be judged to occupy the lowest maturity level; this would be a youth, according to the scale, primarily concerned with "demands that the world take care of him. . . . He behaves impulsively, unaware of anything except the grossest effects of his behavior on others." A youth like this would be placed in a supportive environment such as a foster home; the goals of his therapy would be to meet his dependency needs and help him gain more accurate perceptions about his relationship to others. At the other end of the three-tier classification a youth might exhibit high maturity. This would be a youth who had internalized "a set of standards by which he judges his and others' behavior. . . . He shows some ability to understand reasons for behavior, some ability to relate to people emotionally and on a long-term basis." These high-maturity youths could come in several varieties—a "neurotic acting out," for instance, a "neurotic anxious," a "situational emotional reactor," or a "cultural identifier." But the appropriate treatment for these youths was individual psychotherapy, or family or group therapy for the purpose of reducing internal conflicts and increasing the youths' awareness of personal and family dynamics.

"Success" in this experiment was defined as favorable discharge by the Youth Authority; "failure" was unfavorable discharge, revocation, or recommitment by a court. Warren reported an encouraging finding: Among all but one of the "subtypes," the experimentals had a significantly lower failure rate than the controls. The experiment did have certain problems: The experimentals might have been performing better because of the enthusiasm of the staff and the attention lavished on them; none of the controls had been *directly* released to their regular supervision programs instead of being detained first; and it was impossible to separate the effects of the experimentals' small caseloads from their specially designed treatments, since no experimental youths had been assigned to a small caseload with "inappropriate" treatment, or with no treatment at all. Still, none of these problems were serious enough to vitiate the encouraging prospect that this finding presented for successful treatment of probationers.

This encouraging finding was, however, accompanied by a rather more disturbing clue. As has been mentioned before, the experimental subjects, when measured, had a lower *failure* rate than the controls. But the experimentals also had a lower *success* rate. That is, fewer of the experimentals as compared with the controls had been judged to have successfully completed their program of supervision and to be suitable for favorable release. When my colleagues and I undertook a rather laborious reanalysis of the Warren data, it became clear why this discrepancy had appeared. It turned out that fewer experimentals were "successful" because the experimentals were actually committing more offenses than their controls. The reason that the experimentals' relatively large number of offenses was not being reflected in their failure rates was simply that the experimentals' probation officers were using a more lenient revocation policy. In other words, the controls had a higher failure rate because the controls were being revoked for less serious offenses.

So it seems that what Warren was reporting in her "failure" rates was not merely the treatment effect of her small caseloads and special programs. Instead, what Warren was finding was not so much a change in the behavior of the experimental youths as a change in the behavior of the experimental *probation officers,* who knew the "special" status of their charges and who had evidently decided to revoke probation status at a lower than normal rate. The experimentals continued to commit offenses; what was different was that when they committed these offenses, they were permitted to remain on probation.

The experimenters claimed that this low revocation policy, and the greater number of offenses committed by the special treatment youth, were *not* an indication that these youth were behaving specially badly and that policy makers were simply letting them get away with it. Instead it was claimed, the higher reported offense rate was primarily an artifact of the more intense surveillance that the experimental youth received. But the data show that this is not a sufficient explanation of the low failure rate among experimental youth; the difference in "tolerance" of offenses between experimental officials and control officials was much greater than the difference in the rates at which these two systems detected youths committing new offenses. Needless to say, this reinterpretation of the data presents a much bleaker picture of the possibilities of intensive supervision with special treatment.

'Treatment Effect' Versus 'Policy Effects'

This same problem of experimenter bias may also be present in the predecessors of the Warren study, the ones which had also found positive results from intensive supervision on probation; indeed, this disturbing question can be raised about many of the previously discussed reports of positive "treatment effects."

This possibility of a "policy effect" rather than a "treatment effect" applies, for instance, to the previously discussed studies of the effects of intensive supervision on juvenile and youthful probationers. These were the studies, it will be recalled, which found lower recidivism rates for the intensively supervised.[6.]

One opportunity to make a further check on the effects of this problem is provided, in a slightly different context, by Johnson (1962a). Johnson was measuring the effects of intensive supervision on youthful *parolees* (as distinct from probationers). There have been several such studies of the effects on youths of intensive parole supervision plus special counseling and their findings are on the whole less encouraging than the probation studies; they are difficult to interpret because of experimental problems, but studies by Boston University in 1966, and by Van Couvering in 1966, report no significant effects and possibly some bad effects from such special programs. But Johnson's stud-

ies were unique for the chance they provide to measure both treatment effects and the effect of agency policy.

Johnson, like Warren, assigned experimental subjects to small caseloads and his experiment had the virtue of being performed with two separate populations and at two different times. But in contrast with the Warren case, the Johnson experiment did not engage in a large continuing attempt to choose the experimental counselors specially, to train them specially, and to keep them informed about the progress and importance of the experiment. The first time the experiment was performed, the experimental youths had a slightly lower revocation rate than the controls at six months. But the second time, the experimentals did *not* do better than their controls; indeed, they did slightly worse. And with the experimentals from the first group—those who *had* shown an improvement after six months—this effect wore off at 18 months. In the Johnson study, my colleagues and I found, "intensive" supervision did not increase the experimental youths' risk of detection. Instead, what was happening in the Johnson experiment was that the first time it had been performed—just as in the Warren study—the experimentals were simply revoked less often per number of offenses committed, and they were revoked for offenses more serious than those which prompted revocation among the controls. The second time around, this "policy" discrepancy disappeared; and when it did, the "improved" performance of the experimentals disappeared as well. The enthusiasm guiding the project had simply worn off in the absence of reinforcement.

One must conclude that the "benefits" of intensive supervision for youthful offenders may stem not so much from a "treatment" effect as from a "policy" effect—that such supervision, so far as we now know, results not in rehabilitation but in a decision to look the other way when an offense is committed. But there is one major modification to be added to this conclusion. Johnson performed a further measurement (1962b) in his parole experiment: He rated all the supervising agents according to the "adequacy" of the supervision they gave. And he found that an "adequate" agent, whether he was working in a small *or* a large caseload produced a relative improvement in his charges. The converse was not true: An inadequate agent was more likely to produce youthful "failures" when he was given a *small* caseload to supervise. One can't much help a "good" agent, it seems, by reducing his caseload size; such reduction can only do further harm to those youths who fall into the hands of "bad" agents.

So with youthful offenders, Johnson found, intensive supervision does not seem to provide the rehabilitative benefits claimed for it; the only such benefits may flow not from intensive supervision itself but from contact with one of the "good people" who are frequently in such short supply.

Intensive Supervision of Adults

The results are similarly ambiguous when one applies this intensive supervision to adult offenders. There have been several studies of the effects of intensive supervision on adult parolees. Some of these are hard to interpret because of problems of comparability between experimental and control groups (general risk ratings, for instance, or distribution of narcotics offenders, or policy changes that took place between various phases of the experiments), but two of them (California, 1966; Stanton, 1964) do not seem to give evidence of the benefits of intensive supervision. By far the most extensive work, though, on the effects of intensive supervision of adult parolees has been a series of studies of California's Special Intensive Parole Unit (SIPU), a 10-year-long experiment designed to test the treatment possibilities of various special parole programs. Three of the four "phases" of this experiment produced "negative results." The

first phase tested the effect of a reduced caseload size; no lasting effect was found. The second phase slightly increased the size of the small caseloads and provided for a longer time in treatment; again there was no evidence of a treatment effect. In the fourth phase, caseload sizes and time in treatment were again varied, and treatments were simultaneously varied in a sophisticated way according to personality characteristics of the parolees; once again, significant results did not appear.

The only phase of this experiment for which positive results were reported was Phase Three. Here, it was indeed found that a smaller caseload improved one's chances of parole success. There is, however, an important caveat that attaches to this finding: When my colleagues and I divided the whole population of subjects into two groups—those receiving supervision in the North of the state and those in the South—we found that the "improvement" of the experimentals' success rates was taking place primarily in the North. The North differed from the South in one important aspect: Its agents practiced a policy of resuming both "experimental" and "control" violators to prison at relatively high rates. And it was the North that produced the higher success rate among its experimentals. So this improvement in experimentals' performance was taking place only when accompanied by a "realistic threat" of severe sanctions. It is interesting to compare this situation with that of the Warren studies. In the Warren studies, experimental subjects were being revoked at a relatively *low* rate. These experimentals "failed" less, but they also committed more new offenses than their controls. By contrast, in the Northern region of the SIPU experiment, there was a policy of *high* rate of return to prison for experimentals; and here, the special program *did* seem to produce a real improvement in the behavior of offenders. What this suggests is that when intensive supervision *does* produce an improvement in offenders' behavior, it does so not through the mechanism of "treatment" or "rehabilitation," but instead through a mechanism that our studies have almost totally ignored the mechanism of *deterrence*. And a similar mechanism is suggested by Lohman's study (1967) of intensive supervision of probationers. In this study intensive supervision led to higher total violation rates. But one also notes that intensive supervision combined the highest rate of technical violations with the lowest rate for *new* offenses.

The Effects of Community Treatment

In sum, even in the case of treatment programs administered outside penal institutions, we simply cannot say that this treatment in itself has an appreciable effect on offender behavior. On the other hand, there is one encouraging set of findings that emerges from these studies. For from many of them there flows the strong suggestion that even if we can't "treat" offenders so as to make them do better, a great many of the programs designed to rehabilitate them at least did not make them do *worse*. And if these programs did not show the advantages of actually rehabilitating, some of them did have the advantage of being less onerous to the offender himself without seeming to pose increased danger to the community. And some of these programs—especially those involving less restrictive custody, minimal supervision, and early release—simply cost fewer dollars to administer. The information on the dollar costs of these programs is just beginning to be developed but the implication is clear: *that if we can't do more for (and to) offenders, at least we can safely do less.*

There is, however, one important caveat even to this note of optimism: In order to calculate the true costs of these programs, one must in each case include not only their administrative cost but also the cost of maintaining in the community an offender population increased in size. This population might well not be committing new offenses at any greater rate; but the offender population might, under some of these plans, be larger in absolute *numbers*. So the total number of offenses committed might rise, and our chances of victimization might therefore rise too. We need to be able to make a judgment about the size and probable duration of this effect; as of now, we simply do not know.

Does Nothing Work?

7. *Do all of these studies lead us irrevocably to the conclusion that nothing works, that we haven't the faintest clue about how to rehabilitate offenders and reduce recidivism? And if so, what shall we do?*

We tried to exclude from our survey those studies which were so poorly done that they simply could not be interpreted. But despite our efforts, a pattern has run through much of this discussion—of studies which "found" effects without making any truly rigorous attempt to exclude competing hypotheses, of extraneous factors permitted to intrude upon the measurements, of recidivism measures which are not all measuring the same thing, of "follow-up" periods which vary enormously and rarely extend beyond the period of legal supervision, of experiments never replicated, of "system effects" not taken into account, of categories drawn up without any theory to guide the enterprise. It is just possible that some of our treatment programs *are* working to some extent, but that our research is so bad that it is incapable of telling.

Having entered this very serious caveat, I am bound to say that these data, involving over two hundred studies and hundreds of thousands of individuals as they do, are the best available and give us very little reason to hope that we have in fact found a sure way of reducing recidivism through rehabilitation. This is not to say that we found no instances of success or partial success; it is only to say that these instances have been isolated, producing no clear pattern to indicate the efficacy of any particular method of treatment. And neither is this to say that factors *outside* the realm of rehabilitation may not be working to reduce recidivism—factors such as the tendency for recidivism to be lower in offenders over the age of 30; it is only to say that such factors seem to have little connection with any of the treatment methods now at our disposal.

From this probability, one may draw any of several conclusions. It may be simply that our programs aren't yet good enough—that the education we provide to inmates is still poor education, that the therapy we administer is not administered skillfully enough, that our intensive supervision and counseling do not yet provide enough personal support for the offenders who are subjected to them. If one wishes to believe this, then what our correctional system needs is simply a more full-hearted commitment to the strategy of treatment.

It may be, on the other hand, that there is a more radical flaw in our present strategies—that education at its best, or that psychotherapy at its best, cannot overcome, or even appreciably reduce, the powerful tendency for offenders to continue in criminal behavior. Our present treatment programs are based on a theory of crime as a "disease"—that is to say, as something foreign and abnormal in the individual which can presumably be cured. This theory may well be flawed, in that it overlooks—indeed, denies—both the normality of crime in society and the personal normality of a very large proportion of offenders, criminals who are merely responding to the facts and conditions of our society.

This opposing theory of "crime as a social phenomenon" directs our attention away from a "rehabilitative" strategy, away from the notion that we may best insure public safety through a series of "treatments" to be imposed forcibly on convicted offenders. These treatments have on occasion become, and have the potential for becoming, so draconian as to offend the moral order of a democratic society; and the theory of crime as a

social phenomenon suggests that such treatments may be not only offensive but ineffective as well. This theory points, instead, to decarceration for low-risk offenders—and, presumably, to keeping high-risk offenders in prisons which are nothing more (and aim to be nothing more) than custodial institutions.

But this approach has its own problems. To begin with, there is the moral dimension of crime and punishment. Many low-risk offenders have committed serious crimes (murder, sometimes) and even if one is reasonably sure they will never commit another crime, it violates our sense of justice that they should experience no significant retribution for their actions. A middle-class banker who kills his adulterous wife in a moment of passion is a "low-risk" criminal; a juvenile delinquent in the ghetto who commits armed robbery has, statistically, a much higher probability of committing another crime. Are we going to put the first on probation and sentence the latter to a long term in prison?

Besides, one cannot ignore the fact that the punishment of offenders is the major means we have for *deterring* incipient offenders. We know almost nothing about the "deterrent effect," largely because "treatment" theories have so dominated our research, and "deterrence" theories have been relegated to the status of a historical curiosity. Since we have almost no idea of the deterrent functions that our present system performs or that future strategies might be made to perform, it is possible that there is indeed something that works—that to some extent is working right now in front of our noses, and that might be made to work better—something that deters rather than cures, something that does not so much reform convicted offenders as prevent criminal behavior in the first place. But whether that is the case and, if it is, what strategies will be found to make our deterrence system work better than it does now, are questions we will not be able to answer with data until a new family of studies has been brought into existence. As we begin to learn the facts, we will be in a better position than we are now to judge to what degree the prison has become an anachronism and can be replaced by more effective means of social control.

Study Questions

1. What was the original impetus for Martinson's study of the effectiveness of rehabilitation programs?

2. Discuss the methodology (research design, data collection methods, sample, and measures) used by the author.

3. Many times, authors citing the Martinson Report erroneously state that his conclusion was that "nothing works." What was his actual conclusion? Does this differ from the one stated above?

4. What exactly were the author's conclusions about community treatment programs?

Notes

1. Following this case, the state finally did give its permission to have the work published; it will appear in its complete form in a forthcoming book by Praeger.

2. All studies cited in the text are referenced in the bibliography which appears at the conclusion of the article.

3. The net result was that those who received less prison education—because their sentences were shorter or because they were probably better risks—ended up having better chances than those who received more prison education.

4. A similar phenomenon has been measured indirectly by studies that have dealt with the effect of various parole policies on recidivism rates. Where parole decisions have been liberalized so that an offender could be released with only the "reasonable assurance" of a job rather than with a definite job already developed by a parole officer (Stanton, 1963), this liberal release policy has produced no worsening of recidivism rates.

5. It will be recalled that Empey's report on the Provo program made such a finding.

6. But one of these reports, by Kawaguchi (1967), also found that an intensively supervised juvenile, by the time he finally "failed," had had more previous detentions while under supervision than a control juvenile had experienced.

References

Adams, Stuart. "Effectiveness of the Youth Authority Special Treatment Program: First Interim Report." Research Report No. 5. California Youth Authority, March 6, 1959. (Mimeographed.)

Adams, Stuart. "Assessment of the Psychiatric Treatment Program: Second Interim Report." Research Report No. 15. California Youth Authority, December 13, 1959. (Mimeographed.)

Adams, Stuart. "Effectiveness of Interview Therapy with Older Youth Authority Wards: An Interim Evaluation of the PICO Project." Research Report No. 20. California Youth Authority, January 20, 1961. (Mimeographed.)

Adams, Stuart. "Assessment of the Psychiatric Treatment Program, Phase I: Third Interim Report." Research Report No. 21. California Youth Authority, January 31, 1961. (Mimeographed.)

Adams, Stuart. "An Experimental Assessment of Group Counseling with Juvenile Probationers." Paper presented at the 18th Convention of the California State Psychological Association, Los Angeles, December 12, 1964. (Mimeographed.)

Adams, Stuart, Rice, Rogert E., and Olive, Borden. "A Cost Analysis of the Effectiveness of the Group Guidance Program." Research Memorandum 65–3. Los Angeles County Probation Department, January 1965. (Mimeographed.)

Adams, Stuart. "Development of a Program Research Service in Probation." Research Report No. 27 (Final Report, NIMH Project MH007 18.) Los Angeles County Probation Department, January 1966. (Processed.)

Adamson, LeMay, and Dunham, H. Warren. "Clinical Treatment of Male Delinquents. A Case Study in Effort and Result," *American Sociological Review*, XXI, 3 (1956), 312–320.

Babst, Dean V., and Mannering, John W. "Probation versus Imprisonment for Similar Types of Offenders: A Comparison by Subsequent Violations," *Journal of Research in Crime and Delinquency*, II, 2 (1965), 60–71.

Bernsten, Karen, and Christiansen, Karl O. "A Resocialization Experiment with Short-term Offenders," *Scandinavian Studies in Criminology*, I (1965), 35–54.

California Adult Authority, Division of Adult Paroles. "Special Intensive Parole Unit, Phase I: Fifteen Man Caseload Study." Prepared by Walter I. Stone. Sacramento, CA, November 1956. (Mimeographed.)

California, Department of Corrections. "Intensive Treatment Program: Second Annual Report." Prepared by Harold B. Bradley and Jack D. Williams. Sacramento, CA, December 1, 1958. (Mimeographed.)

California, Department of Corrections. "Special Intensive Parole Unit, Phase II: Thirty Man Caseload Study." Prepared by Ernest Reimer and Martin Warren. Sacramento, CA, December 1958. (Mimeographed.)

California, Department of Corrections. "Parole Work Unit Program: An Evaluative Report." A memorandum to the California Joint Legislative Budget Committee, December 30, 1966. (Mimeographed.)

California, Department of the Youth Authority. "James Marshall Treatment Program: Progress Report." January 1967. (Processed.)

Cambridge University, Department of Criminal Science. *Detention in Remard Homes*. London: Macmillan, 1952.

Craft, Michael, Stephenson, Geoffrey, and Granger, Clive. "A Controlled Trial of Authoritarian and Self-Governing Regimes with Adolescent Psychopaths," *American Journal of Orthopsychiatry*, XXXIV, 3 (1964), 543–554.

Empey, LeMar T. "The Provo Experiment: A Brief Review." Los Angeles: Youth Studies Center, University of Southern California. 1966. (Processed.)

Feistman, Eugene G. "Comparative Analysis of the Willow-Brook-Harbor Intensive Services Program, March 1, 1965 through February 28, 1966." Research Report No. 28. Los Angeles County Probation Department, June 1966. (Processed.)

Forman, B. "The Effects of Differential Treatment on Attitudes, Personality Traits, and Behavior of Adult Parolees." Unpublished Ph.D. dissertation, University of Southern California, 1960.

Fox, Vernon. "Michigan's Experiment in Minimum Security Penology," *Journal of Criminal Law, Criminology, and Police Science*, XLI, 2 (1950), 150–166.

Freeman, Howard E., and Weeks, H. Ashley. "Analysis of a Program of Treatment of Delinquent Boys," *American Journal of Sociology*, LXII, 1 (1956), 56–61.

Garrity, Donald Lee. "The Effects of Length of Incarceration upon Parole Adjustment and Estimation of Optimum Sentence: Washington State Correctional Institutions." Unpublished Ph.D. dissertation, University of Washington, 1956.

Gearhart, J. Walter, Keith, Harold L., and Clemmons, Gloria. "An Analysis of the Vocational Training Program in the Washington State Adult Correctional Institutions." Research Review No. 23. State of Washington, Department of Institutions, May 1967. (Processed.)

Glaser, Daniel. *The Effectiveness of a Prison and Parole System*. New York: Bobbs-Merrill, 1964.

Goldberg, Lisbeth, and Adams, Stuart. "An Experimental Evaluation of the Lathrop Hall Program." Los Angeles County Probation Department, December 1964. (Summarized in Adams, Stuart. "Development of a Program Research Service in Probation," pp. 19–22.)

Great Britain. Home Office. *The Sentence of the Court: A Handbook for Courts on the Treatment of Offenders*. London: Her Majesty's Stationery Office, 1964.

Guttman, Evelyn S. "Effects of Short-Term Psychiatric Treatment on Boys in Two California Youth Authority Institutions." Research Report No. 36. California Youth Authority, December 1963. (Processed.)

Hammond, W.H., and Chayen, E. *Persistent Criminals: A Home Office Research Unit Report*. London: Her Majesty's Stationery Office, 1963.

Harrison, Robert M., and Mueller, Paul F. C. "Clue Hunting About Group Counseling and Parole Outcome." Research Report No. 11. California Department of Corrections, May 1964. (Mimeographed.)

Havel, Joan, and Sulka, Elaine. "Special Intensive Parole Unit: Phase Three." Research Report No. 3. California Department of Corrections, March 1962. (Processed.)

Havel, Joan. "A Synopsis of Research Report No. 10, SIPU Phase IV—The High Base Expectancy Study." Administrative Abstract No. 10. California Department of Corrections, June 1963. (Processed.)

Havel, Joan. "Special Intensive Parole Unit—Phase Four: 'The Parole Outcome Study.'" Research Report No. 13. California Department of Corrections, September 1965. (Processed.)

Hood, Roger. Homeless Borstal Boys: *A Study of Their After-Care and After Conduct.* Occasional Papers on Social Administration No. 18. London: G. Bell & Sons, 1966.

Jacobson, Frank, and McGee, Eugene. "Englewood Project: Re-education: A Radical Correction of Incarcerated Delinquents." Englewood, CO: July 1965. (Mimeographed.)

Jesness, Carl F. "The Fricot Ranch Study: Out-comes with Small versus Large Living Groups in the Rehabilitation of Delinquents." Research Report No. 47. California Youth Authority, October 1, 1965. (Processed.)

Johnson, Bertram. "Parole Performance of the First Year's Releases, Parole Research Project: Evaluation of Reduced Caseloads." Research Report No. 27. California Youth Authority, January 31, 1962. (Mimeographed.)

Johnson, Bertram. "An Analysis of Predictions of Parole Performance and of Judgements of Supervision in the Parole Research Project," Research Report No. 32. California Youth Authority, December 31, 1962. (Mimeographed.)

Kassebaum, Gene, Ward, David, and Wilnet, Daniel. Prison Treatment and Parole Survival: An Empirical Assessment. New York: Wiley, 1971.

Kawaguchi, Ray M., and Siff, Leon, M. "An Analysis of Intensive Probation Services—Phase II." Research Report No. 29. Los Angeles County Probation Department, April 1967. (Processed.)

Kettering, Marvin E. "Rehabilitation of Women in the Milwaukee County Jail: An Exploration Experiment." Unpublished Master's Thesis, Colorado State College, 1965.

Kovacs, Frank W. "Evaluation and Final Report of the New Start Demonstration Project." Colorado Department of Employment, October 1967. (Processed.)

Lavlicht, Jerome, et al., in Berkshire Farms Monographs, I, 1 (1962), 11–48.

Levinson, Robert B., and Kitchenet, Howard L. "Demonstration Counseling Project." 2 vols. Washington, DC: National Training School for Boys, 1962–1964. (Mimeographed.)

Lohman, Joseph D., et al., "The Intensive Supervision Caseloads: A Preliminary Evaluation." The San Francisco Project: A Study of Federal Probation and Parole. Research Report No. 11.

School of Criminology, University of California, March 1967. (Processed.)

McClintock, F.H. *Attendance Centres.* London. Macmillan, 1961.

McCord, William and Joan. "Two Approaches to the Cure of Delinquents," *Journal of Criminal Law, Criminology and Police Science*, XLIV, 4 (1953), 442–467.

McCorkle, Lloyd W., Elias, Albert, and Bixby, F. Lovell. *The Highfields Story: An Experimental Treatment Project for Youthful Offenders.* New York: Holt, 1958.

McCravy, Newton, Jr., and Delehanty, Dolores S. "Community Rehabilitation of the Younger Delinquent Boy, Parkland Non-Residential Group Center." Final Report, Kentucky Child Welfare Research Foundation, Inc., September 1, 1967. (Mimeographed.)

Mandell, Wallace, et al. "Surgical and Social Rehabilitation of Adult Offenders." Final Report. Montefiore Hospital and Medical Center, With Staten Island Mental Health Society. New York City Department of Correction, 1967. (Processed.)

Massimo, Joseph L., and Shore, Milton F. "The Effectiveness of a Comprehensive Vocationally Oriented Psychotherapeutic Program for Adolescent Delinquent Boys," *American Journal of Orthopsychiatry*, XXXIII, 4 (1963), 634–642.

Minet, Joshua, III, Kelly, Francis J., and Hatch, M. Charles. "Outward Bound, Inc.: Juvenile Delinquency Demonstration Project, Year End Report." Massachusetts Division of Youth Service, May 31, 1967.

Narloch, R. P., Adams, Stuart, and Jenkins, Kendall J. "Characteristics and Parole Performance of California Youth Authority Early Release." Research Report No. 7. California Youth Authority, June 22, 1959. (Mimeographed.)

New York State Division of Parole, Department of Correction. "Parole Adjustment and Prior Educational Achievement of Male Adolescent Offenders, June 1957–June 1961." September 1964. (Mimeographed.)

O'Brien, William J. "Personality Assessment as a Measure of Change Resulting from Group Psychotherapy with Male Juvenile Delinquents." The Institute for the Study of Crime and Delinquency, and the California Youth Authority, December 1961. (Processed.)

Persons, Roy W. "Psychological and Behavioral Change in Delinquents Following Psychotherapy," *Journal of Clinical Psychology*, XXII, 3 (1966), 337–340.

Pilnick, Saul, et al. "Collegefields: From Delinquency to Freedom." A Report . . .on Collegefields Group Educational Center. Laboratory for Applied Behavioral Science, Newark State College, February 1967. (Processed.)

Robison, James, and Kevotkian, Marinette. "Intensive Treatment Project: Phase II. Parole Outcome: Interim Report." Research Report No. 27. California Department of Corrections, Youth and Adult Correctional Agency, January 1967. (Mimeographed.)

Rudoff, Alvin. "The Effect of Treatment on Incarcerated Young Adult Delinquents as Measured by Disciplinary History." Unpublished Master's thesis, University of Southern California, 1960.

Saden, S.J. "Correctional Research at Jackson Prison," *Journal of Correctional Education*, XV (October 1962), 22–26.

Schnur, Alfred C. "The Educational Treatment of Prisoners and Recidivism," *American Journal of Sociology*, LIV, 2 (1948), 142–147.

Schwitzgebel, Robert and Ralph. "Therapeutic Research: A Procedure for the Reduction of Adolescent Crime." Paper presented at meetings of the American Psychological Association, Philadelphia, August 1963.

Schwitzgebel, Robert and Kolb, D.A. "Inducing Behavior Change in Adolescent Delinquents." *Behavior Research Therapy*, I (1964), 297–304.

Seckel, Joachim P. "Experiments in Group Counseling at Two Youth Authority Institutions." Research Report No. 46. California Youth Authority, September 1965. (Processed.)

Seckel, Joachim P. "The Fremont Experiment, Assessment of Residential Treatment at a Youth Authority Reception Center." Research Report No. 50. California Youth Authority, January 1967. (Mimeographed.)

Shelley, Ernest L.V., and Johnson, Walter F., Jr. "Evaluating an Organized Counseling Service for Youthful Offenders." *Journal of Counseling Psychology*, VIII, 4 (1961), 351–354.

Shoham, Shlomo, and Sandberg, Moshe. "Suspended Sentences in Israel: An Evaluation of the Preventive Efficacy of Prospective Imprisonment," *Crime and Delinquency*, X, 1 (1964), 74–83.

Stanton, John M. "Delinquencies and Types of Parole Programs to Which Inmates Are Released." New York State Division of Parole, May 15, 1963. (Mimeographed.)

Stanton, John M. "Board Directed Extensive Supervision." New York State Division of Parole, August 3, 1964. (Mimeographed.)

Stuerup, Georg K. "The Treatment of Sexual Offenders," *Bulletin de la societe internationale de criminologie* (1960), pp. 320–329.

Sullivan, Clyde E., and Mandell, Wallace. "Restoration of Youth Through Training: A Final Report." Staten Island, NY: Wakoff Research Center, April 1967. (Processed.)

Taylor, A.J.W. "An Evaluation of Group Psychotherapy in a Girls Borstal," *International Journal of Group Psychotherapy*, XVII, 2 (1967), 168–177.

Truax, Charles B., Wargo, Donald G., and Silber, Leon D. "Effects of Group Psychotherapy with High Adequate Empathy and Nonpossessive Warmth upon Female Institutionalized Delinquents." *Journal of Abnormal Psychology*, LXXXI, 4 (1966), 267–274.

Warren, Marguerite, et al. "The Community Treatment Project after Five Years." California Youth Authority, 1966. (Processed.)

Warren, Marguerite, et al. "Community Treatment Project, An Evaluation of Community Treatment for Delinquents: A Fifth Progress Report." C.T.P. Research Report No. 7. California Youth Authority, August 1966. (Processed.)

Warren, Margeurite, et al. "Community Treatment Project, An Evaluation of Community Treatment for Delinquents: Sixth Progress Report." C.T.P. Research Report No. 8. California Youth Authority, September 1967. (Processed.)

Wilkins, Leslie T. "A Small Comparative Study of the Results of Probation," *British Journal of Criminology*, VIII, 3 (1958), 201–209.

Zivan, Morton. "Youth in Trouble: A Vocational Approach." Final Report of a Research Demonstration Project, May 31, 1961–August 31, 1966. Dobbs Ferry, NY, Children's Village, 1966. (Processed.) ✦

22
Does Correctional Treatment Work?

A Clinically Relevant and Psychologically Informed Meta-Analysis

D. A. Andrews

Ivan Zinger

Robert D. Hoge

James Bonta

Paul Gendreau

Francis T. Cullen

As we have read, Martinson was actually more cautious in his conclusions than many believe. The message, however, was interpreted as "nothing works." Although some have criticized Martinson for his methodology and his public pronouncements, the real value of his work comes from others who answered the challenge. Scholars like Don A. Andrews and his associates began focusing on determining "what works" with offenders. Using a relatively new technique, meta-analysis, researchers have been able to demonstrate that correctional treatment can indeed have an appreciable effect on recidivism rates, provided that certain principles are met. The prin-

Excerpted from "Does Correctional Treatment Work? A Clinically Relevant and Psychologically Informed Meta-Analysis" by Don A. Andrews, Ivan Zinger, Robert D. Hoge, James Bonta, Paul Gendreau, and Francis T. Cullen. Criminology, 28(3): 369–404. Copyright © 1990 by American Society of Criminology. Reprinted by permission.

ciples of effective intervention identified by the authors include the risk principle (targeting higher risk offenders), the need principle (targeting crime producing needs), and the responsivity principle (matching cognitive and behavioral treatment with offender need and learning styles). As these authors show, clinically relevant and appropriate treatment services demonstrate significant and substantive effect sizes when compared with unspecified and vague unstructured programs.

During the 1970s, the ideological hegemony of the individualized treatment ideal suffered a swift and devastating collapse (Rothman, 1980). Previously a code word for "doing good," rehabilitation came to be seen by liberals as a euphemism for coercing offenders and by conservatives as one for letting hardened criminals off easily. Although the public's belief in rehabilitation was never eroded completely (Cullen et al., 1988), defenders of treatment were branded scientifically and politically naive apologists for the socially powerful, self-serving human service professionals, or curious relics of a positivistic past. Thus, a number of jurisdictions in the United States (Cullen and Gilbert, 1982) and Canada (Andrews, 1990; Leschied et al., 1988) embarked on sentencing reforms that undercut the role of rehabilitation in justice and corrections.

The decline of the rehabilitative ideal cannot be attributed to a careful reading of evidence regarding the effectiveness of rehabilitative treatment. As will be shown, reviews of the effectiveness literature routinely found that a substantial proportion of the better-controlled studies of rehabilitative service reported positive effects, and did so for programs that operated within a variety of conditions established by criminal sanctions, such as probation or incarceration. We will also show that criminal sanctions themselves were typically found to be only minimally related to recidivism. Thus, rather than a rational appreciation of evidence, the attack on rehabilitation was a reflection of broader social and intellectual trends. This is evident upon consideration of the particular historical timing and intensity of the attack on rehabilitation.

First, the rapidly changing sociopolitical context of the decade preceding the mid-1970s propelled conservatives to seek "law and order," while liberals attached to class-based perspectives on crime became discouraged about the benevolence of the state and the promise of direct intervention (Allen, 1981; Cullen and Gendreau, 1989). Second, an emerging social science, informed by labelling and critical/Marxist approaches, embraced antipsychological and often antiempirical themes (Andrews, 1990; Andrews and Wormith, 1989). These emergent perspectives played an important role in legitimating the decision of many academic criminologists and juridical policymakers to declare rehabilitation fully bankrupt. Most noteworthy was Robert Martinson's (1974: 25) conclusion that "the rehabilitative efforts that have been reported so far have had no appreciable effect on recidivism." In short order, with the blessing of a major academy of science (Sechrest et al., 1979), the notion that "nothing works" became accepted doctrine (Walker, 1989). "Nothing works" satisfied conservative political reactions to the apparent disorder of the 1960s, liberal sorrow over perceived failures of the Great Society, and the ideological persuasions of those academicians whose truly social visions of deviance asserted that only radical social change could have an impact on crime.

In the 1980s, however, rehabilitation and respect for evidence made at least a modest comeback. As will be noted, a number of revisionist scholars have observed that the marriage of conservative politics and leftist social science—in both its "discouraged liberal" and "critical/Marxist" versions—has neither improved justice nor increased crime control. In any case, it is our thesis that evidence of effective treatment was there from the earliest reviews, now is

mounting, and constitutes a persuasive case against the "nothing works" doctrine.

Even so, criticisms of rehabilitation are not in short supply. As Walker (1989:231) comments: "It is wishful thinking to believe that additional research is going to uncover a magic key that has somehow been overlooked for 150 years." Other scholars—as exemplified most notably and recently by Whitehead and Lab (1989; Lab and Whitehead, 1988)—continue to participate in the scientific exchange on intervention and to present evidence ostensibly bolstering the "nothing works" message.

Whitehead and Lab's (1989) report is very much in the tradition of the reviews and conclusions that are challenged in this paper. Before detailing our position, however, we note that the Whitehead and Lab review is important for several reasons. First, having searched the psychological, sociological, and criminological journals, they produced an impressively complete set of controlled evaluations of juvenile treatment for the years 1975 to 1984. They coded the setting of treatment and distinguished among diversion programs (within and outside the juvenile justice system), probation and other community-based programs, and residential programming. Moreover, they coded type of treatment within these settings as either behavioral or nonbehavioral and considered recency year of publication) and quality of research design. Focused exclusively upon evaluations employing recidivism as an outcome variable, their conclusions actually had to do with crime control. Clearly then, the negative conclusion of Whitehead and Lab is worthy of serious consideration by those in criminal justice.

Most serious, and unlike most earlier reviews—including the Martinson (1974) review—portions of the Whitehead and Lab (1989) paper support a very firm version of "nothing works." That is, the methodological, clinical, and sampling caveats typically listed by earlier reviewers were discounted systematically in Whitehead and Lab (1989). Regarding quality of the research, the more rigorous studies were reported to find correctional treatment to have effects even more negative than did the less rigorous studies. As to standards of effectiveness, Whitehead and Lab advised that their standard (a phi coefficient of .20 or greater) was so generous that evidence favorable to treatment would certainly have emerged had positive evidence, in fact, existed. In regard to type of treatment, they admitted that behavioral forms of intervention may be effective with outcomes other than recidivism, but they found behavioral treatment to be no more effective than nonbehavioral approaches in the control of recidivism.

Our meta-analysis includes, but is not confined to, the Whitehead and Lab (1989) sample of studies. Challenging sweeping conclusions regarding program ineffectiveness, we reaffirm a line of analysis for developing meaningful conclusions on the conditions under which programs will work. Our challenge is informed by considerations of research and theory on the causes of crime and by research and theory on behavioral influence processes. In particular, a growing number of scholars and practitioners now agree with what was always the starting point of the Gluecks (1950), the Grants (1959), Glaser (1974), and Palmer (1975): The effectiveness of correctional treatment is dependent upon what is delivered to whom in particular settings. Certainly that has been our view[1] and the view of many other reviewers and commentators.[2]

Clinically Relevant and Psychologically Informed Programming, Evaluation, and Meta-Analysis

The psychology of criminal conduct recognizes multiple sources of variation in criminal recidivism (Andrews, 1980, 1983; Andrews and Kiessling, 1980; Andrews et al., 1990; Cullen and Gendreau, 1989; Hoge and Andrews, 1986; Palmer, 1983; Warren, 1969).

These major sources of variation are found through analyses of the main and interactive effects of (a) preservice characteristics of offenders, (b) characteristics of correctional workers, (c) specifics of the content and process of services planned and delivered, and (d) intermediate changes in the person and circumstances of individual offenders. Logically, these major sources of variation in outcome reside within the conditions established by the specifics of a judicial disposition or criminal sanction. Thus, there is little reason to expect that variation among settings or sanctions will have an impact on recidivism except in interaction with offender characteristics and through the mediators of intervention process and intermediate change. We develop this "criminal sanction" hypothesis first and then compare it with hypotheses regarding the effectiveness of a correctional service approach that attends to preservice case characteristics, to the process and content of intervention, and to intermediate change within particular sanctions.

In Theory, Why Should Criminal Sanctioning Work?

A focus upon variation in official disposition is a reflection of one or more of the three sets of theoretical perspectives known as *just deserts, labelling,* and *deterrence.* The just deserts or justice set is not overly concerned with recidivism, but on occasion the assumption surfaces that unjust processing may motivate additional criminal activity (Schur, 1973:129). It appears, however, that the devaluation of rehabilitation—in the interest of increasing "just" processing—has been associated with increased punishment and decreased treatment but not with reduced recidivism (Cullen and Gilbert, 1982; Leschied et al., 1988).

The labelling and deterrence perspectives actually yield conflicting predictions regarding the outcomes of different dispositions (Rausch, 1983). Labelling theory suggests that less involvement in the criminal justice system is better than more (because the stigma is less), while deterrence theory suggests the opposite (because fear of punishment is greater). The assumptions of both labelling (Andrews and Wormith, 1989; Wellford, 1975) and deterrence (Gendreau and Ross, 1981) have been subjected to logical and empirical review, and neither perspective is yet able to offer a well-developed psychology of criminal conduct. Basic differentiations among and within levels and types of sanctions have yet to be worked out (Smith and Gartin, 1989), type of offender is likely a crucial moderating variable (Klein, 1986), and the social psychology of "processing" is only now being explored (Link et al., 1989).

In Fact, Does Criminal Sanctioning Work?

To our knowledge, not a single review of the effects of judicial sanctioning on criminal recidivism has reached positive conclusions except when the extremes of incapacitation are tested or when additional reference is made to moderators (e.g., type of offender) or mediators (e.g., the specifics of intervention). Reading Kirby (1954), Bailey (1966), Logan (1972), and Martinson (1974) reveals the obvious but unstated fact that their negative conclusions regarding "treatment" reflected primarily the negligible impact of variation in sanctions such as probation and incarceration. Thus, we agree with Palmer (1975): The main effects of criminal sanctions on recidivism have been slight and inconsistent.

This hypothesis is extended to judicial "alternatives," because there are no solid reasons for expecting alternative punishments, such as community service or restitution, to have an impact on recidivism. Any anticipated rehabilitative benefit of "alternatives" is based on the hope that offenders will learn that crime has negative consequences, and yet the enhancement of cognitive and inter-personal skills (e.g., future-orientation and perspective-taking) are dependent upon systematic modeling, reinforcement, and graduated practice (Ross and Fabiano, 1985). Given little reason to expect much from the incidental learning opportunities provided by such sanctions as restitution, correctional treatment service is a crucial supplement to a criminal justice approach that is preoccupied with avoiding stigma while delivering "just" and "innovative alternative" punishment.

Correctional Treatment Services

Reviewers of the literature have routinely found that at least 40% of the better-controlled evaluations of correctional treatment services reported positive effects (Andrews et al., 1990). For example, considering only the better-controlled studies, the proportion of studies reporting positive evidence was 75% (3/4) in Kirby (1954), 59% (13/22) in Bailey (1966), 50% (9/18) in Logan (1972), 78% (14/18) in Logan when Type of Treatment × Type of Client interactions are considered, 48% (39/82) in Palmer's (1975) retabulation of studies reviewed by Martinson (1974), 86% (82/95) in Gendreau and Ross (1979), and 47% (40/85) in Lab and Whitehead (1988). This pattern of results strongly supports exploration of the idea that some service programs are working with at least some offenders under some circumstances, and we think that helpful linkages among case, service, and outcome are suggested by three principles known as risk, need, and responsivity (Andrews et al., 1990).

The Risk Principle and Selection of Level of Service

The risk principle suggests that higher levels of service are best reserved for higher risk cases and that low-risk cases are best assigned to minimal service. In the literature at least since the Gluecks (1950), the risk principle has been restated on many occasions (e.g., Glaser, 1974). Although the parameters remain to be established, evidence favoring the risk principle continues to grow (Andrews et al., 1990). In brief, when actually explored, the effects of treatment typically are found to be greater among higher risk cases than among lower risk cases. This is expected unless the need and/or responsivity principles are violated.

The Need Principle and Selection of Appropriate Intermediate Targets

Risk factors may be static or dynamic in nature, and psychology is particularly interested in those dynamic risk factors that, when changed, are associated with *subsequent* variation in the chances of criminal conduct. Clinically, dynamic risk factors are called *criminogenic needs*, and guidelines for their assessment are described elsewhere (Andrews, 1983; Andrews et al., 1990).

The most promising intermediate targets include changing antisocial attitudes, feelings, and peer associations; promoting familial affection in combination with enhanced parental monitoring and supervision; promoting identification with anticriminal role models; increasing self-control and self-management skills; replacing the skills of lying, stealing, and aggression with other, more prosocial skills; reducing chemical dependencies; and generally shifting the density of rewards and costs for criminal and noncriminal activities in familial, academic, vocational, and other behavioral settings.[3] Theoretically, modifying contingencies within the home, school, and work by way of an increased density of reward for noncriminal activity may reduce motivation for crime and increase the costs of criminal activity through having more to lose (Hunt and Azrin, 1973).

Less-promising targets include increasing self-esteem without touching antisocial pro-

pensity (e.g., Wormith, 1984), increasing the cohesiveness of antisocial peer groups (e.g., Klein, 1971), improving neighborhood-wide living conditions without reaching high-risk families (the East Side, Midcity, and other community projects in Klein, 1971, and Schur, 1973), and attempts to focus on vague personal/emotional problems that have not been linked with recidivism (Andrews and Kiessling, 1980).

The Responsivity Principle and Selection of Type of Service

The responsivity principle has to do with the selection of styles and modes of service that are (a) capable of influencing the specific types of intermediate targets that are set with offenders and (b) appropriately matched to the learning styles of offenders. We begin with the general literature on the treatment of offenders and then turn to specific Responsivity × Service interactions.

Responsivity: General principles of effective service. Drawing upon our earlier review (Andrews et al., 1990), appropriate types of service typically, but not exclusively, involve the use of behavioral and social learning principles of interpersonal influence, skill enhancement, and cognitive change. Specifically, they include modeling, graduated practice, rehearsal, role playing, reinforcement, resource provision, and detailed verbal guidance and explanations (making suggestions, giving reasons, cognitive restructuring). Elsewhere (Andrews and Kiessling, 1980), we describe the applications of these practices as (a) use of authority (a "firm but fair" approach and definitely not interpersonal domination or abuse), (b) anticriminal modeling and reinforcement (explicit reinforcement and modeling of alternatives to procriminal styles of thinking, feeling, and acting), and (c) concrete problem solving and systematic skill training for purposes of increasing reward levels in anticriminal settings. High levels of advocacy and brokerage are also indicated as long as the receiving agency actually offers appropriate service. Finally, Andrews and Kiessling (1980) recommended that service deliverers relate to offenders in interpersonally warm, flexible, and enthusiastic ways while also being clearly supportive of anticriminal attitudinal and behavioral patterns. Interestingly, social learning approaches receive strong, albeit indirect, support from the prediction literature on the causal modeling of delinquency (Akers and Cochran, 1985; Jessor and Jessor, 1977).

Responsivity: Ineffective service. Some types and styles of services should be avoided under most circumstances (Andrews et al., 1990). Generally, programming for groups is to be approached very cautiously because the opening up of communication within offender groups may well be criminogenic (Andrews, 1980). In group and residential programming, clinicians must gain control over the contingencies of interaction so that anticriminal, rather than procriminal, patterns are exposed and reinforced (Buehler et al., 1966). For example, Agee's (1986) programmatic structures supporting positive change may be contrasted with the failure of unstructured, peer-oriented group counseling and permissive, relationship-oriented milieu approaches. The failure of these unstructured approaches is well documented in open community settings (e.g., Faust, 1965; Klein, 1971), in group homes operating according to the essentially nondirective guidelines of "guided group interaction" (Stephenson and Scarpitti, 1974:Ch. 8), in hospitals (Craft et al., 1966), and in prisons (Kassebaum et al., 1971; Murphy, 1972). There are also no convincing theoretical grounds for believing that young people will be "scared straight" (Finckenauer, 1982). Fear of official punishment is not one of the more important correlates of delinquency (Johnson, 1979), and yelling at people is counter to the relationship principle of effective service (Andrews, 1980).

Finally, traditional psychodynamic and nondirective client-centered therapies are to be avoided within general samples of offenders (Andrews et al., 1990). These therapies are designed to free people from the personally inhibiting controls of "superego" and "society," but neurotic misery and over control are not criminogenic problems for a majority of offenders. Authorities such as Freud (in his introductory lectures on psychoanalysis, 1953) and the Gluecks (in their classic *Unraveling*, 1950) warned us about evocative and relationship-dependent psychodynamic approaches with antisocial cases.

Specific responsivity considerations. The success of highly verbal, evocative, and relationship-dependent services seems to be limited to clients with high levels of interpersonal, self-reflective, and verbal skills. The "I-Level" (Harris, 1988) and "Conceptual Level" (Reitsma-Street and Leschied, 1988) systems provide guidance regarding the types of offenders who may respond in positive ways to services that are less structured than those we have been describing as appropriate for antisocial samples in general.

Summary

Our clinically relevant and psychologically informed principles of treatment predict that criminal sanctioning without attention to the delivery of correctional service will relate to recidivism minimally. Additionally, we suggest that the delivery of services, regardless of criminal sanction or setting, is unproductive if those services are inconsistent with the principles of risk, need, and responsivity. Positively, we predict that appropriate treatment—treatment that is delivered to higher risk cases, that targets criminogenic need, and that is matched with the learning styles of offenders—will reduce recidivism.

Method

Samples of Studies

We subjected 45 of the 50 studies included in the Whitehead and Lab (1989) review to content and meta-analysis.[4] The Whitehead and Lab sample included only studies of juvenile treatment that appeared in professional journals between 1975 and 1984 and that presented effects of treatment on binary (less-more) measures of recidivism. Studies that focused on imprisonment or the treatment of substance abuse were not included.

We also explored a second sample of studies in order to check on the generalizability of any findings based on the Whitehead and Lab sample. Sample 2 included 35 studies in our research files as of February 1989 that were not included in the Whitehead and Lab set but had employed binary measures of recidivism. Studies in sample 2 date from the 1950s through 1989, but they are not purported to be a representative sample of any particular time period. Sample 2 provides a convenient means of exploring, albeit tentatively, how well conclusions based on the Whitehead and Lab sample may generalize to adult samples.

Estimates of Treatment Effect

The Whitehead and Lab sample yielded a total of 87 2 X 2 contingency tables reflecting the strength and direction of the association between two levels of treatment and recidivism-nonrecidivism. Whitehead and Lab, on the other hand, tabled a single phi coefficient for each study. With our approach, distinct phi coefficients were computed when distinct samples and distinct treatments were reported in a paper (e.g., Klein et al., 1977), and rather than compare two "appropriate" styles of service, we compared each service with its respective control (e.g., Jesness, 1975; Mitchell, 1983; in the latter study we estimated that the experimental recidivists were averaging twice the number of new offenses found among control recidivists). Tests of Type of Offender X Type of Treatment interactions were represented only incidentally in Whitehead and Lab. In our report, services to higher and lower risk cases yield separate estimates of treatment effects.

Sample 2 yielded 67 treatment-recidivism tables, 44 based on studies of juveniles and 23 based on adults. (Romig's 1976 analysis of parole supervision is entered as part of the Whitehead and Lab sample, and the analysis of months incarcerated is entered as part of sample 2). . . .

Content Analysis

The potential covariates of phi estimates were coded as follows:

1. Setting: The Whitehead and Lab codes for setting were accepted uncritically: nonsystem diversion, system diversion, probation/parole/community corrections, and institutional/residential. Preliminary analyses confirmed that the effects on phi coefficients of the three different community settings were statistically indistinguishable. Hence, setting was employed as a two-level, community-residential factor in further analyses. . . .

2. Year of publication: before the 1980s/in the 1980s.

3. Quality of research design: Studies employing random assignment were coded "stronger design." Nonrandom assignment was coded "weaker design," except when information on risk factors (e.g., prior offense or "bad attitude") allowed the computation of separate treatment comparisons for lower and higher risk cases. When risk was so controlled, the design was coded "stronger."

4. Sample of studies: Whitehead and Lab/ sample 2.

5. Justice system: Juvenile system/adult system.

6. Behavioral intervention: Programs described as behavioral by the authors of an evaluation study were coded "behavioral," as were those that systematically employed behavioral techniques. [5]

7. Type of treatment: Following the principles discussed above, the four levels of type of treatment were as follows:

a. Criminal sanctions: This code involved variation in judicial disposition, imposed at the front end of the correctional process and not involving deliberate variation in rehabilitative service (e.g., restitution, police cautioning versus regular processing, less versus more probation, and probation versus custody).

b. Inappropriate correctional service: Inappropriate service included (1) service delivery to lower risk cases and/or mismatching according to a need/responsivity system, (2) nondirective relationship-dependent and/or unstructured psychodynamic counseling, (3) all milieu and group approaches with an emphasis on within-group communication and without a clear plan for gaining control over procriminal modeling and reinforcement, (4) nondirective or poorly targeted academic and vocational approaches, and (5) "scared straight."

c. Appropriate correctional service: Appropriate service included (1) service delivery to higher risk cases, (2) all behavioral programs (except those involving delivery of service to lower risk cases), (3) comparisons reflecting specific responsivity-treatment comparisons, and (4) nonbehavioral programs that clearly stated that criminogenic need was targeted and that structured intervention was employed.[6]

d. Unspecified correctional service: Unspecified service was a residual set for those comparisons involving treatments that we could not confidently label appropriate or inappropriate.

Hypotheses

Our first hypothesis is that Type of Treatment is the major source of variation in estimates of effect size (phi coefficients).[7] Specifically, the contributions of Type of Treatment to the prediction of effect size will exceed the predictive contributions of year of publication, quality of design, setting, behavioral-nonbehavioral intervention, justice system (juvenile or adult), and sample of studies examined.

Our second hypothesis is that appropriate correctional service will yield an average estimate of impact on recidivism that is positive and exceeds those of criminal sanctions, unspecified service, and inappropriate service.

Results and Discussion

A preliminary comparison of the two samples of studies was conducted on various control variables. The comparisons reflected an obvious concern that any systematic differences between the Whitehead and Lab sample and sample 2 be documented. Overall, apart from the inclusion of studies of adult treatment in sample 2, the two samples of studies were found to be reasonably comparable across the various potential predictors of treatment effect size explored in this paper (see row 2 of the intercorrelation matrix in Table 22.1).[8]

Hypothesis 1: Relative Predictive Potential of Type of Treatment

Inspection of the first column of Table 22.1 reveals that the correlation between Type of Treatment and phi coefficients was strong (Eta = .69) and, with simultaneous control introduced for each of the other variables through analysis of covariance techniques in a multiple classification analysis, the correlation increased to .72 (Beta). The only other significant unadjusted predictor of phi coefficients was Sample of Studies (.18, unadjusted; .15, adjusted). With controls for Type of Treatment introduced, the magnitude of correlation with phi coefficients increased to significant levels for Year of Publication (from .09 to .18) and for Setting (from −.07 to −.16).

Table 22.1
Intercorrelation Matrix, Correlations with Phi Coefficients (N = 154), and Mean Phi Coefficients at Each Level of Each Variable

	A Type of Treatment	B Sample of Studies	C Justice System	D Year of Publication	E Quality of Design	F Setting
A.		.08	.01	−.14	.10	.11
B.			.48**	.11	.14	.21*
C.				.23*	.15	−.01
D.					−.10	−.33**
E.						−.17
Simple Unadjusted Correlation with Phi (Mean Phi = .104, SD = .234)						
	.69**	.18*	.02	.09	−.03	−.07
Unadjusted Mean Phi Coefficient (n) at Each Level of Each Variable						
1 −.07(30)		.07(87)	.10(131)	.08(76)	.11(81)	.11(119)
2. −.06(38)		.15(67)	.11(23)	.13(78)	.10(73)	.07(35)
3. .13(32)						
4. .30(54)						
F Values for Unadjusted Effects						
45.62**		5.27*	0.49	1.33	0.11	0.74
Partial Correlation with Phi, Controlling for Other Variables						
.72**		.15*	.02	.18*	−.07	−.16*
Adjusted Mean Phi Coefficient (n) at Each Level of Each Variable						
1. −.08(30)		.07(87)	.10(131)	.06(76)	.11(81)	.12(119)
2. −.07(38)		.14(67)	.11(23)	.14(78)	.08(73)	.03(35)
3. .10(32)						
4. .32(54)						
F Values for adjusted Effects						
57.13**		6.99*	0.33	9.80**	1.18	7.43**

*p <.05   **p <.01

Note: The levels of the variables are as follows: Type of Treatment (criminal sanctions, inappropriate service, unspecified service, appropriate service), Sample of Studies (Whitehead and Lab, sample 2), Justice System (juvenile, adult), Year of Publication (before 1980, 1980s), Quality of Research Design (weaker, stronger), and Setting (community, institutional/residential).

Comparisons from sample 2, recency of publication and community-based treatment, were each associated with relatively positive effects of treatment. These trends, however, were overwhelmed by Type of Treatment. In a stepwise multiple regression, the only variables contributing significantly ($p < .05$) to variation in phi estimates were Type of Treatment (beta = .69) and Year of Publication (beta = .19), F $(^2/_{151})$ = 68.01, $p < .000$, adjusted R square = .47. In summary, our first hypothesis was strongly supported: Type of Treatment was clearly the strongest of the correlates of effect size sampled in this study.

Hypothesis 2: The Importance of Appropriate Correctional Service

As described above, the main effect of Type of Treatment on phi estimates was strong and positive, with or without adjustment for control variables. Scheffe tests confirmed that the mean phi coefficient for appropriate correctional service (.30, n = 54) was significantly ($p < 0.05$) greater than that for criminal sanctions (−.07, n = 30), inappropriate service (−.06, n = 38), and unspecified service (.13, n = 32). In addition, Scheffe tests revealed that the average effect of unspecified correctional service significantly exceeded the mean phi coefficients for criminal sanctions and inappropriate service.

Mean phi coefficients for each of the four types of treatment are presented in Table 22.2 at each of the two levels of the various control variables. Inspection reveals a robust correlation between Type of Treatment and effects on recidivism at each level of Sample of Studies, Justice System, Year of Publication, Design, and Setting.

The only variable to interact significantly ($p < 0.05$) with Type of Treatment was Year of Publication. It appears that criminal sanctions yielded more negative phi estimates in the earlier literature than in the more recent literature −.16 versus −.02, F [$^1/_{28}$] = 8.98. $p <$ .006. This reflects a greater representation of residential studies in the earlier years (the negative implications of residential programs will be discussed below). More interestingly, studies of appropriate correctional treatment in the 1980s yielded a much higher mean phi estimate than did earlier studies of appropriate treatment (.40 versus .24, F[$^1/_{52}$] = 8.40, $p <$ .005). Most likely, this reflects three trends. First, the earlier studies included what are now recognized to be unsophisticated applications of token economy systems (see Ross and McKay, 1976). Second, studies of the 1980s paid greater attention to cognitive variables (Ross and Fabiano, 1985). Third, the positive effects of short term behavioral family counseling have been replicated in the 1980s (Gordon et al., 1988). In summary, Hypothesis 2 was supported to a stronger degree than was initially anticipated: Both appropriate and unspecified correctional services were significantly more effective in reducing recidivism than were criminal sanctions and inappropriate service.

Note on Behavioral Intervention

The use of behavioral methods was a major element in the coding of appropriateness according to the principle of responsivity. Not surprisingly, in view of our coding rules, 95% ($^{38}/_{41}$) of the behavioral treatments were coded as appropriate treatment and 70% ($^{38}/_{54}$) of the appropriate treatments were behavioral. Thus, the correlation between Behavioral Intervention and Type of Treatment was substantial ($r = .62$). As expected, Behavioral Intervention, on its own, yielded a significantly greater mean phi coefficient than did nonbehavioral treatment. The mean phi coefficients were .29 (SD = .23, n = 41) and .04 (SD = .20, n = 113) for behavioral and nonbehavioral interventions, respectively (F [$^1/_{152}$] = 46.09, $p <$ .000, Eta = .48). Once controls were introduced for Type of Treatment, however, the contribution of Behavioral Intervention was reduced to nonsignificant levels, F ($^1/_{151}$) < 1.00, Beta = .07. It appears, then, that use of behavioral methods contributes to the reduction of recidivism, but those contributions are subsumed by the broader implications of risk, need, and responsivity as represented in our Type of Treatment variable.

Note on Residential Programming

The minor but statistically significant adjusted main effect of setting is displayed in column six of Table 22.1. This trend should not be overemphasized, but the relatively weak performance of appropriate correctional service in residential facilities is notable from Table 22.2 (mean phi estimate of .20 compared with .35 for treatment within community settings, F[$^1/_{52}$] = 5.89, $p <$ .02). In addition, inappropriate service performed particularly poorly in residential settings compared with community settings (−.15

Table 22.2

The Effect of Type of Treatment on Recidivism at Each Level of the Control Variables: Mean Phi Coefficients (N)

	Criminal Sanctions	Correctional Service		
		Inapp.	Unspec.	Appropriate
Sample of Studies				
Whitehead and Lab	−.04(21)	−.11(20)	.09(16)	.24(30)
Sample 2	−.13(9)	−.02(18)	.17(16)	.37(24)
Justice System				
Juvenile	−.06(26)	−.07(31)	.13(29)	.29(45)
Adult	−.12(4)	−.03(7)	.13(3)	.34(9)
Year of Publication				
Before the 1980s	−.16(10)	−.09(22)	.17(11)	.24(33)
1980s	−.02(20)	−.03(16)	.11(21)	.40(21)
Quality of Research Design				
Weaker	−.07(21)	−.04(10)	.15(18)	.32(26)
Stronger	−.07(9)	−.08(22)	.11(14)	.29(28)
Setting				
Community	−.05(24)	−.14(31)	.12(27)	.35(37)
Institution/Res.	−.14(6)	−.15(7)	.21(5)	.20(17)
Behavioral Intervention				
No	−.07(30)	−.06(36)	.13(31)	.27(16)
Yes	—	−.09(2)	.23(1)	.31(38)
Overall Mean Phi	−.07(30)	−.06(38)	.13(32)	.30(54)
S.D.	.14	.15	.16	.19
Mean Phi Adjusted for Other Variables	−.08(30)	−.07(38)	.10(32)	.32(54)

versus −.04, $F[1/36] = 3.74$, $p < .06$). Thus, it seems that institutions and residential settings may dampen the positive effects of appropriate service while augmenting the negative impact of inappropriate service. This admittedly tentative finding does not suggest that appropriate correctional services should not be applied in institutional and residential settings. Recall that appropriate service was more effective than inappropriate service in all settings.

Conclusions

The meta-analysis has revealed considerable order in estimates of the magnitude of the impact of treatment upon recidivism. As predicted, the major source of variation in effects on recidivism was the extent to which service was appropriate according to the principles of risk, need, and responsivity. Appropriate correctional service appears to work better than criminal sanctions not involving rehabilitative service and better than services less consistent with our a priori principles of effective rehabilitation. This review has convinced us that the positive trends that we and others detected in the literature of the 1960s and early 1970s were indeed worthy of serious application and evaluation. There is a reasonably solid clinical and research basis for the political reaffirmation of rehabilitation (Cullen and Gilbert, 1982).

The importance of clinical and theoretical relevance in programming and in meta-analysis has been demonstrated—the sanction and treatment services should be differentiated, and the action in regard to recidivism appears to reside in appropriate treatment. Much, however, remains to be done. We look forward to critiques and revisions of the principles of risk, need, and responsivity as stated and applied herein. What comparisons were assigned to what analytic categories is described in our report and is thereby easily and appropriately the focus of critical review. . . . Reserved for future reports are the many issues surrounding therapeutic integrity (Gendreau and Ross, 1979), the measurement of recidivism (Andrews, 1983), and methodological issues such as sample size (Lipsey, 1989). Similarly, we anticipate exploring in detail the value of alternatives to ordinary least squares analyses. . . . Gender effects and the treatment of sex offenders, substance abusers, and inmates of long-term institutions require detailed analyses. Toward these ends, our meta-analytic data base is being extended. Our focus here, however, remains on type of service and effect size.

Of immediate concern is the meaning of an average phi coefficient of .30 for comparisons involving appropriate correctional service. First, until convinced otherwise, we will assume that an average phi of .30 is more positive, clinically and socially, than the mean effects of the alternatives of sanctioning without regard for service or servicing without regard to the principles of effective correctional service. Casual review of recidivism rates will reveal that, on average, appropriate treatment cut recidivism rates by about 50% (in fact, the mean reduction was 53.06%, SD = 26.49). Thus, we do not think that the positive effects are "minimal." Second, the correlation between effect size estimates and type of treatment approached .70. Correlations of this magnitude are unlikely to reflect "lucky outliers" (Greenwood, 1988), although more systematic sources of error may indeed inflate correlation coefficients. Third, issues surrounding the assessment of the clinical and social significance of diverse measures of effect size are indeed

worthy of ongoing research. Future reports on our expanding data bank will compare various estimates of effect size, including some direct estimates of clinical/ social significance. For now, we are interested in discovering ethical routes to strengthened treatment effects, but we are not talking about magical cures.

Critics of rehabilitation are correct when they note that the average correlation between treatment and recidivism is not 1.00. At the same time, critics might be asked to report on the variation that their "preferred" variable shares with recidivism. For example, if their preferred variable is social class, they may be reminded that some reviewers have estimated that the average correlation between class and crime is about –.09 (Tittle et al., 1978). If their preferred approach is incapacitation or community crime prevention, they may be reminded of the minimal effects so far reported for these strategies (Rosenbaum, 1988; Visher, 1987). Critics, be they supporters of social class or incapacitation, likely will respond with examples of particular studies that yielded high correlations with indicators of crime. We remind them that the largest correlations are no better estimates of the average effect than are the least favorable estimates. We also remind them that the positive evidence regarding appropriate rehabilitative service comes not from cross-sectional research—the typical research strategy of critics of rehabilitation—but from deliberate and socially sanctioned approximations of truly experimental ideals. Finally, we remind the critics that one can be interested in the effects of class, punishment, and prevention programs on individual and aggregated crime rates while maintaining multiple interests and without letting one interest justify dismissal of the value of another.

This meta-analysis has done more than uncover evidence that supported our a priori biases regarding the importance of appropriate correctional service. The finding that the effects of inappropriate service appeared to be particularly negative in residential settings while the positive effects of appropriate service were attenuated was something of a surprise. While sensitive to the difficulties of working with antisocial groups, we did not predict this incidental affirmation of a widely shared preference for community over residential programming. Institutions and group homes, however, remain important components of correctional systems and hence active but thoughtful service is indicated. The literature should be carefully scrutinized in order to avoid inappropriate service, and follow-up services in the community may be necessary in order to maximize effectiveness. Finally, the suppressive impact of residential programming suggests that the negative effects of custody are better established than we anticipated.

The effect of the quality of the research design on estimates of effect size was relatively minor. Even if some design problems do inflate effect size estimates (Davidson et al., 1984; Lipsey, 1989), the interesting finding was that comparisons involving more and less rigorous research designs agreed as to what types of treatment were most effective. Program managers and frontline clinicians who find truly randomized groups to be practically or ethically impossible may consider conducting an evaluation that approximates the ideals of a true experiment. In particular, we strongly endorse the use of designs that introduce controls for the preservice risk levels of clients and that actually report on risk × service interactions. In addition, even evaluations that rely upon comparisons of clients who complete or do not complete treatment may be valuable.

Finally, the number of evaluative studies of correctional service should increase dramatically over the next decade. Although millions of young people were processed by juvenile justice systems during the past decade, the total number of papers in the Whitehead and Lab (1989) set that involved systematic study of appropriate service was 21. Were it not for behavioral psychologists, the number of papers involving appropriate

service would have been nine. From a positive perspective, there is renewed interest, vigor, and sensitivity in the study of the psychology of criminal conduct (Andrews and Wormith, 1989; Loeber and Stouthamer-Loeber, 1987; Wilson and Hernstein, 1985) and of correctional service and prevention (e.g., Andrews et al., 1990; Cullen and Gendreau, 1988; Currie, 1989; Gendreau and Ross, 1987). There are solid reasons to focus in ethical and humane ways on the client and the quality of service delivered within just dispositions.

Study Questions

1. According to the authors, does criminal sanctioning work?

2. Explain the risk, need, and responsivity principles.

3. Describe the methods, research design, data collection methods, sample, and measures used by the authors to study correctional treatment programs.

4. Summarize the findings and conclusions reached by the authors.

Notes

1. Andrews (1980, 1983, 1990), Andrews and Kiessling (1980), Andrews et al. (1990), Cullen and Gendreau (1989), Gendreau and Ross (1979, 1981, 1987).

2. Basta and Davidson (1988), Currie (1989), Garrett (1985), Geismar and Wood (1985), Greenwood and Zimring (1985), Izzo and Ross (1990), Lipsey (1989), Martinson (1979), Mayer et al. (1986), Palmer (1983), Ross and Fabiano (1985).

3. For example, Andrews et al. (1990), Andrews and Wormith (1989), Glueck and Glueck (1950), Johnson (1979), Loeber and Stouthamer-Loeber (1987), Wilson and Hernstein (1985).

4. Douds and Collingwood (1978) and Collingwood and Genthner (1980) were excluded because their samples appeared to overlap those of either Collingwood et al. (1976) or Williams (1984). Similarly, Fo and O'Donnell (1975) was dropped because of overlap with

O'Donnell et al. (1979). The Baer et al. (1975) report on Outward Bound was excluded because the independent variable did not involve variation in service. Beal and Duckro (1977) was dropped because the outcome seemed to be court proceedings on the offense that led to a program referral.

5. The interventions of Hackler and Hagan (1975) were coded as nonbehavioral. William's (1984) Dallas program was coded behavioral in our study, in line with Whitehead and Lab's coding of the Collingwood et al. (1976) report on the same program as behavioral. Both studies of restitution were coded nonbehavioral in our study (only one of which was coded nonbehavioral by Whitehead and Lab). The Ross and Fabiano behavioral skills program was coded as unspecified because it was a comparison condition for a more appropriate program.

6. Treatments admitted to the "appropriate" category by criterion "4" were appropriate according to the principles of need and responsivity (although some readers might disagree): Kelly et al. (1979) encouraged delinquents to explore alternative values and behavior patterns; the transactional program (Jesness, 1975) established individualized targets based on criminogenic need; the family counseling program of McPherson et al. (1983) targeted discipline and self-management; Bachara and Zaba (1978) focused on specific learning problems; Shore and Massimo (1979) studied very intensive, highly individualized, vocationally oriented counseling. Some difficult calls, which we ultimately coded as unspecified, included the following: Druckman's (1979) family counseling, which hinted at a nondirective client-centered approach but lacked a clear statement of same; the paraprofessional advocacy program of Seidman et al. (1980), Wade et al.'s (1977) family program, and Sowles and Gill's (1970) counseling programs all included references to both d. Unspecified correctional service: Unspecified service was a residual set for those comparisons involving treatments that we could not confidently label appropriate or inappropriate. Some "treatments" in Rausch (1983) may have involved unspecified service components, but they were assigned to the criminal sanction set in the spirit of the Rausch analysis of labelling and deterrence theory.

7. Reliability and validity in coding the type of treatment are obvious concerns. One of our ongoing research efforts involves building a psychometrically sound instrument that can be used to assess the correctional appropriateness not simply of printed program descriptions but also of ongoing programs. The psychometrics of this instrument will be the focus of future reports. . . .

8. The Whitehead and Lab sample (n = 87) and sample 2 (n = 67) were virtually identical in the proportion of tests falling in the three categories of treatment services: inappropriate ($20/87$ vs. $16/67$), unspecified ($16/87$ vs. $16/67$), and appropriate ($30/87$ vs. $24/67$). The nonsignificant trend was an underrepresentation of comparisons involving criminal sanctions in sample 2 ($21/87$ vs. $9/67$, r = .08). Because the Whitehead and Lab sample was limited to studies of juveniles, there was an expected and substantial correlation between Justice System and Sample of Studies (phi = .48, $p < 0.01$). Not as obviously deducible from the descriptions of the samples provided in the methods section, sample 2 included a statistically significant overrepresentation of institution-based treatments (phi = .21, $p < .05$).

References

Adams, R. and H.J. Vetter, 1982, Social structure and psychodrama outcome: A ten-year follow-up. Journal of Offender Counseling, Services, and Rehabilitation 6:111–119.

Agee, V.L., 1986, Institutional treatment programs for the violent juvenile. In S. Apter and A. Goldstein (eds.), Youth Violence: Program and Prospects. Elmsford, N.Y.: Pergamon.

Akers, R.L. and J.K. Cochran, 1985, Adolescent marijuana use: A test of three theories of deviant behavior. Deviant Behavior 3:323–346.

Alexander, J.F., B. Cole, R.S. Schiavo, and B.V. Parsons, 1976, Systems-behavioral intervention with families of delinquents: Therapist characteristics, family behavior, and outcome. Journal of Consulting and Clinical Psychology 44:556–664.

Allen, F.A., 1981, The Decline of the Rehabilitative Ideal: Penal Policy and Social Purpose. New Haven: Yale University Press.

Andrews, D.A., 1980, Some experimental investigations of the principles of differential association through deliberate manipulations of the structure of service systems. American Sociological Review 45:448–462.

Andrews, D.A., 1983, The assessment of outcome in correctional samples. In M.L. Lambert, E.R.

Christensen, and S.S. DeIulio (eds.), The Measurement of Psychotherapy Outcome in Research and Evaluation. New York: John Wiley & Sons.

Andrews, D.A., 1990, Some criminological sources of antirehabilitation bias in the Report of the Canadian Sentencing Commission. Canadian Journal of Criminology. Forthcoming.

Andrews, D.A. and J.J. Kiessling, 1980, Program structure and effective correctional practices: A summary of the CaVIC research. In R.R. Ross and P. Gendreau (eds.), Effective Correctional Treatment. Toronto: Butterworth.

Andrews, D.A. and J.S. Wormith, 1989, Personality and crime: Knowledge destruction and construction in criminology. Justice Quarterly 6: 289–309.

Andrews, D.A., J.J. Kiessling, D. Robinson, and S. Mickus, 1986, The risk principle of case classification: An outcome evaluation with young adult probationers. Canadian Journal of Criminology 28:377–396.

Andrews, D.A., J. Bonta, and R.D. Hoge, 1990, Classification for effective rehabilitation: Rediscovering psychology. Criminal Justice and Behavior 17:19–52.

Bachara, G.H. and J.N. Zaba, 1978, Learning disabilities and juvenile delinquency. Journal of Learning Disabilities 11:242–246.

Baer, D.J., P.J. Jacobs, and F.E. Carr, 1975, Instructors' ratings of delinquents after Outward Bound survival training and their subsequent recidivism. Psychological Reports 36:547–553.

Bailey, W.C., 1966, Correctional outcome: An evaluation of 100 reports. Journal of Criminal Law, Criminology and Police Science 57:153–160.

Baird, S.C., R.C. Heinz, B.J. Bemus 1979, Project Report # 14: A Two Year Follow-up. Bureau of Community Corrections. Wisconsin: Department of Health and Social Services.

Barkwell, L.J. 1976, Differential treatment of juveniles on probation: An evaluative study. Canadian Journal of Criminology and Corrections 18:363–378.

Barton, C., J.F. Alexander, H. Waldron, C.W. Turner, and J. Warburton, 1985, Generalizing treatment effects of functional family therapy: Three replications. The American Journal of Family Therapy 13:16–26.

Basta, J.M. and W.S. Davidson, 1988, Treatment of juvenile offenders: Study outcomes since 1980. Behavioral Sciences and the Law 6:355–384.

Beal, D. and P. Duckro, 1977, Family counseling as an alternative to legal action for the juvenile status offender. Journal of Marriage and Family Counseling 3:77–81.

Berman, J.J., 1979, An experiment in parole supervision. Evaluation Quarterly 2:71–90.

Buckner, J.C. and M. Chesney-Lind 1983, Dramatic cures for juvenile crime: An evaluation of a prisoner-run delinquency prevention program. Criminal Justice and Behavior 10:227–247.

Buehler, R.E., G.R. Patterson, and J.M. Furniss, 1966, The reinforcement of behavior in institutional settings. Behavioral Research and Therapy 4:157–167.

Byles, J.A., 1981, Evaluation of an attendance center program for male juvenile probationers. Canadian Journal of Criminology 23:343–355.

Byles, J.A. and A. Maurice, 1979, The Juvenile Services Project: An experiment in delinquency control. Canadian Journal of Criminology 21:155–165.

Clarke, R.V.G. and D.B. Cornish, 1978, The effectiveness of residential treatment for delinquents. In L.A. Hersov, M. Berger, and D. Shaffer (eds.), Aggression and Anti-social Behavior in Childhood and Adolescence. Oxford: Pergamon.

Collingwood, T.R. and R.W. Genthner, 1980, Skills trainings as treatment for juvenile delinquents. Professional Psychology 11:591–598.

Collingwood, T.R., A.F. Douds, and H. Williams 1976, Juvenile diversion: The Dallas Police Department Youth Services Program. Federal Probation 40:23–27.

Craft, M., G. Stephenson, and C. Granger, 1966A, controlled trial of authoritarian and self-governing regimes with adolescent psychopaths. American Journal of Orthopsychiatry 34:543–554.

Cullen, F.T. and P. Gendreau 1989, The effectiveness of correctional rehabilitation. In L. Goodstein and D.L. MacKenzie (eds.), The American Prison: Issues in Research Policy. New York: Plenum.

Cullen, F.T. and K.E. Gilbert, 1982, Reaffirming Rehabilitation. Cincinnati: Anderson.

Cullen, F.T., J.B. Cullen and J.F. Woznick, 1988, Is rehabilitation dead? The myth of the punitive public. Journal of Criminal Justice 16:303–317.

Currie, E., 1989, Confronting crime: Looking toward the twenty-first century. Justice Quarterly 6:5–25.

Davidson, W.S. and T.R. Wolfred, 1977, Evaluation of a community-based behavior modification program for prevention of delinquency. Community Mental Health Journal 13:296–306.

Davidson, W.S., L. Gottschalk, L. Gensheimer, and J. Mayer, 1984, Interventions with Juvenile Delinquents: A Meta-analysis of Treatment Efficacy. Washington, D.C.: National Institute of Juvenile Justice and Delinquency Prevention.

Davidson, W.S., R. Redner, C. Blakely, C. Mitchell, and J. Emshoff, 1987, Diverson of juvenile offenders: An experimental comparison. Journal of Consulting and Clinical Psychology 55:68–75.

Douds, A.F. and T.R. Collingwood, 1978, Management by objectives: A successful application. Child Welfare 57:181–185.

Druckman, J.M., 1979A, Family-oriented policy and treatment program for female juvenile status offenders. Journal of Marriage and the Family 41:627–636.

Dutton, D.G., 1986, The outcome of court-mandated treatment for wife assault: A quasiexperimental evaluation. Violence and Victims 1:163–175.

Empey, L.T. and M.L. Erickson, 1972, The Provo Experiment: Evaluating Community Control of Delinquency. Lexington, Mass.: Lexington Books.

Farrington, D.P. and T. Bennett, 1981, Police cautioning of juveniles in London. British Journal of Criminology 21:123–135.

Faust, D., 1965, Group counseling of juveniles by staff without professional training in group work. Crime and Delinquency 11:349–354.

Finckenauer, J.O., 1982, Scared Straight and the Panacea Phenomenon. Englewood Cliffs, N.L: Prentice Hall.

Fo, W.S.O. and C.R. O'Donnell, 1975, The buddy system: Effect of community intervention on delinquent offenses. Behavior Therapy 6:522–524.

Freud, S., 1953A, General Introduction to Psychoanalysis. Reprint ed. New York: Permabooks.

Garrett, C.J., 1985, Effects of residential treatment of adjudicated delinquents: A meta-analysis. Journal of Research in Crime and Delinquency 22:287–308.

Geismar, L.L. and K.M. Wood, 1985, Family and Delinquency: Resocializing the Young Offender. New York: Human Sciences Press.

Gendreau, P. and R.R. Ross, 1979, Effectiveness of correctional treatment: Bibliotherapy for cynics. Crime and Delinquency 25:463–489.

Gendreau, P. and R.R. Ross 1981, Correctional potency: Treatment and deterrence on trial. In R. Roesch and R.R. Corrado (eds.), Evaluation and Criminal Justice Policy. Beverly Hills, Calif.: Sage.

Gendreau, P. and R.R. Ross, 1987, Revivification of rehabilitation: Evidence from the 1980s. Justice Quarterly 4:349–408.

Gensheimer, L.K., J.P. Mayer, R. Gottschalk, and W.S. Davidson, 1986, Diverting youth from the juvenile justice system: A meta-analysis of intervention efficacy. In S.J. Apter and A. Goldstein (eds.), Youth Violence: Programs and Prospects. Elmsford, N.Y.: Pergamon.

Gilbert, G.R., 1977, Alternate routes: A diversion project in the juvenile justice system. Evaluation Quarterly 1:301–318.

Glaser, D., 1974, Remedies for the key deficiency in criminal justice evaluation research. Journal of Research in Crime and Delinquency 11:144–153.

Glueck, S. and E.T. Glueck 1950, Unraveling Juvenile Delinquency. Cambridge, Mass.: Harvard University Press.

Gordon, D.A., J. Arbuthnot, K.E. Gustafson, and P. McGreen. 1988, Home-based behavioral systems family therapy with disadvantaged juvenile delinquents. Unpublished paper, Ohio University.

Grant, J.D., 1965, Delinquency treatment in an institutional setting. In H.C. Quay (ed.), Juvenile Delinquency: Research and Theory. Princeton, N.J.: Van Nostrand.

Grant, J.D. and M.Q. Grant, 1959A, Group dynamics approach to the treatment of nonconformists in the navy. Annals of the American Academy of Political and Social Science 322:126–135.

Greenwood, P.W., 1988, The Role of Planned Interventions in Studying the Desistance of Criminal Behavior in Longitudinal Study. Santa Monica, Calif.: Rand.

Greenwood, P.W. and F.E. Zimring, 1985, One More Chance: The Pursuit of Promising Intervention Strategies for Chronic Juvenile Offenders. Santa Monica, Calif.: Rand.

Gruher, M., 1979, Family counseling and the status offender. Juvenile and Family Court Journal 30:23–27.

Hackler, J.C. and J.L. Hagan, 1975, Work and teaching machines as delinquency prevention tools: A four-year follow-up. Social Service Review 49:92–106.

Harris, P.W., 1988, The interpersonal maturity level classification system: I-level. Criminal Justice and Behavior 15:58–77.

Hoge, R.D. and D.A. Andrews, 1986A, Model for conceptualizing interventions in social service. Canadian Psychology 27:332–341.

Horowitz, A. and M. Wasserman, 1979, The effect of social control on delinquent behavior: A longitudinal test. Sociological Focus 12:53–70.

Hunt, G.M. and N.H. Azrin, 1973A, Community-reinforcement approach to alcoholism. Behavior Research and Therapy 11:91–104.

Izzo, R.L. and R.R. Ross, 1990, Meta-analysis of rehabilitation programs for juvenile delinquents. Criminal Justice and Behavior 17:134–142.

Jackson, P.C., 1983, Some effects of parole supervision on recidivism. British Journal of Criminology 23:17–34.

Jesness, C.F., 1975, Comparative effectiveness of behavior modification and transactional analysis programs for delinquents. Journal of Consulting and Clinical Psychology 43:758–779.

Jessor, R. and S.L. Jessor, 1977, Problem Behavior and Psychosocial Development: A Longitudinal Study of Youth. New York: Academic Press.

Johnson, R.E., 1979, Juvenile Delinquency and Its Origins: An Integrative Theoretical Approach. New York: Cambridge University Press.

Johnson, B.D. and R.T. Goldberg, 1983, Vocational and social rehabilitation of delinquents. Journal of Offender Counseling, Services, and Rehabilitation 6:43–60.

Kassebaum, G., D. Ward, and D. Wilner, 1971, Prison Treatment and Parole Survival: An Empirical Assessment. New York: John Wiley & Sons.

Kelley, T.M., A.K. Hawa, and R.A. Blak, 1979, The effectiveness of college student companion therapists with predelinquent youths. Journal of Police Science and Administration 7:186–195.

Kirby, B.C., 1954, Measuring effects of treatment of criminals and delinquents. Sociology and Social Research 38:368–374.

Kirigin, K.A., C.J. Braukman, J.D. Atwater, and M.W. Montrose, 1982, An evaluation of Teaching Family (Achievement Place) Group Homes for juvenile offenders. Journal of Applied Behavior Analysis 15:1–16.

Klein, M.W., 1971, Street Gangs and Street Workers. Englewood Cliffs, N.J.: Prentice-Hall.

——. 1986, Labeling theory and delinquency policy: An experimental test. Criminal Justice and Behavior 13:47–79.

Klein, N.C., J.F. Alexander, and B.V. Parsons, 1977, Impact of family systems intervention on recidivism and sibling delinquency: A model of primary prevention and program evaluation. Journal of Consulting and Clinical Psychology 3:469–474.

Kratcoski, P.C. and L.D. Kratcoski, 1982, The Phoenix Program: An educational alternative for delinquent youths. Juvenile and Family Court Journal 33:17–23.

Kraus, J., 1978, Remand in custody as a deterrent in juvenile jurisdiction. British Journal of Criminology 18:17–23.

——. 1981, Police caution of juvenile offenders: A research note. Australian and New Zealand Journal of Criminology 14:91–94.

Lab, S.P. and J.T. Whitehead, 1988, An analysis of juvenile correctional treatment. Crime and Delinquency 34:60–83.

Leschied, A.W., G.W. Austin, and P.G. Jaffe, 1988, Impact of the Young Offenders Act on recidivism rates of special needs youth: Clinical and policy implications. Canadian Journal of Behavioural Science 20:322–331.

Lewis, R.V., 1983, Scared straight—California style: Evaluation of the San Quentin Program. Criminal Justice and Behavior 10:209–226.

Link, B.G., F.T. Cullen, E. Struening, P.E. Shrout, and B.P. Dohrenwend, 1989A, Modified labeling theory approach to mental illness. American Sociological Review 54:400–423.

Lipsey, M.W., 1989, The efficacy of intervention for juvenile delinquency: Results from 400 studies. Paper presented at the 41st annual meeting of the American Society of Criminology, Reno, Nev.

Lipsey, M.W., D.S. Cordray, and D.E. Berger, 1981, Evaluation of a juvenile diversion program using multiple lines of evidence. Evaluation Review 5:283–306.

Loeber, R. and M. Stouthamer-Loeber, 1987, Prediction. In H.C. Quay (ed.), Handbook of Juvenile Delinquency. New York: John Wiley & Sons.

Logan, C.H., 1972, Evaluation research in crime and delinquency: A reappraisal. Journal of Criminal Law, Criminology and Police Science 63:378–387.

Martinson, R., 1974, What works? Questions and answers about prison reform. The Public Interest 35:22–54.

Martinson, R., 1979, New findings, new views: A note of caution regarding prison reform. Hofstra Law Review 7:243–258.

Maskin, M.B., 1976, The differential impact of work vs communication-oriented juvenile correction programs upon recidivism rates in delinquent males. Journal of Clinical Psychology 32:432–433.

Mayer, J.P., L.K. Gensheimer, W.S. Davidson, and R. Gottschalk, 1986, Social learning treatment within juvenile justice: A meta-analysis of impact in the natural environment. In S.J. Apter and A. Goldstein (eds.), Youth Violence: Programs and Prospects. Elmsford, N.Y.: Pergamon.

McPherson, S.J., L.E. McDonald, and C.W. Ryder, 1983, Intensive counseling with families of juvenile offenders. Juvenile and Family Court Journal 34:27–33.

Mitchell, C.M., 1983, The dissemination of a social intervention: Process and effectiveness of two types of paraprofessional change agents. American Journal of Community Psychology 11:723–739.

Mott, J., 1983, Police decisions for dealing with juvenile offenders. British Journal of Criminology 23:249–262.

Murphy, B.C., 1972A, Test of the Effectiveness of an Experimental Treatment Program for Delinquent Opiate Addicts. Ottawa: Information Canada.

O'Donnell, C.R., R. Lydgate, and W.S.O. Fo, 1979, The buddy system: Review and follow-up. Child Behavior Therapy 1:161–169.

Ostrum, T.M., C.M. Steele, L.K. Resenblood, and H.L. Mirels, 1971, Modification of delinquent behavior. Journal of Applied Social Psychology 1:118–136.

Palmer, T., 1975, Martinson revisited. Journal of Research in Crime and Delinquency 12:133–152.

——. 1983, The effectiveness issue today: An overview. Federal Probation 46:3–10.

Palmer, T. and R.V. Lewis, 1980A, Differentiated approach to juvenile diversion. Journal of Research in Crime and Delinquency 17:209–227.

Persons, R., 1967, Relationship between psychotherapy with institutionalized boys and subsequent adjustments. Journal of Consulting Psychology 31:137–141.

Petersilia, J., S. Turner, and J. Peterson, 1986, Prison versus Probation in California: Implications for Crime and Offender Recidivism. Santa Monica, Calif.: Rand.

Phillips, E.L., E.A. Phillips, D.L. Fixen, and M.W. Wolf, 1973, Achievement Place: Behavior shaping works for delinquents. Psychology Today 6:75–79.

Quay, H.C. and C.T. Love, 1977, The effect of a juvenile diversion program on rearrests. Criminal Justice and Behavior 4:377–396.

Rausch, S., 1983, Court processing vs. diversion of status offenders: A test of deterrence and labeling theories. Journal of Research in Crime and Delinquency 20:39–54.

Redfering, D.L., 1973, Durability of effects of group counseling with institutionalized females. Journal of Abnormal Psychology 82:85–86.

Regoh, R., E. Wilderman, and M. Pogrebin, 1985, Using an alternative evaluation measure for assessing juvenile diversion. Children and Youth Services Review 7:21–38.

Reitsma-Street, M. and A.W. Leschied, 1988, The conceptual level matching model in corrections. Criminal Justice and Behavior 15:92–108.

Romig, D.A, 1976, Length of institutionalization, treatment program completion, and recidivism among delinquent adolescent males. Criminal Justice Review 1:115–119.

Rosenbaum, D.P., 1988, Community crime prevention: A review and synthesis of the literature. Justice Quarterly 4:513–544.

Ross, R.R. and E.A. Fabiano, 1985, Time to Think. A Cognitive Model of Delinquency Prevention and Offender Rehabilitation. Johnson City, Tenn.: Institute of Social Sciences and Arts.

Ross, R.R. and H.B. McKay, 1976A, Study of institutional treatment programs. International Journal of Offender Therapy and Comparative Criminology 21:165–173.

Ross, R.R., E.A. Fabiano, and C.D. Ewles, 1988, Reasoning and rehabilitation. International Journal of Offender Therapy and Comparative Criminology 32:29–35.

Rothman, D.J., 1980, Conscience and Convenience: The Asylum and Its Alternatives in Progressive America. Boston: Little, Brown.

Sarason, I.G. and V.J. Ganzer, 1973, Modeling and group discussions in the rehabilitation of juvenile delinquents. Journal of Counseling Psychology 20:442–449.

Schneider, A.L. and P.R. Schneider, 1984A, Comparison of programmatic and ad hoc restitution in juvenile court. Justice Quarterly 1:529–547.

Schur, E.M., 1973, Radical Nonintervention: Rethinking the Delinquency Problem. Englewood Cliffs, N.J.: Prentice Hall.

Sechrest, L., S.O. White, and E.D. Brown, 1979, The Rehabilitation of Criminal Offenders: Problems and Prospects. Washington, D.C.: National Academy Press.

Seidman, E., J. Rappaport, and W.S. Davidson, 1980, Adolescents in legal jeopardy: Initial success and replication of an alternative to the criminal justice system. In R.R. Ross and P. Gendreau (eds.), Effective Correctional Treatment. Toronto: Butterworth.

Shichor, D. and A. Binder, 1982, Community restitution for juveniles: An approach and preliminary investigation. Criminal Justice Review 7: 46–50.

Shore, M.F. and J.L. Massimo, 1979, Fifteen years after treatment: A follow-up study of comprehensive vocationally-oriented psychotherapy. American Journal of Orthopsychiatry 49:240–245.

Shorts, I.D., 1986, Delinquency by association. British Journal of Criminology 26:156–163.

Smith, D.A. and P.R. Gartin, 1989, Specifying specific deterrence. American Sociological Review 54:94–105.

Sorenson, J.L., 1978, Outcome evaluation of a referral system for juvenile offenders. American Journal of Community Psychology 6:381–388.

Sowles, R.C. and J. Gill, 1970, Institutional and community adjustment of delinquents following counseling. Journal of Consulting and Clinical Psychology 34:398–402.

Stephenson, R.M. and F.R. Scarpitti, 1974, Group Interaction as Therapy: The Use of the Small Group in Corrections. Westport, Conn.: Greenwood Press.

Stringfield, N., 1977, The impact of family counseling in resocializing adolescent offenders within a positive peer treatment milieu. Offender Rehabilitation 1:349–360.

Stuart, R.B., S. Jayaratne, and T. Tripodi, 1976, Changing adolescent deviant behaviour through reprogramming the behaviour of parents and teachers: An experimental evaluation.

Canadian Journal of Behavioural Science 8: 132–143.

Tittle, C.R., W.J. Villimez, and D.A. Smith, 1978, The myth of social class and criminality: An empirical assessment of the empirical evidence. American Sociological Review 43:643–656.

Viano, E.C., 1976, Growing up in an affluent society: Delinquency and recidivism in suburban America. Journal of Criminal Justice 3:223–236.

Vinglis, E., E. Adlap, and L. Chung, 1982, The Oshawa Impaired Drivers Programme: An evaluation of a rehabilitation program. Canadian Journal of Criminology 23:93–102.

Visher, C.A., 1987, Incapacitation and crime control: Does a "lock 'em up" strategy reduce crime? Justice Quarterly 4:513–544.

Vito, G.V. and H.E. Allen, 1981, Shock probation in Ohio: A comparison of outcomes. International Journal of Offender Therapy and Comparative Criminology 25:70–76.

Wade, T.C., T.L. Morton, J.E. Lind, and N.R. Ferris, 1977A, Family crisis intervention approach to diversion from the juvenile justice system. Juvenile Justice Journal 28:43–51.

Walker, S., 1989, Sense and Nonsense about Crime: A Policy Guide. Pacific Grove, Calif.: Brooks/Cole.

Walsh, A., 1985, An evaluation of the effects of adult basic education on rearrest rates among probationers. Journal of Offender Counseling, Services and Rehabilitation 9:69–76.

Walter, T.L. and C.M. Mills, 1980A, Behavioral-employment intervention program for reducing juvenile delinquency. In R.R. Ross and P. Gendreau (eds.), Effective Correctional Treatment. Toronto: Butterworth.

Warren, M.Q., 1969, The case for differential treatment of delinquents. Annals of the American Academy of Political and Social Science 381:47–59.

Wellford, C., 1975, Labelling theory and criminology: An assessment. Social Problems 22:332–345.

Whitaker, J.M. and L.J. Severy, 1984, Service accountability and recidivism for diverted youth: A client and service-comparison analysis. Criminal Justice and Behavior 11:47–74.

Whitehead, J.T. and S.P. Lab, 1989A, Meta-analysis of juvenile correctional treatment. Journal of Research in Crime and Delinquency 26:276–295.

Williams, L., 1984A, Police diversion alternative for juvenile offenders. Police Chief (Feb), 54–56.

Willman, M.T. and J.R. Snortum, 1982A, Police program for employment and youth gang members. International Journal of Offender Therapy and Comparative Criminology 26: 207–214.

Wilson, J.Q. and R.J. Hernstein, 1985, Crime and Human Nature. New York: Simon & Schuster.

Winterdyk, J. and R. Roesch, 1982A, Wilderness Experimental Program as an alternative for probationers. Canadian Journal of Criminology 23:39–49.

Wormith, J.S., 1984, Attitude and behavior change of correctional clientele: A three year follow up. Criminology 22:595–618.

Wright, W.E. and M.C. Dixon, 1977, Community prevention and treatment of juvenile delinquency. Journal of Research in Crime and Delinquency 14:35–67.

Zeisel, H., 1982, Disagreement over the evaluation of a controlled experiment. American Journal of Sociology 88:378–389. ✦

23
Substance Abuse Treatment in US Prisons

Roger H. Peters

Marc L. Steinberg

One of the reasons for the increase in the U.S. prison population is an increase in drug-related crimes, combined with current "get tough" policies. Having more inmates with substance abuse problems leads one to easily conclude that substance abuse needs to be addressed if offenders are going to be successfully reintegrated into the community.

Providing treatment in prison has been offered as an important ingredient to successful rehabilitation. Roger H. Peters and Marc L. Steinberg briefly review the history of substance abuse treatment in corrections and provide an overview of efforts in prisons. The authors discuss a number of programmes and initiatives from across the country. Perhaps more importantly, they reiterate that programmes meeting certain principles appear to be more effective than those that do not. In summary, these authors conclude that inmates who participate and complete substance abuse programmes in prisons are more likely than others to experience post-release success.

Excerpts from "Substance Abuse Treatment in US Prisons" by Roger H. Peters and Marc L. Steinberg, in D. Shewan and J. Davies (Eds.), *Drugs and Prisons* (pp. 89–116). London, UK: Harwood Academic Publishers. Copyright © 2000 by Harwood Academic Publishers. Reprinted by permission.

Us federal and state prisons have grown dramatically in the last decade, and now include over a million male inmates and 68,000 female inmates (US Department of Justice, 1996). During the 1980s, state prisoner populations increased by 237 per cent and federal prisoner populations increased by 311 per cent. Due to prison overcrowding, many states have begun to house prisoners in local jails, including eight states that currently hold more than 10 per cent of their prison population in jails. Prison populations are expected to continue growing by 24 per cent from 1995 to 2000 (US General Accounting Office, 1996), a figure that does not include more than 500,000 state and federal inmates held in local jails. Rates of prison incarceration (number of prisoners per 100,000 US residents) have also been rising steadily. From 1980 to 1995, incarceration rates increased by 191 per cent for state prisoners and 245 per cent for federal prisoners. The prison incarceration rate in 1995 was 428 inmates per 100,000 US residents (US General Accounting Office, 1996), and 600 per 100,000 US residents for incarceration in either jails or prisons, which is the highest rate for any developed country in the world.

Several factors contributing to the rapid increase in the US population include changes in law enforcement practices, sentencing law and policy, and in policies regarding release from incarceration. An increase in drug-related crime has also been linked to the surge of cocaine use that began in the mid-1980s and that has continued steadily since that time. Major law enforcement practices that have influenced arrest and incarceration rates include drug 'stings' and 'reverse sting' operations that target street-level users and sellers.

Several legislative changes have also contributed to the rise in US prison populations. The Sentencing Reform Act of 1984 abolished parole for federal offenders and limited time off for good behaviour to 54 days per year. Many state and federal prisoners incarcerated for drug offences (e.g., drug sales)

311

are no longer eligible for parole and must serve mandatory minimum sentences as a result of legislation such as the AntiDrug Abuse Act passed in 1986. Mandatory minimum sentences have led to increases in time served in federal prisons for drug offences from an average of 22 to 33 months (US Department of Justice, 1995a). Changes in legislation and law enforcement strategies have led to an increase in the proportion of prisoners incarcerated for drug-related charges, from 8 per cent in 1980, to 26 per cent in 1993. Significantly more federal prisoners are drug offenders than state prisoners (60 per cent *vs.* 22 per cent; US General Accounting Office, 1996). . . .

Standards and Guidelines for Prison Treatment Services

The following section reviews the legal contours and professional standards that have emerged over the last 20 years to guide the development of substance abuse treatment services in prisons. As described in this section, the courts have been reluctant to prescribe specific aspects of correctional substance abuse treatment services, but have been much more active in identifying required areas of correctional mental health services. As a result, it is the professional rather than legal standards that have provided the most guidance to prison-based substance abuse treatment programmes in the US.

There are currently no legal mandates for providing a broad scope of substance abuse treatment services in jails or prisons (Peters, 1993). In Marshall *vs.* United States (1974), the Supreme Court ruled that a prisoner did not have a constitutional right to drug treatment. In Pace *vs.* Fauver (1979), a district court in New Jersey found that the Eighth Amendment was not violated by failing to provide treatment for alcoholism in a corrections setting. In this case, the court interpreted the Estelle *vs.* Gamble (1976) ruling to mean that the relevant medical condition

must be of sufficient seriousness, and must be easily recognisable by a lay person or diagnosed by a physician.

The US Supreme Court has determined that prisons cannot ignore the 'serious medical needs' of an inmate (see the 'deliberate indifference' requirement of Estelle *vs.* Gamble, 1976). The Fourth Circuit Court of Appeals also ruled that there is no distinction between the right to medical treatment for prisoners and the right to mental health treatment (Bowring *vs.* Godwin, 1977). Another Court of Appeals (McCuckin vs. Smith, 1992) determined that a *serious medical need* would exist if non-treatment of the condition could result in further significant injury or unnecessary infliction of pain, impairment in daily activities, or presence of chronic and substantial pain. Substance use disorders would not ordinarily fit these court-described conditions unless there were acute and life-threatening consequences (e.g., acute withdrawal symptoms, suicidal behaviour, or other acute physical conditions related to alcohol or drug toxicity; Cohen, 1993). Thus, constitutionally required substance abuse services for prison inmates appear to be quite circumscribed, and include screening, assessment, and treatment (e.g., crisis intervention, medically supervised detoxification) of acute and life-threatening physical symptoms related to substance use.

In two separate cases, the Court of Appeals of New York (Griffin vs. Coughlin, 1996);[1] and the Seventh Circuit Court of Appeals (Kerr *vs.* Farrey, 1996) have recently restricted US prisons from creating special privileges (e.g., family visitation, placement in minimum security facilities, opportunity to earn parole) that are contingent upon participation in self-help programmes such as Alcoholics Anonymous (AA) or Narcotics Anonymous (NA). The courts determined that these programmes contained 'explicit religious content', and that mandatory involvement in such programmes violates constitutional provisions for separation of church and state. As a result of these rulings, and to encourage wider inmate participation in treatment services, many prison systems are exploring the use of alternative self-help programmes, such as Secular Organization for Sobriety (SOS), SMART Recovery, and Rational Recovery, (National Commission on Correctional Health Care, 1997).

In the absence of legal standards for providing substance abuse treatment in prisons, several sets of professional standards and guidelines have been developed. However, agencies that have developed these standards do not currently perform regulatory functions to insure that standards related to substance abuse treatment or other health care services have been implemented as intended. The American Correctional Association (ACA; 1990a), in co-operation with the Commission on Accreditation for Corrections has developed several standards for correctional institutions that are relevant to substance abuse treatment services. The ACA recommends written policies and procedures for clinical management of inmates with substance use disorders in the following areas:

- Diagnosis of chemical dependency by a physician.
- Determination by a physician as to whether an individual requires non-pharmacologically or pharmacologically supported care.
- Individualised treatment plans developed and implemented by a multidisciplinary team.
- Referrals to specified community resources upon release when appropriate.

The ACA and NCCHC standards also identify several items related to the substance abuse history that should be included in preliminary screenings.

The Report of the National Task Force of Correctional Substance Abuse Strategies (US Department of Justice, 1991), the National Institute on Corrections (NIC) describes several general guidelines for substance abuse treatment services provided in prison and other correctional settings. In 1993, the Substance Abuse and Mental Health Services Administration, Centre for Substance Abuse Treatment published a set of guidelines for implementing correctional substance abuse treatment programmes, developed through Project RECOVERY (Wexler, 1993). The guidelines called for the creation of comprehensive state plans for substance abuse treatment services within corrections systems, and planning at the institutional level. Several components of correctional treatment programmes that are recommended by CSAT and NIC include the following:

- Standardised screening and assessment approaches.
- Matching to different levels or types of treatment services.
- Individual treatment plans.
- Case management services.
- Use of cognitive-behavioural/social learning and self-help approaches, including interventions that address criminal beliefs and values.
- Relapse prevention services.
- Self-help groups (e.g., AA, NA).
- Use of therapeutic communities.
- Isolated treatment units.
- Drug testing.
- Continuity of services, including linkages to parole and community-based treatment services.
- Programme evaluation.
- Cross-training of staff.

Overview of the Correctional Treatment Literature

Although Martinson long ago retracted his conclusion that 'nothing works' in correctional treatment (1979), this belief has persisted over time among policymakers and administrators. A significant number of studies conducted since the time of Martinson's work have provided consistent evidence of positive outcomes associated with correctional treatment programmes. Several literature reviews and meta-analyses have reviewed findings from these studies (Andrews, et al., 1990; Gendreau, 1996; Gendreau and Goggin, 1997; Gendreau and Ross, 1984), and have identified principles of effective correctional treatment programmes. Although these reviews include several programmes that are not dedicated to substance abuse treatment, they are instructive in identifying common principles which are likely to enhance the effectiveness of correctional treatment settings. Across different types of therapeutic programmes developed and tested in correctional settings, those based on social learning, cognitive-behavioural models, skills training, and family systems approaches have proven to be the most effective (Cullen and Gendreau, 1989). Programmes based on non-directive approaches, the medical model, or involving a focus on punishment or deterrence have proven to be 'ineffective'. In reviewing the correctional treatment literature, Gendreau (1996) has identified eight key principles of effective programmes:

1. Intensive services are behavioural in nature. Services should occupy from 40–50 per cent of offenders time, and should be of 3–9 months in duration. Programmes should use token economies, modelling, and cognitive-behavioural interventions designed to change offenders' 'cognitions, attitudes, values, and expectations that maintain antisocial behaviour'.

2. Programmes should target the 'criminogenic needs of high-risk offenders' including substance abuse, antisocial attitudes and behaviours, peer associations, and self-control. Risk assessment measures should be provided to identify these 'criminogenic needs'.

3. Treatment programmes should be multimodal, and should match services according to the learning style and personality characteristics of the offender, and to

the characteristics of the therapist/counselor.

4. Programmes should include a structured set of incentives and sanctions. This system must be developed and maintained by staff, with ongoing monitoring of antisocial behaviours within treatment units, and positive reinforcers exceeding negative sanctions 1), in approximate 4:1 ratio.

5. Therapists or counselors should be selected on the basis of effective counseling and interpersonal skills. Staff should have at least an undergraduate degree or equivalent, training in criminal behaviour and offender treatment, and on-the-job training in use of behavioural interventions. Quality of counseling services should be monitored regularly.

6. Programmes should provide a prosocial treatment environment that reduces negative peer influences.

7. Relapse prevention strategies should be provided that provide skills in anticipating and avoiding problem situations, and rehearsing prosocial responses to these situations. Training should be provided to family and friends to reinforce prosocial behaviours, and booster sessions should be provided following release to the community.

8. Linkage and referral to community services should be provided.

These principles of effective correctional treatment reflect several key components of professional standards and guidelines that have been developed by ACA, CSAT, NCCHC, and NIC, including the need for treatment matching, staff training, cognitive-behavioural interventions, relapse prevention services, isolated treatment units, and linkage and referral to community services. However, these principles also point to several new areas that are not incorporated within the standards and guidelines, and/or that have not been implemented widely in prison treatment programmes. These new areas include the following: (1) targeting inmates with significant risk for recidivism and relapse, (2) use of cognitive-behavioural interventions, (3) a focus on criminal thinking, values, behaviours, and impulse control issues, and (4) minimum education requirements for staff of at least a college degree. A major challenge for US prison treatment programmes over the next several decades will be to closely examine principles of effective correctional treatment and to begin to implement these within the context of new or existing substance abuse treatment programmes.

Prison-Based Substance Abuse Treatment Programmes

The following section describes several new substance abuse treatment initiatives developed within US federal and state prison systems during the last 15 years. Several of the programmes described in this section have thrived over a long period of time, while several other programmes have just recently been developed (Chaiken, 1989; Lipton, 1995). Research findings from these programmes demonstrate the effectiveness of correctional substance abuse treatment programmes in reducing substance abuse and criminal recidivism following release from prison (Falkin, Wexler, and Lipton, 1992).

Federal Bureau of Prisons Drug Abuse Programmes

The Federal Bureau of Prisons was one of the first agencies to respond to the recent drug abuse epidemic by developing a comprehensive system of treatment services for prison inmates (Murray, 1992; 1996). The Bureau's Drug Abuse Programmes (DAP's) include four different levels of treatment services (Lipton, 1995; Federal Bureau of Prisons, 1996a,b; 1997). The first level includes a 40-hour drug education programme attended by all prisoners who meet admission criteria. The second level of treatment involves 'non-residential' drug abuse treat-

ment, in which treatment participants are not isolated from the general prison community. Residential treatment services are provided in the third level, in which participants are isolated from the general inmate population. Thirty four of the Bureau's prisons have a residential treatment programme, which are of varying length (6, 9, or 12 months), and include a minimum of 500 hours of treatment services (Federal Bureau of Prisons, 1996b; Weinman and Lockwood, 1993).

The Bureau's programmes also include transitional services following release from prison. Inmates may be released either to the US Probation Office or to a Community Corrections Centre, which are privately contracted, supervised halfway houses. Transitional treatment services are similar to those obtained in prison, and include ongoing counseling, regular drug testing, and assistance to obtain employment. A comprehensive longitudinal study is underway to examine long-term treatment outcomes for participants in the Bureau of Prisons treatment programmes.

California's Amity Prison Therapeutic Community

California's Amity Prison Therapeutic Community is a 200-bed unit located at the R. J. Donovan Correctional Facility [and] is based on the Stay'n Out programme in New York. The prison treatment programme consists of three phases, including a 2 to 3 month orientation phase. In the second phase, participants assist in daily operations of the therapeutic community and act as role models to newer participants. The third phase of treatment lasts for 1–3 months and involves decision-making skills related to recovery, and developing a plan for re-entry to the community. Following release from the prison, graduates are offered up to one year of aftercare treatment in a therapeutic community programme that serves up to 40 residents.

A recent evaluation of California's Amity prison programme indicated favourable outcomes associated with participation in prison treatment (Lipton, 1995, 1996; Simpson *et al.*, 1996). Rates of reincarceration during a one year follow-up period after release from prison were 43 per cent for those who completed the treatment programme, compared to 63 per cent for prisoners not participating in the programme, and 50 per cent for those who dropped out of the programme (Lipton, 1995). Only 26 per cent of individuals who were placed in an aftercare programme following graduation from the in-prison treatment programme were reincarcerated during the same period. Similar patterns of follow-up outcomes were found in relation to participant drug use.

Delaware's Key-Crest Programme

The 'Key' Programme was established in 1987 by the Delaware Department of Corrections (Hooper, Lockwood, and Inciardi, 1993; Inciardi, 1996; Inciardi, *et al.*, 1992; Pan, Scarpiti, Inciardi, and Lockwood, D., 1993). One year of treatment services are provided for male prisoners in a 140-bed therapeutic community that is modelled after New York's Stay'n Out programme. The Key Programme is unique in that a 6 month transitional phase (Crest Outreach Centre) is provided following completion of the in-prison programme, which includes 'Key' participants and other offenders who are supervised in the community. In the Crest programme, prisoners may hold jobs in the community while residing in the therapeutic community programme (Inciardi, 1996). A six month aftercare component is included as the last phase of the Crest programme.

In a recent evaluation of the Key and Crest programmes, researchers compared four groups who had participated in varying levels of programme services: (1) Key programme only, (2) Crest programme only, (3) combined Key-Crest programmes, and (4) an HIV prevention/education 'control' programme. Six month follow-up results indicated that individuals participating in the Crest programme (only) and the combined Key and Crest programmes were significantly less likely to use drugs or to be arrested than participants in the Key (only) and the control group (Martin, Butzin, and Inciardi, 1995). Positive outcomes associated with the Crest (only) and combined Key/Crest programmes were still evident after controlling for the effects for time spent in treatment.

Florida's Tier Programmes

The Florida Department of Corrections (FDOC) has a long history of supporting innovative prison-based substance abuse treatment. In the early 1970s, with funding through the Law Enforcement Assistance Act (LEAA), FDOC developed several of the first prison therapeutic communities in the country, in addition to specialised treatment programmes for female inmates and youthful offenders (Chaiken, 1989; Florida Department of Corrections, 1995; 1996). Comprehensive Substance Abuse Treatment Programmes are provided in 46 major correctional institutions, 31 community correctional centres, and 7 community facilities.

Inmates are placed in several 'tiers' of treatment services. Tier I services consist of 40 hours of drug education services per week, including an orientation to the importance of substance abuse treatment, and group counseling. Tier II programmes provide treatment for approximately 40 inmates at a time over a period of 4–6 months. Tier III programmes provide 4 months of treatment in an intensive therapeutic community setting and include orientation, treatment, and reentry phases. Tier IV services include 6–12 months of treatment ill a residential therapeutic community in 12 institutions, and in seven community based facilities, including a 54-bed treatment programme for inmates placed on work release.

New York's Stay'n Out Programme

One of the longest operating correctional treatment programmes in the US is the Stay'n Out Programme in New York, which provides a highly structured therapeutic community (Wexler and Williams, 1986). In 1989, the New York legislature appropriated $1 billion to augment drug abuse treatment efforts in New York state prisons, which included one 750-bed and seven 200-bed substance abuse treatment facilities (Lipton, 1995).

Outcomes from the Stay'n Out programme were compared to those from milieu treatment, short-term counseling services, a waiting list, and a no-treatment control group (Wexler, Falkin, and Lipton, 1990; Wexler, Falkin, Lipton, and Rosenblum, 1992). Significantly fewer Stay'n Out participants were arrested during follow-up on supervised parole (lasting an average of 3 years) in comparison to other groups (27 per cent *vs.* 35 per cent in milieu treatment, 40 per cent in group or individual counseling, and 41 per cent in a no-treatment comparison group). However, there was no evidence that the Stay'n Out programme delayed the time to arrest during follow-up. Positive outcomes were correlated with increasing time in treatment up to one year; but after this duration, positive outcomes began to decline.

Oregon Department of Corrections

Oregon's Cornerstone Programme opened in 1976, and was modelled after the Stay'n Out programme in New York, but with a higher proportion of professionals and trained correction officers (Lipton, 1994; 1995). The Cornerstone programme is housed in a 32-bed residential unit in the Oregon State Hospital. Four phases of treatment are provided over a period of 10–12 months, followed by 6 months of aftercare/transitional services while under parole supervision (Field, 1989).

Several other modified therapeutic community programmes have recently been developed by the Oregon Department of Corrections, including the Turning Point Alcohol and Drug Programme at the Columbia River Correctional Institution, and the Powder River Alcohol and Drug (PRAD) Programme at the Powder River Correctional Facility. The Turning Point programme provides a 50-bed unit for females and a similar unit for males, while the PRAD Programme provides a 50-bed male unit. The Turning Point treatment programme serves as a pre-release institution for female inmates. In 1989, the Parole Transition Release (PTR) Project was initiated by the Oregon Department of Corrections in Washington County, Oregon, with funding from several federal agencies. Treatment services are provided for 35 offenders over a period of approximately 9 months. Treatment begins prior to release from prison, and continues in the community (Field and Karecki, 1992).

An evaluation of the Cornerstone Programme indicates that treatment participants experience significant reductions in re-arrest and recommitment to prison, in comparison to other groups of inmates. Field (1989; 1992) found that rates of re-arrest and reincarceration during follow-up were inversely related to the time spent in the treatment programme. Only 26 per cent of Cornerstone Programme graduates were recommitted to prison during a three year follow-up period, as compared to 85 per cent of individuals who dropped out of the programme after less than 2 months of participation, 67 per cent of nongraduates who completed from 2–5 months of treatment, and 63 per cent of non-graduates who completed at least 6 months of treatment.

The Texas Criminal Justice Treatment Initiative

In 1991, under the stewardship of Texas Governor Ann Richards, legislation was enacted to create the Texas Criminal Justice Treatment Initiative, the largest state prison treatment programme in the country at that time. This initiative originally provided $95 million for development of Substance Abuse Felony Punishment (SAFP) programmes and In-Prison Therapeutic Community Treatment (ITC) programmes. The initiative also provided funding for alternatives to incarceration programmes and Transitional Treatment Centres, which are community-based facilities for offenders who have completed a SAFP or ITC programme.

As originally enacted, legislation in Texas authorised the development of 12,000 secure treatment beds within the SAFP programme and corresponding space in community residential and non-residential programmes. The scope of SAFP and ITC programmes have since been substantially reduced by the legislature (Texas Department of Criminal Justice, 1997).

The Substance Abuse Felony (SAFP) System allows those with substance abuse problems who are convicted of non-violent felonies to enter long term (6–12 months) substance abuse treatment as a condition of parole or probation. Programme graduates then participate in 15 months of transitional services. State prisoners are eligible to participate in the In-Prison Therapeutic Community Treatment (ITC) programme, which provides drug treatment services for inmates who are within 9–10 months of parole.

Knight *et al.* (1997) report that ITC graduates are significantly less likely to be involved in criminal activity (7 per cent *vs.* 16 per cent arrested; 28 per cent *vs.* 47 per cent reported drug-related offences; and 41 per cent *vs.* 55 per cent involved in criminal activity as determined by any source), are less likely to have a parole violation 6 months after leaving prison (29 per cent vs. 48 per cent), and were less likely to use alcohol or other drugs, in contrast to an untreated comparison group. ITC graduates who went on to complete the TTC aftercare programme within the 6 month follow-up time frame were found to have lower recidivism rates than non-completers and a comparison group consisting of parolees, and fewer ITC

completers used cocaine than the untreated comparison group.

The National Treatment Improvement Evaluation Study

The National Treatment Improvement Evaluation Study (NTIES; Centre for Substance Abuse Treatment, 1997) was conducted by CSAT to determine the long range outcomes of individuals involved in federally funded treatment programmes. Outcome data were obtained for over 4411 individuals, including 709 individuals from the 'correctional' sample, which consisted of 56 per cent prison inmates and 44 per cent offenders from other criminal justice settings. Participants in correctional treatment experienced the greatest reductions in self-reported criminal behaviour (e.g., 81 per cent reduction in selling drugs) and in arrests (66 per cent reduction in drug possession arrests, 76 per cent reduction in all arrests) among all other types of treatment settings/modalities examined in the NTIES study. Reduced drug use and enhanced mental health and physical health functioning were also observed during follow-up among the correctional sample.

Correctional Treatment of Special Needs Populations

Co-occurring Mental Health and Substance Use Disorders

Rates of both mental health disorders and substance use disorders are significantly higher among offenders than in non-incarcerated populations in the community (Keith, Regier, and Rae, 1991; Weissman, Bruce, Leaf, Florio, and Holzer, 1992; Robins and Regier, 1991). For example, rates of mental health disorders are four times higher among prisoners than in the general population, and rates of substance use are four to seven times higher (Robins and Regier, 1991). In the absence of epidemological data, it is estimated that 3–11 per cent of prison inmates have co-occurring mental health and substance use disorders (Peters and Hills, 1993). Over 600,000 US prison inmates have either a serious mental illness or a substance use disorder, and approximately 130,000 inmates have co-occurring disorders (National GAINS Centre, 1997).

As in community settings, co-occurring disorders are often undetected or untreated in correctional settings. One survey found that many correctional systems had not developed procedures for compiling information regarding the rates of co-occurring disorders in their institutions (Peters and Hills, 1993). Non-detection of co-occurring disorders often leads to misdiagnosis, over-treatment of mental health symptoms with medications, neglect of appropriate interventions, inappropriate treatment planning and referral, and poor treatment outcomes (Drake, Alterman, and Rosenberg, 1993; Hall, Popleis, Stickney, and Gardner, 1978; Teague, Schwab, and Drake, 1990). There are several reasons for the non-detection of mental health and substance use disorders within correctional systems. These include negative consequences perceived by inmates for disclosing symptoms, lack of staff training in diagnosis and management of mental health disorders, and cognitive and perceptual difficulties associated with severe mental illness or toxic effects of recent alcohol or drug use.

Inmates with co-occurring disorders present a number of challenges in correctional settings, and manifest more severe psychosocial problems than other inmates (Peters, Kearns, Murrin, and Dolente, 1992) related to employment, family relationships, and physical health. Offenders with co-occurring disorders are more likely to drop out of treatment or to be terminated from treatment, are more likely to be hospitalised, and are thought to be at greater risk for suicide and criminal recidivism (Peters and Bartoi, 1997). Individuals with co-occurring disorders often do not fit well into existing treatment programmes (Carey, 1991). Once involved in treatment, these individuals do not respond as well as others with single diagnoses (Bowers, Mazoure, Nelson, and Jatlow, 1990).

Integrated approaches should be used in screening and assessment of co-occurring disorders among prison inmates (Peters and Bartoi, 1997). Relevant criminal justice, mental health, and substance use information should be reviewed in both screening and assessment of co-occurring disorders. Screening is useful in determining the relationship between co-occurring disorders and prior criminal behaviour, the interaction of these disorders, and motivation for treatment. Because of the high rates of co-occurring disorders in prisons, detection of a single disorder (i.e., either mental health or substance use) should immediately 'trigger' screening for the other type of disorder. Screening and assessment should include an interview, use of self-report and diagnostic instruments as needed, and review of archival records. In the absence of integrated instruments for examining co-occurring disorders, screening and assessment in prisons should include a combination of mental health and substance abuse instruments.

A number of recent initiatives in jails and prisons have been developed to address the treatment needs of this population, including several programmes developed within state prisons in Alabama, Colorado, Delaware, Oregon, and Texas, and one programme in the Federal Bureau of Prisons (*et al.*, 1997). The in-prison dual diagnosis programmes share several features. First, programme staff have experience and training in both mental health and substance abuse treatment. Second, although the disorders were not always addressed simultaneously, both are treated as 'primary' disorders. In addition, each of the programmes utilise psychopharmacological and self-help services, and individual counseling is provided to supplement prisoners' involvement in several standard 'phases' or 'levels' of treatment. Lastly, each of the correctional treatment programmes provide a longterm focus, and recognise the importance of continued treatment following release from prison.

Most programmes for dually diagnosed inmates include a set of structured 'phases' or 'levels' of treatment, which are progressively less intensive over time. Phases of treatment often include an orientation phase focusing on motivation and engagement in treatment, intensive treatment, and relapse prevention and transition services. Aftercare, or linkage to other services is especially important to dually diagnosed prisoners due to their increased vulnerability to relapse (Peters and Hills, 1993). Most existing correctional dual diagnosis programmes provide reentry services to facilitate the transition to aftercare treatment services, work release programmes, or halfway houses (Edens *et al.*, 1997). Several modifications made to correctional dual diagnosis programmes include smaller client caseloads, use of psycho-educational groups, shorter duration of treatment sessions, and more streamlined content of didactic and process group sessions. These programmes also tend to provide less peer confrontation than in most substance abuse treatment programmes (McLaughlin and Pepper, 1991; Sacks and Sacks, 1995).

Treatment of Female Inmates

From 1986 to 1991, the population of female prisoners increased by 75 per cent (Kline, 1993). The growth rate of female prisoners has exceeded that of males, rising at a rate of 12 per cent per year since 1980 (Bureau of Justice Statistics, 1994). This growth reflects a substantial influx of individuals arrested for drug-related crimes. According to the Bureau of Justice Statistics (1994), more than half of incarcerated females committed their crimes under the influence of drugs or alcohol.

Female offenders were found to have higher scores on several scales of the Addiction Severity Index (ASI; McLellan *et al.*, 1992; Peters, Strozier, Murrin, and Kearns, 1997), reflecting significantly more impairment than males related to drug use, employment, legal status, and psychiatric/psychological functioning (males were more impaired on the scale related to alcohol use). Female offenders were also more likely to report psychiatric problems such as serious depression and anxiety (Peters, *et al.*, 1997).

Fewer than 11 per cent of female offenders are involved in substance abuse treatment (Wellisch, Anglin, and Prendergast, 1993a), although a recent survey (American Correctional Association, 1990b) of state prisons indicated that over 40 per cent of female inmates needed substance abuse treatment. Specialised and intensive services for female offenders are less likely to be offered in programmes that serve both men and women, in comparison to those serving female inmates exclusively (Wellisch, Prendergast, and Anglin, 1994). Correctional treatment programmes for women are often of limited intensity and duration, do not assess the full range of psychosocial problems among substance abusing female inmates, and do not have sufficient resources to treat the majority of these problems (e.g., sexual abuse, domestic violence; Wellisch, Prendergast, and Anglin, 1994).

Several recommendations for developing correctional substance abuse treatment programmes for women are provided by Wellisch, Anglin, and Prendergast, (1993b). These include: (1) developing support for specialised female treatment programmes within the corrections system and in the community, (2) providing a continuum of care, (3) transition planning prior to release from prison, (4) ongoing supervision following release to the community, and (5) procedures for data collection and programme evaluation. Some have called for adoption of a 'co-occurring disorders' treatment model in developing services for substance abusing female inmates, based on the multiple and interrelated psychosocial problems manifested by this population (Peters, *et al.*,

1997). The authors recommend that several key principles in treating co-occurring disorders be considered in developing substance abuse services for female inmates. These principles include the following:

- Mental health services should be a central component of treatment, and not isolated from correctional substance abuse services for women.
- When multiple psychosocial problems are present, each should be treated as equally important as the foci of clinical interventions.
- Co-occurring problems should be treated simultaneously rather than sequentially.
- Integrative assessment and treatment approaches should be used that consider the interactive nature of different problems.
- The sequence of treatment services for female inmates should be determined by areas of more severe functional disturbance. These areas should be addressed earlier in the course of treatment.
- An extended assessment 'baseline' should be provided, reflecting the complexity of psychosocial problems among substance abusing female inmates.
- Correctional and treatment staff should receive training regarding the nature of co-occurring problems/disorders, and their interactive effects.

As with other correctional substance abuse treatment services, programmes for female inmates should be geographically isolated from the general prison population, whenever possible. Roles of correctional officers and treatment staff should be easily distinguishable to reduce conflicts regarding security and treatment issues, and to enhance confidentiality of clinical information shared with staff during treatment. Wellisch *et al.* (1993b) describe the importance of clearly defining staff roles for dealing with particular rule infractions. Flexibility should be provided in responding to these situations. Correctional treatment programmes should be staffed by females with professional training, and who can serve as role models.

Optimally, correctional treatment programmes for females should include means for participants to maintain contact with their children, since separation from children may greatly influence recovery goals and engagement in treatment (Wellisch *et al.*, 1993b). Female prisoners often are released to the community as the primary financial provider for their children, yet often do not have adequate job training. Vocational training and job readiness services should be a major component of correctional substance abuse programmes for women. Proper health care is also especially important for female inmates, since many have histories of physical or sexual abuse. They may also have recently given birth, or may be pregnant at the time of incarceration (Wellisch *et al.*, 1993a, 1993b).

One exemplary substance abuse treatment programme for female inmates is the Passages Programme for Women, developed by the Wisconsin Department of Corrections (Wellisch, *et al.*, 1993b). This programme was created in 1988, through funding by the US Department of Justice. The Passages Programme is a 12 week programme, involving 8 hours of treatment programming per day, 5 days per week in the Women's Correctional Centre (WCC). Programme services are provided for 15 inmates in an isolated treatment unit.

The 12 week Passages Programme includes three phases. The first phase is based on the 12-step approach, but also addresses relapse issues and personal values. The second phase of the programme promotes development of interpersonal skills, while the third phase uses role playing and other techniques to develop coping skills such as assertiveness training, conflict resolution, and communication skills. Programme participants are required to attend at least two AA/

NA/CA meetings per week, and receive random drug testing throughout their involvement in the programme. After completion of treatment, inmates are provided re-entry services, or are enrolled in a work/study release programme.

Summary

US prison populations have swelled to over a million inmates since the mid-1980's, due to an ongoing drug epidemic that has been fuelled by decreasing prices of cocaine and availability of relatively cheap synthetic drugs (e.g., 'crystal' methamphetamine), law enforcement efforts targeting street level drug sales, and legislation that has provided more severe penalties for drug-related offences. As traditional punitive approaches have failed to stem the tide of illicit drug use and drug related crime in the community, administrators and policymakers have begun to consider the expansion of treatment and rehabilitative services in prisons. Approximately 55 per cent of US prisoners have an alcohol or drug use disorder at the time of incarceration, although only about 10 per cent of prisoners currently receive any form of substance abuse treatment. Many of these existing prison treatment programmes are not comprehensive in scope, although several exemplary and intensive initiatives have been developed in recent years.

The history of correctional substance abuse treatment in the US is characterised by significant variability in support and funding. Federal involvement in correctional treatment was encouraged by the Porter Act in 1929 and the Narcotic Addict Rehabilitation Act of 1966, while various state commitment laws enacted in the 1960s encouraged broad use of hospitalisation for narcotic addicts. Although Martinson's bleak review of the correctional treatment literature (1974) summoned a new era of pessimism and decreased funding with regard to prison substance abuse programmes, the 1980s brought a resurgence of interest and support for these programmes. Specialised projects funded by the US Department of Justice and the Substance Abuse and Mental Health Administration have provided significant technical assistance to prison substance abuse treatment programmes, and encouraged dissemination of information regarding effective treatment approaches. Standards and guidelines for implementation of prison treatment programmes have been developed by these and other agencies during the 1980s and 1990s, which provide recommended parameters for screening, assessment, treatment, supervision, evaluation, and other key activities. The courts have not actively defined requirements for correctional substance abuse treatment services, other than providing screening and treatment of acute and life-threatening symptoms such as withdrawal from dependency on alcohol or opiates. The courts recently have enjoined prisons from providing privileges that are contingent on involvement in religious-based treatment (e.g., 12-step programmes).

A number of substance abuse treatment programmes have been developed in US prisons during the past 20 years. These efforts have been supported by federal initiatives such as the CSAT Model Programmes for Correctional Populations, the Byrne Formula Grant Programme, and the more recent Residential Substance Abuse Treatment Formula Grant Program. As described in previous sections, many of the correctional substance abuse treatment programmes share common elements and programme structures. In many cases, programme similarities have emerged as a result of federal initiatives such as Project REFORM and RECOVERY, which encouraged adoption of common elements of treatment through co-ordinated training and consultation activities. Examples of programme similarities include the widespread use of therapeutic communities, that emphasise accountability to peers and treatment staff, involvement in daily operations and governance of the treatment community, development of prosocial behaviours through a social learning model, and graduated levels of responsibility and privileges.

Each of the US correctional substance abuse treatment programmes that are profiled in this chapter endorse the goal of major lifestyle change, pursuant to abstinence. Most programmes also isolate treatment participants from general population inmates to reduce the potentially disruptive effects to the treatment community. Common admission criteria used by correctional treatment programmes include (1) classification as 'low' to 'medium' security risk, (2) no history of institutional violence, (3) at least moderate substance abuse problems, and (4) sufficient time remaining on the sentence to complete the inprison treatment programme (and in some cases, sufficient time on parole to complete an aftercare programme).

Most of the existing US correctional treatment programmes include different phases of treatment. An orientation phase, followed by an intensive treatment phase and transition phase are common to many of these programmes. Within the various phases of treatment, there are several common types of treatment activities offered, including drug and alcohol education, individual and group counseling, life skills training, job training, and relapse prevention. Several programmes offer cognitive-behavioural interventions and activities designed to reduce criminal thinking errors. Transition services are also a central component to many correctional treatment programmes, and include development of a re-entry plan, linkages with aftercare treatment providers, parole, and other community services.

Evaluations of correctional substance abuse treatment programmes provide consistent support for the effectiveness of these initiatives. Conclusions from several recent empirical reviews of the correctional treatment literature (Gendreau, 1996; Gendreau and Goggin, 1997) depart significantly from the 'nothing works' doctrine that emerged from Martinson's earlier work. These 'meta-analyses' indicate consistently positive outcomes associated with correctional treatment programmes, with more favourable results obtained from programmes that address criminogenic needs of 'high-risk' offenders, that use cognitive-behavioural techniques, that provide relapse prevention activities, that provide a focus on linkage and referral, and that are intensive, of lengthy duration, and multi-modal in approach.

Findings from the large multi-site NTIES study conducted by the Centre for Substance Abuse Treatment (1997) also support the efficacy of correctional treatment, and indicate that participants in these programmes experience greater post-treatment reductions in criminal behaviour than non-offenders enrolled in several different types of community-based programmes. Controlled treatment outcome studies conducted in five state prison systems surveyed in this chapter all point to significant reductions in post-treatment criminal behaviour and improvements in other areas of psychosocial functioning (e.g., reduced drug use, employment). Length of treatment has also been found to be directly related to treatment outcome in these studies, although there appears to be diminishing effects of treatment beyond one year. Inmates who participate in prison treatment that is followed by an aftercare programme in the community have significantly better outcomes (e.g., lower rates of re-arrest and reincarceration) than inmates who receive only the in-prison treatment. Additional research is needed to examine correctional treatment outcomes among samples that include untreated inmates. Moreover, this research should provide extended follow-up periods, and should examine substance abuse, unreported criminal activity, sanctions received while under community supervision, employment, and use of community services, in addition to more traditional measures of arrest and recommitment to prison.

Study Questions

1. According to Peters and Steinberg, what are three reasons that the prison population has increased?

2. What are the guidelines for prisoners' substance abuse treatment services offered by the Centre for Substance Abuse Treatment and the National Institute of Corrections?

3. According to Gendreau, what are the eight key principles of effective programmes?

4. What are co-occurring disorders, and what do the authors recommend with regard to treatment?

Note

1. In Coughlin v. Griffin (1997), the US Supreme Court subsequently denied certiori, allowing the decision to remain standing

References

American Correctional Association. (1990a) *Standards for adult correctional institutions, 3rd edition.* Washington, D.C.: St. Mary's Press.

American Correctional Association. (1990b) *The female offender: What does the future hold?* Washington, D.C.: St. Mary's Press.

Andrews, D. A., Zinger, I., Hoge, R. D., Bonta, J., Gendreau, P, and Cullen, F. T. (1990) Does correctional treatment work? A clinically relevant and psychologically informed meta-analysis. Criminology, 28, 369–404.

Ball, J. C., (1986) The hyper criminal opiate addict. In B. D. Johnson and F. Wish (Eds.), *Crime rates among drug abusing offenders. Final Report to the National Institute of Justice. (pp.81–104). New York: Narcotic and Drug Research, Inc.*

Ball, J. C., Shaffer, J. W., and Nurco, D. N. (1983) Day-to-day criminality of heroin addicts in Baltimore: A study of the continuity, of offense rates. *Drug and Alcohol Dependence., 12, 119–142.*

Bowers, M. B., Mazure, C. M., Nelson. C. J., and Jatlow, P. I. (1990) Psychotogeme drug use and neurodeptic response. *Schizophrenia Bulletin, 16, 81–85.*

Bowring v. Godwin, 551 F.2d 44 (4th Cir. 1977).

Carey, K. G. (1991) Research with dual diagnosis patients: Challenges and recommendations. *The Behaviour Therapist, 14, 5–8.*

Centre for Substance Abuse Treatment (1997) *NTIES: The National Treatment Improvement Study-Final Report.* Substance Abuse and Mental Health Services Administration, US Department of Health and Human Services. Rockville, MD.

Chaiken, M. (1986) Crime rates and substance abuse among types of offenders. In B. Johnson and E. Wish (Eds.), *Crime rates among drug-abusing offenders,* 12–54. *Final Report to the National Institute of Justice.* New York: Narcotic and Drug Research, Inc.

Chaiken, M. (1989) *In-prison programmes for drug-involved offenders.* Issues and Practices series, National Institute of Justice. Washington, D.C.: US Department of Justice.

Collins, J. J., Hubbard, R. I., and Rachal, J. V. (1985) Expensive drug use in illegal income: A test of explanatory hypothesis. *Criminology,* 23,(4), 743–764.

Cohen, F. (1993) Captives' legal rights to mental health care. *Law and Psychology Review,* 17, 1–39.

Coughlin v. Griffin, 117 US 681 (1997).

Cullen, E. T., and Gendreau, P. (1989) The effectiveness of rehabilitation. In L. Goodstein and D. MacKenzie (Eds.), *The American prison: Issues in research policy* (pp. 23–44). New York: Plenum.

Drake, R. E., Alterman, A. I., and Rosenberg, S. R. (1993) Detection of substance use disorders in severely mentally ill patients. *Community Mental Health,* 29 (2), 175–192.

Edens, J. F., Peters, R. H., and Hills, H. A. (1997). Treating prison inmates with co-occuring disorders: An integrative review of existing programmes. *Behavioural Sciences and the Law.* 15, 439–457.

Estelle v. Gamble, 429 US 97 (1976).

Falkin, G. P., Wexler, H. K., and Lipton, D. S. (1992) Drug treatment in state prisons. In D.R. Gerstein and H.J. Harwood (Eds.), *Treating drug problems, volume II* (pp. 89–131). Washington, DC: National Academy Press.

Federal Bureau of Prisons (1996a) [On-line] Federal Beareau of Prisons Quick Facts Available: http:/www.bop.gov/facts.html#population.

Federal Bureau of Prisons (1996b) *Drug abuse programme options in the Federal Bureau of*

Prisons: Third annual report to Congress. Washington, D.C.: US Department of Justice.

Federal Bureau of Prisons (1997) *Federal Bureau of Prisons Drug Abuse Treatment Programmes*. Washington, D.C.: US Department of Justice.

Field, G. (1989) *A study of the effects of intensive treatment on reducing the criminal recidivism of addicted offenders*. Salem, Oregon: Oregon Department of Corrections.

Field, G. (1992) Oregon Prison Drug Treatment programmes. In C. Leukefeld and F. Tims (Eds.), *Drug abuse treatment in prisons and jails* (pp. 142–155). Research Monograph Series, Vol. 118. Rockville, MD: National Institute on Drug Abuse.

Field, G., and Karecki, M. (1992) *Outcome study of the Parole Transition Release project*. Salem, Oregon: Oregon Department of Corrections.

Florida Department of Corrections (1995) *Substance Abuse Programme Services Office: Comprehensive report. 1995*. Tallahassee, Florida.

Florida Department of Corrections (1996) *1995–96 annual report: The guidebook to corrections in Florida*. Tallahassee, Florida.

Gendreau, P. (1996) The principles of effective intervention with offenders. In A. Harland (Ed.), *Choosing correctional options that work*. Newbury Park, CA: Sage Publications.

Gendreau, P., and Goggin, C. (1997) Correctional treatment: Accomplishments and realities. In P. VanVourbis, M. Braswell, and D. Lester (Eds.), *Correctional counseling and rehabilitation*. Cincinnati, Ohio: Anderson.

Gendreau, P, and Ross, R. R. (1984) Correctional treatment: Some recommendations for successful intervention. *Juvenile and Family Court Journal*, 34, 31–40.

Griffin v. Coughlin. 88 N.Y. 2d 674 (1996).

Hall, R. C., M. K. Popleis, Stickney, S. K., and Gardner, E. E. (1978) Covert outpatient drug abuse. *Journal of Nervous and Mental Disease*, 166, 343–348.

Henneberg, M. (1994) *Bureau of Justice Statistics Fiscal Year 1994 Progam Plan*. Rockville, MD: National Institute of Justce.

Hooper, R. M., Lockwood, D. L., and Inciardi, J. A. (1993) Treatment techniques in corrections based therapeutic communities. *Prison Journal*, 73, 290–306.

Hubbard. R. L., Marsden, M. E., Rachal, J. V., Harwood, H. J., Cavanaugh, E. R., and Ginzburg, H. M. (1989) *Drug abuse treatment: A national study of effectiveness*. Chapel Hill: University of North Carolina Press.

Inciardi, J. A. (1993) Introduction: A response to the War on Drugs. In J. Inciardi, (Ed.), *Drug treatment and criminal justice*. Newbury Park, CA: Sage Publications.

Inciardi, J. A. (1996) The therapeutic community: An effective model for corrections-based drug abuse treatment. In K. Early (Ed.), *Drug treatment behind bars. Prison-based strategies for change*. Westport, CT: Praeger Publishers/ Greenwood Publishing Group.

Inciardi, J. A. (1996) *A corrections-based continuum of effective drug abuse treatment*. National Institute of Justice. Research Preview. Washington, D.C.: US Department of Justice.

Inciardi, J. A., Martin, S. S., Lockwood, D. L., Hooper, R. M., and Wald, B. M. (1992) Obstacles to the implementation and evaluation of drug treatment programmes in correctional settings: Reviewing the Delaware KEY experience. In C. Leukefeld and F. Tims (Eds.), *Drug treatment in prisons and jails* (pp. 176–191). Research Monograph Series, Vol. 118. Rockville, MD: National Institute on Drug Abuse.

Johnson, B. D., Lipton, D. S., and Wish, E. D. (1986) *Facts about the criminality about heroin and cocaine abusers and some new alternatives to incarceration*. New York: Narcotic and Drug Research, Inc.

Keith, S. J., Regier, D. A., and Rae, D. S. (1991) Schizophrenic disorders. In D. N. Robins and D. A. Regier (Eds.), *Psychiatric disorders in America*. New York: MacMillan.

Kerr v. Farrey, 95 F.3d 472 (1996).

Kline, S. (1993) A profile of female offenders in state and federal prisons. In M. D. Laurel, (Ed.), *Female offenders: Meeting needs of a neglected population*. American Correctional Association.

Knight, K., Simpson, D. D., Chatham, L. R., and Camacho, L. M. (1997) An assessment of prison-based drug treatment: Texas' in-prison therapeutic community programme. *Journal of Offender Rehabilitation*, 2(3/4), 75–100.

Leukefeld, C. G. (1985) The clinical connection: Drugs and crime. *International Journal of the Addictions*, 20(6/7), 1049–1064.

Lipton, D. S. (1994) The correctional opportunity: Pathways to drug treatment for offenders. *The Journal of Drug Issues*, 24(2), 331–348.

Lipton, D. S. (1995) *The effectiveness of treatment for drug abusers under criminal justice supervision*. National Institute of Justice Research Report.

Lipton, D. S. (1996) Prison-based therapeutic communities: Their success with drug abusing offenders. *National Institute of Justice Journal,* 12–20.

Lipton, D. S., Martinson, R., and Wilks, J. (1975) *The effectiveness of correctional treatment.* New York: Praeger Publishers.

Marshall v. United States, 414 US 417 (1974).

Martin, S. S., Butzin, C. A., and Inciardi, J. A. (1995) Assessment of a multistage therapeutic community for drug-involved offenders. *Journal of Psychoactive Drugs,* 27,(1), 109–116.

Martinson, R. (1974) What works? Questions and answers about prison reform. *The Public Interest,* 35, 22–54.

Martinson, R. (1979) New findings, new views: A note of caution regarding prison reform. *Hofstra Law Review,* 7, 243–258.

McCuckin v. Smith, 974 F.2d 1050 (9th Cir. 1992).

McLaughlin, P., and Pepper, P. (1991) Modifying the therapeutic community for the mentally ill substance abuser. *New Directions for Mental Health Services,* 50, 85–93.

McLellan, A. T., Kushner, H., Metzger, D., Peters, R., Smith, L., Grissom, G., Pettinati, H., and Argeriou, M. (1992) The fifth edition of the Addiction Severity Index. *Journal of Substance Abuse Treatment,* 9, 199–213.

Murray, D. W. (1992) Drug abuse treatment programmes in the Federal Bureau of Prisons: Initiatives for the 1990's. In C. Leukefeld and F. Tims (Eds.), *Drug treatment in prisons and jails* (pp. 62–83). Research Monograph Series. Vol. 118. Rockville, MD: National Institute on Drug Abuse.

Murray, D. W. (1996) Drug abuse treatment in the Federal Bureau of Prisons: A historical review and assessment of contemporary initiatives. In K. Early (Ed.), *Drug treatment behind bars: Prison-based strategies for change.* Westport, CT: Praeger Publishers/Greenwood Publishing Group.

National Commission on Correctional Health Care (1997) *CorrectCare,* 11,(2), 1–17.

National GAINS Centre (1997) *The prevalence of co-occuring mental and substance abuse disorders in the criminal justice system. Just the Facts series.* Delmar, New York: The National GAINS Centre.

O'Donnell, J. A., and Ball, J. C. (1966) *Narcotic addiction.* New York: Harper and Row.

Pace v. Fauver, 479 F Supp. 456 (D. N. J. 1979).

Palmer, I. (1996) Growth-centered intervention: An overview of changes in recent decades. In K. Early (Ed.), *Drug treatment behind bars: Prison-based strategies for change.* Westport, CT: Praeger Publishers/Greenwood Publishing Group.

Pan, H., Scarpiti, F. R., Inciardi, J. A., and Lockwood, D. (1993) Some considerations on therapeutic communities in corrections. In J. Inciardi (Ed.), *Drug treatment and criminal justice.* Newbury Park, CA: Sage Publications.

Peters, R. H. (1993) Substance abuse services in jails and prisons. *Law and Psychology Review,* 17, 86–116.

Peters, R. H., and Bartoi, M. G. (1997) *Screening and assessment of co-occurring disorders in the justice system.* Delmar N.Y.: The National GAINS Centre.

Peters, R. H., and Greenbaum, P. E., Edens, J. F., Carter, C. R., and Ortiz, M. M. (1998) Prevalence of DSM-IV substance abuse and dependence disorders among prison inmates, *American Journal of Drug and Alcohol Abuse,* 24(1), 573–587.

Peters, R. H., and Hills, H. A. (1993) Inmates with co-occurring substance abuse and mental health disorders. In H. J. Steadman and J. J. Cocozza (Eds.), *Providing services for offenders with mental illness and related disorders in prisons* (pp. 159–212). Washington, D.C.: The National Coalition for the Mentally Ill in the Criminal Justice System.

Peters, R. H., Kearns, W. D., Murrin, M. R., and Dolente, A. S. (1992) Psychopathology and mental health needs among drug involved inmates. *Journal of Prison and Jail Health,* 11(1), 3–25.

Peters, R. H., Strozier, A. I., Murrin, M. R., and Kearns, W. D. (1997) Treatment of substance-abusing jail inmates: Examination of gender differences. *Journal of Substance Abuse Treatment,* 14(4), 339–349.

Robins, D. N., and Regier, D. A. (1991) *Psychiatric disorders in America: The Epidemologic Catchment Area Study.* New York: Free Press.

Sacks, S., and Sacks, J. (1995) *Recent advances in theory, prevention, and research for dual disorder.* Paper presented at the Middle Eastern institute on Drug Abuse, Jerusalem, Israel.

Simpson, D. D., Joe, G. W., and Bracy, S. (1982) Six-year follow-up of opioid addicts after admission to treatment. *Archives of General Psychiatry,* 39, 1318–1323.

Simpson, D. D., Knight, K., and Pevoto, C. (1996) *Research summary: Focus on drug treatment in criminal justice settings.* Ft. Worth, TX: Institute of Behavioural Research, Texas Christian University.

Speckart, G., and Anglin, D. M. (1986) Narcotics use and crime: A causal modeling approach. *Journal of Quantitative Criminology*, 2, 3–28.

Teague, G. B., Schwab, B., and Drake, R. E. (1990) *Evaluating services for young adults with severe mental illness and substance use disorders.* Arlington, VA.: National Association of State Mental Health Programme Directors.

Texas Department of Criminal Justice (1997) *Department of Criminal Justice.* [On-Line]. Available: http://www.lbb.state.tx.us/lbb/members/reports/fiscal/fspscj/FS696.htm.

US Department of Justice (1988) *Drug use and crime: Special report (NCJ.111940).* Washington, D.C.: Bureau of Justice Statistics.

US Department of Justice (1991) *Intervening with substance-abusing offenders: A framework for action. Report of the National Task Force on Correctional Substance Abuse Strategies.* Washington, D.C.: National Institute of Corrections.

US Department of Justice (1992) *A national report: Drugs, crime, and the justice system.* Washington, D.C.: Bureau of Justice Statistics.

US Department of Justice (1994) *Women in prison.* Washington, D.C.: Bureau of Justice Statistics.

US Department of Justice (1995a) *Prisoners in 1994.* Washington, D.C.: Bureau of Justice Statistics.

US Department of Justice (1995b) *Drugs and crime facts, 1994.* Rockville, MD: Bureau of Justice Statistics.

US Department of Justice (1996a) *Prison and Jail Inmates, 1995.* Washington, D.C.: Bureau of Justice Statistics.

US Department of Justice (1996b) *Crime in the United States, 1995: Uniform Crime Reports.* Washington, D.C.: Federal Bureau of Investigation.

US Department of Justice (1997a) *Violent Crime Control and Law Enforcement Act of 1994.* [On-line]. Available: http://gopher.usdoj.gov/crime/crime.html

US Department of Justice (1997b) *Grant Programmes for 1995.* [On-line]. Available: http://gopher.usdoj.gov/crime/ojp_brf.html

US General Accounting Office. (November, 1996) *Federal and State Prisons: Inmate Populations, Costs, and Projection Models.* Report to the Subcommittee on Crime, Committee on the Judiciary, House of Representatives. Washington, D.C.

Weinman, B. A., and Lockwood, D. (1993) Inmate drug treatment programming in the federal bureau of prisons. In J. Inciardi (Ed.), *Drug treatment and criminal justice* (pp. 194–208). Newbury Park, CA: Sage Publications.

Weissman, M. M., Bruce, M. L., Leaf, P. J., Florio, L. P., and Holzer, C. (1992) Affective disorders. In L. N. Robins and D. A. Regier (Eds.), *Psychiatric disorders in America* (pp. 53–80). New York: Macmillan.

Wellisch, J., Anglin, M. D., and Prendergast, M. I. (1993a) Numbers and characteristics of drug using women in the criminal justice system: Implications for treatment. *Journal of Drug Issues*, 23, (1), 7–30.

Wellisch, J., Anglin, M. D., and Prendergast, M. L. (1993b) Treatment strategies for drug-abusing women offenders. In J. Inciardi (Ed.), *Drug treatment and criminal justice* (pp. 5–29). Newbury Park, CA: Sage Publications.

Wellisch, J., Prendergast, M. L., and Anglin, M. D. (1994) *Drug-abusing women offenders: Results of a national survey.* Washington, D.C.: Office of Justice Programmes, National Institute of Justice: Research In Brief, US Department of Justice.

Wexler, H. K. (1993) *Establishing substance abuse treatment programmes in prisons: A practitioner's handbook.* Rockville, MD: Centre for Substance Abuse Treatment.

Wexler, H. K., Falkin, G. P., and Lipton, D. S. (1990) Outcome evaluation of a prison therapeutic community for substance abuse treatment. *Criminal Justice and Behaviour*, 17(1), 71–92.

Wexler, H. K., Falkin, G. P., Lipton, D. S., and Rosenblum, A. B. (1992) Outcome evaluation of a prison therapeutic community for substance abuse treatment. In C. Leukefeld and F. Tims (Eds.), *Drug abuse treatment in prisons and jails* (pp.156–175). Research Monograph Series, Vol. 118. Rockville, MD: National Institute on Drug Abuse.

Wexler, H. K., Lipton, D. S. (1993) From reform to recovery: Advances in prison drug treatment, in J. Inciardi (Ed.), *Drug treatment and criminal justice* (pp. 209–227). Newbury Park, CA: Sage Publications.

Wexler, H. K., and Williams, R. (1986) The Stay'n Out therapeutic community: Prison treatment for substance abusers. *Journal of Psychoactive Drugs*, 18, 221–331). ✦

24

Practicing Penal Harm Medicine in the United States

Prisoners' Voices From Jail

Michael S. Vaughn

Linda G. Smith

Corrections is often said to be a field of misery. Nowhere is this more evident than in the medical care arena. Providing adequate medical care is difficult under ideal conditions, but when faced with severe crowding, an aging prison population, limited budgets, and rural locations, medical treatment in America's prison system is, with little wonder, often criticized. Michael S. Vaughn and Linda G. Smith provide a look inside a mega-jail and uncover systematic neglect and abuse of inmates. There are six areas of ill-treatment that the authors identify: (1) using medical care to humiliate prisoners, (2) withholding medical care from inmates with HIV/AIDS, (3) withholding medical care from other inmates, (4) exposing inmates to temperature extremes and sleep deprivation, (5) torturous dental care, and (6) falsification of inmate medical records. Perhaps most damning is their claim that some correctional health care providers abdicate their ethical obligation.

Excerpted from "Practicing Penal Harm Medicine in the United States: Prisoners' Voices From Jail" by Michael S. Vaughn and Linda G. Smith, *Justice Quarterly*, 16(1):175–231. Copyright © 1999 by Academy of Criminal Justice Sciences. Reprinted by permission.

. . . I will use treatment to help the sick according to my ability and judgment, but I will never use it to injure or wrong them. . . . Into whatsoever houses I enter, I will do so to help the sick, keeping myself free from all intentional wrongdoing and harm. . . .

From the Hippocratic Oath
(Trager 1979:17)

From the "deprivation of liberty" perspective of punishment, the sole purpose of incarceration is to restrict the freedoms of those incarcerated (Council of Europe 1987, 1995; Reynaud 1986; Wilson 1993). That is, the "Prisoner's punishment is being sent to prison"; "punishing prisoners once they're inside is not the point" (Peters 1992:250). Advocating the deprivation of liberty perspective, Penal Reform International (1990:5) argues that prison managers must be "concerned with ensuring prisoners' personal dignity, their physical and mental well-being, education and recreational facilities, religious provisions, and standards of hygiene and medical and psychiatric care." The Council of Europe (1987:34) contends that the "philosophy and management of any [correctional] system [must be] based on . . . principles of humanity, morality, justice, and respect for human dignity that are essential to a modern civilized society." This perspective is "aimed principally at the re-education and re-socialization of the offender" in which "prisons must show respect for the fundamental rights of individuals" (Neale 1991:207).

Opposed to the deprivation of liberty model is the "penal harm" movement, an emerging alternative perspective in American penology (see Clear 1994; Cullen 1995). Penal harm advocates contend that the incarceration experience should inflict pain and make conditions of confinement as harsh as possible (see Allen and April 1997; Bright 1996, 1997). Because "criminals are commonly associated with slime, darkness, and foul odors, their places of punishment must reflect these qualities" (see Duncan 1996:144). Proponents of penal harm call for a system of punishment that embraces imprisonment because it embodies conscious infliction of pain (see Christie 1981, 1993) and recognizes that the "essence of the penal sanction is to harm" (Clear 1994:4). From this perspective, incarceration is a "planned government act, whereby a citizen" is banned intentionally. This justifies the purpose of incarceration: offender suffering (Clear 1994:4). Correctional facilities serve as "factories for the manufacture of psychophysical handicaps," providing the conditions of confinement that harm, damage, and debilitate those confined (Gallo and Ruggiero 1991:278). In recent years, the penal harm movement has gained currency, making the conditions of correctional confinement harsh and punitive, whereas the human rights-oriented "deprivation of liberty" model has been deemphasized (McCoy 1997).

For many years, the workplace culture of corrections was said to be divided into two irreconcilable camps. On one side were custodial personnel who identified with the penal harm movement and wished to inflict pain on prisoners (Fogel 1979). On the other side were the health-oriented medical staff members who focused on the prisoners' welfare and treated them with compassion, dignity, and humanity (Kratcoski 1989). Once correctional systems are committed to implementing the mandates of penal harm, the line between acceptable punishment and ill-treatment becomes blurred. When applied to correctional health care, the implementation of mandates for penal harm challenges the existence of the dichotomy between custody and treatment.

In this article we explore how the implementation of the penal harm movement within a correctional health care system can lead to the ill-treatment and torture of prisoners. Our thesis is that the reported philosophical breach between custodians and some medical staff members is more imagined than real. Because correctional medical personnel work in a system that subordinates their professional canons to the utilitarian rationality of the new penology and the ethical relativism of the penal harm movement, we conclude that some correctional health providers sympathetic to the custodial subculture abdicate their ethical obligations, and that the result is the ill-treatment and torture of prisoners. . . .

Methodology

Research Site

The jail is classified as a mega jail and is located in a large metropolitan area. Like other mega jails, it houses both pretrial detainees and sentenced felons and misdemeanants; some pretrial detainees await trial as long as two years. Some convicted state inmates are incarcerated here because the state penitentiary is overcrowded. The jail traditionally is structured with a top-down, militaristic bureaucracy in which the sheriff, the chief executive officer, dispenses authority downward throughout the organizational hierarchy.

The jail complex consists of several buildings that house maximum-, medium-, and minimum-security male and female prisoners, both pretrial detainees and sentenced inmates. Although a high-rise building serves as the maximum-security facility for male prisoners, it also contains booking and holding cells for males and females, the primary medical unit, the kitchen, several housing units for males, and administrative offices. Another building houses maximum-security female prisoners; this facility contains a small medical clinic for women prisoners. A separate building houses medium-security male prisoners, and two barrack-style buildings houses minimum-security males and females. Work-release centers are located in two separate buildings; one temporarily houses minimum-security females, and the other holds minimum-security male work-release prisoners. Separate buildings hold additional administrative offices, a visitors' center, a kitchen and dining area for staff and prisoners, and the laundry. As jail populations fluctuate, however, the housing unit assignments frequently shift to accommodate changing needs.

The primary medical unit is located in the high-rise maximum-security facility, where a wing is dedicated for male prisoners under suicide watch and those requiring constant medical supervision. Because of growing demand for medical services, some of the regular housing units have been designated as medical housing units; thus some prisoners are remote from the nurses' stations located in the primary medical unit. In the primary medical unit, prisoners report for sick call, dental services, and psychiatric evaluation. Prisoners who suffer minor medical mishaps are treated in the jail's medical unit, but those with major emergencies are transported to local hospitals that have contracted with the jail to accept these individuals. Some prisoners requiring special medical care such as ophthalmology, dermatology, or oncology, are transported to external medical providers for treatment. In 1995 an area within the woman's maximum-security facility was created to house female prisoners requiring medical supervision; this eliminated the need to transport them to the primary medical facility in the high-rise building.

The jail has a history of failing to maintain the facility in accordance with constitutional standards and consent decree requirements. In November 1979 the county entered into a consent decree to remedy unconstitutional conditions of confinement, including unacceptable medical facilities and health care at the jail. . . . From November 1979 to January 1998, when the consent decree was terminated, the jail's medical facilities were never in full compliance with the consent decree's mandates, although the jail remained accredited by the NCCHC (Federal Court Monitor 1992–1996).

As part of the 1979 agreement, the supervising federal court appointed a "court monitor" to assess the jail's compliance with the consent decree. The consent decree mandated that a copy of the agreement be "continuously posted in each prebooking or holding cell and in each cell block" ("Final Proposal" 1979:14). Ten copies of the consent decree were also to be placed in the jail library, and all prisoners were to be "advised in writing of the availability of [the] consent decree and the method to be used in securing a copy" ("Final Proposal" 1979:14). Moreover, the consent decree stated that the federal court monitor's "name and address shall be provided to all [prisoners] upon entering the . . .jail and they shall be advised that [the court monitor] may be contacted in regard to any violation of this agreement" ("Final Proposal" 1979:14). A mailbox was established in each housing unit so that prisoners could drop off letters written to the court monitor. Prisoners who wished to communicate with the court monitor were provided with writing materials to compose letters. Prisoners who did not write a letter but who desired to communicate with the court monitor received the opportunity to do so during quarterly jail inspections.

From October 1992 to September 1997, the jail's medical facilities were managed by three separate private managed-care corporations. Despite the turnover in contract providers, the medical personnel who staffed the facilities remained largely unchanged because the contract providers retained existing health care workers.

Although the medical staff did not work directly for the county, they were required to fulfill the county's legal obligation for the health care of prisoners incarcerated at the jail.

Data Collection and Analysis

The primary units of analysis were letters written by prisoners to the jail monitor to complain about medical facilities and health care personnel. Although prisoners raised many other constitutional and consent decree-related issues in their letters, we focus here on the medical concerns because the court monitor believed that "medical services were the most problematic area of concern under the consent decree" (Federal Court Monitor 1994). Allegations in prisoners' letters were corroborated by independent information gathered from several sources including the federal court monitor (Federal Court Monitor 1992–1996), medical and legal documents (*Nelson v. Prison Health Services* 1997), medical and custodial personnel who worked in the jail, and individuals with detailed knowledge of the consent decree.

In addition to analyzing prisoners' letters, we became familiar with the jail's delivery of medical services by reading sick call slips submitted by prisoners seeking medical treatment, grievance forms filed by prisoners claiming inadequate treatment, reports filed by the jail monitor to the federal judge overseeing the consent decree, internal policies promulgated by the medical provider, and memoranda written by jail staff in response to sick call requests and medical grievances filed by prisoners. We reviewed prisoners' medical records, toured the facility, and interviewed the prisoners' attorney. He brought the original suit that resulted in the consent decree and remained the plaintiffs' attorney for the 18-year life of the case. We also interviewed staff members who worked for the federal judge overseeing the consent decree, prisoners at the jail, the sheriff charged with maintaining the jail, the lieutenant who acted as a liaison between the jail and the federal court monitor, the medical care contract monitor who worked for the sheriffs office, and numerous other custodial staff members at the jail. In addition, we interviewed jail physicians, nurses, physician's assistants, and medical technicians responsible for delivering health care. In all, we spent more than 1,000 hours evaluating the health care system at the jail.

The court monitor provided critical information about the internal dynamics of the jail and the daily operations of the jail's medical unit. Prisoners' letters represented only the "tip of the iceberg" of actual medical ill-

treatment and torture at the jail; through routine jail inspections, the court monitor also took many medical complaints verbally in the cell blocks. During these conversations, the court monitor learned that many prisoners who suffered from medical abuses never wrote letters because the health and custodial staff harassed, intimidated, and retaliated against letter writers. Moreover, the court monitor indicated that a substantial amount of prisoners' legal mail was "lost" and/or "disappeared" at the jail (Federal Court Monitor 1992–1996).

Over the life of the consent decree, three separate federal court monitors were assigned to watch over the jail's compliance with the consent decree. In this article we focus on letters written to the third monitor, whose appointment began in October 1992. The letters were organized chronologically and numbered sequentially by date of postmark. The length and quality of the letters varied markedly. Some prisoners submitted handwritten letters of only two or three sentences; others crafted typed, single-spaced, multiple-page narratives that painted a vivid picture of medical practices at the jail. Several prisoners wrote rambling, stream-of-consciousness diatribes. A few, however, wrote sophisticated, highly developed, well-organized letters consistent with a college education.

Throughout this article, we identify letter writers as prisoners if we could not determine whether the writer was a pretrial detainee or a convicted inmate. We exclude names and other identifying characteristics when referring to specific prisoners and staff members. We employ interpretive/inductive analysis, a form of "content-based methods of analysis" (Denzin 1997:242), to organize and present the letters written to the jail monitor from October 1992 to September 1997. This methodology allows users to make "valid inferences from text" (Weber 1990:9). It "classifies textual material, reducing it to more relevant, manageable bits of data" (Weber 1990:5). Because interpretive/inductive analysis is an excellent tool for analyzing "small groups as microcosms of society" (Weber 1990:11), we seek to provide an understanding of ill-treatment and torture in the medical unit at the jail. . . .

Findings and Discussion

From October 1992 to September 1997, prisoners wrote more than 250 letters to the federal court monitor; 103 of these letters pertained to medical care. During this time, the jail incarcerated approximately 2,400 prisoners per day. According to the federal court monitor, the majority of the prisoners writing letters were pretrial detainees, although most writers did not disclose whether they were pretrial detainees or sentenced inmates. Only 11 (11%) letters were identified as written by pretrial detainees, but the jail monitor believed this figure to be a gross underestimate.

Seventy-four different prisoners (72%) wrote the 103 letters to the federal court monitor complaining of health-related issues. Sixty-five of these writers (88%) were men; nine (12%) were women. Most of the letters were written by different prisoners: 59 (57%) prisoners, 51 (50%) men and 8 (8%) women, wrote one letter each. Eight men wrote two letters each, two men wrote three each, and three men wrote four each. One male and one female prisoner wrote five letters each to the court monitor. Although only a few prisoners wrote multiple letters, their correspondence made up 43% of all medical letters written to the court monitor.

Table 24.1 shows the specific medical provisions of the consent decree that were addressed in the prisoners' letters. Table 24.2 summarizes the methods of ill-treatment and torture identified in these letters, and Table 24.3 displays the number of letters pertaining to various practices of ill-treatment and torture of prisoners at the jail. Although the number of cases was small, these practices are difficult to document and represent the most egregious violations of medical ethics.

Table 24.1

Provisions in the Consent Degree Pertaining to Medical Care Addressed in Prisoners' Letters Written to the Federal Court Monitor

Provision of the Consent Decree	N	%
Access to Physicians	18	17.5
Evaluation of Prisoners' Complaints	10	9.7
Emergency Medical Service	2	1.9
Treatment within 24 Hours	39	37.9
Medical Diet	3	2.9
Hospitalize Infections/Contagious	13	12.6
Custodial Personnel Handling Medication	0	.0
Dental Care	15	14.6
Health Screening	3	2.9
Total	103	100.0

Previous studies on ill-treatment and torture of prisoners also reported a small number of cases documenting the most alarming deviations from medical protocols. The Danish Rehabilitation Center surveyed 200 torture survivors from 18 countries and reported that 41 described the involvement of medical personnel in their torture (Rasmussen 1990). In Chile, a team of physicians affiliated with Amnesty International examined 18 former detainees who alleged that they had been tortured; 15 of those claimed that medical officials examined them before and after their torture (Stover 1987). Researchers studying apartheid medicine in South Africa gained access to only six former detainees who described various forms of medical ill-treatment and torture (Nightingale et al. 1990). Finally, Physicians for Human Rights were allowed to examine only a convenience sample of 86 medical reports of detainees allegedly subjected to medical maltreatment in Turkish correctional facilities (Iacopino et al. 1996). In regard to sample size, our 103 letters written by 74 different prisoners compare favorably with

Table 24.2

Methods of Medical Ill-Treatment and Torture Identified in Prisoners' Letters to the Federal Court Monitor, by Category

Categories of Ill-Treatment and Torture	Methods of Ill-Treatment and Torture
Using Medical Care to Humiliate Prisoners	Betray Prisoners' Confidence
	Verbally Disclose HIV-Positive/AIDS Status
	Policies/Actions That Disclose HIV-Positive/AIDS Status
	Break Prisoners' Will by Exploiting Known Weaknesses
	Force Prisoners to Grovel/Beg for Health Care
Withholding Medical Care from HIV-Positive/ AIDS Prisoners	Make Prisoners Wait Months to See Physician
	Fail to Follow Through with Approved Free-World Medical Treatment
	Refuse to Administer Medication
	Delay Treatment for Infections and Fever
Withholding Medical Care from Other Prisoners	Deny Prisoners Pain Medication
	Administer Inadequate/Wrong Medication
	Delay Care Until Released from Custody
	Refuse to Believe/Treat Medical Complaints
	Fail to Implement Recommended Treatment by Free-World Medical Specialists
Exposing Prisoners to Temperature Extremes and Sleep Deprivation	Prevent Sleep through Intentional Noise/Light
	Expose Prisoners under Suicide Watch to Extreme Cold
	Promise Acute Care in Return for Declaration of Suicidal Intent, but Deny Appropriate Care
Using Dental Care as an Instrument of Ill-Treatment and Torture	Delay Care for Abscessed Teeth for Weeks/Months
	Extract Wrong Teeth
	Extract Teeth as Only Method of Dental Treatment
	Inadequate Pain Control for Dental Discomfort
	Fail to Provide Routine Preventive Dental Care
Falsifying Prisoners' Medical Records	Omit Health Conditions from Files
	Monitor Physical Abuse but Not Record It
	Refuse to Maintain Records
	Document Medication Not Administered
	Record Examinations Not Given
	Document Procedures Not Performed

samples in other studies on medical ill-treatment and torture.

Using Medical Care to Humiliate Prisoners

When prisoners enter correctional systems, they frequently experience degradation ceremonies designed to transform them from being complete persons to "discredited ones" (Goffman 1962, 1963; Irwin 1985; Toch 1992a). Because "there is no confidentiality between prisoner and doctor" (Hudson 1987:958), medical conditions of HIV-positive prisoners and those with AIDS are used as an instrument to label, stigmatize, and cast them out of the general prisoner population (Gostin and Lazzarini 1997:111; Greenspan 1996:115; Turnbull, Dolan, and Stimson 1993:204). In the United States (Carroll 1992; Vaughn and Carroll 1998) and in Uruguay (Bloche 1987), some medical officials disclose prisoners' confidential medical conditions to custodial personnel, who use the health information to punish prisoners. Nightingale et al. (1990:2100) reported that the practice of apartheid medicine in South Africa routinely involved "release of medical records to prison officials without the detainee's consent." Such practices directly contradict guidelines established by the WMA (1976), which forbid punitive use of professional knowledge about prisoners' medical conditions (Jayawardena 1996; Jurgens and Gilmore 1994).

Letters written to the jail monitor and the monitor's subsequent inspections showed an extensive process of degradation, humiliation, and subjugation of prisoners by medical personnel (Federal Court Monitor 1992, 1996). Some jail medical officials disclosed prisoners' HIV-positive/AIDS status to everyone in the facility, including custodial staff, noncustodial staff, and other prisoners (Letter 028).

In one instance a correctional officer, in the presence of three prisoners, ordered the jail barber to wear rubber gloves while cut-

Table 24.3

Practices of Medical Ill-Treatment and Torture Identified in Prisoners' Letters to the Federal Court Monitor

Categories of Ill-Treatment and Torture	N	%
Using Medical Care to Humiliate Prisoners	21	20.4
Withholding Medical Care from HIV-Positive/AIDS Prisoners	15	14.6
Withholding Medical Care from Other Prisoners	36	34.9
Exposing Prisoners to Temperature Extremes and Sleep Deprivation	5	4.8
Using Dental Care as an Instrument of Ill-Treatment and Torture	15	14.6
Falsifying Prisoners' Medical Records	8	7.8
Other Unethical Medical Practices	3	2.9
Total	103	100.0

ting the hair of an HIV-positive prisoner (Letter 021), even though the barber did not routinely wear rubber gloves while cutting prisoners' hair. When the prisoner told the officer that he wanted to file a grievance because the officer had divulged his confidential medical history to nonmedical and noncustodial personnel, the officer refused to provide the prisoner with a grievance form, remarking "to another [prisoner] that those AIDS-infected motherfuckers want to file a grievance against me" (Letter 021).

Because the jail barber had no chance of contracting HIV by cutting the HIV-positive prisoner's hair (Blumberg 1990; Gostin and Lazzarini 1997; Kappeler, Blumberg, and Potter 1996), the correctional officer violated the NCCHC's "Confidentiality of Health Records" standard, which states clearly that prisoners' health records are not to be used for nonmedical or punitive purposes. Moreover, the actions of jail personnel violated the "Sharing of Health Information" standard, which limits the use of information in medical records to situations that "preserve the health and safety of the inmate, other inmates, or the correctional staff" (NCCHC 1996:76). Confidentiality provisions specify that "health care information [should only be available to] employees or correctional staff who need to know" (Gannon 1997:137). "Need-to-know" staff members include "those medical and correctional staff providing clinical services to the prisoner" (Gannon 1997:137). Staff members' behavior also violated the "grievance mechanism" standard, which mandates that accredited facilities have a "grievance mechanism . . .to address inmates' complaints about health services" (NCCHC 1996:11).

According to the court monitor, HIV-positive/AIDS prisoners were identified by a large blue dot placed above their cells (Federal Court Monitor 1992). This symbol revealed who was HIV-positive to everyone in the jail. A detainee with AIDS (Letter 041) complained that "detainees' medical conditions and privacy rights are violated every day [at] the jail. All known HIV-positive/AIDS detainees are separated and isolated from other detainees, even if they are completely healthy." HIV-positive/AIDS prisoners, both pretrial detainees and convicted inmates, have segregated recreation and exercise times; their food trays are specially marked and are used only for HIV-positive/AIDS offenders. As a result, "HIV-positive/AIDS detainees have been humiliated, threatened, discriminated, isolated, teased, and constantly asked, 'Are you dying from AIDS?" (Letter 041). Letters to the jail monitor and the monitor's jail inspections confirmed that custodial staff members and some medical personnel identified HIV-positive prisoners to noncustodial staff members, security personnel, and other prisoners by leaking confidential information contained in health care records.

In Chile and Uruguay, medical personnel commonly participate in torture of prisoners by betraying prisoners' confidence (Nightingale 1990; Nightingale et al. 1990). Under a guise of confidentiality, some medical personnel coax prisoners to divulge secrets; then they betray that confidence by sharing the information with the custodial staff, even if the information has little bearing on institutional safety. The purpose of the betrayal is to retaliate against and punish the prisoner.

This idea was expressed in Letter 179, where a prisoner told the jail mental health counselor that the custodial staff used excessive force against him; the counselor assured the prisoner confidentiality and promised to investigate the matter. After the prisoner talked with the counselor, custodial officers "knew every thing [the prisoner] told the counselor." Thereafter the officers harassed, threatened, and taunted the prisoner, attempting to provoke him to violence. In a letter to the court monitor, the prisoner lamented "I'm in fear of my life from these officers," who are "trying to get me to loose [sic] control so [they can] retaliate and be justified in what they will do to me." Medical officials' gaining prisoners' confidence and then using information gained from that confidence to punish them is a staple of totalitarian regimes (Wei 1997; Wu 1994).

Totalitarian regimes use extreme forms of psychological suffering to punish prisoners (Tindale 1996). During World War II, the "Japanese maintained a policy of submitting Allied prisoners of war to violence, insults, and public humiliation" to inflict severe psychological damage (Roling and Ruter 1977: 420). Among the psychological torture techniques developed by the Central Intelligence Agency (CIA) ("Psychological Torture" 1997), coercive methods designed to render a prisoner powerless and to induce "psychological regression" shatter the prisoner's ability to cope with stressful events (Bierma 1994; Burkhalter 1995; Foster, Sandler, and Davis 1987:113).

Using medical care to break prisoners' will and to exploit known weaknesses was a theme in letters written to the jail monitor. In Letter 098, a Vietnam veteran who suffered from posttraumatic stress disorder (PTSD), manifested in insomnia, combat flashbacks, and anxiety attacks, was diagnosed as 100% disabled by the Department of Veterans Affairs (VA) and was under medical supervision and treatment by VA physicians. When the vet was incarcerated at the jail on a probation violation, his VA-prescribed medication was discontinued. Although the inmate was classified, where he fully disclosed his medical condition and his ongoing treatment, and made repeated requests to continue his Lithium (to control mania) and Xanax (to control anxiety), he never saw a physician during his 16 days of incarceration.

Eleven days into his incarceration, the inmate was examined by a psychiatric nurse, who said "We don't give your type of medication here" and reminded the inmate that jails are "very stressful places and [to] just get use[d] to" being without the medication. When the inmate asked the nurse "why it took so long to see medical" personnel at the jail, the nurse replied, "I've been on vacation." The inmate suffered medication withdrawal, nightmares, and combat flashbacks, saying "[E]very time a helicopter landed . . ., I felt I was in combat back in Vietnam." Letter 098 illustrates abdication of medical responsibility by the psychiatric nurse, whose callousness was aimed at inflicting pain, not at alleviating suffering. According to the *Nursing97 Drug Handbook* (1997:440), Xanax "should not be withdrawn abruptly after long-term use; withdrawal symptoms may occur"; the handbook also warns patients and caregivers to "not stop [Lithium] abruptly" (p. 506).

In a system of medical depravity, prisoners are made to wallow in their own excrement (Cockburn 1997) in an attempt to humiliate them and break their will (La Forte, Marcello, and Himmel 1994:177–88; Roth et al. 1987; Silver et al. 1986). One pregnant prisoner, who suffered a miscarriage at the jail, waited "six or seven hours before [medical personnel] sent [her] to the hospital even though [she] was bleeding profusely" (*Nelson v. Prison Health Services* 1997:1456). According to the court monitor, another female detainee was booked at the jail under the influence of alcohol and/or drugs. Because health care personnel failed to provide proper supervision, the detainee experienced alcohol/drug withdrawal, suffered from hallucinations, removed all of her clothes, and ate her own menstrual flow in view of other prisoners. "Despite the fact that she should have been placed in a medical unit because she was at high risk of withdrawal (D.T.'s), she was left unattended for five days by medical staff" (Federal Court Monitor 1994). The detainee received medical attention only after it was requested by the court monitor, in violation of the consent decree.

Wallowing in excrement is profoundly "humiliating because contact typically demonstrates powerlessness" and lack of environmental control, from which humans draw comfort (Silver et al. 1986:272). These emotions were expressed by another female prisoner; she was under treatment by free-world physicians for a disease known as "short bowel syndrome," from which she suffered "chronic diarrhea 10 to 20 times a day" (Letter 225). Because of the prisoner's condition, she was unable to eat solid food; consequently, free-world physicians had surgically inserted a feeding tube into her stomach, where specially prepared food was pumped into her digestive system.

When the prisoner entered the jail, the medical department threw her "infusion pump . . .and bag of supplies . . .out with the garbage." As her diarrhea worsened, she "was housed in maximum security, not because of [her] behavior, but because" of the foul odor that accompanied her illness. The illness, a "form of cancer, is not contagious, but some staff said she had AIDS, . . .treating her like she had the plague." Although many medical personnel were "rude and very crude, one [counselor] in particular [was] exceptionally offensive." The counselor "threatened to quit her job because of the odor, [and] claimed the smell made her so sick that she had to miss days from work" (Letter 225). As a result, the prisoner was never placed in the jail's medical dormitory but was "moved . . .many times throughout the jail for the convenience of the other prisoners with no regards to [her] own feelings or sickness." Clearly at the breaking point, the prisoner concluded her letter, "[I'm] so sick and tired of being tossed around."

Another tactic used by jail medical staff members to humiliate prisoners and break their will involved the misrepresentation of treatment options available to prisoners; seriously ill prisoners were forced to plead for health care (Federal Court Monitor 1995). Letter 085 was written by a pregnant prisoner who had not been examined by a physician after several weeks of incarceration. The prisoner, who had a history of pregnancy problems, said that the medical staff told her they did not treat pregnant prisoners. She suffered "pain so much at times [she couldn't] even eat and keep food down." Moreover, the prisoner reported that she was "scared of loosing [sic] the baby, depressed, and crying most of the time." She concluded "We are human beings, not animals, and . . .animals get better treatment than what we have been receiving. Please, help me with this problem, as I'm going to be here for at least 3 more months."

A similar scenario was reported in Letter 190, in which a pregnant prisoner, jailed for two months, received no treatment for a vaginal discharge that "looks and feels like chlamydia" (Federal Court Monitor 1995). According to the prisoner, the "discharge feels awful and has a terrible odor—everyone can tell, [which is] embarrassing. I go through over 10 pads a day." The prisoner reported that she saw an obstetrician one month into her incarceration, but remained untreated one month after being examined. At sick call, the jail physician refused to see the prisoner. Humiliated and exasperated, the prisoner wrote "[N]ow I sit going on 2 months with this 'mystery illness,' untreated, getting worse everyday! . . .I'm constantly having headaches, stomach cramps, and can't sleep . . .I'm very scared for my baby and myself . . .This medical condition is aw-

ful . . .I'm going crazy with this medical problem . . .I'm at the verge of tears everyday over it, and the medical staff treat me as a pain-in-the-ass! Please help me!! Help my baby!" The degrading and humiliating medical practices that these pregnant prisoners described in their letters to the jail monitor have been reported in the historical (Butler 1997:163–68) as well as the contemporary literature as a common "correctional response to the health needs of pregnant women" (Acoca 1998:55).

Solzhenitsyn (1974:103) reported that "the actual boundaries of human equilibrium are very narrow, and it is not really necessary to use a rack or hot coals to drive the average human being out of his mind." Letters to the jail monitor illustrated how prisoners with serious medical needs were humiliated and forced to grovel before health care was forthcoming. In the jail, medical care was used to "break prisoners' spirits," and the prisoners in Letters 085, 098, 190, and 225 appeared to be at the breaking point. Prisoners' letters and the jail monitor's inspections (Federal Court Monitor 1992–1996) also indicated that some jail medical personnel violated a basic provision of the consent decree, which mandated that "all [prisoners'] complaints shall result in treatment within 24 hours of the complaint." Reflecting the effects of a total institution, the letters show prisoners' helplessness and dependence; prisoners no longer believed that they were in control of their lives or medical conditions.

Withholding Medical Care From HIV-Positive Prisoners and Those With AIDS

Although torture involves physicians overtly punishing prisoners, more subtle forms of ill-treatment include the withholding of medical treatment from suffering prisoners (Burkhalter 1995; MacPherson 1989; Nightingale et al. 1990; Sagan and Jonsen 1976). During the prosecution of Japanese war criminals in the aftermath of World War II, the International Military Tribunal for the Far East (1946–1948:49, 691) reported that Japanese medical personnel failed to provide "any medical supplies to all theaters of war and contributed to the deaths of thousands of prisoners and internees." In a more recent study, Belknap (1996:36) reported that prisoners in the United States were denied access to a physician for as long as eight months. In these circumstances, it is not the application of medical care but the omission of care that inflicts pain, (Laborde 1989).

Indeed, because "mankind's most fundamental beliefs are those that concern life, suffering, and death" (Bankowski 1996:147), perhaps the cruelest example, in the jail, of the custodial-medical implementation of penal harm involved lack of care for prisoners who were dying and near death. Letters to the jail monitor showed a disregard for the health condition of HIV-positive prisoners: They were made to wait to see a physician, which caused their health to deteriorate rapidly. Research in the United States (Committee on the Judiciary 1991:86; Griffin et al. 1996) and in Great Britain (Turnbull, Dolan, and Stimson 1993) also shows that HIV-positive prisoners and those with AIDS experience more rapid declines in health than do free-world outpatients because they receive little high-quality health care.

When prisoners are admitted to correctional facilities, health care received before admittance is stopped until correctional medical personnel can assess their medical needs (Anno 1997). Correctional health care personnel practicing apartheid medicine in South Africa, for example, implemented penal harm mandates by waiting as long as possible before conducting a medical evaluation, and thereby extended the time in which prisoners received no medical treatment (Nightingale 1990; Rayner 1987). Prisoners in our sample reported that this technique was adapted somewhat by some jail physicians: They promised HIV-positive/AIDS prisoners treatment from free-world medical providers, but ordered all in-jail medical

treatment to stop before the free-world health care was available. As a result, some severely ill AIDS prisoners went months without medical care.

One extremely ill prisoner with AIDS, who suffered from Kaposi's sarcoma, received medical care and medication for HIV/AIDS at the jail (Letter 028). Because of his advanced AIDS and his deteriorating health, the prisoner requested and received permission from jail medical officials for medical treatment in the free-world community. After the external referral was approved but before the prisoner received any treatment by a nonjail physician, the jail medical staff discontinued all of his medical treatment and medication for two months, which caused his condition to deteriorate rapidly. The Federal Court Monitor (1994) confirmed that "orders for outside consultation continues to be a problem with failure by the [jail's] medical staff to follow-up on these [free-world] consultations."

Letter 041 revealed a similar situation. A pretrial detainee wrote the court monitor in February 1993, describing his rapidly declining health status. A long-term AIDS survivor (since 1981), the detainee had Kaposi's sarcoma and was slowly going blind. He had been able to control HIV/AIDS in the free world for more than a decade, but was near death after six months in the jail. Even though he was never examined by an external medical provider, the detainee was told for four months that he would be examined by a free-world physician. The detainee lamented "I haven't been found guilty of anything, but it seems like I have already been sentenced to die in the jail."

In one letter the writer reported that even when jail medical personnel possessed medication to treat seriously ill prisoners with AIDS, they refused to distribute it. A prisoner with end-stage AIDS (Letter 147; Letter 148) did not receive the medication prescribed by his free-world physician during his seven weeks of incarceration at the jail, even though jail officials possessed the 18 medications prescribed by physicians at the

Veterans Affairs Hospital. A month into the prisoner's incarceration, the supervisor at the jail medical unit wrote him a letter saying "I received today your 107 bottles of pills at the sheriffs office, and I will ask [the doctor] to review this list with you . . .when he returns from his vacation." When the prisoner urged jail medical officials to distribute the medication, staff members told the prisoner that AIDS medication was too much trouble, and commented "[Y]ou are in jail not a hotel; if you don't like it bond out." . . .

Withholding Medical Care from Other Prisoners

HIV-positive/AIDS prisoners were not the only inmates at the jail who suffered from the effects of the withdrawal of medical care. Some prisoners in severe pain also were denied medication (Letter 199; Letter 209). In some cases, jail medical staff members delayed implementation of a health care regimen, hoping to stall long enough to allow the prisoner to be released from jail or transferred to another facility before any health care was delivered in the jail (Federal Court Monitor 1992, 1996; Letter 183; Letter 190).

Letter 110 was written by a prisoner with leukemia, who lost all sensation in the left side of his body and the right side of his face but was denied all medical care during his three months in jail. When the prisoner repeatedly asked for treatment, medical personnel told him that they were still evaluating his records. Another prisoner, who suffered from a painful hernia, waited three weeks to see a physician (Letter 168). When he finally was examined, medical staff members told him that hernias "could be all right for a year or so"; therefore no treatment would be provided for the hernia while he was incarcerated at the jail. The medical literature suggests that this cavalier attitude toward prisoners with hernias may be dangerous because early treatment reduces morbidity, mortality, and life-threatening complications (Chung et al. 1997; Naude and Bongard 1997; Witherington 1987).

A third prisoner was denied medical care for four months despite bleeding sores in his mouth (Letter 054). Jail medical personnel told him that he was not receiving health care because "you will be moved soon and not [our] problem anymore." Although he filed numerous requests for treatment with medical personnel, the physician responded "I was told you were gone up the road." A fourth prisoner informed health staff members at intake that she suffered from rectal bleeding and blood in her stool (Federal Court Monitor 1996). Three months later, medical personnel told the prisoner to "see a doctor when [you get] out." Finally, in a lawsuit involving a pretrial detainee, a jail nurse admitted that she had said the jail's medical unit saves "money because we skip the ambulance and bring them right to the morgue" (*Nelson v. Prison Health Services* 1997:1458).

A form of "cherry picking" or "selection bias" (Glazier 1997; Light 1997), the practice of releasing prisoners to avoid medical expenditures, has also been reported. One jail in the United States housed a prisoner with a "grapefruit-sized hernia that was definitely incarcerated and perhaps strangulated." Although the prisoner was in "obvious need of immediate surgical evaluation," he was released so that the health care costs did not "come out of the detention center's budget" (Saunders 1993:132).

An account by the Chief Physician Assistant in the United States Federal Bureau of Prisons indicated that because the Bureau "ensures" that correctional health care "does not exceed that care that is available to the [free-world] community, . . .many elective procedures are deferred until [prisoners] are released from custody" (Vause, Beeler, and Miller-Blanks 1997:67). These practices personify the principle of less eligibility. They implement the sterile utilitarian rationality of the new penal managerialism (Garland 1997; Vaughn and Carroll 1998), in which the drive for efficiency is a product of ideology (Winn 1996).

In the United States, some correctional medical personnel either provide inadequate pain medication to prisoners or place a prisoner suffering intense pain on a mild over-the-counter analgesic and then deny him or her stronger pain medication when it is requested (Vaughn 1995, 1997). Such practices were confirmed in the court monitor's investigations (Federal Court Monitor 1996) and were reported in Letter 115, in which a prisoner, who injured his back falling in the jail shower, was examined by the jail physician and placed on pain medication. After two weeks, he reported severe pain and sought alternative therapies for pain relief. When the prisoner asked for stronger pain medication, the doctor removed him from all medication and refused to prescribe further treatment.

Another detainee (Letter 125) was brought to the hospital, where he was diagnosed with a fractured neck vertebra. At the jail, the physician prescribed aspirin; a few weeks later, however, despite the detainee's protests, he was denied all medical care, including the aspirin. He remained in jail for 90 days with no medical care, medication, or therapy for the fractured neck vertebra. . . .

As in other areas of correctional health care, the monitor's jail inspections and the prisoners' letters to the court monitor provide evidence that some jail health providers withhold medical therapy and treatment as a means to inflict pain. Moreover, prisoners' letters show complicity between some medical and custodial staff members to deny medical care, to prisoners, in violation of the consent decree and the accreditation criteria established by the NCCHC.

Exposing Prisoners to Temperature Extremes and Sleep Deprivation

Storr (1990:305) asserted that "sensory deprivation techniques could be used to produce what was equivalent to a temporary episode of insanity." In fact, isolating prisoners in segregated cells decreases their ability to cope and increases their psychological distress (Cooke, Baldwin, and Howison 1990; Holtz 1998:30; Members of the Special International Tribunal 1991:395–96; Miller and Young 1997). Segregated isolation, combined with temperature extremes and sleep deprivation, produces extreme suffering among prisoners (Lippman 1979; Power, McElroy, and Swanson 1997; Weinstein and Cummins 1996).

Prolonged exposure to cold temperatures is a form of segregated detention developed by Nazi (Lippman 1993; Taylor 1992) and Japanese (Tanaka 1996; Williams and Wallace 1989) doctors, implemented in Soviet gulags (Solzhenitsyn 1974), and perfected by Israeli security police (Human Rights Watch/Middle East 1994), in which prisoners are required to "strip down and sleep in cold cells with very little bedding" (King 1994:76). Solzhenitsyn (1974) reported that the purpose of cold therapy was to impair prisoners' health and break their spirit. In very cold cells, prisoners' normal sleep patterns are disrupted; this disruption undermines their concentration and self-control (Human Rights Watch/Middle East 1994) and compounds their inability to adjust and cope ("Psychological Torture" 1997). At the Pelican Bay State Prison in California, naked prisoners were locked in telephone booth-sized cages and exposed to very cold temperatures "as if animals in a zoo." According to the United States District Court for the Northern District of California, such practices failed to "serve any legitimate penological purpose"; "the fact that it occurred at all exhibit[ed] a callous and malicious intent to inflict gratuitous humiliation and punishment" (*Madrid v. Gomez* 1995:1172).

In our study, letters to the jail monitor revealed that prisoners were exposed to temperature extremes and sleep deprivation as part of the medical regimen. One problem that prisoners continually faced was lack of immediate medical care for acute health problems. Some prisoners with acute conditions, who were targeted for punishment, were refused medical treatment, but staff members offered them a Hobson's choice: To receive prompt medical care, they must be suicidal.

In January 1993, for example, a prisoner suffered a broken jaw as a result of a prisoner-to-prisoner assault (Letter 025). Despite severe pain and a jaw the size of a "softball," he was denied prompt medical treatment. A correctional officer, however, informed the prisoner that emergency medical care was available only for prisoners who claimed they were "going to hurt themselves." The prisoner said he would "hurt himself if . . .that's what it would take . . .to be seen by a doctor and be treated." Moments later he was escorted to "Bravo Wing," where suicidal prisoners were placed under a 24-hour suicide watch. Once in Bravo Wing, these prisoners were stripped, given a sleeveless paper gown, and placed in a cell in which cold air conditioning blew constantly. The cell contained only a metal bed that was "filled with germs and bacteria," and it reeked of "old dried-up food and human waste." Under suicide watch, prisoners were checked every few minutes with a flashlight, which prevented meaningful sleep or rest. Under appropriate medical care, a flashlight is shined on truly suicidal prisoners every 20 minutes to ensure that they do not harm themselves (Danto 1997; Hayes 1997). This standard medical procedure, however, becomes a means of ill-treatment and torture when nonsuicidal prisoners are placed on suicide watch and are prevented from sleeping for extended periods.

In October 1994, a prisoner who had been diagnosed in the free world with posttraumatic stress disorder (PTSD) was awakened abruptly at 2 a.m. by a correctional officer (Letter 159). Upset and surprised by the sudden awakening, the prisoner "assumed a combative stance," which infuriated the officer. When the jail psychiatrist was summoned, the prisoner explained his combative reaction as symptomatic of PTSD: When awakened quickly from a deep sleep, PTSD sufferers may exhibit a "hyper-alertness and exaggerated startle response."

As a result of this exchange and after input from custodial officers, the psychiatrist believed that the prisoner "was going to hurt" himself. Although he vehemently denied that he was suicidal, he was medically committed to Bravo Wing under suicide watch. There he suffered "nakedness, sleeplessness, no mattress, no pillow, no cover, and the cold temperatures for three days." . . .

Using Dental Care as a Means of Ill-Treatment and Torture

Two types of dental ill-treatment and torture were identified in the letters to the jail monitor and in the monitor's jail inspections (Federal Court Monitor 1994–1996). In the first type, prisoners were forced to wait weeks or months for dental care for abscessed teeth; when care finally was available, the correctional dentist pulled the wrong teeth (Walens 1997:86). This practice was implemented at the jail, when a dentist pulled a good tooth, from a prisoner's mouth while leaving the abscessed tooth to be pulled weeks or months later (Letter 104). Several hours after the procedure, when the prisoner complained that the wrong tooth had been pulled, a dental assistant altered his dental chart to make it appear that the prisoner had asked the dentist to pull the good tooth (Letter 106).

In the second practice, the medical staff provided only extractions but no routine preextraction dental maintenance (Letter 236). "Most dentists will agree that it is the object of dentistry to retain as many teeth as possible for as long as possible. One interested in good oral hygiene does not extract teeth indiscriminately" (Schaller 1996:86). According to Murton (1971:27), however, correctional practitioners historically were paid on the basis of the number of teeth they pulled, not on routine dental maintenance (Murton and Hyams 1969:99). Apparently little has changed since that practice was reported: Rasmussen (1990:37) and Belknap (1996:36) observed more recently that preventive dental care was rare and that correctional dental "services are limited to pulling teeth."

Similar practices were reported in the letters to the jail monitor and in the monitor's jail inspections (Federal Court Monitor 1992, 1994, 1995). In Letter 047, for example, a prisoner stated that he suffered from "unbearable pain" due to two abscessed teeth. Jail officials informed him that they did not fill cavities, and scheduled him for an extraction. The prisoner waited over six weeks for the tooth to be pulled. In the interim, jail officials treated him with two Tylenol tablets twice a day. Such efforts at pain control raise questions of compliance with the "medication administration training" standard established by the NCCHC (1996:27), which mandates that the "right drugs are [to be] administered at the right time in the right dose by the right method to the right person." A regimen of four Tylenol tablets a day for a prisoner in "unbearable pain" due to two abscessed teeth raises questions of whether the "right drugs" were administered at the "right time" in the "right dose."

In Letters 124 and 149, a prisoner with a severe toothache was examined by the jail dentist seven days after submitting a request for treatment. The dentist X-rayed the tooth and informed the prisoner that it was infected. After "prescribing Advil for pain and antibiotics for an infection," the dentist "advised [him] that [the] tooth would need to be extracted or have root canal performed." The jail dentist said "that root canal therapy was the best option" for the prisoner; yet, because the "jail would not pay for root canal work," extraction was the prisoner's only option (Letter 149).

Themes in the letters to the jail monitor and in the monitor's subsequent investigations, which question whether the jail's dental care fell below acceptable levels, are corroborated by research reporting that the practice of correctional medicine frequently falls below professional standards of care commonly available in the free world (Vaughn and Carroll 1998). Although the consent decree provided that "extraction should be utilized only as a last resort" ("Final Proposal" 1979:9), prisoners in Letters 047, 124, 138, and 149 were told that extraction was the only dental service offered at the jail. The tactics used by the jail also forced prisoners to wait for dental services; typically the appointment for extraction was made early in the consulting process, but the actual extraction required a wait of weeks or months (Federal Court Monitor 1994, 1995).

Falsifying Prisoners' Medical Records

Medical personnel are uniquely qualified to document abuse of prisoners because they are "often the first to interview [prisoners] who have been ill-treated or tortured" (Audet 1995:609; Beret 1989:501–02; Shenson 1996). Although ethical medical practice requires the keeping of accurate and comprehensive health records (BMAWP 1992; Thomsen and Voigt 1988), Nazi pediatricians and psychiatrists during World War II, falsified death certificates of mentally ill and retarded children and adults to mask their own involvement in medical experimentation, euthanasia, and extermination (Grodin, Armas, and Glantz 1993; Lifton 1986; Taylor 1992). Japanese doctors used prisoners of war as "human guinea pigs" and disposed of their remains by burning the bodies in an "electric furnace to leave no trace" (Williams and Wallace 1989:32). Health professionals practicing apartheid medicine in South Africa falsified prisoners' medical records and autopsy reports to hide ill-treatment and torture (Nightingale et al. 1990:2100). At the infamous Cummins and Tucker Prison Farms in Arkansas, medical files reported that prisoners with glass eyes possessed "normal" vision (Murton and Hyams 1969:111).

More recently, criminal justice personnel have been implicated in destroying and/or altering incriminating documents to thwart investigation of official lawlessness (*Harris v. Roderick* 1997; Kappeler, Sluder, and Alpert

1998). Perjury commonly is recognized as the most widespread form of official wrongdoing in criminal justice agencies (Barker and Carter 1994; Commission to Investigate 1994). In correctional medical facilities, health care personnel in Chile, Nazi Germany, the United States, and Uruguay have been identified as forging medical records by falsely registering incidents of staff brutality as accidental injuries (Danish Medical Association 1987:190; Nightingale 1990; Sheleff 1987; Stover 1987; Stover and Nightingale 1985). Physicians for Human Rights report that correctional medical providers in Turkey are "under extraordinary pressure by law enforcement officials to misrepresent or ignore evidence of torture in their examinations and certify that there are no physical signs of torture" (Iacopino et al. 1996:397; Iacopino 1996). In the 1960s, at one correctional facility in the United States, prisoners returning from the prison hospital were accompanied by thick medical files, but most of these consisted of blank sheets of paper (Murton and Hyams 1969:111). At this facility, the state pathologist concluded that deceased prisoners showed no "evidence of trauma or a violent death . . .[despite] the fact that two of the bodies had been decapitated prior to burial and the skull of the third had been crushed to the size of a grapefruit" (Murton 1971:29).

Although conspiracies involving forged health records are difficult to sustain, prisoners' letters to the jail monitor and the monitor's subsequent investigations showed that some medical personnel at the jail falsified medical documents to hinder detection of ill-treatment and torture of prisoners (Federal Court Monitor 1992–1996). The prisoner author of Letter 052 stated "I have personally seen medical employees watch prisoners on Bravo-Wing get brutally beat [by custodial officers] and then consistently go along with a false report. . . . Usually, officers are walking around looking for an opportunity to roll a cell door and beat the hell out of someone, while a nurse is waiting . . .to come in and shoot the prisoner with a sedative." Letter 052 repeats a theme prevalent in the ill-treatment and torture literature: Health care workers observe and monitor physical abuse, and provide treatment only to cover up atrocities committed by the custodial staff (Nightingale 1990).

Accounts from Chile, Kenya, South Africa, and Turkey report that medical complicity in ill-treatment and torture of prisoners frequently involves falsification of medical records through omission of relevant health information (Berat 1989; Bunce 1997; Danish Medical Association 1987:192; Goldstein and Breslin 1986; Iacopino et al. 1996). According to prisoners' correspondence with the jail monitor, in keeping with the jail's environment of penal harm, custodial staff members used excessive force against prisoners, while some jail medical officials refused to document and treat prisoners' injuries.

In Letter 027, a prisoner reported hearing two correctional officers say they were going to "take care" of him. Minutes later, when one of the officers was escorting the prisoner to a holding area within the jail, the officer struck his head, knocking a gold tooth from his mouth. Then the officer slammed his head to the floor; as a result, the prisoner suffered severe headaches, swelling of the brain, and nerve damage to the right hand. When he sought medical treatment for his injuries, the health care staff refused him an examination by a physician. The nurse called the prisoner a "punk," saying "I hope you rot to death" (Letter 027). More important, no notes or entries were made in the medical records to document the injuries. Because the outward physical manifestations of the assault healed while the prisoner was jailed, the medical files held-no record of these injuries. Thus it was "exceptionally difficult subsequently to prove that torture occurred and [to] prosecute the torturers" (Iacopino et al. 1996:397).

Maintenance of prisoners' medical records in some U.S. correctional facilities is so inadequate as to border on criminal negligence (Vaughn and Carroll 1998). Inadequate health records result in "chaotic medical files that impede the work of even the most conscientious physicians" (King 1979:277). In such situations, prisoners' medical conditions, symptoms, and care are neither recorded nor documented; therefore subsequent caregivers are uninformed about prisoners' medical histories and the success or failure of previous treatments (Hudson 1987; Sparks, Bottoms, and Hay 1996). The United States District Court for the Northern District of California called the "medical record system" at the Pelican Bay Maximum Security Prison "nothing short of disastrous," saying that the court "record was replete with examples of charts without medical histories, with no record of examinations, no management plan, orders for tests with no record of results, and test results with no record of why, when, or by whom the test was ordered" (*Madrid v. Gomez* 1995:1203–1204).

One way in which the jail falsified medical records was to systematically omit prisoners' health complaints from bookkeeping processes; this omission resulted in failure to document and record prisoners' illnesses and injuries (Iacopino et al. 1996). In 1994 the Federal Court Monitor wrote "[T]here isn't any system (such as a numbering system) which would allow a tracking of [prisoners' requests for medical care]. There isn't any doubt that there are [prisoners' requests for medical care] missing out of the [prisoners'] medical records, casting suspicion that not all of [these requests] . . .actually are processed." Then, in 1996, the Federal Court Monitor wrote "[The] method [of medical record keeping at the jail] is not working. The [prisoners' medical] requests are being ignored by medical staff, medical staff are not signing the [medical] forms, correctional officers are picking up the . . .forms, and the [forms] are not being answered in a timely manner or they are not being answered at all. . . . At this point, I don't think that [the medical provider] has any plans to correct this problem." . . .

Conclusion

Correctional medical personnel operate in an occupational subculture where issues of treatment and issues of custody compete for their loyalties. The Hippocratic Oath mandates that health care professionals must not harm patients; penal harm advocates contend that prisoners should be punished, and reject therapeutic measures as pro-offender or antivictim. Just as Nazi doctors participated in "psychic numbing," a reasoning process that made their Jewish victims "less than human and therefore not capable of evoking empathy or moral restraint" (Lifton 1986:442; Markusen 1992:153), correctional medical personnel find "themselves in morally ambiguous circumstances, without sharp limits or clear moral boundaries to restrain them" (Brown 1987:158). In this environment, some of the medical workers identify with custodial mandates and pattern their behavior after "the perceived collective needs of society, not the rights of individual 'subhuman'" prisoners (Brown 1987:158). Nazi doctors were able to abandon the Hippocratic Oath because they believed that their actions served the "larger purpose of bettering human life" (Markusen 1992:152). Similarly, dehumanization of prisoners permits correctional medical personnel to engage in ethical relativism and to abandon allegiance to the Hippocratic Oath.

From an organizational perspective, collective demonization of prisoners allows individual medical workers to deviate from ethical canons. Obedience to the pain-inflicting mandates of the custodial subculture overwhelms the ethical standards and humanistic obligations that the medical professional is sworn to uphold. The practice of penal harm medicine also fits the new penal managerialism or the new penology, whereby individual prisoners' rights are deemphasized and the efficient control of aggregate prisoner populations predominates. In this environment, it is acceptable to harm "subhuman" prisoners. Correctional health care systems committed to implementing the penal harm movement and the rationality of the new penal managerialism do not appear to favor institutional treatment settings ideally based on morality, justice, and respect for human dignity.

Prisoners' letters to the jail monitor and the monitor's subsequent investigations showed that some of the health care staff members in the jail had a custodial-punishment orientation. Advocates of penal harm predict the merging of custodial and medical functions because imprisonment is intended to personify pain: "[The] penal sanction is to harm" (Clear 1994:4). Letters and the monitor's investigations supported our thesis that for some health care employees, practicing in an environment dominated by a philosophy of penal harm led to ill-treatment and torture of prisoners.

Ill-treatment and torture at the jail included psychological methods such as taunting, humiliating, and threatening prisoners, as well as physical methods such as withholding medical care, exposing prisoners to temperature extremes and sleep deprivation, and falsifying medical records. Some medical practices in the jail were similar to brutalization techniques of terror found in Soviet gulags, China's Laogai prison camps, and other tyrannical correctional regimes around the world.

Because the jail still is accredited by the NCCHC, it appears that clear statements of ethical standards and high-principled moral boundaries to guide correctional medical personnel have failed to eradicate ill-treatment and torture there. Judicial intervention also has failed to eliminate all ill-treatment and torture, although the jail was under a federally supervised consent decree from 1979 to 1998. This does not mean, however, that judicial intervention and agency accreditation should be eliminated: Without external supervision of correctional medical care, we believe that ill-treatment and torture would be a far greater problem. Rather, our findings call for stringent implementation of accreditation standards, strict judicial enforcement of existing consent decrees and

constitutional doctrines, and professional conformity to ethical obligations.

Although we have presented the voices of prisoners alleging medical ill-treatment and torture in a county mega jail located in the United States, several limitations restrict our findings and indicate the need for additional research. Multiple letters written months and years apart by different prisoners reported similar practices, and the court monitor's investigations corroborated allegations of medical ill-treatment and torture. Even so, the potential for fabrication by prisoners renders our conclusions tentative. Investigations of medical ill-treatment and torture are rarely as detailed as we would like. Usually the findings are more appropriately "understood as snapshots in time, partial rather than complete accounts or prevalence reports of human rights violations" (Geiger and Cook-Deegan 1993:619–20; Jaranson 1995:255).

During the 5-year period of study, thousands of prisoners were incarcerated at the jail. We do not attempt here to assess all of these prisoners' collective experience with the jail's health care staff. Nor do our data support claims that all health providers at the jail were practicing penal harm medicine. Many correctional health workers are dedicated professionals performing a difficult job in a less-than-ideal environment.

Having said that, we found a persistent pattern of medical ill-treatment and torture at the jail, which extended over the entire five-year period. Given the explosion of correctional populations, the penal harm movement, and the disturbing (although tentative) nature of our findings, penologists, criminologists, and criminal justicians should more fully investigate medical ill-treatment and torture in correctional facilities throughout the United States. Although the secretive, insular world of corrections poses obstacles to access, ethnographic studies in correctional health care systems, uncovering the epidemiology of ill-treatment and torture of prisoners, are in great demand.

More researchers must rely on the methodological technique advanced by constitutive criminology, in which discourses of traditionally oppressed individuals are examined by penologists, criminologists, and criminal justicians. Because one of our findings implicated some correctional health care personnel in falsifying documents to hide medical ill-treatment and torture, it is imperative to investigate prisoners' personal narratives before their stories are filtered and sanitized by the justice system. It is also methodologically beneficial to analyze the local voices of individual prisoners rather than the study and management of aggregates in the new penology. These individual voices and personal narratives contain a wealth of potential data for researchers seeking the empirical reality of correctional health care systems.

Although only a few of the prisoners who wrote to the jail monitor disclosed whether they were pretrial detainees or convicted inmates, the jail monitor maintained that most of the writers were pretrial detainees. Such detainees are presumed innocent until proven guilty and cannot legally be subject to punishment (*Bell v. Wolfish* 1979). Researchers should explore in greater detail the legal, moral, ethical, and philosophical ramifications of punishing these detainees, and how these ramifications relate to the presumption of innocence in the era of penal harm.

A standard remedy for systemic problems in correctional health care systems has been to accredit jail and prison medical facilities. Yet we know little about the political, economic, and professional value of accreditation and the internal dynamics of accreditation agencies (see Keve 1996). Because the jail under study here was accredited by the National Commission on Correctional Health Care, future researchers should evaluate adherence to minimal guidelines in accredited facilities, the value of accreditation itself, disciplinary actions taken against accredited facilities when they violate accreditation criteria and standards, and the sanctions imposed on medical officials who engage in unprofessional behavior. We need the type of analyses of accreditation agencies and processes that Platt (1971) conducted on riot commissions.

Finally, because the medical profession adheres to the Hippocratic Oath and because the American Medical Association (AMA), the American Nursing Association (ANA), and the American Academy of Physician Assistants (AAPA) are the primary professional associations representing physicians, nurses, and physician assistants, future researchers should examine the role of these organizations in the practice of ethical correctional medicine (Summerfield 1997; White 1996). Health care workers who participate in the punishment of prisoners but have pledged to treat the injured, help the sick, and alleviate pain and suffering are violating the most basic precepts of medicine. Here we question whether all correctional health care personnel are truly committed to the Hippocratic Oath and whether such an oath can survive the ravages of the penal harm movement.

Study Questions:

1. Briefly describe the historical ill-treatment and torture of prisoners. What was the "Tucker telephone" used for in Arkansas?

2. Describe the research design, data collection methods, sample, and measures used by the authors in this article. What are some of the issues of reliability and validity that threaten this type of research?

3. What are the major findings of this study?

4. What are some of the steps that need to be taken to remedy the problem of inadequate medical care in correctional facilities?

References

Acoca, L. 1998. "Defusing the Time Bomb: Understanding and Meeting the Growing Health Care Needs of Incarcerated Women in America." *Crime and Delinquency* 44:49–69.

Alderslade, R. 1995. "Human Rights and Medical Practice, Including Reference to the Joint Oslo Statements of September 1993 and March 1994." *Journal of Public Health Medicine* 17: 335–42.

Allen, H.E. and J.C. April. 1997. "The New Chain Gang: Corrections in the Next Century." *American Journal of Criminal Justice* 22:1–12.

American Correctional Association. 1997. *Jail Directory.* Laurel, MD: American Correctional Association.

American Psychiatric Association. 1994. *Diagnostic and Statistical Manual of Mental Disorders.* 4th ed. Washington, DC: American Psychiatric Association.

Amnesty International. 1975. *Report on Torture.* New York: Farrar, Straus and Giroux.

———. 1984a. *Codes of Professional Ethics.* 2nd ed. London: Amnesty International.

———. 1984b. *Torture in the Eighties.* London: Amnesty International.

———. 1988. *Amnesty International Report.* London: Amnesty International.

———. 1990. *Amnesty International Report.* London: Amnesty International.

Angell, M. 1988. "Ethical Imperialism? Ethics in International Collaborative Clinical Research." *New England Journal of Medicine* 319:1081–83.

Anno, B.J. 1991. *Prison Health Care: Guidelines for the Management of an Adequate Delivery System.* Chicago: National Commission on Correctional Health Care.

———. 1997. "Correctional Health Care: What's Past Is Prologue." *Correct Care* 11(3):6–11.

Arrigo, B.A. 1996a. "Subjectivity in Law, Medicine, and Science: A Semiotic Perspective on Punishment." Pp. 69–92 in *Punishment: Social Control and Coercion,* edited by C.T. Sisters. New York: Peter Lang.

———. 1996b. *The Contours of Psychiatric Justice: A Postmodern Critique of Mental Illness, Criminal Insanity, and the Law.* New York: Garland.

Asad, T. 1996. "On Torture, or Cruel, Inhuman, and Degrading Treatment." *Social Research* 63: 1081–1109.

Audet, A.M. 1995. "The Role of the Physician and the Medical Profession in the Prevention of International Torture in the Treatment of Its Survivors." *Annals of Internal Medicine* 122:607–13.

Bankowski, Z. 1996. "Ethics and Human Values in Health Policy." *World Health Forum* 17:146–49.

Barak, G. 1990. "Crime, Criminology, and Human Rights: Towards an Understanding of State Criminality." *Journal of Human Justice* 2(1):11–28.

Barker, T. and D.L. Carter. 1990. "Fluffing Up the Evidence and Covering Your Ass: Some Conceptual Notes on Police Lying." *Deviant Behavior* 11:61–73.

———. 1994. "Police Lies and Perjury: A Motivation-Based Typology." Pp. 139–53 in *Police Deviance,* 3rd ed., edited by T. Barker and D.L. Carter. Cincinnati: Anderson.

Beaman-Hall, L. 1996. "Legal Ethnography: Exploring the Gendered Nature of Legal Method." *Critical Criminology* 7(1):53–54.

Belknap, J. 1996. "Access to Programs and Health Care for Incarcerated Women." *Federal Probation* 60(4):34–39.

Bell, R.A. 1997. "Prison Conditions at the Extreme: Legal and Political Issues in the Closing of West Virginia's Prisons for Men and Women." *Journal of Contemporary Criminal Justice* 13:55–72.

Benffeldt-Zachrisson, F. 1985. "Special Report on Torture as a Medical Problem—State (Political) Torture: Some General, Psychological, and Particular Aspects." *International Journal of Health Services* 15:339–49.

Bennett, K. and R.V. Del Carmen. 1997. "A Review and Analysis of Prison Litigation Reform Act Court Decisions: Solution or Aggravation?" *Prison Journal* 77:405–55.

Beret, L. 1989. "Doctors, Detainees, and Torture: Medical Ethics v. the Law in South Africa." *Stanford Journal of International Law* 25:499–542.

Bernheim, J. 1993. "Medical Ethics in Prison." *Criminal Behavior and Mental Health* 3:85–96.

Bierma, P. 1994. "Torture behind Bars: Right Here in the United States of America." *Progressive* 58(7):21–27.

Blanco, E. 1989. "Torture in Emergency Situations." *Leiden Journal of International Law* 2: 209–28.

Bloche, M.G. 1987. *Uruguay's Military Physicians: Cogs in a System of State Terror.* Washington, DC: American Association for the Advancement of Science.

Blumberg, M. 1990. AIDS. *The Impact on the Criminal Justice System.* Columbus, OH: Merrill.

Blumberg, M. and C. Mahaffey-Sapp. 1997. "Health Care Issues in Correctional Institutions." Pp. 333–44 in *Corrections: An Issues Approach*, 4th ed., edited by M.D. Schwartz and L.P. Travis. Cincinnati: Anderson.

Bonta, J. and P. Gendreau. 1990. "Reexamining the Cruel and Unusual Punishment of Prison Life." *Law and Human Behavior* 14:347–72.

Breed, A.F. 1998. "Corrections: A Victim of Situational Ethics." *Crime and Delinquency* 44:9–18.

Brewer, T.F. and J. Derrickson. 1992. "AIDS in Prison: A Review of Epidemiology and Preventive Policy." *AIDS* 6:623–28.

Bright, S.B. 1996. "The Electric Chair and the Chain Gang—Choices and Challenges for America's Future." *Notre Dame Law Review* 71: 845–60.

——. 1997. "Casualties of the War on Crime: Fairness, Reliability, and the Credibility of Criminal Justice Systems." *University of Miami Law Review* 51:413–24.

British Medical Association Working Party. 1986. *The Torture Report*. London: British Medical Association.

——. 1992. *Medicine Betrayed: The Participation of Doctors in Human Rights Abuses*. London: British Medical Association.

Browde, S. 1989. "Doctors, Ethics and Torture." *Social Science and Medicine* 28:766.

Brown, T.M. 1987. "Doctors in Extremity." *Law, Medicine, and Health Care* 15(3):156–59.

Buchanan, A. 1996. "Judging the Past—The Case of the Human Radiation Experiments." *Hastings Center Report* 26(3):25–30.

Bunce, C. 1997. "Doctors Involved in Human Rights Abuses in Kenya." *British Medical Journal* 314:166.

Burger, T. 1987. *Max Weber's Theory of Concept Formation: History, Laws, and Ideal Types*. Expanded ed. Durham: Duke University Press.

Burkhalter, H.J. 1995. "Barbarism behind Bars: Torture in U.S. Prisons." *Nation* 261(1):17–18.

Butler, A.M. 1997. *Gendered Justice in the American West: Women Prisoners in Men's Penitentiaries*. Urbana: University of Illinois Press.

Carroll, L. 1992. "AIDS and Human Rights in the Prison: A Comment on the Ethics of Screening and Segregation." Pp. 162–77 in *Correctional Theory and Practice*, edited by C.A. Hartjen and E.E. Rhine. Chicago: Nelson-Hall.

——. 1998. *Lawful Order: A Case Study in Correctional Crisis and Reform*. New York: Garland.

Cassese, A. 1996. *Inhuman States: Imprisonment, Detention, and Torture in Europe Today*. Cambridge, UK. Polity.

Center for Human Rights. 1988. *Human Rights: A Compilation of International Instruments*. New York: United Nations.

——. 1994. *Human Rights and Pre-Trial Detention: A Handbook of International Standards Relating to Pre-Trial Detention*. New York: United Nations.

Chilton, B.S. 1991. *Prisons under the Gavel: The Federal Court Takeover of Georgia Prisons*. Columbus: Ohio State University Press.

Christie, N. 1981. *Limits to Pain*. Oxford: Martin Robertson.

——. 1993. *Crime Control as Industry*. London: Routledge.

Chung, C.C., C.O. Mok, K.H. Kwong, E.K. Ng, W.Y. Lau, and A.K. Li. 1997. "Obturator Hernia Revisited: A Review of 12 Cases in 7 Years." *Journal of Royal College of Surgeons of Edinburgh* 42:82–84.

Clark, E.B. 1995. "The Sacred Rights of the Weak: Pain, Sympathy, and the Culture of Individual Rights in Antebellum America." *Journal of American History* 82:463–93.

Clear, T.R. 1994. *Harm in American Penology*. Albany: SUNY Press.

Cockburn, A. 1997. "The Torture of Susan McDougal." *Nation* 265(2):9.

Commission to Investigate Allegations of Police Corruption and the Anti-corruption Procedures of the Police Department (Mollen Commission). 1994. *Commission Report*. New York: Commission to Investigate Allegations of Police Corruption and the Anti-Corruption Procedures of the Police Department.

Committee on the Judiciary, House of Representatives. 1991. *Medical Care for the Prison Population*. Washington, DC: U.S. Government Printing Office.

Cooke, D.J., P.J. Baldwin, and J. Howison. 1990. *Psychology in Prisons*. London: Routledge.

Council of Europe. 1987. *European Prison Rules*. Strasbourg: Council of Europe.

——. 1995. *Human Rights in Prison: The Professional Training of Prison Officials*. Strasbourg: Council of Europe.

Crouch, B.M. and J.M. Marquart. 1989. *An Appeal to Justice: Litigated Reform of Texas Prisons*. Austin: University of Texas Press.

Cullen, F.T. 1995. "Assessing the Penal Harm Movement." *Journal of Research in Crime and Delinquency* 32:338–58.

Danish Medical Association/International Rehabilitation and Research Center for Torture Victims. 1987. "Doctors, Ethics, and Torture: Proceedings of an International Meeting, Copenhagen, August 1986." *Danish Medical Bulletin* 34(4):185–216.

Danto, B.L. 1997. "Suicide Litigation as an Agent of Change in Jail and Prison: An Initial Report." *Behavioral Sciences and the Law* 16:415–25.

Denzin, N.K. 1997. *Interpretive Ethnography: Ethnographic Practices for the 21st Century.* Thousand Oaks, CA: Sage.

Downie, R.S. 1993. "The Ethics of Medical Involvement in Torture." *Journal of Medical Ethics* 19:135–37.

Drob, S.L. 1992. "The Lessons from History: Physicians' Dual Loyalty in the Nazi Death Camps." Pp. 167–71 in Review of Clinical Psychiatry and the Law, Vol. 3, edited by R.I. Snow. Washington, DC: American Psychiatric Press.

DuBose, E.R. 1996. "Prison Infirmary Nurses: Professionalism and Principles." *Making the Rounds* 1(21):1–4.

Duncan, M.G. 1996. *Romantic Outlaws, Beloved Prisons: The Unconscious Meanings of Crime and Punishment.* New York: New York University Press.

Engdahl, B.E. and R.E. Eberly. 1990. "The Effects of Torture and Other Maltreatment: Implications for Psychology." Pp. 31–47 in *Psychology and Torture*, edited by P. Suedfeld. New York: Hemisphere.

"Ex-F.B.I. Man Sentenced in Ruby Ridge Case." 1997. *New York Times*, October 11, p. A–8.

Federal Court Monitor. 1992–1996. *Court Monitoring Reports: Davis v. Roberts* 75–411–Civ–TGC.

Feeley, M. and J. Simon. 1992. "The New Penology: Notes on the Emerging Strategy of Corrections and Its Implications." *Criminology* 30:449–74.

———. 1994. "Actuarial Justice: The Emerging New Criminal Law." Pp. 173–201 in *The Futures of Criminology*, edited by D. Nelken. London: Sage.

"Final Proposal for Entry of Consent Decree." 1979. *Davis v. Roberts* 75-411-Civ-TGC.

Fleisher, M.S. and R.H. Rison. 1997. "Health Care in the Federal Bureau of Prisons." Pp. 327–34 in *Correctional Contexts: Contemporary and Classical Readings*, edited by J.M. Marquart and J.R. Sorensen. Los Angeles: Roxbury.

Fogel, D. 1979. *We Are the Living Proof: The Justice Model for Corrections.* 2nd ed. Cincinnati: Anderson.

Foster, D.H., D. Sandler, and D.M. Davis. 1987. "Detention, Torture, and the Criminal Justice Process in South Africa." *International Journal of the Sociology of Law* 15:105–20.

Gallo, E. and V. Ruggiero. 1991. "The Immaterial Prison: Custody as a Factory for the Manufacture of Handicaps." *International Journal of the Sociology of Law* 19:273–91.

Gannon, C.C. 1997. *Health Records in Correctional Health Care: A Reference Manual.* Chicago: National Commission on Correctional Health Care.

Garland, D. 1997. "Governmentality and the Problem of Crime: Foucault, Criminology, Sociology." *Theoretical Criminology* 1:173–214.

Geiger, H.J. and R.M. Cook-Deegan. 1993. "The Role of Physicians in Conflicts and Humanitarian Crises: Case Studies from the Field Missions of Physicians for Human Rights, 1988 to 1993." *Journal of the American Medical Association* 279:616–20.

Genefke, I. 1993. "Torture, the Most Destructive Power against Democracy." *International Journal of the Humanities* 10(1):73.

Gibbons, D.C. and D.L. Garrity. 1959. "Some Suggestions for the Development of Etiological and Treatment Theory in Criminology." *Social Forces* 38:61–58.

———. 1962. "Definition and Analysis of Certain Criminal Types." *Journal of Criminal Law, Criminology, and Police Science* 53:27–35.

Gill, G.V. and I.A. MacFarlane. 1989. "Problems of Diabetics in Prison." *British Medical Journal* 298:221–23.

Glazier, A.K. 1997. "Genetic Predispositions, Prophylactic Treatments, and Private Health Insurance: Nothing Is Better Than a Good Pair of Genes." *American Journal of Law and Medicine* 23:45–68.

"Glossary of Terms in Health Care." 1995. *Business Journal Serving Southern Tier, CNY, Mohawk Valley, Finger Lakes, North*, December 11, p. 23B.

Goffman, E. [1957]1997. "Characteristics of Total Institutions." Pp. 97–108 in *Correctional Contexts: Contemporary and Classical Readings*, edited by J.M. Marquart and J.R. Sorensen. Los Angeles: Roxbury.

———. 1962. *Asylums: Essays on the Social Situation of Mental Patients and Other Inmates.* Chicago: Aldine.

———. 1963. *Stigma: Notes on the Management of Spoiled Identity.* New York: Aronson.

Goldstein, R.H. and P. Breslin. 1986. "Technicians of Torture: How Physicians Become Agents of State Terror." *Sciences* 26(2):14–19.

Gostin, L.O. and Z. Lazzarini. 1997. *Human Rights and Public Health in the AIDS Pandemic.* New York: Oxford University Press.

Goulet, D. 1977. "Prolegomenon to a Policy: Thinking about Human Rights." *Christianity and Crisis* 37(8):100–104.

Greenspan, J. 1996. "Prisoners Respond to AIDS." Pp. 115–23 in *Criminal Injustice: Confronting the Prison Crisis,* edited by E. Rosenblatt. Boston: South End.

Griffin, M.M., J.G. Ryan, V.S. Briscoe, and K.M. Shadle. 1996. "Effects of Incarceration on HIV-Infected Individuals." *Journal of the National Medical Association* 88:639–44.

Grodin, M.A., G.J. Armas, and L.H. Glantz. 1993. "Medicine and Human Rights: A Proposal for International Action." *Hastings Center Report* 23(4):8–12.

Haritos-Fatouros, M. 1988. "The Official Torturer: A Learning Model for Obedience to the Authority of Violence." *Journal of Applied Social Psychology* 18:1107–20.

Harris, M.K. and D.P. Spiller. 1977. *After Decision: Implementation of Judicial Decrees in Correctional Settings.* Washington, DC: U.S. Government Printing Office.

Hayes, L.M. 1997. "From Chaos to Calm: One Jail System's Struggle with Suicide Prevention." *Behavioral Sciences and the Law* 16:399–413.

Henry, S. and D. Milovanovic. 1996. *Constitutive Criminology: Beyond Postmodernism.* London: Sage.

Holtz, T.H. 1998. "Refugee Trauma versus Torture Trauma: A Retrospective Controlled Cohort Study of Tibetan Refugees." *Journal of Nervous and Mental Disease* 186:24–34.

Hornblum, A.M. 1997. "They Were Cheap and Available: Prisoners as Research Subjects in Twentieth Century America." *British Medical Journal* 315:1437–41.

Howard League for Penal Reform. 1991. *Suicides and Strip Cells.* London: Howard League for Penal Reform.

Hudson, B. 1987. "Prison Medical Service: Serving Health from Behind Bars." *Health Service Journal* 97:958–59.

Human Rights Watch/Middle East. 1994. *Torture and Ill-Treatment. Israel's Interrogation of Palestinians from the Occupied Territories.* New York: Human Rights Watch.

Iacopino, V. 1996. "Turkish Physicians Coerced t Conceal Systematic Torture." *Lancet* 348:1500

Iacopino, V., M. Heisler, S. Pishevar, and R.F Kirschner. 1996. "Physician Complicity in Mi representation and Omission of Evidence (Torture in Postdetention Medical Examina tions in Turkey." *Journal of the American Med cal Association* 276:396–402.

International Military Tribunal for the Far Eas 1946–1948. Record of Proceedings. Tokyo: I ternational Military Tribunal for the Far Eas

Irwin, J. 1985. *The Jail: Managing the Undercla: in American Society.* Berkeley: University (California Press.

Jacobs, F.G. and R.C.A. White. 1996. *The Eur(pean Convention on Human Rights.* 2nd e(New York: Oxford University Press.

Jaranson, J.M. 1995. "Government-Sanctione Torture: Status of the Rehabilitation Mov ment." *Transcultural Psychiatric Research R(view* 32:253–86.

Jayawardena, H. 1996. "AIDS and Profession; Secrecy in the United States." *Medicine, S(ence, and Law* 36:37–42.

Jones, G.E. 1980. "On the Permissibility of To ture." *Journal of Medical Ethics* 6:11–15.

Jonsen, A.R. and L.A. Sagan. 1985. "Torture an the Ethics of Medicine." Pp. 30–44 in *Tl Breaking of Bodies and Minds: Torture, Psych atric Abuse, and the Health Professions,* edite by E. Stover and E.O. Nightingale. New Yor Freeman.

Jurgens, R. and N. Gilmore. 1994. "Divulging (Prison Medical Records: Juridical and Leg; Analysis." *Criminologie* 27(2):127–63.

Kappeler, V.E., M. Blumberg, and G.W. Potte 1996. *The Mythology of Crime and Crimin; Justice,* 2nd ed. Prospect Heights, II Waveland.

Kappeler, V.E., R.D. Sluder, and G.P. Alpert. 199 *Forces of Deviance: Understanding the Da(Side of Policing,* 2nd ed. Prospect Heights, II Waveland.

Kelman, H.C. 1995. "The Social Context of To ture: Policy Process and Authority Structure Pp. 19–34 in *The Politics of Pain: Torturers an Their Masters,* edited by R.D. Crelinsten an A.P. Schmid. Boulder: Westview.

Kemp-Geneike, I. 1991. "Perspective on the Pre ent and the Future." *Journal of Medical Ethi(17(Supplement):11–12.

Keve, Paul W. 1996. *Measuring Excellence: Tl History of Correctional Standards and Accre, tation.* Lanham, MD: American Correction; Association.

King, L.N. 1979. "Public Policy and Administrative Aspects of Prison and Jail Health Services." *Prison Law Monitor* 1(11):265, 277–79.

King, R.D. 1994. "Russian Prisons after Perestroika: End of the Gulag?" *British Journal of Criminology* 34(Special Issue):62–82.

Kooijmans, P.H. 1995. "Torturers and Their Masters." Pp. 13–18 in *The Politics of Pain: Torturers and Their Masters*, edited by R.D. Crelinaten and A.P. Schmid. Boulder: Westview.

Kratcoski, P.C. 1989. *Correctional Counseling and Treatment*, 2nd ed. Prospect Heights, IL: Waveland.

Laborde, J.M. 1989. "Torture: A Nursing Concern." *Image: Journal of Nursing Scholarship* 21(1):31–33.

La Forte, R.S., R.E. Marcello, and R.L. Himmel. 1994. *With Only the Will to Live: Accounts of Americans in Japanese Prison Camps 1941–1945*. Wilmington, DE: Scholarly Resources.

Laing, J.M. 1996. "The Police Surgeon and the Mentally Disordered Suspects: An Adequate Safeguard?" *Web Journal of Current Legal Issues 1*. [Online]. Available at http://www.ncl.ac.uk/-nlawwww/1996/issueIAaingl.html.

Laurence, R. 1992. "Part I: Torture and Mental Health: A Review of the Literature." *Issues in Mental Health Nursing* 13:301–10.

Liebling, A. and P. Hall. 1993. "Seclusion in Prison Strip Cells." *British Medical Journal* 307:399–400.

Lifton, R.J. 1982. "Medicalized Killing in Auschwitz." *Psychiatry* 45:283–97.

———. 1986. *The Nazi Doctors. Medical Killing and the Psychology of Genocide*. New York: Basic Books.

Light, D.W. 1997. "The Real Ethics of Rationing." *British Medical Journal* 315:112–15.

Lindlof, T.R. 1995. *Qualitative Communication Research Methods*. Thousand Oaks, CA. Sage.

Lippman, M. 1979. "The Protection of Universal Human Rights: The Problem of Torture." *Universal Human Rights* 1(4):26–55.

———. 1993. "The Nazi Doctors Trial and the International Prohibition on Medical Involvement in Torture." *Loyola of Los Angeles International and Comparative Law Journal* 15:395–441.

———. 1997. "Crimes against Humanity." *Boston College Third World Law Journal* 17:171–278.

Loeb, G.H. 1993. "Protecting the Right to Informational Privacy for HIV-Positive Prisoners." *Columbia Journal of Law and Social Problems* 27:269–318.

Logan, C.H. and G.G. Gaes. 1993. "Meta-Analysis and the Rehabilitation of Punishment." *Justice Quarterly* 10:245–63.

Machan, T.R. 1990. "Exploring Extreme Violence (Torture)." *Journal of Social Philosophy* 21:92–97.

MacPherson, P. 1989. "In a Padlocked Society, Good Health Care Remains an Elusive Goal." *Governing* 2(April):50–54.

Maeve, M.F. 1997. "Nursing Practice with Incarcerated Women: Caring within Mandated [sic] Alienation." *Issues in Mental Health Nursing* 18:495–510.

Magill, F.N. 1996. *International Encyclopedia of Psychology*, Vol. 2. London: Fitzroy Dearborn.

Markusen, E. 1992. "Comprehending the Cambodian Genocide: An Application of Robert Jay Lifton's Model of Genocidal Killing." *Psychohistory Review* 20:145–69.

Marquart, J.W., D.E. Merianos, S.J. Cuvelier, and L. Carroll. 1996. "Thinking about the Relationship between Health Dynamics in the Free Community and the Prison." *Crime and Delinquency* 42:331–60.

Marquart, J.W., D.E. Merianos, J.L. Hebert, and L. Carroll. 1997. "Health Condition and Prisoners: A Review of Research and Emerging Areas of Inquiry." *Prison Journal* 77:184–208.

Mastrofski, S.D. 1998. "Police Agency Accreditation: A Skeptical View." *Policing: An International Journal of Police Strategies and Management* 21:202–205.

McCoy, C. 1997. "Review Essay: Sentencing and the Underclass." *Law and Society Review* 31:589–612.

Melamed, B.G., J.L. Melamed, and J.C. Bouhoutsos. 1990. "Psychological Consequences of Torture: A Need to Formulate New Strategies for Research." Pp. 13–30 in *Psychology and Torture*, edited by P. Suedfeld. New York: Hemisphere.

Members of the Special International Tribunal. 1991. "Verdict of the Special International Tribunal: On the Violation of Human Rights of Political Prisoners and Prisoners of War in United States Prisons and Jails." *Humanity and Society* 15:375–99.

Meyer-Lie, A. 1986. "Ethics in Prison Health Care." Pp. 63–69 in *Health and Human Rights*, edited by International Commission of Health Professionals. Geneva: International Commission of Health Professionals.

Miller, H.A. and G.R. Young. 1997. "Prison Segregation: Administrative Detention Remedy or Mental Health Problem?" *Criminal Behavior and Mental Health* 7:85–94.

Milovanovic, D. 1996. "Postmodern Criminology: Mapping the Terrain." *Justice Quarterly* 13: 567–610.

Moore, J.M. 1986. "Prison Health Care: Problems and Alternatives in Delivery of Health Care to the Incarcerated—Part 1." *Journal of the Florida Medical Association* 73:531–35.

Morgan, R. and M. Evans. 1994. "Inspecting Prisons: The View from Strasbourg." *British Journal of Criminology* 34(Special Issue):141–59.

Moynihan, D.P. 1997. "The Culture of Secrecy." *The Public Interest* 128(Summer):55–72.

Murton, T. 1971. "Prison Doctors." *Humanist* 310: 24–29.

Murton, T. and J. Hyams. 1969. *Accomplices to the Crime*. New York: Grove.

National Commission on Correctional Health Care. 1996. *Standards for Health Services in Jails*. Chicago: National Commission on Correctional Health Care.

Naude, G. and F. Bongard. 1997. "Obturator Hernia Is an Unsuspected Diagnosis." *American Journal of Surgery* 174:72–75.

Neale, K. 1991. "The European Prison Rules: Contextual, Philosophical, and Practical Aspects." Pp. 203–18 in *Imprisonment: European Perspectives*, edited by J. Muncie and R. Sparks. London: Harvester.

Nightingale, E.O. 1990. "The Role of Physicians in Human Rights." *Law, Medicine, and Health Care* 18(1–2):132–39.

Nightingale, E.O. and J.C. Chill. 1994. "The Health Professions and Human Rights." *Family and Community Health* 17(2):30–37.

Nightingale, E.O., Y. Hannibal, H.J. Geiger, L. Hartmann, R. Lawrence, and J. Spurlock. 1990. "Apartheid Medicine: Health and Human Rights in South Africa." *Journal of the American Medical Association* 264:2097–2102.

Nursing97 Drug Handbook. 1997. Springhouse, PA: Springhouse.

"Order Granting Defendants' Motion to Dissolve Consent Decree." 1998. *Davis v. Roberts* 75–411–Civ–T–21(c).

Osofsky, H.M. 1997. "Domesticating International Criminal Law: Bringing Human Rights Violators to Justice." *Yale Law Journal* 107: 191–226.

Paden, R. 1984. "Surveillance and Torture: Foucault and Orwell on the Methods of Discipline." *Social Theory and Practice* 10:261–71.

Parmentier, S. 1992. "Book Review: The International Fight against Torture." *Human Rights Quarterly* 14:568–72.

Pellegrino, E.D. 1993. "Societal Duty and Moral Complicity: The Physician's Dilemma of Divided Loyalty." *International Journal of Law and Psychiatry* 16:371–91.

Penal Reform International. 1990. *International Instruments on Imprisonment: Briefing No. 1*. London: Penal Reform International.

Peters, E. 1986. *Torture*. New York: Basil Blackwell.

Peters, T. 1992. *Liberation Management*. New York: Knopf.

Petersen, H.D. and O.V. Rasmussen. 1992. "Medical Appraisal of Allegations of Torture and the Involvement of Doctors in Torture." *Forensic Science International* 53:97–116.

Platt, A. 1971. "The Politics of Riot Commissions, 1917–1970: An Overview." Pp. 3–64 in *The Politics of Riot Commissions, 1917-1970. A Collection of Official Reports and Critical Essays*, edited by A. Platt. New York: Macmillan.

Power, K., J. McElroy, and V. Swanson. 1997. "Coping Abilities and Prisoners' Perception of Suicidal Risk Management." *Howard Journal of Criminal Justice* 36:378–92.

"Psychological Torture, CIA-Style." 1997. *Harper's* 94(1763):23–25.

Punamaki, R.L. 1988. "Experiences of Torture, Means of Coping, and Level of Symptoms among Palestinian Political Prisoners." *Journal of Palestine Studies* 17:81–96.

Ramsbotham, S.D. 1996. "Patient or Prisoner? A New Strategy for Health Care in Prisons." *Discussion Paper*, Home Office, London.

Rasmussen, O.V. 1990. "Medical Aspects of Torture: Torture Types and Their Relation to Symptoms and Lesions in 200 Victims, Followed by a Description of the Medical Profession in Relation to Torture: A Monograph." *Danish Medical Bulletin* 37(Supplement 1):1–88.

Rayner, M. 1987. *Turning a Blind Eye? Medical Accountability and the Prevention of Torture in South Africa*. Washington, DC: American Association for the Advancement of Science.

Reed, J. and M. Lyne. 1997. "The Quality of Health Care in Prison: Results of a Year's Program of Semistructured Inspections." *British Medical Journal* 315:1420–24.

Renzetti, C.M. 1997. "Confessions of a Reformed Positivist." Pp. 131–43 in *Researching Sexual Violence against Women: Methodological and Personal Perspectives*, edited by M.D. Schwartz. Thousand Oaks, CA. Sage.

Reyes, H. 1995. "The Conflicts between Medical Ethics and Security Measures." Pp. 41–47 in *Torture: Human Rights, Medical Ethics, and the Case of Israel*, edited by N. Gordon and R. Marton. London: Zed Books.

Reynaud, A. 1986. *Human Rights in Prisons*. Strasbourg: Council of Europe.

Rodley, N.S. 1987. *The Treatment of Prisoners under International Law*. Paris: United Nations Educational, Scientific, and Cultural Organization.

Roling, B.V.A. and C.F. Ruter. 1977. *The Tokyo Judgment: The International Military Tribunal for the Far East*, 29 April 1946–12 November 1948. Amsterdam: APA-University Press Amsterdam.

Rosalki, J. 1993. "The Hippocratic Contract." *Journal of Medical Ethics* 19:154–56.

Rosenberg, T. 1997. "To Hell and Back." *New York Times Magazine*, December 28, pp. 32–36.

Ross, J.I. 1995. "Controlling State Crime: Toward an Integrated Structural Model." Pp. 3–33 in *Controlling State Crime: An Introduction*, edited by J.I. Ross. New York: Garland.

Roth, E.F., I. Lunde, G. Boysen, and I. Kemp-Genefite. 1987. "Torture and Its Treatment." *American Journal of Public Health* 77:1404–1406.

Rynerson, B.C. 1989. "Cops and Counselors." *Journal of Psychosocial Nursing and Mental Health Services* 27(2):12–17.

Sagan, L.A. and A. Jonsen. 1976. "Medical Ethics and Torture." *New England Journal of Medicine* 294:1427–30.

Saunders, J.L. 1993. "When Your Patients Are Murderers and Thieves." *Medical Economics* 70(4):131–35.

Savage, S.P., G. Moon, K. Kelly, and Y. Bradshaw. 1997. "Divided Loyalties? The Police Surgeon and Criminal Justice." *Policing and Society* 7: 79–98.

Schaller, N.L. 1996. *Dental Malpractice: Legal and Medical Handbook, Vol. 1.* 3rd ed. New York: Wiley.

Scroggy, G.A. 1993. "Managing Conflicts between Custody and Health Care Staff." Pp. 130–32 in *The State of Corrections: Proceedings ACA Annual Conference 1992*. Laurel Lakes, MD: American Correctional Association.

Sheleff, L.S. 1987. *Ultimate Penalties: Capital Punishment, Life Imprisonment, Physical Torture.* Columbus: Ohio State University Press.

Shenson, D. 1996. "A Primary Care Clinic for the Documentation and Treatment of Human Rights Abuses." *Journal of General Internal Medicine* 11:533–38.

Shichor, D. 1997. "Three Strikes as a Public Policy: The Convergence of the New Penology and the McDonaldization of Punishment." *Crime and Delinquency* 43:470–92.

Shields, Y.E. and D. de Moya. 1997. "Correctional Health Care Nurses' Attitudes toward Inmates." *Journal of Correctional Health Care* 4: 37–59.

Shue, H. 1978. "Torture." *Philosophy and Public Affairs* 7:124–43.

Silver, M., R. Conte, M. Miceli, and I. Poggi. 1986. "Humiliation: Feeling, Social Control, and the Construction of Identity." *Journal for the Theory of Social Behavior* 16:269–83.

Simon, J. and M. Feeley. 1995. "True Crime: The New Penology and Public Discourse on Crime." Pp. 147–80 in *Punishment and Social Control*, edited by T.G. Blomberg and S. Cohen. New York: Aldine.

Slee, V.N., D.A. Slee, and H.J. Schmidt. 1996. *Health Care Terms.* 3rd ed. St. Paul: Tringa.

Solzhenitsyn, A.I. 1974. *The Gulag Archipelago, 1918-1956. An Experiment in Literary Investigation, 1–11.* New York: Harper and Row.

Sorensen, B. 1992. "Modern Ethics and International Law." Pp. 511–19 in *Torture and Its Consequences: Current Treatment Approaches*, edited by M. Basoglu. Cambridge, UK: Cambridge University Press.

Sparks, R. 1996a. "Prisons, Punishment, and Penalty." Pp. 197–247 in *Controlling Crime*, edited by E. McLaughlin and J. Muncie. London: Sage.

——. 1996b. "Penal Austerity: The Doctrine of Less Eligibility Reborn?" Pp. 74–93 in *Prisons 2000*, edited by R. Matthews and P. Francis. New York: St. Martin's.

Sparks, R., A. Bottoms, and W. Hay. 1996. *Prisons and the Problem of Order.* New York: Oxford University Press.

Steadman, H.J., D.W. McCarthy, and J.P. Morrissey. 1989. *The Mentally Ill in Jail. Planning for Essential Services.* New York: Guilford.

Steadman, T.L. 1995. *Steadman's Medical Dictionary.* 26th ed. Baltimore: Williams and Wilkins.

Stein, G.L. and L.D. Headley. 1996. "Forum on Prisoners' Access to Clinical Trials: Summary of Recommendations." *AIDS and Public Policy Journal* 11:3–20.

Storr, A. 1990. *Churchill's Blackbox, Kafka's Mice, and Other Phenomena of the Human Mind*. New York: Ballantine.

Stover, E. 1987. *The Open Secret: Torture and the Medical Profession in Chile*. Washington, DC: American Association for the Advancement of Science.

Stover, E. and E.O. Nightingale. 1985. "Introduction: The Breaking of Bodies and Minds." Pp. 1–26 in *The Breaking of Bodies and Minds: Torture, Psychiatric Abuse, and the Health Professions*, edited by E. Stover and E.O. Nightingale. New York: Freeman.

Summerfield, D. 1997. "Medical Ethics: The Israeli Medical Association." *Lancet* 350:63–64.

Tanaka, Y. 1996. *Hidden Horrors: Japanese War Crimes in World War II*. Boulder: Westview.

Taylor, T. 1992. "Opening Statement of the Prosecution December 9, 1946." Pp. 67–93 in *The Nazi Doctors and the Nuremberg Code: Human Rights in Human Experimentation*, edited by G.J. Annas and M.A. Grodin. New York: Oxford University Press.

Tesoriero, J.M. and M.L. McCullough. 1996. "Correctional Health Care Now and into the Twenty-First Century." Pp. 214–36 in *Visions for Change: Crime and Justice in the Twenty-First Century*, edited by R. Muraskin and A.R. Roberts. Upper Saddle River, NJ: Prentice Hall.

Thomas, J. 1988. *Prisoner Litigation: The Paradox of the Jailhouse Lawyer*. Totowa, NJ: Rowman and Littlefield.

Thomsen, J.L. and J. Voigt. 1988. "Forensic Medicine and Human Rights." *Forensic Science International* 36:147–51.

Tindale, C.W. 1996. "The Logic of Torture: A Critical Examination." *Social Theory and Practice* 22:349–74.

Toch, H. 1992a. *Living in Prison: The Ecology of Survival*. 2nd. ed. Washington, DC: American Psychological Association,

———. 1992b. *Mosaic of Despair: Human Breakdowns in Prisons*. 2nd. ed. Washington, DC: American Psychological Association.

Tomasevski, K. 1992. *Prison Health: International Standards and National Practices in Europe*. Helsinki: Helsinki Institute for Crime Prevention and Control.

Trager, J. 1979. *The People's Chronology: A Year-by-Year Record of Human Events from Prehistory to the Present*. New York: Holt, Rinehart, and Winston.

Trevelyan, J. 1988. "Agents of Repression." *Nursing Times* 84(42):45–47.

Turnbull, P.J., K.A. Dolan, and G.V. Stimson. 1993. "HIV Testing, and the Care and Treatment of HIV-Positive People in English Prisons." *AIDS Care* 5:199–206.

Turner, S. and C. Gorst-Unsworth. 1990. "Psychological Sequelae of Torture: A Descriptive Model." *British Journal of Psychiatry* 157:475–80.

Ugalde, A. and R.R. Vega. 1989. "Review Essay: State Terrorism, Torture, and Health in the Southern Cone." *Social Science and Medicine* 28:759–67.

Van Heerden, J. 1995. "Issues Affecting the Reform of Prison Health Care in South Africa." *South African Medical Journal* 85:345–46.

Van Maanen, J. and B.T. Pentland. 1994. "Cope and Auditors: The Rhetoric of Records." Pp. 53–90 in *The Legalistic Organization*, edited by S.B. Sitkin and R.J. Bies. Thousand Oaks, CA: Sage.

Van Willigen, L.H.M. 1992. "Organization of Care and Rehabilitation Services for Victims of Torture and Other Forms of Organized Violence: A Review of Current Issues." Pp. 277–98 in *Torture and Its Consequences: Current Treatment Approaches*, edited by M. Basoglu. Cambridge, UK: Cambridge University Press.

Vaughn, M.S. 1995. "Section 1983 Civil Liability of Prison Officials for Denying and Delaying Medication and Drugs to Prison Inmates." *Issues in Law and Medicine* 11:47–76.

———. 1996. "Prison Civil Liability for Inmate-against-Inmate Assault and Breakdown/Disorganization Theory." *Journal of Criminal Justice* 24:139–52.

———. 1997. "Civil Liability against Prison Officials for Prescribing and Dispensing Medication and Drugs to Prison Inmates." *Journal of Legal Medicine* 18:315–44.

Vaughn, M.S. and L. Carroll. 1998. "Separate and Unequal: Prison versus Free-World Medical Care." *Justice Quarterly* 15:3–40.

Vaughn, M.S. and R.V. Del Carmen. 1997. "The Fourth Amendment as a Tool of Actuarial Justice: The Special Needs Exception to the Warrant and Probable Cause Requirements." *Crime and Delinquency* 43:78–103.

Vause, R.C., A. Beeler, and M. Miller-Blanks. 1997. "Seeking a Practice Challenge? PAs in Federal Prisons." *JAAPA/Official Journal of the American Academy of Physician Assistants* 10(2):59–67.

Veatch, R.M. 1987. "Nazis and Hippocratists: Searching for the Moral Relation." *Psychohistory Review* 16:15–31.

Vesti, P. and N.J. Lavil. 1995. "Torture and the Medical Profession: A Review." *International Journal of the Humanities* 11(1):95–99.

Veysey, B.M., H.J. Steadman, J.P. Morrissey, and M. Johnsen. 1997. "In Search of the Missing Linkages: Continuity of Care in U.S. Jails." *Behavioral Sciences and the Law* 15:383–97.

Walens, S. 1997. *War Stories: An Oral History of Life behind Bars*. Westport, CT: Praeger.

Waring, T. 1996. "Prisoners with Diabetes: Do They Receive Appropriate Care?" *Nursing Times* 92(16):38–39.

Weber, R.P. 1990. *Basic Content Analysis*. 2nd ed. Newbury Park, CA: Sage.

Wei, C.S. 1997. *Courage to Stand Alone: Letters from Prison and Other Writings*. New York: Viking.

Weinert, F. 1996. "Weber's Ideal Types as Models in the Social Sciences." Pp. 73–93 in *Verstehen and Humane Understanding*, edited by A. O'Hear. Cambridge, UK: Cambridge University Press.

Weinstein, C. and E. Cummins. 1996. "The Crime of Punishment: Pelican Bay Maximum Security Prison." Pp. 308–21 in *Criminal Injustice: Confronting the Prison Crisis*, edited by E. Rosenblatt. Boston: South End.

Welsh, W.N. 1995. *Counties in Court: Jail Overcrowding and Court-Ordered Reform*. Philadelphia: Temple University Press.

Wessner, D.W. 1996. "From Judge to Participant: The United States as Champion of Human Rights." *Bulletin of Concerned Asian Scholars* 28(2):29–45.

White, L.W. 1996. "The Nazi Doctors and the Medical Community: Honor or Censure? The Case of Hans Sewering." *Journal of Medical Humanities* 17(2):119–35.

Williams, P. and D. Wallace. 1989. *Unit 731: Japan's Secret Biological Warfare in World War II*. New York: Free Press.

Wilson, C.R.M. 1993. "Going to Europe: Prisoners' Rights and the Effectiveness of European Standards." *International Journal of the Sociology of Law* 21:245–64.

Winn, R.G. 1996. "Ideology and the Calculation of Efficiency in Public and Private Correctional Enterprises." Pp. 21–30 in *Privatization and the Provision of Correctional Services: Context and Consequences*, edited by G.L. Mays and T. Gray. Cincinnati: Anderson.

Witherington, R. 1987. "The Acute Scrotum: Lesions That Require Immediate Attention." *Postgraduate Medicine* 82:207–16.

World Medical Assembly. 1976. "Declaration of Tokyo: Guidelines for Medical Doctors Concerning Torture and Other Cruel, Inhuman, or Degrading Treatment or Punishment in Relation to Detention and Imprisonment." *World Medical Journal* 22:87, 90.

Wu, H.H. 1994. *Bitter Winds: A Memoir of My Years in China's Gulag*. New York: Wiley.

Yackle, L.W. 1989. *Reform and Regret: The Story of Federal Judicial Involvement in the Alabama Prison System*. New York: Oxford University Press.

Zupan, L.L. 1991. *Jails: Reform and the New Generation Philosophy*. Cincinnati: Anderson.

Cases Cited

Bell v. Wolfish 441 U.S. 520 (1979).

Estelle v. Gamble 429 U.S. 97 (1976).

Harris v. Roderick 126 F.3d 1189 (9th Cir. 1997).

Harris v. Thigpen 727 F.Supp. 1564 (M.D. Ala. 1990), affd in part and vacated and remanded in part, 941 F.2d 1495 (11th Cir. 1991), on remand, *Onishea v. Hopper* No. 87-VII09-N, Slip Opinion (M.D. Ala. 1995), vacated and remanded, 126 F.3d 1323 (11th Cir. 1997).

Howard v. City of Columbus 466 S.E.2d 51 (Ga. App. 1995).

Madrid v. Gomez 889 F.Supp. 1146 (N.D. Cal. 1995).

Nelson v. Prison Health Services 991 F.Supp. 1452 (M.D. Fla. 1997). ✦

25
Sexual Offender Recidivism Revisited

A Meta-Analysis of Recent Treatment Studies

Gordon C. Nagayama Hall

With the exception of the violent offender, no type of criminal offender evokes more concern from the public than the sex offender. Recent laws have required sex offender registration and public notification. These strategies are designed to keep better track of sex offenders in the community. Although these risk management techniques provide limited assurances that offenders will not recidivate, more important is whether risk reduction can take place through effective treatment.

For many years, it was believed that treatment was ineffective in reducing recidivism among this group of offenders. Using meta-analysis, Gordon C. Nagayama Hall examines twelve studies of treatment with sexual offenders. Hall finds a small, but robust overall treatment effect. The effect sizes were larger in studies that had higher base rates of recidivism, had follow-up periods longer than five years, included outpatients, and involved cognitive behavioral or hormonal treatments. This study confirms what others have found: targeting higher risk offenders with effective treat- ment strategies can have a significant effect on recidivism rates.

Excerpts from "Sexual Offender Recidivism Revisited: A Meta-Analysis of Recent Treatment Studies" by Gordon C. Nagayama Hall, *Journal of Consulting and Clinical Psychology*, 63(5):802–809. Copyright © 1995 by American Psychological Association, Inc. Reprinted by permission.

Sexual aggression is a serious societal problem that demands an effective solution. Unlike many other psychological treatments for highly repetitive problems, such as addictive behaviors (e.g., smoking, alcohol, drugs), in which some recidivism may be expected and even tolerable, the expectation of psychological treatments for sexual offenders is no recidivism because of the serious effects of even a single act of sexually aggressive behavior. Every act of sexual aggression adversely affects a person other than the perpetrator, whereas the effects of other repetitive problems may often be restricted to the individual experiencing the problem. Between 1 in 10 and 1 in 4 adult women are raped or sexually assaulted during adulthood (Koss, 1993) and prevalence figures are similar for child victims of sexual aggression (Finkelhor, 1984). . . .

The purpose of the present study was to perform a meta-analysis of all treatment outcome studies with sexual offenders since the Furby et al. (1989) review. Although limited, there have been a sufficient number of sexual offender treatment outcome studies since the Furby et al. (1989) review that are methodologically adequate for inclusion in a meta-analysis. In this meta-analysis, the following issues are addressed: (a) Have the outcome studies since the Furby et al. (1989) review demonstrated the effectiveness of treatment with sexual offenders? (b) Is sexual offender treatment more effective for any particular type of sexual offender? and (c) Is any particular type of treatment more effective than other types of treatment with sexual offenders? . . .

Only published studies were considered in the present meta-analysis. Studies that are published typically report statistically significant effects (Rosenthal, 1991). However, sexual offender treatment studies without statistically significant treatment effects are often published (e.g., Hanson, Steffy, & Gauthier, 1993; Maletzky, 1991; Marques, Day, Nelson, & West, 1994; Marshall, Eccles, & Barbaree, 1991; McConaghy, Blaszczynski, & Kidson, 1988; Meyer, Cole, & Emory, 1992; Rice, Quinsey, & Harris, 1991). Perhaps studies on sexual offender treatment without statistically significant effects are more commonly published than studies on other types of treatment because of the importance of any information, positive or negative, about the effects of sexual offender treatment. Nevertheless, the number of studies averaging null results required to change the overall significance level from statistical significance to nonsignificance was determined (Rosenthal, 1991).

Method

Ninety-two published studies since the Furby et al. (1989) review listed in PsycLIT, PsycBOOKS, or reported in previous literature reviews that provided outcome data on treatment of male sexual offenders were considered for the meta-analysis. Although the Furby et al. review was published in 1989, some treatment outcome studies that were published in 1988 and 1989 were not included in Furby et al. (1989). Of the 92 published studies, 32 were eliminated because they were case studies of fewer than 10 participants and 48 were eliminated because they had no comparison or control group or did not report recidivism data. The 12 studies listed in Table 25.1 that compared sexual offender treatment with a comparison condition (alternative treatment or no treatment) and provided recidivism data for sexual offenses were selected for the current meta-analysis.

Eleven of the 12 studies included in the current meta-analysis involved men over the age of 17, and one study involved adolescents (Borduin, Henggeler, Blaske, & Stein, 1990). Ten of the 12 studies included male participants who had committed sexual offenses against children (Borduin et al., 1990;

Fedoroff, Wisner-Carlson, Dean, & Berlin, 1992; Hanson et al., 1993; Hildebran & Pithers, 1992; Maletzky, 1991; Marques et al., 1994; Marshall & Barbaree, 1988; Marshall, Eccles, & Barbaree, 1991; McConaghy et al., 1988; Meyer et al., 1992; Rice et al., 1991). Male participants who had committed sexual offenses against women were included in 6 of the 12 studies (Hildebran & Pithers, 1992; Maletzky, 1991; Marques et al., 1994; Meyer et al., 1992; Rice et al., 1991; Wille & Beier, 1989). One of the 12 studies exclusively involved exhibitionists; (Marshall et al., 1991), and male participants who had committed "hands-off" sexual offenses, including exhibitionism and voyeurism, constituted a minority of the participants in 5 other studies (Borduin et al., 1990; Fedoroff et al., 1992; Maletzky, 1991; McConaghy et al., 1988; Meyer et al., 1992). Half of the studies were of outpatients (Borduin et al., 1990; Fedoroff et al., 1992; Maletzky, 1991; Marshall & Barbaree, 1988; Marshall, Eccles, & Barbaree, 1991; Meyer et al., 1992), and the other half involved institutionalized participants (Hanson et al., 1993; Hildebran & Pithers, 1992; Marques et al., 1994; McConaghy et al., 1988; Rice et al., 1991; Wille & Beier, 1989).

Procedure

The individual study was the unit of analysis, with one effect size estimate obtained per study to prevent any single study from disproportionately contributing to the results. When outcome data on the same participants were reported in multiple published studies, only the results of the most recently published study were included in the meta-analysis. Experimental treatments were compared with alternative treatments in studies in which there was not a no-treatment condition. . . .

Table 25.1

Exclusion Criteria and Description of Final Samples and Definition of Recidivism

Study	Exclusion criteria	Sample and recidivism definition
Borduin et al. (1990)	None	Adolescents: 6 arrested for rape or attempted rape, 5 for sexual assault, 4 for sodomy, and 1 for exhibitionism; random assignment to outpatient multisystemic or interpersonal therapy; recidivism = juvenile court, adult court, state police records
Fedoroff et al. (1992)	In treatment <5 years (n = 210); arrested before follow-up (after 5 years of treatment) began (n = 38); died (n = 7); moved or unable to contact (n = 22); organic brain syndrome or incomplete records (n = 9)	Adults who met criteria for pedophile, exhibitionism, voyeurism, or other paraphilias; 27 volunteered for MPA and outpatient group therapy; 19 received outpatient group therapy only because they did not volunteer for MPA; recidivism = police and legal reports of known sexual offenses + self-report
Hanson et al. (1993)	No recidivism data (n = 33)	Adult child molesters incarcerated in maximum security institutions: 106 in inpatient behavioral treatment, 31 in an institution before treatment was offered; 60 were not offered treatment because of insufficient sentence length insufficient space, relative already in treatment program, too old, major mental illness, security risk; recidivism = reconviction for sexual or violent offenses or both based on official (Royal Canadian Mounted Police) records
Hildebran & Pithers (1992)	Withdrawal from program or screened by program staff (n = 65)	Adult child molesters and rapists: 50 who completed inpatient and outpatient relapse prevention program; 40 who left treatment without program staff's approval; recidivism official records
Maletzky (1991)	Participants who received MPA but had inadequate follow-up data (n = 7); participants who did not receive MPA (n = 4,925)	Adult rapists, child molesters, exhibitionists, voyeurs, other paraphilias; 75% referred through judicial channels, 25% referred by professionals, family, or self. 100 who received outpatient MPA and behavioral, cognitive, group, family therapy; 100 who did not receive MPA matched with MPA group on age, marital status, employment status; recidivism = police records, self-report, significant-other interview

Table 25.1
Continued

Study	Exclusion criteria	Sample and recidivism definition
Marques et al. (1994)	Accomplice to sex offense (*n* = ?); incest (*n* = ?); <14 or >30 months until release (*n* = ?); >2 previous felony convictions (*n* = ?); deny committing offenses (*n* = ?); have pending holds or felony warrants (*n* = ?); IQ < 80 (*n* = ?); not English speaking (*n* = ?); required skilled nursing care (*n* = ?); severe management problems in prison (*n* = ?); withdrew consent for treatment (*n* = 26)	Hospitalized adult sexual offenders: 83 child molesters and 23 rapists who volunteered and were randomly assigned to inpatient and outpatient relapse prevention treatment; 79 child molesters and 18 rapists who volunteered and were randomly assigned to no treatment condition; (236 child molesters and 137 rapists who refused treatment not analyzed in current meta-analysis); recidivism = official records from California Department of Justice and parole records
Marshall & Barbaree (1988)	Deny committing offenses (*n* = ?); refused treatment (*n* = ?); brain damage or psychosis (*n* = ?), at risk < 1 year after treatment (*n* = ?)	Adult child molesters referred by Children's Aid Societies, legal-judicial system, physicians, community, or self; agencies, 68 completed outpatient cognitive-behavioral treatment; 34 who desired treatment but did not participate because of distance from treatment center and were referred to other treatment, 18 child molesters participated assessment or in some form of treatment while incarcerated, 6 were incarcerated and did not receive treatment; recidivism = self-report + official records (Royal Canadian Mounted Police) + unofficial estimates by social agencies (police, Children's Aid Societies)
Marshall, Eccles, et al. (1991)	Untreated men who were not processed, (*n* = ?)	Adult exhibitionists referred by probation officers, lawyers, physicians, hospitals: 40 received cognitive-behavioral treatment; 21 did not participate because of distance from treatment center and were referred to other treatment; recidivism = official records (Royal Canadian Mounted Police) + unofficial estimates by social agencies (police, Children's Aid Societies)

Table 25.1
Continued

Study	Exclusion criteria	Sample and recidivism definition
McConaghy et al. (1988)	Psychotic (*n* = ?); withdrawal from program (*n* = 1); withdrew from MPA treatment (*n* = 5)	Adolescents and adults who voluntarily sought treatment and met *DSM-III* criteria for exhibitionism, pedophilia, fetishism, transvestism, or voyeurism (some participants met criteria for more than one paraphilia): 10 randomly assigned to inpatient ID, 10 randomly assigned to inpatient MPA, 10 randomly assigned to inpatient ID + MPA (5 participants withdrew from the MPA or MPA + ID groups); recidivism = reports from patients' legal representatives, self-report
Meyer et al. (1992)	No data (*n* = 92)	Adolescents and adults referred because of sexual offending: 23 child molesters, 7 rapists, 10 exhibitionists who accepted MPA and outpatient individual and group psychotherapy; 14 child molesters, 6 exhibitionists, and 1 voyeur who refused MPA but received outpatient individual and group psychotherapy; recidivism = official records or self-report
Rice et al. (1991)	Participants who could not be matched on offense history and phallometric preference for children (*n* = 95)	29 child molesters who participated in aversion therapy to alter sexual preferences + institutional programs; 29 child molesters who participated in institutional programs without aversion therapy; recidivism = conviction of a sexual offense
Wille & Beier (1989)	Psychosis (*n* = 2); not traceable (*n* = 7); not released to community (*n* = 8)	99 adult sex offenders who were voluntarily castrated, 36 adult sex offenders who volunteered for castration but were not granted castration by a committee of two physicians and a lawyer; 39% of participants were incarcerated, 46% of participants were in psychiatric hospitals or security detention, 15% of participants were outpatients; recidivism = sexual offenses recorded in criminal records

Note. MPA = medroxyprogesterone acetate; *DSM-III* = *Diagnostic and Statistical Manual of Mental Disorders* (3rd ed.); ID = imaginal desensitization.

Results

The exclusion criteria, a description of the final sample, and the definition of recidivism for each study are included in the meta-analysis are reported in Table 25.1. A comparison of the participants excluded and the final samples in each study suggest that at least 80.9% (5,552 of 6,865) of the participants initially available for study were excluded from analyses. Most of the excluded participants (N = 4,932) were from a single study in which most participants were excluded if they were not matched with participants who received hormonal treatment (Maletzky, 1991). Excluding the Maletzky (1991) study, 35.8% (620 of 1,733) of the initially available participants were excluded. In that some

studies excluded unspecified numbers of participants, 35.8% is a conservative estimate. In general the most pathological participants were excluded from samples (e.g., extensive offense history, psychotic, organic brain syndrome, denied offenses, management problem in prison, withdrew from treatment program).

Table 25.2 presents the treatment modalities, treatment length, and follow-up period after treatment in the 12 studies included in the meta-analysis. The mean length of treatment across studies was 18.54 months (SD = 20.304), and the mean follow-up period across studies was 6.85 years (SD = 5.95).

Recidivism rates and effect sizes for each of the 12 studies are reported in Table 25.3. The overall treatment effect size of .12 is con-

Table 25.2
Treatment Modalities, Treatment Length, and Follow-Up Period After Treatment

Study	Modality[a]	Length (months)	Mean follow-up (years)
Borduin et al. (1990)	CB/I	4.5/6.75	CB = 1.6/I = 2.98
Fedoroff et al. (1992)	H + G/G	60	7
Hanson et al. (1993)	B/C	5	B = 19, C1 = 28, C2 = 20
Hildebran & Pithers (1992)	CB/C	Unspecified	7
Maletzky (1991)	H + C + B + F + G/ C + B + F + G	4.7 (MPA)	3
Marques et al. (1994)	CB/C	36	CB = 2.92, C = 3.08
Marshall & Barbaree (1988)	CB/C	Unspecified	CB = 2.82, C = 2.79
Marshall, Eccles, et al. (1991)	CB/C	6	CB1 8.65, CB2 = 3.97, C = 8.89
McConaghy et al. (1988)	B/H/B + H	7	1
Meyer et al. (1992)	H + P + G/P + G	24	10
Rice et al. (1991)	B/IN	20 sessions	B = 3.81, C = 2.52
Wille & Beier (1989)	H/C	Surgery	11

Note. The follow-up data for the Marshall and Barbaree (1988) and the Meyer et al. (1992) studies are estimates. Dosages of medroxyprogesterone acetate (MPA) in Fedoroff et al. (1992), Maletzky (1991), and Meyer et al. (1992) were 300-500 mg/week, 250 mg/week, and 400 mg/week, respectively. The MPA dosage in McConaghy et al. (1988) was 150 mg biweekly for 4 weeks, followed by 150 mg monthly for 4 months. Treatment modalities were B = behavioral; C = no-treatment comparison; CB = cognitive-behavioral; CB1 cognitive-behavioral treatment in Study 1 of Marshall et al. (1991); CB2 = cognitive-behavioral treatment in Study 2 of Marshall et al. (1991); F = family therapy; G = group psychotherapy; H = hormonal (antiandrogen drug or castration); I = interpersonal; IN = institutional programs; P = individual psychotherapy. (All abbreviations represent treatment modalities.)

[a]The first treatment modality listed for each study is the experimental treatment and the subsequent treatment modalities are the comparison conditions.

Table 25.3
Recidivism Rates and Treatment Effect Sizes

		Recidivism rate and ratio			
Study	*n*	Treatment	Comparison	*r*	*d*
Borduin et al. (1990)	16	.12(1/8)	.75(6/8)	.55	1.32
Fedoroff et al. (1992)	46	.15(4/27)	.68(13/19)	.55	1.32
Hanson et al. (1993)	197	.44(47/106)	.38(35/91)	−.14	−0.28
Hildebran & Pithers (1992)	90	.06(3/50)	.33(13/40)	.22	0.45
Maletzky (1991)	200	.10(10/100)	.06(6/100)	−.07	−0.14
Marques et al. (1994)	299	.08(9/106)	.13(25/193)	.07	0.14
Marshall & Barbaree (1988)	126	.13(9/68)	.34(20/58)	.23	0.47
Marshall, Eccles, et al. (1991)	61	.32(13/40)	.57(12/21)	.27	0.56
McConaghy et al. (1988)	25	.20(2/10)	.13(2/15)	−.09	−0.18
Meyer et al. (1992)	61	.42(17/40)	.57(12/21)	.14	0.28
Rice et al. (1991)	58	.38(11/29)	.31(9/29)	−.07	−0.14
Wille & Beier (1989)	134	.03(3/99)	.45(16/35)	.53	1.25
Total	1,313	.19 (129/683)	.27 (169/630)	.12	−0.24

Note. Recidivism rate is for sexual offenses only.

sidered a small effect size (Cohen, 1988). The fail-safe statistic suggests that this finding is robust in that 88 studies would be required to bring the overall *p* value to nonsignificance.

The treatment effect sizes across studies were significantly heterogeneous, X^2 (11, 1313) = 70.9 1, *p* < .00001. One possible source of this heterogeneity is the base rate of recidivism across studies. The zero-order correlation between the recidivism rates among the comparison groups and the effect size for each study is .76, which suggests that the highest treatment effect sizes were in studies with the highest base rates of recidivism. Thus, low participants who completed treatment, in that the mean effect size for studies that used random assignment to treatment and comparison conditions to control for participant motivation did not differ from the mean effect size for studies that did not use random assignment. Moreover, the mean effect size for studies in which the comparison condition involved treatment was not significantly different from the mean effect size for studies in which the comparison condition involved no treatment.

Treatment effects were largest in samples having high base rates of recidivism and treatment effects appear to have been attenuated in studies having low base rates of recidivism. An effective treatment may not produce a statistically significant reduction in recidivism if the base rate is low.

The mean treatment effect size for studies having follow-up periods of longer than 5 years was significantly greater than the mean treatment effect size for studies having follow-up periods of less than 5 years. Long-term follow-up data suggest that sexual offenders may continue to be at risk for recidivism for over 20 years (Furby et al., 1989; Gibbens, Soothill, & Way, 1981; Hanson et al., 1993). It appears that effective treatments may influence the recidivism curve to become relatively asymptotic beyond 5 years after treatment, whereas the effects of less effective treatments may wear off within 5 years.

Among studies of institutionalized samples, there was a small effect size for treatment, whereas there was a medium effect size for treatment in studies of outpatient samples. Sexual offenders typically are institutionalized as a function of psychopathology and perceived risk for recidivism. These differential treatment effects as a function of psychopathology attest to the heterogeneity of sexual aggressors (Hall & Hirschman, 1991). However, the effect sizes in treatment studies that included only nonrapists were not significantly different from the effect sizes in treatment studies that included rapists.

It is encouraging that one of the two studies yielding the largest effect sizes was with adolescent sexual offenders (Borduin et al., 1990). Interventions during adolescence before sexual offenders develop chronic patterns of sexual aggression may have promise as an effective method of prevention. However, the long-term effectiveness of such interventions is unknown, in that the Borduin et al. (1990) study had a relatively short follow-up period.

Both cognitive-behavioral and hormonal treatments appear superior to behavioral treatments. Medium effect sizes were obtained for hormonal treatments and cognitive-behavioral therapy, but cognitive-behavioral and hormonal treatments were not significantly different in their effectiveness in preventing recidivism. However, the reduction of sexual arousal alone may be effective for some sexual offenders, in that the lowest recidivism rate (.03) and one of the largest treatment effect sizes in the present meta-analysis ($r = .53$) occurred in a study of castrated participants, most of whom apparently did not receive additional treatment (Wille & Beier, 1989).

Hormonal treatment programs in the present meta-analysis were not significantly more effective than cognitive-behavioral treatment programs. Insofar as one to two thirds of participants refuse hormonal treatment (Fedoroff et al., 1992; Meyer et al., 1992) and 50% who begin hormonal treatment discontinue it (Langevin et al., 1979), whereas the refusal and dropout rates for

cognitive-behavioral treatment are about one third (Abel et al., 1988; Chaffin, 1992), there appears to be a practical advantage of cognitive-behavioral treatment. Perhaps this differential compliance rate is a function of the invasiveness of hormonal treatments (i.e., intramuscular injections) and their suppressant effect on both deviant and appropriate forms of sexual arousal, at least with medroxyprogesterone acetate (Hall et al., 1993). Moreover, sexual offenders with abnormally high hormonal levels may constitute a minority (Barbaree, 1990) and reduced testosterone in participants with high or normal testosterone levels base rates of recidivism may preclude statistically significant treatment effects.

Another possible source of the effect size heterogeneity is methodological differences among studies. Orthogonal contrasts (Rosenthal, 1991) between studies in which random (Borduin et al., 1990; Marques et al., 1994; McConaghy et al., 1988) versus nonrandom assignment to treatment was used ($Z < 1$) and between studies in which the comparison condition involved treatment (Borduin et al., 1990; Fedoroff et al., 1992; Maletzky, 1991; McConaghy et al., 1988; Meyer et al., 1992; Rice et al. 1991) versus studies in which the comparison condition involved no treatment (Hanson et al., 1993; Hildebran & Pithers, 1992; Marques et al., 1994; Marshall & Barbaree, 1988; Marshall, Eccles, et al., 1991; Wille & Beier, 1989; $Z < 1$) were not significant. However, the effect sizes in studies that had follow-up periods longer than 5 years (Fedoroff et al., 1992; Hanson et al., 1993; Hildebran & Pithers, 1992; Marshall, Eccles, et al., 1991; Meyer et al., 1992; Wille & Beier, 1989) were significantly greater than the effect sizes in studies that had follow-up periods shorter than 5 years (Borduin et al., 1990; Maletzky, 1991; Marques et al., 1994; Marshall & Barbaree, 1988; McConaghy et al., 1988; Rice et al., 1991; $Z = 2.09, p < .02$). Mean effect sizes for studies with follow-up periods of 5 versus years are presented in Figure 25.1.

A third potential source of the heterogeneity of effect sizes is participant pathology. Effect sizes were significantly greater in studies of outpatient participants (Borduin et al., 1990; Fedoroff et al., 1992; Maletzky, 1991; Marshall & Barbaree, 1988; Marshall, Eccles, et al., 1991; Meyer et al., 1992) than in studies of institutionalized participants (Hanson et al., 1993; Hildebran & Pithers, 1992; Marques et al., 1994; McConaghy et al., 1988; Rice et al., 1991; Wille & Beier, 1989; Z = 2.50, *p* < .01). Figure 25.1 presents the mean effect sizes for studies of outpatient participants versus studies of institutionalized participants. However, effect sizes in studies that did (Borduin et al., 1990; Hildebran & Pithers, 1992; Maletzky, 1991; Marques et al., 1994; Meyer et al., 1992; Rice et al., 1991; Wille & Beier, 1989) and did not include rapists (Fedoroff et al., 1992; Hanson et al., 1993; Marshall & Barbaree, 1988; Marshall, Eccles, et al., 1991; McConaghy et al., 1988) were not significantly different (Z < 1).

An additional potential source of effect size heterogeneity is differential treatment effects. Studies in which cognitive-behavioral (Borduin et al., 1990; Hildebran & Pithers, 1992; Marques et al., 1994; Marshall & Barbaree, 1988; Marshall, Eccles, & Barbaree, 1991; Z = 3.46, *p* < .0005) or hormonal treatments (Fedoroff et al., 1992; Maletzky, 1991; Meyer et al., 1992; Wille & Beier, 1989; Z = 3.99, *p* < .00005) were used yielded significantly larger effect sizes than studies in which behavioral treatments (Hanson et al., 1993; McConaghy et al., 1988; Rice et al., 1991) were used. However, effect sizes in studies that used cognitive-behavioral versus hormonal treatments were not significantly different (Z < 1). Mean effect sizes for studies of cognitive-behavioral, hormonal, and behavioral treatments are presented in Figure 25.1.

Discussion

Of the sexual offenders who completed treatment in the studies in the present meta-analysis, 19% committed additional sexual offenses, whereas over 27% of sexual offenders in comparison conditions committed ad-

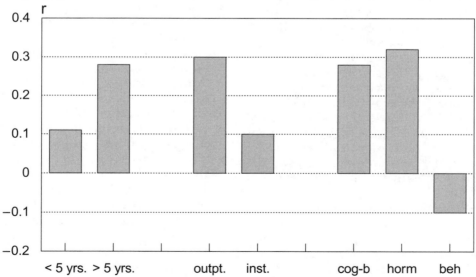

Figure 25.1 Mean effect sizes for treatment as a function of follow-up length, institutional status, and treatment modality. Output. = outpatient participants; Inst. = institutionalized participants; Cog-b = cognitive-behavioral treatment; Horm = hormonal treatment; Beh = behavioral treatment.

ditional sexual offenses. Although the present results should be viewed somewhat cautiously because only 12 studies are included and the overall treatment effect size is small, the findings are robust in that 88 unpublished studies would be required to bring the overall p value to nonsignificance.

Treatment effect sizes across studies were heterogeneous. Variables contributing to this heterogeneity were (a) base rates of recidivism, (b) length of follow-up after the treatment period, (c) participant pathology, and (d) type of treatment. The effect of treatment in the present meta-analysis does not appear to be solely a function of greater motivation to avoid relapse among is not associated with decreased sexual offense recidivism in some individuals (Marshall, Jones, et al., 1991).

In most studies in the present meta-analysis, over one third, and in one study over 80%, of the available participants were screened, primarily on the basis of psychopathology (e.g., extensive offense history, psychotic, organic brain syndrome, denied offenses, management problem in prison, withdrew from treatment program). Thus, the currently reviewed treatments may be less effective with the most pathological sexual offenders. However, among the participants who were not screened, the largest treatment effects were in samples with the highest rates of recidivism.

A possible criticism of the present study is that it overestimates the effectiveness of treatment because of its use of official recidivism data, which may underestimate actual sexually aggressive behavior. Nevertheless, all studies in the present meta-analysis included comparison samples and any inaccurate estimation of recidivism should apply to both treatment and comparison samples. However, the recidivism data in this meta-analysis are for sexual offenses only, and most of the currently reviewed studies did not report data on the effectiveness of treatments in reducing recidivism for nonsexual offenses.

Is the small overall treatment effect clinically significant? The net effect of the sexual offender treatment programs examined in this meta-analysis is 8 fewer sexual offenders per 100, compared with comparison treatments or no treatment. It has been argued that any reduction in recidivism is significant, in terms of harm to victims and costs to society (Marshall, Jones, et al., 1991; Prentky & Burgess, 1990; Quinsey et al., 1993). The results of the present meta-analysis suggest the effect of treatment with sexual offenders is robust, albeit small, and that treatment is most effective with outpatient participants and when it consists of hormonal or cognitive-behavioral treatments.

This meta-analysis includes studies of men who primarily had engaged in sexually aggressive behavior that was sufficiently serious or repetitive to get them into legal trouble. These men are among the most pathological types of sexual aggressors and are the most difficult to effectively treat (Hall & Hirschman, 1991). However, most sexually aggressive men, particularly acquaintance rapists, are not apprehended by the legal system (Koss, 1993). Given that the treatments reviewed in the present meta-analysis were more effective with outpatient than with institutionalized sexual offenders, it follows that the effective treatments may also have promise with sexual aggressors who are not apprehended by the legal system and presumably are less pathological than those that are. Effective treatments directed toward the most common forms of sexual aggression may indeed be a better deterrent of sexually aggressive behavior than those treatments that are restricted to legally apprehended sexual offenders, who may constitute a minority of all sexual aggressors.

Study Questions

1. Describe the research design, data collection methods, sample, and measures used by the author in conducting this study.

2. What are the major findings of this study, and how are they in conflict with previous research?

3. Why is cognitive behavioral treatment more practical than hormonal treatment with sex offenders?

4. What is a methodological criticism of this study?

References

References preceded by an asterisk indicate studies included in the meta-analysis.

Abel, O. G., Mittelman, M., Becker, J. V., Rathner, J., & Rouleau, J. (1988). Predicting child molesters' response to treatment. In R. A. Prentky & V. L. Quinsey (Eds.), *Human sexual aggression: Current perspectives* (pp. 223–234). New York: The New York Academy of Sciences.

Barbaree, H. E. (1990). Stimulus control of sexual arousal: Its role in sexual assault. In W. L. Marshall, D. R. Laws, & H. E. Barbaree (Eds.), *Handbook of sexual assault: Issues, theories, and treatment of the offender* (pp. 115–142). New York: Plenum Press.

*Borduin, C. M., Henggeler, S. W., Blaske, D. M., & Stein, R. J. (1990). Multisystemic treatment of adolescent sexual offenders. *International Journal of Offender Therapy and Comparative Criminology*, 34,105–113.

Chaffin, M. (1992). Factors associated with treatment completion and progress among intrafamilial sexual abusers. *Child Abuse & Neglect*, 16, 251–264.

Cohen, J. (1988). *Statistical power analysis for the behavioral sciences* (2nd ed.). Hillsdale, NJ: Erlbaum.

*Fedoroff, J. P., Wisner-Carlson, R., Dean, S., & Berlin, F. S. (1992). Medroxy-progesterone acetate in the treatment of paraphilic sexual disorders: Rate of relapse in paraphilic men treated in long-term group psychotherapy with or without medroxy-progesterone acetate. *Journal of Offender Rehabilitation*, 18, 109–123.

*Finkelhor, D. (1984). *Child sexual abuse: New theory and research*. New York: The Free Press.

Furby, L., Weinrott, M. R., & Blackshaw, L. (1989). Sex offender recidivism: A review. *Psychological Bulletin*, 105, 3–30.

Gibbens, T. C. N., Soothill, K. L., & Way, C. K. (1981). Sex offenses against young girls: A long-term record study. *Psychological Medicine*, 11, 351–357.

Hall, G. C. N., & Hirschman, R. (1991). Toward a theory of sexual aggression: A quadripartite model. *Journal of Consulting and Clinical Psychology*, 59, 662–669.

Hall, G. C. N., Shondrick, D. D., & Hirschman, R. (1993). Conceptually-derived treatments for sexual aggressors. *Professional Psychology: Research and Practice*, 24, 62–69.

Hanson, R. K., Steffy, R. A., & Gauthier, R. (1993). Long-term recidivism of child molesters. *Journal of Consulting and Clinical Psychology*, 61, 646–652.

*Hildebran, D. D., & Pithers, W. D. (1992). Relapse prevention: Application and outcome. In W. O'Donohue & J. H. Geer (Eds.), *The sexual abuse of the children: Clinical issues* (Vol. 2, pp. 365–393). Hillsdale, NJ: Erlbaum.

Koss, M. P. (1993). Rape: Scope, impact, interventions, and public policy responses. *American Psychologist*, 48, 1062–1069.

Langevin, R., Paitich, D., Hucker, S. J., Newman, S., Ramsay, G., Pope, S., Geller, G., & Anderson, C. (1979). The effect of assertiveness training, Provera, and sex of therapist in the treatment of genital exhibitionism. *Journal of Behavior Therapy and Experimental Psychiatry*, 10, 275–282.

*Maletzky, B. M. (1991). The use of medroxyprogesterone acetate to assist in the treatment of sexual offenders. *Annals of Sex Research*, 4, 117–129.

*Marques, J. K., Day, D. M., Nelson, C., & West, M. A. (1994). Effects of cognitive-behavioral treatment on sex offender recidivism: Preliminary results of a longitudinal study. *Criminal Justice and Behavior*, 21, 28–54.

*Marshall, W. L., & Barbaree, H. E. (1988). The long-term evaluation of a behavioral treatment program for child molesters. *Behaviour Research and Therapy*, 26, 499–511.

*Marshall, W. L., Eccles, A., & Barbaree, H. E. (1991). The treatment of exhibitionists: A focus on sexual deviance versus cognitive and relationship features. *Behaviour Research and Therapy*, 29, 129–135.

Marshall, W. L., Jones, R., Ward, T., Johnston, P., & Barbaree, H. E. (1991). Treatment outcome with sex offenders. *Clinical Psychology Review*, 11, 465–485.

*McConaghy, N., Blaszczynski, A., & Kidson, W. (1988). Treatment of sex offenders with imaginal desensitization and/or medroxyprogesterone. *Acta Psychiatrica Scandinavica, 77,* 199–206.

*Meyer, W. J., Cole, C., & Emory, E. (1992). Depoprovera treatment for sex offending behavior: An evaluation of outcome. *Bulletin of the American Academy of Psychiatry and the Law, 20,* 249–259.

Prentky, R., & Burgess, A. W. (1990). Rehabilitation of child molesters: A cost-benefit analysis. *American Journal of Orthopsychiatry, 60,* 108–117.

Quinsey, V. L., Harris, G. T., Rice, M. E., & Lalumiére, M. L. (1993). Assessing treatment efficacy in outcome studies of sex offenders. *Journal of Interpersonal Violence, 8,* 512–523.

*Rice, M. E., Quinsey, V. L., & Harris, G. T. (1991). Sexual recidivism among child molesters released from a maximum security psychiatric institution. *Journal of Consulting and Clinical Psychology, 59,* 381–386.

Rosenthal, R. (1991). *Meta-analytic procedures for social research* (rev. ed.). Newbury Park, CA: Sage.

*Wille, R., & Beier, K. M. (1989). Castration in Germany. *Annals of Sex Research, 2,* 103–133. ✦

26
What Works for Female Offenders
A Meta-Analytic Review

Craig Dowden

D. A. Andrews

Most of the correctional research that exists focuses on male offenders. Over the years crime has been considered a young man's game. However, while males comprise the largest number of inmates, females are the fastest growing segment of the correctional population. Recent attention has been focused on the neglect that females have experienced, both in terms of research and correctional programming. Some have argued that risk factors for female offenders are different than those of males, and therefore what works for males will not work for females. While there has been considerably less research on correctional treatment programs for females, Craig Dowden and Don Andrews examine the research that is available and conclude that the most effective treatment for females is the same as that for males. Those programs that meet the principles of effective intervention demonstrate the strongest reductions in recidivism. These findings are similar to other research studies that have focused on male offenders.

Excerpted from "What Works for Female Offenders: A Meta-Analytic Review" by Craig Dowden and Don A. Andrews, *Crime and Delinquency*, 45(4):438–452. Copyright © 1999 by Sage Publications, Inc. Reprinted by permission.

Considerable debate has occurred regarding the effectiveness of correctional interventions. Although the notion that nothing works (Martinson 1974) predominated in the 1970s, the advent of meta-analytic research has swung the pendulum to a what works perspective (McGuire 1995). Several meta-analytic reviews have been conducted on the rehabilitation literature and, for the most part, have suggested that some types of correctional interventions can effectively reduce recidivism (Andrews, Dowden, and Gendreau forthcoming; Andrews, Zinger, Hoge, Bonta, Gendreau, and Cullen 1990; Dowden 1998; Hill, Andrews, and Hoge 1991; Izzo and Ross 1990; Lipsey 1989, 1995; Losel 1996).

Although the effectiveness of rehabilitation for general offender populations has received widespread attention (Gibbons 1999), research dedicated to female offender populations has been quite limited (Koons, Burrow, Morash, and Bynum 1997). Morash, Bynum, and Koons (1995) identified 67 studies that reported promising intervention strategies for female offenders, but only 12 included an outcome measure, and none linked recidivism to program components.

A qualitative survey study conducted by Koons and her colleagues (1997) also attempted to identify promising intervention strategies for female offenders. In their report, correctional administrators identified treatment needs that they believed were related to successful treatment outcome. These needs included substance abuse education and treatment and the development of parenting and life skills as well as interpersonal and basic education skills. Interestingly, these program targets only partially overlapped with the list of more promising targets for change (i.e., criminogenic needs) outlined by a number of scholars in the correctional treatment literature (Andrews and Bonta 1998; Andrews, Bonta, and Hoge 1990).

Koons and her colleagues (1997) argued that female offenders have several unique needs and concerns such as childcare, pregnancy, and sexual or physical abuse victimization. Nonetheless, their survey results and introductory overview of the what works literature suggested that the principles of effective correctional treatment (i.e., risk, need, and responsivity) may apply regardless of the gender of the treatment population. At the same time, the authors stated that "the question of whether or not these findings (i.e., principles of effective correctional treatment) can be generalized to the female offender population still is very much in need of an answer" (p. 517).

What Are the Principles of Risk, Need, and Responsivity?

Essentially, the risk principle is concerned with identifying those clients who should receive the most intensive allocation of correctional treatment resources and those who require less attention. In other words, this principle states that the amount of intervention that an offender receives must be matched to his or her risk level to reoffend. The highest levels of service should be reserved for the higher risk cases, whereas the minimal levels of service and supervision should be provided for the lower risk cases (Andrews and Bonta 1998; Andrews, Bonta, et al. 1990).

The need principle, on the other hand, is concerned with the targets for change identified within the treatment program. More specifically, theory and some research have demonstrated that when certain risk factors have been altered, reductions in recidivism for offenders have occurred. These more promising targets or dynamic risk factors have been commonly referred to as criminogenic needs (Andrews and Bonta 1998; Andrews, Bonta, et al. 1990), and they are different from other less promising targets that are classified as noncriminogenic needs. Past research has suggested that programs that targeted these latter needs have not led to significant reductions in recidi-

vism (Andrews and Bonta 1998; Andrews, Bonta, et al. 1990). Accordingly, the need principle states that if the primary goal of treatment is reduced recidivism, the criminogenic needs of offenders must be emphasized and targeted.

Although the need principle has received empirical support within a number of meta-analytic reviews (Cleland, Pearson, and Lipton 1996; Dowden 1998), research has been sorely lacking regarding the applicability of this principle to female offenders. More specifically, research has not focused on whether the criminogenic needs of female offenders are the same as those for general offender populations. For example, one of the promising treatment targets identified within the Koons, Burrow, Morash, and Bynum (1997) study involved focusing on issues of victimization and targeting an offender's level of self-esteem. Traditionally, self-esteem has been classified as a noncriminogenic need (Andrews and Bonta 1998). One of the main goals of the present meta-analytic investigation was to determine whether the list of criminogenic and noncriminogenic needs identified by Andrews and his colleagues (Andrews and Bonta 1998; Andrews, Bonta, et al. 1990) was valid when applied to female offenders.

A third principle of effective correctional treatment is responsivity. This principle is directly concerned with the characteristics of program delivery, and it states that the styles and modes of service used within a treatment program should be matched to the learning styles of offenders. Both general and specific responsivity considerations are encompassed within the responsivity principle. General responsivity states that the most effective types of service are based on cognitive-behavioral and social learning approaches. Specific responsivity focuses on offender characteristics such as interpersonal sensitivity, interpersonal anxiety, and verbal intelligence to name a few. For example, Andrews, Zinger, Hoge, Bonta, Gendreau, and Cullen (1990) stated that "the success of highly verbal, evocative, and relationship-dependent services seems to be limited to clients with high levels of interpersonal, self-reflective, and verbal skill" (p. 376). However, the meta-analytic evidence to date has only examined the effectiveness of the general responsivity principle and has suggested that the most powerful treatment approaches are those that have used concrete social learning and behavioral strategies.

Support for the clinical effectiveness of these three principles was derived from the Andrews, Zinger, Hoge, Bonta, Gendreau, and Cullen (1990) meta-analysis, in which a four-level type-of-treatment variable was used to identify effective correctional treatment programs. This four-level variable consisted of criminal sanctions, inappropriate service, unspecified service, and appropriate service. The results revealed that the appropriate service category (programs that adhered to each of the principles of risk, need, and responsivity) was associated with significantly larger reductions in reoffending when compared to each of the remaining categories. Based on these results, the authors concluded that the most effective correctional interventions were ones that incorporated the principles of effective correctional treatment within their program framework.

Methodology

Sample of Studies

The present study combined two distinct samples of studies. The first was taken directly from Andrews, Zinger, Hoge, Bonta, Gendreau, and Cullen (1990), whereas the second (*n* = 220) was composed of additional studies reported by Andrews (1996), Andrews and Bonta (1998: Resource Note 10.1), and Dowden (1998). Studies selected to be included in the present meta-analysis possessed the following characteristics:

(1). The study was composed predominantly or entirely of female offenders.

(2). The study included a follow-up period. If several follow-up periods were reported, data from the longest follow-up period were coded to ensure the maximum time at risk in the community.

(3). The study compared a group of offenders who received some form of intervention to a control group who did not receive the primary intervention. Individual control groups could have received a diluted form of the treatment program and could even have received alternate services as long as these services could be differentiated from those received by the treatment group.

(4). A measure of recidivism was included in the report. Recidivism was defined in several ways. Acceptable definitions included rearrest, reconviction, and parole failures or revocations. The preferred measure of recidivism was reconviction.

Variables Included in the Analysis

Risk. Andrews, Zinger, Hoge, Bonta, Gendreau, and Cullen (1990) directly coded the risk principle only when the primary study reported outcome data for high- and low-risk groups separately. Consequently, an overall examination of the risk principle for their entire sample was not available. For the present meta-analysis, an aggregate approach to coding risk (Lipsey 1989) was introduced. In other words, each study was coded as involving higher or lower risk offenders, depending on whether the majority of those in the study had penetrated the justice system at the time of the study or had a previous criminal offense. The study was coded as involving high-risk cases if either of these characteristics were present. The advantage of this approach over the one originally used by Andrews, Zinger, Hoge, Bonta, Gendreau, and Cullen (1990) was that it allowed a risk score to be entered for each study included in the meta-analysis.

General responsivity. Andrews, Zinger, Hoge, Bonta, Gendreau, and Cullen (1990) only coded for general responsivity within their meta-analysis. To ensure consistency and facilitate comparison of the findings, this method of coding the responsivity principle was maintained. More specifically, social learning or cognitive-behavioral programs that used modeling, role-playing, reinforcement, and graduated practice were considered to be appropriately addressing general responsivity.

Need. Each individual treatment program was examined to determine whether any of the more or less promising targets for intervention outlined by Andrews and Bonta (1998) had been included within it. Once all of the needs within a particular treatment program were identified, an overall need variable was constructed by considering the difference score between the number of criminogenic and noncriminogenic needs targeted within the treatment program of interest. The variable was a binary measure (0 = the difference score was less than or equal to 0 and 1 = the difference score was greater than or equal to 1). This variable was used as the overall test of the need principle. In other words, programs targeting more criminogenic than noncriminogenic needs were considered to be appropriately addressing the need principle; conversely, programs that targeted an equal or greater number of noncriminogenic needs than criminogenic ones were considered to be inappropriately addressing the need principle.

Type of treatment. Because, in the present investigation, the principles of risk, need, and responsivity were examined separately, the next logical step involved the development of a type-of-treatment variable similar to the one used by Andrews, Zinger, Hoge, Bonta, Gendreau, and Cullen (1990). This variable had to do with how well the principles of risk, need, and responsivity were incorporated within a particular treatment program, and it was an objective extension of the original coding procedures used by Andrews, Zinger, Hoge, Bonta, Gendreau, and Cullen (1990). The scoring for the variable was based on the composite risk, need, and responsivity scores, with a simple count to determine the number of principles that the treatment program appropriately addressed. This score determined the type-of-treatment rating received by each particular treatment program.

The possible range of scores for this variable ranged from 0 to 3. Criminal sanctions without the provision of human service were automatically coded 0. The four categories, in order of appropriateness, were *inappropriate service, weak service, promising service,* and *most promising service.* For example, a human service program that incorporated only two of the three principles of risk, need, and responsivity was coded as a promising service.

Procedure

Because the meta-analysis was conducted on a subsample of studies taken from a larger meta-analytic review and the same set of variables was used, we assumed that the interrater agreement ratings would remain the same; therefore, the results for the interrater reliability reported below were based on those presented in the original meta-analysis (Dowden 1998).

The first author coded all of the studies that met the inclusion criteria for the present meta-analysis, using the previously mentioned coding procedures. An honors student in psychology was also trained to use the coding manuals and was given a preliminary sample of five studies to code. Once the student had finished coding these studies, any discrepancies in scoring were discussed with the first author. This procedure ensured that the other rater fully understood the underlying constructs presented within the coding manuals. Once the other coder felt comfortable with the coding manuals, the first author provided him with a random sample of 29 studies, equally drawn from the justice, inappropriate, unspecified, and appropriate categories identified by Andrews, Zinger, Hoge, Bonta, Gendreau, and Cullen (1990).

The interrater reliability ratings were calculated by dividing the total number of correct classifications by the total number of classified variables. The rates of agreement for the core variables were 100 percent (any treatment, $r = 1.00$) and 90 percent for behavioral ($r = .79$), risk level ($r = .79$), and criminogenic need ($r = .79$). The interrater agreement was 76 percent ($r = .88$) on the four-level type-of-treatment variable.

Calculation of effect sizes. The effect-size measure used in the current study was the phi coefficient. Phi was used as the measure of treatment effect because it provides the magnitude and direction of the association between two binary variables (treatment participation and recidivism) and it is equivalent to the Pearson product-moment correlation coefficient. A valuable characteristic of phi is that it can be translated into the Binomial Effect Size Display (BESD; Rosenthal 1991). The BESD converts this statistic into a value that reflects the difference between the recidivism rates of the treatment group and the control group (assuming a base rate of recidivism of 50 percent and an equal number of cases in each group). For example, using the BESD, a mean correlation coefficient of .20 translates into a recidivism rate of 40 percent for the treatment group (i.e., 50 percent - 20/2) and a corresponding recidivism rate of 60 percent for the control group (50 percent + 20/2).

It should be noted that the analyses were conducted on the unweighted effect-size estimates. Both weighted and unweighted effect-size estimates have been reported in the literature, and we decided to use the unweighted estimates for several reasons. Most importantly, the least-square approaches that can be conducted on the unadjusted estimates allow for a more sophisticated and effective exploration of the hypotheses. For example, several potential moderating variables can be identified, and their independent and joint contributions to effect size can be determined.

Analyses. Two sets of analyses were conducted for each of the major variables. The first set focused on the entire sample of treatment outcome studies in which female offenders predominated to ensure that the maximum number of effect sizes contrib-uted to the analyses. The second set of analyses was conducted on only those studies that were composed entirely of female offender populations. This set of analyses provided an opportunity to examine whether any serious discrepancies existed between the predominantly and entirely female offender studies.

Results and Discussion

What Works: A Focus on Risk, Need, Responsivity, and the Most Promising Service

The present meta-analysis consisted of 45 effect sizes extracted from 26 unique studies that examined the effectiveness of correctional treatment programs for female offenders. Sixteen of the studies were composed entirely of female offenders and contributed 24 effect sizes to the analysis. The small number of studies contributing to the meta-analysis highlighted the relative lack of research that has been conducted on the effectiveness of correctional treatment for female offenders.

A wide range of effect sizes was found within the entire sample of studies. More specifically, these varied from -0.43 to +0.82. The overall, mean effect size for the sample was +0. 14 ($SD = .24$) with a 95 percent confidence interval of +0.07 to +0.21. Using the BESD introduced earlier, this value represented a recidivism rate of 43 percent for the treatment group and 57 percent for the control group. Interestingly, when the analysis focused exclusively on female offenders, the mean effect size was +0. 17 ($SD = .24$).

We hypothesized that human service in a justice context would yield greater reductions in recidivism than criminal sanctioning. Although the mean effect size for criminal sanctions was mildly positive (+0.01; $k = 10$; $SD = .07$), analysis of variance revealed that the mean effect size for human service interventions (+0.18; $k = 35$; $SD = .25$) was associated with a significantly greater mean reduction in recidivism ($\eta = .31$, $p < .04$).

Table 26.1
Mean Effect Size for Each Level of Human Service, Risk, Need, and Responsivity

Variable Label	No (k[a])	Adheres to Principle Yes (k)	η
Human service			
Predominantly female	.01(10)	.18 (35)	.31*
Solely female	.02 (4)	.20 (20)	.29
Risk			
Predominantly female	−.04 (g)	.19 (36)	.40**
Solely female	−.04 (6)	.24 (18)	.51**
Need			
Predominantly female	.04 (24)	.26 (21)	.49**
Solely female	.09 (11)	.23 (13)	.32
Responsivity			
Predominantly female	.08 (30)	.27 (15)	.38**
Solely female	.12 (16)	.25 (8)	.26

[a] k refers to the number of studies that contributed to the mean effect size of interest.
*$p < .05$. **$p < .01$.

Using the BESD, the mean correlation coefficient for human service studies translated into a recidivism rate of 41 percent for human service programs and 59 percent for the control/companion group. The magnitude of this trend was maintained when the analyses focused exclusively on female offenders (see Table 26.1).

These results suggested that human service programs played an important role in determining the therapeutic potential of a particular intervention. Further analyses were conducted to examine whether the principles of risk, need, and responsivity provided additional information concerning what works for female offenders.

Risk, need, and responsivity principles. Strong support was found for each of the principles of risk, need, and responsivity in the meta-analysis (see Table 26.1). More specifically, stronger treatment effects were revealed in programs that targeted higher versus lower risk cases ($\eta = .31$), predominantly focused upon criminogenic versus noncriminogenic needs ($\eta = .49$), and used behav-

ioral-social learning versus nonbehavioral treatment strategies ($\eta = .38$).

Type of treatment. The mean effect sizes for each level of the type-of-treatment variable are presented in Table 26.2. Using the Scheffe correction, the appropriate treatment category yielded a significantly higher mean effect size compared to the weak and inappropriate programs ($p \leq .05$). These findings replicated the results of Andrews, Zinger, Hoge, Bonta, Gendreau, and Cullen (1990) and suggested that programs that appropriately implemented the principles of risk, need, and responsivity within their framework were associated with reductions in reoffending.

Supplementary analyses of need. The percentage distributions for each of the more and less promising targets for intervention are listed in Tables 26.3 and 26.4, respectively. The mean effect size for each need, when it was and was not targeted, and the magnitude of the association with effect size is presented in these tables.

The categorizations used for each of the criminogenic and noncriminogenic need

Table 26.2
Mean Effect Sizes for Each Level of Type of Treatment

Level of Type of Treatment	Predominantly Female (k[a])	Solely Female (k)
Inappropriate service	.02 (14)	.03 (6)
Weak service	.03 (10)	.10 (5)
Promising service	.17 (9)	.18 (7)
Most promising service	.36 (12)	.34 (6)

[a] *k* refers to the number of studies that contributed to the mean effect size of interest.

Table 26.3
Criminogenic Needs and Their Magnitude of Correlation With Effect Size Percentage of Tests With Need Targeted, Mean Effect Size When and When Not Targeted, and Correlation With Effect Size

		Mean Phi (k)[a]		
Need Area Targeted	Percentage	Not a Target	Targeted	Correlation With Phi
Personal criminogenic targets				
Antisocial cognition and skill deficits	18	.11 (37)	.31 (8)	.32*
Antisocial cognition	11	.11 (40)	.38 (5)	.36*
Self-control deficits	11	.13 (40)	.22 (5)	.12
Interpersonal criminogenic targets				
Family and peers	31	.07 (31)	.30 (14)	.45**
Family process	20	.08 (36)	.38 (9)	.51***
Antisocial associates	14	.09 (36)	.35 (9)	.45**
School/work	18	.15 (38)	.10 (7)	−.08
Substance abuse	11	.14 (40)	.14 (5)	−.01

Note: Two targets occurred in less than 5 percent of the studies: Relapse prevention ($k=1$, $r=$N/A) and barriers to treatment ($k=3$, $r=.52$***). Components of antisocial cognition include antisocial attitudes ($k=1$ $r=$N/A) and anger ($k=4$, $r=.34$*). Components of family process include affection ($k=9$, $r=.51$***) and supervision ($k=4$, $r=.62$***). Components of antisocial associates include increase contact with prosocial ($k=8$, $r=.39$**) and decrease contact with antisocial ($k=3$, $r=.08$ n.s.). Components of schoolwork include school ($k=6$, $r=-.04$ n.s.) and vocational skills ($k=1$, $r=$N/A). Components of substance abuse include treatment ($k=4$, $r=.03$ n.s.) and information ($k=3$, $r=.08$ n.s.).

[a] *k* refers to the number of studies that contributed to the mean effect size of interest.
*$p<.05$. **$p<.01$. ***$p<.001$.

targets were derived directly from a recent meta-analysis of the need principle conducted by Andrews, Dowden, and Gendreau (forthcoming). They combined similar criminogenic and noncriminogenic need factors to create composite need categories. These categories and their subcomponents are presented in Tables 26.3 and 26.4.

Regarding criminogenic needs, Table 26.3 reveals that 31 percent of the treatment programs focused on interpersonal criminogenic need targets, defined as family process

Table 26.4

Noncriminogenic Needs Rank Ordered by Magnitude of Correlation With Effect Size: Percentage of Tests With Need Targeted, Mean Effect Size When and When Not Targeted, and Correlation With Effect Size

Need Area Targeted	Percentage	Mean Phi (k)[a]		Correlation With Phi
		Not a Target	Targeted	
Personal noncriminogenic targets	24	.15 (34)	.13 (11)	−.03
Vague emotional/personal problems	20	.14 (36)	.15 (6)	.02
Interpersonal noncriminogenic targets	13	.16 (39)	.01 (6)	−.23
Family (other)	11	.17 (40)	−.06 (5)	−.32*

Note: Low frequency targets include targeting of respect for criminal thinking (k=1, r=N/A) and cohesive peers (k=1, r=N/A). Components of personal noncriminogenic targets include fear of official punishment (k=2, r=−.10) and respect criminal thinking (k=1, r=12). Components of interpersonal noncriminogenic targets include increase cohesiveness of antisocial peer groups (k=1, r=N/A).

[a] k refers to the number of studies that contributed to the mean effect size of interest.

*p <.05.

or antisocial associate variables. These need targets yielded the strongest positive association with reduced reoffending (η = .45). The other category of criminogenic needs, personal criminogenic need targets, included focusing on either antisocial cognition or self-control deficits. This category also yielded a significant positive correlation with effect size (η = .37).

An interesting pattern of results emerged when the analyses shifted to the school/work and substance abuse variables and their corresponding relationships with recidivism. More specifically, both school/work (−.08) and substance abuse (−.01) had slightly negative correlations with reduced reoffending.

Personal and interpersonal noncriminogenic need targets were also examined. The results revealed that almost one quarter of the effect sizes targeted personal noncriminogenic needs. Not surprisingly, personal noncriminogenic needs had a slightly negative correlation with effect size (−.03). On the other hand, interpersonal noncriminogenic needs were targeted in only 13 percent of the cases and yielded a moderate negative association with reduced recidivism (−.23). An even more interesting finding appeared when analyses focused on other noncriminogenic forms of family interventions. Although the family-functioning variables classified as criminogenic needs were associated with enhanced reductions in reoffending, vague forms of family intervention (i.e., providing family counseling without specifically identifying the targets for intervention) had a significant negative relationship with effect size (−.32). Clearly, the specific targets of family intervention were important indicators of the therapeutic potential of these particular programs.

Methodological considerations. Several important methodological factors were also considered to determine their relationship with effect size. The majority of these were taken directly from the strongest methodological variables identified by Andrews, Dowden, and Gendreau (forthcoming) in their examination of the strongest potential threats to validity (see Table 26.5). The remaining two variables, age and randomness of design, were included due to their importance within both meta-analytic and treatment outcome research. The simple and par-

Table 26.5
The Most Important Methodological and Control Variables and Their Relationships With Effect Size

Variable	Frequency (percentage)	Simple r	Partial r
CJ[a] sponsor	84	−.29	−.08
CJ[a] referral	87	.34	.21
Nonresidential	71	−.08	.25
Small sample	58	.26	.12
Now program	38	.26	−.17
Involved evaluator	18	.64***	.53***
Older (age 18+)	22	.03	.17
Random assignment	31	−.02	−.10

[a] CJ stands for criminal justice.
***p < .001.

tial correlation coefficients (with type of controlled treatment) for each of these variables are presented in Table 26.5.

Only the involved evaluator variable was significantly correlated with effect size. Although some individuals have claimed that an involved evaluator is a biasing factor in rehabilitation research, we share Lipsey's (1995) view that an involved evaluator may not be a sign of bias but a sign of increased therapeutic integrity. In other words, having an involved evaluator in the implementation and evaluation of the program increases the likelihood that the program will be correctly implemented. Evaluators who are not so involved may not take the same time and consideration in the preliminary stages of program implementation.

Conclusion

The meta-analysis reported here indicated that the principles of risk, need, and general responsivity were important contributors to treatment outcome for female offenders. These results support previous theoretically derived viewpoints (Andrews and Bonta 1998; Andrews, Bonta, et al. 1990; Andrews, Zinger, et al. 1990).

However, some more specific findings should be emphasized. One of these was that the most promising targets for intervention (i.e., substance abuse and basic education skills) that were identified by a national sample of correctional administrators (Koons et al. 1997) did not emerge as important in our study, rather, the strongest predictors of treatment success were interpersonal criminogenic need targets and, in particular, family process variables. Furthermore, it is clear that personal and interpersonal noncriminogenic needs were not related to treatment outcome; in fact, they were associated with recidivism increases within the treatment group.

Although only a moderate number of effect sizes contributed to the present meta-analysis, it is significant that the principles of risk, need, and responsivity survived all of the strongest threats to validity documented within previous meta-analytic research (Andrews, Dowden, et al. forthcoming). In addition, treatment programs that appropriately addressed these principles were associated with enhanced reductions in recidivism.

The Koons, Burrow, Morash, and Bynum (1997) study suggested that programs that focused on dealing with past victimization issues and targeted self-esteem are promising targets for change for female offenders. Because none of the studies discussed here focused on these treatment targets, it remains unclear as to whether these are criminogenic or noncriminogenic needs for female offenders. These are matters for future study.

Despite these overall findings, one final point should be made. Although the present investigation explored the effectiveness of the principles of risk, need, and responsivity for female offender populations, it did not look at gender as a specific responsivity consideration. More specifically, we did not examine whether making the treatment program more responsive to the specific learning styles of women offenders (i.e., relationship-oriented treatment) had any impact on recidivism. Exploring the effects of gender as a specific responsivity consideration will be the focus of a future meta-analysis.

In conclusion, although promising evidence was uncovered for each of the principles of risk, need, and responsivity, more work needs to be done.

Study Questions

1. Describe the research design, data collection methods, sample, and measures used by the authors in conducting this study.

2. What are the principles of risk, need, and responsivity?

3. Summarize the findings from this study. Why do you think they are important for correctional officials?

Appendix

The following studies were included in the meta-analysis. Studies that were composed predominantly or entirely of female offenders met our inclusion criteria. This standard was adopted to ensure that the maximum number of effect sizes contributed to the meta-analysis. Please note the similarities between the trends for the entire set of studies and those that solely involved female offenders in Table 26.1 and Table 26.2.

Alexander, James F., Cole Barton, R. Steven Schiavo, and Bruce V. Parsons. 1976. "Systems-Behavioral Intervention With Delinquents: Therapist Characteristics, Family Behavior, and Outcome." *Journal of Consulting and Clinical Psychology* 44:556–664.

Borduin, Charles M., Barton J. Mann, Lynn T. Cone, Scott W. Henggeler, Bethany R. Fucci, David M. Blaske, and Robert A. Williams. 1995. "Multisystemic Treatment of Serious Juvenile Offenders: Long-Term Prevention of Criminality and Violence." *Journal of Consulting and Clinical Psychology* 63:569–78.

Buckner, John C. and Meda Chesney-Lind. 1983. "Dramatic Cures for Juvenile Crime: An Evaluation of a Prisoner-Run Delinquency Prevention Program." *Criminal Justice and Behavior* 10:227–47.

Davidson, William S. and Timothy R. Wolfred. 1977. "Evaluation of a Community-Based Behavior Modification Program for Prevention of Delinquency." *Community Mental Health Journal* 13:296–306.

Davies, Jean and Nancy Goodman. 1972. *Girl Offenders Aged 17 to 20 Years*. London, UK: H.M. Stationary Office.

Deng, Xiaogang. 1997. "The Deterrent Effects of Initial Sanction on First-Time Apprehended Shoplifters." *International Journal of Offender Therapy and Comparative Criminology* 41:284–97.

Druckman, Joan M. 1979. "A Family-Oriented Policy and Treatment Program for Female Juvenile Status Offenders." *Journal of Marriage and the Family* 41:627–36.

Gordon, Donald A., Jack Arbuthnot, Kathryn E. Gustafson, and Peter McGreen. 1988. "Home-Based Behavioral Systems Family Therapy With Disadvantaged Juvenile Delinquents." *The American Journal of Family Therapy* 16:243–55.

Gruber, Martin. 1979. "Family Counseling and the Status Offender." *Juvenile and Family Court Journal* 30:23–7.

Johnson, David C., Ronald W. Shearon, and George M. Britton. 1974. "Correctional Education and Recidivism in a Women's Correctional Center." *Adult Education* 24:121–9.

Klein, Nancy C., James F. Alexander, and Bruce V. Parsons. 1977. "Impact of Family Systems Intervention on Recidivism and Sibling Delinquency: A Model of Primary Prevention and Program Evaluation." *Journal of Consulting and Clinical Psychology* 3:469–74.

Meyer, Henry J., Edgar F. Borgotta, and Wyatt C. Jones. 1965. *Girls at Vocational High: An Experiment in Social Work Intervention.* New York: Russell Sage.

Moo, Joy. 1983. "Police Decisions for Dealing With Juvenile Offenders." *British Journal of Criminology* 23:249–62.

O'Donnell, Clifford R., Tony Lydgate, and Walter S. O. Fo. 1979. "The Buddy System: Review and Follow-Up." *Child Behavior Therapy* 1:161–9.

Prendergast, Michael L., Jean Wellisch, and Maimee M. Wong. 1996. "Residential Treatment for Women Parolees Following Prison-Based Drug Treatment: Treatment Experiences, Needs, Services, and Outcomes." *The Prison Journal* 76:253–74.

Rausch, Sharla. 1983. "Court Processing Versus Diversion of Status Offenders: A Test of Deterrence and Labeling Theories." *Journal of Research in Crime and Delinquency* 20:39–54.

Redfering, David L. 1973. "Durability of Effects of Group Counseling With Institutionalized Females." *Journal of Abnormal Psychology* 82:85–6.

Ross, Robert R. and H. Bryan McKay. 1976. "A Study of Institutional Treatment Programs." *International Journal of Offender Therapy and Comparative Criminology* 21:165–73.

Sowles, Richard C. and John H. Gill. 1970. "Institutional and Community Adjustment of Delinquents Following Counseling." *Journal of Consulting and Clinical Psychology* 34:398–402.

Spergel, Irving A., Frederic G. Reamer, and James P. Lynch. 1981. "Deinstitutionalization of Status Offenders: Individual Outcomes and System Effects." *Journal of Research in Crime and Delinquency* 18:4–33.

Stewart Mary J., Edward L. Vockell, and Rose E. Ray. 1986. "Decreasing Court Appearances of Juvenile Status Offenders." *Social Casework* 67:74–9.

Vito, Gennaro F., Ronald M. Holmes, and Deborah G. Wilson. 1985. "The Effect of Shock and Regular Probation Upon Recidivism: A Comparative Analysis." *American Journal of Criminal Justice* 9:152–62.

Wade, Terry C., Tern L. Morton, Judith E. Lind, and Newton R. Ferris. 1971. "A Family Crisis Intervention Approach to Diversion From the Juvenile Justice System." *Juvenile Justice Journal* 28:43–51.

Wexler, Harry K., Gregory P. Flaken, and Douglas S. Lipton. 1990. "Outcome Evaluation of a Prison Therapeutic Community for Substance Abuse Treatment." *Criminal Justice and Behavior* 17:71–92.

Young, Mark C., John Gartner, Thomas O'Connor, David Larson, and Kevin Wright. 1995. "Long-Term Recidivism Among Federal Inmates Trained as Volunteer Prison Ministers." *Journal of Offender Rehabilitation* 22:97–118.

Zeisel, Hans. 1982. "Disagreement Over the Evaluation of a Controlled Experiment." *American Journal of Sociology* 88:378–89.

References

Andrews, D. A. 1996. "Behavioral, Cognitive Behavioral and Social Learning Contributions to Criminological Theory." Presented at the American Society of Criminology annual meeting, November 20, Chicago, IL.

Andrews, D. A. and James Bonta. 1998. *The Psychology of Criminal Conduct.* 2d ed. Cincinnati, OH: Anderson.

Andrews, D. A., James Bonta, and Robert D. Hoge. 1990. "Classification for Effective Rehabilitation: Rediscovering Psychology." *Criminal Justice and Behavior* 17:19–52.

Andrews, D. A., Craig Dowden, and Paul Gendreau. Forthcoming. "Clinically Relevant and Psychologically Informed Approaches to Reducing Criminal Recidivism: A Meta-Analytic Study of Human Service, Risk, Need, Responsivity and Other Concerns in Justice Contexts." Manuscript submitted for publication.

Andrews, D. A., Ivan Zinger, Robert D. Hoge, James Bonta, Paul Gendreau, and Francis T. Cullen. 1990. "Does Correctional Treatment Work? A Clinically Relevant and Psychologically Informed Meta-Analysis." *Criminology* 28:369–404.

Cleland, Charles M., Frank Pearson, and Douglas S. Lipton. 1996. "A Meta-Analytic Approach to the Link Between Needs-Targeted Treatment and Reductions in Criminal Offending." Presented at the American Society of Criminology annual meeting, November 20, Chicago, IL.

Dowden, Craig. 1998. "A Meta-Analytic Examination of the Risk, Need and Responsivity Principles and Their Importance Within the Rehabilitation Debate." Masters thesis, Department of

Psychology, Carleton University, Ottawa, Ontario, Canada.

Gibbons, Don C. 1999. "Review Essay: Changing Lawbreakers—What Have We Learned Since the 1950's?" *Crime & Delinquency* 45:272–93.

Hill, James K., D. A. Andrews, and Robert D. Hoge. 1991. "Meta-Analysis of Treatment Programs for Young Offenders: The Effect of Clinically Relevant Treatment on Recidivism, With Controls Introduced for Various Methodological Variables." *Canadian Journal of Program Evaluation* 6:97–109.

Izzo, Rhena L. and Robert R. Ross. 1990. "Meta-Analysis of Rehabilitation Programs for Juvenile Delinquents." *Criminal Justice and Behavior* 17:134–42.

Koons, Barbara A., John D. Burrow, Merry Morash, and Tim Bynum 1997. "Expert and Offender Perceptions of Program Elements Linked to Successful Outcomes for Incarcerated Women." *Crime & Delinquency* 43:512–32.

Lipsey, Mark W. 1989. "The Efficacy of Intervention for Juvenile Delinquency: Results from 400 Studies." Presented at the 41st annual meeting of the American Society of Criminology, November, Reno, NV.

——. 1995. "What Do We Learn From 400 Research Studies on the Effectiveness of Treatment with Juvenile Delinquents?" Pp. 63–78 in *What Works: Reducing Reoffending—Guidelines From Research and Practice*, edited by J. McGuire. Winchester, UK: Wiley.

Losel, Friedrich. 1996. "Effective Correctional Programming: What Empirical Research Tells Us and What It Doesn't." *Forum on Corrections Research* 8:33–6.

Martinson, Robert. 1974. "What Works? Questions and Answers About Prison Reform." *The Public Interest* 10:22–54.

McGuire, James, ed. 1995. *What Works: Reducing Reoffending—Guidelines From Research and Practice*. Winchester, UK: Wiley.

Morash, Merry, Tim S. Bynum, and Barbara A. Koons. 1995. *Findings From the National Study of Innovative and Promising Programs for Women Offenders*. East Lansing: Michigan State University, School of Criminal Justice.

Rosenthal, Robert. 1991. *Meta-Analytic Procedures for Social Research*. Rev. ed. Newbury Park, CA: Sage. ✦

27
Identifying and Treating the Mentally Disordered Prison Inmate

Eliot S. Hartstone

Henry J. Steadman

Pamela Clark Robbins

John Monahan

During the 1950s, mental hospitals housed hundreds of thousands of mentally ill Americans. Today, those hospitals have given way to penal institutions. The exact number of mentally ill prisoners is unknown; however, there is little question that the mentally ill pose a significant problem for the correctional system. Providing safe and secure facilities, meeting the needs of special populations, and operating within a budget, are all challenges that must be met. Eliot S. Hartstone and his associates offer a glimpse into the scope of mental health problems in prisons. By examining procedures in five states, they provide an overview of how mentally ill prisoners are handled in the United States.

Excerpts from "Identifying and Treating the Mentally Disordered Prison Inmate" by Eliot S. Hartstone, Henry J. Steadman, Pamela Clark Robbins, and John Monahan, in Linda A. Teplin (eds.) *Mental Health and Criminal Justice* pp. 279–296. Copyright © 1999 by Sage Publications, Inc. Reprinted by permission.

M entally disordered offenders" can be considered as an umbrella term embracing four distinct legal categories: defendants who are incompetent to stand trial or not guilty by reason of insanity, persons adjudicated as "mentally disordered sex offenders," and convicted prisoners who are transferred to mental hospitals (Steadman et al., 1982; Monahan and Steadman, 1983a, 1983b). Public attention has focused on the first three of these categories, perhaps because of a belief that they constitute a form of "beating the system." That is, the offenders in these cases committed what would popularly be considered a crime, yet have escaped criminal conviction. Notorious cases that have raised these issues (although not always successfully), such as John Hinckley, Patricia Hearst, David Berkowitz, and Mark Chapman, no doubt contribute to this public attention.

The media, the public, and legislators, however, have yet to show comparable interest in the fourth category of mentally disordered offenders—persons first convicted of a crime, incarcerated, and later found to be in need of transfer to a mental health facility. It is likely that this lack of interest in mentally disordered inmates reflects the fact that these individuals did not "get away" with their crimes since they have already been convicted and sentenced to prison. Social scientists have also, for the most part, limited their research efforts to "incompetency" (Roesch and Golding, 1980; Mowbrey, 1979; Steadman, 1979) or "insanity" (Rogers and Bloom, 1982; Petrila, 1982; Pasewark et al., 1979; Pasewark and Lanthorn, 1977; Steadman, 1980; Cook and Sigorski, 1974; Morrow and Peterson, 1966) and "mentally disordered sex offender" status (Konecni et al., 1980; Sturgeon and Taylor, 1980). Researchers rarely study the less publicized situation where the prisoner's mental health problems were not manifest, or at least not identified, until after placement in prison (Gearing et al., 1990; Halleck, 1961).

Despite the meager public and research attention garnered by mentally disordered inmates, they constitute the largest category of mentally disordered offenders in the U.S.—54% of all mentally disordered offenders, and 68% of all *male* mentally disordered offenders admitted to mental health facilities in the United States in 1978 (Steadman et al., 1982). In fact, 10,831 inmates were transferred from state prisons into separate mental health units or facilities in 1978 (Steadman et al., 1982). This number does not include those inmates who were experiencing mental health problems but received care (or at least remained) in the general prison population.

It also appears that for at least two reasons, the number of mentally disordered inmates may increase in coming years. First, there is a movement in a number of states to do away with the insanity defense in favor of a "guilty but insane" verdict, which may have the effect of mandating mental health services for specified inmates who previously would have been acquitted by reason of insanity. Second, current trends in criminal sentencing seem likely to result in placing more offenders into state prisons for longer periods. In 1981, the largest annual increase in U.S. history in the number of prison inmates (41,292) was recorded (Gardner, 1982). Thus, even if the proportion of inmates who were mentally disordered remained constant, the absolute number of inmates requiring care would have skyrocketed. Using a low estimate of the proportion (15%) of inmates who are mentally disordered there would have been nearly 6200 more inmates needing mental health services in U.S. prisons in 1982 than in 1981.

The level of management problems that these mentally disordered inmates pose has been demonstrated by Uhlig (1976). Examining a group of 356 offenders throughout New England prisons who had been identified as special management problems, he found that 195 (53%) were diagnosed as having current psychiatric disturbances. Clearly, a major source of conflict in volatile prison settings are mentally disordered inmates. These inmates present problems with which prison officials usually are not prepared or trained to cope. Further, these inmates would appear to create additional management problems for prison officials by generating disruptive behavior among inmates who do not know how to respond to the unusual and inappropriate behavior displayed by the mentally disordered, and who tend to victimize these more vulnerable inmates. It is also important to note that an additional series of problems results from those inmates who are withdrawn or excessively depressed but who may not be disruptive or create management problems (Hartstone et al., 1982).

Programmatic responses to mentally disordered inmates in the United States have been cyclical: (1) responsibility for mentally disordered prison inmates repeatedly has shifted back and forth from corrections to mental health departments; and (2) the appropriateness of mixing convicted mentally disordered persons in civil mental hospitals has been viewed very differently from one era to another (Steadman and Cocozza, 1974). The experiences in New York illustrate these long-standing issues.

The first move in New York to separate civil mental patients from mentally disordered persons charged with or convicted of crimes occurred in 1782. An "Act Respecting Lunatics" was passed that prevented the overseers of the poor, who were responsible for the mentally disordered, from housing the mentally disordered in jails or "in the same room with any person charged or convicted of an offense" (N.Y. Laws 1827, Ch. 294, Sec. 2). They could be kept only in poorhouses. When the state's first asylum for the mentally disordered was opened in 1842 in Utica, however, the legislative provisions allowed for the mixing of mentally disordered convicts, those confined under indictments or criminal charge, those acquitted by reason of insanity, and patients committed under any civil process. Thus, the mental health system, rather than the more general social welfare system or corrections, came to care for mentally disordered inmates.

By 1855, there was movement again toward separating patients who were convicted or alleged criminals from civil patients. This movement culminated with the 1859 opening of an Asylum for Insane Convicts at Auburn Penitentiary, the first institution of its kind in the United States. In 1861 the state legislature directed that all mentally disordered male prisoners be transferred from Utica to Auburn. In 1869, Auburn was directed to house those persons acquitted because of insanity as well as defendants charged with murder, attempted murder, or arson who became mentally disordered prior to trial or sentencing. Thus, convicted and unconvicted patients were again confined in the same facility, separate from civil patients, as they had been before Auburn Asylum opened.

A legislative commission established in 1886 located a site in Matteawan to replace the Auburn Asylum, which would be large enough to allow for the separation, within a single facility, of unconvicted patients awaiting trial from mentally disordered convicts. As a *New York Times* article reporting the opening noted, "The two classes of patients differ widely, the criminals giving the officials much anxiety at times. They are frequently dangerous and destructive." As had happened with Auburn soon after its opening, the number of patients at Matteawan quickly increased. While the patient population continued to burgeon at Matteawan, pressure also built for the separation of the "convict insane" from the other criminally insane patients, such as insanity cases. In 1894, the State Lunacy Commission noted that separate institutions were beneficial because the presence of insane convicts "was very objectionable to the ordinary inmates" of state hospitals.

A new facility, Dannemora State Hospital, opened in northern New York in January, 1900, under the auspices of the Department of Corrections. By this time, Matteawan was overcrowded with 719 patients in a building whose capacity was 500. All inmates in the state who were determined to be mentally disordered after a felony conviction would be housed in Dannemora. All other convicted patients and pretrial cases would go to Matteawan. Between 1900 and 1966, the patient population at Matteawan and Dannemora climbed steadily, with Matteawan reaching a patient census of over 2000 in the early 1960s. At the same time, Dannemora reached a peak of about 1400 patients. However, in these 66 years little changed in either the statutes or the two facilities.

Throughout the late 1960s and early 1970s, there was a dramatic decrease in the patient census at Matteawan and Dannemora, and a gradual shift for all mental health treatment for all classes of mentally disordered offenders to the Office of Mental Health (OMH). Dannemora was closed in 1972 and Matteawan in 1977, removing the Department of Corrections (DOC) from any direct mental health care responsibilities. Instead, the OMH opened a maximum-security hospital for incompetent defendants and defendants not guilty by reason of insanity in 1972 and one for mentally disordered inmates in 1977. Thus, over this 150-year period, care of mentally disordered inmates in New York shifted from welfare, to mental health, to corrections, and back to mental health.

History appears to be again repeating itself as states continually tinker with their treatment arrangements for mentally disordered inmates, sometimes charging departments of mental health with the responsibility, either by themselves or in concert with departments of corrections, and sometimes mandating treatment by the departments of corrections themselves. Based on our 1978 national survey (Steadman et al., 1982), there appears to be little consensus on the most appropriate arrangements for mentally disordered inmates. This survey revealed that 16 states transferred most (at least 75%) of their mentally disordered inmates into mental health facilities or units administered by the DOC;[1] 28 states transferred the majority into hospitals or units run by the DMH; and six states utilized a combination of DOC and DMH units.

It may be that the lack of consensus across states on how to handle mentally disordered inmates reflects in part a lack of empirical data. There are no data on whether there is a type of arrangement that is optimal for both inmates and facilities, what such an arrangement might look like, and under what circumstances one arrangement is to be preferred over others. As prison populations climb, as the number of beds in state mental hospitals continues to be limited, and as legal rights to minimum health and mental health treatment are confirmed by the courts, more information is needed to facilitate the development of appropriate programs for mentally disordered inmates.

In an effort to provide some empirical data on the needs of these inmates and how the correctional and mental health systems respond to them, this chapter utilizes data from 67 interviews with a wide range of correctional staff in five states. Specifically, these data focus on the placement options available for mentally disordered inmates, the adequacy of procedures used to identify the inmates and transfer them to mental health facilities, and the extent to which the procedures used meet the needs of these inmates.

Methods

Our data are drawn from a national study of the movement of offenders between prisons and mental hospitals funded by the National Institute of Justice. As part of this effort, six states—Arizona, California, Iowa, Massachusetts, New York, and Texas—were identified for an intensive examination of the confinement and criminal careers of inmates and mental patients, and of the practices and processes of transferring prison inmates to mental health facilities. Five of these six states (New York excluded) were found to use Department of Corrections

(DOC) mental health settings as the main placement for mentally disordered inmates. It is these five states with their use of *intra*-agency transfers for mentally disordered inmates that are the focus of this chapter.

While approximately two-thirds of the states in the United States transfer most of their mentally disordered inmates to state departments of mental health (DMH), since the larger states tend to use DOC options, 71% of all prison inmates transferred for mental health services in 1978 were placed in DOC-operated mental health facilities. Any effort to generalize from the data reported here should be limited to those states that transfer the majority of their inmates to DOC mental health settings. The issues discussed here focus only on procedures for dealing with male inmates, since 95.8% of all inmates transferred in our 1978 study were males. Women's programs require specialized study for what are often more haphazard, less formal service arrangements.

Structured interviews were conducted with a wide range of DOC personnel in the five target states between October 1, 1980, and January 31, 1981. The interviews were primarily open-ended, with some Likert-type items, and averaged 90 minutes. A two-person interview team completed interviews with 67 persons employed by the DOC. Interviews were conducted at the DOC central office, the state prison transferring the most inmates, and the mental health setting receiving the most inmate transfers. At the DOC central office, the DOC Commissioner (or Deputy Commissioner) and the mental health treatment director were interviewed. At the prison transferring the most inmates in each state, we interviewed the warden, the treatment director, two direct clinical service providers, and a correctional officer. Hospital or Treatment Center interviews consisted of the facility or unit director, the chief of security, two clinical staff members, and a line staff representative. In instances where there were a number of people in a particular position, we interviewed the person nominated by the facility director. Thus, the information obtained from the interviews reflects a wide range of staff locations and job responsibilities.

Scope of Mental Health Problems in Prisons

The first issue of interest was the perception of the various DOC staff of the scope of the problem and how their estimates compared with prior research. All respondents were asked what percentage of the DOC inmates they believed to be either seriously mentally disordered (that is, psychotic) or suffering from a psychological problem that warranted mental health treatment. The mean responses, separated by staff location, are presented in Table 27.1. It is clear that a sizeable number of state prisoners were suffering from serious mental health problems. As seen in Table 27.1, the respondents in our five target states estimated on average that 5.8% of state DOC inmates were "seriously mentally ill," and that an additional 37.7%, while not psychotic, were suffering from a psychological problem that would significantly benefit from mental health treatment. This table also shows that, when compared to central office administrators, the people actually working in the institutions (that is, prisons and DOC mental hospitals) thought considerably more DOC inmates were psychotic (6.1% versus 4.3%) or experiencing other psychological problems (38.7% versus 30.6%). While the differences may appear at first glance to be small, one must consider that given the size of the total prison populations in these five states, this translates into a difference of 6389 inmates defined as in need of mental health services.[2]

In general, the overall estimates of the respondents are similar to the best estimates of true prevalence of mental disorder that Monahan and Steadman's (1983a) literature review found:

> One is left from these studies with true prevalence rates for serious mental illness (i.e., psychoses) among offenders incarcerated

in prison or jails varying from 1 percent (Guze, 1976) to 7 percent (Bolton, 1976). True prevalence rates for less severe forms of mental illness (nonpsychotic mental disorders and personality disorders) vary greatly, ranging up to 15–20 percent (Roth, 1980).

When staff were asked whether they believed there had been any change over the past ten years in the percentage of inmates suffering from a "serious mental illness," 43% of the staff said they believed the percentage of disordered inmates had gone up. In contrast, only 7% of those responding said the number had gone down. Those prison and correctional mental health facility staff persons who felt this problem was becoming increasingly severe offered a variety of explanations. Most respondents cited one of three factors: conditions in the prison, the deinstitutionalization movement in state mental hospitals, and general societal conditions. A prison guard concerned that the prisons themselves were generating the problem stated:

> The environment here in prison is changing for the worse. It is becoming more and more crowded, causing a lot of problems. There are now three to four inmates in one cell; they are in the cell for 12–14 hours at a stretch.

A clinician at a DOC-operated mental hospital blamed the problem there on DMH deinstitutionalization of mental hospitals:

> The main cause of deinstitutionalization by (DMH). A lot of these persons are getting criminalized. It is easier for a cop to take John Doe to a lock-up—end up here—than to send him to a state hospital.

A social worker in a state prison stated that she felt there were mental health problems in prison because of general societal conditions:

> There has been an increase in societal population, a breakdown of the families, a pressure packed society. It is a societal problem.

Table 27.1

Percentage of Inmates in State Prisons Perceived as Having Mental Health Problems (by staff location)

	Mental Health Need			
	Seriously Mentally Ill		Psychological Problem Warranting Treatment	
Staff Location	Mean %	(N)	Mean %	(N)
DOC central office	4.3	(9)	30.6	(8)
Mental health facility to which inmates were transferred	6.2	(25)	42.3	(29)
Prison from which inmates were transferred	5.9	(23)	34.4	(24)
Total	5.8	(57)[a]	37.7	(61)[b]

[a] Missing data for 10 cases.
[b] Missing data for 6 cases.

Due to these perceived problems, DOC staff expressed concern that there are sizeable numbers of inmates in the DOC who are experiencing serious psychiatric or psychological problems warranting some form of clinical intervention. The remainder of this chapter examines what is happening to those prison inmates who are mentally disordered—where can they receive treatment, and are they identified and placed in the designated mental health settings?

Placement Options and Procedures

While all five state DOCs treated mentally disordered inmates within the agency, these agencies did not all have the same philosophy regarding mental disorder, nor did they establish the same placement options. California had substantially more beds available and transferred more inmates than any of the other states. Within the California Department of Corrections, two major placement options were used for inmates suffering mental health problems. The California Medical Facility at Vacaville (CMF) received those inmates who were most disordered

and dangerous, and the California Men's Colony (CMC) utilized one of their prison quadrants usually for less disordered and less violent mentally disordered inmates. Over 3000 inmates are transferred into either the CMF or CMC annually. Prior to 1980, some inmates were transferred to DMH's Atascadero State Hospital, but DOC staff said that since January 1980 it was practically impossible to get an inmate into Atascadero. As indicated by the number of DOC beds that were available for mental health care, the California DOC approach clearly reflects a philosophy that stresses the importance of recognizing the mentally disordered offender and placing such inmates in a separate facility or unit for treatment.

In three states (Arizona, Iowa, and Massachusetts) there was a single DOC-operated mental hospital. In these three states, the hospitals admitted all categories of "mentally disordered offenders" (transfers, insanity acquittals, and incompetency cases). The hospitals varied considerably in size and transfer admissions. There were 442 beds at Bridgewater State Hospital (Massachusetts), 80 beds at the Iowa Medical Facility, and 40 beds at Alhambra (Arizona). The Massachusetts and Iowa hospitals both admitted approximately 225–275 transfers annually, while the Arizona facility admitted fewer than 15.

The Texas Department of Corrections (TDC) operated with the philosophy that all TDC inmates are TDC's responsibility and should, whenever possible, be maintained in the general population. While a maximum security unit at Rusk State Hospital (operated by DMH) was a potential placement option, the use of this unit decreased from 65 inmates in 1978, to 37 in 1979, to 9 in 1980. Typically, when an inmate's condition caused the TDC to move an inmate out of the general population, the inmate was transferred to the Huntsville Treatment Center (HTC), located within the Huntsville prison. This unit contained 90 beds, an average census of 67, and admitted 20–25 inmates each month. The HTC was used primarily for short-term stabilization and medication, followed by the inmate's immediate transfer back to the general population. On rare and extreme occasions, inmates have been transferred from the HTC to Rusk State Hospital. The number of inmates placed in neither the HTC or Rusk State Hospital seems particularly low given the large number of inmates (approximately 30,000) residing with the Texas Department of Corrections.

In all five study states, the initial identification of the mentally disordered inmate usually resulted from observations made by a correctional officer and a referral to a prison psychologist or psychiatrist. At that point, however, considerable procedural variations occurred in the role of the prison, the mental hospital, the DOC central office, and the courts in determining which inmates were transferred. In only one state (Massachusetts) was judicial approval required. In two states (Arizona, California), transfer decisions were routinely made or approved by representatives of the DOC central office. The mental health receiving facility had an active role in the transfer decisions in two states (Iowa and Arizona), while in Texas the prison psychologist's recom-

mendations were followed without any review. Whatever the means used to review recommendations made by the prison clinician (such as the court or DOC central office), the review appeared to be perfunctory and virtually all inmates recommended for transfer were, in fact, transferred.

An examination of available placement options and transfer procedures implemented in our five study states reveals that, although each of these states transferred most of their inmates into facilities operated within the DOC, variation occurred in the type of placements available, the extent to which they were used, and the procedures implemented for transferring an inmate to one of these facilities.

Adequacy of Identification and Transfer Procedures

Identification

In order to ascertain which inmates were selected for transfer to mental health facilities, we asked all respondents whether transfers occurred primarily for clinical reasons (that is, mental health difficulties) or behavioral reasons (management problems), and what types of inmates were identified for referral to mental hospitals. The majority of our respondents (52.6%) reported that persons were identified for behavioral reasons, 33.3% felt that identification was usually brought about due to clinical reasons, and 14% stated that identification could occur for either reason. In only one state (California) did more respondents attribute identification to clinical reasons (52.6%) more often than to behavioral reasons (36.8%). In each of the other four states, 50% or more of the respondents said inmates were primarily identified for behavioral reasons.

When asked for specific reasons why inmates were identified for referral to mental health facilities, the respondents focused primarily on mental health problems. As presented in Table 27.2, our 67 respondents

Table 27.2

Reasons Why Inmates Are Transferred to Mental Health Facility

	Staff Work Location							
	Central Office		**Mental Health Facility**		**Prison**		**Total**	
Reason for Transfer	**%**	**(N)**	**%**	**(N)**	**%**	**(N)**	**%**	**(N)**
Psychotic	25.0	(6)	15.4	(10)	14.0	(8)	16.4	(24)
Other mental illness[a]	45.8	(11)	66.2	(43)	72.0	(41)	65.1	(95)
Management problem/violent	25.0	(6)	15.4	(10)	10.5	(6)	15.1	(22)
Other	4.2	(1)	3.0	(2)	3.5	(2)	3.4	(5)
Total							100.0	(146)

[a] Other mental illness includes (1) DSM 11 diagnostic classification that do not fall under the heading of psychotic; (2) more general references to mental illness (for example, crazy, flaky, bizarre, mentally ill, unstable); and (3) mentally ill and dangerous.

produced 146 responses: 16.4% of the responses referred to psychosis, 65.1% referred to other mental health reasons, and 15.1% focused solely on violence or management problems. The fact that behavior was felt to be a more important determinant than clinical factors in deciding whether an inmate was identified for transfer would seem to indicate that some inmates who were mentally disordered were not identified because their behavior was not particularly visible or disruptive, and that other inmates may have been identified for transfer due to behaviors which were unacceptable, but not necessarily indicators of real clinical symptomatology. However, given the high percentage of responses citing mental health problems as a reason for transfer, it appears that, while the initial identification may have been precipitated by behavior, the transfer decision typically was based on mental health problems. Thus, while it would seem that there may be some inmates transferred who are only behavior problems (not mentally disordered), the potentially more important problem is the lack of early identification of those mentally disordered inmates whose behavior does not either annoy the

DOC staff or disrupt prison operations. It seems likely that there are a number of disordered inmates who go unnoticed and, therefore, untreated.

This interpretation is supported by responses to questions about the appropriateness of the number of inmates transferred and the major weaknesses in the identification of inmates for transfer. Staff were asked how they felt about the number of inmates transferred to a mental health facility or unit. Table 27.3 shows the staff responses by staff location and state. As seen in the table, almost half of the staff members responding felt that "too few" inmates were transferred (47.6%). This compares to the small number of staff (7.9%) who felt that "too many" were transferred. Staff in three states[3] clearly were quite concerned that too few mentally disordered inmates were placed in mental health settings. When examining responses by work location of staff responding, it is interesting to note that while concern over underidentification occurred in all three locations (prisons, 62.5%; mental hospitals, 41.4%; and central office, 30.0%), the percentage of prison staff who felt that not enough inmates were transferred more than

Table 27.3

**Staff Perception of the Appropriateness of the Number
of Inmates Transferred (by staff location and state)**

| | Number of Inmates Transferred | | | | | |
| | Too Few | | Just Right | | Too Many | |
Staff Location	%	(N)	%	(N)	%	(N)
Central office	30.0	(3)	60.0	(6)	10.0	(1)
Mental hospital	41.1	(12)	48.3	(14)	10.3	(3)
Prison	62.5	(15)	33.3	(8)	4.2	(1)
			State			
A	20.0	(2)	70.0	(7)	10.0	(1)
B	62.5	(5)	25.0	(2)	12.5	(1)
C	70.0	(14)	25.0	(5)	5.0	(1)
D	30.8	(4)	69.2	(9)	0.0	(0)
E	41.7	(5)	41.7	(5)	16.7	(2)
Total	47.6	(30)	44.4	(28)	7.9	(5)

doubled the percentage of central office administrators who had that concern. While it is unclear whether this distinction reflects a lack of first-hand knowledge by the administrative staff or the lack of mental health expertise of the prison staff (or both), it is apparent that the prison staff felt they were handling inmates whom they were incapable of treating in the general prison population.

Respondents also were asked to name what they perceived to be the major strengths and weaknesses in the identification of mentally disordered inmates. While most respondents did find some strengths, frequently the strength cited was merely a reiteration of the fact that the system did exist and did identify and place mentally ill inmates. More meaningful strengths that were cited with some regularity by the corrections staff were the quality of the clinical staff, the ability of staff to work together, and the efforts made by prison guards.

Efforts to specify weaknesses in identification were more informative. As seen in Table 27.4, many of the responses dealt directly with the problem of prisons "under-identifying" mentally disordered inmates (miss some mentally disordered inmates, 30%; insufficient number of clinical staff, 17.8%; lack of mental health assessment, 4.5%). Additional responses (such as the lack of clinical training of prison staff) at least indirectly dealt with the same concern. Some examples of responses noting the "under-identification" of mentally disordered inmates were:

There are not enough professional staff; I fear the quietly crazy are not identified. That is what concerns me [prison psychologist].

Problems of spotting someone who needs to be there. We have only 30–40 correctional officers for 2000 inmates. Not enough of us to keep up on what's going on. Inmates usually have to show exceptional behavior before being identified. They could have problems, and not be identified [prison correctional officer].

Table 27.4
Major Weaknesses in Identifying Inmates for Transfer

Weakness	% of Responses	(N)
Miss some mentally ill inmates	30.0	(27)
Lack of clinical staff in prison	17.8	(16)
Seek to transfer management problems	11.1	(10)
Inadequate training of prison staff	8.9	(8)
Manipulation of staff by inmates	5.6	(5)
Lack of mental health assessment	4.5	(4)
Other	22.1	(20)
Total	100.0	(90)

We primarily have a disturbance identification process rather than a patient need identification [process] [Correctional mental hospital psychiatrist].

Procedures

Once an inmate was identified by the prison staff as being mentally disordered, each state had formal procedures for reviewing the transfer of the inmate to a mental health facility. All respondents were asked how well they thought the procedures were working. Almost 85% of those interviewed said the procedures were working either "very well" or "well," and in only one state was there considerable concern over how these procedures were operating (33% said "poorly" or "very poorly"). However, a significant difference was revealed in how staff at different locations (central office, mental hospital, prison) assessed the effectiveness of these procedures. Only one respondent across the five states working either at the central office or the mental health facility said the procedures were operating "poorly" or "very poorly" (2.6%). On the other hand, 36% of the prison staff interviewed viewed the operation of transfer procedures as so problematic as to define them as operating "poorly" or "very poorly." This view was found to be limited to two states. Some of the specific criticisms made by prison staff in these two states were:

> No one's going anywhere. There are a lot of mentally ill people here, but they are not housed as if they're mentally ill. Not treated any differently than other inmates [prison psychologist].

> Bed space problems at (the CMH) and their unwillingness to take our inmates. If they are both psychotic and management problems, they [CMH] keep them only a short period of time and say the inmate is only a management problem and send them back [prison administrator].

> Takes too much time! Courts' fault, always getting involved when they know nothing about it. Afraid we will put people there (the CMH) for punishment. Delay in getting hold of "shrink" and taking care of paper work. Delay is at central office . . .[the mental health facility] sends them back too soon, when they shouldn't be housed here at all. The inmates go back and forth [correctional officer].

While DOC staff from the other three states typically stated that procedures were operating well overall, staff in these states frequently said there were still some major weaknesses in the procedures. In one state the concerns frequently focused around the extent to which the procedures protected inmates from being transferred inappropriately:

Procedures are not terribly tight, staff could conspire to place a person who is not mentally ill into a mental hospital. Lack of legal safeguards. Not forced to confront the man and say he is crazy [corrections administrator].

[The Supreme Court] requires there should be an independent review of hospitalization. We don't have this. A good law requires judicial commitment. We don't have this [corrections administrator].

In another state, the issue involved the decision-making process. As seen below, some DOC staff (usually prison staff) felt too much decision-making control was left in the hands of hospital staff. Others (typically hospital staff) felt that too much control was given to the prison and DOC central office.

If _____ [the CMH director] doesn't want someone he doesn't have to take him. He is scared and doesn't want to be bothered by this type of person. He fears they will be disruptive to their program. His power to make this decision is the major weakness in the procedures [correctional officer].

Formal decision is left in the hands of a lay person [central office]. This is a medical facility and he [DOC director] has the ultimate authority. . . . Not a real problem, as long as mental hospital director has right to discharge.

Despite the specific concerns noted above, the respondents were, in general, satisfied with the transfer procedures. The respondents also expressed satisfaction with the receptivity displayed by the DOC mental health facilities to mentally disordered inmates referred by the prison. Almost 90% of the staff interviewed defined the state correctional mental health facility or facilities as either "very" or "somewhat" receptive. The prison staff were considerably more likely to define the mental health facilities as "somewhat" or "very" nonreceptive (22.7%) than the staff at the mental health facilities (3.3%). Almost 75% of the staff responding in each of the five states defined the correctional mental health facility as receptive.

Thus, in general, DOC staff appear to be satisfied with the procedures for inmate transfers from the general prison population into mental health facilities and the receptivity of these facilities to mentally disordered inmates.

One area that generated little concern by the prison staff, DOC central office staff, or mental health staff was the inmate's ability to prevent transfer through procedural safeguards. When asked whether inmates prevented transfer too frequently, as often as they should, or not often enough, 92% of the DOC staff responding said "as often as should be the case." In no state did a sizable percentage of staff express concern that inmates either prevented too many transfers or were unable to prevent transfers often enough. It is not clear whether these responses reflect procedures that gave inmates an optimal amount of input into this decision or whether it more accurately reflects the frequently stated belief of DOC staff that "inmates have no control over these decisions and they shouldn't."

Conclusion

This chapter has used 67 interviews conducted with DOC staff in five states to describe the process of identifying state prisoners suffering from mental disorders and the transferring of these inmates into designated DOC mental health facilities. The major conclusions drawn from these interviews are:

- DOC staff perceive a sizable number of state prisoners to be suffering from a serious psychotic mental disorder (5.8% of all inmates) or psychological problems warranting treatment (37.7%).

- Different states operate with different philosophies on how to handle mentally disordered inmates and therefore identify widely divergent percentages of their inmates as warranting placement in a mental health facility.

- Once the prison psychiatrist or psychologist recommends that an inmate be transferred, it is the rare exception when a review system (prison, DOC, court) reverses that decision.

- Inmates are typically identified in the prison for behavioral management reasons, thereby making it likely that a sizable number of mentally disordered inmates remain in the general population because their behavior is insufficiently visible, annoying, or disruptive.

- A sizable percentage of staff (47.6%) stated they felt "too few" inmates were transferred to mental health settings.

- Staff typically felt that the procedures used to transfer those inmates identified as mentally disordered were working well (84.4%) and that the DOC mental health facilities were receptive to these inmates (85.5%). However, staff working at the prisons were considerably less satisfied with both the procedures and the receptivity of the mental health facilities than were the staff at either the DOC central office or the DOC mental hospitals and treatment centers.

As prison populations continue to burgeon, the problem of mentally disordered inmates will only be exacerbated. Even if the proportion of the inmate population with mental disorders remains constant, the scope of the problem within any given growing prison system will become more acute in terms of absolute human service needs (see Monahan and Steadman, 1983a). While the descriptive work discussed in this chapter is a major first step toward building knowledge in this area, it is essential that more research be devoted to studying mentally disordered inmates. Further research is needed both on inmates themselves and on the system and agencies responsible for their care and treatment.

More information is needed on the prevalence, causes, and correlates of mental disorders within the state prison inmate popula-

tion. A systematic, multistate study is needed that utilizes an objective instrument across states to assess the extent to which prison inmates suffer from mental disorders. Inmates identified as mentally disordered should be studied for purposes of examining causes and correlates of both the criminal behavior and mental disturbance. Included in this assessment should be an examination of how incarceration and prison conditions contribute to inmate mental health problems and in what ways the prison experience may combine with preprison factors to generate serious inmate symptomatology.

Study Questions

1. What are the two reasons the authors give for the likelihood that the number of mentally ill offenders will increase in coming years?

2. Describe the research design, data collection methods, sample, and measures used by the authors in conducting this study.

3. What is the scope of mental health problems in prisons that the authors describe?

4. What are the conclusions reached by the authors of this study? Why do you think they are important for correctional officials?

Notes

1. According to 1978 admission data, there were 16 states in the country which transferred most (at least 75%) of their mentally disordered inmates to mental health settings within the DOC. They are California, Idaho, Illinois, Iowa, Massachusetts, Michigan, Missouri, Nevada, North Carolina, Oregon, South Carolina, Tennessee, Texas, Utah, and West Virginia. In addition, Arizona changed the agency responsible for the mental hospital treating mentally ill inmates from DMH to DOC at the end of 1978.

2. Information contained in the Bureau of Justice Statistics Bulletin (Department of Jus-

tice, 1982) showed that at the end of 1980 the state prison censuses in the five states discussed in this chapter were as follows: Arizona, 4,372; California, 24,569; Iowa, 2,513; Massachusetts, 3,191; Texas, 29,892; total: 64,537.

3. Throughout the remainder of this chapter, we do not identify any of the states by name. We felt that to do so would betray both the confidence and trust the states had in us and risk the anonymity we promised to individual respondents.

References

Cook, G. and C. Sigorski (1974) "Factors affecting length of hospitalization in prisoners adjudicated not guilty by reason of insanity." Bulletin of the American Academy of Psychiatry and Law 2: 251–261.

Department of Justice (1982) Bureau of Justice Statistics Bulletin (NCJ 82262). Washington, DC: Author.

Gardner, R. (1982) "Prison population jumps to 369,725." *Corrections Magazine*, 8(4):6–11, 14, 46.

Gearing, M., R. Hecker, and W. Matthey (1990) "The screening and referral of mentally disordered inmates in a state correctional system." Professional Psychology 11: 849.

Halleck, S. (1961) "A critique of current psychiatric roles in the legal process." Wisconsin Law Review 00: 379–401.

Hartstone, E., H.J. Steadman, and J. Monahan (1982) "*Vitek* and beyond: The empirical context of prison to hospital transfers." Law and Contemporary Problems 45, 3.

Konecni.V., E. Mulcahy, and E. Ebbesen (1980) "Prison or mental hospital: Factors affecting the processing of persons suspected of being mentally disordered sex offenders," in P. Lipsitt and B. Sales (eds.) New Directions in Psychological Research. New York: Van Nostrand Reinhold.

Monahan, J. and H.J. Steadman (1983a) "Crime and mental disorder: An epidemiological analysis," in N. Morris and M. Tonrey (eds.) Annual Review of Criminal Justice. Chicago: University of Chicago Press.

——. [eds.] (1983b) Mentally Disordered Offenders: Perspectives from Law and Social Science. New York: Plenum.

Morrow, W.R. and D.B. Peterson (1966) "Follow-up on discharged offenders—'not guilty by reason of insanity' and 'criminal sexual psychopaths.'" Journal of Criminal Law, Criminology and Police Science 57: 31–34.

Mowbrey, C.T. (1979) "A study of patients treated as incompetent to stand trial." Social Psychiatry 14:31–39.

New York Laws (1827) Chapter 294, Section 2.

New York Times (1892) November 3, p. 9 col. 4.

Pasewark, R.A. and B.W. Lanthorn (1977) "Dispositions of persons utilizing the insanity defense." Journal of Humanistics 5:87–98.

——. M.L. Pantle, and H.J. Steadman (1982) "Detention and rearrest rates of persons found not guilty by reason of insanity and convicted felons." American Journal of Psychiatry 139, 7: 892–897.

——. (1979) "Characteristics and disposition of persons found not guilty by reason of insanity in New York State, 1971–76." American Journal of Psychiatry 136:655–660.

Petrila, J. (1982) "The insanity defense and other mental health dispositions in Missouri." International Journal of Law and Psychiatry 5, 1: 81–102.

Roesch, R. and S. Golding (1980) Competency to Stand Trial. Champaign: University of Illinois Press.

Rogers, J. and J. Bloom (1982) "Characteristics of persons committed to Oregon's Psychiatric Security Review Board." Bulletin of the American Academy of Psychiatry and the Law 10, 3: 155–164.

Steadman, H.J. (1980) "Insanity acquittals in New York State, 1965–1978." American Journal of Psychiatry 137:321–326.

——. (1979) Beating a Rap: Defendants Found Incompetent to Stand Trial. Chicago: University of Chicago Press.

——. and J.C. Cocozza (1974) Careers of the Criminally Insane. Lexington, MA: D. C. Heath.

Steadman, H.J., J. Monahan. E. Hartstone, S.K. Davis, and P.C. Robbins (1982) "Mentally disordered offenders: A national survey of patients and facilities." Law and Human Behavior 6, 1.

Sturgeon, V. and J. Taylor (1980) "Report of a five-year follow-up of mentally disordered sex offenders released from Atascadero State Hospital in 1973." Criminal Justice Journal of Western State University 4:31–64.

Uhlig, R.H. (1976) "Hospitilization experience of mentally disturbed and disruptive, incarcerated offenders." *Journal of Psychiatry and Law.* 4(1):49–59.

This work was done under partial support from the National institute of Justice (79-NI-AX-0126). The assistance of Sharon Kantorowski Davis in the data collection phase of this project is gratefully acknowledged. ✦

28
Adult Academic and Vocational Correctional Education Programs

A Review of Recent Research

Jurg Gerber

Eric J. Fritsch

Does increasing the educational and vocational levels and skills of inmates help reduce recidivism? Many correctional officials believe so as evidenced by the wide availability of such programs in prisons. Despite the commonly held belief that education is an important ingredient to reducing recidivism, the empirical evidence has been sparse and inconsistent. Jurg Gerber and Eric J. Fritsch review the research on this important subject. Their findings suggest that education and vocational programming leads to fewer disciplinary problems among prisoners and, later, reductions in recidivism and increases in employment opportunities. Furthermore, inmates who participated in these types of programs are more likely to participate in educational opportunities upon release from prison.

Excerpts from "Adult Academic and Vocational Correctional Education Programs: A Review of Recent Research" by Jurg Gerber and Eric J. Fritsch, *Journal of Offender Rehabilitation*, 22(1/2): 119–142. Copyright © 1995 by Hayworth Press. Reprinted by permission.

Correctional education programs have existed since the 1800s, but initially the programs focused on religious instruction. It was believed that rehabilitative efforts could be enhanced if the incarcerated offender sought spiritual enlightenment (Linden & Perry, 1983). Not until the 1930s did educational programs begin to play a primary role in the rehabilitative process and to receive broad acceptance for their potential effect on offenders. These programs focused primarily on academic and vocational education. In the 1960s, postsecondary programs began to be offered in correctional settings (Linden & Perry, 1983). Today correctional education programs are prevalent, but observers have questioned the impact of these programs on inmates, both during incarceration and upon release.

Writing about two decades ago, and after thoroughly reviewing 231 studies of prison programs aimed at rehabilitating inmates, Martinson concluded that

> [w]ith few and isolated exceptions, the rehabilitative efforts that have been reported so far have had no appreciable effect on recidivism (1974 [1976]:25).

This finding, which was picked up by the mass media (e.g., "Big Change in Prisons" 1975), was used by critics of prison programs to argue against rehabilitation as a primary justification for incarceration. Soon, however, Martinson's critics pointed out that he was premature in dismissing all forms of intervention. Although few programs can succeed in rehabilitating all inmates, more moderate successes may be possible:

> Rather than ask, "What works for offenders as a whole?" we must increasingly ask "Which methods work best for which types of offenders, and under what conditions or in what types of setting?" (Palmer, 1976: 150).

Our goal is to identify research that assesses the effects of correctional education on inmates. We focus on the following possible outcomes:

- Do inmates who participate in educational programs while incarcerated have lower recidivism rates than nonparticipants?
- Are participants more likely than nonparticipants to enroll in educational programs upon release from incarceration?
- After release do participants have better employment records than nonparticipants?
- While incarcerated do participants exhibit fewer disciplinary problems than nonparticipants?

Adult education in prison could lead to a reduction in criminal behavior, to postrelease enrollment in education, to better postrelease employment history, and to fewer disciplinary problems in two ways.

First, inmates could become more conscientious as a result of moral development due to exposure to the liberal arts (Gordon & Arbuthnot, 1987). The following claim, for instance, concerns inmates' behavior in prison:

> The prisons will benefit because intellectually challenged minds tend to maintain clean institutional records since the inmate, trained at a higher cognitive level, will acquire the ability to respond to situations intellectually and verbally rather than physically (O'Neil, 1990:29).

Second, and alternatively, inmates may benefit because they have better educational credentials upon release, which lead to more opportunities. Thus they may suffer less strain (Merton, 1938). These possibilities seem plausible, but must be supported by experience and observation. Although education may have positive influences on an inmate upon release, extraneous variables also may affect these outcomes. These variables include various social, psychological, and environmental factors. . . .

Review of Literature

The great variety of programs administered in prisons makes evaluation difficult, but we can distinguish between *academic, vocational,* and *social* education. Furthermore, some studies focus on the outcomes of participation in college education; others examine high school or below-high school education. Some studies analyze the outcomes of educational programs for juveniles; others concentrate on programs for adults. We will discuss separately the literature dealing with each of these programs. Our discussion focuses on academic and vocational education for adults.

For comparison, we also present findings from research on social education programs for adults, but we do not emphasize these findings. Social education programs focus primarily on providing inmates with "coping skills," as distinct from marketable skills or credentials. Also, we do not present research on intervention programs for juveniles because it does not pertain to adult correctional education.

Adult Academic Education

Basic and secondary education. Research findings concerning basic and secondary education are fairly clear. A few researchers found no evidence that adult academic education has any positive effects on recidivism, but the most common finding, shown in Table 28.2, is that inmates exposed to education programs have lower recidivism rates than nonparticipants.

Martinson (1974; also see Lipton, Martinson, & Wilks, 1975) claimed to find no evidence of a relationship between adult academic education and lower recidivism rates. A close reading of Martinson's discussion, however, shows that the studies he cited do not support his conclusions. Martinson claimed that six studies analyzed this relationship and that three showed no correlation. Unfortunately, he failed to identify two of these studies [Note 2]. Of the remaining

Table 28.1
Selection and Evaluation Criteria for Studies Reviewed

Selection

EMPIRICAL DATA. Does the study report empirical data, or is it merely a "thought" piece? Generally, we omitted thought pieces.

Evaluation

CONTROL GROUP. Did the studies include control groups? Some studies reported only on an experimental group, that is, participants in an educational program—without including a comparison group of inmates who did not participate. We included a few such studies in our review because they are cited often in the literature, but generally we excluded them (see Babbie [1992] for a discussion of control groups).

MATCHING vs. RANDOM ASSIGNMENT OF SUBJECTS. If control groups were used, did the researchers assign subjects randomly to control and experimental groups, did they match subjects, or did they simply compare participants in a program with nonparticipants? Statisticians consider random assignment best, matching second best, and simple comparisons of participants with nonparticipants least desirable (Hagan, 1993; Kalton, 1983), but our review of the literature shows that research constraints rarely allow for random assignment.

STATISTICAL CONTROLS. If the researchers did not assign subjects randomly to control and experimental groups, did they control statistically for background differences? As a rule, more faith can be placed in research that controls for some of the generally accepted correlates of successful postrelease adjustment: for example, prior convictions, age at first conviction, or opiate use (Pritchard, 1979).

TESTS OF STATISTICAL SIGNIFICANCE. Are differences between experimental and control groups due to chance or are they statistically significant? Statisticians warn against the use of differences between samples unless it can be shown that they are not due to chance alone (Ott, 1993).

three, he acknowledged that two (Saden, 1962; Schnur, 1948) *did* show a correlation between adult education and a reduction in recidivism; he dismissed the final study, Glaser (1964), as difficult to interpret.

The great majority of studies focusing on adult basic and secondary education show an inverse relationship between participation and recidivism. Anderson, Anderson, and Schumacker (1988:1–2) found in Illinois that "those who completed a GED/High School or higher, upon release, had a higher employment rate, lower unemployment rate, and lower criminal activity rate at twelve months than those releasees who had less than a GED" (also see Schumacker, Anderson, & Anderson, 1990). Similarly, a study in Florida showed that among inmates released between 1986 and 1988, those who completed an academic program while in prison were much less likely to recidivate than members of the general prison population (Correctional Education School Authority, 1990). In earlier studies in Delaware (Zink, 1970) and in Ohio (Cochran, 1965), participants in correctional education programs fared significantly better on release than did nonparticipants. More recently, studies in Alabama (Cogburn, 1988) and in New York (New York State, 1989, 1992) produced similar findings [Note 3].

Along somewhat different lines, Anderson (1981:22) found in Illinois that "parolees who were enrolled in academic course work while at the institution were significantly more likely to take vocational or further academic course work while on parole." Similar findings were discovered in Texas in a prison program titled "Reading to Reduce Recidivism." Nearly 75 percent of the participants in this program continued to participate in the community program after release, as compared with 15 to 20 percent of parolees in other programs. The success of the program was credited to the design of the prison program: it could be followed up easily in the community. With respect to recidivism, preliminary reports suggest that this program *may* be successful (State of Texas, 1992).

Table 28.2
Summary of Findings of Studies That Address Precollege Education

Consequence

Citation	Relationship Found	Methodology Rating
• POSTRELEASE RECIDIVISM		
Anderson 1981	=	3
Anderson, Anderson & Schumacker 1988	+	2
Cochran 1965	+	3
Cogburn 1988	+	1
Correctional Education School Authority 1990	+	2
Johnson et al. 1974	=	3
New York State Department of Correctional Services 1989, 1992	+	3
Saden 1962	+	2
Schnur 1948	+	2
Schumacker, Anderson & Anderson 1990	+	2
Rogers 1980	=	?
Roundtree, Edwards & Dawson 1982	=	3
Zink 1970	+	3
• POSTRELEASE EMPLOYMENT		
Anderson 1981	=	3
Anderson, Anderson & Schumacker 1988	+	2
Correctional Education School Authority 1990	+	2
Schumacker, Anderson & Anderson 1990	+	2
• POSTRELEASE PARTICIPATION IN EDUCATION		
Anderson 1981	+	3
State of Texas 1992	+	2

LEGEND: + Relationship between correctional program and consequence is in the desirable direction.
  – Relationship between correctional program and consequence is in the undesirable direction.
  = No relationship between correctional program and consequence.
  0 Methodologically weakest studies: no control group, statistical controls, or significance tests.
  1 Research includes one of the above.
  2 Research includes two of the above.
  3 Methodologically strongest studies: research included all three of the above.
  ? Adequacy of research methodology cannot be ascertained.

Since Martinson's publication, however, we find few studies that show no correlation between prison education and recidivism. Johnson, Shearon, and Britton (1974), whose study was not included in Martinson's review, discovered that female inmates who earned the GED while in prison were no less likely to recidivate than inmates who did not participate in prison education. In a study conducted in Canada, Rogers (1980) found no differences in recidivism between inmates who participated in prison adult education and those who did not. Roundtree, Edwards, and Dawson (1982) studied the impact of education on male inmates' self-esteem. Although the authors implied that improvement in mathematical skills increased self-esteem, the results were not statistically significant [Note 4].

As Table 28.2 shows, the methodological adequacy of the studies did not systematically influence their outcomes. We reviewed seven recidivism studies that received a 3, our highest rating (the authors received one point each for using a control group, statistical controls, and tests of significance). Three of these studies (Anderson, 1981; Johnson et al., 1974; Roundtree et al., 1982) revealed no correlation between education and recidivism; the remaining four (Cochran, 1965; Cogburn, 1988; New York State, 1989, 1992) showed strong correlations.

Only one of the studies that merited a 3 for methodological rigor (Anderson, 1981) focused on the correlation between precollege academic correctional education and (1) postrelease employment and (2) postrelease participation in education. Participation in correctional education did not increase the probability of success in postrelease employment, but it did lead to greater participation in education after release. Yet the other studies we found that focused on these two relationships generated consistent findings (i.e., inverse correlations between education and recidivism) and were relatively sound methodologically (each received a rating of 2). Therefore, we conclude, most empirical research indicates that precollege education leads to more favorable patterns of employment and postrelease education among participants.

At the same time, however, we found no research that focused on the relationship between precollege education and a reduction in disciplinary problems during incarceration.

College education. Like high school education, participation in college correctional programs is likely to produce benefits for inmates and (by implication) for society. Numerous studies have shown a clear and fairly consistent correlation between collegiate studies and recidivism, and between college and variables measuring personal growth. At the same time, some critics have pointed out methodological weaknesses in the research, and caution against overoptimistic interpretations:

> Studies of the relationship between prison higher education and recidivism give mixed reviews of the impact of prison college programs on recidivism. Some of the studies are flawed by serious methodological problems. Control groups are sometimes not well-matched, sample sizes are often small, and "time at risk" often differs for the subjects in the research. Given a collection of studies of such disparate quality, the question of the efficacy of prison higher education remains (Lockwood, 1991:188).

Most studies report an inverse relationship between college education and recidivism. Reporting on a study of a prison program of the University of Victoria (British Columbia), Duguid (1981; also see Ayers et al., 1980) reported that only 14 percent of the inmates who participated in the program returned to prison within three years; the rate for nonparticipants was 51 percent. Furthermore, the former students "showed impressive sophistication in their thinking on law and politics, criminal behavior, and family relations" (Duguid, 1981:65).

Inmates in Maryland who had earned at least 12 credits in a community college prison program were much less likely than nonstudents to recidivate (Blackburn, 1981). Several studies conducted in New York State generated similar results. For instance, inmates who earned a college degree while incarcerated were less likely to recidivate, but, as the authors point out, their success may have been due only partly to their participation in college. These inmates also may have succeeded because they were "more motivated and/or competent than those who do not complete these programs . . .these same factors are related to their future adjustments on parole" (Thorpe, MacDonald, & Bala, 1994:87). In another statewide study in New York, 26 percent of inmates who earned a college degree in 1986–1987 had been returned to state custody by February 1991; the corresponding figure for nongraduates was 45 percent (New York State, 1991:1) [Note 5].

In addition to these studies, research in Alabama found relative success with respect to recidivism (O'Neil, 1990); studies conducted in Ohio revealed lower recidivism and better employment history upon release (Holloway & Moke, 1986). Again, in Maryland, lower recidivism was the result of participation in a college education program (Hagerstown Junior College, 1982; State of Maryland, 1989). In Oklahoma, lower recidivism rates were observed, but inmates in education programs were not involved in fewer disciplinary actions than nonparticipants during their incarceration (Langenbach et al., 1990). In Wisconsin, college attendees were found generally to adjust better to parole conditions (Knepper, 1990).

A few studies, however, found no support for the hypothesis that college education leads to reduction in recidivism and to other outcomes. In one Canadian study, researchers discovered no difference in recidivism rates between former students and other inmates, but reported, according to prison staff members, that

> [p]rogram inmates had better disciplinary records than they had before starting school. Some administrators felt that the program had a stabilizing effect on the prison because of the commitment which the inmates had to make to their studies (Linden et al., 1984:72).

At the same time, Gendreau and his associates (1985) showed that participation in the University of Victoria program at Matsqui Penitentiary did not lead to improved disciplinary records among inmates. They dismiss this finding by arguing that the rate of misconduct in that particular prison is so low that any reduction cannot be statistically significant, instead, alternative measures of institutional adjustment should be used (e.g., the frequency of inmates' grievances). Similarly, in a study conducted in

New York State, researchers found little support for the theory that college education reduces recidivism, indeed, persons with more than 60 college credits were *more* likely to be reincarcerated than those with fewer than 30 credits (Lockwood, 1991) [Note 6].

As in the case of precollege academic prison education, the methodological rigor of studies does not invariably predict the outcomes of the studies. As shown in Table 28.3, we gave six studies our highest methodology rating; of these six, four (Blackburn, 1981; New York State, 1991, 1992; O'Neil, 1990) showed a strong inverse relationship between college education and recidivism, while two (Knepper, 1990; Linden et al., 1984) showed no relationship. The findings thus are somewhat mixed, but the methodological weaknesses identified by critics cannot explain, in themselves, why some programs succeeded and others did not.

The available studies on the relationship between college education and postrelease employment and education are methodologically weak, but consistently show positive consequences for society. We recommend reserving judgment on these two outcomes until more rigorous studies are conducted.

No definite conclusions can be drawn concerning the relationship between correctional participation in college programs and prerelease disciplinary problems. Of the three studies we found on this subject, two were methodologically sound but generated contradictory findings. Linden et al. (1984) showed the expected inverse correlation; Langenbach et al. (1990) disclosed no correlation between enrollment in prison-based college programs and prisoners' misconduct.

Vocational Education

In his "nothing works" article, Martinson (1974) claimed that vocational education produces no positive consequences. Again, however, his conclusion was based on little evidence. Indeed, in the single study discussed by Martinson that addresses the issue

Table 28.3
Summary of Findings of Studies That Address College Education

Consequence

Citation	Relationship Found	Methodology Rating
• POSTRELEASE RECIDIVISM		
Ayers et al. 1980	+	?
Blackburn 1981	+	3
Duguid 1981	+	?
Hagerstown Junior College 1982	+	1
Holloway & Moke 1986	+	2
Knepper 1990	=	3
Langenbach et al. 1990	+	3
Linden et al. 1984	=	3
Lockwood 1991	=	2
New York State Department of Correctional Services 1991	+	3
New York State Department of Correctional Services 1992	+	3
O'Neil 1990	+	3
Thorpe et al. 1994	+	2
Wolf & Sylves 1981	+	0
• POSTRELEASE EMPLOYMENT		
Duguid 1981	+	?
Holloway & Moke 1986	+	2
Wolf & Sylves 1981	+	0
• DISCIPLINARY PROBLEMS		
Gendreau et al. 1985	=	2
Langenbach et al. 1990	+	3
Linden et al. 1984	+	3
• POSTRELEASE PARTICIPATION IN EDUCATION		
Duguid 1981	+	?
Wolf & Sylves 1981	+	0

LEGEND: + Relationship between correctional program and consequence is in the desirable direction.

– Relationship between correctional program and consequence in the undesirable direction.

= No relationship between correctional program and consequence.

0 Methodologically weakest studies: no control group, statistical controls, or significance tests.

1 Research includes one of the above.

2 Research includes two of the above.

3 Methodologically strongest studies: research included all three of the above.

? Adequacy of research methodology cannot be ascertained.

most directly, Gearhart and his associates (1967) found a correlation between vocational training and lower recidivism but only "when a trainee succeeded in finding a job related to his area of training" (Martinson, 1974:13). Martinson interprets this finding as evidence that "skill development programs fail because what they teach bears so little relationship to an offender's subsequent life outside prison" (1974:13).

Most of the research conducted in recent years shows a correlation between vocational training and a variety of outcomes generally considered positive for either society or correctional institutions: lower recidivism rates, lower parole revocation rates, better postrelease employment patterns, and better institutional disciplinary records. Studying determinants of parole success in a midwestern state, Anderson and his associates (1991) showed that among several other factors, participation in academic and vocational programs was correlated positively with successful parole. These researchers (Schumacker, Anderson, & Anderson, 1990) also found that "completers" of vocational programs had better employment rates and fewer arrests than noncompleters. In an earlier study, Anderson (1981) found that vocational training leads to longer postrelease employment, fewer arrests, and fewer parole revocations.

Alston (1980) studied the impact of vocational programs in Texas, and found evidence for lower recidivism rates among inmates who participated. Participants also broke fewer rules while incarcerated, a finding that Alston explains as the result of "more positive impulse control" (1980:9). Saylor and Gaes (1992) reported very similar findings in research on federal penitentiaries: inmates who received vocational training while in prison showed "better institutional adjustment" (fewer rule violations) than those who did not receive such training, were more likely to complete stays in a halfway house, were less likely to have their paroles revoked, and were more likely to be employed. Three other studies, however, contradict these findings. In a study involving inmates released from correctional facilities in Oklahoma, graduates of vocational programs recidivated sooner than members of the control group, namely inmates who did not participate in any of the programs (Davis & Chown, 1986). Unfortunately, the authors did not report results of tests of statistical significance.

Downes, Monaco, and Schreiber (1989) and Markley, Flynn, and Bercaw-Dooen (1983) conducted similar studies, but they, unlike Davis and Chown, made statistical tests to determine the significance of differences between groups. Further, the study by Markley and his associates is noteworthy because their control and experimental groups were more closely matched than those in many other studies. Their experimental group included inmates who completed at least three-fourths of the skills training program for which they were selected; the control group consisted of inmates who had been selected for training but could not participate because not enough training slots were available.

By using such inmates as the control group, the authors were able to control more precisely for differences in the study participants' backgrounds. In this way they eliminated some of the competing factors that could affect the outcome of the research. They found that vocational-technical training did not increase postrelease employment success, nor did it reduce recidivism rates. Furthermore, they found that only 40 percent of the training participants found work related to their training.

In sum, most of these studies indicate reductions in rates of recidivism, better employment histories, and fewer disciplinary problems among inmates who receive vocational training, but at least two recent and well-designed studies show that training does not produce these results. It is conceivable that in the future, all methodologically rigorous studies will find support for the latter finding. Such an outcome, however, is highly unlikely: We found several recent studies of sound design that revealed strong inverse correlations between participation in vocational education and the various outcomes. Anderson (1981) received our highest rating and showed a decrease in recidivism, as did Cochran (1965) and Anderson, Schumacker, and Anderson (1991; see Table 28.4). Similarly, Saylor and Gaes (1992) found better postrelease employment patterns and fewer prerelease disciplinary problems among vocational trainees.

We found no studies focusing on vocational education and post-release participation in education. Research on this issue is needed.

Social Education

Some educational programs in correctional institutions deal with the acquisition of skills that sometimes are called "life skills" and that fall under the heading of "social education." Although social education is defined in various ways (and many different skills are included under "life skills"), advocates of such programs agree that inmates are deficient in the skills needed for coping with daily stresses:

> Social education as we define it is an organized effort to furnish factual information to the individual in those areas of social and emotional interaction in which his past faulty attitudes have caused him difficulty and to suggest methods by which he can effect a more satisfying and socially acceptable way of living (Baker, 1973:241).

Inmates must be taught these skills in order to adjust to the pressures of life after release; if they do not acquire these skills, recidivism will result (Burchard & Lane, 1982).

A few studies examine the relationship between education in social skills and various outcomes. Marshall, Turner, and Barbaree (1989) show that inmates who received training in problem-solving skills. assertiveness and interpersonal functioning, and practical skills in living developed greater self-esteem, became more assertive, less concerned about being evaluated negatively, and more socially skilled. Furthermore, these researchers reported that the programs made participants more empathetic and reduced psychopathy. No data were available, however, to allow us to determine whether these changes led to lower recidivism rates upon release.

Moral development, say some observers, is related to development of social skills. According to this argument, inmates must be encouraged in moral development in order to reduce recidivism; in this way they learn to make moral rather than hedonistic decisions (Duguid, 1986; Fox, 1989; Michalek, 1988; Tope & Warthan, 1986). Unfortunately, most of the available writing on this topic is based more on reasoning than on research. An argument for this training can be made on logical grounds, but opposing arguments are easily constructed (Minahan, 1990). According to research conducted in Canada, however, inmates who were exposed to the Living Skills program of the Correctional Service of Canada adjust to life after release better than other inmates [Note 7].

Finally, Hamm (1991) reported some encouraging results from a prison intervention program aimed at reducing violence against women. Men who had committed such acts of violence participated in a program whose purpose was to teach that "women must not, under any circumstance, become the victims of violence" (Hamm, 1991:67). Hamm reports that 80 percent of the graduates of this program were not rearrested during the 18-month period following their release; unfortunately, however, his study did not include a control group of abusers who were not exposed to the program.

Discussion

In an overview of the effectiveness of prison education programs, Linden and Perry (1983) pointed out that the 1950s and 1960s were a period of optimism, whereas the 1970s were characterized by Martinson's assessment that nothing works. On the basis of an additional decade of research, they argued that prison education can produce desirable results:

> Most evaluations have shown that inmates make substantial improvements in learning, but this does not necessarily have an impact on rates of post-release employment

Table 28.4
Summary of Findings of Studies That Address Vocational Education

Consequence

Citation	Relationship Found	Methodology Rating
• POSTRELEASE RECIDIVISM		
Alston 1980	+	1
Anderson 1981	+	3
Anderson, Anderson & Schumacker 1988	+	2
Anderson, Schumacker & Anderson 1991	+	3
Cochran 1965	+	3
Cogburn 1988	+	1
Correctional Education School Authority 1990	+	2
Davis & Chown 1986	−	1
Downes et al. 1989	=	3
Gearhart at al. 1967	+	?
Markley et al. 1983	=	3
Saylor & Gaes 1992	+	3
Schumacker, Anderson & Anderson 1990	+	2
• POSTRELEASE EMPLOYMENT		
Anderson 1981	+	3
Anderson, Anderson & Schumacker 1988	+	2
Correctional Education School Authority 1990	+	2
Downes et al. 1989	−	3
Markley et al. 1983	=	3
Saylor & Gaes 1992	+	3
Schumacker, Anderson & Anderson 1990	+	2
• DISCIPLINARY PROBLEMS		
Alston 1981	+	1
Saylor & Gaes 1992	+	3

LEGEND: + Relationship between correctional programs and consequence is in the desirable direction.

− Relationship between correctional program and consequence is in the undesirable direction.

= No relationship between correctional program and consequence.

0 Methodologically weakest studies: No control group, statistical controls, or significance tests.

1 Research includes one of the above.

2 Research includes two of the above.

3 Methodologically strongest studies: research included all three of the above.

? Adequacy of research methodology cannot be ascertained.

and recidivism. The review of the literature suggests that programs will be most likely to succeed if they are intensive, if they can establish an alternative community within the prison, and if they offer post-release services to inmates (Linden & Perry, 1983:43).

Our own assessment, based on yet another decade of research, is quite similar. Numerous studies show a correlation between participation in correctional education and various outcomes. Further, even though the methodologically less rigorous studies (e.g., those without control groups or with inadequate matches between control and experimental subjects) are likely to show a correlation, there also exist enough scientifically sound studies to make us confident that these positive findings are not statistical artifacts.

Drawing from Linden and Perry's (1983) review of the literature, from Rice and his associates' (1980) review of 10 successful correctional vocational programs, and from our own review, we can identify several factors that explain why some programs are more successful than others in achieving their stated goals:

- The more extensive the educational program, the more likely it is to achieve its stated objectives. For instance, research in New York State showed that inmates who earned the GED were less likely to recidivate than those who attended GED classes but did not earn the diploma (New York State, 1989).

- Programs that are separate from the rest of the prison are more likely to succeed. "Successful programs had a designated area for providing vocational education and *only* vocational education" (Rice et al., 1980:12; emphasis in original).

- Programs that provide follow-up after release are more likely to succeed. With respect to vocational education, "successful programs had systematic procedures for providing placement services that emphasized employer contact" (Rice et al., 1980:12).

- Programs that are successful in attracting an appropriate audience are more likely to achieve their intended objectives. For instance, the "Reading to Reduce Recidivism" program in Texas was hampered because it was designed for inmates who would serve short sentences and would be released quickly into the community, whereas the median sentence served by program partic-

ipants was 15 years (State of Texas, 1992).

- With respect to vocational education, programs that provide skills relevant to the contemporary job market are more likely to achieve their stated objectives. Administrators claim that their programs offer inmates "salable skills which will enhance their probability of obtaining and maintaining employment in the free world" (Windham School System, no date: 12), but critics often maintain that vocational training programs fail because "what they teach bears so little relationship to an offender's subsequent life outside of prison" (Martinson, 1976:13).

As we explained earlier in this report, it is probably unrealistic to expect prison education to offset all social and psychological reasons for recidivating, for being unable to find or keep a job, for not continuing educational progress after release, or for having disciplinary problems in prison. In an overview of 71 studies that analyzed predictors of recidivism, Pritchard found that

[a]n offense of auto theft, the presence of prior convictions, stability of employment, age at first arrest, living arrangements, current income, history of opiate use, and history of alcohol abuse appear to be the most stable predictors of recidivism (1979:19).

These findings are supported by a 1991 study of recidivism patterns conducted by the Texas Department of Criminal Justice. With respect to demographic traits, releasees who were young when released, who were black, male, and single, who had little formal education, who were raised by people other than their natural parents, and who had family members involved in crime were more likely to recidivate than their demographic counterparts. Furthermore, the younger they were at first arrest, conviction, and incarceration, the more likely they were to recidivate (Eisenberg, 1991).

In sum, the research shows a fair amount of support for the hypotheses that adult academic and vocational correctional education programs lead to fewer disciplinary violations during incarceration, reductions in recidivism, to increases in employment opportunities, and to increases in participation in education upon release. Future research, however, must employ more precise controls for extraneous variables that may have an independent effect on the various outcomes. Without adequate control techniques, it is difficult to speak definitively about the impact of correctional education programs. In addition, future research should focus on questions not addressed or answered in the literature. This research primarily should analyze the relationships between precollege and college education and disciplinary problems during incarceration, between college education and postrelease employment and education, and between vocational education and postrelease participation in education. Finally, research that compares the outcomes of correctional education programs for men and women should be conducted and evaluated.

Study Questions

1. What are the research questions addressed by this study?
2. Describe the research design, data collection methods, sample, and measures used by the authors in their study of education and vocational programs.
3. What are the major findings of this study?

Research Notes

1. For an excellent example of a study whose authors control for this problem, see the various reports on the *Post Release Employment Project* (PREP) of the Federal Bureau of Prisons (Federal Bureau of Prisons, 1985, especially pp. 9–12; Saylor & Gaes, 1987, 1992).

2. The study that Martinson identified, by Gearhart and associates (1967), deals more with vocational education than with academic education, and is discussed below.

3. The correlation between adult secondary education and recidivism also has been observed among probationers. Walsh (1985) found that probationers participating in GED preparation programs were less likely than nonparticipants to be rearrested; if rearrested, they were less criminally involved (fewer and less serious crimes).

4. For a recent review of literature that criticizes the presumed positive effects of education on correctional outcomes, see Jengeleski (1984).

5. For another, earlier study in New York State showing support for the recidivism hypothesis, see Wolf & Sylves (1981).

6. According to the author, this research proves that education does not lead to an increase in inmates' moral development—at least, not enough to prevent recidivism.

7. Numerous articles, reports, and books have been published on this research. For an overview consult Fabiano (1991), Ross & Fabiano (1985), and Ross, Fabiano, & Ross (1988).

References

Alston, J. G. (1980). Preparation for life after incarceration. *ERIC Microfiche ED 202 559.*

Anderson, D. B. (1981). The relationship between correctional education and parole success. *Journal of Offender Counseling, Services and Rehabilitation,* 5, 13–25.

Anderson, D. B., Schumacker. R. E., & Anderson, S. L (1991). Releasee characteristics and parole success. *Journal of Offender Rehabilitation,* 17, 133–45.

Anderson, S. L., Anderson, D. B., & Schumacker, R. E. (1988). *Correctional education: A way to stay out.* Springfield: Illinois Council on Vocational Education.

Ayers, D., Duguid, S., Montague, C., & Wolowidnyk, S. (1980). Effects of University of Victoria program: A post release study. Report to the Correctional Service in Canada, Ottawa.

Babbie, E. (1992). *The practice of social research*, 6th ed. Belmont, CA: Wadsworth.

Baker, J. E. (1973). Social education in a penitentiary. In A. R. Roberts (ed.), *Readings in prison education*, pp. 240–50. Springfield, IL: Thomas.

Big change in prisons: Punish—Not reform (1975). *U.S. News & World Report*, August 25, pp. 21–25.

Blackburn, F. S. (1981). The relationship between recidivism and participation in a community college associate of arts degree program for incarerated offenders. Paper presented at the Thirty-sixth Annual Conference of the Correctional Association, Costa Mesa, CA.

Burchard, J. D., & Lane, T. W. (1982). Crime and delinquency. In A. S. Bellack, M. Herson, and A. E. Kazdin (eds.), *International handbook of behavior modification and therapy*. New York: Plenum.

Cochran, A. W. (1965). Is education of value to the parolee? *Journal of Correctional Education*, 17(2), 22–24.

Cogburn, H. E. (1988). *Recidivism study: Positive terminations from J. F. Ingram State Technical College, 1976–1986*. Deatsville, AL: J. F. Ingram State Technical College.

Correctional Education School Authority (1990). *Academic and vocational program completers released from prison during fiscal year 1986–1988: Employment, recidivism and cost avoidance*. Tallahassee: Correctional Education School Authority, Planning, Research and Evaluation.

Davis, S., & Chown, B. (1986). Recidivism among offenders incarcerated by the Oklahoma department of corrections who received vocational-technical training: A survival data analysis of offenders released January 1982 through July 1986. *ERIC Microfiche ED 312 506*.

Downes, E. A., Monaco, K. R., & Schreiber, S. O. (1989). Evaluating the effects of vocational education on inmates: A research model and preliminary results. In S. Duguid (ed.), *The yearbook of correctional education*, Pp. 249–62. Burnaby, BC, Canada: Simon Fraser University.

Duguid, S. (1981). Rehabilitation through education: A Canadian model. *Journal of Offender Counseling, Services and Rehabilitation*, 6(1–2), 53–67.

Duguid, S. (1986). Selective ethics and integrity: Moral development and prison education. *Journal of Correctional Education*, 37, 61–64.

Eisenberg, M. (1991). *Five year outcome study: Factors associated with recidivism*. Austin: Texas Department of Criminal Justice.

Enocksson, K. (1981). Correctional programs: A review of the value of education and training in penal institutions. *Journal of Offender Counseling, Services and Rehabilitation*, 6, 5–18.

Fabiano, E. A. (1991). How education can be correctional and how corrections can be educational. *Journal of Correctional Education*, 42(2):100–106.

Federal Bureau of Prisons (1985). PREP: Post Release Employment Project—Interim report. Mimeographed report, Office of Research and Evaluation.

Fox, T. (1989). The necessity of moral education in prisons. *Journal of Correctional Education*, 39, 174–81.

Gearhart, J. W., Keith, H. L., & Clemmons, G. (1967). An analysis of the vocational training program in the Washington state adult correctional institutions. *Research Review, 23*. State of Washington, Department of Institutions.

Gendreau, R., Ross, R., & Izzo, R. (1985). Institutional misconduct: The effects of the UVIC program at Matsqui Penitentiary. *Canadian Journal of Criminology*, 27, 209–17.

Glaser, D. (1964). *The Effectiveness of a Prison and Parole System*. New York: Bobbs-Merrill.

Gordon, D. A., & Arbuthnot, J. (1987). Individual, group, and family fly interventions. In H. C. Quay (ed.), *Handbook of juvenile delinquency*, pp. 290–324. New York: Wiley.

Hagan, F. E. (1993). *Research methods in criminal justice and criminology*, 3rd ed. New York: Macmillan.

Hagerstown Junior College (1982). Hagerstown junior college prison program operations manual. *ERIC Microfiche ED 215 745*.

Hamilton, L. C. (1990). *Modern data analysis: A first course in applied statistics*. Pacific Grove, CA: Brooks/Cole.

Hamm, M. S. (1991). Batterers anonymous: Toward a correctional education to control romantic violence. *Journal of Correctional Education*, 42(2), 64–73.

Holloway, J., & Moke, P. (1986). Post secondary correctional education: An evaluation of parolee performance. *ERIC Microfiche ED 269 578.*

Jengeleski, J. L. (1984). Reintegrating the ex-offender: A critique of education and employment programs. *Journal of Offender Education,* 35(3):90–95.

Johnson, D. C., Shearon, R. W., & Britton, G. M. (1974). Correctional education and recidivism in a woman's correctional center. *Adult Education,* 24, 121–29.

Kalton, G. (1983). *Introduction to Survey Sampling.* Newbury Park, CA: Sage.

Knepper, P. (1990). Selective participation, effectiveness, and prison college programs. *Journal of Offender Counseling, Services and Rehabilitation,* 14:109–35.

Langenbach. M., North, M. Y., Aagaard, L., & Chown, W. (1990). Televised instruction in Oklahoma prisons: A study of recidivism and disciplinary actions. *Journal of Correctional Education,* 41(2):87–94.

Linden, R., & Perry, L. (1983). The effectiveness of prison education programs. *Journal of Offender Counseling, Services and Rehabilitation,* 6(4):43–57.

Linden, R., Perry, L., Ayers, D., & Parlett, T. A. A. (1984). An evaluation of a prison education program. *Canadian Journal of Criminology,* 26: 65–73.

Lipton, D., Martinson, R., & Wilks, J. (1975). *The effectiveness of correctional treatment: A survey of treatment evaluation studies.* New York: Praeger.

Lockwood, D. (1991). Prison higher education and recidivism: A program evaluation. *Yearbook of Correctional Education 1991,* pp. 187–201.

Markley, H., Flynn, K., & Bercaw-Dooen, S. (1983). Offender skills training and employment success: An evaluation of outcomes. *Correctional and Social Psychiatry and Journal of Behavior Technology Therapy,* 29, 1–11.

Marshall, W. L., Turner, B. A., & Barbaree, H. E. (1989). An evaluation of life skills training for penitentiary inmates. *Journal of Offender Counseling, Services and Rehabilitation,* 14(2), 41–59.

Martinson, R. (1974 [1976]). What works? Questions and answers about prison reform. *The Public Interest,* 35, 22–54. Reprinted in R. Martinson, T. Palmer, and S. Adams (eds.), *Rehabilitation, Recidivism. and Research,* pp. 7–39. Hackensack, NJ: National Council on Crime and Delinquency.

Merton, R. (1938). Social structure and anomie. *American Sociological Review,* 3, 672–82.

Michalek, W. (1988). Correctional education: Skill acquisition and moral enterprise. *Journal of Correctional Education,* 39(1), 6–10.

Minahan, J. (1990). Mapping the world: Some thoughts on teaching the humanities in prison. *Journal of Correctional Education,* 41(1):14–19.

New York State, Department of Correctional Services (1989). *Follow-up study of a sample of offenders who earned high school equivalency diplomas while incarcerated.* Albany: Department of Correctional Services.

New York State, Department of Correctional Services (1991). *Analysis of return rates of the inmate college program participants.* Albany: Department of Correctional Services.

New York State, Department of Correctional Services (1992). *Overview of department follow-up research on return rates of participants in major programs—1992.* Albany: Department of Correctional Services.

O'Neil, M. (1990). Correctional higher education: Reduced recidivism. *Journal of Correctional Education,* 41(1), 28–31.

Ott, R. L. (1993). *An introduction to statistical methods and data analysis,* 4th ed. Belmont, CA: Duxbury Press.

Palmer, T. (1976). Martinson revisited. In R. Martinson, T. Palmer, and S. Adams (eds.), *Rehabilitation, Recidivism, and Research,* pp. 41–62. Hackensack, NJ: National Council on Crime and Delinquency.

Pritchard, D. A. (1979). Stable predictors of recidivism. *Criminology,* 17:15–21.

Rice, E., Poe, J. R., Jr., Hawes, J. R. B., Jr., & Nerden, J. (1980). Assessment of quality vocational education in state prisons. Executive summary. Final report. *ERIC Microfiche ED 203 032.*

Rogers, S. (1980). *An examination of adult training centers in Ontario: Community follow-up.* Province of Ontario: Ministry of Correctional Services.

Ross, R. R., & Fabiano, E. (1985). *Time to think: A cognitive model of delinquency prevention and offender rehabilitation.* Johnson City, TN: Institute of Social Sciences and Arts.

Ross, R. R., Fabiano, E., & Ross, R. (1988). (Re)habilitation through education: A cognitive model for corrections. *Journal of Correctional Education,* 39(2):44–47.

Roundtree, G. A., Edwards, D. W., & Dawson, S. H. (1982). The effects of education on self-esteem of male prison inmates. *Journal of Correctional Education*, 32(4):12–18.

Saden, S. J. (1962). Correctional research at Jackson prison. *Journal of Correctional Education*, 15 (October):22–26.

Saylor, W. G., & Gaes, G. G. (1987). *PREP-Post Release Employment Project: The effects of work skills acquisition in prison on post-release employment*. Paper presented at the Annual Meeting of the American Society of Criminology, Montreal.

Saylor, W. G., & Gaes, G. G. (1992). *PREP study links UNICOR work experience with successful post-release outcome*. Washington, DC: U.S. Department of Justice.

Schnur, A. (1948). The educational treatment of prisoners and recidivism. *American Journal of Sociology*, 54:142–47.

Schumacker, R. E., Anderson, D. B., & Anderson, S. L. (1990). Vocational and academic indicators of parole success. *Journal of Correctional Education*, 41(1):8–13.

Sharp, J. (1992). *Schools behind bars: Windham school system and other prison education programs*. Austin: Texas Comptroller of Public Accounts.

State of Maryland, Department of Public Safety and Correctional Services (1989). *Implementation of system to measure recidivism and statistical information on recidivism*. Baltimore.

State of Texas, Criminal Justice Policy Council (1992). *An evaluation of the reading to reduce recidivism program: Final report to Texas Department of Commerce*. Austin: Author.

Thorpe. T., MacDonald, D., & Bala, G. (1994). Follow-up of offenders who earn college degrees while incarcerated in New York State. *Journal of Correctional Education*, 35(3):86–88.

Tope, E. R., & Warthan, R. J. (1986). Correctional education: Igniting the spark of moral maturation. *Journal of Correctional Education*, 37(2): 75–78.

Walsh, A. (1985). An evaluation of the effects of adult basic education on rearrest rates among probationers. *Journal of Offender Counseling, Services and Rehabilitation*, 9(4):69–76.

Windham School System, Texas Department of Criminal Justice, Institutional Division (no date). *Annual performance report: 1989–90 school year*. Huntsville, TX: Texas Department of Criminal Justice.

Wolf, J. G., & Sylves, D. (1981). The impact of higher education opportunity programs. Post prison experience of disadvantaged students: A preliminary follow-up of HEOP ex-offenders. Final report. *ERIC Microfiche ED 226 073*.

Zink, T. M. (1970). A study of the effect of prison education on societal adjustment. *Journal of Correctional Education*, 22(2):18–20. ✦

Part VI

Release From Prison and Parole

Despite one's opinions about incarceration and punishment, the fact remains that the vast majority of prisoners will one day be released. Some will complete all of their time and "max" out, while many others will receive a conditional release, traditionally called parole.

Parole from prison, like the prison itself, is primarily an American innovation. It emerged from a philosophical revolution and a resulting tradition of penal reform, established in the late eighteenth century in the newly formed United States. As with many other ideas that emerged in early America, parole had its roots in the practices of English and European penal systems. Alexander Maconochie is usually credited as the father of parole. In 1840, Captain Maconochie was put in charge of the English penal colony in New South Wales at Norfolk Island, about 1,000 miles off the coast of Australia. To this colony were sent the criminals who were twice condemned. They had been shipped from England to Australia and then from Australia to Norfolk. Conditions were allegedly horrible, and it was under these conditions that Maconochie devised parole. Although the roots of parole spring from Australia, it was the prison reform movement in the United States that embraced the concept and developed and expanded its use.

Perhaps no aspect of the correctional system has come under more attack than parole. Liberals questioned the secretiveness of the process and the arbitrariness of the release decision. Conservatives questioned both the wisdom of releasing offenders after only a portion of their sentence had been served as well as the effectiveness of parole supervision in protecting the public. Despite these attacks, parole has survived in many states and remains a vehicle for release and supervision of offenders in the community.

The failure of prisons to rehabilitate offenders has often been attributed to a lack of support and transitional care and services. However, transition from prison to the community is made more effective through community correctional facilities, often called halfway houses. Halfway houses have a long history in the United States and are considered by many to be essential to the civic reintegration of offenders. Substance abuse treatment, housing, employment training, counseling, and family services are some examples of such community correctional programs. Giving support and assistance to those in need is only one role these programs play. Protecting the community and increased cost effectiveness are also critical aspects that need to be factored in when considering the effectiveness of correctional programs such as halfway houses. ✦

29
History of the Federal Parole System
Part 2 (1973–1997)

Peter B. Hoffman

Although parole has its roots in Australia, it was not until the concept spread to the United States that parole gained widespread acceptance. Over the years, the U.S. Federal Parole System has been considered at the forefront of parole practices. For example, as a result of criticisms of parole release, the 1970s saw the development and spread of guidelines designed to structure the discretion and nature of parole. Along with these changes came new instruments, such as the salient factor score, which were designed to measure the probability of reoffending. By the 1980s, many jurisdictions had begun experimenting with sentencing guidelines. As before, the U.S. Federal Parole Commission led the way for these significant changes. Peter B. Hoffman provides a chronological description of these changes over a 24-year period.

Chronological History

Significant events are shown corresponding to the date above each entry. At the end of the entry, an abbreviation for the source material used is shown in brackets; the full citation is given in the references at the end of the article. The few entries without a bracketed citation are based either on the source

Excerpted from "History of the Federal Parole System: Part 2 (1973–1997)," by Peter B. Hoffman. *Federal Probation*, 61(4): 49–57. Copyright © 1997. Reprinted by permission.

described in the entry itself or on the personal knowledge of the author.

1973

In May 1973, Maurice Sigler, Chairman of the U.S. Board of Parole, submitted a proposal for a reorganization of the parole board and revision of the parole board's procedures to the Department of Justice. Key features of this proposal were the use of explicit guidelines for parole decision-making; the decentralization of the parole board into five regions (each headed by a board member) with the Chairman and two other members forming a National Appeals Board in Washington, DC; hearings conducted by panels of two hearing examiners with review by the regional parole board member on the record; the provision of written reasons for parole decisions; the opportunity for prisoners to have representatives at parole hearings; and an administrative appeal process. In July 1973, this proposal was approved by Attorney General Elliot Richardson. [EUSBPR]

The explicit paroling policy guidelines adopted by the parole board were published in the *Federal Register*. These guidelines were developed in cooperation with a project funded by the Law Enforcement Assistance Administration and conducted by the National Council on Crime and Delinquency. The guidelines were in the form of a two-dimensional grid. The seriousness of the prisoner's current offense (offense severity) was considered on the vertical axis with six categories (later increased to seven and then eight categories). The prisoner's likelihood of recidivism (parole prognosis) was considered on the horizontal axis with four categories. The dimension of parole prognosis was determined by use of a "salient factor score," an empirically derived parole prediction instrument. The intersections of the vertical and horizontal axes formed a grid containing time ranges (such as 12–18 months). The time range set forth the parole board's policy on the customary time to be served before release for a prisoner having that offense seriousness and parole prognosis, assuming good institutional conduct. Decisions outside the guidelines may be made for good cause and upon the provision of case-specific written reasons. For example, misconduct in the institution might warrant a decision above the applicable guideline range, and exceptionally good participation in institutional programs might warrant a decision below the applicable guideline range. [PDMR]

The Research Center of the National Council on Crime and Delinquency published a 14-volume set of reports on the Federal Parole Decision-Making Project. [PDMR]

1974

Regional offices were established in Philadelphia, Pennsylvania; Atlanta, Georgia; Dallas, Texas; Kansas City, Missouri; and Burlingame, California. Each regional office included a parole board member, five hearing examiners, two case analysts, and clerical staff. [EUSBPR].

The parole board's budget for fiscal year 1974 was $2,025,000, up from $1,391,000 in fiscal year 1973 and from approximately $500,000 in 1965. The increase from fiscal year 1973 to fiscal year 1974 included the cost of implementing the reorganization. Personnel increased from 48 positions in fiscal year 1965 to 125 positions in fiscal year 1974. [EUSBPR]

1975

Each regional office has approximately 20 employees. A typical regional office is staffed with a board member acting as the regional director, an administrative hearing examiner and four hearing examiners, a pre-release analyst, a post-release analyst, and administrative and clerical support personnel. [EUSBPR]

Hearing examiner panels, each consisting of two persons, conduct parole interviews at each institution within the region. At the conclusion of each interview, the examiners

inform the prisoner of the recommended (tentative) parole decision. If the recommendations of the examiners differ, the prisoner is informed of both recommendations. All panel decisions are reviewed in the regional office by an administrative hearing examiner and the regional board member. It is the regional board member who makes the final decision, subject to certain limitations (if the regional board member wishes to alter a panel recommendation by more than 6 months, the case must be sent to the national board members for review). After a decision is made, a Notice of Action is mailed to the prisoner within 15 working days of the hearing. If the prisoner is not granted parole at that time, the reasons are given as part of the Notice of Action. If the prisoner is dissatisfied with the decision, he or she has available a two-step administrative appeal process. [EUSBPR]

According to a report of field visits by Department of Justice Management Programs and Budget staff, the average hearing lasted 30 minutes. Revocation hearings took anywhere from 45 to 90 minutes. The hearing began with a review of the inmate's file by one hearing examiner while the other examiner dictated the results of the last hearing. The review usually took 10 to 15 minutes. The offender's prior criminal history was closely examined during the file review. After the file was reviewed by one examiner, that examiner provided a brief summary of the file to the other examiner, who had completed dictating the results of the previous hearing.

Before the interview with the inmate, the hearing panel discussed the inmate's progress with the institutional case manager. At the beginning of the interview with the inmate, the hearing examiner carefully explained the board's procedures to the inmate and the inmate's right to appeal the decision. The principal discussion points initiated by the hearing examiners were: the validation of the salient factor score, the inmate's offense and the surrounding circumstances of the crime, and the inmate's institutional behavior and program participation.

The inmate's remarks usually began with a description of the mitigating circumstances of the offense and past criminal behavior. This most often was followed by the inmate's statements regarding his participation in institutional programs and his motivation to become a better citizen. The inmate usually made some reference to his parole release plan. The period of time for the discussion with the inmate ranged from 5 to 16 minutes. When an inmate's representative was present, the discussion period required as much as one half hour.

Following the inmate's discussion, he was asked if he had any questions he would like to ask the panel. If not, he left the room and the hearing examiners discussed the case. In most instances, the decision-making process, which takes from 2 to 5 minutes, was a straightforward application of the guidelines and salient factors to the individual case.

The inmate returned to the hearing room and was advised of the panel's tentative decision. When parole was approved, the discussion continued on the completion and validation of the release plan. When parole was denied, the examiners advised the inmate of the reasons and the right to appeal the decision. The process of advising the inmate of the decision required approximately 5 minutes.

Most representatives who were observed by the evaluation teams were institutional staff, however, relatives, prospective employers, and educators have appeared at a number of hearings. Generally, hearing examiners and Bureau of Prisons institutional staff agree that the inmate representative does not have a major effect on parole decisions; however, the representatives can have a positive effect on the inmate's attitude. Cases have occurred in which Bureau of Prisons institutional staff members serving as inmates' representatives have directly contradicted the observations and recommendations of the inmate's caseworker. In these instances, the examiner stated that the rep-

resentative can have a major impact on the decision. [EUSBPR]

1976

The Parole Commission and Reorganization Act (Public Law 94–233) became effective on May 14, 1976. A major revision of the statutes pertaining to parole, this act retitled the agency as the United States Parole Commission. The primary provisions of this act are listed below.

- The U.S. Parole Commission is created with a membership of nine Commissioners. The Youth Correction Division was eliminated and its duties absorbed within the new Commission.

- No fewer than five regions are mandated; a Regional Commissioner is placed in charge of each. Three Commissioners are assigned to a National Appeals Board. Authority and responsibilities of the Commission, the Chairman, and the Regional Commissioners are set forth.

- Eligibility for parole for prisoners with long sentences, including life terms, is reduced to 10 years from the previous 15 years.

- Explicit guidelines for decision-making are mandated.

- Reasons for denial of parole must be provided to the prisoner in writing. Decisions outside the guidelines must be for "good cause" and must contain specific written reasons for such departure.

- Parole applicants have a right to examine their own case file (with limited exceptions) before the hearing.

- Parole applicants may be accompanied at their hearings by a representative of their choice, who may make a statement on the applicant's behalf.

- If a prisoner's sentence is less than 7 years, he must be reviewed no later than at 18-month intervals after the initial hearing. If this sentence is 7 years or more, he must be reviewed no later than at 24-month intervals following the initial hearing.

- Prisoners with terms of 5 years or more and satisfactory institutional conduct must be paroled after service of two-thirds of the term, unless the Commission finds that there is a "reasonable probability" of further crime.

- A two-level appeal system is mandated.

- Regular and special conditions of release set by the Commission may be modified only after an opportunity has been offered to the releasee to comment on the proposed modifications. Such modifications also are appealable.

- The Commission must review a parolee's progress under supervision after 2 years and at least annually thereafter and may terminate supervision before completion of the sentenced term. Termination of supervision ends the jurisdiction of the Commission over the releasee.

- After 5 years of supervision in the community, the Commission must terminate jurisdiction unless it finds, after a hearing, that there is a likelihood of further crime. Such decision is appealable.

- At the discretion of the Commission, alleged violators may be summoned to a hearing in lieu of being arrested on a warrant and may be released under supervision pending a revocation hearing.

- Reviews of parole violation warrants placed as a detainer, while a prisoner is serving a subsequent sentence, must be reviewed within 180 days and a decision made with regard to disposition of the warrant.

- Alleged parole violators have the right to confront "adverse" witnesses at a preliminary interview and any revocation hearing held in the local community. At such interview or at any revocation hearing, the prisoner may be represented by an attorney (either retained or appointed). Voluntary witnesses also may be present.

- A preliminary interview is not necessary if the releasee has been convicted of a crime while under supervision.

- The Commission may subpoena witnesses in revocation proceedings.

- Following revocation, the parolee receives credit for time under supervision in the community unless he has been convicted of a crime committed while under supervision. If he absconded from supervision, he is credited with the time from the date of release to supervision to the date of such absconding.

- Attorney representation, privately retained or court appointed, is permitted in any revocation proceeding and at any termination hearing scheduled after 5 years on parole. [ARUSPC (1976–78)]

1977

The Parole Commission modified the permissible grounds for a prisoner's appeal to make them more specific. The modified grounds for appeal are:

- That the guidelines were incorrectly applied.

- That a decision outside the guidelines was not supported by the reasons of facts as stated.

- That especially mitigating circumstances justify a different decision.

- That a decision was based on erroneous information and the actual facts justify a different decision.

- That the Commission did not follow correct procedure in deciding the case, and a different decision would have resulted if the error had not occurred.

- There was significant information in existence but not known at the time of the hearing.
- There are compelling reasons why a more lenient decision should be rendered on grounds of compassion. [ARUSPC (1976–78)]

Mexico and the United States signed a treaty for the mutual exchange of prisoners incarcerated for crimes while transient aliens within each nation's jurisdiction. The Commission's legal staff participated with the State Department and other units of the Department of Justice in the development of prisoner transfer treaties and implementing legislation. In December 1977, 154 U.S. citizens convicted of crimes in Mexico were transferred to the United States. A special docket was set up to provide prompt parole hearings to these cases. Shortly thereafter, Canada and Bolivia followed this precedent by establishing similar treaties with the United States. [ARUSPC (1976–78)]

After a pilot test of the concept in the Parole Commission's Western Region, the Commission implemented a new procedure that has come to be called "presumptive parole." The purpose of the presumptive parole procedure is to provide the prisoner at the beginning of his sentence a date on which it is presumed that release will take place, provided the prisoner maintains a good institutional adjustment and has developed adequate release plans. This procedure is designed to remove much of the dysfunctional uncertainty and anxiety surrounding the parole process while retaining the flexibility to deal with substantial changes in circumstances. Presumptive parole procedures went into effect in September 1977. All prisoners with 7 years or less (regardless of sentence procedure) and all prisoners with no minimum sentences are heard within 120 days of commitment or as soon thereafter as practicable. A presumptive release date may be set up to 4 years from the date of the initial hearing (previously, parole dates were set up to 6 months from the date of the hearing).

If a presumptive release date is not set within 4 years from the date of the initial hearing, the prisoner will be continued to a reconsideration hearing 4 years from the date of the initial hearing (a "four-year reconsideration hearing"). In addition, interim hearings are conducted as required by statute to consider whether there are any substantial positive or negative changes in circumstances (e.g., outstanding institutional program achievement, disciplinary infractions) that may warrant modifying the presumptive release date originally set. In addition, a prerelease record review is conducted to ensure that the conditions of the presumptive release date (good institutional conduct and a suitable release plan) have been satisfied. Failure to satisfy these conditions may result in retardation of the release date or the scheduling of a rescission hearing. [ARUSPC (1976–78)]

1978

The Parole Commission published *Federal Parole Decision Making: Selected Reprints*, Volume I. [PDMSR (1)]

In October 1978, the Commission began a periodic review of its paroling policy guidelines at 28 C.F.R. 2.20 and 2.21. In addition to usual publishing and posting of the proposal, copies were sent to over 1,000 interested persons. Public hearings were held in Atlanta, Denver, and Washington, DC, and at the Atlanta and Englewood facilities of the Bureau of Prisons. Testimony was received from 69 witnesses, generating over 3,000 pages of transcript. Those giving their views included representatives from the judiciary, defense and prosecution attorneys, federal prisoners, enforcement agencies, the Bureau of Prisons, the probation system, state correctional systems, and scholars. As a result of this effort, certain listed offense behaviors were defined more specifically, certain previously unlisted offense behaviors were added to the guidelines, and certain offense behaviors were moved from one category to another or subdivided. The revised paroling policy guidelines became effective June 4, 1979. [ARUSPC (1978–80)]

1979

Decision guidelines were established for decisions to retard or rescind a parole on account of institutional misconduct. These guidelines are set forth at 28 C.F.R. 2.36. [ARUSPC (1978–80)]

Decision guidelines were established to reward sustained superior program achievement by a reduction from a previously established presumptive release date. The advancement for superior program achievement under these guidelines was deliberately kept modest. It is the intent of the Commission to encourage voluntary program participation, not superficial attendance in programs merely in an attempt to impress the parole decision-makers. These guidelines are set forth at 28 C.F.R. 2.60. [ARUSPC (1978–80)]

1980

The Parole Commission's presumptive release date procedures were expanded. Under the revised procedures, presumptive release dates are set up to 10 years from the date of the initial hearing. A defendant who does not receive a presumptive release date will be scheduled for a 10-year reconsideration hearing. Procedures for interim hearings, as required by statute, to review the case for any significant changes in circumstances are unchanged. [ARUSPC (1978–80)]

From April 9–11, 1980, the Parole Commission, in joint sponsorship with the National Institute of Corrections, conducted the Third National Parole Symposium. The conference was held at the University of Maryland at College Park. United States District Judge Frank A. Kaufman, Governor Brendan T. Byrne of New Jersey, and Charles Silberman, author of *Criminal Violence, Criminal Justice*, were featured speakers. Approximately 250 persons attended. The proceedings of the conference were published as *Parole in the 1980s: Proceedings of the Na-*

tional Parole Symposium. [ARUSPC (1978–80)]

The Parole Commission published *Federal Parole Decision Making: Selected Reprints*, Volume II. [PDMSR (2)]

1981

The Parole Commission published *Federal Parole Decision Making: Selected Reprints*, Volume III. [PDMSR (3)]

Effective August 31, 1981, the Parole Commission, as a result of a research study, revised its Salient Factor Score, an actuarial device used in determining risk of recidivism. The new Salient Factor Score (SFS 81) includes six items which, when added together, produce a score with a range from zero to 10 points. The higher the score, the higher is the likelihood of favorable outcome. SFS 81 demonstrates predictive validity and stability equivalent to that of the seven-item predictive device previously used by the Commission. Of prime importance, the revised device holds promise for greater scoring reliability and ease of scoring. [ARUSPC (1980–83)]

1982

The Parole Commission published the first *Rules and Procedures Manual*, which consolidated the Parole Commission's rules (28 C.F.R. 2.1 *et seq.*) with the accompanying procedures. Previously, these had been published separately.

The Parole Commission published *Federal Parole Decision Making: Selected Reprints*, Volume IV. [PDMSR (4)]

1983

Effective January 31, 1983, the Parole Commission revised its offense severity scale. The revision, which used the format of the proposed revision of the federal criminal code, was designed to make the severity scale more comprehensive, to improve its clarity and organization, and to reflect changes in Commission policy for particular offenses. [ARUSPC (1980–83)]

1984

The Comprehensive Crime Control Act of 1984 (Public Law 98–473, October 12, 1984) was passed. This legislation provided for the creation of a United States Sentencing Commission to promulgate explicit decision guidelines (by May 1, 1986) to be used by federal judges in making sentencing decisions. The Chairman of the Parole Commission serves as an *ex officio*, non-voting member of the Sentencing Commission. The Parole Commission was to be abolished 5 years from the date the sentencing guidelines took effect. During the 5-year transition period, the Parole Commission was to continue in existence to handle cases of parole-eligible defendants convicted of offenses committed before November 1, 1987. Cases sentenced under the new law would serve determinate sentences with limited reduction for good time (about 15 percent). For such cases, post-release supervision would be called supervised release rather than parole, and decisions regarding the conditions of supervised release and revocation would be made by the courts rather than by the Parole Commission. This legislation also abolished the Youth Corrections Act. [ARUSPC (1985–86)]

The Comprehensive Crime Control Act of 1984 also eliminated the Parole commission's intermediate administrative appeal (regional appeal), providing a one-step rather than a two-step administrative appeal. [ARUSPC (1986–87)]

The Parole Commission published *Federal Parole Decision Making: Selected Reprints,* Volume V. [PDMSR (5)]

1985

Due to a delay in the appointment of the first members of the Sentencing Commission, legislation was enacted that extended the date for the first sentencing guidelines by 1 year (until May 1, 1987).

1986

The Parole Commission sought various legislative initiatives to facilitate the transition between the current and new systems. Legislation was enacted (Public Law 99–646, November 10, 1986) containing two provisions that afforded the Parole Commission flexibility to facilitate its phase out. First, the legislation eliminated the requirement for no less than five regions. Second, the legislation authorized the use of single hearing examiners to conduct hearings (with the requirement of a panel of two hearing examiners met by a review on the record by the second examiner). [ARUSPC (1985–86)]

The Parole Commission also provided assistance to the newly created Sentencing Commission. As the move toward the establishment of federal sentencing guidelines was based, in large part, on the successful development and use of federal parole guidelines, much of the research conducted and experience gained in the parole context was directly relevant to the sentencing guidelines effort. The Parole Commission provided a number of databases for the Sentencing Commission's use, and staffs of both agencies met regularly to examine the data, review the documentation, and discuss the empirical findings. [ARUSPC (1985–86)]

The Parole Commission published *Federal Parole Decision Making: Selected Reprints,* Volume VI. [PDMSR (6)]

In March 1986, the Parole Commission implemented an experimental program, called Special Curfew Parole, to provide a substitute for Community Treatment Center residence for the 60-day period preceding the otherwise scheduled parole release date. This program, a joint effort of the Parole Commission, the U.S. Bureau of Prisons, and the U.S. Probation System, was designed for prisoners who were transferred to Community Treatment Centers for a 30- to 120-day period before parole, but who no longer required the support services provided there. Under this program, a qualified prisoner could have his release date advanced by up to 60 days on the condition that he remain at his place of residence between the hours of 9 p.m. and 6 a.m. each night unless given permission in advance by his probation officer. The probation system provided high-activity supervision of the parolee during this period (at least weekly in-person contact, as well as monitoring compliance with the curfew by random telephone calls). Failure to comply with this special condition could result in imposition of Community Treatment Center residence as a condition of parole or revocation of parole and return to prison. Implemented as a cost-reduction procedure through which the Bureau of Prisons could reduce the number and expense of inmates confined in Community Treatment Centers, this project saved over $1 million in its first 18 months of operation. [ARUSPC (1985–86)]

In collaboration with the Bureau of Prisons and the National Institute of Justice, the Parole Commission initiated an experimental program in which selected prisoners would have their parole dates advanced if they volunteered to complete 400 hours of "reparative work." Reparative work is defined as unpaid volunteer work for public or nonprofit private agencies (such as the Volunteers of America, the Salvation Army, or Goodwill Industries). The purpose of the project was to develop an alternative form of punishment that returned something of value to the community and, at the same time, saved prison bed space. During the first phase of the project, 100 prisoners in selected cities each completed the 400 hours of reparative work while residing in halfway houses. These prisoners logged 38,481 hours of unpaid service, work which would have cost the participating agencies over $168,000 for paid employees to perform. In return, release dates were advanced by 5,538 days, providing a substantial savings in prison bed space. Upon release, some parolees were offered full-time paid positions

with the agencies they had worked for in the program. A second phase of the program was begun at the Federal Correctional Institution at Forth Worth. In this phase, a limited number of prisoners performed reparative work in the community while still residing at the institution. [ARUSPC (1985–86)]

The Anti-Drug Abuse Act of 1986 enacted long, mandatory minimum sentences for many drug offenders.

1987

On April 14, 1987, the U.S. Sentencing Commission transmitted its initial sentencing guidelines to Congress. These guidelines took effect, as scheduled, on November 1, 1987, and applied to all defendants whose offenses were committed on or after that date.

The Bureau of Prisons reported that the cumulative savings from the Special Curfew Parole Project exceeded $2 million and requested that the program be extended indefinitely. [ARUSPC (1986–87)]

The Parole Commission initiated a "Community Control Project," a joint effort with the Bureau of Prisons and U.S. probation system, using electronic monitoring to ensure compliance with a curfew. Because of population pressures, the Bureau of Prisons was placing offenders in halfway houses up to 6 months before release even if there was no treatment need for such placement. Under this experimental program, selected low-treatment-need offenders were released to the community up to 180 days before their normally scheduled parole date with a curfew, electronic monitoring, and intensive supervision substituted for Community Treatment Center placement. Two districts (Southern District of Florida and Central District of California) were selected for this project. [ARUSPC (1986–87)]

The Reparative Work Project was terminated. During the two phases, 132 offenders each performed 400 hours of reparative work and had their parole dates advanced by up to 60 days. A total of 51,281 hours of unpaid community service work was completed and participants had their parole dates advanced by a total of 7,458 days. The value of the work done was estimated to be over $225,000 (for paid employees to have done the same work), and the project was well received by the nonprofit agencies involved. Despite these positive findings, the project was terminated because the Bureau of Prisons did not believe that the staff time needed to monitor the project could be spared given the level of overcrowding. [ARUSPC (1986–87)]

1988

The cumulative number of offenders participating in the Special Curfew Parole Project reached 3,000. Very few problems were reported; the revocation rate for violations on curfew parole was less than 3 percent. [ARUSPC (1987–88)]

The Community Control Project was expanded to four additional districts. To date, 120 offenders have participated in this project. [ARUSPC (1987–88)]

The Anti-Drug Abuse Act of 1988 broadened the scope of the mandatory minimum sentences for drug offenders enacted by the Anti-Drug Abuse Act of 1986. The Anti-Drug Abuse Act of 1988 gave the Parole Commission jurisdiction over new-law transfer treaty cases (transfer treaty cases in which the offense was committed on or after November 1, 1987). In such cases, the Parole Commission is to determine the release date by applying the sentencing guidelines promulgated by the U.S. Sentencing Commission. [ARUSPC (1987–88)]

The Anti-Drug Abuse Act of 1988 also gave the Parole Commission continuing responsibility over all state defendants who are accepted into the U.S. Marshals Service Witness Protection Program. Once a state defendant is accepted into this program, the Parole Commission assumes jurisdiction over the case.

Fifty percent of the initial hearings conducted in fiscal year 1988 involved offenders with drug-related convictions, 26 percent involved property crimes, and another 11 percent involved crimes of violence (murder, kidnaping, arson, robbery, and assault). [ARUSPC (1987–88)]

1989

The Parole Commission began an Intensive Supervision Project with the U.S. Probation Office for the District of Maryland for high risk cases. [ARUSPC (1988–89)]

The number of hearings conducted by the Parole Commission began to decline as the sentencing guidelines took effect for defendants who committed offenses on or after November 1, 1987. In fiscal years 1987 and 1988, the Commission conducted 19,796 and 20,465 hearings, respectively. In fiscal year 1989, the number of hearings declined to 16,619. [ARUSPC (1988–89)]

1990

The Judicial Improvements Act of 1990 extended the life of the Parole Commission by an additional 5 years until November 1, 1997, because the Comprehensive Crime Control Act of 1984 had failed to make adequate provision for handling old-law cases. Retrospective abolition of parole consideration (for defendants who had already committed their offenses) would raise a serious constitutional issue under the *ex post facto* clause. [ARUSPC (1989–90)]

The Parole Commission has jurisdiction over the following cases: (1) "Old Law" Cases (persons sentenced to prison terms of more than 1 year for offenses committed before November 1, 1987, unless sentenced under a statute expressly prohibiting parole eligibility); (2) Transfer Treaty Cases (persons transferred to the United States from foreign countries to complete service of a foreign sentence, regardless of the date of the offense); (3) State Witness Protection Cases (probationers and parolees serving state sentences who are transferred to federal jurisdiction because of participation in the Federal Witness Protection Program, regardless of the date of the offense); (4) D.C. Code Cases in Federal Institutions (persons sentenced under the District of Columbia Code who are confined in correctional facilities of the U.S. Bureau of Prisons, regardless of the date of the offense); and (5) Military Prisoners in Federal Institutions (persons convicted of military offenses who are confined in correctional facilities of the U.S. Bureau of Prisons, regardless of the date of the offense). The number of Parole Commission hearings continued to decline. There were 13,568 hearings conducted in fiscal year 1990, including 903 hearings for D.C. Code offenders housed in federal institutions. [ARUSPC (1989–90)]

1991

In August 1991, as part of its phase-down effort, the Parole Commission closed its Philadelphia and Atlanta Regional Offices and consolidated these operations in a new Eastern Regional Office co-housed with the Headquarters Office in Chevy Chase, Maryland. [ARUSPC (1990–91)]

The Special Curfew Parole Project, which had started in 1986, reached a cumulative total of 3,500 cases. As electronic monitoring (started under the Community Control Project) became available in each judicial district, it replaced the curfew parole project. [ARUSPC (1990–91)]

1992

The Parole Commission, in cooperation with the U.S. probation system, developed an experimental project to place technical parole violators in "sanction centers," rather than return them to prison. In 1992, two sanction centers were opened, one in the Baltimore, Maryland, area and one in the Washington, DC, area. [ARUSPC (1991–92)]

The Parole Commission's Intensive Supervision Project in Hyattsville and Baltimore, Maryland, which had started in 1988, was terminated due to the downsizing of the Commission. An evaluation of the Hyattsville project, prepared by the National Center on Institutions and Alternatives, concluded that the early intervention and increased surveillance of the project provided a tool for preventing escalating criminal behavior. [ARUSPC (1991–92)]

1993

The number of hearings conducted in fiscal year 1993 was 6,769, down from 10,720 hearings in fiscal year 1991 and 9,307 hearings in fiscal year 1992, and slightly less than one-half of the 13,568 hearings conducted in fiscal year 1990. [ARUSPC (1992–93)]

1994

As part of its phase-down effort, the Commission closed its Dallas Regional Office and consolidated that operation in its Eastern Regional Office co-housed with the Headquarters Office in Chevy Chase, Maryland. This closing resulted in a savings of more than $1 million in operating funds and reduced the number of Commission personnel by 22 positions. The Commission also eliminated a number of mid-management positions. [ARUSPC (1993–94)]

Given the requirement for the downsizing of the Commission, the Commission began using single hearing examiners to conduct parole hearings. From 1974 to 1994, hearings had been conducted by two-person panels of hearing examiners. Under the revised procedure, a second examiner would review the case record and hearing summary at the Commission's office. [ARUSPC (1993–94)]

1995

The Parole Commission modified the Salient Factor Score by adding an additional item for older offenders (offenders at least 41 years of age on the date of the current offense). The revised Salient Factor Score is designated as SFS 95.

The Parole Commission published a 16-chapter *Desk Book on Training and Reference Materials* as part of a program of staff training.

1996

The Parole Commission closed its Kansas City Regional Office and consolidated that operation in its Eastern Regional Office co-housed with the Headquarters Office in Chevy Chase, Maryland. This action resulted in a savings of more than $1 million in operating funds and reduced the number of Commission personnel by 22 positions. With the closing of this office, all Commission functions will be conducted from its Chevy Chase, Maryland, office.

Congress passed the Parole Commission Phaseout Act of 1996. This act extended the life of the Parole Commission by an additional 5 years (until November 1, 2002). In addition, it reinstated the 12-year limitation on total service as a Parole Commissioner and provided for the reduction in the number of Parole Commissioners to two Commissioners on December 31, 1999, and to one Commissioner on December 31, 2001. Furthermore, it required the Attorney General to report to the Congress annually, beginning in May 1998, as to whether it is more cost effective for the Parole Commission to remain a separate agency or whether its functions should be transferred elsewhere. If the Attorney General recommends incorporating the Commission's functions in another component of the Department of Justice, the Attorney General's plan shall take effect in November of the year in which it is submitted unless Congress, by law, provides otherwise. If the Commission's functions are transferred to another component within the Department of Justice, all laws remaining to these functions remain in effect notwithstanding the November 1, 2002, termination date for the Commission set forth elsewhere in the legislation.

The Parole Commission, with the assistance of a grant from the Office for Victims of Crime, established two victim/witness coordinator positions and developed a program to enhance the Commission's responsiveness to victims and witnesses at revocation hearings.

The Parole Commission had 48 positions at the end of 1996, a substantial reduction from 145 positions in 1992. At the beginning of 1996, there were six Parole Commissioners. By the end of 1996, this number was reduced to three due to resignations and the provisions of the Parole Commission Phaseout Act of 1996.

1997

The Parole Commission began an experimental project in which parole hearings are conducted using video-conferencing equipment. In February 1997, the first hearings in this project were conducted for prisoners at the Federal Correctional Institution in Oakdale, Louisiana.

Study Questions

1. Federal parole guidelines were designed to structure the discretion of the parole board. What were the two components of these guidelines? When were they replaced by sentencing guidelines?

2. Describe the Reparative Work Project. Why was this project terminated?

3. Briefly discuss the changes in the Federal Parole Commission since the early 1970s.

References

[ARUSBP] *Annual Report of the United States Board of Parole* (various years). Washington, DC: U.S. Board of Parole.

[ARUSPC] *Annual Report of the United States Parole Commission* (various years). Washington, DC [Chevy Chase, MD, beginning in 1981]: U.S. Parole Commission.

[EUSBPR] *An Evaluation of the U.S. Board of Parole Reorganization.* (1975). Management Programs and Budget Staff, Office of Management and Finance. Washington, DC: U.S. Department of Justice.

[HUSBP] *History of the United States Board of Parole.* (undated, circa 1976). Washington, DC: U.S. Board of Parole. [A mimeographed document prepared by James C. Neagles, Staff Director of the U.S. Board of Parole.]

[PDMR] *Parole Decision-Making Reports.* (1973). Davis, CA: Research Center of the National Council on Crime and Delinquency. [A set of 14 reports describing the Parole Decision-Making Project.]

[PDMSR] *Parole Decision Making: Selected Reprints,* Volume I (1978), II (1980), III (1981), IV (1982), V (1984), VI (1986). Washington, DC [Chevy Chase, MD, beginning in 1981]: U.S. Parole Commission. [The volume number is shown in parentheses.]

This, the second part of a two-part article, provides a chronology from 1973 to the present. Part 1, which was published in the September 1997 issue *Federal Probation*, presented the chronology from the origin of the federal parole system through 1972. The views expressed in this article are the personal views of the author and do not necessarily reflect the official position of the U.S. Parole Commission or the Department of Justice. This article was abstracted from a report, entitled *History of the Federal Parole System*, prepared for the United States Parole Commission. ✦

30
Save Parole Supervision

Robert Martinson

Judith Wilks

In the 1970s, parole came under intense scrutiny and criticism. Liberals believed that parole release was a secretive, capricious, and unfair process, while conservatives believed that it undermined the effects of punishment and was ineffective in reducing recidivism. Robert Martinson, best known as the author of the "nothing works" doctrine, conducted a review of parole with Judith Wilks and argued that the evidence supported the retention of parole as an effective way to release and supervise offenders in the community. In the years that followed, a number of states and the federal government abolished parole. However, despite these developments, many states have retained the release and supervision practice known as parole.

The increasing attacks on the institution of parole in the United States today fail to distinguish between parole as a method for releasing offenders from (or returning offenders to) imprisonment and parole as a method for supervising offenders in the community. These two distinct functions need to be separately evaluated for an overall assessment of the usefulness of parole and its fairness in our system of criminal justice.

The parole release (and revocation) decision is inseparable from the indeterminate sentence. Decision-making is a quasi-judicial process carried on by small groups of appointed officials organized into Parole Boards. Parole supervision, on the other hand, is not dependent on the indeterminate sentence. It is a method for controlling, helping, or keeping track of offenders in the community. For hundreds of thousands of convicted offenders, it is a major institutional alternative to extended periods of imprisonment. The supervision functions of parole are carried on by an extended network of thousands of agents organized into parole district offices and divisions.

The essential criterion of parole as a quasi-judicial process is simple fairness and equity. Such issues are especially critical when unreviewed discretion involves deprivation of liberty. Many critics have rightly argued that the parole decision-making process is lamentably brief for such an important decision, lacking in essential elements of due process, frequently arbitrary and subject to political interference, and based in part on a myth that parole boards have the ability to accurately predict when a particular offender is "ready" for parole.

The usual criterion for assessing parole supervision has been how *effective* it is in reducing the criminal behavior of those under supervision. Such effectiveness need not be gained at the price of unfairness. On the contrary, since the consequence of engaging in criminal behavior is to be reimprisoned, supervision which is effective directly contributes to fairness in the sense that fewer offenders are deprived of their liberty. By preventing or inhibiting criminal behavior, effective parole supervision insures that fewer offenders will be rearrested, convicted, and returned to prison.

Unfortunately, in their haste to restrict or eliminate the Parole Board decision-making function (and the indeterminate sentence on which it rests), some critics propose to throw the baby out with the bath water. Yet there is no reason why a mandatory and definite parole sentence could not be substituted for the present system of parole board discretion

Excerpts from "Save Parole Supervision" by Robert Martinson and Judith Wilks, *Federal Probation*, 42(3): 23–27. Copyright © 1978 by the National Institute of Justice. Reprinted by permission.

and conditional release under threat of revocation for rule-breaking.[1] And those who propose such radical surgery would do well not to speak in the name of the offender for there is grave danger that the overall consequence of abolishment of parole supervision would be to consign larger numbers of offenders to prison.

One critical empirical question that must be answered is: Would the abolition of the present system of parole supervision increase or decrease the rates at which persons released from incarceration would be reprocessed into the criminal justice system? Previous research has not addressed this question. Such research deals primarily with variants of parole supervision within the existing system.[2] Inferences from such research are speculative and do not permit a " . . .direct comparison of offenders under parole supervision with offenders set entirely free."[3]

Parole has never been a universal method for releasing offenders from incarceration, and therefore in most jurisdictions in the United States some persons are released on parole supervision while others are released at the expiration of their terms, i.e., "set entirely free." Clearly, the most obvious research method, available to researchers since parole was established in the United States, would be controlled comparisons of persons released under parole supervision with comparable persons released directly from imprisonment without parole supervision. This is the method to be used in the present analysis.

The Survey

The data presented in Table 30.1 are taken from a larger survey of criminal justice research. The survey was designed to provide a standard procedure for maximizing the accumulation of existing information so that substantive questions can be answered and decisions taken on matters of public policy. For a description of the search procedure,

the classification of documents received, and the variables coded, it is necessary to read the preliminary report.[4] The present substudy illustrates the utility of the procedure adopted.

Two key concepts were employed in collecting, coding, and organizing the data taken from more than 600 recent documents: the "batch" and the "computable recidivism rate."

Batch.—A "batch" is any number of persons at some specifiable location in the criminal justice system for whom a "proper" recidivism rate is computable. A proper recidivism rate must specify what *proportion* of a batch are recidivists. The term "Parent batch" refers to a universal set which contains two or more batches. For example, a universal set of, say 1,000 male and female parolees may be broken into one batch of 800 *male* parolees and one batch of 200 *female* parolees. Each of these batches is coded as "exclusive" since together they exhaust the parent batch and have no members in common. All batches in Table 30.1 are exclusive batches with an N of 10 or more.

Recidivism Rate.—The primary unit of analysis in the survey is the computable recidivism rate. Each such rate specifies what proportion of any batch shall be identified as "recidivists" according to whatever operational definition of recidivism is utilized by the researcher. Such an operational definition will normally specify the length of time which the batch was followed up in addition to the criminal justice action (arrest, suspension, conviction, return to prison, and so forth) which led to the decision to classify a particular person as a "recidivist." All such definitions were coded into seven categories. Three of these categories—arrest, conviction, and return to prison with a new conviction—were judged to be appropriate for a comparison of parolees and persons released from incarceration with no supervision ("max out").[5]

The term "system re-processing rate" specifies precisely what is being measured in Table 30.1. An "arrest," for example, is an event that can occur to a person under the jurisdiction of criminal justice, and an arrest *rate* simply reports what proportion of any batch included in Table 30.1 were reported as being reprocessed in this way in the documents coded in the survey.

Each recidivism rate in the survey has been coded with additional items of information. The coding system developed was guided by the primary aim of the accumulation of knowledge based on the existing state of the art in criminal justice research. Codes were designed to maximize the information produced by the standard procedures now used in the body of documents encountered. Many of the items specify critical methodological features of the study, such as whether the batch is a population or a sample, the type of research design utilized, months in followup, months in treatment, the type of population or sample (e.g., "termination" sample), and so forth. Since studies report information on the characteristics of batches in a bewildering variety of ways, a standard attribute code was developed so as to maximize the reporting of such information as educational attainment, current offense, race, class position, family status, and so forth.[6] In addition, it was possible to code a considerable number of batches (and therefore rates) with such information as mean age, months in incarceration, sex, whether the batch consisted primarily of narcotics cases or persons with alcohol problems, and so forth.

Procedure

The procedure adopted was to exhaust the survey data base of all meaningful comparisons between adult offenders released from incarceration to parole supervision and comparable groups of adult offenders not released to parole supervision ("max out"). This was a simple sorting operation with an IBM counter-sorter. From a total pool of 5,804 recidivism rates for batches of adult persons in the United States and Canada re-

leased under parole supervision, those rates which fell in the category of "arrest" (N=235), "conviction" (N=135), and "return to prison with a new conviction" (N=738) were sorted out. A similar sort for adult max out rates resulted in 44 arrest rates, 26 conviction rates, and 73 return-to-prison-with-new-conviction rates. The total number of rates produced by these initial sorts are found at the bottom of Table 30.1.

The cards were then sorted on the variables which had been coded in the survey making no distinction between items which were primarily methodological (e.g., time in followup) and those which were primarily descriptive of a batch (e.g., mean age, sex, percent property offenders). All code categories for which at least two rates were reported for both parole and max out were located. Mean rates for these code categories were computed, and are presented in Table 30.1.[7]

Discussion

Item 1 can be used to illustrate how the table should be read. For parole, there were 84 recidivism rates where "arrest" was the measurement of recidivism and for which the batch size fell between 100 and 499. The mean of these 84 rates was 26.9. For this same batch size (100–499), there were 12 max out rates, and the mean of these rates was 32.8. The difference between these two means is 5.9.

Reading across the table, for the "conviction" definition the mean rates for parole and max out were 20.5 and 25.9, respectively. For the "return to prison with new conviction" definition these means were 11.0 and 14.7. Turning to a different batch size of 50–99 (item 24), one notes that comparisons could only be made for two of the three definitions. For some variables comparisons were possible for only one definition.

This table presents data in a manner which is similar to the procedure of simultaneously controlling for adulthood, definition of recidivism, place in the criminal justice

Table 30.1
Mean Recidivism Rates

Batch Characteristics	Definition: Arrest Parole X	N*	Max X	N	Out D**	Conviction Parole X	N	Max X	N	Out D	New Prison Sentence Parole X	N	Max X	N	Out D
1. Batch N=100–499	26.9	84	32.8	12	5.9	20.5	68	25.9	22	5.4	11.0	227	14.7	44	3.7
2. Male	25.2	174	39.5	32	14.3	19.1	85	29.6	21	10.5	11.3	393	14.3	58	3.0
3. % White=0–24.9	20.8	38	31.0	17	10.2	12.8	18	22.8	6	10.0	13.3	24	22.8	6	9.5
4. Total Population	20.8	62	37.7	22	16.9	13.9	31	28.1	25	14.2	9.7	593	14.5	67	4.8
5. Termination Sets	24.4	206	42.1	25	17.7	21.3	79	35.7	17	15.4	10.9	603	14.9	71	4.0
6. After-Only Research Design	25.2	96	42.3	27	17.1	21.8	60	28.9	25	7.1	10.9	581	14.8	73	3.9
7. Research done in 1970's	24.0	178	43.6	42	19.6	18.1	66	28.9	25	10.8	9.8	543	14.8	73	5.0
8. Standard Treatment	27.4	129	43.0	39	15.6	19.3	96	29.9	26	10.6	10.3	584	14.9	72	4.6
9. 7–12 Months Follow-up	24.6	85	43.7	12	19.1	15.6	66	22.8	6	7.2	8.7	250	5.2	15	-3.5
10. 19–24 Months Follow-up	28.4	41	57.5	10	29.1	20.9	11	32.5	5	11.6	11.0	170	11.2	15	.2
11. 25–36 Months Follow-up	28.9	25	49.5	4	20.6	17.8	15	27.5	10	9.7	15.5	79	18.9	16	3.4
12. Measured Only After Treatment	28.3	8	43.4	36	15.1	46.3	11	33.2	15	-13.1	14.9	48	13.9	62	-1.0
13. % Property Offenders 50–74.9	16.6	39	34.5	6	17.9	13.0	70	22.8	6	9.8					
14. % First Offenders 0–24.9	29.5	32	37.5	10	8.0	13.8	14	22.8	6	9.0					
15. Not Primarily Narcotic Users	32.5	5	32.5	5	0	5.9	7	22.8	6	16.9					
16. Not Primarily Alcohol Problems	43.4	9	36.2	6	-7.2	13.7	12	22.8	6	9.1					
17. % White 25–49.9	27.8	39	51.2	9	23.4	44.5	7	30.7	13	-13.8					
18. Mean Age 25–34.9	22.2	51	40.5	25	18.3	20.9	28	23.1	7	2.2					
19. % High School Graduates 0–24.9	25.5	67	41.2	9	15.7	19.8	17	22.8	6	3.0					
20. Measured over Same Time at Risk	22.6	26	44.0	19	21.4	18.7	55	18.9	9	.2					
21. Months Incarcerated = 12–17	17.3	36	40.8	8	23.5	17.5	10	28.2	19	10.7					
22. % From Broken Families 50–74.9	32.3	93	2.5	5	.2	19.3	23	22.8	6	3.5					
23. Comparison Group	28.3	70	42.5	15	14.2						9.9	126	14.5	9	4.6
24. Batch N=50–99	20.9	53	64.5	4	43.6						12.6	62	15.5	10	2.9
25. Sample	25.9	62	48.1	22	22.2						14.0	145	16.3	11	2.3
26. "E" Group	23.7	84	42.5	5	18.8										
27. % Property Offenders 25–49.9	21.1	29	48.5	10	27.4										
28. Batch N=10–49	22.8	72	44.1	28	21.3										
29. Primarily Narcotics Users	29.0	20	29.5	6	.5										
30. Mixed Sex Batch	28.6	39	61.7	9	23.1										
31. % From Broken Families 0–24.9	29.3	31	51.2	3	21.9										
32. % High School Graduates 25–49.9	33.5	10	37.0	4	3.5										
33. Lowest Class	34.1	22	45.8	8	11.7										
34. Non-Random Research Design	24.4	93	43.9	17	19.5										
35. 1–6 Months Follow-up	15.5	61	29.5	12	14.0										
36. 13–18 Months Follow-up	30.1	16	32.5	5	2.4										
37. Months Incarcerated=24–29	29.5	32	31.2	8	1.7										
38. Months Incarcerated=30–36	86.2	6	59.5	6	23.3										
39. % Property Offenders 0–24.9						20.5	15	30.5	10	10.0					
40. Highest Class						20.8	19	22.8	6	2.0					
41. Batch N=500											9.3	378	13.9	18	4.6
42. 37–60 Months Follow-up											13.5	87	18.4	18	4.9
43. 60+ Months Follow-up											14.1	22	25.4	7	11.3
TOTAL	24.5	235	42.9	44	18.4	19.7	185	29.9	26	10.2	10.6	738	14.8	73	4.3

*N=Number of Rates   **D=Max Out Mean Minus Parole Mean

system (i.e., parole vs. max out), and at least one additional variable. Given the number of rates available, it would have been possible to have controlled for one (or even more) variables in addition to the four specified above. For reasons of time, these additional controls were not attempted.

It is interesting to note that in *74 of the 80 comparisons contained in Table 30.1, the mean of the recidivism rates for parole is lower than for max out.* This is the case whether the final variable controlled is methodological or sociodemographic. For the arrest definition, the differences *in favor of* parole range from a low of 0.2 (item 22) to a high of 43.6 (item 24). For conviction, the differences in favor of parole range from 0.2 (item 20) to 16.9 (item 15). For new prison sentence, the differences in favor of parole range from 0.2 (item 10) to 11.3 (item 43).

In 6 of the 80 comparisons, the mean of the rates for max out is equal to or lower than the mean for parole. These six cases are unsystematically distributed throughout the table. In three instances the final control variable is methodological; in three it is sociodemographic. Two cases fall under the arrest definition; two under conviction; and two under return to prison. These six exceptions do not suggest to us any particular set of conditions which might be further explored to discover subgroups of offenders, or contexts, for which max out would be a superior policy for criminal justice.

Data contained in our Preliminary Report provided a starting point for this analysis. This initial data (based on 3,005 rates coded at that time) indicated that the mean of the rates for parole (25.4) was somewhat lower than the mean of the rates for max out (31.6). This six percentage point difference resulted from a comparison which did not further control for the definition of recidivism, for adult vs. juvenile, or for any of the other variables utilized in Table 30.1. Increasing the total number of rates, and simultaneously controlling for four additional variables has led to the discovery of larger mean differences between parole and max out.[8]

Summary

Those who propose the abolition of parole supervision in this country often speak of "fairness to the offender." It is difficult to detect in Table 30.1 evidence of such fairness. On the contrary. The evidence seems to indicate that the abolition of parole supervision would result in substantial increases in arrest, conviction, and return to prison. Those who wish to eliminate the unfairness of parole board decision-making might well concentrate on finding a specific remedy for this problem, a remedy which would not increase the very "unfairness" they deplore.

At the very least, the data in Table 30.1 should give pause to those policymakers and legislators who have been operating on the unexamined assumption that parole supervision *makes no difference*. In face of the evidence in Table 30.1 such an assumption is unlikely.

Study Questions

1. Martinson and Wilks discuss some of the major criticisms leveled against parole in the 1970s. What were they and are these criticisms still valid today?

2. Discuss the methods, data collection, and samples used by the authors for their study of parole.

3. What are the conclusions reached by the authors concerning parole?

Notes

1. See, J. Wilks and R. Martinson, "Is the Treatment of Criminal Offenders Really Necessary?" *Federal Probation*, March 1976, pp. 3–9.

2. See, for example, D. Lipton, R. Martinson, and J. Wilks, *The Effectiveness of Correctional Treatment*. New York: Praeger Publishers, 1975, sections on Probation and Parole.

3. D.T. Stanley, *Prisoners Among Us: The Problem of Parole*, The Brookings Institution, Washington, D.C., 1976, pp. 181–2.

4. See, R. Martinson and J. Wilks, *Knowledge in Criminal Justice Planning, A Preliminary Report*, October 15, 1976, p. 58 (processed).

5. The other four categories were: 100% minus "success" rate; short of arrest (i.e., AWOL, absconding, suspension, and similar); return to prison for technical violation; and return to prison for technical plus new conviction. Three of these categories were eliminated because they cannot happen to max out groups. The fourth—100% minus "Success" rate—was eliminated because of possible problems in interpreting the meaning of the measure.

6. The proportion in which any attribute was present in a batch was coded as follows: 1—0–24.9%; 2—25–49.9%; 3—50–74.9%; and 4—75–100%.

7. Multiplying the total number of coding categories (97) by the three definitions gives a total of 291 possible comparisons if sufficient data had been present. Eliminating 39 cases where data were reported as "unknown," 38 cases in which there were less than two rates in a category of either parole or max out, and 134 cases in which no data were reported, leaves the 80 comparisons reported in Table 30.1.

8. This method is an application of standard research procedures. See, for example, P.P. Lazersfeld, "Interpretation of Statistical Relations as a Research Operation," in: *The Language of Social Research* (P.F. Lazersfeld and M. Rosenberg, eds.), Glencoe, Ill.: The Free Press, 1955.

Editors' note: An extensive bibliography of the studies from which the data in Table 30.1 were taken is available from the authors at The Center for Knowledge in Criminal Justice Planning, 38 East 85th Street, New York, NY 10028. ✦

31
Residential Community Correctional Programs

Edward J. Latessa

Lawrence F. Travis III

Many people believe that providing offenders released from prison with support and assistance can mean the difference between them remaining out of or returning to prison. No correctional program offers more reintegrative opportunities than community residential programs, often called halfway houses. Edward J. Latessa and Lawrence F. Travis III trace the historical development of halfway houses and review the models under which they operate. Some halfway houses provide minimal services and support—a warm meal and a place to sleep—while others offer a wide range of services and treatment. Whether their program is considered "three hots and a cot" or a full service facility, halfway houses play an important role in the supervision and rehabilitative efforts of the correctional system. As the authors point out, numerous measures of effectiveness can be applied to halfway houses. Cost savings, social adjustment, the humane treatment of offenders, and recidivism are among the more important measures that researchers can examine.

Excerpts from "Residential Community Correctional Programs" by Edward J. Latessa and Lawrence F. Travis III, in James M. Bryne, Arthur L. Lurigio, and Joan Petersilia (eds.), *Smart Sentencing: The Emergence of Intermediate Sanctions.* Copyright © 1992 by Sage Publications, Inc. Reprinted by permission.

Community residential programs for criminal offenders have a long history in the United States (Allen, Carlson, Parks, & Seiter, 1978; Latessa & Travis, 1986). In the past, the typical use of community residential facilities was as "halfway houses." These programs were designed as transitional placements for offenders to ease the movement from incarceration to life in the free society. In time, some programs developed as alternatives to incarceration, so that the "halfway" aspect could mean either halfway *into* prison, or halfway *out of* prison.

Between 1950 and 1980, the number and use of such halfway houses grew considerably. In the last 10 to 15 years, residential placements for criminal offenders have also undergone considerable role expansion. Increasingly, the population served by these programs has come to include large numbers of probationers and persons awaiting trial. In many jurisdictions, placement in a residential facility is available as a direct sentencing option to the judge. These changes in the role and population of residential programs supported the replacement of the traditional halfway house notion with the broader title of *community corrections residential facility.*

This chapter reviews the history, purposes, and structure of residential community corrections programs. It includes an assessment of the types and effectiveness of programs, and concludes by describing emerging trends and future directions for residential programs.

What's in a Name?

Until recently, community corrections residential programs were subsumed under the general title of halfway houses. This label, however, has proven to be inadequate as a description of the variety of residential programs used with correctional populations today. The International Halfway House Association, founded in 1964, has itself changed its name to reflect more accurately the variety of purposes and persons served by residential programs.

The contemporary name given to such programs, community corrections residential facilities, is a broader title that reflects the role expansion of the traditional halfway house that has occurred in recent years. Rush (1991) defines a residential facility as "a correctional facility from which residents are regularly permitted to depart, unaccompanied by any official, for the purposes of using community resources, such as schools or treatment programs, and seeking or holding employment" (p. 265).

This definition is free of any reference to incarceration that was implicit in the term *halfway*. Further, it does not necessitate the direct provision of any services to residents within the facility, and clearly identifies the program with a correctional mission. Thus, unlike the traditional halfway house, the community residential facility serves a more diverse population and plays a broader correctional role. Traditional halfway houses are included within the category of residential facilities, but their ranks are swelled by newer adaptations, such as community corrections centers, prerelease centers, and restitution centers.

The Development of Community Residential Programs

Halfway houses as transitional programming for inmates released from prisons are not a new phenomenon (Latessa & Allen, 1982). Their origins can be traced at least as far back as the early nineteenth century in England and Ireland (Keller & Alper, 1970). In the United States, the exact origin of halfway houses is not clear, but one such program was started in New York City in 1845, the Isaac T. Hooper Home (Rush, 1991, p. 143). A halfway house for released female prisoners was opened in Boston, Massachusetts, in 1864. For nearly 100 years, halfway houses tended to be operated by charitable organizations for the benefit of released inmates. Halfway house programs did not begin a period of expansion until after World War II (Beha, 1977).

In the 1950s, specialized residential programs desired to deal with substance-abusing offenders were added to the traditional halfway house programs. Residential programs for alcoholic or drug addicted offenders opened and spread throughout this period, and into the 1960s. For typical criminal offenders, however, halfway house placements were rare.

In the middle 1960s, the President's Commission on Crime and Administration of Justice (1967) signaled a change in correctional philosophy toward the goal of reintegration. Reintegration placed increased emphasis on the role of the community in corrections, and on the value of keeping offenders in the community, rather than in prison, whenever possible. This ideology of community corrections supported the notion of residential placements for convicted offenders, and halfway houses began a period of unprecedented expansion, supported by federal funds from programs as diverse as the Office of Economic Opportunity and the Law Enforcement Assistance Administration (Hicks, 1987, p. 6).

During the early 1980s, however, support for halfway house programs dwindled. The effects of recession, demise of LEAA, and a general hardening of public attitudes toward offenders worked against the continued growth and development of halfway houses or other residential programs. This period of retrenchment was, however, shortlived. The same forces that temporarily halted the growth of residential programs soon added their weight to continued development.

In the last decade, community corrections residential facilities have grown in response to the crisis of prison crowding. Allen et al. (1978, p. 1) attribute an increased use of halfway houses with parole populations to three factors: the philosophy of reintegration, success with such programs in the mental health field, and the lower costs of halfway houses compared with prisons. To these was added the need to respond to prison crowding in the 1980s.

The lack of prison capacity, coupled with an increasing emphasis on risk control and retributive sentencing, spurred a search for intermediate sanctions. Over the last several years, a number of observers have called for the creation of penal sanctions that range in severity between incarceration and traditional probation supervision (McCarthy, 1987). They suggest that such sanctions will allow the correctional system to meet the punitive and risk-control goals of sentencing, especially with those persons diverted from prison or jail because of crowding.

The list of intermediate sanctions includes house arrest, electronic monitoring, and intensive supervision (*Federal Probation*, 1986; Petersilia, 1987). DuPont (1985) explicitly identifies a role for community residential facilities as an adjunct to traditional probation or parole supervision. Such facilities would serve to increase both the punitive severity and public safety of traditional community-based corrections.

In an era when both correctional costs and populations grow yearly, planners, practitioners, and policymakers have supported a wide range of correctional alternatives. As Guynes (1988) has observed, one effect of prison and jail crowding has been a dramatic increase in probation and parole populations. Further, Petersilia (1985), among others, suggests that these larger supervision populations are increasingly made up of more serious and more dangerous offenders. Community residential facilities have come to be seen as an important option for the management and control of these growing and more dangerous offender populations.

A result has been the redefinition of the role of community residential facilities. The traditional role of transitional placement for offenders, or as a response to special needs populations such as substance abusers, has been expanded. Residential placement has emerged as a correctional alternative in its own right.

Hicks (1987) observes that the use of residential placement as an alternative to incarceration or traditional community supervision has engendered some changes in operations and philosophy. She terms this a movement "toward supervision rather than treatment." Thus in many cases residential facilities provide little more than a place to live and access to community resources. The emphasis in these programs is upon custody and control rather than counseling and correction.

Prison on the Cheap?

Unable or unwilling to underwrite the costs of prison for large numbers of convicted offenders, several jurisdictions have supported community residential facilities. As Hicks (1987) notes, "Budget weary legislators often view halfway houses as an inexpensive lunch" (p. 7). Residential programs, they hope, will provide public safety as well as incarceration, but at a fraction of the cost. As substitute prisons, however, the atmosphere of these programs has changed. Traditional halfway houses, where staff and programs are designed for the provision of direct services to residents, still continue. These programs provide counseling, substance abuse treatment, educational and vocational training, and a variety of social services. In other, newer programs, especially those operated by corrections departments, the atmosphere is closer to that of a minimum-security prison than a rehabilitative community.

This addition of residential programs as "bed space" to the traditional use of such programs as treatment modalities has led to a schizophrenic field of practice. In most facilities, rules and regulations are stricter, and enforcement more rigid, than in earlier days. Additionally, a number of "large" facilities, housing hundreds of residents, have been added. Typically "prerelease" centers, these larger facilities house prison inmates eligible for parole, or in the final months before their release.

The recent growth in community residential facilities has complicated the picture. These facilities serve a variety of clients, ranging from as-yet-unconvicted offenders diverted from court through prison inmates. Facility sizes range from those housing fewer than 10 residents to those with populations in the hundreds. Treatment services range from programs providing full services to those in which few, if any, direct services are available to residents. The one constant is that residents live in the facilities for a period of time, and are generally free to leave the facilities during approved hours, for approved purposes, without escort.

Residential Facilities in Contemporary Corrections

As the foregoing discussion illustrates, it is not possible to describe the average residential facility. Diversity in population, program, size, and structure is the rule. It is, unfortunately, also not possible to know for certain how many such facilities are in operation today, or the number of offenders served by them. As Hicks (1987) observes, "There are no national figures, only educated guesses" (p. 2).

The International Halfway House Association published a directory of residential facilities in 1981 that lists almost 2,300 facilities with a combined capacity of nearly 100,000 beds (Gatz & Murray, 1981). Not all of these facilities, however, serve correctional populations. Five years earlier, Seiter et al. (1977) estimated that approximately 400 facilities existed that served correctional populations, with a capacity of about 10,000 beds. In 1978, a survey of parole authorities revealed the existence of nearly 800 facilities, with almost 15,000 inmates being paroled to halfway house placements. More recently, the National Institute of Corrections supported a survey that identified 641 community corrections residential facilities. The

identification was based on the characteristics of residents as under correctional supervision, among other criteria.

While the methods and definitions employed in these different studies varied considerably, the results are fairly consistent. Given these admittedly incomplete data, it is possible to estimate that there are in excess of 600 residential facilities in operation today. Further, it appears that the number of facilities has grown as much as 50% in the last decade.

It is not possible to estimate the number of offenders served by these facilities with any certainty. Length of residence is typically short, on the order of three to four months, meaning that a facility with 50 beds may serve 150 to 200 individuals annually. Based on the probability that a halfway house would serve three to four times as many residents as it has beds in each year, Allen and his colleagues (1978, p. 2) estimate that roughly 10,000 beds equals 30,000 to 40,000 residents each year. Further, many of those in residential facilities are included in the totals of other correctional population counts, such as the number of prison inmates or persons under parole supervision. Still, it is clear that the total number of residents in these facilities each year is substantial.[1]

Types of Facilities

The large number of facilities and their differing traditions, populations, and services render it difficult to assess the impact of residential programs. Beyond noting that these programs have played an important role in the provision of services to convicted offenders, and that their importance as alternatives to imprisonment has increased, the variety of facilities means that questions of effectiveness must be narrowly drawn.

Allen and his colleagues (1978), for example, have developed a four-class typology of halfway houses, using two dimensions to yield four possible types of facilities. Halfway houses can be either public or private, and they can be either interventive or supportive in program. Public or private, of course, relates to the organization of the facility as either a government entity or not. Program types are based on whether the services of the facility are designed to intervene in problem areas of the residents' lives, such as substance abuse counseling, or to provide a supportive environment in which residents use community resources.

This simple typology indicates that different facilities must be assessed differently. For example, a residential facility designed to provide supportive services would not be well evaluated on the basis of direct service provision. Similarly, a program aimed at intervention would not be well understood solely in terms of resident length of stay. Rather, the type of program offered in a facility must form an important base of any assessment effort.

What Do We Know About the Effectiveness Question?

Despite the long tradition of residential community correctional programs, the research literature concerned with them is sparse and inconclusive. There appear to be a number of reasons that residential programs have been largely ignored by correctional researchers.

First, residential facilities represent a relatively small part of the correctional system, and, as mentioned above, it is often difficult to distinguish between residential facilities that serve only correctional clientele and those that serve a broader constituency. Second, many programs are operated by private entities, and are either unwilling or unable to facilitate research. Third, generalization is a problem, because these programs are often markedly different from locale to locale, in terms of both the treatment offered and the types of clients they accept. Finally, it is often difficult to develop an adequate comparison group and to conduct a follow-up of residents. Despite these obstacles, there have

been some notable attempts to evaluate the effectiveness of residential programs.

As correctional interventions, residential community correctional programs seem to meet two objectives: a reduction in postprogram criminality (recidivism) and an increase in prosocial behavior on the part of clients. Outcome assessments of residential programs then should assess both of these dimensions of program effectiveness. The literature indicates that recidivism has generally been the focus of most outcome evaluations, with varying definitions of recidivism.

In the first systematic evaluation of correctional halfway houses, Allen et al. (1976) reviewed 35 studies of halfway houses. Of these, 17 used quasi-experimental designs in comparing postprogram recidivism rates, 2 utilized true experimental designs, and 16 relied on nonexperimental designs. Based on the experimental and quasi-experimental studies, the researchers concluded that the evidence was about equally divided between lower recidivism rates for halfway house residents and no difference in recidivism rates when compared with a control group. They also found no evidence that halfway houses improved socially acceptable adjustment behaviors of residents, but that they were cheaper to operate than prisons, while more expensive than parole and probation.

Focusing on parolees, Latessa and Allen (1982) reported on evaluations of halfway house programs providing an overview of evaluations of programs throughout the United States. They rated 44 such studies as being characterized by sufficient methodological rigor to allow assessment of postrelease outcome. Of these, only 2 studies were found to have employed true experimental designs, involving random assignment to either an "experimental" (halfway house placement) or "control" (incarceration or other placement) group. Neither study indicated that halfway house clients performed significantly better than did subjects in the control conditions. An additional 23 studies employed quasi-experimental designs. There were also 19 nonexperimental studies that reported outcome data.

In general, the results were mixed, with some reports showing significantly lower recidivism among halfway house residents, some showing no significant differences, and others showing that the halfway house clients did significantly worse on release than did their counterparts in the control groups. In their conclusions, Latessa and Allen suggest that the literature indicates that halfway house programs are at least as effective as parole, especially given that halfway house clients are generally characterized by having higher risk and greater needs than those in a traditional parole population. Similarly, Seiter et al. (1977) conclude that prior evaluations "suggest that halfway house programs may more effectively reintegrate prisoners returning to the community than direct release to parole" (p. 160).

In an attempt to compare "recidivism" rates, some research has indicated that certain social, demographic, and criminal history characteristics must be controlled. Those with less education, who are younger, and who have less successful employment records, longer prior criminal records, and generally less stability in their social and personal lives are more likely to recidivate (Beha, 1977; Beran, McGruder, & Allen, 1974; Donnelly & Forschner, 1984; Dowell, Klein, & Kirchmar, 1985; Moczydlowski, 1980; Moran, Kass, & Muntz, 1977; Seiter, Petersilia, & Allen, 1974).

In a recent study, Donnelly and Forschner (1987) used discriminant function analysis and found that a similar set of factors serve to distinguish between residents who completed or failed to complete a halfway house program. Thus it appears that in order to determine if a residential program has been effective it is necessary to ensure that any differences between the treatment and control groups on these dimensions are known.

In addition to recidivism, however defined, it is important that improved prosocial behavior or social adjustment be measured. One of the earliest examples of this type of measurement was done by Seiter et al. (1974), using a scale of social adjustment. This scale allowed a cumulative score of the subject's involvement in employment, education, residence, interpersonal relations, and the like to be computed. The scale yielded a continuous score for each subject, thereby allowing comparisons. Based on their measure of recidivism *and* social adjustment, Seiter et al. conclude in their study of Ohio halfway houses that "halfway houses are more effective at assisting ex-offenders in their reintegration to the community than traditional modes of assistance."

Several other studies of halfway house program effectiveness have also attempted to address this dimension of outcome. Beck (1979) evaluated federal community treatment centers (CTCs) with measures of both recidivism and social adjustment, measured as days employed and money earned. He concluded that CTC clients fared better in social adjustment than did control subjects. Toborg, Center, Milkman, and Davis (1978) report similar effects in social adjustment in their review and assessment of more than 250 community assistance programs.

Finally, as Donnelly and Forschner (1987) have observed, "The success or failure of a halfway house is often defined in terms of the number or percent of the residents who complete the halfway house program" (p. 5). While they note that completion of the program may not satisfy those who define the "real goal" of correctional intervention as reduced recidivism, they argue that program completion is both an important organizational goal of the halfway house agency and inversely related to recidivism. These characteristics of program completion, they suggest, make it an appropriate criterion of outcome.

In a recent study of halfway house programs that examined both recidivism and social adjustment, we studied 132 probationers who resided in three halfway houses during 1983 (Latessa & Travis, 1986). A comparison group was composed of a sample of 140 felony probationers selected from the county probation department. We conducted a three-year follow-up through the use of official criminal records.

The results of this study illustrate the similarities and differences between the two groups. While there were a number of similarities between the halfway house and probation samples with regard to demographics, criminal history, and special problems/ needs, some notable differences existed. Those in the halfway house sample were less educated and less likely to have been married. Those in the probation group had more prior convictions, and the halfway house subjects exhibited more prior involvement in drugs, alcohol treatment, and psychiatric problems. These data support other studies that have found that residential populations are in need of more intensive treatment than regular probationers. We also found that the halfway house group received significantly more services and treatment than the probation sample. This was true in almost every area examined.

Finally, the factors examined for the follow-up showed no significant differences between the two groups in terms of new crime convictions or social adjustment. Simply stated, the halfway house group did no better and no worse than the probation sample with regard to convictions or positive adjustment.

In addition to the outcome analysis, we conducted discriminant analyses of factors associated with outcome (both recidivism and program completion). The results revealed few surprises. Prior criminal history, measured by the number of prior adult convictions, filing of technical probation violations, and the presence of a drug problem predicted recidivism in expected ways. Similarly, the provision of employment training was associated with fewer new convictions. In regard to program completion, higher scores on a social adjustment scale, enrollment in an educational program, and the absence of drug or psychiatric problems were associated with success. The provision of

group counseling, however, was associated with failure.

While further research is required if we are to understand the relationships fully, the data from our study and from the studies of other researchers tend to support the following observations:

1. Residential community correctional groups display greater service needs than do regular probation or parole groups.

2. Many of these needs, such as psychiatric and drug/alcohol abuse history, are related both to positive adjustment and to new criminal convictions.

3. Offenders in residential facilities are more likely to receive a variety of treatment and counseling services.

4. When these observations are combined with the finding of no significant differences in recidivism and social adjustment outcomes between groups, the possibility of a treatment effect is raised. That is, from these studies it would appear that halfway house residents receive services commensurate with their needs.

5. Based on group characteristics at intake, an a priori assumption that the halfway house group would demonstrate a higher rate of recidivism and lower social adjustment seems reasonable. That, generally, no such differences in outcome have been observed and that residential groups have received considerably more treatment interventions may indicate that program participation is beneficial for this group.

The obvious implication of these conclusions is that placement into a residential program should be considered a dispositional option for convicted offenders. A general assessment of risk alone, however, may not adequately identify those most likely to benefit from such placement. That is, rather than viewing residential placement as a punitive (more intrusive) or incapacitative (more controlling) sanction for convicted offenders, placement in a program should be guided by an assessment of an offender's needs. It is possible that residential intervention can reduce the likelihood of negative outcome through meeting the treatment needs of clients.

There is also little evidence that successful completion of a residential program is a prerequisite of successful completion of probation or parole. Indeed, this suggests that residential programs, perhaps by virtue of their more rigorous rules and expectations of program participation, may not be appropriate for some offenders.

Most of the research has revealed that residential placement has been used with those offenders presenting higher needs and a priori risk, in general, than the regular probation/parole population. Even among this group, however, such placement may not always be necessary. Future research should address case classification issues. Such efforts could help identify the types of features within this high-risk/high-needs group who are most likely to benefit from placement in a particular residential program.

As is clear from the evaluation studies summarized above, most of the research on residential facilities has focused on halfway houses or similar placements with an interventive design. As yet, little is known about the use and effects of residential placements in facilities designed to provide closer surveillance of offenders, without interventive treatments. For these programs, the primary criteria of evaluation would appear to be protection of public safety and cost considerations. Extrapolating from what we have learned about interventive programs, it is reasonable to expect that residents in such facilities will pose no greater danger to the community than those under probation or parole supervision. They are no more likely to "recidivate" than those who are imprisoned.

And, when compared with imprisonment, residential facility costs should be lower.

The Future of Residential Facilities

What does the future hold for residential community correctional facilities? First, in many ways they will remain an enigma to correctional researchers. Residential facilities that evolved from traditional halfway houses are now becoming multiservice agencies. The evolution will continue, but, unfortunately, so will our lack of understanding of these facilities, their effectiveness, and their role in the correctional process.

Second, residential community correctional facilities will continue to grow and develop new programs. In large part this will be a response to the crowding of local and state correctional institutions. Many traditional residential facilities will seize the opportunity and will diversify and offer a wider range of programs and services, such as victim assistance programs, family and drug counseling, drunk driver programs, work release centers, and house arrest, electronic monitoring, and day programs for offenders.

Finally, while there has been an increase in public sector operation of residential facilities, particularly prerelease and reintegration centers, it will be the private sector that will continue to play a dominant role in the development and operation of residential correctional programs. A number of arguments support private provision of community-based correctional services. Principal among these is cost-effectiveness. Proponents argue that the private sector will contain costs and thus, for the same dollar amount, provide more, or at least better, service. Government agencies, it is suggested, cannot achieve the same level of cost-efficient operation as can private, especially for-profit, companies.

As Clear, Hairs, and Record (1982) succinctly summarize: "Due to 'domestication' (characterized by a lack of competition and critical self-assessment), corrections officials often are inadvertently rewarded by taking a budget-administration approach rather than a cost-management stance." The attraction of private involvement in community corrections is the promise of a free market, or, as Greenwood (1981) put it, "They would be free to innovate, to use the latest technology and management techniques as in any profit service industry."

Another, perhaps more compelling, reason for the continued development of private community residential programs is that they can offer what Gendreau and Ross (1987) call "therapeutic integrity." That is, because of their accountability to the contractor and the possibility of competition, privately operated programs may provide more intensive and higher-quality service provision than might government agencies. Indeed, many who have studied public community correctional agencies have lamented the increasingly bureaucratic role of the change agent (Clear & Latessa, 1989), noting the large number of staff who are simply "putting in time" for retirement or who are encumbered by paperwork and red tape. It often seems that organizational goals outweigh concerns about effective treatment and service delivery.

Of course, this is really an issue of accountability that involves some nonmonetary value questions. This is one of the fundamental differences between the private and public sectors. Private enterprise often measures outcome in terms of profit, while the public sector measures it in terms of social value and benefits. While there is no empirical evidence that the private sector is "better" at providing services, reducing recidivism, and so forth, there is a growing sentiment that it ought to at least be given a chance. Privately run facilities may also be in a better position to lobby for more services, staff, and programs. One need only look at the typical adult probation department, where caseloads range from 150 to 300, to see how ineffective they have been in garnering additional resources. Private providers may, because of contractual agreements, be better able to advocate for additional support.

Of more importance than the simple dichotomy between public and private operation is the future evolution of the mission of community corrections residential facilities. The traditional halfway house had a charitable, quasi-volunteer, and service-oriented mission (Wilson, 1985). The contemporary multiservice community agency or department of corrections-operated facility is more formal, legalistic, and control oriented. As correctional agencies contract with both new private sector vendors and older, charitable programs, the emphasis in residential facilities may change from treatment to custody. Further, as the importance of correctional contracts for the support and spread of residential facilities grows, the "community" nature of these programs may increasingly be replaced by a more formal, governmental administrative style. That is, the forces that currently support the development of programs may ultimately change them in fundamental ways.

The traditional halfway house operated by a civic-minded reform group for the purpose of assisting offenders may be replaced by for-profit or nonprofit contractors working for the government. Thus, rather than a focus on the needs and interests of the community and the offender, the emphasis may be placed on the needs of the correctional system for bed space.

Of course, it is also entirely likely that the current confusion in residential programs will continue. There will continue to be traditional halfway houses focused on the needs of residents, with deep roots in the community. There will also be a variety of custody and crowding-control facilities designed to provide minimal direct services. Only time will tell what the future of community corrections residential facilities will be. The one thing that is clear is that some form of such facilities will exist in the future.

Study Questions

1. Briefly sketch the history of halfway houses. Why did halfway houses experience a setback in the 1980s?

2. What are the four class types of halfway houses?

3. What is the difference between a supportive and an interventive halfway house?

4. What are some of the dimensions that can be used to gauge effectiveness of halfway houses? What does the research tell us about how halfway houses perform on each of these performance measures?

5. According to the authors, what does the future hold for halfway houses?

Note

1. Estimating the size of the community corrections residential facility population is hazardous at best. In her 1987 article, however, Hicks reported interviews with representatives of California, Texas, and the Federal Bureau of Prisons. These officials estimated that by 1988, the combined total of offenders served in residential facilities for these three jurisdictions would exceed 7,000. Given that these numbers do not include probationers or misdemeanants; in all three jurisdictions, a conservative, extrapolation yields an estimated 70,000 offenders in residential facilities during 1988. This represents about 10% of the prison population for that year.

References

Allen, H. E., Carlson, E. W., Parks, E. C., & Seiter, R. P. (1978). *Program models: Halfway houses.* Washington, DC: U.S. Department of Justice.

Allen, H. E., Seiter, R. P., Carlson, E. W., Bowman, H. H., Grandfield, J. J., & Beran, N. J. (1976). *National Evaluation Program Phase I: Residential inmate aftercare, state of the art summary.* Columbus: Ohio State University, Program for the Study of Crime and Delinquency.

Beck, J. L. (1979). An evaluation of federal community treatment centers. *Federal Probation,* 43(3), 36–40.

Beha, J. A. (1977). Testing the functions and effects of the parole halfway house: One case study. *Journal of Criminal Law and Criminology,* 67, 335–350.

Beran, N. J., McGruder, J. L., & Allen, H. E. (1974). *The community reintegration centers of Ohio: A second year evaluation.* Columbus: Ohio State University, Program for the Study of Crime and Delinquency.

Clear, T., Hairs, P. M., & Record, A. L. (1982). Managing the cost of corrections. *Prison Journal,* 53, 1–63.

Clear, T., & Latessa, E. J. (1989, March). *Intensive surveillance versus treatment.* Paper presented at the annual meeting of the Academy of Criminal Justice Sciences, Washington, DC.

Donnelly, P. G., & Forschner, B. (1984). Client success or failure in a halfway house. *Federal Probation,* 48(3), 38–44.

Donnelly, P. G., & Forschner, B. (1987). Predictors of success in a co-correctional halfway house: A discriminant analysis. *Journal of Crime and Justice,* 10(2), 1–22.

Dowell, D., Klein, C., & Kirchmar, C. (1985). Evaluation of a halfway house for women. *Journal of Criminal Justice,* 13, 217–226.

DuPont, P. (1985). *Expanding sentencing options: A governor's perspective.* Washington, DC. National Institute of Justice.

Federal Probation. (1986). Intensive probation supervision [Special issue]. Vol. 50, No. 2.

Gatz, N., & Murray, C. (1981). An administrative overview of halfway houses. *Corrections Today,* 43, 52–54.

Gendreau, P., & Ross, R. R. (1987). Revivification of rehabilitation: Evidence from the 1980's. *Justice Quarterly,* 4, 349–407.

Greenwood, P. (1981). *Private enterprise prisons? Why not?* Santa Monica, CA: RAND Corporation.

Guynes, R. (1988). *Difficult clients, large caseloads plague probation, parole agencies.* Washington, DC: U.S. Department of Justice.

Hicks, N. (1987). A new relationship: Halfway houses and corrections. *Corrections Compendium,* 12(4), 1, 5–7.

Keller, O. J., & Alper, G. (1970). *Halfway houses: Community centered correction and treatment.* Lexington, MA: D. C. Heath.

Latessa, E. J., & Allen, H. E. (1982). Halfway houses and parole: A national assessment. *Journal of Criminal Justice,* 10(2), 153–163.

Latessa, E. J., & Travis, L. F. (1986, October). *Halfway houses versus probation: A three year follow-up of offenders.* Paper presented at the annual meeting of the Midwestern Criminal Justice Association, Chicago.

McCarthy, B. R. (Ed.). (1987). *Intermediate punishments: Intensive supervision, home confinement, and electronic surveillance.* Monsey, NY: Criminal Justice Press.

Moczydlowski, K. (1980). Predictors of success in a correctional halfway house for youthful and adult offenders. *Corrective and Social Psychiatry and Journal of Behavior Technology, Methods and Therapy,* 26, 59–72.

Moran, E., Kass, W., & Muntz, D. (1977). In-program evaluation of a community correctional agency for high risk offenders. *Corrective and Social Psychiatry and Journal of Behavior Technology, Methods and Therapy,* 23, 48–52.

Petersilia, J. (1985). *Probation and felon offenders.* Washington, DC: U.S. Department of Justice.

Petersilia, J. (1987). *Expanding options for criminal sentencing* (Publication No. R-3544-EMC). Santa Monica, CA: RAND Corporation.

President's Commission on Law Enforcement and Administration of Justice. (1967). *Taskforce report: Corrections.* Washington, DC: Government Printing Office.

Rush, G. E. (1991). *The dictionary of criminal justice* (3rd ed.). Guilford, CT: Dushkin.

Seiter, R. P., Carlson, E. W., Bowman, H., Grandfield, H., Beran, N. J., & Allen, H. E. (1977). *Halfway houses.* Washington, DC: Government Printing Office.

Seiter, R. P., Petersilia, J. R., & Allen, H. E. (1974). *Evaluation of adult halfway houses in Ohio* (Vol. 2). Columbus: Ohio State University, Program for the Study of Crime and Delinquency.

Toborg, M. A., Center, L. J., Milkman, R. H., & Davis, D. W. (1978). *The transition from prison to employment: An assessment of community-based assistance programs.* (National Evaluation Program Phase I report). Washington, DC: U.S. Department of Justice.

Wilson, G. P. (1985). Halfway house programs for offenders. In L. F. Travis (Ed.), *Probation, parole, and community corrections* (pp. 151–164). Prospect Heights, IL: Waveland. ✦

32
Work Release
Recidivism and Corrections Costs in Washington State

Susan Turner

Joan Petersilia

Allowing inmates to work in the community has a long tradition in the United States. The benefits of work release are many: maintaining ties to the community, providing financial support, reducing the costs of incarceration, and developing work skills and a work ethic, for example. Despite obvious advantages, many states have cut back or reduced significantly the number of inmates under work release status. The reasons for this shift away from work release are varied, but generally they center on concern for public safety. In this article, Susan Turner and Joan Petersilia examine the state of Washington's work release program. Findings from their research show who was successful on work release and some of the benefits derived from the program.

Each year U.S. prisons release more than 400,000 criminal offenders to their communities. Most of those released will not remain crime free, and national statistics show that within 3 years of release, 40 percent will be returned to prison or jail. Experts debate the reasons for such high recidivism rates, but

Excerpts from "Work Release: Recidivism and Corrections Costs in Washington State" by Susan Turner and Joan Petersilia, *National Institute of Justice, Research in Brief.* Copyright © December 1996. Reprinted with permission.

all agree that the lack of adequate job training and work opportunities is a critical factor. Offenders often have few marketable skills and training and, as a result, have a difficult time securing legitimate employment. With no legitimate income, many resort to crime.

Since the early 1920s, corrections officials have attempted to remedy the problem through prison work release programs. Work release programs permit selected prisoners nearing the end of their terms to work in the community, returning to prison facilities or community residential facilities in nonworking hours. Such programs are designed to prepare inmates to return to the community in a relatively controlled environment, while they are learning how to work productively. Work release also allows inmates to earn income, reimburse the State for part of their confinement costs, build up savings for their eventual full release, and acquire more positive living habits.

During the 1970s prison work release programs expanded considerably, but they have declined in recent years. Although 43 States have existing statutes authorizing work release, only about one third of U.S. prisons report operating such programs, and fewer than 3 percent of U.S. inmates participate in them.

Despite public disenchantment with work release (see "Reasons for the Decline of Work Release"), the State of Washington has maintained its commitment to the program since initiating it in 1967. The Washington work release program permits selected inmates to serve the final 4 to 6 months of their prison sentences in privately run, community residential facilities, where they are required to be employed, submit to drug testing, and abide by curfews and numerous program rules.

It is not that Washington has been immune to the challenges faced by other states. Washington's prison population has jumped 71 percent since 1980, while the State's general population has grown just 13 percent. Citizens are frustrated with high levels of crime and violence, as is evidenced by their legislature's enactment of the nation's first "three strikes" law—in part a reaction to a felon's committing a rape while on parole. Observers have wondered how the program can continue to operate successfully when the emphasis is on punitive policies and politics.

This Research in Brief presents findings from two studies of Washington's work release program, conducted under a National Institute of Justice (NIJ) grant between 1991 and 1994. In sponsoring the studies, NIJ hoped that results might add to the growing body of research on intermediate sanctions and provide guidance to other states that were looking for effective and less costly corrections programs.

Study 1 analyzed a cohort of all males released ($n=2,452$) from Washington prisons in 1990. Data pertaining to their criminal and social background and their participation and performance in work release were analyzed to describe how work release was implemented in Washington and how well inmates performed in the program. Estimated costs of work release versus prison were based on analysis not only of the cost of the program but on costs incurred if the work release participant was returned to prison for violation of program rules or for committing a crime.

Study 2 evaluated the impact of work release on recidivism and on corrections costs by comparing a sample of inmates who participated in work release with a comparable sample of inmates who completed their sentences in prison. Investigators collected information about program implementation and recidivism at 6 and 12 months following the inmates' assignment to the study.

Overall, the studies found that the program achieved its most important goal: preparing inmates for final release and facilitating their adjustment to the community. The program did not cost the state more than it would have if the releasees had remained in prison. The public safety risks were nearly nonexistent because almost no work releasee committed new crimes, and when they committed rule violations they were quickly returned to prison.

While in the program these inmates maintained employment, paid room and board, reconnected with their communities, and most remained drug free. Less than 5 percent committed new crimes while on work release, and 99 percent of those crimes were less serious property offenses, such as forgery and petty theft. Moreover, offenders who participated in work release were somewhat less likely to be rearrested, but the results were not statistically significant. One could reasonably conclude from these results that work release in Washington is a program "that works."

Reasons for the Decline of Work Release

One reason work release programming has declined pertains to funding. Many work release programs begun in the 1970s were paid for by the Federal Government using funds from the Law Enforcement Assistance Administration. When Federal funding ceased, many programs were discontinued. And as the rehabilitation ideal—of which work release was very much a part—started to fade, the public embraced imprisonment as the only sure way to forestall crime. Programs that focused on rehabilitation, job training, and transitional services seemed hopelessly out of touch with the public.

Moreover, a few highly publicized and sensational failures convinced the public that early-release programs, such as work release or furlough, threatened public safety. The most extreme example was Willie Horton, the Massachusetts inmate who absconded and committed serious and violent crimes while on furlough. (Horton was actually on work furlough, not work release, but the two terms are often used interchangeably.) The case became an issue in the 1988 presidential campaign, and the negative publicity helped further erode community support for work release programs. ✦

How Washington's Work Release Program Operates

Washington's work release program, created by legislative action in 1967, gave the state permission to allow inmates to serve sentences in the community for the purpose of work training and experience. In 1970 the first community-based program was established in Seattle under a contract agreement with Pioneer Cooperative, a private, nonprofit corporation (now Pioneer Human Services—see "A Partnership With Private Industry").

Staffing and costs. The work release program is the responsibility of the Division of Community Corrections within the State Department of Corrections (DOC). Division staff establish guidelines governing the selection of offenders for placement in work release, work with contractors to provide food and shelter in a halfway house arrangement, and supervise the correctional officers who are assigned to work release facilities.

The actual operation of the work release facilities is done on a contractual basis, with contracts renegotiated every 2 years. DOC contracts with providers for the buildings, plus the day-to-day activities, including staff, meals, shelter, inmate sign-in and sign-out procedures, urinalysis, and job checks. Contracts are negotiated on a per bed, per day basis, regardless of whether the bed is actually occupied. In 1992, at the time of the study, the average work release contract costs were between $32 and $35 per day, per bed.

DOC contracts with 15 residential work release facilities, which house more than 350 offenders (mostly adult males) on any single day throughout the state. The facilities can handle a range of approximately 15 to more than 100 residents, but most accommodate between 20 and 40 inmates. Small numbers of beds are available to female offenders and mentally ill or developmentally disabled offenders.

In the 1991–1993 biennium, approximately $115 million of the $312-million DOC budget was allocated to community corrections. About 38 percent (or $43 million) of the community corrections budget was for work release. These funds pay primarily for DOC staff to administer the statewide program and monitor participants at the work release centers.

Admission criteria and process. Washington's work release program is governed by the stipulations set forth in the Sentencing Reform Act (SRA) of 1981, which significantly altered the state's criminal sentencing practices as well as the guidelines for work release. The SRA stipulates that an inmate may not enter work release sooner than 6 months prior to discharge. The exact time depends on the length of the offender's original sentence. Inmates generally apply for work release within 12 to 17 months prior to their release date. The application is screened by the correctional counselor, the unit supervisor, and finally by the current DOC facility superintendent.

Inmates can apply for work release only if:

- They have a minimum security status.

- They have less than 2 years to serve on their minimum term, including anticipated good time credits.

- They have not been convicted of rape in the first degree or, if so, are beyond the first 3 years of confinement.

- They have not been convicted of murder in the first degree or, if so, have the written approval of the Secretary of Corrections.

Inmates who meet these initial screening criteria may be subsequently denied work release by DOC if (1) they have exhibited assaultive behavior while in prison, (2) the offender's victim resides in the area, (3) the offender has made threats to the victim during incarceration, or (4) the offender has two or more prior work release failures during the current commitment.

A Partnership With Private Industry

Washington's work release program has benefited enormously from a particularly close working partnership with private industry, particularly Pioneer Human Services (PHS). PHS has been contracting with DOC to operate work release facilities since its inception nearly 30 years ago. It now operates 4 such facilities, housing about 1,200 work releasees annually (or about one-third of all Washington's work releasees). Over the years, PHS has grown to a full-service organization, providing job training at a manufacturing facility it runs, prerelease and postrelease employment in a food service business it founded, housing for offenders with special needs, and electronic monitoring of state and federal offenders. PHS is highly regarded nationally and in the state and was recognized by former President Bush in 1992 as one of the Nation's "Points of Light." ✦

Once DOC judges an offender eligible for work release, the work release facilities' Community Screening Board, consisting of work release staff and local citizens, must agree to accept the inmate for admission to their local work release center. In most cases the Community Screening Board accepts DOC's recommendations.

Daily operations. After being accepted for a particular residential facility, inmates receive a set of standard rules. These rules specify that they are to abide by their work plan, remain in the work release facility at all times except those approved for work and other appointments, remain alcohol and drug free, be employed or have resources in order to meet financial needs, report all earnings to DOC community corrections officers (CCOs), and obey all federal, state, and local laws.

Offenders must obtain gainful employment or training and must pay about $10 a day for room and board. Participants are ultimately responsible for finding work in the community, although CCOs and staff provide referrals. Residents also pay support to their families and court-ordered restitution. The average length of stay in the work re-

lease facility is about 4 months but varies according to the length of the original court imposed sentence.

The CCOs work at the work release facilities a minimum of 8 hours a day. Their primary role is to provide case management services, which includes providing informal advice and conducting intake interviews. For example, they review each client's progress as well as discuss personal problems, such as substance abuse. CCOs can require offenders to participate in special treatment or may initiate procedures for sending them back to prison. Residents fill out "Offender Schedule Plans" listing place of employment, immediate supervisor, and rate of pay; CCOs check with employers to verify these facts.

Study 1: A Statewide Analysis of Work Release

Study 1 was designed to answer the following research questions:

- What are the characteristics of prisoners placed on work release? How have these characteristics differed from those of the general prison population?

- How many offenders placed on work release have successfully completed their programs? Why have some not succeeded?

- What characteristics distinguish those who have been successful from those who have been unsuccessful on work release?

- What are the costs associated with a prison term that includes a work release sentence compared to those of a prison sentence without work release?

The data for study 1 were supplied by DOC research staff. They identified all male inmates released from prison (to the streets) during calendar year 1990. For each of the 2,452 offenders in this cohort, background and criminal record information was obtained from DOC's computerized Offender Based Tracking System (OBTS). OBU lists the inmate's age, race, prior criminal record, most serious conviction, sentence length imposed, and date admitted and discharged from DOC. It also records transfers to jail, prerelease, and work release and work release application and performance information. To this information was added more detailed data from DOC files on the exact reason for return (e.g., new crime, drug possession) for work releasees who had been returned to custody.

Study 1 Findings

The data reveal that almost half (48.8 percent) of the inmates in the 1990 release cohort applied for work release during their prison term, and 39.4 percent were placed in work release facilities at some point during their sentence.

An average of 7.1 months elapsed between the time an inmate was admitted to prison and when he applied for work release. Once the application was submitted, it took just over 3 weeks before a decision was made to accept or reject him for the program. After an additional 56 days, the inmate actually entered a work release facility; this time was used to prepare the inmate for work release and to locate a suitable and available residential placement. These inmates served an average sentence of 15 months. With an average application process of 10 months, the inmates spent approximately 5 months in work release.

Participant characteristics. One would expect work release participants to differ from the general prison population since the law and DOC policies indicate that only certain offenses and offenders (generally the less serious) are eligible. After meeting these legal standards, inmates are free to decide if they want to apply for work release. Incentives to participate include the opportunity to live in the community, be closer to family and friends, and obtain some practical work experience. But some inmates do not plan to be released to a location where a work facility exists, and some inmates judge the requirements and closer supervision of work release too bothersome. They choose instead to serve out their full terms in prison.

Several background characteristics distinguished inmates who did not choose work release from those who did:

- Younger and older inmates were *less* likely than middle-aged inmates to go to work release.
- Hispanics were *less* likely to go to work release than either whites or blacks.
- Inmates with no prior criminal record were *less* likely to go to work release.
- Inmates convicted of property offenses (burglary, theft, and forgery) were the *most* likely to go to work release.

At least one of these differences may reflect the screening procedures for work releases. For example, policies deny work release to offenders convicted of certain violent offenses—hence their lower representation in the work release sample. There could be another explanation for the finding that inmates with no prior criminal records were less likely to participate in work release. These lower risk inmates had other program options for decreasing their prison length of stay (such as a "work ethic" camp for nonviolent offenders).

Although Hispanics were disproportionately underrepresented in the work release cohort, this did not appear to result from their having fewer of the characteristics that would have made them eligible. In fact, Hispanics were overrepresented as drug offenders—which indicates their representation among work releasees should have been much higher than observed. DOC staff suggested one reason for fewer than expected Hispanics is that some may have had Immigration and Naturalization Service detainers, making them ineligible for work release.

Who was successful? Each inmate was classified according to performance:

- *Successful* inmates were those who completed work release without any type of rule infraction or new crimes having been noted in their official corrections record and who returned directly into the community from the work release facility.

- *Moderately successful* inmates were those who had committed an infraction but one not judged serious enough to remove them permanently from work release.

- *Unsuccessful* inmates committed some type of infraction, either a rule violation or new criminal conduct, and were returned to prison to serve out the remainder of their term.

Of the 965 work releasees in the cohort, 544 (or 56 percent of participants) were judged successful in work release. If one considers that nearly 40 percent of the original cohort were placed on work release to begin with, and that about two-thirds succeeded, it is clear that almost one out of four inmates in Washington made a successful transition to the community through work release.

An additional 131 inmates (or 13.5 percent of participants) were moderately successful, and 290 inmates (or 30 percent of participants) were judged unsuccessful in work release and were returned to prison to complete their terms.

The most frequent reasons for return to prison from work release were failure to abide by curfews or absconding from the program, drug possession, and other program rule infractions (see exhibit 32.1). New crimes or law violations accounted for a very small percentage (3.6 percent) of those returned. In fact, in the entire cohort of 965 work releasees studied, records indicate that no offender committed a violent felony while in the program: the few crimes committed were thefts and forgeries. These findings suggest that Washington's work release program poses very little risk to the surrounding community.

Exhibit 32.1
Most Serious Infraction for "Unsuccessful" Work Release Participants

Reason for Return	Percent of 290 Offenders
Law Violation	**3.6**
Forgery	0.7
Theft	1.4
Other, unspecified	1.5
Medical Condition	**3.6**
Drug Possession	**34.9**
Program Rule Violation	**57.8**
Alcohol possession	12.2
Escape/curfew	20.1
Fighting	3.2
Failure to work	4.3
Failure to report income	2.5
Miscellaneous	15.5

Predicting success. Variables indicating race, education level, occupation before imprisonment, marital status, employment status at arrest, previous work stability, conviction offense type, prior criminal record, substance abuse dependency, and length of current sentence were each cross-tabulated with the three success-level variables, revealing that:

- Older offenders were more successful at work release than younger offenders.

- Whites were more successful than Hispanics and blacks. More than 40 percent of Hispanic and black work releasees were returned to prison compared with 25 percent of white offenders.

- Offenders with no prior criminal record were more successful than those with a prior record. Almost two thirds of inmates with no prior record were successful compared with fewer than half the offenders with a prior conviction.

- Offenders convicted of person crimes (e.g., robbery and assault) were more successful than offenders convicted of property or drug crimes.

Comparing work release costs with prison costs. A recent survey of prison administrators reported that, while they recognized the rehabilitative potential of work release, they were most interested in using work release to reduce prison crowding and associated costs. Community-based facilities are much less expensive to operate than prisons, and so allowing inmates to serve the last several months of their prison sentence in the community can reduce corrections costs. According to national estimates, for example, work release costs about $34 a day, and prison costs $54 a day (operational costs only). In addition, inmates who work can be required to help pay for their room and board, support their families, and pay taxes.

Unfortunately, the cost savings accrued through work release and other community-based programs have not been as substantial as proponents had hoped. For example, Minnesota recently implemented an Intensive Supervision Program designed to release prisoners early from prison on the condition that they participate in an enhanced community supervision program. Fewer offenders than expected actually participated in early release, reducing the potential for large cost savings. Similar results have been seen in New Jersey, Florida, Arizona, Texas, and Oregon.

It is therefore clear that community-based sanctions are not necessarily less expensive than prison. It all depends on how offenders behave in the program and how program administrators choose to punish infractions (particularly drug use). If infractions and rule violations are punished with incarceration, initial cost savings are reduced or eliminated as a result of the additional dollars required to incarcerate program failures. In effect, close surveillance may end up generating many program failures who are eventually returned to prison. In that case, the state incurs the cost of their work release program in addition to eventual reuse of a prison cell. The community-based sanction may actually end up costing more than a single term of incarceration uninterrupted by work release. Previous work release evaluations have not provided a complete accounting of total costs, which at a minimum must include the cost of rehousing unsuccessful work release offenders in jail or prison.

For each of the 2,452 inmates in the work release cohort, files on their movements since coming to prison were available. The data made it possible to record how much time each inmate spent in work release and nonwork release institutions as well as in local jails.

DOC then provided statewide estimates of the daily cost of different sanctions; by combining this information, researchers were able to calculate the average cost of a prison sentence that included work release and one that did not (see exhibit 32.2).

When all incarceration time served is taken into account, inmates who participated in work release served, on average, about 4 months less time in a prison or prerelease facility than inmates who did not participate. However, for every 3 days in work release, offenders spend about 1 day back in an institution—either prison or a prerelease center.

Exhibit 32.2 suggests that inmates who participated in work release cost the State about $4,000 less than inmates who did not. However, the cost comparison does not account for crime and background differences between work releasees and nonwork releasees, which have already been shown to be considerable. It is known that nonwork releasees were, on average, convicted of more serious crimes. As such, one would expect that they would serve longer prison terms and cost the state more as a result. To make credible cost comparisons among sanctions, one must compare offenders who are similar in background characteristics and conviction crimes. Study 2 was designed to do exactly that.

Exhibit 32.2
Costs of Prison Sentence That Includes
Work Release vs. Prison Without Work Release

Program Type	Daily Cost	Prison Without Work Release		Prison With Work Release	
		Average Number of Days	Cost	Average Number of Days	Cost
Before Work Release					
Prison	$68.60	440	$30,185	240	$16,464
Prerelease	$50.36	11	$ 554	48	$ 2,417
Jail	$51.00	1	$ 51	0	0
After Work Release					
Prison	$68.60	—	—	25	$ 1,715
Prerelease	$50.36	—	—	11	$ 554
Work release	$48.07	—	—	104	$ 4,999
Jail	$51.00	—	—	5	$ 255
Total Costs			**$30,790**		**$26,404**

Note: Prison, prerelease, and work release costs are averages of 1991–1992 and 1992–1993 costs. For jail costs, $51/day is the figure that would be charged to an outside contractor for a jail bed in King County, Washington (the largest county). Work release costs reflect "recovery" costs of inmates' room and board payments.

Study 2: The Impact of Work Release on Recidivism and on Corrections Costs

This evaluation of the effects of work release was designed as an experiment in which eligible offenders were to be randomly assigned to participate or not to participate in work release. In a randomized experiment, one has more confidence that any observed differences result from participating in work release rather than from preexisting background differences.

The experiment was conducted in Seattle, which is Washington's largest city and home to more than 50 percent of the work release offenders. The study had the full cooperation of the Washington DOC, the DOC Community Corrections Division, and the various managers of the six individual work release facilities serving males in Seattle.

Identifying the sample. The study required a fairly large sample size in order to

detect the relatively small outcome differences that were expected between experimental and control offenders. Based on prior evaluations, it was estimated that the work release effects (e.g., recidivism reduction) would not be large, with perhaps 10- to 20-percent differences between experimental and controls. Procedures were devised that would yield expected sample sizes of several hundred offenders during the time frame of the study.

Offenders who were deemed eligible for work release by DOC were randomly assigned to either the experimental group (who progressed toward work release using normal procedures) or the control group (who were removed from the work release eligibility list and remained in prison to complete their full prison terms).

To avoid seriously disrupting the flow of inmates into Seattle work release facilities, investigators assigned 1 out of every 10 eligible inmates to the control group and 1 to the experimental group. The remaining 8 eligible offenders did not participate in the study but instead maintained their status on the waiting list and were handled according to normal DOC operating procedures. Based on analysis of available DOC data, these procedures were estimated to yield approximately 200 study offenders a year.

However, the flow of offenders entering the DOC pool of work release "eligibles" was too slow to permit reaching an adequate sample size during the study's assignment period. A year after the random assignment procedures were put in place, only 125 offenders had been assigned to the study. It is unclear why the inmate flow did not meet expectations, but DOC officials suggest it resulted from fewer applications to the program (not from rejecting more applicants).

To increase the study's sample size, researchers supplemented the randomized assignment with offenders who during the study period had been part of the 8 out of every 10 offenders who were not included in the initial randomized assignment procedures. Forty-eight offenders were randomly selected from this initial pool of work release eligibles and placed in the experimental study group. In addition, DOC identified 45 additional control offenders who for reasons unrelated to eligibility criteria had not actually participated in work release prior to their release from prison, primarily because they had "maxed out" on their sentences before all the administrative procedures had been completed or work release beds had become available. These offenders were used to supplement the control group. Thus, the final sample totaled 218 offenders, of whom 125 had been randomly assigned to the study and an additional 93 had been chosen as a matched comparison group.

Data collection. For each of the 218 study participants, a number of data collection forms were completed by the researchers' onsite staff. The background review captured information about the inmate's demographics (e.g., age, race, education, marital status), prior employment history, drug use information, current offense information, and prior criminal history.

At 6 months and again at 12 months after assignment, a series of other forms were completed that recorded such information as time spent in different institutions and work release centers, contacts made and services received, and the number of days on postdischarge status. Finally, recidivism information was obtained for each offender based on State-level criminal history "rap sheets." The date, nature of arrest, disposition, and sentence were recorded for each offense occurring during the 1-year follow-up period after study assignment.

Characteristics of the Seattle Sample

The Seattle sample closely resembled the statewide sample, which was to be expected since about one-third of Washington's DOC population comes from the Seattle area. As shown in exhibit 32.3, the study work release offenders averaged about 30 years of age. About half of the offenders in the sample were white, and 43 percent were black. More than half of the sample were convicted of drug offenses, and 84 percent were classified as dependent on alcohol, with almost three-quarters dependent on cocaine. About two-thirds of the offenders in the sample had never worked or had worked only occasionally (6.2 percent and almost 60 percent, respectively).

One can see that the characteristics of work release participants were not significantly different from those of nonwork release participants, except in three instances: number of prior arrests, occupational history, and type of current offense. This suggests that the randomization and matching strategy used was successful in that it was desired that the two groups be similar in background characteristics so that any observed differences in recidivism could be attributed to participation in work release.

Work Release Program Activities

The investigators sought to learn what actually transpired when offenders were placed in work release. What kinds of jobs did they get, and what types of monitoring activities were imposed? How well did inmates perform, and how long did they stay in the program? To answer those questions, the work release offenders were "followed" into their individual site placements, and information was coded about the kinds of jobs they obtained, how much money they earned, the number of times they were seen by CCOs, how often they were tested for drugs, and the kinds of rehabilitation programs they participated in.

As expected, most of the program's focus was on obtaining a job. In fact, if offenders did not have a job within the first few weeks, they might be returned to the institution. Generally, offenders had one or two jobs during their 3- to 4-month work release stay. Many more interviews were attempted with employers than were actually completed. The analysis of offenders' first jobs showed that most were either in the restaurant or construction industries, with a median pay of $8 an hour. More than half of the offenders were still working at their first jobs when they left work release (discharged from DOC or placed on postrelease supervision) or when the review of their files was completed.

Work releasees were tested for drugs at the work release facility an average of once a month. The tests revealed very low percentages of drug use. Only 8 percent of work release participants tested positive for drugs, usually for cocaine. On average, work releasees participated in outpatient drug and alcohol counseling sessions (usually Alcoholics Anonymous and Narcotics Anonymous meetings) about once every 2 months. In addition, they had face-to-face meetings with their CCO about once a week.

Recidivism Outcomes During 12-Month Follow-up

It is generally believed that recidivism rates are the key factor in determining the effectiveness of work release. This study included a 1-year follow-up period, which began at the point of random assignment. Work releasees were not immediately placed in the community following random assignment, since several weeks often passed between approval for the program and actual transfer to the work release facility. Thus, the 12-month follow-up included an average of 2 months initial time in an institution, followed by an average of 10 months in the community for work release study offenders. During the follow-up period, control offenders were "on the street" an average of just un-

Exhibit 32.3
Characteristics of Control vs. Experimental Work Release Sample

	Control (N=106) (Percent)	Experimental (N=112) (Percent)
Average Age (years)	31.4	30.4
Race		
White	63.2	49.6
Black	30.2	43.2
Hispanic	3.8	1.8
Other	2.8	5.4
Education[a]		
High school	45.9	48.4
High school graduate	39.3	48.4
Post high school graduate	13.1	3.1
Occupation[a]		
Clerical/sales/teacher	4.6	4.7
Service	13.1	14.1
Skilled labor	26.2	25.0
Semiskilled	13.1	17.2
Unskilled	19.7	31.2
Marital Status[a]		
Single	62.3	67.2,
Married	18.0	6.2
Divorced/separated	16.4	23.4
Employed at Time of Arrest[a]	34.4	25.0
Yes		
Work Stability[ab]		
Never worked	16.4[b]	6.2
Occasionally	36.1	59.4
About half the time	4.9	10.9
Worked most of the time	16.4	9.4
Continuous employment	21.3	9.4
Unknown	4.9	4.0

Exhibit 32.3 (continued)
Characteristics of Control vs. Experimental Work Release Sample

	Control (N=106) (Percent)	Experimental (N=112) (Percent)
Most Serious Current Offense[b]		
Homicide	2.9	3.6
Rape/sex	16.2	1.8
Robbery	5.7	12.6
Assault	7.6	8.1
Burglary	24.8	15.3
Theft	11.4	8.1
Drugs	31.4	50.4
other	0.0	0.0
Average Sentence Length	(months)	(months)
	25.5	18.0
Average Number of	(number)	(number)
Prior arrests[b]	7.2	4.5
Prior felony convictions	2.8	2.4
Prior miscellaneous convictions	2.9	2.1
Prior jail terms	2.3	2.1
Prior prison terms	0.9	0.5
Prior adult person criminal convictions	0.3	0.3
Prior adult drug convictions	0.5	0.5
Prior adult property convictions	1.7	1.4
Prior adult other convictions	1.0	1.0
Dependency on[a]		
Alcohol	78.7	84.4
Marijuana	62.3	70.3
LSD	3.3	7.8
Amphetamines	1.6	1.6
Cocaine	59.0	73.4
Crack	29.5	28.1
Heroin	16.4	12.51
Participated in Drug Treatment[a]		
Yes	67.2	68.8

[a]Indicates data were available for randomly assigned subjects only.

[b]Indicates controls and experimentals were significantly different at $p<.05$. Chi-square tests were used for categorical variables; t-tests were used for continuous variables.

der 7 months after being released from prison.

Investigators obtained each offender's State rap sheet and recorded all arrests (felony and misdemeanor), convictions, and incarcerations occurring during the follow-up period. Information on infractions during work release and prison was obtained from the DOC OBTS computer and work release

folders. Events that occurred while the offender was in prison or on work release were separated from events that occurred afterward (including postdischarge).

The results (see exhibit 32.4) show significant differences. Infractions (mostly rule violations and drug possession and use) were recorded for 58 percent of work releasees, but for only 4.7 percent of nonwork releasees. As a result, about a quarter of all work releasees were returned to prison, compared to 1 percent of nonwork releasees. However, when looking at infractions while offenders were in an institution, one finds that nonwork releasees incurred significantly more infractions during their time in prison. When one adds together infractions during work release and while in prison (in analyses not reported in exhibit 32.4), work release offenders were twice as likely to incur a violation when compared to nonwork releasees (67.3 percent versus 33.6 percent).

In terms of new crimes, although work releasees were less likely to be arrested during the follow-up period, the difference was not statistically significant. As in study 1, a very small percentage of work releasees were arrested for new crimes while on work release (less than 3 percent). By the end of the 1-year follow-up period, which included an average of about 3 months after discharge from DOC, 30 percent of nonwork releasees (controls) had been arrested, compared to 22 percent of work releasees (experimentals). As a result, about 4 percent of both groups were returned to prison for a new crime during the year.

Overall, if one combines all the returns to prison (for either a rule infraction or new crime), one finds that 29.5 percent of work releasees were returned to prison during the 1-year follow-up, compared to 5.7 percent for nonwork release participants.

The returns to prison were mostly for short stays, however. By the end of the 1-year follow-up period, 71.4 percent of control offenders and 52.7 percent of experimental offenders had been discharged. Nine percent of work release participants were institutionalized, contrasted with 2.9 percent of controls, a marginally significant difference. These differences suggest that the length of time under correctional supervision may actually have been longer for those participating in work release.

Costs of Work Release Versus Prison

Is work release less expensive than serving a complete term in prison? To answer this question, one must determine the relevant period of time for which costs are to be estimated. Since about 26 percent of work releasees were returned to prison as a result of a work release infraction, the costs of rehousing them in prison needed to be considered in the overall cost calculation.

If one considers only costs before the inmates either leave prison or work release for the first time, one ignores "reprocessing" for offenders who are returned to prison from work release facilities or the community. However, if one wants to include costs following first release, one must make some decision about how far in the future to extend the window for analysis. Not all the study offenders were discharged during the study time period; thus, one cannot estimate costs for the entire sentence served in the institution plus time in the community before discharge for all offenders. The analysis reflects the costs associated with completed sentences for 70 percent of controls and 50 percent of experimentals.

Washington corrections officials furnished the daily cost of each of the correctional programs, making it possible to compute the total costs of supervising each inmate during the initial sentence and the follow-up period. By averaging these cost estimates across inmates in the control and experimental groups, one can compare the costs of a prison term that includes work release to one that does not.

The analysis (see exhibit 32.5) shows basically no difference in costs between work

Exhibit 32.4

Recidivism During 1-Year Follow-up for Study 2 Participants

	Control (N=106) (Percent)	Experimental (N=112) (Percent)
In-Prison Infractions		
Any infraction	29.8*	11.8
Assault/sex crime	5.8*	0.9
Weapon possession	1.0	0.0
Possession of drugs, alcohol	3.8	3.6
Rules	17.3*	5.4
Work Release Infractions		
Any infraction	4.7*	58.0
Assault/sex crimes	0.0	0.0
Weapon possession	0.0	0.0
Possession of drugs, alcohol	1.0*	18.8
Escape	0.0	8.9
Rules	2.8*	42.3
Sanctions for Infractions		
Jail pending a hearing	1.0	1.8
Returned to prison	1.0*	25.9
Arrests During Work Release		
Any arrest	0.0	2.7
Homicide/rape	0.0	0.0
Assault	0.0	0.0
Robbery	0.0	0.9
Theft	0.0	0.9
Drugs	0.0	0.9
Arrests After Release		
Any arrest	30.2	22.3
Homicide/rape	0.0	0.0
Assault	8.5	2.7
Robbery	0.9	1.8
Burglary	3.8	2.7
Theft	3.8	7.1
Drugs	7.6	8.9
Sanctions for Arrests		
Any conviction	7.6	7.1
Any jail	0.0*	3.4
Any prison	4.7	3.6

*Indicates control and experimental groups were significantly different at $p<.05$ using chi-square tests.

releasees and inmates completing their full terms in prison. If one considers the costs associated with work release from the time an inmate was admitted to prison until his discharge, the estimated cost would average $25,883 per inmate. This is in contrast to the estimated $25,494 it would have cost per inmate, on average, to serve out his time in prison.

The two studies thus produced similar findings regarding the costs of work release.

Exhibit 32.5

Study 2 Work Release vs. Prison Costs, for Initial Sentence and 1 Year After Assignment to Study

	Daily Cost	Control		Experimental	
		Average Number of Days	Cost	Average Number of Days	Cost
Before First Release to Community					
Prison	$68.60	290	$19,894	240	$16,464
Prerelease	$50.36	95	$ 4,784	48	$ 2,417
Work release	$48.07	6	$ 288	88	$ 4,230
After Release (i.e. reprocessing cost)					
Prison	$68.60	3	$ 206	25	$ 1,715
Prerelease	$50.36	2	$ 101	11	$ 554
Work release	$48.07	1	$ 48	104	$ 4,999
Community custody inmate	$ 2.03	55	$ 112	80	$ 162
Postrelease supervision	$ 2.03	30	$ 61	14	$ 28
Discharge	$ 0	108	0	80	0
Total Costs		**592**	**$25,494**	**592**	**$25,883**

Note: For controls, "after release" refers to the follow-up time after an offender first leaves his initial prison term and returns "to the street." For experimentals, "after release" refers to the follow-up time after an offender first leaves his first placement in a work release facility and returns either "to the street" or back to an institution.

Other findings related to success, failure, and recidivism lead to several conclusions.

Who Is Successful on Work Release?

Although work release might not reduce the overall recidivism rates of participants, there may be subgroups for whom the program could produce more successful outcomes. Similar to the analysis in study 1, an attempt was made to identify factors that were related to three recidivism outcomes: any infraction during work release; any arrest during the 1-year follow-up; and any return to prison (as a result of infraction or arrest) during the 1-year follow-up. A number of background characteristics of offenders were considered, such as age, race, education, prior employment, drug involvement, and current offense.

It was not possible to find characteristics of offenders, or a profile of an offender, who appeared to do better on work release than in prison. However, a few characteristics were related to success, regardless of condition. For example, offenders with a prior history of cocaine or crack dependence were more likely to have committed an infraction than others; those whose most serious current offense was for a theft charge were more likely to be rearrested; and white offenders were less likely than others to commit an infraction.

Summary and Conclusions

Washington's work release program has been successful on several fronts: nearly a quarter of *all* prisoners released in Washington under current statutes made a successful transition to the community through work release. While in the program, these inmates maintained employment, reconnected with their local communities, paid for their room and board, and most remained drug free. Given that in most states fewer than 5 percent of prisoners even participate in work release, this is quite an accomplishment.

However, the work release program did not reduce offender recidivism rates or corrections costs. Critics of community corrections often argue that such programs should deliver all of the above services while showing a reduction in recidivism and costs. Such expectations, are unrealistic. Prison programs should not assume the goals and functions of other social institutions such as schools and welfare agencies.

Realistic measures of corrections programs' effectiveness should account for daily activities and the constraints under which the programs operate. Realism, however, does not mean easy to achieve. Most participants in Washington's work release program had lengthy criminal histories, serious substance abuse problems, and possessed limited education and job skills. Yet, when supervised in this work release program, they found jobs, paid rent, and refrained from crime.

Although most corrections evaluations adopt recidivism as their primary outcome measure, few corrections officials believe that what they do chiefly determines recidivism rates. As John J. DiIulio, Jr., recently wrote: "Most justice practitioners understand that they can rarely do for their clients what parents, teachers, friends, neighbors, clergy. . .or economic opportunities may have failed to do." Adopting more realistic outcome measures may make it more possible to bridge the wide gap between public expectations for the justice system and what most practitioners recognize as the system's actual capability to control crime. By documenting what corrections programs can accomplish, we can move toward integrating programs like work release into a more balanced corrections strategy. Such a strategy would successfully return low-risk inmates to the community, thereby making room to incarcerate the truly violent offenders.

Study Questions

1. What is work release, and what are some of the advantages to the program? What are some disadvantages?

2. Briefly describe how Washington State's work release program works.

3. Summarize the major findings from the author's study of work release in Washington State.

4. What are the conclusions reached by the authors concerning work release? ✦

Part VII
New Directions

The final section of this book focuses on America's obsession with "getting tough" on offenders. Three strikes and you're out, increased use of incarceration and the death penalty, and the disturbing consequences of these policies make it difficult to be optimistic about the direction of corrections. However, while some may view the future of corrections with pessimism, we choose to end this book with an article that shows the public's support for treatment and rehabilitation.

Clearly, the public has grown more punitive over the years, but the evidence also shows that what citizens want most is a reasonable approach to dealing with offenders. Research suggests that the public continues to support treatment, with rehabilitation being a primary purpose of prison. Many people believe criminals should not be coddled, nor should support go to programs that do not work. Sensible approaches, however, are widely supported by the public, who outright reject monolithically punitive approaches.

Unfortunately, get-tough policies are politically expedient, and policy makers and politicians have often over-estimated the public's punitiveness. The question for the future is how corrections will respond to the challenge of maintaining public safety while reducing recidivism rates of the offenders it serves. Ultimately, public safety is best served when offenders leave the correctional system and lead crime-free, prosocial lives. ✦

33
Three Strikes and You're Out
The Political Sentencing Game

Peter J. Benekos

Alida V. Merlo

"Three strikes and you're out." This phrase is now being used throughout the country in reference to particular criminal sanctions. The analogy to baseball is not accidental; it has appeal as an all-American slogan. But, as this selection by Peter J. Benekos and Alida V. Merlo shows, the new three-strikes laws are just that: slogans. The only benefit of these laws is in political rhetoric. Unlike most other topics in corrections, there is little debate about the utility of the three-strikes laws. Nearly all penologists agree that such laws are ineffective. The authors here clearly demonstrate how the politicalization of crime control translates into poor public policy.

The "WAR on crime" has added another weapon to the arsenal of getting tough on crime: "three strikes and you're out." From the slogans of "just say no" to "if you can't do the time, don't do the crime," it is ironic that the latest metaphor for crime policy parallels the baseball players' strike of 1994. The re-

Excerpts from "Multisite Evaluation of Shock Incarceration" by Doris Layton MacKenzie and Claire Souryal, *National Institute of Justice Research Report*, Copyright © 1994 by the National Institute of Justice. Reprinted by permission.

cent initiatives to mandate life sentences for three-time convicted felons are responses to the public's fear of crime and frustration with the criminal justice system and indicate the continuation of politicized crime policy.

In the 30 states that have introduced "three-strikes" legislation and in the 10 that have passed tougher sentencing for repeat offenders (*Criminal Justice Newsletter*, 1994c, p. 1), politicians have demonstrated quick-fix responses to the complex and difficult issues of crime, violence, and public anxiety over the disorder and decline in America. The United States Congress also finally overcame differences to legislate a new get-tough crime bill that not only includes a provision of life imprisonment for a third felony conviction but also authorizes the death penalty "for dozens of existing or newly created federal crimes" (Idelson, 1994, p. 2138).

Notwithstanding the critics of these sentencing policies (Currie, 1994; Gangi, 1994; Gladwell, 1994; Kramer, 1994; Lewis, 1994; Raspberry, 1993) politicians have rushed to embrace the "get even tougher" sentencing proposals because they have learned that "politically, it still works" (Schneider, 1993, p. 24). "Crime used to be the Republicans' issue, just as the economy was the Democrats'. No more" (Schneider, 1993, p. 24). In his commentary on how the "misbegotten" three-strikes piece of legislation became part of the crime bill, Lewis writes that "the answer is simple: politics. Democrats wanted to take the crime issue away from Republicans. Republicans responded by sounding 'tougher'" . . .and "President Clinton wanted something—anything—labeled 'crime bill'" (Lewis, 1994, p. A13).

This [chapter] reviews the ideological and political context of these sentencing reforms, examines get-tough legislation in three states and on the Federal level, and considers the consequences of increasing sentencing severity. The review suggests that baseball sentencing will further distort the distribution of punishments and will contribute to an escalation of political posturing on crime policies.

Politicalization of Crime

In a sense, this is what baseball sentencing is about: using the fear factor as a political issue; relying on what Broder calls "bumper sticker simplicity" to formulate crime policy (1994b, p. 6), and taking a tough stance on sentencing criminals as symbolic of doing something about crime. The politicizing of crime as a national issue can be traced to the 1964 Presidential election when Barry Goldwater promoted the theme of "law and order" and challenged Lyndon Johnson's "war on poverty" as a soft-headed response to crime and disorder (Cronin, Cronin, & Milakovich, 1981).

Thirty years ago the voters chose "social reform, civil rights, and increased education and employment opportunities" over a "get-tough response to crime that included expanding police powers and legislating tougher laws" (Merlo & Benekos, 1992a, p. x). Today's election results reflect a reversal of policy and the expansion of the Federal role in crime control (Congressional Digest, 1994).

Even though Johnson won the 1964 election, the "nationalization" of the crime issue was established and the Federal Government began "a new era of involvement in crime control" (Congressional Digest, 1994, p. 162): "the law and order issue just wouldn't go away" (Cronin et al., 1981, p. 22) and it became embedded in the public's mind and on the national agenda (Merlo and Benekos, 1992a, p. x).

In his 1965 address to Congress, President Johnson "called for the establishment of a blue ribbon panel to probe 'fully and deeply into the problems of crime in our Nation'" (Congressional Digest, 1994, p. 162). This led to the Law Enforcement Assistance Act of 1965, the Omnibus Crime Control and Safe Streets Act of 1968, and more recently to the Comprehensive Crime Control Act of 1984, the Anti-Drug Abuse Act of 1986, the Anti-Drug Abuse Act of 1988, the Crime Control Act of 1990, and finally, the Violent Crime Control and Law Enforcement Act of 1994 (Congressional Digest, 1994, pp. 163, 192), which was signed by President Clinton on September 13, 1994. Since 1965 to 1992, the Federal spending for the "administration of justice" has "risen from $535 million to an estimated $11.7 billion" (Congressional Digest, 1994, p. 162).

From Horton to Davis and McFadden

The lessons of crime and politics were learned again in the Presidential election of 1988 when the then Vice President George Bush invoked the get-tough issue when he challenged Massachusetts Governor Michael Dukakis on his state's correctional policies that allowed a convicted murderer serving a life sentence to participate in the furlough program (Merlo & Benekos, 1992a, p. x).

Willie Horton became the poster child of Republicans and reminded Democrats (as well as doubting Republicans) that appearing to be soft on crime (and criminals) was politically incorrect. The Willie Horton incident "effectively crystalized a complex problem by presenting it as a dramatic case history of one individual" (The Sentencing Project, 1989, p. 3). Ironically, even without the Willie Horton incident, the 1980s were a period of conservative crime policy in which get-tough sentencing reforms were implemented throughout the country (Merlo & Benekos, 1992b). As part of these get-tough, get-fair, just deserts, determinate sentencing reforms, penalties were increased, mandatory sentences were legislated, and prisons became overcrowded (Shover & Einstadter, 1988, p. 51).

Similar to the Willie Horton situation, in 1993 another tragic case also became a "condensation symbol" for the public's perception that crime was increasing, that violent criminals were getting away with murder, that sentences were too lenient, and that offenders were getting out of prison after serving only small portions of their sentences. The California case which outraged the public was the October 1, 1993, abduction and murder of 12-year-old Polly Klaas by a parolee who had been released after serving 8 years of a 16-year sentence for a 1984 kidnapping (*New York Times*, 1993, p. A22).

Richard Allen Davis, who was arrested November 30, 1993, had convictions for two kidnappings, assault, and robbery and had spent "a good part of his adult life in jail" (*New York Times*, 1993, p. A22). At the time of his arrest, he was in violation of a pass from the halfway house that he was released to and therefore was also charged as a parole violator.

This type of crime fuels public fear and outrage and becomes fodder for politicians who respond by calling for tougher sentences to curb the perceived increases in crime and violence. Coincidentally to Davis' arrest, the FBI released its semiannual tabulation of crime which "showed that the rate of crime as a whole declined 5 percent in the first six months of 1993 from the same period the year before and that the rate of violent crime dropped 3 percent" (Lewis, 1993, p. B6).

These data, however, are not comforting to a public which sees the Klaas incident as evidence of the horrific and violent crimes which grip the nation in fear. "The public doesn't rely on statistics to generate their perception of the level of crime. People's perceptions are based on what they see and hear going on around them" (Michael Rand of the Justice Department, cited in Lewis, 1993, p. B6). In reviewing 1994 state political campaigns, Kurtz observed that "although other traditional hot-button issues—welfare, taxes, immigration, personal ethics—also are prominent, crime remains the 30-second weapon of choice, and the charge most often is that an incumbent is responsible for turning dangerous inmates loose." (1994, p. 12).

Recent 'Baseball Sentencing' Legislation

In order to provide a clearer picture of the legislation that is designed to impose mandatory life sentences (without possibility of parole or early release), we examined the recently enacted Violent Crime Control and Law Enforcement Act of 1994 and similar statutes in the states of Washington, California, and Georgia. The Violent Crime Control and Law Enforcement Act of 1994, signed by President Clinton on September 13, 1994, authorizes mandatory life imprisonment for persons convicted on two previous separate occasions of two serious violent felonies or one or more serious violent felonies and one or more serious drug offenses. According to the new Federal code, a "serious violent felony" includes offenses ranging from murder and aggravated sexual abuse to arson, aircraft piracy, car-jacking, and extortion (U.S. Government Printing Office, 1994, pp. 194–195).

In the State of Washington, the "Persistent Offender Accountability Law" was approved by the voters in November 1993 by a 3 to 1 victory and became effective in December 1993 (*Corrections Digest*, 1994a). Under the revised statute, an offender who is categorized as a "persistent offender" must be sentenced to life imprisonment without any hope of parole if he or she has been convicted of a "most serious offense" and has two prior separate convictions for crimes that meet the "most serious offense" definition (Washington Laws, 1994, p. 1). Included in the definition of "most serious offense" are crimes ranging from "manslaughter in the second degree" to "promoting prostitution in the first degree" or any felony defined under any law as a Class A felony or criminal solicitation of or criminal conspiracy to commit a Class A felony (Washington Laws, 1994, p. 13).

In March 1994, Governor Pete Wilson signed California Assembly Bill 971 into law. Its most publicized provision is the requirement that judges impose " . . .an indeterminate sentence of a minimum of 25 years to life, or triple the normal sentence, whichever is greater, on offenders convicted of certain serious or violent felonies if they have two previous convictions for any felony" (Tucker, 1994, p. 7). The offenses included in the category of serious or violent felony range from murder and rape to burglary, any felony using a firearm, and selling or giving drugs such as heroin, cocaine, and PCP to a minor (California Penal Code, s1192.7).

In Georgia the voters approved "The Sentence Reform Act of 1994" which authorizes life imprisonment without possibility of parole, pardon, early release, leave, or any other measure designed to reduce the sentence for any person convicted of a second "serious violent felony." Under Georgia law, a serious violent felony is defined as " . . .murder or felony murder, armed robbery, kidnapping, rape, aggravated child molestation, aggravated sodomy and aggravated sexual battery" (Georgia Statutes, 17-10-6.1).

Despite the fact that this law became effective January 1, 1995, any felony committed before that date in Georgia or in another jurisdiction, which meets the Georgia definition of a "serious violent felony," would count as one of the "strikes." The Federal code and the Washington and California laws contain similar language. The offender's criminal record in the state where the most recent conviction occurs as well as his or her record in other states or on the Federal level determine the number of "strikes." In short, an offender may already have the requisite number of convictions even as the mandatory sentencing provisions first become effective.

When the Federal criminal code and the three-strikes laws are compared, it appears that the Georgia law is the most restrictive. Unlike the others, it contains a "two-strikes" versus a "three-strikes" provision. However, upon closer inspection, Georgia's law is the only one of the four reviewed here that requires mandatory life imprisonment for crimes that can be strictly identified as violent. By contrast, the Federal law and the Washington and California laws include a variety of nonviolent crimes such as burglary, prostitution, and drug trafficking that can result in a mandatory life sentence in prison. In California, for example, a criminal twice convicted of the property crime of burglary may be sentenced to life in prison for a third burglary conviction.

In order to clarify the intent of the legislation—that these offenders serve lengthy prison sentences—some states such as Washington stipulate that the Governor is "urged to refrain from pardoning or granting clemency" to offenders sentenced until the offender has reached the age of 60 (*Final Legislative Report*, 1994, p. 1). In order to discourage the Governor's use of pardons as a way to minimize the effects of the legislation, Washington law mandates that the Governor provide reports twice each year on the status of these "persistent offenders" he or she has released during his or her term of office and that the reports continue to be made for as long as the offender lives or at least 10 years after his or her release from prison (*Final Legislative Report*, 1994, p. 1).

Effects of Baseball Legislation

Thermodynamic Effects of Baseball Punishment

While the get-tough rhetoric continues to capture the public's support, the consequences of increased sentencing penalties are having an unintended but not unanticipated impact on the criminal justice system. In California where the mandatory statute "makes no distinction between 'violent' and 'serious' felonies . . .a superior court judge, Lawrence Antolini, declared the three-strikes law unconstitutional" because it "metes out 'cruel and unusual' jail terms" for nonviolent criminals and "robs justices of the power to evaluate the nuances of individual cases" (Peyser, 1994, p. 63). In an article about the tough California sentencing law, a *New York Times* report indicated that "judges in many California jurisdictions have been indicating their reluctance to follow the new law . . .by changing some felony charges to misdemeanors" (1994c, p. A9). In addition, Supreme Court Justice Anthony Kennedy has also criticized the "increasing use of mandatory minimum sentences, saying the practice was unwise and often unfair" (*New York Times,* 1994a, p. A14).

And, as some judges find fault with the harsher sentencing laws, prosecutors are also raising doubts about the ability of the courts to handle the number of cases which fall under the baseball sentencing provisions. In California, where the District Attorney's Association opposed the three-strikes law, Los Angeles County District Attorney Gil Garcetti voiced concerns that the broad nature of California's sentencing law would expand the number of felons subject to life in prison (*Criminal Justice Newsletter,* 1994a, p. 6). In an interview with National Public Radio, Garcetti stated that Los Angeles County alone would need 40 more prosecutors to handle the increase in the number of cases (National Public Radio, 1994).

What Garcetti was referring to is the potential increase in the number of accused offenders who refuse to plea-bargain and would rather take their chances on a trial (Peyser, 1994, p. 63). For example, a convicted murderer in California, Henry Diaz, originally entered guilty pleas to three counts of child molestation. When he learned that "one of the incidents occurred after the 'three-strikes' law went into effect on March 7 (1994), making (him) eligible for sentencing under the new law," he withdrew his guilty plea and requested a trial (*New York Times,* 1994d, p. A19). Responses such as this give the California Judicial Council reason to "estimate that the new law will require an additional $250 million per year to try more felony cases" (*Criminal Justice Newsletter,* 1994a, p. 7).

These types of judicial responses illustrate a hydraulic, thermodynamic effect where getting tough may in fact result in being softer. For example, "the law allows prosecutors to move to dismiss criminals' prior convictions 'in the furtherance of justice'— namely, if they believe the law mandates an elephantine sentence for a puny offense" (Peyser, 1994, p. 63). Another avenue to circumvent the law is a "wiggle" factor where

district attorneys can "classify certain crimes that straddle the felony-misdemeanor line as misdemeanors" (Peyser, 1994, p. 63).

In addition, some district attorneys have reported "instances in which crime victims had told prosecutors they would not testify if a conviction meant the defendant would fall under the requirements of the new law." (*New York Times,* 1994c, p. A9). As Griset observed in her study of determinate sentence reforms, legislators fail to "recognize the inevitability of the exercise of discretion at all points in the criminal justice system" and as a result develop policies which are incongruent and inconsistent with the reality of the criminal justice system (1991, p. 181). The above examples illustrate her conclusions and also suggest an inverse relationship between the severity of sanctions and the likelihood that those sanctions will be applied (Black, 1976). Police officers are also experiencing the effects of these baseball "swings" at offenders: "suspects who are more prone to use violence when cornered" (Egan, 1994, p. A11). In one case in Seattle, a suspect threatened to shoot police after he was cornered. "After the suspect was taken into custody, the police were told by his acquaintances that he thought he was facing a three-strikes charge. Rather than face life in prison, he decided to confront officers" (Egan, 1994, p. A11).

Prisons and Prisoners: Economic and Social Impact

With crime uppermost in voters' minds, the new Federal crime bill was frequently featured in the 1994 election campaigns. Incumbent members of Congress informed their constituents of the immediate effects of the legislation on their home state. For example, New Jersey has been promised $77 million for new prisons and 3,800 police officers. Pennsylvania is slated for $110 million for prisons and 4,200 new police officers (*The Vindicator,* 1994, p. A5). These tangible results of the crime bill are intended to provide voters with a sense of security and satisfaction. However, the public has not yet focused on the long-term costs of these new initiatives.

There is little doubt that an immediate effect of the legislation will be to increase the already enormous prison population in the United States. According to The Sentencing Project research, there are currently 1.3 million Americans incarcerated (Mauer, 1994a, p. 1). The incarceration rate is 519 per 100,000, making the United States' rate second only to Russia's (Mauer, 1994a, p. 1). In the United States, the incarceration rate of African-Americans (1,947 per 100,000) as compared to the incarceration rate of whites (306 per 100,000) is even more striking; Mauer's analysis illustrates that there are currently more African-American males in prisons and jails in the United States than enrolled in institutions of higher education (Mauer, 1994a, pp. 1–2). In terms of future projections, the National Council on Crime and Delinquency (NCCD) contends that if the remainder of the states follow in the footsteps of the Federal Government and of those states such as Washington and California, the inmate population in American prisons will rise to a minimum of 2.26 million within the next 10 years (*Corrections Digest*, 1994b, p. 1).

An increase of over a million inmates will mandate an increase in the level of funding necessary to accommodate such a large population. According to NCCD estimates, the Federal Government and the states will need an additional $351 billion during the next 10 years (*Corrections Digest*, 1994b, p. 1). In California, the effects of the three-strikes provision are estimated to increase the costs of operating the state prisons by $75 million for fiscal year 1994–1995 (Tucker, 1994, p. 7). The requisite prison construction that will be necessary to fulfill the legislative provisions is estimated to cost California residents $21 billion (Mauer, 1994a, p. 22). The Federal grants that the states are hoping to

receive from the Federal Government will fall far short of these costs.

In addition, there are also the costs associated with providing health care and security for inmates over the age of 50. Based upon demographic data obtained from the California Department of Corrections, NCCD projects that the number of inmates who are 50 years of age or older will increase by 15,300 from 1994 to 1999. Although these older inmates comprised only 4 percent of California's prison population in 1994, it is estimated that they will represent 12 percent of the prison population in 2005 (NCCD, 1994, p. 3). State officials in California expect that the full impact of this legislation will be realized in the year 2020 at which time over 125,000 inmates or 20 percent of the prison population will be 50 years of age or older (NCCD, 1994, p. 3).

The New Jersey Department of Corrections has estimated that a new baseball sentencing bill would have a substantial financial impact on prison costs. In a financial impact statement, the Office of Legislative Services reported that "for every inmate who is not paroled as a result of this bill, an additional $80,000 in construction costs and $1 million in operating costs would be incurred over the lifetime of that inmate . . .that accounting breaks down to $25,000 per year per inmate for operating costs or an additional $3.75 million each year for 30 years, or $1.7 billion" (Gray, 1994, p. B9). In other words, Todd Clear estimates it would cost "$1 million to lock up a 30-year [old] criminal for life" (Clear cited in Levinson, 1994, p. B2).

In his review of the costs of crime and punishment, Thomas not only finds that "the fastest growing segment of state budgets in fiscal 1994 is corrections" but he considers that as more funds are put into public safety and crime control, there are fewer funds for other public and social programs (Thomas, 1994, p. 31). For example, Geiger reports that "70 percent of all the prison space in use today was built since 1985. Only 11 percent of our nation's classrooms were built during the 1980s" (1994, p. 22).

In an assessment of the consequences of baseball sentencing laws on prison costs, The Sentencing Project cautioned that "the most significant impact of these proposals, though, will begin to take place 10–20 years after their implementation, since the prisoners affected by these proposals would generally be locked up for at least that period of time under current practices" (1994, p. 2).

Confronted with the fact that an older inmate population will have a higher incidence of circulatory, respiratory, dietary, and ambulatory difficulties than younger inmates, prison officials need to anticipate and plan for geriatric services and programs now. Another realization is that these inmates pose the least risk in terms of criminal behavior. As a group, they are not a threat to society since crime is primarily an activity of young males. As a result, while the United States will be spending millions of dollars on the incarceration of these older prisoners, this is unlikely to reduce the incidence of crime.

Mauer (1994a) contends that these sentencing policies will have several lasting effects. First, the money spent to build new prisons will represent a commitment to maintain them for at least 50 years. Once the public has invested the requisite capital for construction, the courts will continue to fill the beds. Second, the funds that will be allocated to the increased costs of corrections will not be able to be used for other crime prevention measures. There will be little money available to improve the effectiveness of other components of the system such as juvenile justice, and diversion or early intervention programs will receive only limited funding and support. Third, the incarceration rate of African American males will continue to increase. As a result, there is little reason to believe that the status of young African American males will improve when their representation in American prisons and jails exceeds their representation in college classrooms. Fourth, there will be little opportunity to fully examine and discuss crime in the political arena because prevailing policies will be so dependent upon a limited range of sentencing initiatives (Mauer, 1994a, p. 23). Once the "quick fix" mentality to crime has been adopted, it is less likely to expect a divergence from the "punitive-reactive" response to crime.

Assessing the Effectiveness of Baseball Sentences

While some legislatures and policy wonks would disagree, "there is no reason to believe that continuing to increase the severity of penalties will have any significant impact on crime" (The Sentencing Project, 1994, p. 2). In their critique of incarceration trends, Irwin and Austin observed that political rhetoric has distorted rational sentencing policies and resulted in large increases in the number of prisoners, many of whom are nonviolent, without any corresponding reductions in crime (1994).

In a study of California's get-tough-on-crime strategy, "which quadrupled the prison population between 1980 and 1992," Joan Petersilia concluded "that the much higher imprisonment rates in California had no appreciable effect on violent crime and only slight effects on property crime" (Petersilia, cited in Broder, 1994a, p. 4). Despite such findings that these measures may be ineffective in reducing crime, and notwithstanding the spiraling costs of baseball sentencing, the punishment model continues to prevail.

In her review of retributive justice and determinate sentencing reforms, Griset (1991, p. 186) concludes that

> the determinate ideal arose as a reaction, a backlash against the perceived evil of the reigning paradigm. While the theoretical underpinnings of determinacy attracted a large following, in practice the determinate ideal has not lived up to the dreams or the promises of its creators.

With a similar argument, Robert Gangi, executive director of the Correctional Association of New York, writes that "three strikes and you're out represents extension of a policy that has proven a failure" (1994, p. A14).

With a strong momentum toward tougher sentences and the success of get-tough political posturing on crime issues, it is unlikely that baseball metaphors will fall into disuse. For example, a proposal in Oregon would offer voters a "grand slam" package for crime. This package would require prisoners to work or study, prohibit sentence reductions without a two-thirds legislative vote, make sentencing alternatives to prison more difficult, and impose mandatory minimum sentences for all violent offenders older than 15 (Rohter, 1994, p. A12).

Conclusion

In this review of the recently enacted Federal crime bill and the Washington, California, and Georgia statutes, and in the assessment of the anticipated consequences of recent sentencing statutes, baseball punishment is characterized as the latest episode in the search for the "quick fix" to a complicated and disturbing social problem. These attempts to prevent crime, however, are misguided and will prove to be far more costly and ineffective than their proponents and the public could have anticipated. In the rush to enact "three-strikes legislation," elected officials and the electorate appear to have given little thought to the long-term effects of these provisions.

In terms of additional systemic costs, these laws will have a considerable effect on an already over-burdened court system. The process of justice relies extensively on an offender entering into a plea agreement. Once these laws become enacted, there will be little incentive for an offender to plead guilty to any charges which could result in longer periods of incarceration. If offenders know that pleading guilty will constitute a first or sec-ond strike let alone a third, there is a greater likelihood that they will demand a trial. As a result, such legislation will necessitate additional funding for more prosecutors, judges, and court administrative and support staff.

One of the distressing aspects of these sentencing proposals is that they seem to have far-reaching effects on other offender populations. Included in the newly enacted Federal code is a provision to try as adults those juveniles who are 13 years of age and charged with certain violent crimes. It will be possible for the first strike to have been committed at age 13. This tendency to treat juvenile offenders more harshly is but one manifestation of a trend in juvenile justice mandating waiver into the adult court and sentencing younger juveniles to prison. Efforts to confront the crime problem would be more effective if society addressed the tough issues of gun availability, family violence, and drug prevention (Mauer, 1994c).

The "three-strikes" legislation has also raised public expectations far beyond the likelihood of success. A *Wall Street Journal* NBC News poll found that 75 percent of Americans interviewed believed that enacting such legislation would make a "major difference" in the crime rate (*Criminal Justice Newsletter,* 1994d, p. 1). Apparently, elected officials and the media have succeeded in pandering to the American penchant for oversimplifying the causes of crime.

Despite legislative sentencing changes, the *crime* problem has not been addressed. Absent a commitment to do more than get tough on criminals, the "three-strikes" legislation is just one more costly slogan which will have no appreciable benefit for society. Research and commentary on the consequences of baseball punishment suggest that prison populations will continue to grow, corrections expenditures will consume larger percentages of government budgets, and sentence severity will have "no discernible effect on the crime rate" (Currie, 1994, p. 120). As the rhetoric pushes punitive policies to the margin, baseball metaphors and politicalization of sentencing will continue to divert attention from addressing the antecedents and correlates of crime. It is not surprising that the emotionalizing of policy results in "feel-good bromides, like 'three-strikes' . . .that create the illusion of problem solving" (Kramer, 1994, p. 29).

Study Questions

1. How does the politicalization of crime influence legislation?

2. What are some of the negative effects of "three-strikes laws"?

3. If criminal justice experts agree that this type of legislation is ineffective and politicians know that, then why do you suppose that such legislation continues to be enacted?

References

Allen, Harry. (1994). Personal Communication. (September 17).

Balz, Dan. (1994). "Pete Wilson: Practicing the Politics of Survival." *The Washington Post National Weekly Edition.* (August 29–September 4): 14.

Black, Donald. (1976). The Behavior of Law. New York: Academic Press.

Booth, William. (1994). "Florida Turns Up the Heat on Crime." The Washington Post National Weekly Edition. (February 21–27): 37.

Broder, David. (1994a). "Population Explosion." The Washington Post National Weekly Edition. (April 25–May 1): 4.

——. (1994b). "When Tough Isn't Smart." *The Criminologist.* (July/August) 19: 4, 6.

California Legislative Service. (1994). Chapter 12 (A-B. No. 971) (West) 1994 Portion of 1993–94 Regular Session. "An Act to Amend Section 667 of the Penal Code."

California Penal Code Section 1192.7 *Congressional Digest.* (1994). "The Federal Role in Crime Control." Washington, DC (June–July).

Corrections Digest. (1994a). "Experts Doubt '3 Strikes You're Out' Laws Will Effectively Curb Crime." (February 9): 7–9.

——. (1994b). "Senate Crime Bill Will More Than Double American Prison Population by Year 2005." (March 9): 1–4.

Crime Control Digest. (1994). "'Three-time Loser' Bill to be Introduced in House." (January 24): 5–6.

Criminal Justice Newsletter. (1994a). "California Passes a Tough Three-Strikes-You're-Out Law." (April 4): 6–7.

——. (1994b). "Texas Comptroller Warns of 'Prison-Industrial Complex.'" (May 2): 2–3.

——. (1994c). "State Legislators Moving Toward Tougher Sentencing." (June 15): 1–2.

——. (1994d). "State Chief Justices Oppose Senate Crime Bill Provisions." (February 15): 1–3.

Cronin, Thomas, Tania Cronin, and Michael Milakovich. (1981). *U.S. v. Crime in the Streets.* Bloomington, IN: Indiana University Press.

Currie, Elliot. (1994). "What's Wrong with the Crime Bill." *The Nation.* (January 31) 258: 4, 118–121.

Egan, Timothy. (1994). "A 3-Strike Penal Law Shows It's Not as Simple as It Seems." *New York Times.* (February 15): A1, A11.

Final Legislative Report. (1994). Fifty-Third Washington State Legislature. 1994 Regular Session and First Special Session.

Gangi, Robert. (1994). "Where Three-Strikes Plan Takes Us in 20 Years." *New York Times.* (February 7): A14.

Geiger, Keith. (1994). "Upgrading School Buildings." *The Washington Post National Weekly Edition.* (September 26–October 2): 22.

Georgia Statutes 17-10-6.1 Code of Georgia, Title 17. Criminal Procedure, Chapter 10 Sentence and Punishment, Article 1. Procedure for Sentencing and Imposition of Punishment.

Gladwell, Malcolm. (1994). "The Crime Bill May Not Be the Cure." *The Washington Post National Weekly Edition.* (June 6–12): 33.

Gleason, Bucky. (1994). "Anti-Crime Packages Don't Work." *Erie Times News.* (October 9): A1, A12.

Gray, Jerry. (1994). "New Jersey Senate Approves Bill to Jail 3-Time Criminals for Life." *New York Times.* (May 13): A1, B9.

Griset, Pamala. (1991). *Determinate Sentencing: The Promise and the Reality of Retributive Justice.* Albany, NY: State University of New York Press.

Idelson, Holly. (1994). "Crime Bill's Final Version." *Congressional Quarterly.* (July 30) 52: 30, 2138.

Irwin, John, and James Austin. (1994). *It's About Time: America's Imprisonment Binge.* Belmont, CA: Wadsworth.

Kramer, Michael. (1994). "Tough. But Smart?" *Time.* (February 7): 29.

Kurtz, Howard. (1994). "The Campaign Weapon of Choice." *The Washington Post National Weekly Edition.* (September 19–25): 12.

Levinson, Arlene. (1994). "Three Strikes and You're Out." *Erie Morning News.* (January 25): B2.

Lewis, Anthony. (1994). "Crime and Politics." *New York Times.* (September 16): A13.

Lewis, Neil. (1993). "Crime Rates Decline; Outrage Hasn't." *New York Times.* (December 3): B6.

Mauer, Marc. (1994a). "Americans Behind Bars: The International Use of Incarceration, 1992–1993." The Sentencing Project. Washington, DC.

——. (1994b). "An Assessment of Sentencing Issues and the Death Penalty in the 1990s." The Sentencing Project. Washington, DC.

——. (1994c). "Testimony of Marc Mauer Before the House Judiciary Committee, Subcommittee on Crime and Criminal Justice on 'Three Strikes and You're Out.'" (March 1): 1–13.

Merlo, Alida, and Peter Benekos. (1992a). "Introduction: The Politics of Corrections" in Peter Benekos and Alida Merlo (eds.) *Corrections: Dilemmas and Directions.* Cincinnati, OH: Anderson Publishing.

——. (1992b). "Adapting Conservative Correctional Policies to the Economic Realities of the 1990s." *Criminal Justice Policy Review.* (March) 6: 1, 1–16.

National Council on Crime and Delinquency. (1994). "The Aging of California's Prison Population: An Assessment of Three Strikes Legislation." 1–6.

National Public Radio. (1994). Broadcast on "All Things Considered" (September 30).

Neri, Albert. (1994a). "With Candidates in Dead Heat, Ridge Uses Casey in Ad." *Erie Morning News.* (October 6): A14.

——. (1994b). "Singel Faces Up to His Worst Nightmare." *Erie Times News.* (October 9): B3.

New York Times. (1993). "Hunt for Kidnapped Girl, 12, Is Narrowed to Small Woods." (December 3): A22.

——. (1994a). "Mandatory Sentencing is Criticized by Justice." (March 10): A14.

——. (1994b). "Georgia Voters to Consider '2-Strikes' Law." (March 16): A10.

——. (1994c). "California Judge Refuses to Apply a Tough New Sentencing Law." (September 20): A9.

——. (1994d). "Killer Withdraws Plea in a '3 Strikes' Case." (September 28): A19.

Peyser, Marc. (1994). 'Strike Three and You're Not Out." *Newsweek.* (August 29): 63.

Raspberry, William. (1993). "Digging In Deeper." *The Washington Post National Weekly Edition.* (November 1–7): 29.

Reno, Janet. (1994). "Memorandum from the Attorney General: The Violent Crime Control and Law Enforcement Act of 1994." (September 15): 1–5.

Rohter, Larry. (1994). "States Embracing Tougher Measures for Fighting Crime." *New York Times.* (May 10): A1, A12.

Schneider, William. (1993). "Crime and Politics: Incumbents Got Mugged by Fear in Our Streets." *The Washington Post National Weekly Edition.* (November 15–21): 24.

The Sentencing Project. (1989). "The Lessons of Willie Horton." Washington, DC.

Shover, Neal and Werner Einstadter. (1988). *Analyzing American Corrections.* Belmont, CA: Wadsworth.

——. (1994). "Why '3 Strikes and You're Out' Won't Reduce Crime." Washington, DC.

Thomas, Pierre. (1994). "Getting to the Bottom Line on Crime." *The Washington Post National Weekly Edition.* (July 18–24): 31.

Tucker, Beverly. (1994). "Can California Afford 3 Strikes?" California Teachers Association Action (May): 7; 17.

U.S. Government Printing Office. (1994). "The Violent Crime Control and Law Enforcement Act of 1994." Conference Report. Washington, DC.

The Vindicator. (1994). "Law Will Star in Fall Campaigns." (August 28): A5.

Walker, Samuel. (1994). *Sense and Nonsense About Crime and Drugs: A Policy Guide*, 3rd ed. Belmont, CA: Wadsworth.

Washington Laws. (1994). *1994 Pamphlet Edition Session Laws* Fifty-Third Legislature 1994 Regular Session. Chapter 1 "Persistent Offenders—Life Sentence on Third Conviction." (Statute Law Committee) Olympia, WA. ◆

34
'Infamous Punishment'

The Psychological Consequences of Isolation

Craig Haney

A*nother new trend that nearly equals the "three-strikes" legislation, but is not as politicized, is the use of ultramaximum security prisons. Recalcitrant inmates are often placed into these types of institutions after causing trouble in the general prison population. An extreme example of such prisons is that of Pelican Bay, as described by Craig Haney in the following selection. It is little more than a dungeon with bare floors, in which there is no chance of seeing the outside world nor any opportunity for meaningful human contact. The results of such an experiment were already determined when New York devoted one wing of its prison to total isolation. Beaumont and Tocqueville reported on its disastrous consequences in Chapter 5. Complete isolation can have devastating psychological consequences for inmates, many of whom serve time under horrific conditions because they are mentally disturbed. Although this arrangement makes the job of administering corrections easier, it spells disaster for everyone else involved, including the community into which most of these inmates will ultimately be released.*

Excerpts from "'Infamous Punishment': The Psychological Consequences of Isolation" by Craig Haney, *The National Prison Project Journal*, Spring 1993, pp. 3–7, 21. Copyright © 1993 by *The National Prison Project Journal*. Rerprinted by permission.

Since the discovery of the asylum, prisons have been used to isolate inmates from the outside world, and often from each other. As most students of the American penitentiary know, the first real prisons in the United States were characterized by the regimen of extreme isolation that they imposed upon their prisoners. Although both the Auburn and Pennsylvania models (which varied only in the degree of isolation they imposed) eventually were abandoned, in part because of their harmful effects upon prisoners,[1] most prison systems have retained and employed—however sparingly—some form of punitive solitary confinement. Yet, because of the technological spin that they put on institutional design and procedure, the new super-maximum security prisons are unique in the modern history of American corrections. These prisons represent the application of sophisticated, modern technology dedicated entirely to the task of social control, and they isolate, regulate, and surveil more effectively than anything that has preceded them.

The Pelican Bay SHU

The Security Housing Unit at California's Pelican Bay State Prison is the prototype for this marriage of technology and total control.[2] The design of the Security Housing Unit—where well over a thousand prisoners are confined for periods of six months to several years—is starkly austere. Indeed, Pelican Bay's low, windowless, slate-gray exterior gives no hint to outsiders that this is a place where human beings live. But the barrenness of the prison's interior is what is most startling. On each visit to this prison I have been struck by the harsh, visual sameness and monotony of the physical design and the layout of these units. Architects and corrections officials have created living environments that are devoid of social stimulation. The atmosphere is antiseptic and sterile; you search in vain for humanizing touches or physical traces that human activity takes place here. The "pods" where prisoners live are virtually identical; there is little inside to mark location or give prisoners a sense of place.

Prisoners who are housed inside these units are completely isolated from the natural environment and from most of the natural rhythms of life. SHU prisoners, whose housing units have no windows, get only a glimpse of natural light. One prisoner captured the feeling created here when he told me, "When I first got here I felt like I was underground." Prisoners at Pelican Bay are not even permitted to see grass, trees or shrubbery. Indeed, little or none exists within the perimeters of the prison grounds, which are covered instead by gray gravel stones. This is no small accomplishment since the prison sits adjacent to the Redwood National Forest and the surrounding landscape is lush enough to support some of the oldest living things on earth. Yet here is where the California Department of Corrections has chosen to create the most lifeless environment in its—or any—correctional system.

When prisoners do get out of their cells for "yard," they are released into a barren concrete encasement that contains no exercise equipment, not even a ball. They cannot see any of the surrounding landscape because of the solid concrete walls that extend up some 20 feet around them. Overhead, an opaque roof covers half the yard; the other half, although covered with a wire screen, provides prisoners with their only view of the open sky. When outside conditions are not intolerably inclement (the weather at Pelican Bay often brings harsh cold and driving rain), prisoners may exercise in this concrete cage for approximately an hour-and-a-half a day. Their movements are monitored by video camera, watched by control officers on overhead television screens. In the control booth, the televised images of several inmates, each in separate exercise cages, show them walking around and around the perimeter of their concrete yards, like laboratory animals engaged in mindless and repetitive activity.

Prisoners in these units endure an unprecedented degree of involuntary, enforced idleness. Put simply: prisoners here have virtually nothing to *do*. Although prisoners who can afford them are permitted to have radios and small, regulation size televisions in their cells, there is no *activity* in which they may engage. Except for the limited exercise I have described and showers (three times a week), there are no prison routines that regularly take them out of their cells. All prisoners are "cell fed"—twice a day meals are placed on tray slots in the cell doors to be eaten by the prisoners inside. (Indeed, on my first tour of the institution one guard told me that this was the only flaw in the design of the prison—that they had not figured out a way to feed the prisoners "automatically," thus eliminating the need for any contact with them.) Prisoners are not permitted to do work of any kind, and they have no opportunities for educational or vocational training. They are never permitted out on their tiers unless they are moving to and from showers or yard, or being escorted—in chains and accompanied by two baton-wielding correctional officers per inmate—to the law library or infirmary outside the unit. Thus, with minor and insignificant exceptions, a prisoner's entire life is lived within the parameters of his 80-square-foot cell, a space that is typically shared with another prisoner whose life is similarly circumscribed.

All movement within these units is tightly regulated and controlled, and takes place under constant surveillance. Prisoners are permitted to initiate little or no meaningful behavior of their own. When they go to shower or "yard," they do so at prescribed times and in a prescribed manner and the procedure is elaborate. Guards must first unlock the padlocks on the steel doors to their cells. Once the guards have left the tier (they are never permitted on the tier when an unchained prisoner is out of his cell), the control officer opens the cell door by remote control. The prisoner must appear naked at the front of the control booth and submit to a routinized visual strip search before going to yard and, afterwards, before returning to his cell. Some prisoners are embarrassed by this public display of nudity (which takes place not only in front of control officers and other prisoners, but whomever else happens to be in the open area around the outside of the control booth.) As might be expected, many inmates forego the privilege of taking "yard" because of the humiliating procedures to which they must submit and the draconian conditions under which they are required to exercise. Whenever prisoners are in the presence of another human being (except for those who have cellmates), they are placed in chains, at both their waist and ankles. Indeed, they are chained even *before* they are permitted to exit their cells. There are also special holding cages in which prisoners are often left when they are being moved from one place to another. Prisoners are kept chained even during their classification hearings. I witnessed one prisoner, who was apparently new to the process, stumble as he attempted to sit down at the start of his hearing. Because he was chained with his hands behind his back, the correctional counselor had to instruct him to "sit on the chair like it was a horse"—unstable, with the back of the chair flush against his chest.

The cells themselves are designed so that a perforated metal screen, instead of a door, covers the entrance to the cells. This permits open, around-the-clock surveillance whenever guards enter the tiers. In addition, television cameras have been placed at strategic locations inside the cellblocks and elsewhere within the prison.

Because the individual "pods" are small (four cells on each of two floors), both visual and auditory surveillance are facilitated. Speakers and microphones have been placed in each cell to permit contact with control booth officers. Many prisoners believe that the microphones are used to monitor their conversations. There is little or no personal privacy that prisoners may maintain in these units.

Psychological Consequences

The overall level of long-term social deprivation within these units is nearly total and, in many ways, represents the destructive essence of this kind of confinement. Men in these units are deprived of human contact, touch and affection for years on end. They are denied the opportunity for contact visits of any kind; even attorneys and experts must interview them in visiting cells that prohibit contact. They cannot embrace or shake hands, even with visitors who have traveled long distances to see them. Many of these prisoners have not had visits from the outside world in years. They are not permitted to make phone calls except for emergencies or other extraordinary circumstances. As one prisoner told me: "Family and friends, after the years, they just start dropping off. Plus, the mail here is real irregular. We can't even take pictures of ourselves" to send to loved ones.[3] Their isolation from the social world, a world to which most of them will return, could hardly be more complete.

The operational procedures employed within the units themselves insure that even interactions with correctional staff occur infrequently and on highly distorted, unnatural terms. The institutional routines are structured so that prisoners are within close proximity of staff only when they are being fed, visually searched through the window of the control booth before going to "yard," being placed in chains and escorted elsewhere within the institution. There is always a physical barrier or mechanical restraint between them and other human beings.

The only exceptions occur for prisoners who are double-celled. Yet double-celling under these conditions hardly constitutes normal social contact. In fact, it is difficult to conceptualize a more strained and perverse form of intense and intrusive social interaction. For many prisoners, this kind of forced, invasive contact becomes a source of conflict and pain. They are thrust into intimate, constant co-living with another person—typically a total stranger—whose entire existence is similarly and unavoidably co-mingled with their own. Such pressurized contact can become the occasion for explosive violence. It also fails to provide any semblance of social "reality testing" that is intrinsic to human social existence.[4]

The psychological significance of this level of long-term social deprivation cannot be overstated. The destructive consequences can only be understood in terms of the profound importance of social contact and social context in providing an interpretive framework for all human experience, no matter how personal and seemingly private. Human identity formation occurs by virtue of social contact with others. As one SHU prisoner explained: "I liked to be around people. I'm happy and I enjoy people. They take that away from you [here]. It's like we're dead. As the Catholics say, in purgatory. They've taken away everything that might give a little purpose to your life." Moreover, when our reality is not grounded in social context, the internal stimuli and beliefs that we generate are impossible to test against the reactions of others. For this reason, the first step in any program of extreme social influence—ranging from police interrogation to indoctrination and "brainwashing"—is to isolate the intended targets from others, and to create a context in which social reality testing is controlled by those who would shape their thoughts, beliefs, emotions, and behavior. Most people are so disoriented by the loss of social context that they become highly malleable, unnaturally sensitive, and vulnerable to the influence of those who control the environment around them. Indeed, this may be its very purpose. As one SHU prisoner told me: "You're going to be what the place wants you to be or you're going to be nothing."

Long-term confinement under these conditions has several predictable psychological consequences. Although not everyone will manifest negative psychological effects to the same degree, and it is difficult to specify the point in time at which the destructive consequences will manifest themselves, few

escape unscathed. The norms of prison life require prisoners to struggle to conceal weakness, to minimize admissions of psychic damage or pain. It is part of a prisoner ethic in which preserving dignity and autonomy, and minimizing vulnerability, is highly valued. Thus, the early stages of these destructive processes are often effectively concealed. They will not be apparent to untrained or casual observers, nor will they be revealed to persons whom the prisoners do not trust. But over time, the more damaging parts of adaptation to this kind of environment begin to emerge and become more obvious.[5]

The first adaptation derives from the totality of control that is created inside a place like Pelican Bay. Incarceration itself makes prisoners dependent to some degree upon institutional routines to guide and organize their behavior. However, the totality of control imposed in a place like Pelican Bay is extreme enough to produce a qualitatively different adaptation. Eventually, many prisoners become entirely dependent upon the structure and routines of the institution for the control of their behavior. There are two related components to this adaptation. Some prisoners become dependent upon the institution to *limit* their behavior. That is, because their behavior is so carefully and completely circumscribed during their confinement in lockup, they begin to lose the ability to set limits for themselves. Some report becoming uncomfortable with even small amounts of freedom because they have lost the sense of how to behave without the constantly enforced restrictions, tight external structure, and totality of behavioral restraints.

Other prisoners suffer an opposite but related reaction, caused by the same set of circumstances. These prisoners lose the ability to *initiate* behavior of any kind—to organize their own lives around activity and purpose—because they have been stripped of any opportunity to do so for such prolonged periods of time. Apathy and lethargy set in. They report being tired all the time, despite the fact that they have been allowed to do nothing. They find it difficult to focus their attention, their minds wander, they cannot concentrate or organize thoughts or actions in a coherent way. In extreme cases, a sense of profound despair and hopelessness is created.

The experience of total social isolation can lead, paradoxically, to social withdrawal. That is, some prisoners in isolation draw further into themselves as a way of adjusting to the deprivation of meaningful social contact imposed upon them. They become uncomfortable in the course of the little social contact they are permitted. They take steps to avoid even that—by refusing to go to "yard," refraining from conversation with staff, discouraging any visits from family members or friends, and ceasing correspondence with the outside world. They move from being starved for social contact to being frightened by it. Of course, as they become increasingly unfamiliar and uncomfortable with social interaction, they are further alienated from others and disoriented in their presence.

The absence of social contact and social context creates an air of unreality to one's existence in these units. Some prisoners act out as a way of getting a reaction from their environment, proving to themselves that they still exist, that they are still alive and capable of eliciting a human response—however hostile—from other human beings. This is the context in which seemingly irrational refusals of prisoners to "cuff up" take place—which occur in the Pelican Bay SHU with some regularity, in spite of the knowledge that such refusals invariably result in brutal "cell extractions" in which they are physically subdued, struck with a large shield and special cell extraction baton, and likely to be shot with a taser gun or wooden or rubber bullets before being placed in leg irons and handcuffs.[6]

In some cases, another pattern emerges. The line between their own thought processes and the bizarre reality around them becomes increasingly tenuous. Social contact grounds and anchors us; when it is gone,

there is nothing to take its place. Moreover, for some, the environment around them is so painful and so painfully impossible to make sense of, that they create their own reality, one seemingly "crazy" but easier for them to tolerate and make sense of. Thus, they live in a world of fantasy instead of the world of control, surveillance, and inhumanity that has been imposed upon them by the explicit and conscious policies of the correctional authorities.

For others, the deprivations, the restrictions, and the totality of control fills them with intolerable levels of frustration. Combined with the complete absence of activity or meaningful outlets through which they can vent this frustration, it can lead to outright anger and then to rage. This rage is a reaction against, not a justification for, their oppressive confinement. Such anger cannot be abated by intensifying the very deprivations that have produced it. They will fight against the system that they perceive only as having surrounded and oppressed them. Some will lash out violently against the people whom they hold responsible for the frustration and deprivation that fills their lives. Ultimately, the outward expression of this violent frustration is marked by its irrationality, primarily because of the way in which it leads prisoners into courses of action that further insure their continued mistreatment. But the levels of deprivation are so profound, and the resulting frustration so immediate and overwhelming, that for some this lesson is unlikely ever to be learned. The pattern can only be broken through drastic changes in the nature of the environment, changes that produce more habitable and less painful conditions of confinement.

The magnitude and extremity of oppressive control that exists in these units helps to explain another feature of confinement in the Pelican Bay SHU that, in my experience, is unique in modern American corrections. Prisoners there have repeatedly voiced fears of physical mistreatment and brutality on a widespread and frequent basis. They speak of physical intimidation and the fear of violence at the hands of correctional officers. These concerns extend beyond the physical intimidation that is structured into the design of the units themselves—the totality of restraint, the presence of guards who are all clad in heavy flak jackets inside the units, the use of chains to move prisoners out of their cells, and the constant presence of control officers armed with assault rifles slung across their chests as they monitor prisoners within their housing units. Beyond this, prisoners speak of the frequency of "cell extractions" which they describe in frightening terms. Most have witnessed extractions in which groups of correctional officers (the previously described "cell extraction team") have entered prisoners' cells, fired wooden or rubber bullets and electrical tasers at prisoners, forcibly chained and removed them from their cells, sometimes for the slightest provocation (such as the failure to return food trays on command). And many note that this mistreatment may be precipitated by prisoners whose obvious psychiatric problems preclude them from conforming to SHU rules or responding to commands issued by correctional officers.[7] One prisoner reported being constantly frightened that guards were going to hurt him. The day I interviewed him, he told me that he had been sure the correctional staff was "going to come get him." He stuck his toothbrush in the door of his cell so they couldn't come inside. He vowed "to hang myself or stop eating [and] starve to death" in order to get out of the SHU.

I believe that the existence of such brutality can be attributed in part to the psychology of oppression that has been created in and around this prison. Correctional staff, themselves isolated from more diverse and conflicting points of view that they might encounter in more urban or cosmopolitan environments, have been encouraged to create their own unique worldview at Pelican Bay. Nothing counters the prefabricated ideology into which they step at Pelican Bay, a prison that was designated as a place for the "worst of the worst" even before the first prisoners

ever arrived. They work daily in an environment whose very structure powerfully conveys the message that these prisoners are not human beings. There is no reciprocity to their perverse and limited interactions with prisoners—who are always in cages or chains, seen through screens or windows or television cameras or protective helmets—and who are given no opportunities to act like human beings. Pelican Bay has become a massive self-fulfilling prophecy. Violence is one mechanism with which to accommodate to the fear inevitably generated on both sides of the bars.

Psychiatric Disorders

The psychological consequences of living in these units for long periods of time are predictably destructive, and the potential for these psychic stressors to precipitate various forms of psychopathology is clear-cut. When prisoners who are deprived of meaningful social contact begin to shun all forms of interaction, withdraw more deeply into themselves and cease initiating social interaction, they are in pain and require psychiatric attention. They get little or none.[8] Prisoners who have become uncomfortable in the presence of others will be unable to adjust to housing in a mainline prison population, not to mention free society. They are also at risk of developing disabling, clinical psychiatric symptoms. Thus, numerous studies have underscored the role of social isolation as a correlate of mental illness. Similarly, when prisoners become profoundly lethargic in the face of their monotonous, empty existence, the potential exists for this lethargy to shade into despondency and, finally, to clinical depression. For others who feel the frustration of the totality of control more acutely, their frustration may become increasingly difficult to control and manage. Long-term problems of impulse control may develop that are psychiatric in nature.

This kind of environment is capable of creating clinical syndromes in even healthy personalities, and can be psychologically destructive for anyone who enters and endures it for significant periods of time. However, prisoners who enter these places with *pre-existing* psychiatric disorders suffer more acutely. The psychic pain and vulnerability that they bring into the lockup unit may grow and fester if unattended to. In the absence of psychiatric help, there is nothing to keep many of these prisoners from entering the abyss of psychosis.

Indeed, in the course of my interviews at Pelican Bay, numerous prisoners spoke to me about their inability to handle the stress of SHU confinement. Some who entered the unit with pre-existing problems could perceive that they had gotten worse. Others had decompensated so badly that they had no memory of ever having functioned well, or had little awareness that their present level of functioning was tenuous, fragile, and psychotic. More than a few expressed concerns about what they would do when released—either from the SHU into mainline housing, or directly into free society (as a number are). One prisoner who was housed in the unit that is reserved for those who are maintained on psychotropic medication told me that he was sure that the guards in this unit were putting poison in his food. He was concerned because when released (this year), he told me "I know I won't be able to work or be normal."

Many SHU prisoners also reported being suicidal or self-mutilating. A number of them showed me scars on their arms and necks where they had attempted to cut themselves. One prisoner told me matter-of-factly, "I've been slicing on my arms for years, sometimes four times a day, just to see the blood flow." One suicidal prisoner who is also deaf reported being cell extracted because he was unable to hear the correctional officers call count (or "show skin"—a procedure used so that staff knows a prisoner is in his cell). He now sleeps on the floor of his cell "so that the officers can see my skin." Another prisoner, who has reported hearing voices in the past and seeing "little furry

things," has slashed his wrists on more than one occasion. Instead of being transferred to a facility where he could receive mental health treatment—since obviously none is available at Pelican Bay—he has been moved back and forth between the VCU and SHU units. While in the VCU, he saw a demon who knew his name and frequently spoke to him. As I interviewed him, he told me that the voices were cursing at him for talking to me. In the course of our discussion, he was clearly distracted by these voices and, periodically, he laughed inappropriately. One psychotic SHU prisoner announced to me at the start of our interview that he was a "super power man" who could not only fly, but see through steel and hear things that were being said about him from great distances. He had lived in a board-and-care home and been maintained on Thorazine before his incarceration. Although he had attempted suicide three times while at Pelican Bay, he was confident that when he was placed back in the mainline he would not have to attempt to kill himself again—because he thought he could convince his cellmate to do it for him. Another flagrantly psychotic SHU prisoner talked about a miniature implant that the Department of Corrections had placed inside his head, connected to their "main computer," which they were using to control him electronically, by programming him to say and do things that would continually get him into trouble. When I asked him whether or not he had seen any of the mental health staff, he became agitated and earnestly explained to me that his problem was medical—the computer implant inserted into his brain—not psychiatric. He offered to show me the paperwork from a lawsuit he had filed protesting this unauthorized medical procedure.

When prison systems become seriously overcrowded—as California's is (operating now at more than 180 percent of capacity)—psychiatric resources become increasingly scarce and disturbed prisoners are handled poorly, if at all. Often, behavior that is caused primarily by psychiatric disfunction results in placement in punitive solitary confinement, where little or no psychiatric precautions are taken to protect or treat them. They are transferred from one such punitive isolation unit to another, in what has been derisively labeled "bus therapy."[9] In fact, I have come to the conclusion that the Pelican Bay SHU has become a kind of "dumping ground" of last resort for many psychiatrically disturbed prisoners who were inappropriately housed and poorly treated—because of their psychiatric disorders—in other SHU units. Because such prisoners were unable to manage their disorders in these other units—in the face of psychologically destructive conditions of confinement and in the absence of appropriate treatment—their continued rules violations, which in many cases were the direct product of their psychiatric disorders, have resulted in their transfer to Pelican Bay. Thus, their placement in the Pelican Bay SHU is all the more inappropriate because of the process by which they got there. Their inability to adjust to the harsh conditions that prevailed at these other units should disqualify them for placement in this most harsh and destructive environment, yet, the opposite appears to be the case.

Conclusions

Although I have seen conditions elsewhere that approximate those at the Pelican Bay SHU, and have testified about their harmful psychological effects, I have never seen long-term social deprivation so totally and completely enforced. Neither have I seen prisoner movements so completely regimented and controlled. Never have I seen the technology of social control used to this degree to deprive captive human beings of the opportunity to initiate meaningful activity, nor have I seen such an array of deliberate practices designed for the sole purpose of preventing prisoners from engaging in any semblance of normal social intercourse. The technological structure of this environment adds to its impersonality and anonymity.

Prisoners interact with their captors over microphones, in chains or through thick windows, peering into the shields that hide the faces of cell extraction teams as they move in coordinated violence. It is axiomatic among those who study human behavior that social connectedness and social support are the prerequisites to long-term social adjustment. Yet, persons who have been wrenched from a human community of any kind risk profound and chronic alienation and asociality.

A century and a half ago, social commentators like Dickens and de Tocqueville marveled at the willingness of American society to incarcerate its least favored citizens in "despotic" places of solitary confinement.[10] De Tocqueville understood that complete isolation from others "produces a deeper effect on the soul of the convict," an effect that he worried might prove disabling when the convict was released into free society. Although he admired the power that American penitentiaries wielded over prisoners, he did not have the tools to measure their long-term effects nor the benefit of more than a hundred years of experience and humane intelligence that has led us away from these destructive interventions. Ignoring all of this, places like Pelican Bay appear to have brought us full circle. And then some.

Study Questions

1. Describe the physical environment and social interactions in the SHU at Pelican Bay.

2. How do such brutalizing conditions affect the human psyche?

3. What is the relationship between psychologically disturbed prisoners and treatment of prisoners at SHU?

4. Compare this system of punishment to the early experiments with solitary confinement in the New York system described by Beaumont and Tocqueville in Chapter 5.

Notes

1. In words it appears to have long since forgotten, the United States Supreme Court more than a century ago, characterized solitary confinement as an "infamous punishment" and provided this explanation for its abandonment: "Experience demonstrated that there were serious objections to it. A considerable number of the prisoners fell, after even a short confinement into a semi-fatuous condition, from which it was next to impossible to arouse them, and others became violently insane; others still, committed suicide; while those who stood the ordeal better were not generally reformed, and in most cases did not recover sufficient mental activity to be of any subsequent service . . .[I]t is within the memory of many persons interested in prison discipline that some 30 or 40 years ago the whole subject attracted the general public attention, and its main feature of solitary confinement was found to be too severe." *In re Medley*, 134 U.S. 160, 168 (1890).

2. Its predecessor, the federal prison at Marion, Illinois, is now more than 25 years old and a technological generation behind Pelican Bay. Although many of the same oppressive conditions and restrictive procedures are approximated at Marion, these comments are focused on Pelican Bay, where my observations and interviews are more recent and where conditions are more severe and extreme. In addition to some of the descriptive comments that follow, conditions at the Pelican Bay SHU have been described in Elvin, J. "Isolation, Excessive Force Under Attack at California's Supermax," *NPP JOURNAL*, Vol. 7, No. 4, (1992), and White, L. "Inside the Alcatraz of the '90s," *California Lawyer* 42–48 (1992). The unique nature of this environment has also generated some media attention. E.g., Hentoff, N., "Buried Alive in American Prisons," *The Washington Post*, January 9, 1993; Mintz, H., "Is Pelican Bay Too Tough?" 182 *The Recorder*, p. 1, September 19, 1991; Roemer, J. "High-Tech Deprivation," *San Jose Mercury News*, June 7, 1992; Ross, J. "High-tech dungeon," *The Bay Guardian* 15–17, (1992). The creation of such a unit in California is particularly unfortunate in light of fully 20 years of federal litigation over conditions of confinement in the "lockup" units in four of the state's maximum security prisons (Deuel Vocational institution,

Folsom, San Quentin, and Soledad). E.g., *Wright v. Enomoto*, 462 F. Supp. 397 (N.D. Cal. 1976). In a lengthy evidentiary hearing conducted before judge Stanley Weigel, the state's attorneys and corrections officials were present during expert testimony from numerous witnesses concerning the harmful effects of the punitive solitary confinement they were imposing upon prisoners in these units. Except for some disagreement offered up by Department of Corrections employees, this testimony went unanswered and unrebutted. *Toussaint v. Rusben*, 553 F. Supp. 1365 (N.D. Cal. 1983), *aff'd in part Toussaint v. Yockey*, 722 F.2d 1490 (9th Cir. 1984). Only a few years after this hearing, and while a federal monitor was still in place to oversee the conditions in these other units, the Department of Corrections began construction of Pelican Bay. In apparent deliberate indifference to this extensive record, and seemingly without seeking any outside opinions on the psychological consequences of housing prisoners in a unit like the one they intended to create or engaging in public debate over the wisdom of such a project, they proceeded to commit over $200 million in state funds to construct a prison whose conditions were in many ways worse than those at the other prisons, whose harmful effect had been litigated over the preceding decade.

3. Most corrections experts understand the significance of maintaining social connectedness and social ties for long-term adjustment in and out of prison. See, e.g., Schafer, N. "Prison Visiting: Is It Time to Review the Rules?" *Federal Probation 25–30* (1989). This simple lesson has been completely ignored at Pelican Bay.

4. Indeed, in my opinion, double-celling in Security Housing Units like those at Pelican Bay constitutes a clear form of overcrowding. As such, it can be expected to produce its own, independently harmful effects, as the literature on the negative consequences of overcrowding attests.

5. Although not extensive, the literature on the negative psychological effects of solitary confinement and related situations is useful in interpreting contemporary observations and interview data from prisoners placed in punitive isolation like Pelican Bay. See, e.g., Heron, W. "The Pathology of Boredom," *Scientific American*, 196 (1957); Burney, C. "Solitary Confinement," London: Macmillan (1961); Cormier, B., & Williams, P. "Excessive

Deprivation of Liberty," *Canadian Psychiatric Association Journal* 470–484 (1966); Scott, G., & Gendreau, P. "Psychiatric Implications of Sensory Deprivation in a Maximum Security Prison," 12 *Canadian Psychiatric Association Journal* 337–341 (1969); Cohen, S., & Taylor, L., *Psychological Survival*, Harmondsworth: Penguin (1972); Grassian, S., "Psychopathological Effects of Solitary Confinement" 140 *American Journal of Psychiatry* 1450–1454 (1983); Jackson, M. *Prisoners of Isolation: Solitary Confinement in Canada*, Toronto: University of Toronto Press (1983); Grassian, S. & Friedman, N., "Effects of Sensory Deprivation in Psychiatric Seclusion and Solitary Confinement" 8 *International Journal of Law and Psychiatry* 49–65 (1986); Slater, R. "Psychiatric Intervention in an Atmosphere of Terror," 7 *American Journal of Forensic Psychiatry* 6–12 (1986); Brodsky, S., & Scogin, F., "Inmates in Protective Custody: First Data on Emotional Effects," 1 *Forensic Reports* 267–280 (1988); and Cooke, D. "Containing Violent Prisoners: An Analysis of the Barlinnie Special Unit," 29 *British Journal of Criminology* 129–143 (1989).

6. This description of cell extraction practices is corroborated not only by numerous prisoner accounts of the process but also by explicit Department of Corrections procedures. Once a decision has been made to "extract" a prisoner from his cell, this is how the five-man cell extraction team proceeds: the first member of the team is to enter the cell carrying a large shield, which is used to push the prisoner back into a corner of the cell; the second member follows closely, wielding a special cell extraction baton, which is used to strike the inmate on the upper part of his body so that he will raise his arms in self-protection; thus unsteadied, the inmate is pulled off balance by another member of the team whose job is to place leg irons around his ankles; once downed, a fourth member of the team places him in handcuffs; the fifth member stands ready to fire a taser gun or rifle that shoots wooden or rubber bullets at the resistant inmate.

7. One of the basic principles of any unit premised on domination and punitive control—as the Pelican Bay Security Housing Unit is—is that a worse, more punitive and degrading place always must be created in order to punish those prisoners who still commit rule infractions. At Pelican Bay, that place is termed the "Violence Control Unit" (which the prisoners refer to as "Bedrock"). From my observations and interviews, some of the most psychiatrically disturbed prisoners are kept in the VCU. Prisoners in this unit are not permitted televisions or radios, and they are the only ones chained and escorted to the door of the outside exercise cage (despite the fact that no prisoner is more than four cells away from this door). In addition, there are plexiglass coverings on the entire outside facing of the VCU cells, which results in a significant distortion of vision into and out of the cell itself. Indeed, because of the bright light reflected off this Plexiglas covering, I found it difficult to see clearly into any of the upper-level VCU cells I observed, or even to look clearly into the faces of prisoners who were standing right in front of me on the other side of this plexiglass shield. Inside, the perception of confinement is intensified because of this added barrier placed on the front of each cell.

8. In the first several years of its operation, Pelican Bay State Prison had *one* full-time mental health staff member, and not a single PhD psychologist or psychiatrist, to administer to the needs of the entire prison population, which included over 1,000 SHU prisoners, as well as over 2,000 prisoners in the general population of the prison. Although the size of the mental health staff has been increased somewhat in recent years, it is still the case that no advance screening is done by mental health staff on prisoners admitted to the SHUs to determine pre-existing psychiatric disorders or suicide risk, and no regular monitoring is performed by mental health staff to assess the negative psychological consequences of exposure to this toxic environment.

9. Cf. Toch, H., "The Disturbed Disruptive Inmate: Where Does the Bus Stop?" *10 Journal of Psychiatry and Law* 327–350, (1982).

10. Dickens, C., *American Notes for General Circulation*. London: Chapman and Hall (1842); Beaumont, G., & de Tocqueville, A., *On the Penitentiary System in the United States and Its Application in France*, Montclair, NJ (1833, 1976). ✦

35
'This Man Has Expired'
Witness to an Execution

Robert Johnson

Capital punishment is another long-touted solution to the problem of violent crime. After a decade-long moratorium that ended with the execution of Gary Gilmore in 1977, capital punishment moved into full swing in the 1980s and 1990s. However, a period of readjustment followed the moratorium, in which most death-sentenced cases during and shortly thereafter resulted in life sentences. At that time, the process of review was very slow, but in recent years the likelihood of a death sentence actually being carried out has increased. Reversals are less frequent and cases are moving along at a more rapid pace. There are currently over 3000 inmates awaiting execution on death rows across the United States. In the following article, the work of the execution team described by Robert Johnson has just begun.

The death penalty has made a comeback in recent years. In the late sixties and through most of the seventies, such a thing seemed impossible. There was a moratorium on executions in the U.S., backed by the authority of the Supreme Court. The hiatus lasted roughly a decade. Coming on the heels of a gradual but persistent decline in the use of

Excerpts from "'This Man Has Expired': Witness to an Execution" by Robert Johnson, *Commonweal Foundation*, 66 (1): 9–15. Copyright © 1989 by Commonweal Foundation. Reprinted by permission.

the death penalty in the Western world, it appeared to some that executions would pass from the American scene [cf Commonweal, January 15, 1988]. Nothing could have been further from the truth.

Beginning with the execution of Gary Gilmore in 1977, over 100 people have been put to death, most of them in the last few years. Some 2,200 prisoners are presently confined on death rows across the nation. The majority of these prisoners have lived under sentence of death for years, in some cases a decade or more, and are running out of legal appeals. It is fair to say that the death penalty is alive and well in America, and that executions will be with us for the foreseeable future.

Gilmore's execution marked the resurrection of the modern death penalty and was big news. It was commemorated in a best-selling tome by Norman Mailer, *The Executioner's Song*. The title was deceptive. Like others who have examined the death penalty, Mailer told us a great deal about the condemned but very little about the executioners. Indeed, if we dwell on Mailer's account, the executioner's story is not only unsung; it is distorted.

Gilmore's execution was quite atypical. His was an instance of state-assisted suicide accompanied by an element of romance and played out against a backdrop of media fanfare. Unrepentant and unafraid, Gilmore refused to appeal his conviction. He dared the state of Utah to take his life, and the media repeated the challenge until it became a taunt that may well have goaded officials to action. A failed suicide pact with his lover staged only days before the execution, using drugs she delivered to him in a visit marked by unusual intimacy, added a hint of melodrama to the proceedings. Gilmore's final words, "Let's do it," seemed to invite the lethal hail of bullets from the firing squad. The nonchalant phrase, at once fatalistic and brazenly rebellious, became Gilmore's epitaph. It clinched his outlaw-hero image, and found its way onto tee shirts that confirmed his celebrity status.

Befitting a celebrity, Gilmore was treated with unusual leniency by prison officials during his confinement on death row. He was, for example, allowed to hold a party the night before his execution, during which he was free to eat, drink, and make merry with his guests until the early morning hours. This is not entirely unprecedented. Notorious English convicts of centuries past would throw farewell balls in prison on the eve of their executions. News accounts of such affairs sometimes included a commentary on the richness of the table and the quality of the dancing. For the record, Gilmore served Tang, Kool-Aid, cookies and coffee, later supplemented by contraband pizza and an unidentified liquor. Periodically, he gobbled drugs obligingly provided by the prison pharmacy. He played a modest arrangement of rock music albums but refrained from dancing.

Gilmore's execution generally, like his parting fete, was decidedly out of step with the tenor of the modern death penalty. Most condemned prisoners fight to save their lives, not to have them taken. They do not see their fate in romantic terms; there are no farewell parties. Nor are they given medication to ease their anxiety or win their compliance. The subjects of typical executions remain anonymous to the public and even to their keepers. They are very much alone at the end.

In contrast to Mailer's account, the focus of the research I have conducted is on the executioners themselves as they carry out typical executions. In my experience executioners—not unlike Mailer himself—can be quite voluble, and sometimes quite moving, in expressing themselves. I shall draw upon their words to describe the death work they carry out in our name.

Death Work and Death Workers

Executioners are not a popular subject of social research, let alone conversation at the dinner table or cocktail party. We simply don't give the subject much thought. When we think of executioners at all, the imagery runs to individual men of disreputable, or at least questionable, character who work stealthily behind the scenes to carry out their grim labors. We picture hooded men hiding in the shadow of the gallows, or anonymous figures lurking out of sight behind electric chairs, gas chambers, firing blinds, or, more recently, hospital gurneys. We wonder who would do such grisly work and how they sleep at night.

This image of the executioner as a sinister and often solitary character is today misleading. To be sure, a few states hire freelance executioners and traffic in macabre theatrics. Executioners may be picked up under cover of darkness and some may still wear black hoods. But today, executions are generally the work of a highly disciplined and efficient team of correctional officers.

Broadly speaking, the execution process as it is now practiced starts with the prisoner's confinement on death row, an oppressive prison-within-a-prison where the condemned are housed, sometimes for years, awaiting execution. Death work gains momentum when an execution date draws near and the prisoner is moved to the death house, a short walk from the death chamber. Finally, the process culminates in the death watch, a twenty-four-hour period that ends when the prisoner has been executed.

This final period, the death watch, is generally undertaken by correctional officers who work as a team and report directly to the prison warden. The warden or his representative, in turn, must by law preside over the execution. In many states, it is a member of the death watch or execution team, acting under the warden's authority, who in fact plays the formal role of executioner. Though this officer may technically work alone, his teammates view the execution as a shared responsibility. As one officer on the death watch told me in no uncertain terms: "We all take part in it; we all play 100 percent in it, too. That takes the load off this one individual [who pulls the switch]." The formal executioner concurred. "Everyone on the team can do it, and nobody will tell you I did it. I know my team." I found nothing in my research to dispute these claims.

The officers of these death watch teams are our modern executioners. As part of a larger study of the death work process, I studied one such group. This team, comprised of nine seasoned officers of varying ranks, had carried out five electrocutions at the time I began my research. I interviewed each officer on the team after the fifth execution, then served as an official witness at a sixth electrocution. Later, I served as a behind-the-scenes observer during their seventh execution. The results of this phase of my research form the substance of this [chapter].

The Death Watch Team

The death watch or execution team members refer to themselves, with evident pride, as simply "the team." This pride is shared by other correctional officials. The warden at the institution I was observing praised members of the team as solid citizens—in his words, country boys. These country boys, he assured me, could be counted on to do the job and do it well. As a fellow administrator put it, "an execution is something [that] needs to be done and good people, dedicated people who believe in the American system, should do it. And there's a certain amount of feeling, probably one to another, that they're part of that—that when they have to hang tough, they can do it, and they can do it right. And that it's just the right thing to do."

The official view is that an execution is a job that has to be done, and done right. The death penalty is, after all, the law of the land. In this context, the phrase "done right" means that an execution should be a proper, professional, dignified undertaking. In the words of a prison administrator, "We had to be sure that we did it properly, professionally, and [that] we gave as much dignity to

the person as we possibly could in the process. . . . If you've gotta do it, it might just as well be done the way it's supposed to be done—without any sensation."

In the language of the prison officials, "proper" refers to procedures that go off smoothly, "professional" means without personal feelings that intrude on the procedures in any way. The desire for executions that take place "without any sensation" no doubt refers to the absence of media sensationalism, particularly if there should be an embarrassing and undignified hitch in the procedures, for example, a prisoner who breaks down or becomes violent and must be forcibly placed in the electric chair as witnesses, some from the media, look on in horror. Still, I can't help but note that this may be a revealing slip of the tongue. For executions are indeed meant to go off without any human feeling, without any sensation. A profound absence of feeling would seem to capture the bureaucratic ideal embodied in the modern execution.

The view of executions held by the execution team members parallels that of correctional administrators but is somewhat more restrained. The officers of the team are closer to the killing and dying, and are less apt to wax abstract or eloquent in describing the process. Listen to one man's observations:

> It's a job. I don't take it personally. You know, I don't take it like I'm having a grudge against this person and this person has done something to me. I'm just carrying out a job, doing what I was asked to do. . . . This man has been sentenced to death in the courts. This is the law and he broke this law, and he has to suffer the consequences. And one of the consequences is to put him to death.

I found that few members of the execution team support the death penalty outright or without reservation. Having seen executions close up, many of them have lingering doubts about the justice or wisdom of this sanction. As one officer put it:

I'm not sure the death penalty is the right way. I don't know if there is a right answer. So I look at it like this: if it's gotta be done, at least it can be done in a humane way, if there is such a word for it. . . . The only way it should be done, I feel, is the way we do it. It's done professionally, it's not no horseplaying. Everything is done by documentation. On time. By the book.

Arranging executions that occur "without any sensation" and that go "by the book" is no mean task, but it is a task that is undertaken in earnest by the execution team. The tone of the enterprise is set by the team leader, a man who takes a hard-boiled, nononsense approach to correctional work in general and death work in particular. "My style," he says, "is this: if it's a job to do, get it done. Do it and that's it." He seeks out kindred spirits, men who see killing condemned prisoners as a job—a dirty job one does reluctantly, perhaps, but above all a job one carries out dispassionately and in the line of duty.

To make sure that line of duty is a straight and accurate one, the death watch team has been carefully drilled by the team leader in the mechanics of execution. The process has been broken down into simple, discrete tasks and practiced repeatedly. The team leader describes the division of labor in the following exchange:

The execution team is a nine-officer team and each one has certain things to do. When I would train you, maybe you'd buckle a belt, that might be all you'd have to do. . . . And you'd be expected to do one thing and that's all you'd be expected to do. And if everybody does what they were taught, or what they were trained to do, at the end the man would be put in the chair and everything would be complete. It's all come together now.

So it's broken down into very small steps. . . .

Very small, yes. Each person has *one* thing to do.

I see. What's the purpose of breaking it down into such small steps?

So people won't get confused. I've learned it's kind of a tense time. When you're executin' a person, killing a person—you call it killin', executin', whatever you want—the man dies anyway. I find the less you got on your mind, why, the better you'll carry it out. So it's just very simple things. And so far, you know, it's all come together, we haven't had any problems.

This division of labor allows each man on the execution team to become a specialist, a technician with a sense of pride in his work. Said one man,

My assignment is the leg piece. Right leg. I roll his pants' leg up, place a piece [electrode] on his leg, strap his leg in . . .I've got all the moves down pat. We train from different posts; I can do any of them. But that's my main post.

The implication is not that the officers are incapable of performing multiple or complex tasks, but simply that it is more efficient to focus each officer's efforts on one easy task.

An essential part of the training is practice. Practice is meant to produce a confident group, capable of fast and accurate performance under pressure. The rewards of practice are reaped in improved performance. Executions take place with increasing efficiency, and eventually occur with precision. "The first one was grisly," a team member confided to me. He explained that there was a certain amount of fumbling, which made the execution seem interminable. There were technical problems as well: The generator was set too high so the body was badly burned. But that is the past, the officer assured me. "The ones now, we know what we're doing. It's just like clockwork."

The Death Watch

The death-watch team is deployed during the last twenty-four hours before an execution. In the state under study, the death watch starts at 11 o'clock the night before the execution and ends at 11 o'clock the next night when the execution takes place. At least two officers would be with the prisoner at any given time during that period. Their objective is to keep the prisoner alive and "on schedule." That is, to move him through a series of critical and cumulatively demoralizing junctures that begin with his last meal and end with his last walk. When the time comes, they must deliver the prisoner up for execution as quickly and unobtrusively as possible.

Broadly speaking, the job of the death watch officer, as one man put it, "is to sit and keep the inmate calm for the last twenty-four hours—and get the man ready to go." Keeping a condemned prisoner calm means, in part, serving his immediate needs. It seems paradoxical to think of the death watch officers as providing services to the condemned, but the logistics of the job make service a central obligation of the officers. Here's how one officer made this point:

> Well, you can't help but be involved with many of the things that he's involved with. Because if he wants to make a call to his family, well, you'll have to dial the number. And you keep records of whatever calls he makes. If he wants a cigarette, well, he's not allowed to keep matches so you light it for him. You've got to pour his coffee, too. So you're aware what he's doing. It's not like you can just ignore him. You've gotta just be with him whether he wants it or not, and cater to his needs.

Officers cater to the condemned because contented inmates are easier to keep under control. To a man, the officers say this is so. But one can never trust even a contented, condemned prisoner.

The death-watch officers see condemned prisoners as men with explosive personalities. "You don't know what, what a man's gonna do," noted one officer. "He's liable to snap, he's liable to pass out. We watch him all the time to prevent him from committing suicide. You've got to be ready—he's liable to

do anything." The prisoner is never out of at least one officer's sight. Thus surveillance is constant, and control, for all intents and purposes, is total.

Relations between the officers and their charges during the death watch can be quite intense. Watching and being watched are central to this enterprise, and these are always engaging activities, particularly when the stakes are life and death. These relations are, nevertheless, utterly impersonal; there are no grudges but neither is there compassion or fellow-feeling. Officers are civil but cool; they keep an emotional distance from the men they are about to kill. To do otherwise, they maintain, would make it harder to execute condemned prisoners. The attitude of the officers is that the prisoners arrive as strangers and are easier to kill if they stay that way.

During the last five or six hours, two specific team officers are assigned to guard the prisoner. Unlike their more taciturn and aloof colleagues on earlier shifts, these officers make a conscious effort to talk with the prisoner. In one officer's words, "We just keep them right there and keep talking to them—about anything except the chair." The point of these conversations is not merely to pass time; it is to keep tabs on the prisoner's state of mind, and to steer him away from subjects that might depress, anger, or otherwise upset him. Sociability, in other words, quite explicitly serves as a source of social control. Relationships, such as they are, serve purely manipulative ends. This is impersonality at its worst, masquerading as concern for the strangers one hopes to execute with as little trouble as possible.

Generally speaking, as the execution moves closer, the mood becomes more somber and subdued. There is a last meal. Prisoners can order pretty much what they want, but most eat little or nothing at all. At this point, the prisoners may steadfastly maintain that their executions will be stayed. Such bravado is belied by their loss of appetite. "You can see them going down," said one officer. "Food is the last thing they got on their minds."

Next the prisoners must box their meager worldly goods. These are inventoried by the staff, recorded on a one-page checklist form, and marked for disposition to family or friends. Prisoners are visibly saddened, even moved to tears, by this procedure, which at once summarizes their lives and highlights the imminence of death. At this point, said one of the officers, "I really get into him; I watch him real close." The execution schedule, the officer pointed out, is "picking up momentum and we don't want to lose control of the situation."

This momentum is not lost on the condemned prisoner. Critical milestones have been passed. The prisoner moves in a limbo existence devoid of food or possessions; he has seen the last of such things, unless he receives a stay of execution and rejoins the living. His identity is expropriated as well. The critical juncture in this regard is the shaving of the man's head (including facial hair) and right leg. Hair is shaved to facilitate the electrocution; it reduces physical resistance to electricity and minimizes singeing and burning. But the process has obvious psychological significance as well, adding greatly to the momentum of the execution.

The shaving procedure is quite public and intimidating. The condemned man is taken from his cell and seated in the middle of the tier. His hands and feet are cuffed, and he is dressed only in undershorts. The entire death watch team is assembled around him. They stay at a discrete distance, but it is obvious that they are there to maintain control should he resist in any way or make any untoward move. As a rule, the man is overwhelmed. As one officer told me in blunt terms, "Come eight o'clock, we've got a dead man. Eight o'clock is when we shave the man. We take his identity; it goes with the hair." This taking of identity is indeed a collective process—the team makes a forceful "we," the prisoner their helpless object. The staff is confident that the prisoner's capacity to resist is now compromised. What is left of

the man erodes gradually and, according to the officers, perceptibly over the remaining three hours before the execution.

After the prisoner has been shaved, he is then made to shower and don a fresh set of clothes for the execution. The clothes are unremarkable in appearance, except that velcro replaces buttons and zippers, to reduce the chance of burning the body. The main significance of the clothes is symbolic: they mark the prisoner as a man who is ready for execution. Now physically "prepped," to quote one team member, the prisoner is placed in an empty tomblike cell, the death cell. All that is left is the wait. During this fateful period, the prisoner is more like an object "without any sensation" than like a flesh-and-blood person on the threshold of death.

For condemned prisoners, like Gilmore, who come to accept and even to relish their impending deaths, a genuine calm seems to prevail. It is as if they can transcend the dehumanizing forces at work around them and go to their deaths in peace. For most condemned prisoners, however, numb resignation rather than peaceful acceptance is the norm. By the accounts of the death-watch officers, these more typical prisoners are beaten men. Listen to the officers' accounts:

> A lot of 'em die in their minds before they go to that chair. I've never known of one or heard of one putting up a fight. . . . By the time they walk to the chair, they've completely faced it. Such a reality most people can't understand. Cause they don't fight it. They don't seem to have anything to say. It's just something like "Get it over with." They may be numb, sort of in a trance.

> They go through stages. And, at this stage, they're real humble. Humblest bunch of people I ever seen. Most all of 'em is real, real weak. Most of the time you'd only need one or two people to carry out an execution, as weak and as humble as they are.

These men seem barely human and alive to their keepers. They wait meekly to be escorted to their deaths. The people who come for them are the warden and the remainder of the death watch team, flanked by high-ranking correctional officials. The warden reads the court order, known popularly as a death warrant. This is, as one officer said, "the real deal," and nobody misses its significance. The condemned prisoners then go to their deaths compliantly, captives of the inexorable, irresistible momentum of the situation. As one officer put it, "There's no struggle. . . . They just walk right on in there." So too, do the staff "just walk right on in there," following a routine they have come to know well. Both the condemned and the executioners, it would seem, find a relief of sorts in mindless mechanical conformity to the modern execution drill.

Witness to an Execution

As the team and administrators prepare to commence the good fight, as they might say, another group, the official witnesses, are also preparing themselves for their role in the execution. Numbering between six and twelve for any given execution, the official witnesses are disinterested citizens in good standing drawn from a cross-section of the state's population. If you will, they are every good or decent person, called upon to represent the community and use their good offices to testify to the propriety of the execution. I served as an official witness at the execution of an inmate.

At eight in the evening, about the time the prisoner is shaved in preparation for the execution, the witnesses are assembled. Eleven in all, we included three newspaper and two television reporters, a state trooper, two police officers, a magistrate, a businessman, and myself. We were picked up in the parking lot behind the main office of the corrections department. There was nothing unusual or even memorable about any of this. Gothic touches were notable by their absence. It wasn't a dark and stormy night; no one emerged from the shadows to lead us to the prison gates.

Mundane considerations prevailed. The van sent for us was missing a few rows of seats so there wasn't enough room for all of us. Obliging prison officials volunteered their cars. Our rather ordinary cavalcade reached the prison but only after getting lost. Once within the prison's walls, we were sequestered for some two hours in a bare and almost shabby administrative conference room. A public information officer was assigned to accompany us and answer our questions. We grilled this official about the prisoner and the execution procedure he would undergo shortly, but little information was to be had. The man confessed ignorance on the most basic points. Disgruntled at this and increasingly anxious, we made small talk and drank coffee.

At 10:40 P.M., roughly two-and-a-half hours after we were assembled and only twenty minutes before the execution was scheduled to occur, the witnesses were taken to the basement of the prison's administrative building, frisked, then led down an alleyway that ran along the exterior of the building. We entered a neighboring cell block and were admitted to a vestibule adjoining the death chamber. Each of us signed a log, and was then led off to the witness area. To our left, around a corner some thirty feet away, the prisoner sat in the condemned cell. He couldn't see us, but I'm quite certain he could hear us. It occurred to me that our arrival was a fateful reminder for the prisoner. The next group would be led by the warden, and it would be coming for him.

We entered the witness area, a room within the death chamber, and took our seats. A picture window covering the front wall of the witness room offered a clear view of the electric chair, which was about twelve feet away from us and well-illuminated. The chair, a large, high-back solid oak structure with imposing black straps, dominated the death chamber. Behind it, on the back wall, was an open panel full of coils and lights. Peeling paint hung from the ceiling and walls; water stains from persistent leaks were everywhere in evidence.

Two officers, one a hulking figure weighing some 400 pounds, stood alongside the electric chair. Each had his hands crossed at the lap and wore a forbidding, blank expression on his face. The witnesses gazed at them and the chair, most of us scribbling notes furiously. We did this, I suppose, as much to record the experience as to have a distraction from the growing tension. A correctional officer entered the witness room and announced that a trial run of the machinery would be undertaken. Seconds later, lights flashed on the control panel behind the chair indicating that the chair was in working order. A white curtain, opened for the test, separated the chair and the witness area. After the test, the curtain was drawn. More tests were performed behind the curtain. Afterwards, the curtain was reopened, and would be left open until the execution was over. Then it would be closed to allow the officers to remove the body.

A handful of high-level correctional officials were present in the death chamber, standing just outside the witness area. There were two regional administrators, the director of the Department of Corrections, and the prison warden. The prisoner's chaplain and lawyer were also present. Other than the chaplain's black religious garb, subdued grey pinstripes and bland correctional uniforms prevailed. All parties were quite solemn.

At 10:58 the prisoner entered the death chamber. He was, I knew from my research, a man with a checkered, tragic past. He had been grossly abused as a child, and went on to become grossly abusive of others. I was told he could not describe his life, from childhood on, without talking about confrontations in defense of a precarious sense of self—at home, in school, on the streets, in the prison yard. Belittled by life and choking with rage, he was hungry to be noticed. Paradoxically, he had found his moment in the spotlight, but it was a dim and unflattering light cast before a small and unappreciative audience. "He'd pose for cameras in the chair—for the attention," his counselor had told me earlier in the day. But the truth was

that the prisoner wasn't smiling, and there were no cameras. The prisoner walked quickly and silently toward the chair, an escort of officers in tow. His eyes were turned downward, his expression a bit glazed. Like many before him, the prisoner had threatened to stage a last stand. But that was lifetimes ago, on death row. In the death house, he joined the humble bunch and kept to the executioner's schedule. He appeared to have given up on life before he died in the chair.

En route to the chair, the prisoner stumbled slightly, as if the momentum of the event had overtaken him. Were he not held securely by two officers, one at each elbow, he might have fallen. Were the routine to be broken in this or indeed any other way, the officers believe, the prisoner might faint or panic or become violent, and have to be forcibly placed in the chair. Perhaps as a precaution, when the prisoner reached the chair he did not turn on his own but rather was turned, firmly but without malice, by the officers in his escort. These included the two men at his elbows, and four others who followed behind him. Once the prisoner was seated, again with help, the officers strapped him into the chair.

The execution team worked with machine precision. Like a disciplined swarm, they enveloped him. Arms, legs, stomach, chest, and head were secured in a matter of seconds. Electrodes were attached to the cap holding his head and to the strap holding his exposed right leg. A leather mask was placed over his face. The last officer mopped the prisoner's brow, then touched his hand in a gesture of farewell.

During the brief procession to the electric chair, the prisoner was attended by a chaplain. As the execution team worked feverishly to secure the condemned man's body, the chaplain, who appeared to be upset, leaned over him and placed his forehead in contact with the prisoner's, whispering urgently. The priest might have been praying, but I had the impression he was consoling the man, perhaps assuring him that a forgiving God awaited him in the next life. If he heard the chaplain, I doubt the man comprehended his message. He didn't seem comforted. Rather, he looked stricken and appeared to be in shock. Perhaps the priest's urgent ministrations betrayed his doubts that the prisoner could hold himself together. The chaplain then withdrew at the warden's request, allowing the officers to affix the death mask.

The strapped and masked figure sat before us utterly alone, waiting to be killed. The cap and mask dominated his face. The cap was nothing more than a sponge encased in a leather shell with a metal piece at the top to accept an electrode. It looked decrepit and resembled a cheap, ill-fitting toupee. The mask, made entirely of leather, appeared soiled and worn. It had two parts. The bottom part covered the chin and mouth, the top the eyes and lower forehead. Only the nose was exposed. The effect of a rigidly restrained body, together with the bizarre cap and the protruding nose, was nothing short of grotesque. A faceless man breathed before us in a tragicomic trance, waiting for a blast of electricity that would extinguish his life. Endless seconds passed. His last act was to swallow, nervously, pathetically, with his Adam's apple bobbing. I was struck by that simple movement then, and can't forget it even now. It told me, as nothing else did, that in the prisoner's restrained body, behind that mask, lurked a fellow human being who, at some level, however primitive, knew or sensed himself to be moments from death. The condemned man sat perfectly still for what seemed an eternity but was in fact no more than thirty seconds. Finally the electricity hit him. His body stiffened spasmodically, though only briefly. A thin swirl of smoke trailed away from his head and then dissipated quickly. The body remained taut, with the right foot raised slightly at the heel, seemingly frozen there. A brief pause, then another minute of shock. When it was over, the body was flaccid and inert.

Three minutes passed while the officials let the body cool. (Immediately after the execution, I'm told, the body would be too hot to touch and would blister anyone who did.) All eyes were riveted to the chair; I felt trapped in my witness seat, at once transfixed and yet eager for release. I can't recall any clear thoughts from that moment. One of the death watch officers later volunteered that he shared this experience of staring blankly at the execution scene. Had the prisoner's mind been mercifully blank before the end? I hoped so.

An officer walked up to the body, opened the shirt at chest level, then continued on to get the physician from an adjoining room. The physician listened for a heartbeat. Hearing none, he turned to the warden and said, "This man has expired." The warden, speaking to the director, solemnly intoned: "Mr. Director, the court order has been fulfilled." The curtain was then drawn and the witnesses filed out.

The Morning After

As the team prepared the body for the morgue, the witnesses were led to the front door of the prison. On the way, we passed a number of cell blocks. We could hear the normal sounds of prison life, including the occasional catcall and lewd comment hurled at uninvited guests like ourselves. But no trouble came in the wake of the execution. Small protests were going on outside the walls, we were told, but we could not hear them. Soon the media would be gone; the protestors would disperse and head for their homes. The prisoners, already home, had been indifferent to the proceedings, as they always are unless the condemned prisoner had been a figure of some consequence in the convict community. Then there might be tension and maybe even a modest disturbance on a prison tier or two. But few convict luminaries are executed, and the dead man had not been one of them. Our escort officer offered a sad tribute to the prisoner: "The inmates, they didn't care about this guy."

I couldn't help but think they weren't alone in this. The executioners went home and set about their lives. Having taken life, they would savor a bit of life themselves. They showered, ate, made love, slept, then took a day or two off. For some, the prisoner's image would linger for that night. The men who strapped him in remembered what it was like to touch him; they showered as soon as they got home to wash off the feel and smell of death. One official sat up picturing how the prisoner looked at the end. (I had a few drinks myself that night with that same image for company.) There was some talk about delayed reactions to the stress of carrying out executions. Though such concerns seemed remote that evening, I learned later that problems would surface for some of the officers. But no one on the team, then or later, was haunted by the executed man's memory, nor would anyone grieve for him. "When I go home after one of these things," said one man, "I sleep like a rock." His may or may not be the sleep of the just, but one can only marvel at such a thing, and perhaps envy such a man.

Study Questions

1. Describe the execution process, including the work of the death watch team.

2. What functions are served by the elaborate and impersonal procedures used, and how are they carried out?

3. Do you believe that this impersonal process is more civilized than previous forms of executions (e.g., stoning or hanging)? Would you expect this type of execution to be more or less effective as a form of retribution and deterrence than previous methods? ✦

36
It's About Time
America's Imprisonment Binge

John Irwin

James Austin

Most of the new articles presented in this section are not very optimistic about the future of corrections. So as not to end on a discouraging note, this last selection by John Irwin and James Austin offers a glimmer of hope for the future. The authors begin, however, by recounting their own grim interpretation of the present situation.

Our study of the American prison system revealed that most of the unprecedented numbers of people we are sending to prison are guilty of petty property and drug crimes or violations of their conditions of probation or parole. Their crimes or violations lack any of the elements that the public believes are serious or associates with dangerous criminals. Even offenders who commit frequent felonies and who define themselves as "outlaws," "dope fiends," crack dealers, or "gang bangers" commit mostly petty felonies. These "high-rate" offenders, as they have been labeled by policy makers and criminologists, are, for the most part, uneducated, unskilled (at crime as well as conventional pursuits), and highly disorganized persons who have no access to any form of reward-

Excerpts from *It's About Time: America's Imprisonment Binge* by John Irwin and James Austin, pp. 143–146, 151–153, 156, 157, 159–161, 163–174. Copyright © 1994 by Wadsworth Publishing Company. Reprinted by permission.

ing, meaningful conventional life. They usually turn to dangerous, mostly unrewarding, petty criminal pursuits as one of the few options they have to earn money, win some respect, and avoid monotonous lives on the streets. Frequently, they spend most of their young lives behind bars.

What may be more surprising is that a majority of all persons sent to prison, even the high-rate offenders, aspire to a relatively modest conventional life and hope to prepare for that while serving their prison sentences. This should be considered particularly important because very little in the way of equipping prisoners for a conventional life on the outside is occurring in our prisons. In preceding decades, particularly the 1950s and 1960s, a much greater effort was made to "rehabilitate" prisoners. Whatever the outcome of these efforts (as this is a matter of some dispute), rehabilitation has been all but abandoned. Prisons have been redefined as places of punishment. In addition, rapid expansion has crowded prisoners into physically inadequate institutions and siphoned off most available funds from all services other than those required to maintain control. Prisons have become true human warehouses—often highly crowded, violent, and cruel.

The Financial Cost

We must consider the costs and benefits of increased imprisonment rates. The financial cost is the easiest to estimate. Most people are aware that prisons are expensive to build and operate. Few, however, understand just how expensive. Indeed, previous estimates routinely cited by public officials have dramatically underestimated the amounts of money spent on housing prisoners and building new prisons.

Prison and jail administrators typically calculate operating costs by dividing their annual budget by the average daily prison population. However, this accounting practice is misleading and produces patently low estimates of the true costs of imprisonment. For example, agency budgets often exclude contracted services for food, medical care, legal services, and transportation provided by other government agencies. According to two studies conducted in New York, these additional expenses increased the official operating costs by 20 to 25 percent. An independent audit of the Indiana prison system found that actual expenditures were one-third higher than those reported by the agency. Besides these "hidden" direct expenditures, there are other costs that are rarely included in such calculations. To name only a few, the state loses taxes that could be paid by many of the imprisoned, pays more welfare to their families, and maintains spacious prison grounds that are exempt from state and local real estate taxation. In the New York study conducted by Coopers and Lybrand in 1977, these costs amounted to over $21,000 per prisoner.

Although there is considerable variation among the states, on the average prison officials claim that it costs about $20,000 per year to house, feed, clothe, and supervise a prisoner. Because this estimate does not include indirect costs, the true annual expenditure probably exceeds $30,000 per prisoner.

The other enormous cost is prison construction. Prisons are enclosed, "total" institutions in which prisoners are not only housed, but guarded, fed, clothed, and worked. They also receive some schooling and medical and psychological treatment. These needs require—in addition to cellblocks or dormitories—infirmaries, classrooms, laundries, offices, maintenance shops, boiler rooms, and kitchens. Dividing the total construction costs of one of these institutions by the number of prisoners it houses produces a cost per "bed" of as low as $7,000 for a minimum-security prison to $155,000 for a maximum-security prison.

Instead of using current tax revenues to pay directly for this construction, however, the state does what most citizens do when they buy a house—that is, borrow the money, which must be paid back over several decades. The borrowing is done by selling bonds or using other financing instruments that may triple the original figure. The costs of prison construction are further increased by errors in original bids by contractors and cost overruns caused by delays in construction, which seem to be the rule rather than the exception. A recent survey of 15 states with construction projects revealed that cost overruns averaged *40 percent* of the original budget projections.

Consequently, when a state builds and finances a typical medium security prison, it will spend approximately $268,000 per bed for construction alone. So in the states that have expanded their prison populations, the cost per additional prisoner will be $39,000 a year. This includes the cost of building the new cell amortized 30 years. In other words, the 30-year cost of adding space for one prisoner is more than $1 million.

These enormous increases in the cost of imprisonment are just beginning to be felt by the states. Budgetary battles in which important state services for children, the elderly, the sick, and the poor are gutted to pay for prisons have already begun. In coming years, great cutbacks in funds for public education, medical services for the poor, highway construction, and other state services will occur.

Crime Reduction

Those who are largely responsible for this state of affairs—elected officials who have harangued on the street crime issue and passed laws resulting in more punitive sentencing policies, judges who deliver more and longer prison terms, and government criminal justice functionaries who have supported the punitive trend in criminal justice policies—promised that the great expansion of prison populations would reduce crime in our society. A key U.S. Department of Justice official recently summarized the government's scientific basis for supporting incarceration as the best means for reducing crime as follows: "Statisticians and criminal justice researchers have consistently found that falling crime rates are associated with rising imprisonment rates, and rising crime rates are associated with falling imprisonment rates." Former Attorney General William Barr more recently restated this position, arguing that the country had a "clear choice" of either building more prisons or tolerating higher violent crime rates. This view implies that increasing the government's capacity to imprison is the single most effective strategy for reducing crime. . . .

Demographic Shifts and Crime Rates

There are several reasons to question the interpretation that reductions for NCVS property crimes validate the "imprisonment reduces crime" perspective. First is the failure to incorporate the influence of shifting demographics on crime rates. Most crimes are committed by males between the ages of 15 and 24. As that population grows or subsides, one can expect associated fluctuations in the crime rates. Before changes in crime rates can be attributed to changes in imprisonment rates, the influence of demographic changes must be taken into consideration.

Beginning in the early 1960s, the size of this age group began to grow and continued to grow through the 1970s—the exact period of the rise in crime rates. By the late 1970s, this age group as a percentage of the population began to decline and the crime rate began to ebb by 1980. A recent article by two criminologists found that most of the decline in crime rates observed since 1979–1985 was a direct result of a declining "at-risk" population. When we take into account the influence of this demographic shift, reductions in the NCVS from 1980 to 1988 are largely attributable (60 percent of the crime reduction explained) to reductions in the ages 15–24 high-crime-rate population. The same analysis, when applied to the UCR data, actually shows an increase in UCR during the same time period.

The NCVS rates are also influenced by significant changes that have occurred over the past two decades in the number, characteristics, and location of U.S. households. In the most recent publication on NCVS, the Justice Department acknowledged that, since 1973, the size of the American household has (1) declined, (2) shifted from urban areas to suburban locations, and (3) shifted from the Northeast and Midwest to the South and the West.

The first two conditions automatically reduce crime rate estimates because smaller households located in suburban areas are less likely than larger and urban households to experience crime. The third condition, relocation to the West where crime rates are highest, increases the likelihood of households being victimized. These trends in the NCVS must be more carefully analyzed before conclusions can be made that a tripling of the imprisonment rate is solely responsible for declines in personal and household theft.

Drug Trafficking and Property Crime

A second reason to question the drop in NCVS and UCR property crimes since 1980 is related to the dramatic increase in drug trafficking that began in 1980. It is very possible that the decline in burglary and theft reflected a change in criminal activity from these crimes to the more lucrative and less difficult drug trade business. It is difficult to prove with statistics that this shift has indeed occurred because drug dealing is not reported by the NCVS. But for those criminologists who spend time observing America's deteriorating inner cities, it is obvious that street crime has shifted from household burglaries to drug trafficking.

Prison Versus Other Forms of Punishment

Even if the NCVS figures reflect a true drop in property crime, it cannot be concluded that imprisonment was the cause of the decline. . . . [O]ther and less punitive forms of correctional supervision (probation, parole, and jail populations) grew just as fast as the prison population. Statistically and substantively, it could be argued that NCVS crime rate reductions were related to greater use of probation and short jail terms since they are applied to a far larger number of offenders than prison.

State-by-State Comparisons

The *best* test of the proposition that increasing prison populations has reduced crime is a comparison between the 50 states and the District of Columbia, which serve as experiments on this issue. This is because they not only differ in their crime and imprisonment rates, but they have also undergone dramatically different changes in these over the last fifteen years.

The period 1980 to 1991 is ideal for this comparison. The national crime rate peaked in 1980, as it did individually in all but 13 states. (These peaked in 1981 or 1982.) Also, after increasing slowly for several years, the national rate of incarceration began to rise steeply. . . . All the states increased their prison populations in that 12-year period, but they did so by very different amounts, from 26 to 742 per 100,000. The states and D.C., in a sense, are 51 different "petri dishes" (used in biological experiments), each with its unique array of factors that could be related to changes in crime rates, into which the experimental variable—increases in imprisonment—is introduced. If a causal relationship existed, we would see a consistent pattern—namely, states that increased their imprisonment rates the most would show the largest reductions in crime rates. Conversely, states that increased their imprisonment rates more slowly would show higher increases in crime rates.

Actually, there is no pattern. . . . Most states (34) experienced decline in crime rates. However, there is no tendency for those that increased their prison populations the most to have greater decreases in crime. In fact, the opposite is true. The states that increased their prison populations by less than 100 per 100,000 were more likely to have experienced a decrease in crime than those that increased imprisonment rates by more than 200. . . .

We analyzed this distribution by regression analysis, which establishes the line from which the points deviate the least (whether or not the distribution calls for a line) and measures to what extent the points deviate from it. This is indicated in a coefficient of correlation—*R*. When *R* is 1.0, the points all lie on the line. In our case, *R* was .08179 in the positive direction. This suggests that in the 12-year period, there was a very slight tendency for more incarceration to be related to *increases* in crime. It would be simple minded to conclude that this is a causal relationship. But it is very reasonable to recognize that this state by state comparison strongly indicates that the massive increases in incarceration failed to produce *any* reduction in crime rates.

The California Imprisonment Experiment

If we were to pick a state to test the imprisonment theory, California would be the obvious choice, for this state's prison population has increased from 19,623 in 1977 to over 110,000 by 1992. Former Attorney General William Barr believes California should serve as the model for the rest of the country. California, he states, "quadrupled its prison population during the 1980s and various forms of violent crimes fell by as much as 37 percent. But in Texas, which did not increase prison space, crime increased 29 percent in the decade."

A closer examination of the California data presents a very different picture than that cited by Barr. . . . During this period, the size of the prison population increased by 237 percent (from 29,202 to 97,309) and the jail population increased by 118 percent (34,064 to 74,312). Prison operating costs increased by 400 percent, and jail operating costs increased by 265 percent. As of 1990, Californians were paying nearly $3 billion per year to operate the state's prisons and jails.

What has been the impact of this substantial investment in violent crime? Contrary to the claim that the violent crime rate (homicide, rape, robbery, and assault) has dropped, the rate actually *increased* by 21 percent. Substantial declines did occur, but only for burglary and larceny theft—a phenomenon that, as we noted earlier, was at least partially attributable to growth in illegal drug trafficking and shifts in the at-risk population. More interesting is the fact that after 1984 the overall crime rate, and especially violent crimes and auto theft, have grown despite a continued escalation of imprisonment. . . .

California is now so strapped for funds that it must dramatically reduce the number of its parole officers and has been unable to open two brand new prisons, capable of holding 12,000 inmates. The state now has the most overcrowded prison system in the nation (183 percent of rated capacity) and spends millions of dollars each year on court cases challenging the crowded prison conditions. Despite the billions of dollars now being spent each year in locking up offenders, the public is as fearful of crime as it was a decade ago. Clearly, the grand California imprisonment experiment has done little to reduce crime or the public's fear of crime.

The Costs of Further Escalating the Imprisonment Binge

Many argue that crime has not been reduced in California or nationally simply because we have not incarcerated enough persons. They suggest that if we were willing to imprison many times more people for much longer periods of time, significant reductions in crime would occur, that is, "street crime." (The pervasive and more expensive other forms of crime, e.g., white collar crime, are not and would not be affected by imprisonment.)

This viewpoint is not mere speculation but one that is being regularly advocated by many politicians. Former Attorney General William Barr listed 24 steps the government should take to reduce violent crime including "truth in sentencing" that requires inmates to serve the full amount of their sentences, increased use of mandatory minimum prison sentences, relaxation of evidentiary rules to increase conviction rates, greater use of the death penalty, and increased numbers of police officers. President Clinton campaigned on adding 100,000 police officers to the streets to increase arrests. And, both political parties have formally advocated the need to get even tougher with criminals.

. . .The major components of such a program would be as follows:

Policy 1: Add 100,000 police officers;

Result: Increases the number of felony arrests from 3.6 million to 4.2 million;

Policy 2: Increase the conviction rate from 65 percent to 75 percent;

Result: Increases the number of convictions from 2.3 million to 3.4 million;

Policy 3: Increase the proportion of convictions resulting in a prison sentence from 19 percent to 40 percent;

Result: Increases the number of prison admissions from 475,000 to 1.5 million;

Policy 4: Adopt a "truth in sentencing" policy that would require offenders to serve 80 percent of their prison terms;

Result: Length of stay in prison would increase from 1.6 years to 5 years.

The net result of these reforms would be to create a prison population of 7.5 million. Such a massive expansion of the prison population would undoubtedly have a profound impact on the crime rate. But there would be a heavy price to pay. An additional 6.7 million prison beds would have to be constructed at a cost of at least $376 billion. Annual operating costs would escalate from $15.1 billion to $133 billion.

To do this constitutionally while preserving a semblance of our civil rights would require an expansion of the other parts of the criminal justice system—the jails, courts, and police departments. Assuming that the use of probation and parole would be reduced there would be limited savings on the least expensive components of the correctional system.

The annual price of all this escalation, less the prison construction costs, would probably exceed $220 billion as opposed to the $74 billion now being spent, with most of these costs being borne by state governments to operate large scale prison systems. States now spend only $14 billion on corrections alone (which includes probation and parole services). Total state general fund expenditures in 1990 totaled $300 billion. Consequently, to operate such a massive prison system at the state level would require over one third of all state revenues to be dedicated to prison operations. And these costs would not include the nearly $376 billion in capital construction funds or increases to local government to expand and operate its law enforcement, court systems, and local jails.

Unless we wanted to strip down or abandon many other government enterprises—education, welfare, transportation, medical services—we would have to greatly increase state taxes to pay for this massive experiment in imprisonment. In many ways—the financial costs, the social disruptions, the removal of a very large percent of young males—this policy would be like World War II, prolonged for decades.

Of course there would be other consequences. The nation's incarceration rate would increase from 310 per 100,000 to over 3,000 per 100,000. Since 47 percent of the current prison population is black, it would mean that most of the nation's 5.5 million black males age 18–39 would be incarcerated and we would look a lot like South Africa of the 1950s and 1960s.

It is still not clear what this would do to overall crime rates. Certainly, the removal of such a large portion of young males would reduce the forms of street crime we are presently experiencing. However, it is impossible to anticipate what new forms of social problems, crime, and upheavals this punitive experiment would cause. The massive social disruptions—such as the removal of most young, black males—might result in unanticipated new types of violent, criminal activities. In a few years, millions of parolees, who probably will be considerably socially crippled and embittered by their long prison terms, will be returning to society. They will at least be an enormous nuisance and burden, but also may engage in a lot of crime. Even if we assume that crime would eventually decline, how long would we have to maintain such a large prison system to continually deter and incapacitate each successive generation of potential criminals?

Since we do not believe Americans are ready for this costly solution to the crime problem through imprisonment, we are left with its failure. . . .

Voodoo Criminology

The failure of the massive expansion of prison populations to accomplish its most important objective—the reduction of crime—should come as no surprise because the idea that increased penalties will reduce crime is based on a simplistic and fallacious theory of criminal behavior. It starts with the idea that every person is an isolated, willful actor who makes completely rational decisions to maximize his or her pleasure and to minimize his or her pain. Consequently, individuals only commit crimes when they believe it will lead to more pleasure, gain, or satisfaction and with minimal risk for pain or punishment. If penalties for being caught are small or nonexistent, then many persons who are not restrained by other factors (e.g., strong conventional morals or the disapproval of close friends or family) will commit crimes—indeed, a *lot* of crimes. Only by increasing the certainty and severity of punishment, this thinking goes, will people "think twice" and be deterred.

The punishment/incapacitation/deterrence theory assumes that all individuals have access to the same conventional lifestyles for living out a law-abiding life. This is not true for most of the individuals who are caught up in our criminal justice system. For many, particularly young members of the inner-city underclass, the choice is not between conventional and illegal paths to the good life, but between illegal and risky paths or no satisfaction at all. They are faced with a limited and depressing choice between a menial, dull, impoverished, undignified life at the bottom of the conventional heap or a life with some excitement, some monetary return, and a slim chance of larger financial rewards, albeit with great risks of being imprisoned, maimed, or even killed. Consequently, many "choose" crime despite the threat of imprisonment.

For many young males, especially African Americans and Hispanics, the threat of going to prison or jail is no threat at all but rather an expected or accepted part of life. Most minority males will be punished by the criminal justice system during their lifetime. Deterrence and punishment are effective only when the act of punishment actually worsens a person's lifestyle. For millions of males, imprisonment poses no such threat. As a young black convict put it when Claude Brown told him that his preprison life meant that there was a "60 percent chance he will be killed, permanently maimed, or end up doing a long bit in jail":

"I see where you comin' from, Mr. Brown," he replied, "but you got things kind of turned around the wrong way. You see, all the things that you say could happen to me is dead on the money and that is why I can't lose. Look at it from my point of view for a minute. Let's say I go and get wiped [killed]. Then I ain't got no more needs, right? All my problems are solved. I don't need no more money, no more nothing, right? Okay, supposin' I get popped, shot in the spine and paralyzed for the rest of my life—that could happen playing football, you know. Then I won't need a whole lot of money because I won't be able to go no place and do nothin', right?"

"So, I'll be on welfare, and the welfare check is all the money I'll need, right? Now if I get busted and end up in the joint [prison] pullin' a dime and a nickel, like I am, then I don't have to worry about no bucks, no clothes. I get free rent and three squares a day. So you see, Mr. Brown, I really can't lose."

America's Farm System for Criminals

Most people who engage in crime do so not as isolated individuals, but—like we all are—as participants in various social organizations, groups, or "social systems," each of which has its own rules and values. Some groups in our society (often because of subjection to reduced circumstances such as poverty, idleness, and incarceration over an extended period of time) develop preferences for deviant lifestyles. For example, young males who were abused as children, dropped out of school, lived in poverty, abused drugs, and served many juvenile jail and prison sentences have become immersed in deviant values and are distanced from any set of conventional values. They are most satisfied when engaging in specialized deviant practices related to their unique culture—wild partying involving drug use and sex along with extremely risky behavior involving extreme displays of machismo.

Since crime is not the sole product of individual motives, efforts, especially by the state, to punish the individual without addressing the social forces that produced that individual will fail. Individuals do not decide to sell drugs, purchase drugs, and set up single-proprietor operations on their own. Most street crime involves groups, organizations, and networks. Drug dealers are persons who have been involved in groups and networks of people who use drugs, have connections, know or are dealers. The same is true of gang bangers, hustlers, and thieves.

In effect, America has created a lower-class culture designed to produce new cohorts of street criminals each generation. Similar to organized sports, most of these criminal operations have major leagues, minors leagues, and a bench. Children come up through the ranks, learn the game, and finally move into the starting lineup once they reach their adolescent years. When they are temporarily or permanently removed (that is, arrested, imprisoned, or killed), they are replaced by others from the bench to continue the game. When the bench is depleted, someone comes up from the minors. Much as in professional and college sports, the span of their career is short, with their most active crime years taking place between the ages of 15 and 24.

Our impoverished inner-city neighborhoods (or what is left of them as neighborhoods) have almost unlimited reserves milling about who are kept out of the starting lineup by managers and first-string players. As soon as the police arrest the "kingpin" drug dealer, the leaders of a gang, some of the top pimps or hustlers, new recruits move in to take over these positions.

This characterization of criminal operations also explains why the War on Drugs, which has been going on for at least a decade, has failed. During the 1980s, the government spent billions of tax dollars and arrested millions for drug possession or drug trafficking. Regularly, the media reported that a new large-scale drug operation and some kingpin drug dealers have been caught. Drugs continue to be at least as available as they were before the new arrests, however, as

"new" kingpins quickly and often violently replace the recently departed leaders.

Even if a particular type of criminal operation dies out, new crime games appear. In the late 1980s, the news media and government officials were blaming crack cocaine dealing for unprecedented numbers of homicides in Los Angeles inner city neighborhoods. However, sociologist Jack Katz discovered that, contrary to the media's reports, homicide rates in the crack neighborhoods had not changed over the last decade. Earlier in the 1980s, rival gangs were killing each other over territory. It seems, using the sport analogy, that the number of players available for crime games is related to broader social conditions, such as the existence of a large underemployed population of young males who have the ordinary youthful desires for respect, excitement, and gratification but are confronted with extremely limited access to legitimate means of acquiring them. Thus, the number of potential players remains constant over an extended period. Only the types of games being played change from season to season.

Cutting Our Losses on the Prison Solution

The past decade has witnessed the uncritical adoption of a national policy to reduce crime by increasing the use of imprisonment. That policy has failed. Despite a more than doubling of the correctional industrial complex and a tripling of criminal justice system costs, crime in general has not been reduced. Though there is evidence that property crimes committed against households have declined, all measures of crime are increasing. Moreover, it appears that crime is likely to increase in the near future. This is not news to the American public, which is increasingly apprehensive about personal safety even as their taxes are increased to pay for the failed imprisonment policy.

For these reasons, the grand imprisonment experiment, which has dominated

America's crime reduction policy for the past 15 years, should not only be severely questioned but abandoned. It has simply failed to produce its primary objective—reduced crime. This is not to say that certain offenders should not be imprisoned and, in some cases, for lengthy periods; a few individuals are truly dangerous and need to receive long sentences. But to argue that all offenders should be so treated is misguided and ineffective.

Reducing crime means addressing those factors that are more directly related to crime. This means reducing teenage pregnancies, high school dropout rates, unemployment, drug abuse, and lack of meaningful job opportunities. Although many will differ on how best to address these factors, the first step is to acknowledge that these forces have far more to do with reducing crime than escalating the use of imprisonment.

The "prison reduces crime" theory has not worked. Crime, especially violent crime, is not declining. We need to cut our losses and try crime prevention policies that will work. It may well take a decade before the fruits of such an effort are realized, but we can no longer afford to keep investing in a widespread crime reduction policy that has failed so ubiquitously.

The Social Costs of Imprisonment

The full range and depth of the social costs, which are tremendous, are much more difficult to identify and measure accurately. Though most of the persons in our sample were not contributing significantly to the support of a family, some were. About 40 percent indicated that they were employed at the time of arrest and 25 percent stated that they had been employed most of the time in the period before arrest. Many prisoners sent to prison are married and have children. Moreover, all of them have mothers, fathers, brothers, sisters, uncles, aunts, or cousins. Though it is sometimes true that a prisoner was causing family and friends a great deal of difficulty, usually relatives experience some disruption and pain when persons are sent to prison. The removal of an individual from his social contexts does some harm to his family, friends, and employer, though the amount of this harm is hard to calculate.

Perhaps the highest cost of our careless extension of the use of imprisonment is the damage to thousands of people, most of whom have no prior prison record and who are convicted of petty crimes, and the future consequences of this damage to the society. These persons are being packed into dangerous, crowded prisons with minimal access to job training, education, or other services that will prepare them for life after prison. Some marginally involved petty criminals are converted into hard-core "outlaws"—mean, violence-prone convicts who dominate crowded prison wards.

Making matters worse, a growing number of prisoners are being subjected to extremely long sentences. These long-termers are not only stacking up in prisons and filling all available space, but their long terms, much of which they serve in maximum-security prisons that impose severe deprivation on them, result in more loss of social and vocational skills, more estrangement, and more alienation.

It must be kept in mind that virtually all of these profoundly damaged individuals will be released from prison and will try to pick up life on the outside. For the most part, their chances of pursuing a merely viable, much less satisfying, conventional life after prison are small. The contemporary prison experience has converted them into social misfits and cripples, and there is a growing likelihood that they will return to crime, violence, and other forms of disapproved deviance.

This ultimate cost of imprisonment—that which society must suffer when prisoners are released—continues to be confirmed by research. The Rand Corporation study cited earlier found that convicted felons sent to prison or granted probation had significantly higher rates of rearrest after release than those on probation. In California, which has by far the nation's most overcrowded prison system, the recidivism rate (the rate of reimprisonment of prisoners released on parole), has doubled in the last five years.

Even more tragically, imprisonment is increasingly falling on blacks, Hispanics, and other people of color. Sixty years ago, almost one-fourth of all prison admissions were nonwhite. Today, nearly half of all prison admissions are nonwhite. Nationally, the imprisonment rate of blacks is at least ten times higher than for whites. Hispanics are incarcerated at a rate three times higher than whites. Studies show that a black male American has a 50 percent chance of being arrested once by age 29.

Our Vindictive Society

Crime has incurred another profound cost: the increase of general vindictiveness in our society. Historically, Americans (as compared to Europeans and Japanese, for example) have been highly individualistic, which means, for one thing, that they are prone to blaming individuals for their actions. In America, according to the dominant ideology, everyone is responsible for his or her acts and every act is accomplished by a willful actor. Consequently, every undesirable, harmful, "bad" act is the work of a blameful actor. This belief has resulted in our being the most litigious people in the world and has given us the world's largest legal profession. It has also led us to criminalize more and more behavior and to demand more and more legal action against those who break laws. Today many Americans want someone blamed and punished for every transgression and inconvenience they experience.

Social science should have taught us that all human behavior is only partially a matter of free will and that persons are only par-

tially responsible for their deeds. Everyone's actions are always somewhat influenced or dominated by factors not of one's own making and beyond personal control (with economic situation being the most influential and obvious).

Moreover, seeking vengeance is a pursuit that brings more frustration than satisfaction. It has not only been an obstacle in solving many social problems and in developing cooperative, communal attitudes (the lack of which are one of the important causes of the crime problem), but it is in itself a producer of excessive amounts of anxiety and frustration. Ultimately, vindictiveness erects barriers between people, isolates them, and prevents them from constructing the cooperative, communal social organizations that are so necessary for meaningful, satisfying human existence. Ironically, it is just these social structures that contain the true solution to our crime problem.

The Crime Problem as a Diversion

Our tendency toward vindictiveness is greatly nurtured by the media, politicians, and other public figures who have persistently harangued on the crime issue. They do this largely because the crime issue is seductive. It is seductive to politicians because they can divert attention away from larger and more pressing problems, such as the economy and pollution, whose solution would require unpopular sacrifices, particularly for them and other more affluent segments of the society. Street crime is seductive to the media because it fits their preferred "sound bite" format of small bits of sensational material. Likewise, it is deeply seductive to the public, who, though they fear crime, possess at the same time deep fascination for it.

It's About Time

We *must* turn away from the excessive use of prisons. The current incarceration binge will eventually consume large amounts of tax money, which will be diverted from essential public services such as education, child care, mental health, and medical services—the very same services that will have a far greater impact on reducing crime than building more prisons. We will continue to imprison millions of people under intolerably cruel and dangerous conditions. We will accumulate a growing number of ex-convicts who are more or less psychologically and socially crippled and excluded from conventional society, posing a continuing nuisance and threat to others. We will severely damage some of our more cherished humanitarian values, which are corroded by our excessive focus on blame and vengeance. And we will further divide our society into the white affluent classes and a poor nonwhite underclass, many of them convicts and ex-convicts. In effect, we are gradually putting our own apartheid into place.

We believe that these trends can be reversed without jeopardizing public safety. But how should we accomplish a turnaround of this magnitude? First, we must recognize that crime can, at best, be marginally reduced by escalating the use of imprisonment. If we are to truly reduce crime rates, we as a society must embark on a decade-long strategy that reverses the social and economic trends of the previous decade. In particular, we must jettison the overly expensive and ineffective criminal justice approach and redirect our energies on the next generation of youth, who already are at risk for becoming the generation of criminals.

The "crime reduction" reforms we have in mind have little to do with criminal justice reform. Rather, these reforms would serve to reduce poverty, single-parent families headed by females, teenage pregnancies and abortions, welfare dependency, unemployment, high dropout rates, drug abuse, and inadequate health care. These, and not "slack" imprisonment policies, are the social indicators that have proven to be predictive of high crime rates.

The programs and policies that will work, such as better prenatal health care for pregnant mothers, better health care for children to protect them against life-threatening illnesses, Head Start, Job Corps, and Enterprise Zones, have been well-documented. We will also need a level of commitment from our major corporate leaders to reduce the flight of jobs, especially the so-called blue-collar and industrial jobs, from this country to Third World nations where cheap labor can be exploited for profits but at tremendous cost to this country. Given the current fiscal crisis facing most states and the federal government, however, it will be extremely difficult to continue a traditional and increasingly expensive war against crime and at the same time launch new social and economic policies that will reduce crime rates in the long term.

So how do we go about cutting our losses? We begin by reducing, or at least reducing the rate of growth in, the prison population and reallocating those "savings" to prevention programs targeted [at] at-risk youth and their families. But is it realistic to assume that prison populations and their associated costs can be lowered without increasing crime? How, exactly, should we proceed?

Many methods of reducing prison populations have been advocated. Some argue that certain classes of felony crimes should be reclassified as misdemeanors or decriminalized completely. In the late 1960s, there was a great deal of support to do this for many minor drug offenses. Others claim that a significant number of those convicted of felonies could be diverted from prison to probation and new forms of alternatives to prison, including intensive probation, house arrest, electronic surveillance, and greater use of fines and restitution.

We are persuaded, however, that these "front-end" reforms would not substantially reduce prison crowding. Historically, well-intentioned alternatives have had marginal impact on reducing prison populations. Instead, they have had the unintended consequence of widening the net of criminal justice by imposing more severe sanctions on people who otherwise would not be sentenced to prison. Moreover, they have little support with public officials, who, like the public, are increasingly disenchanted with probation and other forms of community sanctions.

For alternatives to work, legislators, prosecutors, police, judges, and correctional agencies would all have to agree on new laws and policies to implement them. Such a consensus is unlikely to occur in the near future, since these measures are replete with controversy and disagreement. Even if the forces that are presently driving the punitive response to crime abated considerably, it would take several years to work through these disagreements and effect changes in the laws and policies that would slowly produce an easing of prison population growth. Such a slow pace of reform would not allow states to avoid the catastrophe that is rapidly developing in our prisons.

Even diversion of a substantial number of offenders from prison would not have a major impact on prison population growth. "Front-end" diversion reforms are targeted for those few offenders who are already serving the shortest prison terms (usually less than a year). The recent flood of tougher sentencing laws has greatly lengthened prison terms for offenders charged with more serious crimes and repeat property or drug offenders. Consequently, it is this segment of the prison population that is piling up in the prisons. The problem is that inmates with long sentences are unlikely to be candidates for diversion from prison.

For these reasons, we believe the single most direct solution that would have an immediate and dramatic impact on prison crowding and would not affect public safety is to *shorten prison terms*. This can be done swiftly and fairly through a number of existing mechanisms, such as greater use of existing good-time credit statutes and/or accelerating parole eligibility.

Indeed, many states have launched such programs with no impact on crime rates. Between 1980 and 1983, the Illinois Director of Corrections released more than 21,000 prisoners an average of 90 days early because of severe prison crowding. The impact on the state's crime rate was insignificant, yet the program saved almost $50 million in tax dollars. A study of the program found that the amount of crime that could be attributed to early release was less than 1 percent of the total crime of the state. In fact, the state's crime rate actually *declined* while the early release program was in effect. Based on these findings, the state expanded its use of "good time" by another 90 days. A recent study of that expanded program found that the state was now saving over $90 million per year in state funds, even taking into account the costs of early release crimes (which represented less than 1 percent of all crimes committed in Illinois) to crime victims. The governor has declared that no more new prisons will be built in Illinois.

An earlier demonstration of how swiftly and easily prison populations can be reduced occurred in California from 1967 to 1970. When Ronald Reagan became governor, he instructed the parole board to reduce the prison population. The board began shortening sentences, which it had the power to do within the indeterminate sentence system, and in two years lowered the prison population from 28,000 to less than 18,000.

Many other states are following these examples. A recent study of the Oklahoma preparole program found that inmates could be released earlier by three to six months without influencing the state's crime rate and at considerable savings to the state. Specifically, that study found that for each inmate released early, the state saved over $9,000 per inmate, even when taking into account the costs of crimes committed by these offenders had they remained in prison. Texas, Tennessee, and Florida are just a few states that have been required by the federal courts to reduce overcrowded prison systems by shortening prison terms.

For such a policy to work, prison terms would have to be shortened across the board, including inmates serving lengthy sentences for crimes of violence who, because of their age, no longer pose a threat to public safety. Since the average prison stay in the United States is approximately two years, even marginal reductions in the length of stay for large categories of inmates would have substantial effects on population size. Using the 1990 figure of approximately 325,000 new prison sentences, and assuming that 80 percent of those inmates (representing those who are nonviolent and have satisfactory prison conduct records) had their prison terms reduced by 30 days, the nation's prison population would have declined by 27,000 inmates. A 90-day reduction would result in 80,000 fewer prisoners; a six-month reduction, 160,000 fewer prisoners. Assuming a conservative average cost of $25,000 per inmate, the nation would avert as much as $4 billion a year in operating costs and reduce the need to construct new prisons.

Unless such a reform is adopted, prison populations as well as crime rates will continue to rise indefinitely into the twenty-first century. Reducing prison terms by the amounts advocated may only slow the rate of expansion. But it can be done with no cost to public safety and with enormous dollar savings. Most important, these averted costs can be redirected to more promising social reforms targeted at high-risk and disadvantaged youth and their families. Only by cutting our losses on our failed policy of unchecked punishment and imprisonment can we adequately address those social and economic forces that feed America's crime problem.

Study Questions

1. How do the authors determine that crime rates are not reduced by a policy of increased incarceration?

2. What are some of the negative ramifications of a policy of further incarceration?

3. What policies do the authors suggest in place of incarceration? ✦

37
Ten Unintended Consequences of the Growth in Imprisonment

Todd R. Clear

The ever increasing growth in our prison population has a number of unintended fiscal and social consequences. Todd R. Clear discusses how these negative consequences help explain the incredible increase in the U.S. prison population without an equivalent decrease in the amount of crime. This is an important subject, especially because many believe that the most effective way to reduce crime is to increase incarceration. Indeed, there are those who attribute recent reductions in the crime rate to our willingness to incarcerate more and more people for longer periods of time. The author of this article provides a convincing argument that the relationship between the crime rate and the incarceration rate is not as obvious as it would seem.

Imprisonment levels in the United States have grown precipitously for nearly a quarter of a century. Corrections managers are well aware of this fact. They also know the impact this growth has had on the size of corrections budgets: increasing over 1,000% since 1971, over 300 percent in real dollars.[1] About 3 percent of American adults are under some form of corrections supervision—

Excerpts from "Ten Unintended Consequences of the Growth in Imprisonment" by Todd R. Clear, *Correctional Management Quarterly*, 1(2):25–31. Copyright © 1997 by Aspen Publishers. Reprinted by permission.

over 5 million individuals—representing a 400 percent increase over 1973 levels.

The magnitude of this change is difficult to overestimate. Between 1925 and 1973—nearly 50 years—America's incarceration rate was semi-stable, fluctuating between about 90 and 120 per 100,000 citizens. Beginning in 1973, a steady, 23-year increase in imprisonment has brought America's prison population to the second highest in the world.[2]

This increase is the direct result of intentional policy. Lawmakers, convinced that crime needs to be fought by ever-tougher methods, have increased sentence lengths for offenders significantly. Time served by first-time felons has risen from 22 months in 1965 to 27 months today[2]; time served for repeat offenders is far higher.[3]

The premise underlying this policy shift is that tougher policies will reduce crime. It has not been fully achieved, however. While crime rates are declining across the nation,[4] since 1973 the crime rate has gone through two periods of increase and two periods of decrease. Violent crime rates have remained high, while property crime rates have not yet fallen enough to match what the increases in prison population would seem to predict. Studies of the incapacitation effect of imprisonment estimate that these enormous increases have translated into no more than a 10 percent reduction in violent crime[5] and perhaps a 10 percent or less reduction in property crime (compare Spelman[6] to Zimring and Hawkins[7]).

If the intended consequences have been disappointing to the advocates of prison growth, what can be said about the side effects? Unintended consequences are a result of two main components of this enormous growth in the prison system:

1. The growth removes large numbers of people differentially from their communities.

2. The growth requires a large public investment.

These unintended consequences stem from the fact that offenders do not live in a vacuum. Their lives are not only a series of criminal events, but also include the variety of normal, everyday circumstances that occur in all human existence. When an offender is removed from society, it is an attempt to remove those crimes. However, the everyday activities are removed as well. The unintended consequences occur because of the elimination of these activities.

This article identifies ten unintended consequences of incarceration that occur because of the two identified aspects of prison growth. These unintended consequences can be divided into two types. The first type is social consequences, which directly increase the probability of crime. The second type is fiscal consequences, which directly reduce the quality of life by tying up social investment in crime control instead of other services. In short, the article argues that the growth in prison has led to unanticipated increases in crime and decreases in the quality of life.

Social Consequences

Under the dimension of social consequences, the four unintended results are as follows:

1. Replacement of criminal offenders
2. Recruitment of younger offenders
3. Depreciation of the value of punishment
4. Familial deficits

Each is discussed separately in the text that follows.

Replacement of Criminal Offenders

One of the most popular ideas about imprisonment is the common sense that "a thug in jail can't shoot your sister."[8] It is the conventional belief that prison prevents crime through incapacitation. Estimates of incapacitation effects run high—DiIulio and Piehl's survey of prisoners in Wisconsin and New Jersey leads them to estimate the "average" prisoner would commit between 12 and 20 crimes, were he or she on the streets.[9,10] Even higher is Zedlewski's claim that the "average" active offender commits 187 crimes per year.[11] It seems obvious that offenders who are locked up cannot be committing those crimes.

> Locking up offenders does not mean that crimes will not occur.

But locking up offenders does not mean [that] crimes will not occur. Research shows that many offenses are committed by offenders in groups—in fact, a majority of crimes may be group phenomena.[12] When an individual is imprisoned for an offense, the crimes he or she would have been involved in with others may well occur anyway. The group may continue its activity; indeed, it may recruit someone new to take the missing comrade's place in criminal activity. In fact, research suggests that locking up a gang member does not interrupt gang activity, except when the person locked up is a pivotal leader in the gang's criminal activity.[12] Other research shows, however, that most gangs are loosely formed with leaders being selected almost randomly and always changing.[13] This ever-changing group composition fosters an environment where new members can easily participate in the criminal activities of the gang.

The "replacement" hypothesis, as it has been called, helps explain why the large increases in imprisonment have not produced the kinds of reductions in crime one would expect from the incapacitation studies cited previously. Instead of preventing the crimes, they are merely displaced to a different set of participants.

How much crime is "replaced" after an imprisonment? No firm figures exist, but the numbers could be quite high. One third of all prison admissions are for drug offenses,[2] nearly all of which occur in an elastic marketplace that replaces new drug workers.[14] Another quarter of admissions are property offenders, many of whom committed their offenses in groups. If these numbers are any guide, incapacitation is declawed by a great deal of replacement.

Recruitment of Younger Offenders

The replacement of criminal offenses may be worse than a mere crime control wash. Newly recruited offenders can augment overall criminal activity by developing a criminal career that would not have occurred had they not been recruited into criminal activity. For example, it is known that earlier onset of criminality is predictive of longer criminal careers.[15] Moreover, there is broad anecdotal evidence (as well as limited ethnographic work, see Sullivan[16]) that happenstance involvement in criminal activity can draw a peripheral actor in crimes deeper into criminal networks and lead to deeper commitments to crime.

Blumstein alludes to this process when he theorizes that a doubling of rates of violent crime among young males can be accounted for by replacement-augmented criminality.[17] The incarceration of large numbers of drug offenders may have resulted in recruitment of ever-younger replacements who, once armed, become more violent than their predecessors due in part to their younger age.

The full extent of replacement-augmentation is not clear. Until ethnographic studies of offenders' careers are completed, the magnitude of these effects can only be estimated. It remains plausible, however, that nearly every criminal replacement represents a "promotion" from marginal deviance to central criminality.

Depreciation of the Value of Punishment

When penalties deter, they do so, in part, because they are feared. The production of fear of punishment bears a complicated rela-

tionship to actual personal experience with punishment. For example, logic suggests that one way to get someone to fear a punishment is to give him or her a "taste" of its severity. Research and experience question this logic.

Finckenauer's study of the "scared straight" program illustrates the problem.[18] He found that students exposed to the frightening and abusive treatment of Rahway prisoners serving life terms actually did worse after leaving the program than a comparison group not exposed to the program. Finckenauer reasoned that the brutal treatment actually backfired, tending to inure the youth to the brutality of prison life and giving them an experience of survival. Tyler's study of a sample of Chicago citizens found that compliance with the law followed experiences with the legal system deemed "fair" by the citizen, while experiences deemed "unfair" were followed by noncompliance.[19]

Thus, the widespread experience of punishment in some communities may not breed fear of the law as much as contempt for it. It is no secret that many members of minority communities harbor deepseated skepticism about the fairness and justness of the criminal law. There are over a half million African Americans in prisons, and the reach of the punitive hand of the law may be thought as touching not only them, but also their brothers, sisters, children, spouses, fathers, uncles, nephews, and so on. What are these many family members to think of the prison? When a stay in the prison becomes a commonplace experience, would this experience not be expected to diminish the fear and stigma associated with it?

The extended increase in imprisonment represents not a social order triumphant, but a frenzied response to a perception of a social order run amok. It does not inspire confidence in the people who are not its targets, but it enkindles animosity in those who are. The question is not whether people learn to fear (or rationally fear) the system's penalties. Rather, the question is whether the much broadened use of penalties undermines its own importance, both as a symbol and as a practical impediment to conformity.

Familial Deficits

Lynch and Sabol estimate that up to 30 percent of male African Americans between the ages of 20 and 40 from Washington, D.C., are currently incarcerated[20]; this figure represents 7 percent of all adult African American males nationwide.[21] Seventy percent of prisoners in New York's prison system come from seven boroughs in New York City, mostly African Americans and Hispanics.[22] The removal of parent-age males from the home is a government action not evenly distributed across citizens.

There is a wealth of data to suggest that the removal of large numbers of males could have damaging consequences for communities. Removal of males leads to single-parent families and fosters reduced supervision of children, disruption in parenting, and deterioration of family strengths.[23] Each of these consequences can be expected to increase the chance that children will become involved in more serious delinquency.[24,25]

Studies of parenting deficits following incarceration have clearly documented the negative impacts when mothers are sent to prison, but more recent work suggests the consequences can be significant for fathers as well.[26–29] For a majority of males in a jail sample, for example, there were children who experienced a significant interruption in parenting after the incarceration.[30] Such effects are consistent with existing literature on precursors to delinquency,[31] raising questions about the causal connection between parental incarceration and the delinquency of subsequent generations—a statistical relationship well established in the literature.[24,32]

Even if the contribution of incarceration to delinquency is minor, the effects can be great because the numbers are so large. If the father's imprisonment leads to family deficits that increase the net criminality of a child by 10 percent, for example, and there are an average of two children per offender in prison, today's prison and jail populations of 1.5 million accumulate the equivalent of 300,000 additional delinquent careers. Of course, the actual effects are dependent on the offender's length of stay, the resources of the abandoned family, and a host of other factors. But the possibility exists that massive increases in imprisonment can lead to delinquency increases that are not simply marginal.

Fiscal Consequences

Under the dimension of fiscal consequences, the following six results can be found:

1. Movement of economic value from urban to nonurban areas
2. Creation of a corrections industrial complex
3. Reduction in funding of schools and other public services
4. Increased social inequality
5. Growth in "future generation" debt
6. Cultural tolerance of official cruelty

Each consequence is discussed separately.

Movement of Economic Value From Urban to Nonurban Areas

Most offenders come from financially disadvantaged neighborhoods. Their economic lives occur in those neighborhoods. Because offenders tend also to be poor, their removal has little effect on neighborhood resources at an individual level, but when many individuals are imprisoned, there is an effect that matters.

The average offender represents somewhere in the vicinity of $10,000 in local economic activity: local purchases of services and goods from local sources.[16] When this person is removed, some of this activity is removed as well. A store that would have sold him or her a sandwich may not sell the sandwich. A bike or radio that might have been bought for a child is not bought.

But this economic activity is not merely removed, it is transformed and transferred. When the now prisoner is prosecuted, the professionals who carry out this function receive their pay for this task. They seldom live in the local area from which the offender was removed, and their wages are not spent there. When the person is eventually incarcerated, the money spent on this "service" translates into wealth for the communities that serve as home to the prison. Thus, in many states, a city dweller worth $10,000 in economic activity to his or her locality, once arrested becomes transformed into $25,000 worth of economic activity for nicer neighborhoods. Once imprisoned, it is converted into income for the rural locality of the prison.

The mathematics of the prison economy is one of the reasons that local areas bid so furiously for new prison contracts when they are offered. The new prison is industry, and it represents jobs and financial security. The popular NIMBY (not-in-my-backyard) has been replaced with what might be called a wildly successful PIOT (please-in-our-town). Jobs—good jobs with permanence that will not be eliminated by downsizing—have been created by growth in the corrections system, and they have been for the most part located in rural areas.

Creation of a Corrections Industrial Complex

The arrival of big business into the corrections system is one of the untold stories of this decade. Prison building is one of the few remaining monetary spoils in government. With revenues decreasing or staying stable, declining social services, and growing public suspicion of government growth, corrections is the one place where the tax base can be politically directed and made to expand.

> The arrival of big business into the corrections system is one of the untold stories of this decade.

The numbers can be staggering. Before her defeat by George Bush, Jr., Governor Ann Richards was building a new prison every month—with all the siting, contracting, hiring, and favoring each facility allowed. In California, the strongest new labor union comprises corrections officers. Members donate large amounts of money to both parties, and they lobby for ever-harsher penalties leading to ever increasing prison populations and more prison jobs and union members.

Privatization has also made changes in the finances of the corrections system. In Connecticut, a private jail was having trouble locating suitable prisoners (at upwards of $60 per day in fees). Investors therefore lobbied to import offenders from other regions for local incarceration. The concept of people making profits from crime control is questionable from a moral standpoint, but it is not debatable that when those profit margins are superior to other government services, such as schools or health, the marketplace will be pressured to expand its imprisonment spaces and investor dollars will go to imprisonment function instead of other moneymaking ventures.

Reduction in Funding of Schools and Other Public Services

Government revenues are limited. When there is a cap on money available to be spent, but one of the costs is not capped, it is necessary to move dollars from some budget items to that cost item in order to maintain fiscal soundness. Corrections systems demands are placing such a burden on government costs.

In California, recent analyses found that the "three-strikes" legislation would be so expensive as to use up the available, flexible revenues for functions such as education and health services.[33] Increases in corrections costs in California have been almost identical to decreases in spending on higher education. These facts indicate a truism: There is only so much money for government services.

The corrections-industrial complex enters this truism as a lobbyist for particular revenue priorities: prisons. The fact that many people stand to benefit directly from prison expansion means that the services that are less central to personal interests have to compete with ever-more powerful, entrenched commitments. The most obvious targets are "soft" funding priorities such as education (local revenues and tuition can make up for reductions in support, and wealthy families can afford whatever costs are incurred) and social welfare programming.

Increased Social Inequality

Social inequality is not produced by a secret plan, it results from the transfer of wealth from those who have less to those who have more. This pattern has been prevalent in the United States since the 1960s. What does it have to do with imprisonment?

Many of the forces of unintended consequences widen the gulf of wealth. The removal of wage earners reduces the resources of their children; the permanent negative impact on wages of imprisonment[34] punishes offenders long after their sentences have been served. The normalization of incarceration in some communities turns those communities into "prison" cultures by bringing the realities of being locked up into daily life (the baggy, "grunge" look of many adolescents descends from the oversized clothing of training schools, so often worn by young male African Americans).

There is no escaping the fact that inequality breeds crime. It does so from several points of view. Conflict theories say the poor rebel against oppression; strain theories posit the disadvantaged seek illegitimate means for goal attainment; subcultural theories state that isolated members of society develop anti-mainstream normative expectations.[35,36] The point is that all theories of crime, no matter how disparate, would predict increased criminality from increased inequality.

Growth in 'Future Generation' Debt

The prison population is not growing "naturally." That is, the growth is not a result of growth in crime. For instance, in Florida prison intake has been declining steadily for 5 years, but prison populations continue to rise.[37] This rise is a result of increases in sentence length. People being punished for crimes today are more likely to serve time and serve more time than in previous years.

This fact may seem like an anomaly to those who perceive the system of justice to be more lenient than ever before. This common idea is something of a social myth, a collective ignorance. In fact, both the chances of a person going to prison and the chances that the time served will be longer have increased in the last 20 years. The prisons required for today's growing prison population, and the continued incarceration required for those contained there, will have to be paid for by future generations.

"Three strikes" legislation offers a good example of this incurred future debt. A person convicted of a third serious felony might have served 15 years under earlier statutes. Sentenced at the age of 25, he or she would be expected to be on the streets at the age of 40. But legislation will keep him or her in prison until death from old age. The prisoner is locked up after his or her 40th birthday, with an effect of incapacitation that approaches zero, according to all knowledge of the age-crime curve.[38]

But it also costs nothing for 15 years. That is, current policy would already have required that expenditure. The new policy requires no expenditure for those 15 years. Its increased costs only kick in after the original sentence is expired. That is, the costs will not exist until today's 6-year-old children are 21 years old. They will have to pay the taxes to institute the policy change. And its effect is to lock up someone after his or her 40th birthday, a time yielding minuscule crime prevention benefits at best.

The creation of future debt should surprise nobody. Today's politicians and voters have been transferring debt to their children in the form of deficit spending, health care guarantees, and so forth for years. Why would anybody think crime policy would be immune from this trend?

Cultural Tolerance of Official Cruelty

The expanded "toughness" has had a substantive side. Prisoners are no longer allowed recreation, education, affiliation, or rehabilitation. They are forced into labor lines attached by chains. They are subjected to humiliation and defamation. The crime rate has refused to plummet, and its stubbornness in the face of toughness reminds us that social policy is not a simple puzzle.

The unrelenting toughness of our crime policy demeans us, not only because of its ineffectualness, but also because of what it says about our social character. We tolerate extreme forms of cruelty to fellow citizens— even celebrate these actions—in answer to some visceral urge for social harm. We are increasingly defined as a society that encourages disdainful treatments of our neighbors. We read of Singaporian canings and Saudi decapitations of the arm, and we feel envy. Charity, generousness, and restraint are pummeled from official policy and cast out of the collective social heart. We have become a society that invests its money in machinery of penalty, transferring funds inexorably from our schools and hospitals. We have lost track of any perspective on the idea of social peace-making.

Conclusion

Imprisonment is a growth industry in America. It siphons its resources from other endeavors, mostly public services. Americans are sentimental in the extreme. In a world careening toward the future, they seek control over their present. Like the slightly paranoic partygoer who fears contact with anyone else at the party and stays resolutely in the safety of the lonely corner of the room, we engage in the very behavior that feeds our discontent.

Imprisonment has many consequences. It is a profound intervention in a social system, this practice of removing people for periods of time, confining them to unpleasant experience, and then returning them. Some of the results of this policy are not socially cohesive. When we extend the experience more broadly than ever before, we experience the decohesive effects more directly.

Study Questions

1. What are the social consequences of the growth of imprisonment?
2. What are the fiscal consequences of the growth of imprisonment?
3. Discuss two ways that we can reduce the prison population.

References

1. Clear, T.R., and Cole, G. *American Corrections*. Belmont, Calif: Wadsworth, 1997.
2. Bureau of Justice Statistics Reports. *Prisoners in 1994*. Washington, D.C.: U.S. Department of Justice, 1995.
3. Bureau of Justice Statistics. *State Court Sentencing of Convicted Felons*, 1992. Washington, D.C.: U.S. Department of Justice, 1996.
4. Bureau of Justice Statistics. *Crime Victimization Drops Three Percent from 1993–1994*. Washington, D.C.: U.S. Department of Justice, 1996.
5. Reiss, A.J., and Roth, J., eds. *Understanding and Controlling Violence*. Washington, D.C.: National Academy of Sciences Press, 1993.

6. Spelman, W. *Criminal Incapacitation*. New York, N.Y.: Plenum, 1994.

7. Zimring, F., and Hawkins, G. *Incapacitation*. Chicago, Ill.: University of Chicago, 1994.

8. Wattenberg, B. *Values Matter Most*. New York, N.Y.: Free Press, 1995.

9. DiIulio, J., and Piehl, A.M. "Does Prison Pay?" *The Brookings Review* (Fall 1991):28–35.

10. Council on Crime in America. *The State of Violent Crime in America*. Washington, D.C.: Council on Crime in America, 1996.

11. Zedlewski, E. *Making Confinement Decisions: The Economics of Disincarceration*. Washington, D.C.: U.S. Department of Justice, 1987.

12. Reiss, A.J. "Co-offending and Criminal Careers." In *Crime and Justice: An Annual Review of Research* edited by M. Tonry and N. Morris, vol. 10. Chicago, Ill.: University of Chicago, 1988.

13. Spergel, I. *The Youth Gang Problem: A Community Approach*. New York, N.Y.: Oxford University Press, 1995.

14. Reuter, P., and MacCoun, R.J. *Lessons from the Absence of Harm Reduction in American Drug Policy*. Santa Monica, Calif.: Rand, 1996.

15. Blumstein, A. et al. *Criminal Careers and Career Criminals*. Washington, D.C.: National Academy Press, 1986.

16. Sullivan, M. *Getting Paid: Youth, Crime and Work in the Inner City*. Ithaca, N.Y.: Cornell University Press, 1989.

17. Blumstein, A. "Violence by Young People: Why the Deadly Nexus?" *NIJ Journal* 229 (1995): 2–9.

18. Finckenauer, J.O. *Scared Straight: The Panacea Phenomenon*. Englewood Cliffs, N.J.: Prentice Hall, 1982.

19. Tyler, T. *Why People Obey the Law*. New Haven, Conn.: Yale University Press, 1990.

20. Lynch, J., and Sabol, W.J. "Macro-Social Changes and Their Implications for Prison Reform: The Underclass and the Composition of Prison Populations." Paper presented to the American Society of Criminology, New Orleans, 5 November 1992.

21. Mauer, M. *African American Males and the Criminal Justice System*, 1995. Washington, D.C.: The Sentencing Project, 1995.

22. Clines, FX "Ex-Inmates Urge Return to Areas of Crime to Help." *The New York Times*, 23 December 1992, 1 FF.

23. Clear, T.R., and Rose, D.R. "A Thug in Jail Can't Shoot Your Sister: The Unintended Consequences of Incarceration." Paper presented to the American Sociological Association, 18 August 1996.

24. Hagan, J. "The Next Generation: Children of Prisoners." In *The Unintended Consequences of Incarceration* (pp. 22–39). New York, N.Y.: Vera Institute of Justice, 1996.

25. Wilson, W.J. *The Truly Disadvantaged*. Chicago, Ill.: University of Chicago, 1987.

26. Brodsky, S. *Families and Friends of Men in Prison*. Lexington, Mass.: Lexington Books, 1975.

27. Lowstein, A. "Temporary Single Parenthood—The Case of Prisoner's Families." *Family Relations* 35 (1986): 79–85.

28. Gabel, S. "Children of Incarcerated and Criminal Parents: Adjustment, Behavior and Prognosis." *Bulletin of American Academic Psychiatry Law* 20 (1992): 33–45.

29. King, A.E.O. "The Impact of Incarceration on African American Families: Implications for Practice." *Journal of Contemporary Human Service* 73, no. 3 (1993):145–53.

30. Smith, M., and Clear, T.R. *Fathers in Prison: Interim Report*. Draft report to the Edna McConnel Clark Foundation by the Rutgers University School of Criminal Justice.

31. Office of Juvenile Justice and Delinquency Prevention. *Family Strengthening in Delinquency Prevention*. Washington, D.C.: Office of Juvenile Justice and Delinquency Prevention, 1994.

32. Andrews, D. *Effective Treatments for Corrections*. Monograph prepared for the National Institute of Corrections. Washington, D.C., 1996.

33. Greenwood, P. *Estimating the Effects of California's "Three Strikes" Law on Resources and Crime*. Santa Monica, Calif.: Rand, 1995.

34. Freeman, R.B. "Crime and Unemployment of Disadvantaged Youth." In *Drugs, Crime and Social Isolation: Barriers to Urban Opportunity*, edited by A. Harrell and G. Peterson. Washington, D.C.: Urban Institute, 1992.

35. Beime, P., and Messerschmidt, J. *Criminology*. New York, N.Y.: Harcourt, Brace, 1995.

36. Petee, T.A., et al. "Levels of Contextual Integration in Group Contexts and the Effects of

Informal Sanction Threat on Deviance." *Criminology* 32, no. 1 (1994): 85–106.

37. Florida Department of Corrections. *Annual Report*. Tallahassee, Fla.: Florida Department of Corrections, 1995.

38. Gottfredson, M., and Hirschi, T. *A General Theory of Crime*. Stanford, Calif.: Stanford University Press, 1990. ✦

38
Public Support for Correctional Treatment
The Continuing Appeal of the Rehabilitative Ideal

Brandon K. Applegate

Francis T. Cullen

Bonnie S. Fisher

For over thirty years, correctional policy in the United States has centered on "getting tough" with offenders. Many policy makers and legislators enact punitive practices under the mantel of public support. However, as the research by Brandon K. Applegate, Francis T. Cullen, and Bonnie S. Fisher demonstrates, the public is not monolithically punitive in its attitudes toward crime. Support by the public for rehabilitation remains strong and is fairly consistent across demographic groups and across different types of questions used to measure citizens' views. Developing and implementing effective correctional programs are measures clearly consistent with public attitudes and opinions, and these should be a high priority of public officials

Excerpts from "Public Support for Correctional Treatment: The Continuing Appeal of the Rehabilitative Ideal" by Brandon K. Applegate, Francis T. Cullen, and Bonnie S. Fisher, *The Prison Journal*, 77(3): 237–258. Copyright © 1997 by Sage Publications, Inc. Reprinted by permission.

Because of the important role that public opinion plays regarding decisions about punishment and correctional policy, it is critical that we have an accurate appraisal of the public's views. Recently, there has been a "penal harm" movement (Clear, 1994), which involves decreasing amenities for prisoners, the reimplementation of chain gangs, long sentences for habitual offenders, and other punitive measures. Often, policy makers suggest that these policies are implemented in accordance with the public will.

Such assertions are potentially problematic because it is unclear that citizens advocate an approach to corrections that seeks only to punish offenders. As noted below, although research has demonstrated that citizens want criminals to be punished, other studies confirm that the public is not monolithically punitive; most citizens also support the rehabilitation of offenders.

The difficulty for policy makers who might wish to use polls of rehabilitation attitudes to guide their decision making is that few researchers have assessed *recent* opinions. Further, the information that is available from contemporary studies is constrained by various methodological limitations. These studies, for example, typically have drawn samples of respondents from limited geographic areas and have included only a few measures of treatment attitudes. In an effort to improve our understanding of public views of rehabilitation, this study provides an assessment of current attitudes toward correctional treatment. Moreover, we employ a variety of different questions to measure support for rehabilitation among a statewide random sample of adult respondents.

Public Views of Rehabilitation

During the 1970s and 1980s, and particularly following Martinson's (1974) work ostensibly revealing the ineffectiveness of treatment, considerable doubts were raised about the standing of rehabilitation with the public. At least three researchers, for example, asked directly, "Is rehabilitation dead?" (Cullen, Cullen, & Wozniak, 1988; Halleck & Witte, 1977; Serrill, 1975). Studies of public attitudes conducted throughout the 1980s, however, showed that the public continued to believe that rehabilitation should be an integral part of correctional policy.

The most prevalent approach that researchers have taken to evaluate the public's position on rehabilitation has been to provide respondents with a list of goals and ask which one is the most important. We were able to identify 27 studies that have asked respondents to rate, rank, or choose rehabilitation compared to at least one other correctional goal. Rehabilitation received the highest rating in at least one part of 20 of these studies. For example, 73% of respondents chose rehabilitation as the preferred emphasis of prisons in a 1968 Harris poll (Hindelang, Dunn, Aumick, & Sutton, 1975, p. 218). Harris repeated this poll five times, conducting the last survey in 1982. In this final poll, support for rehabilitation had declined to 44%, but it still was rated higher than protection of society (32%) or punishment (19%) (McGarrell & Flanagan, 1985, p. 233). More recently, a 1989 Gallup poll asked whether it was more important to punish offenders or "get them started on the right road" (Maguire & Flanagan, 1991, p. 198). Although 38% chose punishment, 48% said that rehabilitation was more important. In a 1986 poll, the residents of two major Ohio cities also endorsed treatment. When asked what "should be the main emphasis of prisons" they more often chose rehabilitation (55% and 59%) than protection (35% and 30%) or punishment (6% and 7%) (Cullen, Skovron, Scott, & Burton, 1990).

When Gottfredson, Warner, and Taylor (1988) applied a different rating task, their results showed that the public felt that the rehabilitation of offenders was equal in importance to general deterrence and was more important than incapacitation or punishment. Similar high levels of support have been reported by other researchers using a variety of question wordings (Barrum,

Henningsen, & Young, 1983; Brown, Flanagan, & McLeod, 1984; Cullen, Clark, & Wozniak, 1985; Gottfredson & Taylor, 1984; Hindelang et al., 1975; Johnson & Huff, 1987; Knowles, 1987; Langworthy & Whitehead, 1986; Reichel & Gauthier, 1990; Riley & Rose, 1980; Roberts & Edwards, 1989; Steinhart, 1988; Thomson & Ragona, 1987).

Even when rehabilitation is not selected as the primary purpose of corrections, citizens still regard it as an important secondary goal. For example, when asked about the immediate purpose of punishment, 40% of Thomson and Ragona's (1987) respondents answered that it was to punish. The second largest proportion of respondents, however, chose rehabilitation (29%), placing treatment ahead of control (16%), reparation (7%), and "other" (3%). Similarly, Warr and Stafford (1984) explicitly asked their respondents to indicate the first, second, and third most important reasons for sending an offender to prison from a list of six justifications. Although only 17% of those asked said that rehabilitation was the most important goal, 59% chose it as one of the top three. This level of approval was second only to retribution (66%). Further, special deterrence (25%) and rehabilitation (24%) were most often chosen as the second most important correctional goal. Other studies also indicate that although the public sees rehabilitation as somewhat less important than various punitive goals, they still rate treatment as a legitimate and integral part of the correctional enterprise (Cullen, Clark, & Wozniak, 1985; Flanagan & Jamieson, 1988, pp. 158–159; Knowles, 1987; Roberts & Gebotys, 1989; Sundt, Cullen, Applegate, & Turner, 1997).

In addition to asking people to compare correctional goals, researchers also have presented the public with questions about specific types of rehabilitation, the perceived effectiveness of rehabilitation, and expansion of treatment programs. Further, several authors have developed multiple-item scales to measure support for rehabilitative ideology. The wide variety of methods employed in this research makes explaining all relevant studies somewhat unwieldy. Overall, however, the research here shows much the same result as when goals are pitted against each other: Citizens endorse both punishment and treatment (Cullen, Clark, Cullen, & Mothers, 1985; Cullen et al., 1988; Cullen, Golden, & Cullen, 1983; Cullen et al., 1990; Harris, 1968; Hindelang et al., 1975; Johnson, 1994; McCorkle, 1993; McGarrell & Flanagan, 1985; Riley & Rose, 1980; Steinhart 1988).

These findings might appear to make further assessments of the public mood unnecessary. It seems that citizens want offenders to be punished, but that they also want reformation through correctional treatment. Despite this knowledge, the movement to expand the use of penal harm in the United States that began in the 1970s shows little sign of subsiding in the 1990s (Clear, 1994). In fact many of the recent innovations in corrections could be characterized as mean-spirited attempts to humiliate, punish, or control offenders. Some examples of these developments include the reimplementation of chain gangs—teams of inmates shackled together who perform "stoop labor" ("Alabama," 1995; Bragg, 1995; Cohen, 1995; Gavzer, 1995)—the introduction of "three strikes and you're out" legislation in 37 states (Turner, Sundt, Applegate, & Cullen, 1995), and reductions in the amenities afforded prison inmates (Johnson, Bennett, & Flanagan, 1997; Wunder, 1995).

As Cullen (1995) observed, these innovations might be more symbolic than substantive. These are high-publicity policies that may affect most offenders in only marginal ways. Even a cursory examination of recent incarceration rate trends, however, confirms that offenders are being punished more harshly than they were at the beginning of this decade (Bureau of Justice Statistics, 1996). The expansion of attempts to place greater controls on offenders punished in the community also is well documented (Cullen, Wright & Applegate, 1996; Gordon, 1991; Morris & Tonry, 1990).

Given the persistence of the "get tough" or penal harm movement; we might ask whether rehabilitation still is supported by the public. Do citizens support a policy agenda that devotes attention mainly to harming rather than improving offenders? Unfortunately, the existing research conducted during the 1990s is limited in the information that it may provide to correctional policy makers. Most often, studies of rehabilitation attitudes have used samples selected from a single urban area (Brown & Elrod, 1995; Cullen et al., 1990; Johnson, 1994; McCorkle, 1993; Senese, 1992; Sundt et al., 1997). The generalizability of their findings, therefore, is questionable. . . .

Methodology

Sample

For this study, we randomly selected a statewide sample of 1,000 Ohio residents. Questionnaires were mailed to each member of the sample following Dillman's (1978) total design method. The first mailing was distributed in May 1996, with reminder mailings following 1, 3, and 7 weeks later. Questionnaires were returned completed or nearly completed by 559 respondents. In addition, 105 questionnaires were returned unanswered because the intended respondent could not be located, had moved out of the state, was too ill to complete the survey, or was deceased. The resulting response rate for those members of the sample who received a survey and were capable of completing it was 62.4% (559/895).

Based on comparisons with the 1990 census, it appears that our sample overrepresents men (66.7%), Whites (92.5%), people who are older (M = 53.5 years), people who have college educations (27.9%), and people who earn higher incomes (median = $35,000–$49,999) (U.S. Bureau of the Census, 1994). Prior studies indicate that older respondents, White respondents, and those with higher incomes tend to be more punitive and less supportive of rehabilitation; those who are more educated, on the other hand, tend to favor treatment (for a review, see Applegate, 1997). Although these relationships typically are weak, past research suggests that, if any bias exists, support for rehabilitation might be slightly attenuated in the current study.

Measures

Support for rehabilitation was assessed in a variety of ways. First, we replicated the question posed by Harris (see Cullen et al., 1990; Hindelang et al., 1975, p. 218; McGarrell & Flanagan, 1985, p. 233; Sundt et al., 1997):

> Now what do you think *should* be the *main* emphasis in most prisons—punishing the individual convicted of a crime, trying to rehabilitate the individual so that he might return to society as a productive citizen, or protecting society from future crimes he might commit?

The respondents were instructed to choose one main goal and were afforded four response options: "punish" "rehabilitate," "protect society," and "not sure."

Because other research has revealed that rehabilitation may be a secondary correctional goal for many people, we also asked the respondents to indicate how important each goal was to them (see Table 38.2): "very important," "important," "a little important," or "not important." These questions ask for citizens' preferences without referring to any specific offender or situation; therefore, they are used to measure global attitudes.

Specific attitudes were assessed by presenting the respondents with a vignette. This vignette described a specific offender and several aspects of his or her situation—criminal history, drug use, employment history, current offense, sentence, and type of rehabilitation program. . . .

The construction of vignettes invariably requires some choices about what words and phrases to include. These decisions affect the rating task and thus may shape the results. To help minimize these effects, the vignettes were constructed using Rossi's (Rossi & Nock, 1982) factorial survey methodology. Using this approach, the specific characteristics of each vignette are randomly assigned, making it very unlikely that any two of the distributed vignettes were identical. Because we were able to vary a large proportion of the potentially salient attributes, the effects of our choices of phrase may be less pronounced than if we had employed a single vignette.

Each respondent in the sample received one unique, randomly generated vignette to rate. After reading the vignette, the respondents were asked to indicate the extent to which they agreed or disagreed with five statements about the hypothetical offender:

> I support the use of rehabilitation with Gary/Lisa.

> It is right to put people like Gary/Lisa in programs that try to cure the particular problem that caused them to break the law.

> This type of rehabilitation program should be expanded so that more offenders could be involved.

> Trying to rehabilitate Gary/Lisa probably will lessen the chances that he/she will go back into crime.

> If Gary/Lisa successfully completes his/her rehabilitation program, he/she should have the opportunity to have his/her sentence reduced.

The respondents rated each statement on a 6-point Likert-type scale from *disagree strongly* (1) to *agree strongly* (6). An additive index of these statements was developed and showed substantial internal consistency (Cronbach's alpha = .87).

In addition to the global questions on the purpose of prisons and the specific vignette items, we also included a set of statements that probed the respondents' views on particular rehabilitation policies:

It is important to try to rehabilitate juveniles who have committed crimes and are now in the correctional system.

It is important to try to rehabilitate adults who have committed crimes and are now in the correctional system.

We should try to rehabilitate women who have broken the law.

We should try to rehabilitate men who have broken the law.

Rehabilitation programs should be available even for offenders who have been involved in a lot of crime in their lives.

It is a good idea to provide treatment for offenders who are supervised by the courts and live in the community.

It is a good idea to provide treatment for offenders who are in prison.

The best way to rehabilitate offenders is to try to help offenders change their values and to help them with the emotional problems that caused them to break the law.

The best way to rehabilitate offenders is to teach them a skill that they can use to get a job when they are released from prison.

The best way to rehabilitate offenders is to give them a good education.

The respondents indicated their reaction to each statement on the same agree-disagree 6-point Likert-type scale used to rate the vignettes. An index of these items also showed high reliability (Cronbach's alpha = .90).

Most authors have presented the distinction between global and specific attitudinal measures as dichotomous (see Applegate et al., 1996; Brandl, Frank, Worden, & Bynum, 1994; Cumberland & Zamble, 1992; Easton, 1965; Vining & Ebreo, 1992; White & Menke, 1982; Zamble & Kalm, 1990). Kaminski and Jefferis (1997, p. 23), however, suggest that measures of attitudes may be "better conceptualized as lying on a continuum." That is, some items are *more* specific or *less* specific than others. In this vein, the 10 statements presented here appear to be somewhat less global than the questions

about the main emphasis of prisons and less specific than the vignette.

Finally, we measured several respondent characteristics: age, race, sex, education, family income, political party, and political conservatism.

Results

Level of Support

As detailed above, one way we measured citizen support for rehabilitation was to replicate Harris's question about the preferred emphasis of prisons. Table 38.1 reports the percentage of the respondents who chose each goal or indicated that they were "not sure" for our sample and for two of Harris's samples (1968 and 1982). Of the 552 individuals who provided a response in the present study, 41.1% stated that rehabilitation "should be the main emphasis" of imprisonment. This goal was chosen by the largest percentage of the respondents, revealing that a substantial minority of these participants strongly endorsed correctional treatment. It might be argued that less than half of the sample selected rehabilitation as the preeminent correctional goal. Still, the other two options individually garnered less support. Thus, only 31.9% chose protection of society as what should be the most important goal of incarceration, and only 20.3% indicated that they thought it most important to punish offenders. The remaining 6.7% reported that they were not sure of the appropriate aim of prisons.

Notably, the pattern of responses in our 1996 sample is quite similar to Harris's 1982 results. As shown in Table 38.1 nearly the same percentage of respondents chose protection of society and punishment in both samples. More relevant to the present discussion, 44% of Harris's respondents indicated that rehabilitation should be the main emphasis in most prisons. Thus, there is less than a 3% difference in support for rehabilitation between the two surveys. In comparison, support for treatment had declined 28% from 1968 to 1982 (see Table 38.1). Caution must be exercised in comparing the results of Harris's national poll to our findings, which are based on a single state. Still, it seems that support for rehabilitation, which appears to have weakened during the 1970s, may have stabilized in the last decade and a half.

Table 38.1

Percentage of Respondents Reporting Their Preferred Emphasis of Incarceration

Emphasis Should Be	Current 1996 Sample (N = 552)	Harris (1982)	Harris (1968)
Rehabilitate	41.1	44	72
Protect society	31.9	32	12
Punish	20.3	19	7
Not sure	6.7	5	9

Note: Based on the question, "Now what do you think *should* be the *main* emphasis in most prisons— punishing the individual convicted of a crime, trying to rehabilitate the individual so that he might return to society as a productive citizen, or protecting society from future crimes he might commit?"

In addition to inquiring about the main emphasis of incarceration, we also asked the respondents to indicate how important they believed each goal was to prisons. This assessment revealed that the respondents viewed rehabilitation as an important goal, although less important than punishment or protection. As shown in Table 38.2, 60.3% and 54.3% of the respondents said that protection of society and punishment, respectively, were "very important." By comparison, only 37.7% of the respondents chose this level of importance for rehabilitation. Even so, nearly 83% of the respondents felt that rehabilitation was "very important" or "important" and less than 4% thought that it was not important at all. Clearly, citizens believe that prisons should serve multiple goals and that correctional treatment should be an integral component of prison policy.

Table 38.3 reports the level of support for rehabilitation that the respondents expressed in response to the 10 rehabilitation

policy statements. As shown in the table, there was widespread support for correctional treatment. The mean for 8 statements was 4.29 or greater (on a 6-point scale), and for the remaining two statements it was greater than 3.45. When the agree responses are grouped together (i.e., "agree strongly," "agree," "agree slightly"), we see that over 50% of the respondents agreed with each statement, and over 80% agreed with 8 of the 10 statements (see Table 38.3). It is instructive that the respondents firmly favored treatment for offenders of different ages and sexes and for intervention of different types and in different settings. Support for rehabilitation dropped below 80% for only two issues: educational programming and treatment for chronic offenders. Even here, however, a majority of the respondents expressed agreement with these proposals.

Table 38.2

Percentage of Respondents Reporting the Importance of Each Goal of Imprisonment (N = 551)

Importance	Rehabilitation	Protection	Punishment
Very important	37.7	60.3	54.3
Important	45.1	34.3	41.0
A little important	13.6	4.9	4.0
Not important	3.6	0.5	0.7

Note: Based on the question, "Some people believe that prisons should work toward only one goal. Other people believe that many goals are important. You have just told us what you think should be the *main* emphasis in most prisons. We would also like to know how you feel about the other goals. Please show how important you think *each* goal is by circling your answers below."

Turning to the most specific measure of attitudes, Table 38.4 reports the level of support for rehabilitation that the respondents expressed in response to the vignettes. This table presents the percentage of people providing each response without regard for the variations that were introduced across the vignettes. In this way, we are able to examine the approximate average level of support.

When the agree categories are combined, the results in Table 38.4 reveal that a majority of the respondents agreed with each of the five statements. Thus, over 88% agreed with the idea of using rehabilitation with the hypothetical offender, whereas nearly 87% of the respondents agreed that individualized treatment should be employed to "cure the particular problem" of the offender. The respondents also indicated that they favored the expansion of treatment opportunities, and that they thought rehabilitation would reduce the likelihood of recidivism for the offender (see Table 38.4). The respondents were least supportive of basing decisions about the offender's sentence length on his or her progress in treatment. Even here, however, more than 55% of the respondents expressed agreement that successful completion of a rehabilitation program should be considered in reducing an offender's sentence.

Correlates of Support

The previous section revealed substantial support for rehabilitation. It also is important, however, to determine whether any substantial cleavages exist in public views of treatment. Conflicting opinions among identifiable social groups could hamper correctional reform efforts. On the other hand, relative consensus in thinking about crime may provide a foundation for implementing and expanding rehabilitative treatment programs and policies.

In this section, we examine the factors that are related to support for rehabilitation among the various measures. More specifically, we explore the relationship of respondent characteristics with four measures of attitudes toward correctional treatment. First, two dependent variables were constructed from the questions that asked about the goals of incarceration. We divided the responses to the question about the main emphasis of prisons into two categories where 1 equaled rehabilitation and 0 equaled all

other responses. Second, we dichotomized the question about the importance of rehabilitation by collapsing the categories "very important" and "important" (1) to indicate support and "a little important" and "not important" (0) to indicate an absence of support. Because both measures are dichotomous, they were analyzed through logit models.

We also examined the multiple-item measures of support for rehabilitation described in the Methodology section. That is, we looked at the 10-item index that assessed the respondents' views on particular rehabilitation policies and analyzed the five-item vignette index. These variables were analyzed using ordinary least squares (OLS) regression.

Table 38.5 reports the results of logistic and linear multiple regression models of support for rehabilitative ideology and the respondent demographic characteristics. The most notable finding is the consistency of correlates across measures. As shown in the table, 3 of the 7 independent variables are unrelated to any measure of support for rehabilitation. One variable, political party, is related to all four measures of rehabilitation attitudes. The remaining three respondent characteristics—age, sex, and conservatism—are related to 3 of the 4 measures of support. In most cases, therefore, the demographic groups of respondents who favored rehabilitation on one assessment tended to support it on the other assessments.

It also is instructive that there are no large divisions in support for correctional treatment across demographic lines. As shown in Table 38.5, strong Republicans and more conservative respondents consistently felt less favorable toward rehabilitation than their demographic opposites. In addition, males and younger respondents also tended to be less supportive of a treatment approach to offenders. Still, the amount of variation that is explained by the respondent characteristics is small (see Table 38.5).

In a separate analysis, we examined the responses of the Republican males who

Table 38.3
Support for Rehabilitation: Policy Statements (*N* = 551)

Item	Agree Strongly (6)	Agree (5)	Agree Slightly (4)	Disagree Slightly (3)	Disagree (2)	Disagree Strongly (1)	Mean Age of Offender
Age of offender							
It is important to try and rehabilitate juveniles who have commited crimes and are now in the correctional system.	35.9%	47.0%	13.2%	1.6%	1.3%	1.1%	5.11
It is important to try and rehabilitate adults who have commited crimes and are now in the correctional system.	13.8%	41.0%	30.8%	7.2%	5.2%	2.0%	4.48
Sex of offender							
We should try to rehabilitate women who have broken the law.	15.7%	50.8%	23.5%	3.8%	5.1%	1.1%	4.65
We should try to rehabilitate men who have broken the law.	14.8%	45.8%	35.8%	5.4%	5.8%	1.4%	4.55
Chronic offenders							
Rehabilitation programs should have been available for offenders who have been involved in a lot of crime in their lives.	7.4%	23.5%	23.3%	12.7%	19.7%	13.4%	3.46
Location of treatment							
It is a good idea to provide treatment for offenders who are supervised in the courts and live in the community.	17.0%	42.2%	25.0%	6.2%	6.9%	2.7%	4.45
It is a good idea to provide treatment for offenders who are in prison.	11.6%	42.1%	32.2%	6.7%	6.1%	1.3%	4.42
Types of treatment							
The best way to rehabilitate offenders is to help offenders change their values and to help them with emotional problems that caused them to break the law.	18.6%	42.3%	27.4%	5.2%	5.4%	1.1%	4.60
The best way to rehabilitate offenders is to teach them a skill that they can use to get a job when they are released from prison.	12.1%	39.6%	29.5%	4.9%	11.4%	2.5%	4.29
The best way to rehabilitate offenders is to give them a good eduaction.	7.1%	22.8%	31.3%	14.9%	18.3%	5.6%	3.69
Policy statement rehabilitation index[a]	15.3%	39.9%	26.3%	6.8%	8.5%	3.2%	4.37

[a] Average percentages reported.

Table 38.4
Support for Rehabilitation in Response to the Vignette (*N* = 560)

Item	Agree Strongly (6)	Agree (5)	Agree Slightly (4)	Disagree Slightly (3)	Disagree (2)	Disagree Strongly (1)	Mean Age of Offender
I support the use of rehabilitation with Gary/Lisa.	19.6%	50.6%	18.0%	4.0%	5.8%	2.0%	4.68
It is right to put people like Gary/Lisa in programs that try to cure the particular problem that caused them to break the law.	15.6%	50.0%	21.2%	4.9%	6.2%	2.2%	4.57
This type of rehabilitation program should be expanded so that more offenders could be involved.	14.2%	42.1%	27.2%	6.2%	7.1%	3.3%	4.40
Trying to rehabilitate Gary/Lisa will lessen the chances that he/she will go back into crime.	10.3%	40.1%	30.9%	7.1%	9.1%	2.5%	4.28
If Gary/Lisa successfully completes his/her rehabilitation program, he/she should have the opportunity to have his/her sentence reduced.	6.9%	26.7%	22.2%	11.5%	20.7%	12.0%	3.52
Vignette rehabilitation index[a]	13.3%	41.9%	23.9%	6.7%	9.8%	4.4%	4.29

[a] Average percentages reported.

scored above the median (5) on the conservatism scale. Of the 93 respondents falling into this category, 25.8% chose rehabilitation as the most important emphasis of prisons; this response was second to protection but was higher than punishment. More instructive, almost two thirds thought that rehabilitation was an important or very important goal of incarceration.

The index scores for this group of respondents also indicate that they were less enthusiastic than the other respondents about rehabilitation for the offender described in the vignette and about the rehabilitation policy statements. Even so, the means on the vignette index (3.80) and on the policy statements index (3.97) suggested slightly more agreement than disagreement with correctional treatment.

Discussion

Many studies seem to show that the public has grown intolerant of crime and is ready to impose stringent punishment on offenders in pursuit of retribution, deterrence, and incapacitation (see Pettinico, 1994). Research showing that citizens endorse such punitive measures as capital punishment, long sentences, restrictions on early release, harsher courts, and abolishment of plea bargaining is plentiful. Although several scholars have criticized many of these studies for their oversimplification of potentially complex issues (Johnson & Huff, 1987; McCorkle, 1993; Roberts, 1992; Thomson & Ragona, 1987; Zamble, 1990), these punitive opinion-poll results are readily available to policy makers and may shape their understanding of the crime policies favored by the public.

It is noteworthy that policy makers consistently overestimate public punitiveness and consistently underestimate public support for rehabilitation. Gottfredson and Taylor (1984) reported that in a 1980 survey of Maryland citizens and correctional elites, the policy makers believed that less than 40% of the public would support community rehabilitation centers for adults, but over 60% believed that citizens would favor abolishing parole. In fact, when actually polled, more than 70% of the citizen respondents approved of the rehabilitation centers and less than 30% wanted to see an end to paroling offenders. Similarly, the legislators in Johnson and Huff's (1987, p. 125) analysis thought that less than one fourth of the public would select "change their behavior" as the purpose of imprisonment for first-time incarcerates. The actual percentage was 75. Other studies likewise have found a strong yet inaccurate expectation by elites that "the public is predominantly punitive rather than interested in rehabilitative goals" (Gottfredson et al., 1988; Riley & Rose, 1980, p. 354).

The results reported here confirm what less contemporary or more limited assessments of attitudes toward rehabilitation suggest: Despite perceptions to the contrary, the public supports correctional treatment for offenders. Furthermore, our findings dem-

Table 38.5

Correlates of Support for Rehabilitation Across Measures: Unstandardized Regression (Logit or OLS) Coefficients

Variable	Goal of Prisons	Importance of Rehabilitation	Policy Statements Index	Vignette Index
Age	−.018*	−.020*	.004	.008*
Race (1 = White, 0 = non–White)	−.263	.411	−.019	.209
Sex (1 = male, 0 = female)	−.445*	−.938*	−.256*	−.152
Education	.041	.066	.014	.013
Income	−.012	.013	−.030	−.044
Political party (1 = *strong Republican*, 5 *strong Democrat*)[a]	.356*	.392*	.132*	.171*
Conservatism (1 = *extremely liberal*, 0 = *extremely conservative*)	−.133	−.193*	−.101*	−.134*
Constant	−1.220	0.481	4.547	4.081
Chi-square or *F*	41.019*	38.139*	9.746*	10.890*
Pseudo R^2 or *R*	.08	.07	.12	.13

[a] The remaining categories are Republican (=2), Independent (=3), and Democrat (=4). $p \leq .05$.

onstrate that a great deal of consistency exists in attitudes toward rehabilitation. First, comparisons of our results with those of national Harris polls suggest that although public attitudes toward rehabilitation became less favorable during the 1970s, since the early 1980s support for the treatment ideal appears to have stabilized at a moderately high level. Despite the penal harm movement and repeated attacks on liberal crime policies, the public continues to embrace rehabilitation as an integral part of the correctional enterprise.

Second, few demographic differences in attitudes were observed in our sample. Only 1 of the 7 respondent characteristics examined was consistently related to all four measures of correctional attitudes, and even those groups of respondents who were less favorable toward treatment were not opposed to rehabilitating offenders.

A third type of consistency can be observed by noting the responses gathered across the different measures. Straightforward comparisons can be made between the vignette responses and the support expressed for the rehabilitation policies. The mean index score for the vignettes (4.29) is not significantly different than the mean index of the rehabilitation policy statements (4.37). Direct comparisons between these items and the global attitudes are more difficult because of the different response scales employed. We may note, however, that the largest percentage of the respondents chose rehabilitation as the most important aim of prisons, more than 80% thought that rehabilitation was a "very important" or "important" goal, and, on average, more than 80% supported various rehabilitation policies and supported rehabilitating the offender described in the vignette. Thus, regardless of whether we measured global or specific attitudes, the results indicate that the public has not given up on reforming offenders. Again, there is continuing support for the rehabilitative ideal.

Skeptics and those who know of the public's desire for offenders to be punished may ask whether our results are an anomaly. Have we overestimated the public's support for treating offenders? Three aspects of the present study suggest that our estimates of public attitudes are not substantially biased in favor of rehabilitation. First, as we noted in the Methodology section, our sample overrepresents older, White, wealthy, highly educated males. With the exception of respondents' sex, these variables were not related to support for treatment in the present study. Still, the relationships between these characteristics and attitudes toward punishment and rehabilitation that have been reported in previous studies suggest that we may have underestimated support for treatment.

Second, as measured by attitudes toward capital punishment, the punitiveness of the present sample is similar to that of the nation as a whole. The questionnaire included a replication of Gallup's most recent capital punishment question: "Are you in favor of the death penalty for a person convicted of murder?" In response to this question in 1995, 77% of a national sample reported that they favored execution (Moore, 1995). Comparatively, 76% of the present sample supported the death penalty. That these attitudes are consistent with other assessments of punitiveness adds confidence to the representativeness of the results regarding public views toward treatment.

Third, the data for this project were collected using a mailed questionnaire. Farnworth, Bennett, and West (1996) report the results of a mail survey of punitive attitudes and a telephone survey of the same attitudes. The respondents to the mail survey indicated greater support for prison construction and for the death penalty for murder. They also registered greater opposition to shorter sentences for offenders and to increased use of probation than the respondents in the telephone survey. Given consistent findings of a negative relationship between punitiveness and support for treatment, these results suggest that the format of the present survey may provide a conservative estimate of public support for rehabilitation.

Conclusion

After reviewing recent public opinion polls on crime policies, Pettinico (1994) concluded:

> Simply put, Americans are fed up. They see crime rising all around them and, at the same time, they see a criminal justice system that, in their view, is far too lenient lax, and forgiving. In response, the public is demanding a stress on retribution over rehabilitation, long prison terms over early release, increased use of the death penalty, and placing the safety of society over the happiness of the incarcerated. . . . When it comes to criminals, it appears that the American people have run out of checks to turn. (p. 32)

The findings presented here challenge such a pessimistic view of the public mood. We do not deny that the public desires punishment and that people want to be protected from predatory criminals. It appears, however, that the public still is receptive to treating offenders; the appeal of the rehabilitative ideal remains widespread.

The importance of this observation lies in the possibility of a positive direction for correctional policy. Cullen and Gilbert (1992) observed that once rehabilitation is no longer a valid goal, considerations of how best to protect the public can be structured only on the conservative call for harsher, more certain penalties. Since the 1970s, crime policy has followed this path of increasing punitiveness. Continuing to get tough with offenders, however, may shortchange public safety, since it is not clear that deterrent and incapacitative policies can effectively reduce crime (Little, 1992; Paternoster, 1987; Visher, 1987; Zimring & Hawkins, 1995). In contrast, a growing body of literature demonstrates that rehabilitation programs can substantially reduce recidivism, especially when they adhere to principles shown to be effective (Andrews et al., 1990; Garrett, 1985; Gendreau & Ross, 1987; Lipsey, 1992; Lipsey & Wilson, 1997; Palmer, 1992). A melding of this knowledge base on "what works" with evidence that the public still sees rehabilitation as a valid aim of corrections may provide an avenue for positive correctional reform. . . .

Study Questions

1. How have attitudes toward crime changed over the past 30 years?

2. Does the public continue to support rehabilitation as a primary purpose of corrections? Why do you believe this to be the case?

3. What did Applegate and his colleagues find are significant correlates of support?

4. What are your own views toward the purpose of corrections?

References

Alabama to make prisoners break rocks. (1995, July 29). *The New York Times*, p. 5.

Andrews, D. A., Zinger, I., Hoge, R. D., Bonta, J., Gendreau, P., & Cullen, F. T. (1990). Does correctional treatment work? A clinically relevant and psychologically informed meta-analysis. *Criminology, 28,*369-404.

Applegate. B. K. (1997). *Specifying public support for rehabilitation: A factorial survey approach.* Unpublished doctoral dissertation, University of Cincinnati, Cincinnati, OH.

Applegate, B. K., Cullen, F. T., Turner, M. G., & Sundt, J. L. (1996). Assessing public support for three-strikes-and-you're-out laws: Global versus specific attitudes. *Crime & Delinquency,* 42,517-534.

Barrum, J. A., Henningsen, R. J., & Young, J. P. (1983). *Community based corrections.* Huntsville, TX Criminal Justice Center, Sam Houston State University.

Bragg, R. (1995, March 26). Chain gangs to return to roads of Alabama: State hopes revival will deter crime. *The New York Times*, p. Y9.

Brandl, S. G., Frank, J., Worden, R. E., & Bynum, T S. (1994). Global and specific attitudes toward the police: Disentangling the relationship. *Justice Quarterly*, 11, 119–134.

Brown, E. J., Flanagan, T. J., & McLeod, M. (Eds.). (1984). *Sourcebook of criminal justice statistics—1983*. Washington, DC: Government Printing Office.

Brown, M. P., & Elrod, P. (1995). Electronic house arrest: An examination of citizen attitudes. *Crime & Delinquency*, 41, 332-346.

Bureau of Justice Statistics. (1996). *Correctional populations in the United States, 1994*. Washington, DC: U.S. Department of Justice.

Clear, T. K. (1994). *Harm in American penology. Offenders, victims, and their communities*. Albany: State University of New York Press.

Cohen, A. (1995, May 15). Back on the chain gang. *Time*, p. 26.

Cullen, F. T. (1995). Assessing the penal harm movement. *Journal of Research in Crime and Delinquency*, 32,338-359.

Cullen, F. T., & Gilbert; K. E. (1992). *Reaffirming Rehabilitation*. Cincinnati, OH: Anderson.

Cullen, F. T., Clark, G. A., Cullen, L B., & Mothers, R. A. (1985). Attribution, salience, and attitudes toward criminal sanctioning. *Criminal Justice and Behavior*, 12, 305–331.

Cullen, F. T., Clark, O. A., & Wozniak, J. F. (1985). Explaining the get tough movement: Can the public be blamed? *Federal Probation*, 49, 16-24.

Cullen, F. T., Cullen, J. B., & Wozniak, I. F. (1988). Is rehabilitation dead? The myth of the punitive public. *Journal of Criminal Justice*, 16, 303-317.

Cullen, F. T., Golden, K. M., & Cullen, J. B. (1983). Is child saving dead? Attitudes toward juvenile rehabilitation in Illinois. *Journal of Criminal Justice*, 11, 1-13.

Cullen, F. T, Skovron, S. E., Scott J. E., & Burton, V. S., Jr. (1990). Public support for correctional treatment: The tenacity of rehabilitative ideology. *Criminal Justice and Behavior*, 17,6-18.

Cullen, F. T., Wright, J. P., & Applegate, B. K. (1996). Control in the community: The limits of reform. In A. T. Harland (Ed.), *Choosing correctional options that work: Defining the demand and evaluating the supply* (pp. 69-116). Thousand Oaks, CA: Sage.

Cumberland, J., & Zamble, E. (1992). General and specific measures of attitudes toward early release of criminal offenders. *Canadian Journal of Behavioural Science*, 24, 442–455.

Dillman, D. A. (1978). *Mail and telephone surveys: The total design method* New York: John Wiley.

Easton, D. (1965). *A framework for political analysis*. Englewood Cliffs, NJ: Prentice Hall.

Farnworth, M., Bennett K., & West, V. M. (1996). Mail vs. telephone surveys of criminal justice attitudes: A comparative analysis. *Journal of Quantitative Criminology*, 12, 113–133.

Flanagan, T. J., & Jamieson, K. M. (Eds.). (1988). *Sourcebook of criminal justice statistics 1987*. Washington, DC: Government Printing Office.

Flanagan, T. J., & Longmire, D. R. (Eds.). (1996). *Americans view crime and justice: A national public opinion survey*. Thousand Oaks, CA: Sage.

Garrett, C. J. (1985). Effects of residential treatment on adjudicated delinquents: A meta-analysis. *Journal of Research in Crime and Delinquency*, 22, 287-308.

Gavzer, B. (1995, August 13). Serving time in America. *Parade Magazine*, pp. 3-7.

Gendreau, P., & Ross, R. R. (1987). Revivification of rehabilitation: Evidence from the 1980s. *Justice Quarterly*, 4, 349–407.

Gordon, D. (1991). *The justice juggernaught: Fighting street crime, controlling citizens*. New Brunswick, NJ: Rutgers University Press.

Gottfredson, S. D., & Taylor, I. B. (1984). Public policy and prison populations: Measuring opinions about reform. *Judicature*, 68, 190-201.

Gottfredson, S. D., Warner, B. D., & Taylor, R. B. (1988). Conflict and consensus about criminal justice in Maryland. In N. Walker & M. Hough (Eds.), *Public attitudes to sentencing. Surveys from five countries* (pp. 16-55). Brookfield, VT: Gower.

Halleck, S. L., & Witte, A. D. (1977). Is rehabilitation dead? *Crime & Delinquency*, 23,372-382.

Harris, L. (1968). Changing public attitudes toward crime and corrections. *Federal Probation*, 32(4),9-16.

Hindelang, M. J., Dunn, C. S., Aumick, A. L., & Sutton, L. P. (Eds.). (1975). *Sourcebook of criminal justice statistics—1974*. Washington, DC: Government Printing Office.

Hough, M., Lewis, H., & Walker, N. (1988). Factors associated with "punitiveness" in England and Wales. In N. Walker & M. Hough (Eds.), *Public attitudes to sentencing. Surveys from five countries* (pp. 203-217). Brookfield, VT. Gower.

Johnson, B. (1994). To rehabilitate or punish: Results of a public opinion poll. *American Jails*, 8, 41–43.

Johnson, B., & Huff, C. R. (1987). Public opinion and criminal justice policy formulation. *Criminal Justice Policy Review, 2,* 118–132.

Johnson, W. W., Bennett, K., & Flanagan, T. J. (1997). Getting tough on prisoners: Results from the National Corrections Executive Survey, 1995. *Crime & Delinquency, 43,* 24-4.

Kaminski, R. J., & Jefferis, E. (1997, March). *The effect of a violent televised arrest on public perceptions of the police: A partial test of Easton's theoretical framework.* Paper presented at the annual meeting of the Academy of Criminal Justice Sciences, Louisville, KY.

Knowles, J. J. (1987). *Ohio citizen attitudes concerning crime and criminal justice.* Columbus, OH: Governor's Office of Criminal Justice Services.

Langworthy, R. H., & Whitehead, J. T. (1986). Liberalism and fear as explanations of punitiveness. *Criminology, 24,* 575-591.

Lipsey, M. W. (1992). Juvenile delinquency treatment: A meta-analytic inquiry into the variability of effects. In T. D. Cook, H. Cooper, D. S. Cordray, H. Hartmann, L. V. Heges, R. J. Light, T. A. Louis, & F. Mosteller (Eds.) *Meta-analysis for explanation: A casebook* (pp. 83-127), New York: Russell Sage.

Lipsey, M. W., & Wilson, D. B. (1997). *Effective intervention for serious juvenile offenders: A synthesis of research.* Unpublished manuscript, Vanderbilt University, Nashville, TN.

Little, T. A. (1992) *Meta-analysis of the effectiveness of punishment programs for offenders: A preliminary assessment.* Unpublished manuscript, University of New Brunswick, Saint John, Canada.

Maguire, K., & Flanagan, T. J. (Eds.). (1991). *Sourcebook of criminal justice statistics—1990.* Washington, DC: Government Printing Office.

Martinson, R. (1974, Spring). What works? Questions and answers about prison reform. *Public Interest,* pp. 23-54.

McCorkle, R. C. (1993). Research note: Punish and rehabilitate? Public attitudes toward six common crimes. *Crime & Delinquency, 39,*240-252.

McGarrell, E. F., & Flanagan, T. J. (Eds.). (1985). *Sourcebook of criminal justice statistics—1984.* Washington, DC: Government Printing Office.

Moore, D. W. (1995, June). Americans firmly support death penalty. *Gallup Poll Monthly,* pp. 23–25.

Morris, N., & Tonry, M. (1990). *Between prison and probation: Intermediate punishments in a rational sentencing system.* New York: Oxford University Press.

Palmer, T. (1992). *The re-emergence of correctional intervention.* Newbury Park, CA: Sage.

Paternoster, R. (1987). The deterrent effect of perceived certainty and severity of punishment: A review of the evidence and issues. *Justice Quarterly, 4,* 173-217.

Pettinico, G. (1994). Crime and punishment: America changes its mind. *Public Perspective,5*(6), 29–32.

Reichel, P. L., & Gauthier, A. K. (1990). Boot camp corrections: A public reaction. In R. Muraskin (Ed.), *Issues in justice: Exploring policy issues in the criminal justice system* (pp. 73–96). Bristol, IN: Wyndham Hall.

Riley, P. J., & Rose, V. M. (1980). Public vs. elite opinion on correctional reform: Implications for social policy. *Journal of Criminal Justice, 8* 345-356.

Roberts, J. V. (1992). Public opinion, crime, and criminal justice. In M. Tonry (Ed.), *Crime and justice: A review of research*(Vol. 16, pp. 99-180). Chicago: University of Chicago Press.

Roberts, J. V., & Edwards, D. (1989). Contextual effects in judgement of crimes, criminals, and the purposes of sentencing. *Journal of Applied Social Psychology, 19,* 902-917.

Roberts, J. V., & Gebotys, R. J. (1989). The purpose of sentencing: Public support for competing aims. *Behavioral Sciences and the Law, 7* 387-402.

Rossi, P. H., & Nock, S. L. (Eds.). (1982). *Measuring social judgements: The factorial survey approach.* Beverly Hills, CA: Sage.

Sandys, M., & McGarrell, E. F. (1995). Attitudes toward capital punishment: Preference for the penalty or mere acceptance? *Journal of Research in Crime and Delinquency, 32,* 191-213.

Senese, J. D. (1992). Intensive supervision probation and public opinion: Perceptions of community correctional policy and practice. *American Journal of Criminal Justice, 16* 33-56.

Serrill, M. S. (1975, May-June). Is rehabilitation dead? *Corrections Magazine,* pp. 3-12, 21-32. *Sourcebook of criminal justice statistics—1995,* at URL: *http://www.albany.edu/sourcebook/.*

Steinhart, D. (1988). *California opinion poll: Public attitudes on youth crime.* San Francisco: National Council on Crime and Delinquency.

Sundt, J. L., Cullen, F. T., Applegate, B. K., & Turner, M. G. (1997, March). *The tenacity of rehabilitative ideology revisited.* Paper presented at the annual meeting of the Academy of Criminal Justice Sciences, Louisville, KY.

Thomson, D. R., & Ragona, A. J. (1987). Popular moderation versus governmental authoritarianism: An interactionist view of public sentiments toward criminal sanctions. *Crime & Delinquency, 33,*337-357.

Tuchfarber, A. J. (1988). Ohio: Presidential politics in "the heart of it all." *Election Politics,* 5(1), 15-18.

Turner, M. G., Sundt, J. L., Applegate, B. K., & Cullen, F. T. (1995). "Three strikes and you're out" legislation: A national assessment. *Federal Probation,* 59,16-35.

U.S. Bureau of the Census. (1994). *County and city databook: 1994.* Washington, DC: Government Printing Office.

Vining, J., & Ebreo, A. (1992). Predicting recycling behavior from global and specific environmental attitudes and changes in recycling opportunities. *Journal of Applied Social Psychology,* 22, 1580-1607.

Visher, C. A. (1987). Incapacitation and crime control: Does a lock'em up strategy reduce crime? *Justice Quarterly,* 4,513-543.

Warr, M., & Stafford, M. (1984). Public goals of punishment and support for the death penalty. *Journal of Research in Crime and Delinquency,* 21, 95-111.

White, M. F., & Menke, B. A. (1982). On assessing the mood of the public toward the police: Some conceptual issues. *Journal of Criminal Justice,* 10, 211-230.

Wunder, A. (1995). The extinction of inmate privileges. *Corrections Compendium, 26*(6), 5-20.

Zamble, E. (1990). Public support for criminal justice policies: Some specific findings. *Forum on Corrections Research,* 2(1), 14-19.

Zamble, E., & Kalm, K (1990). General and specific measures of public attitudes toward sentencing. *Canadian Journal of Behavioural Science,* 22, 327-337.

Zimring, F., & Hawkins, G. (1995). *Incapacitation: Penal confinement and the restraint of crime.* New York: Oxford University Press. ✦